PENGUIN CLASSICS

EITHER/OR

SØREN AABYE KIERKEGAARD was born in Copenhagen in 1813, the youngest of seven children. His mother, his sisters and two of his brothers all died before he reached his twenty-first birthday. Kierkegaard's childhood was an isolated and unhappy one, clouded by the religious fervour of his father. He was educated at the School of Civic Virtue and went on to enter the university, where he read theology but also studied the liberal arts and science. In all, he spent seven years as a student, gaining a reputation both for his academic brilliance and for his extravagant social life. Towards the end of his university career he started to criticize the Christianity upheld by his father and to look for a new set of values. In 1841 he broke off his engagement to Regine Olsen and devoted himself to his writing. During the next ten years he produced a flood of discourses and no fewer than twelve major philosophical essays, many of them written under *noms de plume*. Notable are *Either/Or* (1843), *Repetition* (1843), *Fear and Trembling* (1843), *Philosophical Fragments* (1844), *The Concept of Anxiety* (1844), *Stages on Life's Way* (1845), *Concluding Unscientific Postscript* (1846) and *The Sickness unto Death* (1849). By the end of his life Kierkegaard had become an object of public ridicule and scorn, partly because of a sustained feud that he had provoked in 1846 with the satirical Danish weekly the *Corsair*, partly because of his repeated attacks on the Danish State Church. Few mourned his death in November 1855, but during the early twentieth century his work enjoyed increasing acclaim and he has done much to inspire both modern Protestant theology and existentialism. Today Kierkegaard is attracting increasing attention from philosophers and writers 'inside' and outside the postmodern tradition.

ALASTAIR HANNAY was born to Scottish parents in Plymouth, Devon, in 1932 and educated at Edinburgh Academy, the University of Edinburgh and University College, London. In 1961 he became a resident of Norway, where he is now Emeritus Professor of Philosophy at the University of Oslo. A Fellow of the Royal Society of Edinburgh, he has been a frequent visiting professor at the University of California, at San Diego and Berkeley. Alastair Hannay has also translated Kierkegaard's *Fear and Trembling*, *The Sickness unto Death* and *Papers and Journals* for Penguin Classics. His other publications include *Mental Images – A Defence*, *Kierkegaard (Arguments of the Philosophers)*, *Human Consciousness*, *Kierkegaard: A Biography*, and *Kierkegaard and Philosophy: Selected Essays*, as well as articles on diverse themes in philosophical collections and journals.

SØREN KIERKEGAARD

Either/Or

A Fragment of Life

Edited by
VICTOR EREMITA
Abridged, Translated and with an Introduction and Notes by
ALASTAIR HANNAY

PENGUIN BOOKS

PENGUIN BOOKS

Published by the Penguin Group
Penguin Books Ltd, 80 Strand, London WC2R ORL, England
Penguin Group (USA), Inc., 375 Hudson Street, New York, New York 10014, USA
Penguin Books Australia Ltd, 250 Camberwell Road, Camberwell, Victoria 3124, Australia
Penguin Books Canada Ltd, 10 Alcorn Avenue, Toronto, Ontario, Canada M4V 3B2
Penguin Books India (P) Ltd, 11 Community Centre, Panchsheel Park, New Delhi – 110 017, India
Penguin Books (NZ) Ltd, Cnr Rosedale and Airborne Roads, Albany, Auckland, New Zealand
Penguin Books (South Africa) (Pty) Ltd, 24 Sturdee Avenue, Rosebank 2196, South Africa

Penguin Books Ltd, Registered Offices: 80 Strand, London WC2R ORL, England

www.penguin.com

This translation first published 1992
Reprinted 2004
031

Copyright © Alastair Hannay, 1992
All rights reserved

The moral right of the author has been asserted

Printed in England by Clays Ltd, St Ives plc

ISBN-13: 978-0-140-44577-0

www.greenpenguin.co.uk

MIX
Paper from
responsible sources
FSC
www.fsc.org   FSC™ C018179

Penguin Books is committed to a sustainable
future for our business, our readers and our planet.
This book is made from Forest Stewardship
Council™ certified paper.

CONTENTS

Translator's Note   vi
Introduction   1

PART ONE: CONTAINING THE PAPERS OF A

Preface   27
1   Diapsalmata   39
2   The Immediate Erotic Stages or the Musical Erotic   59
3   Ancient Tragedy's Reflection in the Modern   137
4   Shadowgraphs   163
5   The Unhappiest One   209
6   Crop Rotation   223
7   The Seducer's Diary   243

PART TWO: CONTAINING THE PAPERS OF B: LETTERS TO A

1   The Aesthetic Validity of Marriage   381
2   Equilibrium between the Aesthetic and the Ethical
    in the Development of Personality   475
3   Last Word   591
4   The Edifying in the Thought that Against God
    We Are Always in the Wrong   595

Notes   610

TRANSLATOR'S NOTE

This abridgement contains two kinds of omission: cuts of varying length in the pieces translated and one essay omitted in its entirety. The former are marked [. . .] in the text, while other, similar indications (e.g. . . . and –) are in the original. By far the greatest number and longest omissions of this kind, some extending to several pages, occur in Part Two. The essay omitted, along with shorter passages which make reference to it, is from Part One. It is 'Den første Kjærlighed, Lystspil i een Act af Scribe, oversat af J. L. Heiberg' ('First Love, Comedy in One Act by Scribe, translated by J. L. Heiberg'). For comments on both kinds of omission, see the introduction.

Paragraph divisions have been added to the original text where appropriate; the original contains often very long paragraphs, sometimes stretching over several pages.

Personal and place (including street) names have largely been left as in the original.

I am deeply grateful to my editor, Christine Collins, for suggesting many stylistic improvements.

INTRODUCTION

> Like the unfortunate madman who says he'll climb down into
> Dovrefjell to blow up the whole world with a syllogism, what
> was needed was someone who could, to everyone's knowledge,
> climb really deep down into the whole world of mediation, medi-
> ocrity, and spiritlessness to plant there, for all to see, the explosive
> either/or.*

WHEN Kierkegaard wrote these words in 1852, nine years after
the publication of *Either/Or*, he was looking back on his working
life as a deed on behalf of Christian awakening. By then his
targets had become the Danish clergy: 'servants of Christianity'
who, in the prevailing tendency to 'idolize mediocrity', had
'shrewdly' exploited the 'pagan optimism' which made Christianity
commensurable with all things finite, and managed to reap the
benefits of a 'both/and' which made being a Christian just another
item on the list.

Either/Or had no such clear-cut target. It was written still some
time before the notion of a 'leap' into a distinctively Christian point
of view crystallized in Kierkegaard's writings. The motivation for
the work was probably a combination of two things: the fateful
choice Kierkegaard had just made in his own life by breaking off an
engagement and his confrontation with the philosophy of Friedrich
Wilhelm Joseph Schelling, from whose lectures in Berlin he sought
a philosophical answer to Hegelianism. Schelling (in lectures pub-

---

* *Søren Kierkegaards Papirer* (20 vols.), Gyldendal, Copenhagen, 1909–48, X⁴, A
665, p. 476. The reference is to a short story by the Danish author S. S. Blicher
(1782–1848).

lished posthumously as *Philosophy of Revelation* and *Philosophy of Mythology*) was presenting reality (or 'actuality') as a free action of a personal God, instead of as the outcome of historical or spiritual necessity. Though at first enthusiastic,* Kierkegaard soon saw that Schelling's was not the promised radical criticism of Hegelian philosophy he had hoped for. What was needed was a 'doubled-edged little dagger' with which he could 'assassinate' the whole of reality: the 'either/or'.†

In March 1842, after four months in Berlin, Kierkegaard returned to Copenhagen. *Either/Or* was published on 20 February the following year. According to Kierkegaard himself it took eleven months to write. Part Two was written first and already completed while he was in Berlin; most of Part One was written after his return.‡ The 'editor's' preface, written last, was ready in November 1842. The official chronology gives approximately 7 December 1841 as the date of completion of the second of the two main sections of Part Two. So, assuming he wrote the sections consecutively and in Berlin, as he must have if eleven months is an accurate estimate, that is a truly astonishing achievement, all the more so in view of the fact that he was at the same time attending lectures at the University. The completion dates of the essays in Part One indicate that these too were written in a different order from that in which they eventually appeared. Thus the concluding 'Seducer's Diary' was completed before the first main essay on the 'Immediate Erotic Stages'. This suggests that the writing itself may not have followed any conscious plan or strategy discernible in the work as we now have it.

This is part of the fascination of *Either/Or*. True to its title, Kierkegaard's classic places many choices in its would-be reader's path and almost as many temptations – mostly, as hinted here, of interpretation. But there are also practical choices and temptations

---

* *Papirer* III, A 179, p. 72.
† *Papirer* III, B 179, 62, p. 207.
‡ *Synspunktet for min Forfatter-Virksomhed: En Ligefrem Meddelelse, Rapport til Historien* ('The Point of View of My Activity as an Author: A Direct Communication, Report to History'), in *Søren Kierkegaard: Samlede Værker*, ed. A. B. Drachmann, J. L. Heiberg and H. O. Lange, Gyldendal, Copenhagen, vol. 18, 1964, p. 89.

to consider, the first prompted by the work's sheer size: Must I really read the whole thing? The standard two-volume format invites a rather handy answer to that question by offering a prior choice: Do I have to buy both volumes?

Vain searches for the first volume among shelves full of copies of the second quickly reveal the outcome of that short-lived choice. Although what this particular preference very likely indicates is the continuing reputation of Kierkegaard's portrayals of the aesthetic way of life, rather than penury, say, or normal human postponement, the author himself would hardly approve. Commenting on the work's critics, Kierkegaard says, 'If someone starts by saying "either" – and doesn't conceal from the listener that the first clause is going to be a very long one, you owe it to him either to ask him not to begin or to listen also to his "or".'* An advantage of the single-volume version offered here is that it ensures that would-be readers give themselves the chance also to read Kierkegaard's 'or'.

Against that, however, we are offering an abridgement, which surely deprives readers of a choice the author would definitely wish them to retain. Indeed Kierkegaard says one should either read the whole or not read it at all. So what justification is there for not merely defying the author's express wishes here, but also for disallowing a privilege any reader of a classic is surely entitled to, namely to read such a work in its entirety?

The original 1843 edition, to whose reception Kierkegaard was reacting, was also in two volumes. Perhaps in view of his comments a second edition, of 1849, appeared in a single volume. But later editions, encumbered with an increasingly demanding annotational apparatus (to say nothing of introductions), have been forced into the two-volume format by plain bulk. The most obvious justification for an abridgement, therefore, is the making available once more of a portable (and readable) single-volume edition able nevertheless to incorporate at least a minimum of annotational material and an introduction. Naturally, if the cuts involve a serious loss of meaning, that is not a satisfactory reason. Since, however, a lengthy discussion of this question would be self-defeating in the present

* *Papirer* IV, B 24, p. 192.

context, we must let the following clarifications and comments suffice.

Besides the omission of a few 'diapsalmata', one shorter essay, 'The First Love', is omitted in its entirety from Part One (as well as short sections in other essays making reference to it). A commentary on a one-act comedy by the French dramatist A. E. Scribe, this was the outcome of an essay Kierkegaard had apparently begun before forming any clear idea of the later project. The comedy was familiar to Copenhagen theatregoers, who would also be among Kierkegaard's readers, and they would be in an excellent position to appreciate this illustration of an important idea in the work. But the commentary undoubtedly loses something in narrative coherence to readers lacking that familiarity, and since the idea itself is discussed copiously elsewhere in the work, it was decided to omit this essay in preference to others.

The omissions from Part Two are of a different kind. Although conveniently contributing to the provision of a slimmer volume, the cuts here are designed primarily to bring the line of Vilhelm's argument into greater relief and thus to help it make a more immediate impact upon the reader. Whatever the purist's misgivings, the result is at least better than the far more drastic abridgements usually resorted to, patched out of passages quoted out of context in textbooks.

As for Kierkegaard's own insistence that the work be read in its entirety or not at all, that too should be read in context. Kierkegaard is complaining that although they have been provided with both an 'either' and an 'or', his critics have shown interest only in the 'either', some only in the 'Seducer's Diary'. By saying 'read it all or not at all', Kierkegaard means first of all 'read at least *both* my "either" *and* my "or"'.

With these practical decisions behind us and a firm reader's commitment to a qualified 'both/and', there remain the choices, and temptations, of interpretation. The situation is less straightforward than it can seem. That is, one cannot immediately assume that the point or significance of *Either/Or* is adequately put by saying that the work provides readers with the opportunity to ask themselves which of the two points of view represented they themselves prefer. Many questions intervene. Just how distinct are the two points of view? Why can't they be combined? What if we don't feel like assenting to either? And isn't it really obvious that we are supposed to assent in the end to the ethical point of view anyway? But then what if I don't feel like doing that? Must I conclude that I've missed something, or is it because something is missing in me?

Later generations are sometimes said to be better placed to make sense of a significant work of literature than its contemporaries. That is claimed particularly in the case of a significantly innovative work, a category to which *Either/Or* clearly belongs. The reason offered is that the contemporary lacks the perspective needed for seeing the work's real significance, and lacks it necessarily since the perspective and its distance are not yet in place.* That may well be true, but time can complicate the picture as much as clarify it. There are two mutually reinforcing factors why this should be especially true of *Either/Or*.

One factor is a general truth about literary classics. They become parts of traditions which they help to sustain but also to change. Readings of them can therefore reflect two quite different points of view: that of their origin and that of their (always provisional) destination. No doubt it is also true that what makes a work a classic (something one of the essays in Part One of *Either/Or* is much concerned with) is in part its ability to perform these functions at the propitious time. Since this factor is bound up in Kierkegaard's case with his reputation as 'the father of existentialism', there is a not unnatural tendency to read *Either/Or* as an expression of such modern existentialist notions as that of radical commitment, of which more in a moment. This perspective obscures the fact that *Either/Or* is Kierkegaard's first main work, and therefore also the possibility that one can read it in a more historical light. There is also the fact – though one might well choose to ignore it, believing an author's works once completed to be self-sufficient – of Kierkegaard's own changing attitudes to the work.

---

* Hans-Georg Gadamer (*Truth and Method*, Sheed & Ward, 1975) claims that we approach contemporary works of art with 'prejudices we are not in control of, presuppositions that have too great an influence over us for us to know about them', and that these can give such works 'a resonance that does not correspond to their true content and their true significance' (p. 265).

Compounding this confusion is the second factor: the author's notorious practice of concealing himself behind a barrage of pseudonyms. *Either/Or* is exemplary in this respect, wrapped as it is in several layers of pseudonymity. The two main parts are assigned to two fictitious authors, the first part containing what is at least made to look like a diary by a third author, and the second containing a sermon by a fourth. On top of that the work is as a whole presented by a pseudonymous editor in a fictitious preface.

Why such subterfuge? Well, of course it wasn't really subterfuge on Kierkegaard's part. Nobody was taken in, at least not for long, and given the pseudonyms Kierkegaard chose it would be ludicrous to suppose he intended that they should be. At most he may have hoped to spread uncertainty for a while as to whether it was he or someone else lurking behind the strange Latinized pseudonyms.

But then again these pseudonyms are not *just* means of concealment. Literal translations can disclose their special signatures in the form of a variety of points of departure, positions, or perspectives. Thus Johannes *de silentio*, the 'author' of *Fear and Trembling*, writes about something of which he himself says one cannot intelligibly speak, namely that Abraham's intention to sacrifice Isaac should be an act of faith.* Of *Either/Or*, Kierkegaard later wrote that when writing the work he was 'already in a cloister, which thought is hidden in the pseudonym: *Victor Eremita*'.† What does that tell us? Kierkegaard says in the same passage that when writing the book he had long given up the thought of a comfortingly marital solution to life. Although it is not clear whether he means life in general or his own, the remark at least indicates that he himself was not prepared to follow Vilhelm's advice; yet that hardly justifies the inference that Kierkegaard himself thought the advice should not be followed. Nor does it justify our saying of Victor Eremita, as does one commentator, that *he* is 'no more taken in by the

---

*   See *Fear and Trembling*, tr. Alastair Hannay, Penguin Classics, Harmondsworth, 1985, translator's introduction, pp. 10ff.
†   *Synspunktet for min Forfatter-Virksomhed* ('The Point of View of My Activity as an Author'), *Samlede Værker*, vol. 18, 1964, p. 90.

aesthete's paean to enjoyment than he is by the Judge's vision of marriage'.*

Yet that is surely an interesting possibility; it would mean that at least from the fictitious editor's point of view, the proper conclusion to draw from reading *Either/Or* is 'neither/nor'. So although the fact that Eremita is looking at things from the coolness of a cloister doesn't indeed force us to assume that he occupies some vantage-point superior to the two he presents, the ultimate 'significance' of *Either/Or* – even in Kierkegaard's mind – might still be that he does occupy that position, and that we should therefore somehow seek in deficiencies of both views the basis of a third.

But then, whether we place Eremita above, below, or behind his two protagonists, we are still one layer away from Kierkegaard himself. So we can still think of him as occupying another position. Or none. This latter is a useful idea. One way of looking at the pseudonymity is to note how it enables Kierkegaard to disown authority for what he writes. It 'scrambles' the author–reader link in a way that allows the writings to enjoy a genuinely independent existence, letting them become considerations in the mind of the reader, to do there whatever work they have it *in themselves* to do.†
Moreover, if dissolving the semblance or pretence of authority inherent in acknowledged authorship is one advantage of pseudonymity, another – the opposite side of the same coin – is that it also absolves a writer of personal responsibility for the views expressed, thus freeing him of the potential restrictions on movement imposed by an accumulating authorial past.

Time can not only make the search for a literary work's meaning complicated, it can positively distort that meaning. This factor is important in assessing a quite common reaction to Part Two. Judge Vilhelm strikes many as a hopeless bore and hypocrite. And there can be no doubt that our modern climate of opinion makes

---

* Josiah Thompson, *Kierkegaard*, Alfred A. Knopf, New York, 1973, p. 165.
† See *Papirer* IV, A 87, p. 33, where Kierkegaard writes that it seems to be his lot to teach the truth, as far as he can find it, but in a way that destroys all his authority. But for someone ready to learn, he says, it doesn't matter whether he is spoken to by 'a Balaam's ass or a guffawing crosspatch or an apostle or an angel' (cf. Numbers 22–24).

his defence of marriage look very like a classic case of male
chauvinism. In deference to the author, those who see Vilhelm in
this light may then suppose that this is what Kierkegaard intended.
But then there are also other negative responses that conflict with
this one. Some see in Vilhelm a fantast, a romantic, playing the
same kind of game as his young friend the aesthete, but with his
dreams being played out in social and family forms. Both these
responses may be due to a cultural cleft. Thus we might surmise
that our modern age has lost (as surely almost by definition it
has) certain kinds of background attitudes necessary for taking Vilhelm's seriousness as seriously as he himself takes it – and as
seriously as he would like the aesthete to take it. If that hypothesis
were true, we would then have to ask whether the modern positions or perspectives from which we make such judgements are
in some universally valid sense superior to those envisioned for
his readers by Kierkegaard. But the possibility would also have to
be faced that we have lapsed into a position already envisioned
by Kierkegaard, indeed into something Vilhelm himself might feel
justified in calling 'despair'. Might not the conclusion we reach
after reading *Either/Or*, then, be that we, or most of us, are 'mere'
aesthetes?

Thus, apart from the possibility of a neither/nor reading, a crucial
question which awaits the person who decides against that reading,
and assumes therefore that Kierkegaard definitely intends one of the
two views presented to be life-affirming, is 'Which?'.

We must be careful to separate that question from another,
namely, 'Which, if either, do *I* take to be life-affirming?'. Whether
due to the cultural cleft or just to a significant shift in climate, it is
of course quite plausible that a reader's response to *Either/Or* should
be quite different from Kierkegaard's own. But that raises another
question that must be answered before the two questions can be
taken to be as different as may at first be supposed. That question is:
'In writing *Either/Or* did Kierkegaard believe it more important that
readers decide for themselves which life-view is life-affirming than
that they should see the matter as he did?' But even there we
haven't reached rock bottom. We can also wonder whether Kierkegaard, had he suspected that Vilhelm's case might lose its appeal,
could have approved of attempts to update his portrait of the ethical

in order to restore that appeal, for example by making Vilhelm a feminist.

Alternatively, in order to escape this plethora of options, the reader may choose another, totally ignoring what Kierkegaard might have meant and simply reading the work as though first published today, and reading it in an altogether open-minded way just to see where the portrait fits and to find out how far the choices can affect one's value-horizon.

Consistently with a negative evaluation of Vilhelm's case for the ethical goes a typically modern predilection for his aesthetic counterpart. Indeed it could be said that the less conviction Vilhelm's portrayal of the supposedly fulfilling life of the ethicist carries, the more plausibly his young friend appears to us in the guise of the modern hero, richly egocentric, tragically melancholic, excitingly nihilistic, daringly imaginative. There is indeed a cultural stereotype of the aesthete that fits well with Kierkegaard's portrait. It is amply represented in both nineteenth- and twentieth-century literature, no better perhaps than in the one-act plays of the Austrian writer Arthur Schnitzler (1862–1931).* Looking at the work in this light, favouring as it does a monocular focusing on Kierkegaard's 'either', we can simply choose to ignore whatever evidence there is that Kierkegaard is conducting a campaign on behalf of his ethical 'or'. We prize instead his contribution to a progressive aesthetic culture. Perhaps we can even broaden the perspective in a binocular direction just enough to reveal the ethicist as representative of a powerful but oppressive tradition unfriendly to life and ready for replacement by some aesthetic alternative, even ripe for some sabotage from the aesthetic camp itself.

The fact that it would not be wholly perverse to choose to look at *Either/Or* in this way is an indication of the work's immense cultural resources. But it also helps us to see more clearly just what kind of war Kierkegaard thought he was waging, against whom, and with what victory in mind. The target or enemy was philosophy. That in itself dictates that the weapons with which he was committed to prosecuting his campaign were literary rather

---

* *Anatol* (1893) is a fine example.

than philosophical. It was the spirit of philosophy itself, incarnate in
Hegel, that Kierkegaard was out to destroy, and in order to break
with Hegel he could not resort to the discursive and systematic
methods of the Hegelians themselves. Kierkegaard had to appeal to
his reader's sensibilities. Hegel was to be destroyed in subsequent
works (notably in *Concluding Unscientific Postscript*) mainly by appeal
to the reader's sense of the ridiculous. But the most important point
to be clear about is that the victory Kierkegaard had in mind was
not merely the destruction of Hegel; it was the retrieval from
philosophy of legitimate human goals (ethical and religious understanding) which he believed philosophy had usurped and dreadfully distorted. This positive appeal, then, had to be first of all to
our senses of fulfilment in life, in pleasure or a sense of beauty,
from which alone the ethically crucial sense of a want of fulfilment could then be elicited in the reader. Kierkegaard was thus
able to put his native literary talent to the edifying task of regener-
ating ethics in the ordinary-life situations that make up a human
life. The means he created are the books of his pseudonymous
authorship.

In an important comment on *Either/Or*, 'leaked' by another of his
pseudonyms, Kierkegaard gives us to understand that the work's
special purpose was to 'exhibit the existential relationship between
the aesthetic and the ethical in an existing individual', the motive
behind this being the need to remind people 'what it means to *exist*,
and what *inwardness* signifies'. This was something that, 'because of
the great increase of knowledge', his age had forgotten. 'Knowledge'
here is an ironic reference to Hegelian philosophy, a 'system' of
thought which accords no ultimate value to subjectivity, sensibility
or inwardness. Of the German philosopher Friedrich Heinrich Jacobi
(1743–1819), criticized for subordinating the realm of knowledge to
that of feeling and faith, this other pseudonym, Johannes Climacus,
says:

Poor Jacobi! Whether anyone visits your grave I do not know, but I
know that the paragraph-plough digs all your eloquence, all your inwardness under, while a few scant words are registered in the System
as what you amount to. It says of him that he represented feeling
with enthusiasm; a reference like that makes fun of both feeling and

enthusiasm, whose secret is precisely that they cannot be reported at second-hand . . .*

Whatever the ethical view of life has to offer, then, it can only direct its appeal to individual sensibility. But that of course means directing it to where the aesthetic view of life also makes its appeal. So aesthetics is where one inevitably has to begin, and that applies equally to the religious view of life, not portrayed in this work but glimpsed in the 'sermon' appended as a 'last word' (*Ultimatum*) to Judge Vilhelm's second letter. In the same passage Climacus comments on the absence of a distinctively religious perspective in *Either/Or*, but says that the fact that his age had forgotten what it is to exist religiously implied also that people had first of all forgotten what it was to exist as human beings. *Either/Or* is the required reminder, a necessary prolegomenon to the reminders to come, about what it is to lead, first, a religious existence and then, secondly, a specifically Christian existence.

We now find ourselves face to face with one final interpretational either/or. As we noted earlier, reading Kierkegaard from within the perspective of modern existentialism, some people interpret the choice between an aesthetic and an ethical view of life in terms of a 'radical choice'. In place of 'radical' the term 'criterionless' is sometimes used; a choice made according to some criterion not exclusively part of the view itself would not be criterionless, and the choice would therefore not be radical enough to cover the transition from the aesthetic to the ethical point of view. Each Kierkegaardian 'stage' or 'sphere' of existence in effect represents an atomically distinctive answer to the question, 'What is it essentially to be a human being?'. The radical nature of the choice lies in the fact that in choosing one of the stages you are also choosing the kinds of reason available to you for defending the choice.

The peculiarly 'modern' touch to this is the belief that the notion of a criterionless choice is a way of expressing an insight the gaining of which marks the coming of age of our culture. It involves recognizing an irreducible multiplicity of cultural traditions,

---

* *Concluding Unscientific Postscript*, tr. David F. Swenson and Walter Lowrie, Princeton University Press, Princeton, 1941, pp. 223–4, quoted with alterations. (*Samlede Værker*, vol. 9, 1963, pp. 208–9.)

irreducible in the sense that there is no general basic principle for deciding between them. If we have to conclude from this, as well we might, that values in general are no more than expressions of habitual and basically arbitrary preferences, we may look on this positively as a release from bad philosophical habits, or else negatively as a cultural nightmare. But some people advocate an 'Aristotelian' solution which (to exploit a not at all inappropriately biological metaphor) would let values grow in specific cultures. Here the notion of 'radicalness' would apply only in the sense that given cultural contexts were what provided values with their 'roots'. Those who advocate such a solution see Existentialists with their 'radical choices' as engaged in a hopeless task, trying with the mere choosing to confer on the choice that substantial quality it can only acquire within a culture to which the chooser also belongs.*

If one considers briefly what this idea of a radical choice implies, the criticism seems justified. It means that the chooser stands outside the options offered, so whichever one is picked is selected as arbitrarily as one picks a chocolate from a box not knowing what kind of centre it has, though here one is not even supposed to care. Since there are no operative preferences upon which the selection is based – they all belong to the alternatives on offer – it would be appropriate to describe this as a case of picking rather than choosing. By the same token there can be no inter-'stage' or inter-'sphere' dialogue. Naturally, there can be dialogue in the sense of conversations about matters of shared interest, swapping of information and so on, as well as disputes about things on which there is disagreement. But there can be no way of settling basic disputes, no shared basis of considerations to which, say, an ethicist can appeal to try to win over an aesthete. So if Vilhelm offers arguments to his friend, these will have no effect if they are arguments sincerely offered in defence of the ethical way of life. If they are to have any effect, either his friend must already have taken leave of the aesthetic world and be able and willing to see the point of arguments based on ethical criteria,

---

* See, for example, Alasdair MacIntyre's *After Virtue: A Study in Moral Theory*, Duckworth, 1981.

or else Vilhelm will have to deliberately phrase his arguments in terms of aesthetic values to which he himself does not subscribe. He will then have to lure his friend into the ethical with arguments that, if he really stood by them, would place him in the aesthetic world alongside his friend.

Yet however radically the views presented in *Either/Or* differ, it is hard not to see the work as having the character of a dialogue. Part One contains implicit arguments against the ethical life-view, which are then rebutted in Part Two. There are also such arguments in Part Two, in the form of objections to ethical ideals that Vilhelm recalls his young friend having voiced and to which he replies. Further, it would be hard to read the two main sections in Part Two otherwise than as a sustained argument in favour of the ethical life-view, which is also continually underpinned by arguments against the aesthetic life-view. So 'either' there is a great deal of indirect persuasion and subterfuge, hardly a good advertisement at least for a supposedly *ethical* life-view, 'or' the radical-choice reading is mistaken.

But since dialogues do nevertheless aim at agreement, if only on some position that turns out to be neither of the original alternatives, and since agreement surely requires some kind of choice on the part of at least one of the participants, there should still be room for an either/or and so for a choice. There are, however, a number of quite different ways in which we might think of a choice occurring in conclusion of a dialogue. One would be where one party convinces the other by making him see how what he says 'stands to reason'. There would, however, be no appeal to 'inwardness' here; the dialogue might be said to occur only at a 'paragraph-ploughing' level. Another way, that did appeal to inwardness and sensibility, could be one in which the convinced party simply goes over to the new position as a matter of course in the light of certain appeals to which he was already attuned but about whose relevance to the case in hand he had not been clear. The function of the dialogue would be to bring about that clarity and the result might still, though only just, be called a kind of choice.

Neither of these captures the sense of choice required by Vilhelm of his young friend's entering upon the ethical life. That choice, as the reader discovers, is said to be 'of oneself'; and part of what that means is precisely that one no longer regards oneself as a being who, as in the second case, moves from one position to another simply from the weight or pressure of argument or circumstance. The ethical life involves rejecting any idea of oneself as just a passive accumulator, or in the case of the mature aesthete also imaginative manipulator, of life's contingent blessings; it requires acceptance of the quite different idea that one is a responsible agent. The 'choice of oneself' is therefore one that cuts short the passivity and imaginative manipulation. It requires, first, that one acknowledge a peculiarly human ability, indeed a need, to ask what it is essentially to be a human being. Second, it requires that one take this ability at its face value, as a genuine freedom to stake out one's own future according to a 'view of life'; and, third, it requires that the view of life one adopts be one in which one is 'revealed' in a context of familial and social responsibilities. 'Revelation' here does not mean the disclosure of a self that was previously hidden; a hidden 'self' is precisely not a self in Vilhelm's sense. The choice of oneself is the choice of visible selfhood, placing the chooser firmly within the area of public morality, and amenable for the first time to the ethical categories of good and bad, praise and blame.

This choice is clearly still a radical one. And its radicalness still lies in the total redefining of the values of a human life. It is important to realize the compass of the redefinition. It isn't a matter simply of turning over a new leaf; the choice of oneself means rewriting the whole book. In choosing oneself, as Vilhelm says, one takes responsibility for one's past and 'repents' for not having taken on this responsibility earlier. The ethicist's task as Vilhelm sees it, then, is to persuade the aesthete of the urgency of the choice. But this task is made the easier by the fact that the mature aesthete's life has already taken a form which an ethical redefinition of values can be seen to fit, as easily in principle as a glove fits a hand, the actual practice requiring only the will to put it on. His aestheticism is driving him out of the world in which his pleasure is sought; it has driven him into a corner from where he has to rely on his ingenuity and imagination to keep things going, on his ability to enjoy things in reflection, to enjoy the idea of things rather than the things themselves. He should be well disposed in principle at least, then, to seeing what Vilhelm is getting at when he describes the aesthete's life as one of 'despair'. But he should be able also to see the point of Vilhelm's advice to 'choose despair' rather than, say, some occupation or marrying, where these would be undertaken as expedients for just the kinds of reasons that an aesthete must give. Finally, then, if that is the case he might also be able to see how both getting a job and marrying might be radically reconceived as vehicles of human fulfilment instead of as expedients.

Getting a job and marrying were things Kierkegaard himself conspicuously failed to do. The background to that fact and a short account of the events in Kierkegaard's life prior and subsequent to the publication of *Either/Or* may help to put its subject-matter in perspective, as well as providing the reader unfamiliar with the details of Kierkegaard's life with the benefit of a brief portrait.

The sequence of events which turned Søren Aabye Kierkegaard to full-time authorship began in 1837 when he met Regine Olsen, daughter of a Copenhagen dignitary. Regine was then fourteen years old. The following year Kierkegaard's father died, aged eighty-one (Kierkegaard was then twenty-five). Kierkegaard's father had exercised a largely oppressive influence on his son from early childhood, and Kierkegaard later said that he had never enjoyed a proper childhood. Two years before the meeting with Regine he had been describing Christianity, associated with his father, as a debilitating influence and, looking about him for some other idea 'to live or die for',* he gave up his studies and led outwardly the life of an aesthete and wit. Entries in his Journal tell a different story. Kierkegaard was undergoing a period of deep and even occasionally suicidal depression. But the year before his father died came the first meeting with Regine, and Kierkegaard effected a reconciliation with his father shortly before the latter's death.

Just one month later Kierkegaard published his first book, *From the Papers of One Still Living*, though the title derives not from his

---

* *Papirer* I, A 75, p. 53. The entry is dated 1 August 1835. The details of Kierkegaard's life are largely gathered from Josiah Thompson's excellently vivid biography, *Kierkegaard*, A. A. Knopf, New York, 1973. The account draws from my own *Kierkegaard*, The Arguments of the Philosophers, Routledge, 1982 (rev. edn 1991), Chapter 1.

father's death but the death in the same year of Søren's teacher and friend, Poul Martin Møller (1794–1838). A little over two years later Kierkegaard became engaged to Regine. He underwent practical training for a career in the State Church and in 1841 published and publicly defended his doctoral thesis, *The Concept of Irony with Constant Reference to Socrates*. Since he had already preached his first sermon, all seemed set for a life of conventional civic virtue. But well before the end of that year Kierkegaard had returned Regine's engagement ring. The reasons for this turn of events are much disputed. The crux, however, seems to have been Kierkegaard's sense of his inability to 'reveal' himself as civic life, and in particular the life of a husband and father, required. By November, soon after the defence of his thesis, the break had become final and Kierkegaard was on his way to Berlin, the first of four visits which were his only journeys outside Denmark. It was from this first visit, ostensibly for the purpose of attending Schelling's lectures, that Kierkegaard brought back the manuscripts containing Judge Vilhelm's defence of romantic love and marriage.

The publication of *Either/Or* in February 1843 was followed in October by two slimmer volumes, *Repetition* and *Fear and Trembling* (both mostly written on a second visit to Berlin not long after the publication of *Either/Or*). All these works deal with the problem of entering society (or 'realizing the universal', an expression introduced by Vilhelm). The same theme was pursued in the substantial *Stages on Life's Way*, published in April 1845, though now with a distinctive religious aspect more in evidence. But almost a year previously, in June 1844, there had appeared two books introducing new topics. *Philosophical Fragments* sought, in subtle and spare language, to offer a Christian alternative to Hegelian philosophy, though without mentioning the latter. The theme was elaborated more explicitly, at great length, and with much irony and humour, almost two years later in *Concluding Unscientific Postscript to the Philosophical Fragments*. Within a few days of *Philosophical Fragments*, however, there had also appeared *The Concept of Dread* (alternatively 'The Concept of Anxiety'), an examination of the psychological background to the experience of sin. Alongside this already impressive production, Kierkegaard also published twenty-one 'edifying' and 'Christian' discourses under his own name, some of them published on the same days as works under pseudonyms.

As its title shows, *Concluding Unscientific Postscript* was supposed to mark the end of Kierkegaard's work as a writer. A few days before the manuscript was delivered to the printer, Kierkegaard provoked a feud with a satiric weekly called *Corsair* (*Corsaren*). In a volume of essays by a well-known literary figure and aesthete, P. L. Møller, he had chanced upon a biting criticism of his own latest work at the time, *Stages on Life's Way*. Not altogether coincidentally, Møller was the reputed model for Johannes, the pseudonymous author of 'The Seducer's Diary'. Kierkegaard, who knew that Møller sustained a connection with *Corsair* which he nevertheless wished to keep secret so as not to spoil his prospects for a Chair at the University, divulged the connection in a newspaper article under a pseudonym from the work criticized, at the same time wondering why the pseudonyms had been singled out for the dubious honour of being spared *Corsair*'s abuse. *Corsair*'s response was immediate. The weekly began mercilessly to pillory, not the pseudonyms, but Kierkegaard in person. Three weeks before *Postscript* was to be published, and while the *Corsair* business was at its height, Kierkegaard wrote in his Journal that he felt his time as an author was over, and even before the feud it appears he had given thought once more to the priesthood. There remained only one more literary chore: the proof-reading of a review of a book called *Two Ages*, a review in which he may have felt that he had properly rounded off his work by spelling out its social and political implications.

By the beginning of the following year, however, Kierkegaard was dismissing these plans as a lapse of nerve and the author was again in full spate. The same year (1847) he published *Edifying Discourses in Different Spirits* and the substantial *Works of Love*, followed in the spring of 1848 by *Christian Discourses* and in 1849 by *The Lilies of the Field and the Birds of the Air* and *Three Discourses at Communion on Fridays*. There then followed two works under a new pseudonym, Anti-Climacus: *The Sickness unto Death* and *Practice in Christianity*.

These later works display a new stringency. Perhaps the *Corsair* affair, which left Kierkegaard an object of public ridicule, enforced a polarization between him and his society. His own suffering for truth was set off against the complacency of a bourgeois public which manifested its self-contentment not least in the manner of its religious observances, and whose religious leaders, formerly close associates of Kierkegaard and friends of his family, struck him as exemplars of self-seeking worldliness. Thus, in a way, the social and political criticism that emerged in what might have been Kierkegaard's final work, the review of *Two Ages*, was a seed that developed in the atmosphere created by the feud with *Corsair* to become a general condemnation of the age in which he lived. *The Sickness unto Death* diagnoses the problem as despair, but as the preface to that work says, this time as the sickness and not, as Vilhelm has it in *Either/Or*, the remedy.*

In the next few years Kierkegaard wrote little until he unleashed a vitriolic attack on the State Church, which he now saw clearly as the real root and bastion of spiritual complacency and compromise. During these years he lived in increasingly straitened circumstances, and the remainder of his inheritance and the modest proceeds of his authorship went to financing the final assault, amongst other things through the publication of his own broadsheet, *The Instant*. This went through nine issues before Kierkegaard fell ill, collapsed in the street, and died in hospital some six weeks later, probably of a lung infection. He was forty-two years old. On his sickbed he confided to Emil Boesen, his friend from boyhood, indeed by that time his only friend, now a pastor and the only member of the Church he would see (including his own brother), that his life had been a 'great and to others unknown and incomprehensible suffering', which looked like 'pride and vanity' but 'wasn't'. Kierkegaard regretted he hadn't married and taken on an official position. His funeral was the occasion of what may have been one of the first student demonstrations, led by his nephew, an early supporter, who protested at the Church's insistence on officiating at the committal proceedings, contrary to the deceased's wishes.

We remarked earlier that since *Either/Or* was an early work we might ask ourselves what Kierkegaard thought about it later. But it

---

* *The Sickness unto Death*, tr. Alastair Hannay, Penguin Classics, Harmondsworth, 1989, p. 36.

was also suggested that this question could quite properly be ignored. Once a literary or a philosophical work has been launched on the world, readers are no more obliged to concern themselves with than to share in whatever embarrassments it may have caused its author. On the other hand, Kierkegaard's deathbed regrets about not having married or occupied an official position kindle one's curiosity. And we still don't really know what Kierkegaard ever thought of Vilhelm. Our comments here, now that we are focusing on the author and not the work, can be treated initially as nothing but an appendix to the biography.

One question relates to selfhood. In a note from the year *Either/ Or* was published, Kierkegaard tells us that the reason Part Two begins with a defence of marriage is that marriage is life's 'deepest form of revelation'.* Might then the later Kierkegaard wish to allow that emerging from the cover of his pseudonyms to conduct a public campaign against the established Church also counted as a form of revelation? Or does his regret at not having married amount to a belief that he remained incompletely revealed and therefore that he failed to attain true selfhood? On the other hand, the later pseudonym Anti-Climacus added a direct God-relationship to Vilhelm's specification of selfhood. So here Kierkegaard may have felt he had the better of Vilhelm in spite of conspicuously failing to live up to the latter's ideal of the ethical. Much of Kierkegaard's working life was spent worrying whether what it accomplished justified his being an 'exception'. One way of putting the problem would be to ask whether there was a 'selfhood' reserved for martyrs. The deeper question would then be whether he deserved that status. One way of construing the *Corsair* affair is to see it as an attempt to hasten the necessary trial by ordeal before it was too late to run the course.

There is also the problem of Vilhelm's portrayal of the relation between the sexes in marriage, and whether the limitations in it so apparent to us today are expressions of Kierkegaard's own views at the time and if so whether these ever changed. The year before his death he wrote that what Vilhelm says about 'the woman' is 'what you could expect from a husband defending marriage with ethical

Papirer IV, A 234, p. 92.

enthusiasm'. Kierkegaard seems to suggest the ethical enthusiasm is somehow false. He says that although man has a lust for life, left to himself he finds no way to awaken it. When the woman, however, in whom this lust is already alive, appears before him she awakens his 'unspecified' lust and specifies it.* So Vilhelm's marriage is really no more than an expression of his own shortcomings and needs, and Vilhelm himself really as much of an egoist as his friend the aesthete. So far so good, but this is where Kierkegaard stops. Or rather, he says that man is constitutionally 'spirit', which as readers of *The Sickness unto Death* will recognize, means that he is fated to exercise what was referred to here earlier as the human ability to ask what it is essentially to be a human being. Two things follow: first that the exercise of this ability deprives man of his lust for life, and second, that the only way for him to supplement this loss is for woman to lack this peculiarly *human* ability. An unholy combination if ever there was one: Vilhelm's stolid chauvinism gives way to a cynical symbioticism. Does Kierkegaard have any better defence of marriage to offer than that of an enthusiastic ethicist?

Our motto, the reader will recall, has Kierkegaard using his either/or to drive out mediocrity and 'spiritlessness', along with the pagan optimism which made Christianity just one more item on the agenda of finitude. Here the either/or makes a clear separation between the finite life we lead, and would like to have a lust for, and the world of spirit for which life as we generally lead it is trivial and not lustworthy. 'Drop all this egoistic trifling which people usually fill their lives with, doing business, marrying, begetting children, being something in the world; drop it, cut it all out – let your life be dedicated to loving God and devotion to humanity . . .'† The 1854 either/or spans an unbridgeable divide between petty bourgeois self-seeking and a life of unspecified self-effacement on behalf of the Good. Just where the things Vilhelm prizes find a place in a world defined by these stark alternatives is unclear, as indeed what it could be about them that gave us any sense of their value. The appeal of our 1841–2 either/or is that its 'either' is

* *Papirer* XI^1, A 164, p. 128.
† *Papirer* XI^1, A 141, p. 97.

precisely not a life of mediocrity or spiritlessness. How Kierkegaard could have handled a spiritless life-view *poetically* is hard to conceive anyway. Such a life has no appeal. Nor does it lead anywhere. An aesthetic 'either' is one that its 'or' can sympathize with because that is where it can have come from; and it has the imagination and depth needed to grasp the force of appeals made to it to choose the 'or'.

PART ONE

CONTAINING THE PAPERS OF A

Are passions, then, the pagans of the soul?
Reason alone baptized?
                              Edward Young[1]

PREFACE

PERHAPS it has sometimes occurred to you, dear reader, to doubt the correctness of the familiar philosophical proposition that the outward is the inward, the inward the outward.[2] You yourself have perhaps nursed a secret which, in its joy or pain, you felt was too precious for you to be able to initiate others into it. Your life has perhaps brought you into touch with people of whom you suspected something of the kind, yet without being able to wrest their secret from them by force or guile. Perhaps neither case applies to you and your life, and yet you are not a stranger to that doubt; it has slipped before your mind now and then like a fleeting shadow. Such a doubt comes and goes, and no one knows where it comes from or to where it hurries on. I, for my part, have always been of a somewhat heretical temper on this point of philosophy and have therefore early accustomed myself to undertaking, as best I may, observations and investigations of my own; I have sought guidance from the authors whose views in this respect I shared; in short, I have done everything in my power to fill the gap left by the philosophical literature.

Little by little, hearing became my favourite sense; for just as it is the voice that reveals the inwardness which is incommensurable with the outer, so the ear is the instrument whereby that inwardness is grasped, hearing the sense by which it is appropriated. Whenever I found a contradiction between what I saw and what I heard, I found my doubt corroborated, and my passion for observation increased. A father-confessor is separated from the penitent by a grille; he does not see, he only hears. Gradually, as he listens, he forms a corresponding exterior. Consequently, he avoids contradiction. It is otherwise, however, when you see and hear at the same time, and yet perceive a grille between yourself and the speaker. As far as results go, my observational efforts in this direction

have met with very varied success. Sometimes I have had fortune
with me, sometimes not, and any returns along this road always
depend on good fortune. However, I have never lost the desire to
continue my investigations. Whenever I have been on the point of
ruing my perseverance, my efforts have been crowned by an unexpected stroke of luck. It was an unexpected stroke of good luck
of this kind that, in a most curious way, put me in possession of the
papers I hereby have the honour of presenting to the reading public.
These papers have given me the opportunity to gain an insight into
the lives of two men which corroborated my suspicion that the
outward was not, after all, the inward. This applies particularly to
one of them. His exterior has been in complete contradiction to his
interior. To some extent it is also true of the other inasmuch as he
concealed a rather significant interior beneath a somewhat ordinary
exterior.

Still, for the record I had better explain how these papers came
into my possession. It is now about seven years since, at a
second-hand dealer's here in town, I noticed an escritoire. It caught
my attention the moment I saw it; it was not of modern work-
manship and rather well used, yet it captivated me. I cannot
possibly explain the reason for this impression, but most people
have experienced something similar in their lives. My daily path
took me past the dealer and his escritoire, and never a day passed
but I fastened my eyes on it as I went by. Gradually that escritoire
acquired a history for me; seeing it became a necessity for me,
and to that end I thought nothing of going out of my way for
its sake when an unaccustomed route called for that. The more I
saw it the more I wanted to possess it. I was quite aware that this
was a curious desire, seeing I had no use for this piece of furniture,
that procuring it was an extravagance on my part. Yet, as we all
know, desire is very sophistical. I found some pretext for going
into the dealer's, asked about other things, and as I was about to
leave, casually made a very low offer for the escritoire. I thought
the dealer might possibly have accepted. Then it would have
fallen into my hands by chance. Certainly it wasn't for the sake
of the money that I behaved in this way, but for the sake of my
conscience. The plan failed. The dealer was uncommonly firm.
For some time again I went by every day, and looked with loving

eyes upon my escritoire. 'You must make up your mind,' I thought, 'for suppose it is sold, then it's too late. Even if you succeeded in getting hold of it again, you would never have the same feeling for it.' My heart pounded when I went into the dealer's. It was bought and paid for. 'This has to be the last time,' I thought, 'that you are so extravagant. Yes, in fact it is lucky you have bought it, for every time you look at it you will think how extravagant you were. With the escritoire a new period of your life is to begin.' Alas, desire is very eloquent and good resolutions are always at hand!

So the escritoire was set up in my apartment, and as my pleasure in the first period of my enamourment had been to look upon it from the street, so now I walked by it at home. Gradually I became familiar with all its rich content, its many drawers and recesses, and I was pleased in every way with the escritoire. But it was not to remain thus. In the summer of 1836 my affairs permitted me a week's trip to the country. The postilion was ordered for five o'clock in the morning. The luggage I needed had been packed the evening before; everything was prepared. I awoke at four, but the picture of the beautiful district I was to visit had such an intoxicating effect upon me that I fell asleep again, or to dreaming. It seems my servant thought he should allow me all the sleep I could get, for it was not until half-past five that he called me. The postilion was already blowing his horn, and although I am not usually inclined to follow the orders of others I have nevertheless always made an exception of the postilion and his evocative leitmotif. I was speedily dressed. I was already at the door when it occurred to me, 'Have you enough money in your pocket-book?' There wasn't much. I unlocked the escritoire to pull out my money drawer and take with me what the house could afford. What do you think! The drawer wouldn't budge. All expedients were in vain. It was all as unfortunate as could be. To stumble just at that moment, when my ears were still ringing with the postilion's inviting tones, on such difficulties! The blood rose to my head, I became indignant. As Xerxes had the sea whipped, I resolved to take a terrible revenge.[3] A hatchet was fetched. With it I dealt the escritoire a tremendous blow. Whether in my wrath I missed or the drawer was as obstinate as I, the effect was not the one intended. The drawer was closed and the drawer remained closed. But something else happened. Whether my blow fell just on that point, or the overall shock to the whole framework of the escritoire was what did it, I don't know; but what I do know is that there sprang open a secret door which I had never noticed before. This enclosed a recess which naturally I hadn't discovered either. Here to my great surprise I found a mass of papers, the papers that form the content of the present work. My resolve remained unaltered. At the first station I would take out a loan. In the greatest haste a mahogany case in which there usually lay a pair of pistols was emptied and the papers placed in it. Pleasure had triumphed and gained an unexpected increase. In my heart I begged the escritoire forgiveness for the harsh treatment, while my mind found its doubt corroborated – that the outward after all is not the inward, and my empirical proposition confirmed – that luck is needed to make such discoveries.

I arrived at Hillerød in the middle of the forenoon, put my finances in order, and let the magnificent countryside make its general impact. Immediately the following morning I began my excursions, which now took on a quite other character than I had intended. My servant followed me with the mahogany case. I sought out a romantic spot in the forest where I was as safe as possible from surprise and then took out the documents. My host, who was not unaware of these frequent peregrinations with the mahogany case, ventured the remark that I was perhaps practising at shooting with my pistols. For this remark I was much obliged to him and left him undisturbed in his belief.

A cursory glance at the new-found papers immediately revealed that they formed two *œuvres* which differed markedly also in externals. One of them was written on a kind of letter-vellum in quarto, with a fairly wide margin. The handwriting was legible, sometimes even a little elegant, just once in a while careless. The other was written on full sheets of foolscap divided into columns, in the way that legal documents and the like are written. The handwriting was clear, rather extended, uniform, and even; it looked as though it belonged to a businessman. The contents, too, proved straightaway to be dissimilar. The one part contained a number of aesthetic essays of varying length, the other consisted of two long inquiries and one shorter, all ethical in content, as it seemed, and in the form of letters. On closer examination this difference proved fully corroborated, for the latter compilation consisted of letters written to the author of the first.

But I must find some briefer way of designating the two authors. To that end I have scrutinized the papers very carefully but have found nothing, or as good as nothing. Regarding the first author, the aestheticist, there is no information at all. As for the other, the letter-writer, one learns that he was called Vilhelm, had been a judge, but of what court is not specified. If I were to go strictly by the historical facts and call him Vilhelm I would lack a corresponding appellation for the first author and have to give him some arbitrary name. I have therefore preferred to call the first author A, the second B.

In addition to the longer essays there were, among the papers, some slips on which were written aphorisms, lyrical effusions, reflections. The handwriting alone indicated that they belonged to A. The contents confirmed this.

The papers themselves I then tried to arrange as best I could. With B's papers that was fairly easily done. One of the letters presupposes the other. In the second letter there is a quotation from the first. The third letter presupposes the two previous ones.

Arranging A's papers was not such an easy matter. I have therefore let chance determine the order, that is to say, I have left them in the order in which I found them, of course without being able to decide whether this order has any chronological value or notional significance. The scraps of paper lay loose in the hiding-place; these I have had to assign a place. I have let them come first because I thought they could best be regarded as preliminary glimpses of what the longer essays develop more connectedly. I have called them 'Diapsalmata',[4] and added as a kind of motto 'ad se ipsum'.[5] This title and this motto are in a way mine and yet not mine. They are mine in so far as they apply to the whole collection; on the other hand they belong to A himself, for the word 'Diapsalmata' was written on one of the scraps, and on two of them the words 'ad se ipsum'. Also a little French verse, which appeared above one of the aphorisms, I have had printed on the reverse of the title page, in a way A himself has frequently done. Since the majority of these aphorisms have a lyrical character, I have thought it quite suitable to use the word 'Diapsalma' in the main title. If the reader should think this infelicitous, then truth demands that I acknowledge it as my own invention and affirm that it was surely good taste on A's part to use it for the aphorism over which it was found. In the arrangement of the individual aphorisms I have let chance prevail. That the individual expressions often contradict one another I found quite in order, for it belongs essentially to the mood. I did not find it worth the trouble adopting an arrangement that made these contradictions less conspicuous. I followed chance, and it is also chance that has drawn my attention to the fact that the first and the last aphorism in a way correspond to one another, in that the one as it were reverberates with the pain of being a poet, while the other savours the satisfaction of always having the laughter on one's side.

As for A's aesthetic essays, I have nothing to remark in their regard. They were all ready for printing. And so far as they contain difficulties I must let these speak for themselves. [. . .]

The last of A's papers is a story entitled 'The Seducer's Diary'. Here there are new difficulties, since A does not acknowledge himself as its author, but only as editor. This is an old short-story writer's trick, to which I should not object further did it not contribute to making my own position so complicated, because it presents the one author as lying inside the other, as in a Chinese-box puzzle. Here is not the place to go further into what confirms me in my opinion; I shall only note that the dominant mood of A's preface in a way betrays the writer. It is really as if A himself had become afraid of his work which, like a restless dream, still continued to frighten him while it was being told. If these were actual events to which he had been witness, it seems strange that the preface bears no stamp of A's joy at seeing the realization of the idea that had often hovered before his mind. This idea of the seducer's is suggested in the essay on the 'Immediate Erotic' as well as in 'Shadowgraphs', namely the idea that the analogue of Don Juan must be a reflected seducer who works within the category of the interesting, where the thing is therefore not how many he seduces but how he does it. I find no trace of such a joy in the preface but rather, as noted, a trembling, a certain horror, which is no doubt due to his poetical relation to this idea. Nor does it surprise me that it has affected A in this way; for I, too, who have nothing at all to do with this tale and am indeed twice removed from the original author, even I have at times felt quite uncomfortable while busying myself with these papers in the still of the night. It was as if the seducer moved like a shadow over my floor, as if he threw a glance at the papers, as if he fastened his demonic eye on me and said, 'So, you mean to publish my papers! That is in any case indefensible of you; you will cause anxiety in the little dears. But then, of course, you think in return to make me and my sort harmless. There you are wrong. I shall simply change my method and then I am even better placed. What flocks of young girls will run straight into my arms when they hear that seductive name, "a seducer"! Give me half a year and I shall provide a story more interesting than everything I have experienced up to now. I imagine a young, vigorous girl with a sharp turn of mind getting the remarkable idea of avenging her sex on me. She thinks she can coerce me, give me a taste of the pangs of unrequited love. That's a girl for me. If she doesn't make a good enough job of it herself, I shall come to her aid. I shall writhe like the Mols people's eel.[6] And when I have brought her to that point, she is mine.'

But perhaps I have abused my position already as editor by burdening the readers with my reflections. The occasion must speak for my pardon, for it was on the occasion of the awkwardness of my position due to A's presenting himself only as editor of this story, and not as author, that I let myself be carried away.

What more I have to add about this story I can only do in my capacity as editor. For I believe I can find in it some clue to the time of its action. Here and there in the diary is a date; what is missing is the year. That makes it look as though I should get no further. However, by examining the individual dates more closely I think I have found a clue. For although every year has a seventh of April, a third of July, a second of August, etc., it by no means follows that the seventh of April falls each year on a Monday. So I calculated accordingly and discovered that this combination fits the year 1834.[7] Whether A has thought of that I cannot determine; I hardly believe so, for otherwise he would surely not have employed as much caution as is his custom. Nor does the diary read 'Monday, April 7th', etc., it says simply 'April 7th'. Indeed the entry itself for that

date begins, 'On Monday, then', which precisely points your mind
in the wrong direction; but reading through the entry under that
date, one sees that it must have been a Monday. In the case of this
story, then, I have a definite date. But all attempts I have made until
now with its help to determine the times of the other essays have
been unsuccessful. I could just as well have placed this story third,
but, as I said above, I have preferred to let chance prevail and
everything remains in the order in which I found it.

As for B's papers, these fall easily and naturally into place. In
their case, however, I have made an alteration inasmuch as I have
allowed myself to furnish them with titles, seeing the letter-form
has prevented the author himself from giving these inquiries a title.
Should the reader, therefore, having become acquainted with the
contents, find that the titles were not happily chosen, I am always
willing to reconcile myself to the pain attached to doing badly what
one wanted to do well. [. . .]

As for B's manuscript, there I have permitted myself absolutely
no changes but have looked upon it scrupulously as a document. I
might perhaps have removed the occasional carelessness, which is
understandable enough when one considers that he is only a letter-
writer. I didn't want to do that, because I was afraid I might go too
far. [. . .]

The point I have now arrived at is the one I had already reached
five years ago. I had arranged the papers in their present order, had
made up my mind to publish them, but then thought it best after all
to wait a while. I considered five years to be an appropriate space of
time. Those five years have now elapsed and I am beginning where
I left off. Presumably it is unnecessary to reassure the reader that I
have left no stone unturned in my efforts to trace the authors. The
dealer kept no books. As everyone knows, the practice is rare
among second-hand dealers. He did not know from whom he had
bought that piece; he seemed to recall that it had been purchased at
a general auction. I shall not venture to narrate to the reader the
many fruitless attempts that have consumed so much of my time,
the less so seeing their recollection is so unpleasant to myself. I can
at least in all brevity let the reader in on the result, for the result was
absolutely nil.

As I was about to carry out my resolve to publish the papers, a single misgiving awoke in me. The reader will perhaps permit me to speak quite frankly. It struck me that I might be guilty of an indiscretion towards the unknown authors. However, the more familiar I became with the papers, the more that misgiving diminished. The papers were of such a nature that, for all my painstaking investigations, they yielded no information. So much less likely in that case that a reader should find any, since I dare measure myself with any reader, not indeed in taste and sympathy and insight, but in industry and tirelessness. Assuming therefore that the unknown authors still existed, that they lived here in town, that they came to make this unexpected acquaintance with their works, then, if they themselves remained silent nothing would come of their publication, for it is true in the strictest sense of these papers what one usually says anyway of all printed matter – they hold their peace.

One other misgiving I had was in itself of less importance, fairly easy to dispel, and has indeed been overcome even more easily than I had thought. It occurred to me that these papers might become a financial proposition. Although it seemed proper that I should receive a small fee for my troubles as editor, an author's fee I had to consider much too excessive. As the honest Scottish farmers in *The White Lady*[8] decide to buy the estate, cultivate it, and then make a present of it to the Counts of Avenel should they ever return, I decided to place the entire fee at interest, so that if the authors should ever turn up I would be able to give them the whole thing with compound interest. If my complete ineptitude has not already convinced the reader that I am no author or scholar who makes publishing his profession, then the naivety of this reasoning should put the matter beyond all doubt. This misgiving was also overcome in a much easier way, since in Denmark even an author's fee is no manor-house, and the unknown authors would have had to stay away for a long time for their fee, even with compound interest, to become a financial proposition.

There remained merely to give these papers a title. I could have called them 'Papers', 'Posthumous Papers', 'Found Papers', 'Lost Papers', etc.; there are many and various possibilities, as we all know. But none of these titles satisfied me. In deciding on a title I have therefore allowed myself a liberty, a deception, which I shall endeavour to answer for. During my constant occupation with these papers it dawned upon me that they could yield a new aspect if regarded as the work of one man. I am quite aware of all that can be objected to in this view, that it is unhistorical, improbable, preposterous that one person should be the author of both parts, notwithstanding the reader might well fall for the conceit that once you have said A you must also say B. However, I have still been unable to give up the idea. Then it would have been someone who had lived through both kinds of experience, or had deliberated on both. For A's papers contain a variety of attempts at an aesthetic view of life; to convey a unified aesthetic life-view is scarcely possible. B's papers contain an ethical life-view. As I let this thought influence my soul, it became clear to me that I might let this guide me into determining the title. This is just what the title I have chosen expresses. If there be any loss in this to the reader, it cannot be much, for he can just as well forget the title while reading the book. Once he has read it he may perhaps then think of the title. Doing so will free him from every finite question as to whether A was actually persuaded and repented, whether B won the day, or whether, perhaps, it ended by B's going over to A's point of view. For in this respect these papers are without an ending. If one thinks this isn't as it should be, it would be unwarranted to say it was mistaken, for one might just as well call it unfortunate. I, for my part, consider it a piece of good fortune. One occasionally comes across novelettes where opposite life-views are expressed through particular persons. It usually ends with one of them convincing the other; rather than insisting on the view's speaking for itself, the reader is enriched with the historical result that the other party was convinced. I consider it a piece of good fortune that these papers provide no information in that regard. Whether A wrote his aesthetic essays after receiving B's letters, whether his soul has continued since then to riot in wild abandon or has calmed down, of this I cannot see myself in a position to pass on a single piece of information since the papers contain none. Nor do they contain any clues as to how things have gone with B, whether he had the strength to stick to his view or not. Once the book has been read, A and B are forgotten; only the views confront each other and await no final decision in particular persons.

I have no further comment to make except that it has occurred to me that the honourable authors, if they were aware of my project, might possibly wish to accompany their papers with a word to the reader. I shall therefore add a few words under their hands' guidance. A would surely have no objection to the publication of the papers; to the reader he would presumably cry out, 'Read them or don't read them, you will regret both.' It is harder to determine what B would say. He might perhaps direct one or another reproach at me, especially regarding the publication of A's papers. He would let me feel that he himself had no part in it, that he could wash his hands of it. Having done that he might perhaps turn to the book with these words: 'Go out into the world, then; avoid if possible the attention of the critics, call on a single reader in a favourable moment, and should you stumble upon a lady reader, I would say: "My fair reader, in this book you will find something you ought perhaps not to know, and something else you might well profit from knowing; so read the first something in such a way that you who have read it can be as though one who has not read it, the other in such a way that you who have read it can be as though one who has not forgotten what has been read."'[9] As editor I will only append the wish that the book meets the reader in a favourable hour, and that the fair lady reader succeeds in scrupulously following B's well-intentioned advice.

November 1842   THE EDITOR

1 DIAPSALMATA

ad se ipsum

DIAPSALMATA

Grandeur, savoir, renommé,
Amitié, plaisir et bien,
Tout n'est que vent, que fumée:
Pour mieux dire, tout n'est rien.[1]

Wʜᴀᴛ is a poet? An unhappy man who hides deep anguish in his heart, but whose lips are so formed that when the sigh and cry pass through them, it sounds like lovely music. His fate is like that of those unfortunates who were slowly tortured by a gentle fire in Phalaris's bull; their cries could not reach the tyrant's ears to cause him dismay, to him they sounded like sweet music.[2] And people flock around the poet and say: 'Sing again soon' – that is, 'May new sufferings torment your soul but your lips be fashioned as before, for the cry would only frighten us, but the music, that is blissful.' And the critics come forward and say: 'That's the way, that's how the rules of aesthetics say it should be done.' Of course, a critic resembles a poet to a hair, except he has no anguish in his heart, no music on his lips. So I tell you, I would rather be a swineherd at Amagerbro and be understood by the swine than a poet and misunderstood by people. [. . .]

I prefer talking with children, with them one can still hope they may become rational beings; but those who have become that – Lord save us!

Aren't people absurd! They never use the freedoms they do have but demand those they don't have; they have freedom of thought, they demand freedom of speech.

I can't be bothered. I can't be bothered to ride, the motion is too violent; I can't be bothered to walk, it's strenuous; I can't be bothered to lie down, for either I'd have to stay lying down and that I can't be bothered with, or I'd have to get up again, and I can't be bothered with that either. In short: I just can't be bothered.

As everyone knows, there are insects which die in the moment of fertilization. Thus it is with all joy, life's supreme and most voluptuous moment of pleasure is attended by death. [. . .]

This is the main defect with everything human, that it is only through opposition that the object of desire is possessed. I shan't speak of the various syndromes that can keep the psychologist busy (the melancholic has the best-developed sense of humour, the most extravagant person is often the one most prone to the picturesque, the dissolute one often the most moral, the doubter often the most religious), but simply recall that it is through sin that one first catches sight of salvation.

Besides my other numerous circle of acquaintances I have one more intimate confidant – my melancholy. In the midst of my joy, in the midst of my work, he waves to me, calls me to one side, even though physically I stay put. My melancholy is the most faithful mistress I have known; what wonder, then, that I love her in return. [. . .]

Old age realizes the dreams of youth; look at Swift: in his youth he built an asylum, in his old age he himself entered it.[3]

It should worry one to see with what hypochondriac profundity a former generation of Englishmen have discovered the ambiguity at the bottom of laughter. Thus Dr Hartley[4] has remarked: 'When laughter first manifests itself in the infant, it is an incipient cry, excited by pain, or by a feeling of pain suddenly inhibited, and recurring at brief intervals.' What if everything in the world were a misunderstanding, what if laughter were really tears?

There are times when one can be so infinitely pained on seeing someone all alone in the world. Thus the other day I saw a poor girl walking all alone to church to be confirmed. [. . .]

I say of my sorrow what the Englishman says of his home: my sorrow is my castle. Many consider sorrow one of life's comforts.

I feel as a chessman must when the opponent says of it: that piece cannot be moved. [. . .]

I'm stunted as a *sheva*, weak and unaspirated as a *dagesh lene*,[5] I feel like a letter written back-to-front in the line, yet rampant as a three-tailed pasha,[6] jealous of myself and my thoughts as the bank is of its printing plates, and generally as self-reflected as any reflexive pronoun. If only it went with misfortune and sorrow as with conscious good deeds, where those who do them have their reward 'taken away'.[7] If that were true of sorrows, I'd be the happiest of men; for I take all my troubles in advance and still they all stay behind.

The tremendous poetic power of folk literature finds expression in, among other ways, its having the strength to desire. Compared to it, the desire of our own time is both sinful and boring because what it covets is the neighbour's. That other desire knows very well that the neighbour no more than itself has what it seeks. And when its desire is sinful it is on such a titanic scale as to make man tremble. It won't let its price be beaten down by the cold probabilities of a sober reason. Don Juan still strides over the stage with his 1,003 mistresses. Out of deference to the tradition no one dares smile. If a writer ventured the like in our own time he would be ridiculed. [. . .]

Alas, the door of fortune does not open inwards so that one can force it by charging at it; it opens outwards and so there is nothing one can do.

I think I have the courage to doubt everything; I think I have the courage to fight everything. But I do not have the courage to know anything, nor to possess, to own anything. Most people complain that the world is so prosaic, that life isn't like a romantic novel where opportunities are always so favourable. What I complain of is that life is not like a novel where there are hard-hearted fathers, and goblins and trolls to fight with, enchanted princesses to free. What are all such enemies taken together compared to the pallid, bloodless, glutinous nocturnal shapes with which I fight and to which I myself give life and being.

How barren is my soul and thought, and yet incessantly tormented by vacuous, rapturous and agonizing birth pangs! Is my spirit to be forever tongue-tied? Must I always babble? What I need is a voice as penetrating as the glance of Lynceus, terrifying as the sigh of the giants, persistent as a sound of nature, mocking as a frost-chilled gust of wind, malicious as Echo's callous scorn,[8] with a compass from the deepest bass to the most melting chest-notes, modulating from the whisper of gentle holiness to the violent fury of rage. That is what I need to get air, to give expression to what is on my mind, to stir the bowels of my wrath and of my sympathy. – But my voice is only hoarse like the cry of a gull, or dying away like the blessing upon the lips of the dumb.

What is to come? What does the future hold? I don't know, I have no idea. When from a fixed point a spider plunges down as is its nature, it sees always before it an empty space in which it cannot find a footing however much it flounders. That is how it is with me: always an empty space before me, what drives me on is a result that lies behind me. This life is back-to-front and terrible, unendurable.

After all, it is the best time of one's life, the first period of falling in love, when with every meeting, every glance, one brings home something new to rejoice over.

My reflection on life altogether lacks meaning. I take it some evil spirit has put a pair of spectacles on my nose, one glass of which magnifies to an enormous degree, while the other reduces to the same degree. [. . .]

Of all ridiculous things in the world what strikes me as the most ridiculous of all is being busy in the world, to be a man quick to his meals and quick to his work. So when, at the crucial moment, I see a fly settle on such a businessman's nose, or he is bespattered by a carriage which passes him by in even greater haste, or the drawbridge is raised, or a tile falls from the roof and strikes him dead, I laugh from the bottom of my heart. And who could help laughing? For what do they achieve, these busy botchers? Are they not like the housewife who, in confusion at the fire in her house, saved the fire-tongs? What else do they salvage from the great fire of life?

I lack altogether patience to live. I cannot see the grass grow, but since I cannot I don't feel at all inclined to. My views are the fleeting observations of a 'travelling scholar'[9] rushing through life in the greatest haste. People say the good Lord fills the stomach before the eyes. I haven't noticed; my eyes have had enough and I am weary of everything, and yet I hunger.

Ask any questions you will, just don't ask me for reasons. A young girl is excused for not being able to give reasons, they say she lives in her feelings. It is different with me. Generally, I have so many and usually mutually contradictory reasons that, for that reason, it is impossible for me to give reasons. Also cause and effect don't seem to hang properly together. At one time huge and powerful causes give rise to tiny and unimpressive little effects, occasionally to none at all; at another a brisk little cause gives birth to a colossal effect. [. . .]

Life has become a bitter drink to me, and yet it must be taken in drops, counted one by one.

No one comes back from the dead, no one has entered the world without crying; no one is asked when he wishes to enter life, nor when he wishes to leave.

Time passes, life is a stream, people say, and so on. I haven't noticed it. Time stands still and I with it. All the plans I form fly straight back at me, when I want to spit in my own face.

When I get up in the morning I go straight back to bed again. I feel best in the evening, the moment I dowse the candle, pull the eiderdown over my head. I raise myself up once more, look about the room with an indescribable peace of mind, and then it's goodnight, down under the eiderdown.

What am I good for? For nothing or everything. That is an unusual capability. I wonder if the world will appreciate it? God knows if the girls get jobs who look for positions as maids-of-allwork or, failing that, as anything at all.

One should be an enigma not just to others but to oneself too. I study myself. When I'm tired of that I light a cigar to pass the time, and think: God only knows what the good Lord really meant with me, or what He meant to make of me. [. . .]

The sorcerer Virgil had himself chopped in pieces and placed in a cauldron to be cooked for eight days, thus to become rejuvenated.[10] He had someone watch out that no intruder peeped into the cauldron. The watchman was unable, however, to resist the temptation. It was too soon. Virgil disappeared with a cry, like a little child. I, too, have probably looked too early into the cauldron, into the cauldron of life and its historical development, and no doubt will never manage to be more than a child. [. . .]

Let others complain that our age is evil; my complaint is that it is paltry. For it is without passion. People's thoughts are thin and flimsy as lace, they themselves are as pitiable as lacemakers. The thoughts in their hearts are too paltry to be sinful. For a worm it might be considered a sin to harbour such thoughts, but not for the human being shaped in the image of God. Their desires are stodgy and sluggish, their passions sleepy. They do their duty, these hucksters, but like the Jews, they let themselves clip the coin just a little; they think that however well the good Lord keeps His books, they can still get away with cheating Him a little. Fie upon them! That's why my soul always reverts to the Old Testament and to Shakespeare. There at least one feels that it's human beings talking. There people hate, people love, people murder their enemy and curse his descendants through all generations, there people sin.

I divide my time thus: half the time I sleep, the other half I dream. When I sleep I never dream; that would be a pity, for sleeping is the height of genius.

Being a perfect human being is after all the highest goal. Now I have corns, that's always a help. [. . .]

The best proof adduced of the wretchedness of life is that derived from contemplating its glory.

Most people are in such a rush to enjoy themselves that they hurry right past it. They are like the dwarf who kept guard over an abducted princess in his castle. One day he took an after-dinner nap. When he woke up an hour later she was gone. Quickly he pulled on his seven-league boots and with one step he had far outstripped her.

My soul is so heavy that no longer can any thought sustain it, no wingbeat lift it up into the ether. If it moves, it only sweeps along the ground like the low flight of birds when a thunderstorm is brewing.

How empty life is and without meaning. — We bury a man, we follow him to the grave, we throw three spades of earth on him, we ride out in a coach, we ride home in a coach, we take comfort in the thought that a long life awaits us. But how long is threescore years and ten? Why not finish it at once? Why not stay out there and step down into the grave with him, and draw lots for who should have the misfortune to be the last alive to throw the last three spades of earth on the last of the dead? [. . .]

Wretched fate! In vain you paint your furrowed face like an old harlot, in vain you make a racket with your fool's bells. You bore me, it's always the same, an *idem per idem*.[11] No variation, always a rehash. Come, sleep and death, you promise nothing, you keep everything. [. . .]

A fire broke out backstage in a theatre. The clown came out to warn the public; they thought it was a joke and applauded. He repeated it; the acclaim was even greater. I think that's just how the world will come to an end: to general applause from wits who believe it's a joke.

Whatever can be the meaning of this life? If we divide mankind into two large classes, we can say that one works for a living, the other has no need to. But working for one's living can't be the meaning of life; to suppose that constantly procuring the conditions of life should be the answer to the question of the meaning of what they make possible is a contradiction. Usually the lives of the other class have no meaning either, beyond that of consuming the said conditions. To say that the meaning of life is to die seems again to be a contradiction.

The real pleasure consists not in what one takes pleasure in but in the mind. If I had in my service a humble spirit who, when I asked for a glass of water, brought me all the world's most expensive wines nicely blended in a goblet, I would dismiss him until he learned that the pleasure consists not in what I enjoy but in having my way.

So it isn't I who am master of my life, I am just one of the threads to be woven into life's calico! Well then, even if I cannot spin, I can at least cut the thread in two. [. . .]

I seem destined to suffer every possible mood, to gain experience in all directions. I lie every moment like a child learning how to swim, out in the middle of the sea. I scream (which I have learned from the Greeks, from whom one can learn what is purely human); for although I have a harness around my waist, I cannot see the pole that is to hold me up. It is a fearful way to gain experience.

It's rather remarkable, one acquires a conception of the eternal from the two most appalling opposites. If I think of that unhappy bookkeeper who lost his mind in despair at ruining a merchant house through saying that seven and six make fourteen; if I think of him repeating seven and six are fourteen to himself, day in and day out, unmindful of all else, I have an image *of* eternity. – If I imagine a voluptuously beautiful woman in a harem, reclining on a sofa in all her allure, not caring for anything in the world, I have another image *for* eternity.

What the philosophers say about reality is often as deceptive as when you see a sign in a second-hand store that reads: Pressing Done Here. If you went in with your clothes to have them pressed you would be fooled; the sign is for sale.

For me nothing is more dangerous than recollection. Once I have recalled some life-situation it ceases to exist. People say that separation helps to revive love. That is quite true, but it revives it in a purely poetic way. A life in recollection is the most perfect imaginable; memory gives you your fill more abundantly than all of reality and has a security which no reality possesses. A life-situation recalled has already passed into eternity and has no more temporal interest.

If anyone should keep a diary it's me, to aid my memory a little. After a while it often happens that I completely forget what reasons motivated me to do this or that, not just in bagatelles, but also in taking the most decisive steps. Should the reason then occur to me, sometimes it seems so strange that I myself refuse to believe it was the reason. This doubt would be removed if I had something written to refer to. In any case a reason is a curious thing; if I concentrate all my passion on it, it grows into a huge necessity that can move heaven and earth; if I lack passion, I look down on it with scorn. – I have speculated for some time as to the real reason why I resigned my post as secondary-school teacher. Thinking it over now, it occurs to me that such a position was the very thing for me. Today it dawned on me: that was precisely the reason, I had to consider myself absolutely fitted for the job. So if I'd continued in it I had everything to lose, nothing to gain. Wherefore I thought it proper to resign my post and seek employment with a travelling theatre, the reason being that I had no talent, and so everything to gain. [. . .]

The social striving and the exquisite sympathy that goes with it, is becoming more and more widespread. In Leipzig a committee has been formed which, out of sympathy for the sad end of old horses, has decided to eat them.

I have only one friend, Echo. And why is Echo my friend? Because I love my sorrow, and Echo does not take it away from me. I have only one confidant, the silence of the night. And why is it my confidant? Because it is silent.

As it happened to Parmeniscus in the legend, who in the cave of Trophonius lost the ability to laugh but got it back on Delos at the sight of the shapeless block which was supposed to be the image of the goddess Leto, so too with me.[12] When I was very young I forgot in the cave of Trophonius how to laugh; when I became older, when I opened my eyes and saw reality, I started to laugh and haven't stopped since. I saw the meaning of life was getting a livelihood, its goal acquiring a titular office,[13] that love's rich desire was getting hold of a well-to-do girl, that the blessedness of friendship was to help one another in financial embarrassment, that wisdom was what the majority assumed it to be, that enthusiasm was to make a speech, that courage was to risk losing ten dollars, that cordiality consisted in saying 'You're welcome' after a dinner, that fear of God was to go to communion once a year. That's what I saw, and I laughed.

What is it that binds me? Of what was the fetter that bound the Fenris wolf formed?[14] It was wrought of the noise of the cat's paws as it walks on the ground, of women's beards, of the roots of rocks, the sinews of the bear, the breath of fish, and the spittle of birds. So, too, am I bound by a fetter formed of dark fancies, of disturbing dreams, of restless thoughts, of dire misgivings, of inexplicable anxieties. This chain is 'very supple, soft as silk, resilient to the strongest tensions, and cannot be torn in two'.[15]

It's rather strange, the same thing preoccupies us at every age in life and we always get just so far, or rather we go backwards. At fifteen when I was in grammar school, I wrote with much unction about the proofs of God's existence and the immortality of the soul, about the concept of faith, about the significance of the miracle. For my *examen artium* I wrote an essay on the immortality of the soul for which I was awarded *prae ceteris*; later I won a prize for an essay on this subject. Who would believe, after such a solid and very promising start, that in my twenty-fifth year I should have reached the point where I cannot produce a single proof of the immortality of the soul. I remember particularly from my school days that an essay of mine on 'The Immortality of the Soul' received exceptional praise from the teacher and was read out by him, as much for the beauty of the style as for the content. Alas! I threw that essay away long ago. How unfortunate! Perhaps my doubting soul would have been captivated by it, as much for the content as for the beauty of the style. So my advice to parents, guardians and teachers is to warn children entrusted to them to set aside the Danish essays written at the age of fifteen. Giving this advice is the only thing I can do for the good of mankind. [. . .]

How true to form human nature runs! With what native genius a small child often shows us a living image of the larger situation. I was greatly amused today at little Ludvig. He sat in his little chair and looked about him with visible pleasure. Then the nanny, Mary, went through the room. 'Mary.' 'Yes, little Ludvig,' she answered with her usual friendliness and came over to him. He leaned his large head slightly to one side, fastened his immense eyes upon her with a touch of roguishness, and then said quite phlegmatically: 'Not this Mary, it was the other Mary.' What do we older people do? We cry out to the whole world, and when it makes a friendly approach, we say: 'It wasn't this Mary.'

My life is like an eternal night; when at last I die, I can say with Achilles:

Du bist vollbracht, Nachtweide meines Daseyns.[16] [. . .]

I am like the Lüneburger pig.[17] My thinking is a passion. I am very good at rooting out truffles for others; I myself take no pleasure in them. I root out the problems with my snout, but all I can do with them is toss them back over my head.

I struggle in vain. My foot slips. My life is still a poet's existence. What could be more unhappy? I am chosen; fate laughs at me when it suddenly shows me how everything I do to resist becomes an element in such an existence. I depict hope so vividly that every hopeful individual will recognize himself in my portrayal; and yet it is a fake, for while I depict it I am thinking of recollection. [. . .]

How terrible is tedium – how terribly tedious. I know no stronger expression, none truer, for like is all that like knows. If only there were a higher expression, a stronger one, then at least there would still be some movement. I lie stretched out, inert; all I see is emptiness, all I live on is emptiness, all I move in is emptiness. I do not even suffer pain. At least the vulture kept on pecking at Prometheus's liver, and Loki had the poison constantly dripping down on him; at least there was an interruption, however monotonous. But even pain has lost its power to refresh me. Were I offered all the world's glories or all its torments, they would affect me indifferently; I would not turn over on the other side either to reach for or to escape them. I die death itself.[18] Is there anything that could divert me? Yes, if I caught sight of a fidelity that stood every trial, an enthusiasm that sustained everything, a faith that moved mountains; if I came by a thought that bound together the finite and the infinite. But my soul's poisonous doubt is all-consuming. My soul is like the dead sea, over which no bird can fly; when it gets halfway, it sinks down spent to its death and destruction. [. . .]

Tautology nevertheless is and remains the supreme principle, the highest law of thought.[19] So no wonder that most people use it. It's not all that impoverished either, and might well fill out a whole life. It has its playful, witty, entertaining form in the infinite judgements.[20] This is the paradoxical and transcendental kind of tautology. It has its serious, scientific and edifying form. The formula for this is: when each of two magnitudes are equal to one and the same third magnitude, they are equal to each other. This is a quantitative inference. This kind of tautology is especially useful for rostrums and pulpits, where one is expected to say something significant.

The disproportion in my build is that my forelegs are too short. Like the Australian kangaroo I have quite short forelegs but infinitely long hind legs. As a rule I sit quite still, but whenever I move I make a huge leap to the horror of all those to whom I am bound by the tender bonds of kinship and friendship.

EITHER/OR
An ecstatic lecture

If you marry, you will regret it; if you do not marry, you will also regret it; if you marry or if you do not marry, you will regret both; whether you marry or you do not marry, you will regret both. Laugh at the world's follies, you will regret it; weep over them, you will also regret it; if you laugh at the world's follies or if you weep over them, you will regret both; whether you laugh at the world's follies or you weep over them, you will regret both. Believe a girl, you will regret it; if you do not believe her, you will also regret it; if you believe a girl or you do not believe her, you will regret both; whether you believe a girl or you do not believe her, you will regret both. If you hang yourself, you will regret it; if you do not hang yourself, you will regret it; if you hang yourself or you do not hang yourself, you will regret both; whether you hang yourself or you do not hang yourself, you will regret both. This, gentlemen, is the sum of all practical wisdom. It isn't just in single moments that I view everything *aeterno modo*, as Spinoza says; I am constantly *aeterno modo*. Many people think that's what they are too when, having done the one or the other, they combine or mediate these opposites. But this is a misunderstanding, for the true eternity lies not behind either/or but ahead of it. So their eternity will also be in a painful succession of moments in time, since they will have the double regret to live on. My practical wisdom is easy to understand, for I have only one principle, which is not even my starting-point. One must distinguish between the successive dialectic in either/or and the eternal dialectic touched on here. In saying that I do not start out from my principle, the opposite of this is not a starting-out from it, but simply the negative expression of my principle, the expression for its grasping itself as in opposition to a starting-out or a not-starting-out from it. I do not start out from my principle, for were I to do so, I would regret it. If I were not to start out from it, I would also regret it. Therefore if it seemed to any of my highly esteemed hearers that there was something in what I was saying, he would only prove that his mind was unsuited to philosophy. If he thought there was movement in what was said, that would prove the same. On the other hand, for those hearers capable of following me, in spite of my not making any movement, I will now unfold the eternal truth whereby this philosophy remains in itself and admits of nothing higher. For if I started out from my principle, I would be unable to stop again; if I didn't stop, I would regret it; if I stopped, I would also regret it, etc. Since I never start, however, I can always stop, for my eternal starting is my eternal stopping. Experience has shown that it isn't at all difficult for philosophy to begin. Far from it: it begins with nothing and can accordingly always begin.[21] What seems so difficult to philosophy and the philosophers is to stop. This difficulty, too, I have avoided. For if anyone believed that in stopping at this point I am really stopping, he proves he has no speculative insight. For I do not stop; I stopped that time I began. My philosophy has, therefore, the advantage of brevity and irrefutability. For if anyone were to contradict it I would surely be justified in pronouncing him insane. Philosophy, then, is constantly *aeterno modo* and does not have, like blessed Sintenis,[22] just single hours which are lived for eternity.

Why wasn't I born in Nyboder, why didn't I die as a small child? Then my father would have laid me in a little coffin, taken me under his arm, carried me out one Sunday morning to the grave, thrown the earth upon the coffin himself, said a few words half aloud that only he could understand. It could only occur to the unhappy days of old to let small children weep in Elysium because they had died so young.[23] [. . .]

My misfortune is this: an angel of death always walks by my side, and it is not the doors of the elect that I am to sprinkle with blood, as a sign that he is to pass them by;[24] no, it is precisely their doors that he enters – for only the love that lives in memory is happy.

Wine no longer gladdens my heart; a little of it makes me sad – much, melancholic. My soul is faint and powerless; I dig the spur of pleasure in vain into its flank, it can no more, it no longer rises up in its royal prance. I have lost all my illusions. In vain I try to abandon myself to the infinity of joy; it cannot raise me up, or rather, I cannot raise myself up. Once it had only to beckon and I rose light of foot, sound in body, and bold. When I rode slowly through the forest, it was as though I flew; now when the horse froths ready to drop, it feels as though I do not budge. I am alone, as I have always been; abandoned not by men, that would not pain me, but by the happy spirits of joy who in countless hosts encircled me, who met everywhere with their kind, pointed everywhere to an opportunity. As an intoxicated man gathers youth's wanton swarm around him, so they flocked about me, the elves of joy, and my smile was due to them. My soul has lost possibility. Were I to wish for anything I would not wish for wealth and power, but for the passion of the possible, that eye which everywhere, ever young, ever burning, sees possibility. Pleasure disappoints, not possibility. And what wine is so sparkling, what so fragrant, so intoxicating! [. . .]

My sorrow is my knight's castle, which lies like an eagle's eyrie high up upon the mountain peaks among the clouds. No one can take it by storm. From it I fly down into reality and seize my prey; but I do not remain down there, I bring my prey home; and this prey is a picture I weave into the tapestries in my palace. Then I live as one dead. In the baptism of forgetfulness I plunge everything experienced into the eternity of remembrance; everything finite and contingent is forgotten and erased. Then I sit thoughtful like an old man, grey-headed, and in a low voice, almost a whisper, explain the pictures; and by my side a child sits and listens, even though he remembers everything before I tell it.

The sun shines into my room so beautiful and bright; in the next room the window is open. In the street everything is quiet; it is Sunday afternoon. I hear clearly a lark, warbling outside a window in one of the neighbouring buildings, outside the window where the pretty girl lives. Far away, from a distant street, I hear a man crying shrimps. The air is so warm, yet the whole city seems dead. – Then I am reminded of my youth and my first love – I longed then, now I only long for my first longing. What is youth? A dream. What is love? The dream's content.

Something wonderful happened to me. I was transported into the seventh heaven. All the gods sat there in assembly. By special grace I was accorded the favour of a wish. 'Will you,' said Mercury, 'have youth, or beauty, or power, or a long life, or the prettiest girl, or any other of the many splendours we have in our chest of knick-knacks? So choose, but just one thing.' For a moment I was at a loss. Then I addressed myself to the gods as follows: 'Esteemed contemporaries, I choose one thing: always to have the laughter on my side.' Not a single word did one god offer in answer; on the contrary they all began to laugh. From this I concluded that my prayer was fulfilled and that the gods knew how to express themselves with taste, for it would hardly have been fitting gravely to answer, 'It has been granted you.'

2 THE IMMEDIATE EROTIC STAGES
OR
THE MUSICAL EROTIC

————

From the moment my soul was first overwhelmed in wonder at Mozart's music, and bowed down to it in humble admiration, it has often been my cherished and rewarding pastime to reflect upon how that happy Greek view that calls the world a cosmos, because it manifests itself as an orderly whole, a tasteful and transparent adornment of the spirit that works upon and in it – upon how that happy view repeats itself in a higher order of things, in the world of ideals, how it may be a ruling wisdom there too, mainly to be admired for joining together those things that belong with one another: Axel with Valborg, Homer with the Trojan War, Raphael with Catholicism, Mozart with Don Juan. A wretched unbelief exists which seems to contain much healing power. It thinks such a connection fortuitous and sees in it no more than a lucky concurrence of the different forces at play in life. It thinks it an accident that the lovers get each other, an accident that they love each other; there were a hundred other girls he could have been just as happy with, whom he could have loved just as deeply. It thinks many a poet has existed who would have been just as immortal as Homer had that marvellous material not been seized on by him, many a composer just as immortal as Mozart had only the opportunity offered. Now this wisdom contains much solace and comfort for all mediocre minds since it lets them and like-minded spirits fancy that the reason they are not as celebrated as the celebrities is some confusion of fate, a mistake on the part of the world. This produces a most convenient optimism. But to every high-minded soul, to every optimate[1] who does not feel bound to save himself in such a pitiable manner as by losing himself in contemplation of the great, it is of course repugnant, while his soul delights and it is his holy joy to see united those things that belong together. This is what fortune is, not in the fortuitous sense, and so it presupposes two factors whereas the fortuitous consists in the inarticulate interjections of fate. This is what historical fortune consists in: the divine conjuncture of historical forces, the heyday of historical time. The fortuitous has just one factor: the accident that the most remarkable epic theme

imaginable fell to Homer's lot in the shape of the history of the
Trojan wars. In good fortune there are two: that the most remarkable epic material came to the lot of Homer. The accent lies here
on Homer as much as on the material. In this lies the profound
harmony that resounds in every work of art we call classic. And
so too with Mozart: it is a piece of good fortune that what in a
deeper sense is perhaps the only true musical subject was granted
– to Mozart.

With his *Don Giovanni* Mozart enters that small, immortal band
of men whose names, whose works, time will not forget, for they
are remembered in eternity. And although, once having entered,
it is a matter of indifference whether one is placed highest or
lowest, because in a sense they are equally, because infinitely, high,
and although it is childish to argue over the highest and the lowest
place here, as if for one's place in line at confirmation, I am still
far too much a child, or rather, I am like a young girl in love
with Mozart and must have him placed highest whatever the cost.
And I shall appeal to the deacon and the priest and the dean and
the bishop and the entire consistory, and I shall beg and beseech
them to grant my prayer, and I shall implore the whole congregation for the same; and if they refuse to hear my prayer, if they
refuse to grant my childish wish, I shall retire from the congregation and renounce its ways of thinking, I shall form a sect that
not only places Mozart highest but simply refuses to accept
anyone besides Mozart; and I shall beg Mozart to forgive me because his music did not inspire me to great deeds but made a fool
of me – I, who through him lost the last grain of reason I possessed, and now spend most of my time in quiet sadness humming
what I do not understand, haunting like a ghost what I cannot
enter into. Immortal Mozart! You, to whom I owe everything,
to whom I owe the loss of my reason, the wonder that overwhelmed my soul, the fear that gripped my inmost being; you,
who are the reason I did not go through life without there being
something that could make me tremble; you, whom I thank for
the fact that I shall not have died without having loved, even
though my love was unhappy. What wonder then that I should
be more jealous of his glorification than of the happiest moment
of my own life, more jealous of his immortality than of my

own existence. Yes, to take him away, to efface his name, would be to overturn the only pillar that hitherto has prevented everything collapsing for me into a boundless chaos, into a fearful nothingness.

Though I have no fear that any age will deny him a place in that kingdom of the gods, I must be prepared for people to think it childish of me to insist that he have the first place. And though I by no means intend to be ashamed of my childishness, although for me that will always be more meaningful and have more worth than any exhaustive meditation precisely because it can be exhausted, I shall nevertheless attempt a considered proof of his legal title.

The happy feature of the classic work, what constitutes its classic nature and immortality, is the way in which the two forces absolutely cohere. This cohesion is so absolute that a later reflective age can hardly separate, even in thought, what is so intimately united without risk of giving rise to or entertaining a misunderstanding. Thus, its being said that it is Homer's good fortune to have acquired the most remarkable epic theme can make us forget that it is always in Homer's grasp of it that this topic comes down to us, and that its seeming to be the most perfect epic subject-matter is clear to us only in and through the transubstantiation that is due to Homer. If, on the other hand, one puts the emphasis on the poetic activity with which Homer penetrated the material, one is in danger of forgetting that the poem would never have become what it is unless the thought with which Homer penetrated it was its own thought, unless the form was that of the matter itself. The poet wants his material; but wanting is no art, as one says, quite rightly and with much truth in the case of a host of impotent poetic wants. To want rightly, on the other hand, is a great art, or rather, it is a gift. It is what is inexplicable and mysterious about genius, just like the divining rod, to which it never occurs to want except in the presence of what it wants. Here, then, wanting is far more profoundly significant than usual; yes, to the abstract understanding it may seem ridiculous, since the latter really thinks of wanting in respect of what is not, not in respect of what is.

There was a school of aesthetics which by one-sidedly stressing the importance of form can be accused of occasioning the opposite misunderstanding.[2] It has often seemed strange to me that these aestheticians unquestioningly adhered to the Hegelian philosophy, seeing that even a general familiarity with Hegel, and not specifically with his aesthetics, makes it clear that above all he places great emphasis in aesthetic respects on the importance of the subject-matter. However, both go essentially together, and to show this it is enough to point to a single fact since otherwise nothing of the kind would be thinkable. It is usually only a single work, or a single set of works, that stamps the individual poet or artist, etc. as a classic. The same individual may have produced many different things which stand in no relation to this. Thus Homer has also written a *Batrachomyomachia*,[3] but has not become a classic or immortal on that account. To say that that is due to the insignificance of the subject is foolish indeed, for it is the balance that makes a work a classic. If what made it a classic lay only in the individual artist, then everything he produced would have to be a classic, in a similar though higher sense as that in which the bee always produces a certain type of cell. Were one then to reply that the reason is that he has been luckier with the one than with the other, one would really not have replied at all. This is in part just a superior tautology, of the kind that all too often enjoy the honour of being taken for answers. In part, considered as an answer, it is the answer given inside another relativity than the one in which the question is posed. For it tells us nothing about the relation between matter and form, and could at best come into consideration when it is a question of the formative activity alone.

Now Mozart's case is similar: there is one work alone of his which makes him a classic composer and absolutely immortal. That work is *Don Giovanni*. Whatever else he has produced may cause pleasure and delight, arouse our admiration, enrich the soul, satisfy the ear, gladden the heart; but it does him and his immortality no service to lump everything together and make everything equally great. *Don Giovanni* is his acceptance piece.[4] With *Don Giovanni* he enters that eternity which lies not outside time but within it, which no curtain conceals from human eyes, into which the immortals are admitted not once and for all but are constantly discovered as one generation passes and turns its gaze towards them, is happy in its contemplation of them, goes to the grave, and the next generation passes in its turn and is transfigured in its contemplation. Through his *Don Giovanni* he enters the ranks of those immortals, of those visibly transfigured ones, whom no cloud ever carried away from the eyes of man.[5] Through *Don Giovanni* he ranks highest among them. It was this, as was said above, that I would try to prove.

All classic works, as earlier remarked, rank equally high because each one ranks infinitely high. Nevertheless, if one tries to introduce some order into this procession, it is evident that one can base it on nothing essential; for if one could, it would follow that there was an essential difference, and from that it would follow in turn that the word 'classic' was incorrectly predicated of them collectively. Thus, to ground a classification on the different nature of the subject-matter would immediately involve one in a misunderstanding which in its wider implications would end in the rescinding of the whole concept of the classic. The subject-matter is an essential factor to the extent that it is one of the factors, but it is not the absolute, since it is indeed just one factor. One could point out that certain kinds of classic in a sense have no subject-matter, whereas with others the subject-matter plays such an important part. The first would be the case with the works we admire as classics in architecture, sculpture, music and painting, especially the first three, and even with painting so far as the subject-matter enters into it, for its importance is really only in providing the occasion. The second would apply to poetry, taking that word in its widest sense to designate all artistic production based on language and the historical consciousness. In itself this observation is quite correct, but if one tries to base a classification on it by seeing the absence of subject-matter or its presence as a help or a hindrance to the productive subject, one goes adrift. Strictly speaking, one would be urging the opposite of what one really intended, as always happens when one operates abstractly in dialectical categories, where it isn't just that we say one thing and mean another but we say the other; we say not what we think we are saying but the opposite. So it is when we make the subject-matter the principle of classification. In talking about this, we talk about something quite different, namely the formative activity.[6] If, on the other hand, we proceed from the formative activity and stress only that, we suffer the same fate. By trying to call on the difference, and thus stress that in some directions the formative activity is creative to the degree that it also creates the subject-matter while in others it receives it, here again, even though we think we are talking about the formative activity, we are really talking about the subject-matter and in fact using that as the basis of our classification. Exactly the same applies to the formative activity as a point of departure as to the subject-matter. It is never possible, therefore, to use just one of them as an ordering principle; it will always be too essential to provide sufficient contingency, too accidental to provide an essential ordering. But this absolute mutual penetration, which implies, if we are to speak plainly, that we can just as well say that the matter penetrates the form as that the form penetrates the matter – this mutual penetration, this 'like for like' in the immortal friendship of the classic, may serve to throw light on a new side of the classic and confine it so that it does not become too ample. For those aestheticians who one-sidedly pressed the case of poetic activity so broadened this concept as to enrich, indeed overburden, that pantheon with classic knick-knacks and trifles, so much so that the natural conception of a cool hall of great figures of individual distinction disappeared altogether, and the pantheon became a junk-room instead. According to this aesthetics, every pretty little piece of artistic perfection is a classic work assured of absolute immortality; in this hocus-pocus admittance indeed was given above all to small trifles of this kind. Although otherwise hating paradox, no one feared the paradox that the least was really art. The error consists in one-sidedly highlighting the formal activity. So an aesthetics of this kind could only sustain itself for a definite time, that is for as long as no one was aware that time mocked it and its classic works. This view was, in the field of aesthetics, a form of the radicalism that has manifested itself similarly in so many spheres; it was an expression of the unbridled subject in its equally unbridled emptiness. This effort, however, like so many, found its suppressor in Hegel. It is, in general, a sad fact with regard to the Hegelian philosophy that it hasn't at all acquired the importance, either for a previous or a present age, that it would have had if the previous one had not been so busy scaring people into it, but on the contrary had given them a little more calm in which to appropriate it, and the present one had not been so tirelessly active in hustling people beyond it. Hegel brought back the subject-matter, the idea in its proper right, and thereby banished all these ephemeral classics, these insubstantial beings – dusk moths from the vaults of classicality. It is far from our intention to deny these works their due value; the point is to ensure that the language here is not confused, the concepts impoverished, as happens in so many other places. A certain eternity one may gladly accord them, and this they deserve; yet this eternity is really only the eternal instant which every true work of art possesses, not that full-bodied eternity in the midst of the vicissitudes of the times. What these products lacked was ideas, and the greater their formal perfection, the more quickly they burnt themselves out. The more their technical proficiency was developed to the highest degree of virtuosity, the more transient this virtuosity became and it had neither courage and strength nor poise to withstand the blows of time, while with an increasingly superior air making ever greater claims to be the most rarefied of spirits. Only where the idea is brought to rest transparently in a definite form can we talk of a classic work, but then it will also be able to stand up to the times. This unity, this inward mutuality, is possessed by every classic work, and thus one easily sees that any attempt at classifying the different classics based on a separation of matter and form, or of idea and form, is by virtue of that very fact a failure.

One might conceive another approach. One could make the object of consideration the medium in which the idea is manifested, and noting how one medium was richer, another poorer, base the classification on the fact that one sees help or hindrance in variations of richness or poverty of the medium. But the medium stands in far too necessary a relation to the whole work for a classification based on it not to get entangled, after a step or two, in the difficulties stressed above.

On the other hand, I believe the following observations will open the way for a classification which will have validity precisely because it is altogether contingent. The more abstract and hence impoverished the idea is, and the more abstract and hence impoverished the medium, the greater the probability that no repetition is conceivable, the greater the probability that having found its expression it has acquired it once and for all. On the other hand, the more concrete and hence richer the idea, and similarly with the medium, the greater the probability of a repetition. If I now arrange all the different classics side by side and, without putting them in any order, am amazed precisely to find that they all rank equally high, then one section may still easily prove to contain more works than another, or if not there is the possibility of its doing so, while such a possibility seems less likely in the case of the other.

This is something I wish to develop in a little more detail. The more abstract the idea, the less the probability. But how does the idea become concrete? By being permeated with the historical. The more concrete the idea the greater the probability. The more abstract the medium the less the probability, the more concrete the greater. But what does it mean to say that the medium is concrete except that it either does or is seen to approximate to language; for language is the most concrete of all media. The idea which manifests itself in sculpture is entirely abstract, it bears no relation to the historical, and the medium in which it manifests itself is similarly abstract; accordingly the probability that the section of classics embracing sculpture will contain only a few works is large. In this I have all the testimony of time and the assent of experience. If, on the other hand, I take a concrete idea and a concrete medium, it proves otherwise. Thus Homer, indeed, is a classic epic poet, but precisely because the idea which comes to light in the epic is a concrete idea, and because the medium is language, the section of classic works embracing the epic can be thought to contain several works all equally classic since history is continually giving us new epic material. In this, too, I have the testimony of history and the assent of experience.

Seeing that my classification is based on this complete contingency, its own contingency can hardly be denied. But if that was what I were to be criticized for, my reply would be that the criticism is misplaced because that is just how it should be. It is a contingent fact that the one section contains, or can contain, a greater number than the other. But because this is a contingency one could clearly just as well place that class highest which does or might have the highest number. I could stick to my previous reasoning at this point and quite evenly reply that this was perfectly correct but that one should only praise my consistency all the more for placing the opposite class highest altogether contingently. However, I shall not do that but appeal on the contrary to something which speaks in my favour, namely that the sections which embrace the concrete ideas are not complete and do not allow of such completion. For that reason it is more natural to place the others first and hold the double-doors constantly open for the latter. But if it were objected that it was an imperfection, a deficiency on the part of that first class, then the objector would be ploughing outside the furrows of my own thought and I cannot heed his speech however profound it may be; for the fixed point is indeed that, seen essentially, everything is equally perfect.

But what is the most abstract idea? Our concern here, of course, is only with an idea that can become the object of an artistic treatment, not with ideas that lend themselves to scientific presentation. Which is the most abstract medium? I shall answer the latter first. The medium farthest removed from language.

Before proceeding to the first question, however, I would call the reader's attention to something that affects the final solution to my problem. It is not always the case that the most abstract medium has as its object the most abstract idea. Thus although the medium used by the architect is the most abstract, the ideas brought to light in architecture are not at all the most abstract. Architecture bears a much closer relation to history than does, for example, sculpture. Yet another choice now presents itself. In our order of ranking I can place in the first class those works whose medium is the most abstract or those whose idea is the most abstract. Here I select the idea, not the medium.

Of course abstract media are the prerogative of sculpture and painting and music as well as architecture. This is not the place to pursue that question. The most abstract idea conceivable is the spirit of sensuality.[7] But in what medium can it be represented? Only in music. It cannot be represented in sculpture, for in itself it is a kind of quality of inwardness. It cannot be painted, for it cannot be grasped in fixed contours; it is an energy, a storm, impatience, passion, and so on, in all their lyrical quality, existing not in a single moment but in a succession of moments, for if it existed in a single moment it could be portrayed or painted. Its existing in a succession of moments indicates its epic character, yet in a stricter sense it is not an epic, for it has not reached the level of words; it moves constantly in an immediacy. Nor can it be represented, therefore, in poetry. The only medium that can represent it is music. For music has an element of time in it yet it does not lapse in time except in an unimportant sense. What it cannot express is the historical in time.

We have the perfect unity of this idea and its corresponding form in Mozart's *Don Giovanni*. But just because the idea is so immensely abstract, so too is the medium abstract, and therefore there is no probability of Mozart's ever having a competitor. Mozart's good fortune was to get hold of a subject that is in itself absolutely musical, and were any other composer to vie with Mozart, all he could do would be to compose *Don Giovanni* over again. Homer found a perfect epic subject, but one can imagine many epic poems because history has more epic material to offer. That is not the case with *Don Giovanni*. What I really mean by this can perhaps best be grasped by pointing to the difference with a related idea. Goethe's *Faust* is a genuine classic, the idea is an historical one, and so every significant historical age will have its *Faust*. *Faust* has language as its medium, and the fact that language is a far more concrete medium is another reason why several works of the same kind can be imagined. *Don Giovanni*, on the other hand, is and will remain the only one of its kind, just as the classic sculptures of Greece. But since the idea in *Don Giovanni* is far more abstract even than that underlying sculpture, one sees easily why we have just one work in music but several in sculpture. One can indeed imagine many more musical classics, yet there still remains just one work of which it can be said that its idea is absolutely musical, so that the music does not enter as an accompaniment but, in bringing the idea to light, reveals its own innermost being. Therefore Mozart with his *Don Giovanni* stands highest among the immortals.

But now I shall abandon this whole inquiry. It is written only for those in love. And just as it takes little to please a child, everyone knows how the most curious things can bring pleasure to people in love. It is like a heated lovers' quarrel over nothing, which neverthe- less has its worth – for the lovers. Although the above remarks have tried in every possible way, conceivable and inconceivable, to secure acknowledgement of Mozart's *Don Giovanni* as first among all classics, virtually no attempt has been made to prove that it is indeed a classic. [. . .] I admit that to do that would be a very appropriate introduction to the real inquiry [. . .] but it could never occur to me to undertake that task, however easily it might come to me. But since I shall all the time be assuming the matter to be beyond question, the sequel will offer many opportunities for, and ways of, shedding light on *Don Giovanni* in this respect, just as what has gone before held several hints.

The task this inquiry has really set itself is to show the significance of the musical erotic, and to that end to indicate in turn the different stages which, all sharing the property of being immediately erotic, agree also in all being essentially musical. What I have to say on this score I owe to Mozart alone. So should anyone be civil enough to concede that I am right in what I say, but have some doubts as to how far what I say relates to Mozart's music or to what I read into it, I can assure him that he will find in the music not only the little that I contrive to present here but infinitely more; indeed, I can assure him that this is precisely the thought that makes me so bold as to hazard an explanation of particular features of Mozart's music. What someone has loved with the infatuation and admired with the enthusiasm of youth, what someone has kept up a clandestine and enigmatic commerce with in his innermost soul, what someone has hidden away in his heart, that is something the like of which one always approaches with a certain shyness, with mixed feelings, when one knows that the intention is to try to understand it. What you have learned to know bit by bit, like a bird gathering every little straw, happier over each small piece than over all the rest of the world; what the loving ear has absorbed, solitary in the great multitude, unremarked in its secret place of hiding; what the greedy ear has snatched up, never gratified, the miserly ear hidden, never secure, that whose softest echo has never deceived the searching ear's sleepless vigil; what you have lived by day, relived by night, what has banished sleep and made it troubled; what you have dreamt of in sleep, what you have woken up to dream of again when awake, what caused you to leap up in the middle of the night for fear of forgetting it; what has come to you in your moments of greatest rapture; what like a woman's embroidery you keep constantly beside you; what has followed you on the clear moonlit nights, in lonely forests by the shores, in the gloomy streets, in the dead of night, at break of day, what has ridden with you on horseback, accompanied you in the carriage, what permeates your home, what your chamber has been witness to, what has echoed in your ear, resounded through your soul, what your soul has spun into its finest web – that now reveals itself to thought. As those mysterious beings in ancient tales rise from the ocean bed invested in seaweed, so it now rises up from the sea of remembrance interwoven with memories. The soul becomes sad and the heart soft, for it is as though one bade it farewell, were parting from it never to meet again, either in time or eternity. One feels as though unfaithful, that one has broken one's covenant, one feels one is no longer the same, not as young, not as childlike; one fears for oneself in case one loses what has made one glad and happy and rich; one fears for what one loves lest it suffer with this change, perhaps prove less perfect, that possibly it will be at a loss for answers to the many questions; and then, alas! all is lost, the spell is gone, and never more can it be evoked. As regards Mozart's music, my soul knows no fear, my confidence no bounds. In part this is because what I have understood so far is so very little and there will always be enough left over hiding in the shadows of presentiment; partly because I am convinced that if Mozart ever became wholly comprehensible to me, he would for the first time become wholly incomprehensible to me.

To maintain that Christianity has brought sensuality into the world seems boldly venturesome. But nothing ventured, nothing gained, as the saying is, and that goes here too, as will be apparent when one considers that in positing something one indirectly posits the other thing which one excludes. Since sensuality in general is what is negated, it first comes into view, is first posited, through the act that excludes it by positing the opposite, positive principle. As a principle, a power, a system in itself, sensuality was first posited with Christianity, and to that extent Christianity has introduced sensuality to the world. However, if one wishes properly to understand the proposition that Christianity has introduced sensuality to the world, it must be understood identically with its opposite, that it is Christianity that has chased sensuality out, kept it out of the world. As a principle, a power, a system in itself, sensuality was first posited with Christianity. I could add a further qualification which perhaps makes my meaning most clear: it was Christianity that first posited sensuality under the category of spirit. That is quite natural, for Christianity is spirit, and spirit the positive principle it has introduced to the world. But when sensuality is considered under the category of spirit, one sees that its significance is that it is to be excluded; but it is precisely by the fact that it is to be excluded that it is defined as a principle, as a power; for what spirit, itself a principle, is to exclude must be something appearing in the form of a principle even though it only appears as a principle the moment it is excluded. That sensuality has existed before Christianity would naturally be a very foolish objection, for it is self-evident that what is to be excluded always pre-exists what excludes it, even if in another sense it first comes into existence through its exclusion. This is due, again, to its coming into existence in another sense, and that is why I said at the start: nothing ventured, nothing gained.

Sensuality has indeed existed previously, but not defined spiritually. In what manner then has it existed? It has existed under the category of soul. That is how it existed in paganism and if one is looking for the most perfect expression of it, that is how it existed in Greece. But under the category of soul, sensuality is not opposition, exclusion, but harmony and accord. Precisely because sensuality is posited under the category of harmony, however, it is not posited as a principle but as an assonant enclitic.[8]

The importance of this consideration is to cast light on the different forms assumed by the erotic in the different steps in the development of the world-consciousness, and so to lead us towards a definition of the immediate erotic as identical with the musical erotic. In the Greek consciousness, sensuality was under control in the beautiful individual, or more properly, it was not under control for it was not indeed an enemy that had to be subdued, a dangerous rebel to be kept in check; it was given freedom of life and joy in the beautiful individual. Sensuality, consequently, was not posited as a principle; the quality of soul that constituted the beautiful individual was inconceivable without the sensual; for that reason neither was sensually based eroticism posited as a principle. Sensual love was everywhere as an element, and present elementally in the beautiful individual. The gods knew its power no less than men; the gods no less than men knew their happy and unhappy love affairs. In none of them, however, is love present as a principle; in so far as it existed in them, in the individual, it was present as an element of love's universal power, which however was present nowhere, and therefore not even for the Greek conception or in the Greek consciousness. It might be objected that Eros was, after all, the god of love; so it must be possible to imagine love present as a principle at least in him. But apart from the fact that here again love does not depend on the erotic, in the sense of deriving from the sensual alone, but on qualities of the soul, there is another factor to note which I shall now go into more closely.

Eros was the god of love but was not in love himself. In so far as the other gods and men sensed the power of love in themselves, they attributed this to Eros, referred it to him, but Eros was not himself in love; and the fact that it did happen to him once[9] must be considered an exception; in spite of being the god of love, he lagged far behind the other gods in the number of his adventures, and far behind men. Indeed, that he did fall in love amounts to saying that he too yielded to the universal power of love, which became in a way a power outside him, and which, being turned away from him, had no place of its own where one could seek it. And his love is not based on sensuality but on qualities of soul. It is a genuinely Greek thought that the god of love is not himself in love while all others owe it to him that they are. Were I to imagine a god or a goddess of longing, it would be genuinely Greek to suppose that while all who felt the sweet unrest or pain of longing referred it to this being, this being itself had no feeling of longing. I know no better way of describing the remarkable nature of this relation than by saying that it is the converse of representation. In the relation of representation all the energy is gathered in a single individual and the particular individuals share in him to the extent that they share in his particular movements. I might also say, this relation is the converse of that upon which the Incarnation is based. In the Incarnation the individual has the whole of life's fullness within him and the other individuals only have access to this from beholding it in the incarnated individual. In the Greek relationship, the opposite is the case. What makes for the power of the god is not in the god but in all the other individuals who refer it to him; it is as though he himself were powerless, impotent, because he communicates his energy to all the rest of the world. The incarnated individual as it were sucks in the energy from all the others and the fullness is then in him and only for the others to the extent that they behold it in that individual. This will have consequences for what follows, just as it is important in itself with regard to the categories which the world-consciousness uses in different epochs. Sensuality as a principle is not to be found in the Greek consciousness, nor do we find the erotic as a principle based on the principle of the sensual; and even if we had found that, we still see – and this is of the greatest importance for this inquiry – that the Greek consciousness lacks the strength to concentrate the whole in a single individual but lets the whole radiate to all the others from a point which lacks it, so that really this constitutive point is to be identified by its being the only point which lacks what it gives to all others.

Sensuality as a principle, then, is posited with Christianity, and similarly the sensual erotic as a principle. The idea of representation was introduced to the world by Christianity. If I imagine the sensual erotic as a principle, as a power, as a realm characterized by spirit, that is to say characterized by being excluded by spirit, if I imagine it concentrated in a single individual, then I have the concept of the spirit of the sensual erotic. This is an idea which the Greeks did not have, which Christianity first introduced to the world, if only in an indirect sense.

If this spirit of the sensual erotic in all its immediacy demands expression, the question is: what medium lends itself to that? What must be especially borne in mind here is that it demands expression and representation in its immediacy. In its mediate state and its reflection in something else it comes under language and becomes subject to ethical categories. In its immediacy it can only be expressed in music. On this score I must ask the reader to recall what was said about this in the platitudinous introduction. This is where the significance of music is revealed in its full validity, and in a stricter sense it also reveals itself as a Christian art, or rather as the art which Christianity posits by shutting it out, as the medium for what Christianity shuts out and thereby posits. In other words, music is the demonic.[10] In the erotic sensual genius, music has its absolute object. This of course by no means implies that music cannot express other things, but this is nevertheless its proper object. Similarly, the art of sculpture can represent much more than human beauty, and yet this is its absolute object; painting can represent much more than celestially transfigured beauty, and still this is its absolute object. The important thing in this respect is to be able to see the concept in each art, and not let oneself be put off by what it can do besides. Man's concept is spirit and we must not allow ourselves to be put off by the fact that he is also able to walk on two legs. Language's concept is thought, and we must not let ourselves be put off by the view of certain sensitive people that its greatest significance is to produce inarticulate sounds.

Here I beg to be allowed a little platitudinous interlude; *praeterea censeo*,[11] that Mozart is the greatest among classical composers, and that his *Don Giovanni* deserves the highest place among all classic works of art.

Now regarding the nature of music as a medium, this will naturally always be a very interesting problem. Whether I am able to say anything adequate on the matter is another question. I am well aware that I have no understanding of music. I freely admit that I am a layman. I do not hide the fact that I am not one of those select people who possess musical expertise, that I am at most a proselyte of the gate,[12] whom a strangely irresistible impulse carried from afar to this point but no further. And yet it could be that the little I have to say contained some particular remark which, if it met with favour and indulgence, might be found to contain some truth even if it concealed itself under a shabby coat. I stand outside music and from this standpoint I observe it. That this standpoint is very imperfect I freely admit; that I am able to see very little in comparison with those fortunate people who stand inside I do not deny; but I still continue to hope that from my standpoint I too may be able to impart some odd piece of enlightenment on the subject, although the initiated could do it much better – yes, to some extent even understand what I say better than I do myself. If I were to imagine two countries bordering on each other, with one of which I was fairly familiar and with the other was quite unfamiliar, and I was not allowed to enter that unknown realm however much I wanted to, I should still be able to form some conception of it. I would travel to the boundaries of the kingdom I knew and follow them constantly, and as I did so my movements would describe the contours of that unknown land; in this way I would form a general idea of it even though I had never set foot in it. And if this was a task that greatly occupied me, and if I was indefatigable in my accuracy, it would no doubt sometimes happen that, as I stood sadly at my own country's boundary and looked longingly into that unknown land which was so near me and yet so far, some little revelation might fall to my lot. And although I feel that music is an art which requires experience to a high degree to justify one's having an opinion about it, still I comfort myself again, as so often, with the paradox that there is experience to be gained in presentiment and in ignorance. I comfort myself by remembering that Diana, who had not herself given birth, nevertheless came to the assistance of the childbearing woman; indeed that she had this as a native gift from childhood so that she came to Latona's assistance in her labour when she herself was born.

The country known to me, to whose furthest boundaries I intend to go in order to discover music, is language. If one wants to arrange the different media according to a definite order of development, one must place music and language next to each other; for which reason it has also been said that music is a language, which is more than just a brilliant remark. If one liked indulging in brilliance one could say that sculpture and painting, too, are a kind of language, in so far as every way of expressing an idea is always a language, since language is the essence of the idea. Brilliant people talk, therefore, of the language of nature, and maudlin clergymen now and then open up the book of nature for us to read something which neither they nor their hearers understand. If the remark that music is a language was in no better shape than this, I should not question it but let it pass and count for what it is. But that is not how it is. It is only when spirit is posited that language comes into its rights; but when spirit is posited, everything that is not spirit is excluded. But this exclusion is a qualification of spirit, and to the degree, then, that what is excluded is to assert itself it needs a spiritually qualified medium, and this is music. But a medium which is spiritually determined is essentially language; then since music is spiritually determined, it has justly been called a language.

As a medium, language is the one absolutely spiritually qualified

medium; it is therefore the proper medium for the idea. To elaborate
this point in more detail goes beyond both my competence and the
scope of this little inquiry. Just one remark, however, which again
brings me back to music. In language the sensual is, as medium,
reduced to the level of mere instrument and constantly negated.
Such is not the case with the other media. Neither in sculpture nor
in painting is the sensual a mere instrument but an integral part, nor
is it constantly negated, for it must continually be part of what is
seen. It would be a peculiarly perverted way of looking at a statue
or a painting to ignore the sensual aspect, thus completely rescinding
its beauty. In sculpture, architecture, painting, the idea is bound up
with the medium; but this fact that the idea neither reduces the
medium to the level of mere instrument, nor constantly negates it,
is as it were an expression of the fact that that medium cannot
speak. So too with nature. Therefore we rightly say that nature is
dumb, and architecture and sculpture and painting; we say it rightly
in spite of all those fine-tuned, sensitive ears that can hear them
speak. It is therefore idiocy to say that nature is a language, as it is
inept to say that the mute is vocal, since it is not even a language in
the sense in which sign-language is. But with language it is different.
The sensual is reduced to mere instrument and thus rescinded. If
when a man spoke one heard the movements of his tongue, etc., he
would speak badly; if when he heard, he heard the air vibrations
instead of the words, he would hear badly; if when reading a book
one constantly saw the individual letters, one would read badly.
Language becomes the perfect medium just at the moment when
everything sensual is negated in it. So also with music; what should
really be heard constantly emancipates itself from the sensual. That
music, as a medium, does not stand as high as language has already
been pointed out, and that is also why I said that only in a certain
sense was music a language.

Language makes its appeal to the ear. No other medium does
that. The ear is the most spiritually determined of the senses. This I
believe most people will admit. Should anyone wish further information on this point, I refer him to the preface of *Karikaturen des
Heiligsten* by Steffens.[13] Beside language, music is the only medium
that addresses the ear. In this we have yet another analogy and
testimony to the way in which music is a language. There is much

in nature which addresses itself to the ear but what affects the ear is the purely sensual, and therefore nature is dumb. And it is a ridiculous fancy that one hears something because one hears a cow moo or, what has perhaps a larger claim in this respect, a nightingale sing; it is mere imagination to think that one hears something, mere imagination that the one is worth more than the other, for it's all six of one and half a dozen of the other.

Language has time as its element; all other media have space as their element. Only music also takes place in time, but the fact that it takes place in time is again a negation of the sensual. With products of the other arts, their sensual character indicates precisely that they have their existence in space. Now, of course, again there is much in nature that takes place in time. Thus when a brook murmurs and continues to murmur it seems to have the character of time. However, that is not so, and were one to insist that there was this character of time, one would have to say that although it was there, it was present in a spatialized way. Music exists only in the moment of its performance, for however skilful one may be at reading notes and however lively one's imagination, it cannot be denied that it is only in an unreal sense that the music exists when read. It exists really only when it is performed. This might seem to be an imperfection in this art as compared with the others, whose works constantly endure because they have their existence in the sensual. Yet that is not so. Rather it is a proof that music is a higher, a more spiritual art.

If I begin with language, in order, by moving through it, to as it were hear my way towards music, the matter appears to be roughly as follows. If I assume that prose is the language-form farthest removed from music, then I detect already in the oratorical style of delivery, in the sonorous structure of periods, a suggestion of the musical which comes more and more strongly to the fore through different levels in the poetic style, in the structure of the verse, in the rhyme, until at last the musical has developed so strongly that language ceases and everything becomes music. This latter is indeed a favourite expression of the poets, who use it to indicate that in a way they disown the idea, the idea drops out of their view, everything ends in music. This might seem to indicate that music is an even more perfect medium than language. However, that is one of

those mawkish misunderstandings which originate only in empty
heads. That it is a misunderstanding will be shown later; here I
would only draw attention to the remarkable circumstance that by
moving through language in the opposite direction I again come up
against music; that is, when I proceed downward from concept-
permeated prose until I land in interjections which again are musical,
just as the child's first babbling is musical. Here, however, it could
hardly be said that music is a more perfect medium than language,
or that music is a richer medium than language, unless one takes
saying 'ugh!' to be worth more than a whole thought. But what
follows from this – that wherever language comes to an end, I run
into the musical? Surely, it is the most perfect expression of the idea
that music always sets limits to language. One sees in addition how
this is connected with the misunderstanding that music is a richer
medium than language. In saying that when language stops, music
begins, and in saying, as people do, that everything is musical, we
are not going onwards but back. That is why I have never had any
sympathy – and here perhaps even the experts will agree with me –
for that purified music which thinks it can do without words. For as
a rule it thinks of itself as being above the word, in spite of being its
inferior. Now one might object as follows: 'If it is true that language
is a richer medium than music, it is incomprehensible why it should
be so hard to give an aesthetic account of the musical, incomprehensible that language should always prove in this connection
a poorer medium than music.' However, it is neither incomprehensible nor beyond explanation. For music always expresses
the immediate in its immediacy. That is also why in relation to
language music comes first and last; but from this one also sees it is a
misunderstanding to say that music is a more perfect medium. In
language there is reflection and therefore language cannot express
the immediate. Reflection kills the immediate and that is why it is
impossible to express the musical in language; but this apparent
poverty of language is precisely its wealth. For the immediate is the
indeterminable and so language cannot apprehend it, but the fact
that it is indeterminable is not its perfection but a defect. This is
indirectly acknowledged in many ways. Thus to cite but one example, we say: 'I can't really explain why I do this or that, in this
way or that; I do it by ear.' In connection with things bearing no

relation to music we frequently use a word taken from music, but what we indicate by its use is the obscure, the unaccountable, the immediate.

Now if the immediate, qualified spiritually, is what is properly expressed in music, one may ask again, more explicitly, what species of the immediate is essentially music's object. The immediate, qualified spiritually, can be specified as falling either within the sphere of the spiritual or outside it. When the immediate, qualified spiritually, is specified as falling within the sphere of the spiritual, it can well find its expression in the musical, but this immediacy cannot be music's absolute object, for so specifying it as to include it within the spiritual suggests that music is in a sphere foreign to it; it forms a constantly cancelled prelude. But if the immediate, qualified spiritually, is so specified as to fall outside the spiritual, we have then music's absolute object. For the former species of the immediate it is not essential that it be expressed in music but essential for it to become spirit, and accordingly to be expressed in language. For the latter it is, on the contrary, essential that it be expressed in music, it cannot be expressed other than in music, it cannot be expressed in language, since spiritually it is so specified as to fall outside the spiritual and accordingly outside language. But the immediacy thus excluded by the spirit is sensual immediacy. This belongs to Christianity. In music it has its absolute medium, and from this can also be explained the fact that music was not properly developed in antiquity but belongs to the Christian era. Music is, then, the medium for that species of the immediate which, qualified spiritually, is specified as lying outside spirit. Naturally, music can express much else, but this is its absolute object. It is also easy to see that music is a more sensual medium than language, much more stress being placed here on the sensual sound than in language.

Sensual genius is thus music's absolute object. Sensual genius is absolutely lyrical, and in music it breaks out in all its lyrical impatience, for it is qualified spiritually and is therefore power, life, movement, constant unrest, continual succession. But this unrest, this succession, does not enrich it; its spirit remains always the same, it does not develop but rages on uninterrupted as if in a single breath. Were I to characterize this lyrical quality with a single predicate, I might say: 'It sounds.' And that takes me back once more to the spirit of sensuality as what manifests itself immediately in music.

I realize that even I could say considerably more on this point. I acknowledge that it would be an easy matter for the experts to make a much better job of clarifying it. But since no one, as far as I know, has made the attempt or even a show of doing so, since they all continue to repeat that Mozart's *Don Giovanni* is the crown of all operas but without elaborating on what they mean by that, although they all say it in a way that clearly shows they mean to say more than just that *Don Giovanni* is the best opera, that there is a qualitative difference between it and all other operas which is nevertheless not to be found in the absolute relation between idea, form, subject-matter and medium; since, I say, that is so, then I have broken the silence. Maybe I have been a little too hasty, maybe I would have succeeded in saying it better had I waited yet a while; I do not know. But what I do know is that I have not hurried in order to have the pleasure of speaking, not hurried because I was afraid in case someone more expert might steal a march on me, but because I feared that if I too kept silent, the stones would take to speaking in Mozart's honour, to the shame of every human being to whom it was given to speak.

What has been said so far I assume is just about enough for this little inquiry, since its main purpose here is to serve to clear the way for the characterization of the immediate erotic stages as we get to know them in Mozart. Before going on to that, however, I would cite a further fact which lets us see the absolute relation between the spirit of sensuality and the musical from another angle. Music, as we know, has always been subject to suspicion on the part of religious zealots. Whether they are right or not does not concern us here since that has only a religious interest. On the other hand, it is not unimportant to consider what has brought this about. If I follow the course of religious zealotry in this regard, I can characterize it quite generally in the following way: the stronger the religiosity, the more one renounces music and stresses the word. The different stages in this respect are represented in world history. The final stage excludes music entirely and abides by the word alone. I could deck out this statement with a multitude of particular observations. I will not do that but simply cite a few words from a Presbyterian in one of Achim von Arnim's stories: 'We Presbyterians regard the organ as the devil's bagpipes which lull serious reflection to sleep, just as dance benumbs good intentions.'[14] This must be considered an exemplary remark. But what reason can one have for excluding music and giving absolute sway to the word? All intelligent sects will admit that, when misused, the word can confuse the emotions just as much as music. So there must be some difference in kind. But what religious zeal wants to give expression to is spirit; so it requires language, which is spirit's proper medium, and rejects music, which, for it, is a sensual medium and so far always an imperfect medium for the expression of spirit. Whether religious zeal is right in excluding music is, as I said, another question; its view of the relation of music to language, on the other hand, may be perfectly correct. Music, therefore, need not be excluded, but we have to realize that in the spiritual realm it is an imperfect medium, and that therefore, specified as spirit, music cannot have its absolute object in the immediately spiritual. From this it by no means follows that one must look upon it as the work of the devil, even if our age provides much fearful evidence of the demonic power with which music can seize hold of an individual, and of how this individual can in turn arouse and captivate the masses, particularly women, in the seductive snares of dread with all the titillation of voluptuous delight. It by no means follows from this that one must regard it as the work of the devil, even if one notes with a secret horror how terribly this art, above all others, often lacerates its votaries, a phenomenon which oddly enough seems to have escaped the attention of psychologists and the multitude, except when they are startled now and then by a despairing individual's shriek of terror. However, one cannot fail to notice that in the folk legends, and thus in the popular consciousness these express, the musical is again the demonic. As an example I can mention the *Irish March of the Elves*.[15]

As for the immediate erotic stages, I owe anything at all I have to say on this subject to Mozart alone, to whom I owe everything. Since, however, the comparisons I shall try to make here are based on combinations other than his and so can only indirectly be ascribed to him, before going to work I have put myself and the comparisons to the test to find out if I might in any way disturb the pleasure I and my reader derive from admiring Mozart's immortal works. Anyone who wants to see Mozart in his true immortal greatness must turn his gaze upon *Don Giovanni*. Compared with that everything else is accidental, unessential. But then if we look at *Don Giovanni* in such a way as to see particular things from Mozart's other operas from the same point of view, I am convinced that we shall neither belittle him nor do any harm to ourselves or our neighbour. We shall then have the chance to rejoice in the fact that music's real potential is exhausted in the music of Mozart.

I should add that in using the word 'stages' in the above, and in continuing to use it in what follows, the idea must not be taken in such a literal way as to imply that each stage exists independently, the one outside the other. I might perhaps more pertinently use the word 'metamorphoses'. The different stages taken together constitute the immediate stage, and this shows that the individual stages are more like disclosures of predicates, so that all the predicates tumble down into the wealth of the last stage, since this is the real stage. The other stages have no independent existence; in themselves they exist only in concept, and from this one may see their contingent character as against the last stage. Since, however, they have found separate expression in Mozart's music, I shall discuss them separately. Above all, however, one must avoid thinking of them as different levels of consciousness, since even the last stage has not yet arrived at consciousness. I am all the time concerned only with the immediate in its sheer immediacy.

Of course, the difficulties always encountered when one considers music aesthetically are not to be avoided here either. The difficulty in the foregoing lay chiefly in the fact that while I wanted to prove through a process of thought that sensual genius is the proper object of music, really this can only be proved with music, just as it is only through music itself that I myself have come to an appreciation of music. The difficulty the following must contend with is really that since what the music under discussion expresses is essentially music's proper object, this music expresses it far more perfectly than does language, which makes a very poor showing in comparison. Of course, if I had been concerned with different levels of consciousness, the advantage would be on my side and that of language, but that is not the case here. So what remains to be explained can only have meaning for the person who has listened and who continues constantly to listen. For him it may perhaps contain a suggestion or two that may move him to listen once more.

First Stage

The first stage is suggested by the Page in *Figaro*. Of course we should not see in the Page a particular individual, as we are so easily tempted to when in imagination or reality we see him represented by a person. For then it would be difficult to avoid – as is also partly true of the Page in the play – the intrusion of something accidental, something not relevant to the idea, his becoming more than he should be; for in a sense that is what he does as soon as he becomes an individual. But in becoming more he becomes less, he ceases to be the idea. For that reason no spoken lines can be given to him, music is the only adequate expression, and one notes accordingly that *Figaro* as well as *Don Giovanni*, as they have come from Mozart's hand, belong to opera seria.[16] But if we look on the Page as a mythical figure we shall find what is characteristic of the first stage expressed in the music.

The sensual awakens, though not to movement but to motionless rest, not to joy and gladness but to deep melancholy. Desire is not yet awake, it is moodily hinted at. In desire there is always the desired, which rises out of it and comes to view in a bewildering twilight. So it is for the sensual: shadows and mists take the object away, yet its reflections in these bring it nearer. Desire possesses what will become its object but does so without having desired it, and in that way does not possess it. That is the painful, but in its sweetness, also captivating and fascinating contradiction which re-sounds with its sadness, its melancholy, through this stage. For the pain of it lies not in there being too little but too much. The desire is a quiet desire, the longing a quiet longing, the infatuation a quiet infatuation, in which the object dawns and is so close to it as to be in it. Desire's object hovers over the desire, sinks down into it, yet without this movement occurring through desire's own power of attraction, or because it is desired. The object of desire does not fade away; it does not extricate itself from desire's embrace, for that would mean that desire was awake; it is desired without being present to desire, which therefore becomes melancholy precisely because it cannot reach the point of desiring. As soon as desire awakens, or rather in and with its awakening, desire and its object are separated; now desire breathes freely and soundly where previously it could not live and breathe for the desired. When desire is not awake, the object of desire enchants and entices, yes, almost frightens it. Desire must have air, it must break out. That happens with their separation; the object of desire flees blushingly, bashful as a woman, a separation occurs between them, the desired object disappears *et apparet sublimis*,[17] or in any case outside the desire. If one paints the ceiling of a room so that it is entirely covered with figures, such a ceiling presses down on us, as the painter says. If, lightly and quickly, one puts just a single figure on it, this ceiling seems higher. Such is the relation between desire and the desired at a first and at a later stage.

Accordingly the desire, which at this stage is only there in a presentiment of itself, is motionless, without disturbance, rocked gently only by an inexplicable inner motion. As the life of the plant is confined to the earth, so is desire lost in the present in a quiet longing, engrossed in contemplation, and yet it cannot evacuate its object, essentially because in a deeper sense no object exists; nor, however, is its object this lack of an object, for then it would straightaway be in motion; it would be specified if in no other way then in sorrow and pain, but sorrow and pain do not have in them that contradiction which is characteristic of melancholy and depression, do not have that ambiguity which is the sweetness of melancholy. Although desire is at this stage not specified as such, although this presentiment of desire, as far as its object goes, is entirely undetermined, still it has one specification, that is, it is infinitely deep. Like Thor, it sucks through a horn whose other end is the ocean,[18] yet the reason why it cannot suck its object up into itself is not that the latter is infinite, but that this infinitude cannot be an object for it. Its sucking therefore does not indicate a relation to the object but is identical with its sigh, and this is infinitely deep.

In harmony with the description given here of the first stage, we will find it very significant that, musically, the part of the Page is pitched to suit a woman's voice. What is contradictory with the stage is as though intimated by this contradiction; the desire is so indeterminate, the object so little separated, that the desired rests androgynously in the desire, just as in plant-life the male and female occupy one blossom. Desire and the object desired are joined in this unity; they are both neuter in gender.

Although the line does not belong to the mythical Page but to the Page in the piece, the poetic figure Cherubino, and although for this reason we cannot consider it in this connection, since for one thing it is not Mozart's and for another it expresses something quite different from what we are talking about here, I would nevertheless highlight one particular line because it allows me to describe this stage in analogy to a later one. Susanna mocks Cherubino because he is also in love, in a way, with Marcellina, and the only answer the Page has to offer is, 'She is a woman'. Regarding the Page in the play, it is essential that he should fall in love with the Countess, unessential that he should fall in love with Marcellina, that being only an indirect and paradoxical expression for the intensity of the passion binding him to the Countess. Regarding the mythical Page, it is equally essential that he should be in love with Marcellina as with the Countess; his object is womanliness, and the Countess and Marcellina have this in common. So when we later hear of Don Giovanni:

> Even coquettes three-score years old
> With joy he adds them to the roll,[19]

we have the perfect analogy to this, except that the intensity and definiteness of the desire are far more developed.

If I were to try to specify in a single predicate the special quality of Mozart's music with regard to the Page in *Figaro*, I would say 'drunk with love'. But like all intoxication, being drunk with love can work in two ways, either making the joy of life increasingly transparent or compressing it into an opaque dejection. The latter is the case with the music here, and rightly so. Music cannot give the reason, that is beyond its power. Words are unable to express the mood itself, it is too heavy, too ponderous, for words to carry; only music can express it. The reason for its melancholy lies in the profound inner contradiction that we have tried to call attention to in the foregoing.

We now leave the first stage, represented by the mythical Page; we let him go on dejectedly dreaming of what he has, continue in his melancholy yearning for what he possesses. He never gets any further, he never gets going, for his movements are illusory and hence he makes none. It is another matter with the Page in the play.

We would like to have a truly and genuinely friendly interest in his future; we congratulate him on having become a captain, we let him kiss Susanna once more in farewell, we shall not let on about the mark on his forehead, which none can see who aren't in the know,[20] but no more than this, my good Cherubino, or we shall call the Count, and he will shout, 'Be off with you, out with you, to your regiment! He's no child, as no one knows better than myself!'

Second Stage

This stage is represented by Papageno in *The Magic Flute*. Here, too, of course we must separate the essential from the accidental, evoke the mythical Papageno and forget the actual person in the play, particularly because this figure has become involved in all sorts of dubious gibberish. In this respect it might be not without interest to go through the whole opera in order to show that, as far as opera is concerned, its subject-matter is deeply flawed. One would then also gain an opportunity to illuminate the erotic from a new angle, through noticing how the attempt to invest it with a deeper ethical view, which allows it to try its hand at all sorts of weighty dialectical ordeals, is a venture that has gone quite beyond the boundaries of music, so that even for a Mozart it has been impossible to lend it any deeper interest. This opera's definitive direction is to be found in that which is not musical about it, and so, in spite of some individually perfect concert numbers and affecting utterances, it is by no means a classic opera. But none of this can occupy us in the present little inquiry. We are concerned only with Papageno; which, however, is a great advantage if for no other reason than that it excuses us from every attempt to explain the meaning of Papageno's relationship to Tamino, a relationship which the plot makes out to be so profound and thoughtful that it becomes well-nigh unthinkable for sheer thoughtfulness.

This treatment of *The Magic Flute* may seem arbitrary to some readers, because it sees both too much in Papageno and too little in the rest of the opera; they may not approve of our procedure. The reason is their disagreement with us on the point of departure for any consideration of Mozart's music. That, in our view, is of course

Don Giovanni, and it is also our conviction that it is by seeing several things from the other operas in relation to it that one shows most piety towards Mozart, although I would not thereby deny the importance of making each individual opera an object of special consideration.

Desire awakens, and as one always first realizes one has been dreaming at the moment of waking, so here too the dream is over. This arousal in which desire awakens, this tremor, separates desire and its object, gives the desire an object. This is a dialectical feature which must be kept sharply in mind; only when the object exists does the desire exist; desire and its object are twins neither of which enters the world a fraction of an instant before the other. Yet though they enter it at exactly the same moment, and not even with the time interval that can separate other twins, the importance of their coming into existence in this way is not that they are united but, on the contrary, that they are separated. But this, the sensual movement, this earthquake, for a moment splits the desire and its object infinitely asunder; but as the principle of motion appears for a moment to separate, so it reveals itself again as wishing to unite the separated elements. The consequence of the separation is that desire is plucked out of its substantial repose within itself, and the object as a result no longer comes under the category of substance, but splits up into a multiplicity.

As the life of the plant is bound to earth, so is the first stage confined in substantial longing. Desire awakens. The object takes flight, revealing its multiplicity, the longing breaks loose from the soil and goes out a-wandering; the flower gets wings and flutters erratically and tirelessly hither and thither. Desire is directed towards the object, at the same time stirring within itself, the heart beats soundly and happily, the objects swiftly vanish and appear, yet before every disappearance is a present enjoyment, a moment of contact, short but blessed, incandescent like a glow-worm, fickle and fleeting like the touch of a butterfly, and as harmless; countless kisses, but so swiftly savoured that it is as if only all that was taken from one object was what was given to the next. Only momentarily is a deeper desire hinted at, but this hint is forgotten. In Papageno desire aims at discoveries. This delight in discovery is what pulsates in it, is its animation. It does not find the real object of this search, but it discovers the multiplicity through searching within it for the object it seeks to discover. Desire is thus awake but not yet specified as desire. If we remember that desire is present in all three stages, we can say that in the first stage it is specified as *dreaming*, in the second as *seeking*, in the third as *desiring*. The seeking desire is not yet desiring; what it seeks is only what it can desire but it does not desire it. So perhaps the most apposite description is, 'It discovers'. If we compare Papageno with Don Giovanni in this respect, the latter's journey through the world is something more than a voyage of discovery; he savours not just the adventure of travelling to discover, he is a knight who goes out to conquer (*veni, vidi, vici*).[21] Discovery and conquest are here identical; indeed in a sense one can say that he forgets the discovery in the conquest, or that the discovery lies behind him, and he therefore leaves it to his servant and secretary Leporello, who keeps a list in a quite different sense from that in which I might imagine Papageno keeping accounts. Papageno picks out, Don Giovanni enjoys, Leporello checks.

I can indeed represent in thought the special character of this, as of every stage, but only in the instant it has ceased to exist. But even if I could describe its peculiarity perfectly and explain the reason for it, there would still always be something left over which I cannot say and yet wants to be heard. It is too immediate to be grasped in words. So, too, with Papageno, it is the same song, the same melody; he sets off again from the beginning as soon as he has finished, and so on continually. It might be objected that it is impossible in any case to express anything immediate. And in a sense that is quite true, but in the first place it is in language that the immediacy of the spirit has its immediate expression, and second, in so far as the intervention of thought brings any change here, being spirit's qualification it nevertheless stays essentially the same. Here, however, it is an immediacy of the sensual, which as such has quite another medium, where consequently the disproportion between the media makes the impossibility absolute.

If I were now to try to indicate in a single phrase the special character of Mozart's music in the part of the work that interests us, I would say that it is merrily chirping, vigorous, sparkling with love. What I would stress in particular are the first aria and the chime of bells. The duet with Pamina, and later with Papagena, fall entirely outside the category of immediate musicality. But if one considers the first aria, one will surely approve of the predicates I have used and, if one pays closer attention to it, find also an opportunity to see what significance the musical element has, how it presents itself as the absolute expression of the idea, and how the latter is accordingly an immediately musical idea. As you know, Papageno accompanies his light-hearted cheerfulness on the flute. Every ear has certainly felt strangely moved by this accompaniment. But the more one considers it, and the more one sees the mythical Papageno in Papageno, the more expressive and characteristic one will find it; one doesn't tire of hearing it again and again, because it is an absolutely adequate expression of Papageno's whole life; Papageno, whose life is an incessant twittering of this kind, who, constantly carefree, chirps on in all idleness, and who is happy and pleased because this is the content of his life, happy in his work and happy in his song. As you know, things are arranged so very profoundly in the opera that the flutes of Tamino and Papageno correspond with each other. Yet what a difference! Tamino's flute, from which the opera nevertheless takes its name, entirely fails of its effect. And why? Because Tamino is simply not a musical figure. This is part of the misconceived plot of the opera as a whole. Tamino becomes exceedingly tiresome and sentimental on his flute; and when one considers the rest of his development, his state of consciousness, one cannot help but think, every time he takes up his flute and plays a piece on it, of the farmer in Horace (*rusticus exspectat, dum defluat amnis*),[22] except that Horace hasn't given his farmer a flute for an unprofitable pastime. As a dramatic figure, Tamino is entirely beyond the musical, just as the spiritual development which the plot aims at realizing is in any case a totally unmusical idea. Tamino, indeed, has reached the point where the musical ceases, so his flute-playing is only a time-waster to drive away thought. For banishing thoughts is something music is supremely capable of, even evil thoughts, as indeed we say of David that his playing exorcised Saul's evil spirit.[23] On the other hand, a big deception lies implicit in this idea, for it does that only in so far as it carries consciousness back into immediacy and lulls it therein. The individual may therefore indeed feel happy in the moment of intoxication, but he only becomes the more unhappy. Quite parenthetically I permit myself an observation here. We have used music to heal the mentally disordered; in a sense we have also achieved our purpose, and yet it is an illusion. For when madness has a mental cause, it is always the result of the hardening of one or another point in consciousness. This hardening must be overcome, but for it truly to be overcome, one must go in quite the opposite direction from music. To employ music is to go altogether the wrong way and make the patient still more insane, even if he seems no longer to be so.

I can just as well let what I have said here about Tamino's flute-playing stand, without fear of seeing it misunderstood. I don't mean to deny what has several times been conceded, that music can have its significance as an accompaniment, entering as it does, in that case, an alien sphere – that of language. The fault in *The Magic Flute*, however, is that the whole work is biased towards consciousness, and its tendency is therefore to do away with music while still remaining an opera; and not even this thought is made clear in the piece. The goal of its plot is ethically qualified love, or married love, and that is where the basic fault of the play lies. For let marriage be, ecclesiastically or secularly, what it will; one thing it is not, it is not musical; indeed it is absolutely unmusical.

So, musically, the first aria has its great significance through being the immediate-musical expression of Papageno's whole life, and any history that finds its absolutely adequate expression in music is history only in a figurative sense. The chime of bells, on the other hand, is the musical expression of his activity, of which again one can only form an idea through music; it is enchanting, tempting, seductive, like the playing of the man who caused the fish to pause and listen.[24]

The lines, for which either Schikaneder or the Danish translator is responsible, are in general so crazy and stupid that it is almost inconceivable that Mozart brought as much out of them as he did. Letting Papageno say 'I am a child of Nature', and thus the same instant make himself a liar, may be taken as an example *instar omnium* ['as good as any']. An exception might be made of the words of the text in the first aria, about him putting the maidens he catches in his cage. That is, if one puts a little more into them than the author himself presumably has, they demonstrate precisely the inoffensive character of Papageno's activity, as we have indicated it above.

We now leave the mythical Papageno. The actual Papageno's fate need not concern us. We wish him joy with his little Papagena, and gladly let him seek his happiness in populating a primitive forest, or an entire continent, with nothing but Papagenos.

Third Stage

This stage is represented by Don Giovanni. Here I have no need, as above, to single out a particular section of the opera. The question here is one of summating, not separating, since the entire opera is essentially an expression of the idea and, except for one or two individual numbers, it pivots essentially upon that, gravitating with dramatic necessity towards the idea at its centre. So there is an opportunity, once again, to see in what sense I can call the preceding 'stages' by that name when I call the third stage *Don Giovanni*. I have already reminded you that they have no separate existence, and when one takes this third stage, which is really the whole stage, as one's point of departure, they are less easily seen as one-sided abstractions or provisional anticipations, but rather as presentiments of *Don Giovanni*, except that there is always something left behind, which more or less justifies my using the expression 'stage', in that they are one-sided presentiments, each of them intimating one side only.

The contradiction in the first stage lay in the fact that desire could acquire no object, but was in possession of its object without having desired it, and therefore could not reach the point of desiring. In the second stage, the object appears in its multiplicity, but since desire seeks its object in this multiplicity, in a deeper sense it still has no object, it is not yet specified as desire. In *Don Giovanni*, on the other hand, desire is specified absolutely as desire, is connotationally and extensionally the immediate unity of the two preceding stages. The first stage desired the One ideally; the second desired the particular under the category of the multiple; the third stage is the unity of these. In the particular, desire has its absolute object, it desires the particular absolutely. Herein lies the seductiveness of which we shall speak later. Desire in this stage is therefore absolutely sound, victorious, triumphant, irresistible, and demonic. It must of course not be forgotten, therefore, that it is not a question here of desire in a particular individual but of desire as a principle, spiritually specified as that which spirit excludes. This is the idea of the spirit of sensuality, as was also intimated above. The expression of this idea is Don Giovanni, and the expression of Don Giovanni is, again, solely music. It is these two considerations in particular which will be constantly highlighted from different angles in what follows, from which also the proof will be indirectly furnished for this opera's classic significance. To make it easier for the reader to keep an overview, however, I shall attempt to collect the scattered considerations under particular headings.

To present some unitary view of this music is not my intention, and in particular I shall, with the support of all good spirits, take care not to scare together a mass of platitudinous but very noisy predicates, or to betray in linguistic lasciviousness the impotence of language, the more so since I do not regard this impotence as an imperfection in language but as a high potency, yet am therefore also the more willing to recognize music within its own limits. What I do want to do, on the other hand, is in part to illuminate the idea from as many angles as possible, and its relation to language, and in this way constantly encompass more and more of the territory in which music has its home, scaring it into breaking cover, as it were, though without my being able to say more about it, once it can be heard, than, 'Listen!' [...] [Nor shall I] give a running commentary on the music, for really that can only contain subjective contingencies and idiosyncrasies and can only appeal to something corresponding in the reader. [...] What I shall do, however, is constantly ferret out the musical in the idea, the situation, etc., hear it out, and when I have brought the reader to the point of being musically receptive enough to seem to hear the music although hearing nothing, I have completed my task, I make myself mute, I say to the reader as to myself: listen! You friendly genii who protect all innocent love, to you I commit all my faculties, watch over the busy thoughts that they may be found worthy of their object, fashion my soul into a euphonious instrument, let the gentle breezes of eloquence pass swiftly over it, send the refreshment and blessing of fruitful moods! You righteous spirits who stand guard at the boundaries in the realm of beauty, watch over me lest, in muddled enthusiasm and a blind zeal to make *Don Giovanni* all, I do not do it injustice, demean it, make it something other than it really is, which is the highest! You powerful spirits who know how to stir the heart of man, stand by me that I may capture the reader, not in the net of passion, nor the artifices of eloquence, but in the eternal truth of conviction.

1. *Sensual Genius Specified as Seduction*

When the Don Juan idea originated is not known;[25] all we know is that it belongs to Christianity, and through Christianity it belongs in turn to the Middle Ages. If one were unable to trace back the idea in human consciousness to that period of world history with any degree of certainty, a consideration of the inner nature of the idea would immediately dispel any doubt. The Middle Ages in general embody the idea of representation, partly consciously, partly unconsciously; the total is represented in a single individual, yet in such a way that only one aspect is determined as totality. The single individual who epitomizes the totality is therefore both more and less than an individual. Alongside this individual stands another individual who just as totally represents another side of life's content, as with the knight and the scholastic, the ecclesiastic and the layman. The grand dialectic of life is thus invariably illustrated by representative individuals, who more often than not confront each other in pairs; life is always presented only in one aspect, and there is no hint of the great dialectical unity which embraces life under both aspects.[26] The oppositions therefore usually stand, indifferently, outside each other. Of all this the Middle Ages knew nothing. Thus they themselves realized the representative idea unconsciously, while only a later reflection sees in them the idea. If the Middle Ages posit for their own consciousness an individual as representative of the idea, then they usually posit at his side another individual in relation to him. This relationship is then generally a comic one, where the one individual as it were compensates for the disproportionate greatness of the other in actual life. Thus the king has his fool by his side, Faust has his Wagner, Don Quixote Sancho Panza, and Don Giovanni Leporello. This arrangement, too, belongs essentially to the Middle Ages.

Thus the idea belongs to the Middle Ages; it is not, in the Middle Ages, the property of a single poet, it is one of those ideas with a primal power that spring from the popular consciousness with primordial aboriginality. The Middle Ages had to make the discord between flesh and spirit, which Christianity introduced to the world, a subject of their consideration, and to that end they made the contending forces individual objects of intuition. So Don Juan is, dare I say, flesh incarnate, or the inspiration of the flesh by the flesh's own spirit. This is already sufficiently emphasized in the foregoing; the question I would call attention to here, however, is whether we ought to refer Don Juan to the earlier or later Middle Ages. That he stands in an essential relation to the Middle Ages is surely evident to everyone. Either he is, then, the dissenting, misunderstood anticipation of the erotic that was manifest in the knight errant, or chivalry is an as yet merely relative contrast to the spirit, and only when the opposition became still sharper did Don Juan appear as the sensual which opposes the spirit at all costs. The erotic of the age of chivalry bears a certain resemblance to that of the Greek consciousness; the latter is, like the former, specified as soul. The difference is that the soul specification here lies within a general specification of the spirit, or a specification of totality. The idea of femininity is constantly in motion, in many ways, which was not the case with the Greeks, where all were simply beautiful individuals with no hint of femininity as such. In the consciousness of the Middle Ages, too, the erotic of the knight had a rather conciliatory relation to the spiritual, even if the spiritual in its jealous austerity held it in suspicion. If one now supposes the principle of the spirit to be posited in the world, one can either imagine that the most glaring contrast, the most titanic disjunction came first, and later was gradually mitigated, in which case Don Juan belongs to the earlier Middle Ages; or, assuming instead that the relation developed progressively into this absolute opposition, as is also more natural, the spirit taking more and more of its shares out of the joint firm so as to act alone, whereupon the real *skandalon*[27] appears, then Don Juan belongs to the later Middle Ages.

We are led on then to that point in time where the Middle Ages are about to come to an end, and where we meet a related idea, namely Faust – except that Don Juan must be placed a little earlier.

As the spirit, exclusively specified as spirit, renounces this world, feels that this is not simply not its home but not even its scene of action, and withdraws up into the higher regions, it leaves the worldly behind as the arena for the power with which it has always lived in conflict and for which it now steps aside. As the spirit then frees itself from the world, sensuality appears in all its power; it offers no objection to the change, it too sees the advantage in being separated, and rejoices that the Church does not prevail on them to stay together, but hews asunder the bond that binds them. Stronger than ever before, sensuality now awakens in all its richness, in all its rapture and exultation, and just as that recluse in nature, the reticent echo that never speaks first to anyone or speaks without being asked, found such great pleasure in the knight's hunting horn and his love ballads, in the baying of hounds, the snorting of horses, that it never tired of repeating these over and over again and, in the end, completely under its breath, so as not to forget them, so the whole world became an abode for sensuality's worldly spirit, echoing from all sides, while the spirit had abandoned the world. The Middle Ages have as much to say of a mountain not found on any map; it is called Venusberg.[28] There the sensual has its home, there it has its wild pleasures, for it is a kingdom, a state. In this kingdom language has no home, nor thought's sobriety, nor the laborious business of reflection. All one hears there is the elemental voice of passion, the play of the appetites, the wild din of intoxication; indulgence, only, in an eternal tumult. The first-born of this kingdom is Don Juan. This is not yet to say that it is the realm of sin, for we must grasp it at the moment when it appears in aesthetic indifference. Not until reflection enters does it present itself as the realm of sin, but then Don Juan is slain, the music comes to an end, one sees only the despairing defiance which impotently casts its negative vote but can find no constituency, not even in musical sounds. When sensuality presents itself as what is to be excluded, as what the spirit will have nothing to do with, though still without the latter's having passed judgement on it or condemned it, then the sensual assumes the form of the demonic in aesthetic indifference. It is just a matter of a moment; soon everything is changed; then the music too has ceased. Faust and Don Juan are the Titans and giants of the Middle Ages, who although no different from those of antiquity in the grandeur

of their endeavours, certainly differ from them in standing in isolation, in not combining their forces before storming heaven. All the
power is gathered in just one individual.

Don Juan, consequently, is the expression of the demonic specified
as the sensual; Faust is the expression of the demonic specified as the
spiritual which the Christian spirit excludes. These ideas are essentially related to each other, and they bear many similarities; one
might therefore expect them to have in common that both are
preserved in legends. We know this is true of Faust. [. . .] But no
such legend is to be found concerning Don Juan. [. . .] There has
probably been a legend all the same, but in all likelihood it has been
confined to just a few hints. [. . .] It is well known that Don
Juan existed far back in time as a booth-theatre piece. Indeed, that
may very likely be its origin. But there the idea was conceived
comically; remarkable as it is in general how proficient the Middle
Ages were in furnishing ideals, they could equally be relied on to
see the comic side of the larger-than-life dimensions of the ideal. To
make Don Juan a braggart who imagined he had seduced every
girl, to let Leporello believe his lies, was surely not an entirely
infelicitous basis for comedy. And even if that is not how it was,
even if that was not the conception, still the comic twist could not
have failed to turn up, since it lies in the contradiction between the
hero and the theatre he moves within. Thus one may also let the
Middle Ages tell of heroes so powerfully built that their eyes were a
foot apart, but if an ordinary person were to come on stage and
pretend to have eyes a foot apart, the comic would be in full swing.

These remarks on the legend of Don Juan would have found no
place here had they not served some closer relation to the subject
under investigation, if they did not serve to direct thought to the
once determined goal. I imagine that the reason why this idea,
compared with that of Faust, has so poor a past has to do with the
fact that so long as nobody realized that music was its proper
medium, there was something mysterious in it. Faust is idea, but an
idea which is also essentially individual. To imagine the spiritual–
demonic concentrated in an individual is the prerogative of thought,
while to conceive the sensual in an individual is impossible. Don
Giovanni constantly hovers between being idea – that is to say,
energy, life – and individual. But this hovering is the vibrating of

music. When the sea is agitated the foaming waves form images, as though creatures, in this upheaval. It is as if these creatures set the waves in motion, and yet it is the contrary action of the waves which creates them. Similarly, Don Giovanni is an image that constantly appears but gains neither form nor substance, an individual who is constantly being formed but not finished, of whose life history one can form no more definite an impression than one can by listening to the tumult of the waves. When Don Giovanni is conceived in this way, there is meaning and profound significance in everything. If I imagine some particular individual, if I see him or hear him speak, it becomes comic that he has seduced 1,003; as soon as he is a particular individual the accent falls in quite another place, for now it is those whom he has seduced, and in what manner, that are highlighted. The naivety of ballads and popular belief can successfully express such things without a suspicion of the comical; for reflection that is impossible. When he is interpreted in music, on the other hand, I do not have a particular individual, I have the power of nature, the demonic, which as little tires of seducing, or is done with seducing, as the wind is tired of raging, the sea of surging, or a waterfall of cascading down from its height. In this respect, the number of the seduced might just as well be any number at all, or a far greater one. Often it is not an easy task, when translating the text of an opera, to do it so exactly that the translation is not merely singable but also harmonizes reasonably with the textual meaning and thus with the music. To illustrate how sometimes this may not matter at all, I can mention the number in the list in *Don Giovanni* without treating the matter as offhandedly as people usually do and taking such things to have nothing to do with the matter. On the contrary, aesthetically I take the matter extremely seriously, and that is the reason I think it unimportant. I would, however, commend one feature of this number 1,003: it is odd and accidental, which is not at all unimportant, for it gives the impression that the list is by no means closed, but on the contrary that Don Giovanni is on the move. One almost begins to pity Leporello who has not only, as he says himself, to stand watch outside the door, but to carry on so complicated a system of book-keeping withal that it could keep a practised departmental secretary busy.

The way in which sensuality is conceived in *Don Giovanni* – as a principle – is one in which it has never been conceived before; for this reason the erotic is also defined by another predicate: the erotic here is *seduction*. Curiously enough, the idea of a seducer is entirely absent in the Greek consciousness. Far be it from me to want to praise the Greeks on that account, for gods as well as men were notoriously indiscreet in their love affairs; nor do I criticize Christianity, for after all it has the idea only as something external to it. The reason why the Greek consciousness lacks this idea is that its whole life is specified as individuality. The aspect of soul is thus predominant or always in harmony with the sensual. Greek love, therefore, was of the soul, not sensual, and it is this that inspires the modesty which rests over all Greek love. They fell in love with a girl, they set heaven and earth in motion to possess her; when they succeeded, perhaps they tired of her and sought a new love. In their inconstancy they may, indeed, bear a certain resemblance to Don Giovanni and, to mention just one example, Hercules could surely produce a fair-sized list, considering that he sometimes helped himself to families numbering up to fifty daughters, and like a family son-in-law, according to some reports, had his way with all of them in a single night. Still, he differs essentially from Don Giovanni; he is no seducer. For when one considers Greek love, it is according to its own lights essentially faithful just because it is of the soul; and it is some accidental factor in the particular individual that he loves many, and with regard to the many he loves, it is again accidental every time he loves a new one; when he is in love with one he does not think of the next. Don Giovanni, on the other hand, is from tip to toe a seducer. His love is not of the soul but sensual, and sensual love is not according to its own lights faithful but absolutely faithless; it loves not one but all, that is to say, it seduces all. For it exists only in the moment, but the moment, in terms of its concept, is the sum of moments, and so we have the seducer.

Chivalrous love, too, is of the soul and, therefore, according to its own lights essentially faithful; only sensual love is, in its own lights, essentially faithless. But this, its faithlessness, manifests itself also in another way; it becomes simply a repetition. Love from the soul is dialectical in a twofold sense. In the first place, it has in it the doubt and disquiet as to whether it will also be happy, see its desire fulfilled, and be requited. This anxiety is something sensual love does not have. Even a Jupiter has doubts about his victory, and this cannot be otherwise; indeed, he himself cannot wish it otherwise. With Don Giovanni this is not the case; he cuts matters short and must always be considered absolutely victorious. This might seem an advantage to him, but it is really an impoverishment. Love from the soul has, secondly, yet another dialectic, for it differs in relation to every single individual who is the object of love. Therein lies its wealth, its full-bodied content. Such is not the case with Don Giovanni. He has no time for this, for him everything is merely a matter of the moment. To catch sight of her and love her, that was one and the same. In a sense one may say the same of love from the soul, but in that there is also just the suggestion of a beginning. For Don Giovanni it is true in a different way. To catch sight of her and to love her are the same thing, that is in the moment; the very same moment everything is over, and the same endlessly repeats itself.

If one imagines Don Giovanni specified as soul, it becomes ridiculous and a self-contradiction, not even in accord with the idea, to posit 1,003 in Spain. It becomes an exaggeration which has a disturbing effect even if one were to entertain the fancy that one was considering him in an ideal way. If then we have no other medium for describing this love than language, we are at a loss, for as soon as we abandon the naivety that can insist, in all innocence, that there were 1,003 in Spain, we need something more, namely the individualization in soul. The aesthetic is not at all satisfied that everything should be thus lumped together, and wants to astonish with numbers. Love from the soul moves precisely in the rich multiplicity of the individual life, where the nuances are what are really significant. Sensual love, on the other hand, can lump everything together. What is essential for it is woman quite in the abstract, and at most distinctions of the more sensual kind. Love from the soul is a continuation in time, sensual love a disappearance in time, but the medium which expresses this is precisely music. This is something music is excellently fitted to accomplish, since it is far more abstract than language and therefore does not express the particular but the general in all its generality, and yet it expresses the general, not in reflective abstraction, but in the concreteness of immediacy.

As an example of what I mean, I shall discuss in a little more detail the servant's second aria: the aria listing the seduced. This may be regarded as Don Giovanni's real epic. So make this experiment if you doubt the truth of what I say! Imagine a poet more happily endowed by nature than any before him, give him an abundance of expression, give him mastery and authority of the forces of language, let everything in which there is the breath of life be obedient to him, deferring to his slightest gesture, let everything wait in readiness for his command, let him be surrounded by a numerous band of light skirmishers, fleet-footed messengers who overtake thought in its swiftest flight, let nothing escape him, not the slightest movement, let there be no secret left for him, nothing unutterable, in all the world – then give him the task of celebrating Don Giovanni epically in song, of unfolding the list of the seduced. What will be the result? He will never be finished! The epic has the defect, if you will, that it can go on as long as needs must; his hero, the improviser, Don Giovanni, can go on as long as needs must. The poet will then enter into the multiplicity, there will always be enough there to give pleasure but he will never achieve the effect that Mozart has obtained. For even if he finally finished, he would not have said the half of what Mozart has expressed in this one piece. Now Mozart has not even embarked upon the multiplicity; what he deals with are certain large configurations of passing events. This has its sufficient reason in the very medium, in music, which is too abstract to express the differences. The musical epic thus becomes something comparatively short, and yet it has in an incomparable manner the epic quality of going on as long as need be, since one can always let it begin again and hear it over and over again, precisely because it expresses the general in the concreteness of immediacy. This is not Don Giovanni as a particular individual that we hear, not his speech, but we hear the voice, the voice of sensuality, and we hear it through the longing for femininity. The only way in which Don Giovanni can become epic is by constantly finishing and constantly starting over again, for his life is the sum of mutually repellent moments that lack any coherence; his life is as moment the sum of moments, as sum of moments the moment.

In this generality, in this hovering between being individual and force of nature, lies Don Giovanni. As soon as he becomes individual the aesthetic acquires quite different categories. Therefore it is quite proper, and has a deep inner significance, that in the seduction that occurs in the piece, that of Zerlina, the girl should be a common peasant girl. Hypocritical aestheticians who, under the show of understanding poets and composers, do all they can to help us misunderstand them, will perhaps instruct us that Zerlina is an uncommon girl. Anyone who thinks that shows that he has totally misunderstood Mozart and is using the wrong categories. That he misunderstands Mozart is clear enough, for Mozart has been at pains to keep Zerlina as insignificant as possible. [. . .] If Don Giovanni's love were specified other than as sensual, if he were a seducer in a spiritual sense (something which will be a subject for consideration later), then it would have been a radical fault in the piece that the heroine in the seduction which dramatically engages us is a little peasant girl. The aesthetic would require that Don Juan be set a more difficult task. But for Don Giovanni these differences are of no importance. If I could imagine him making such a speech about himself, perhaps he'd say, 'You are wrong, I am no husband who needs an ordinary girl for my happiness; every girl has what makes me happy, and so I take them all.' It is in a similar way that we must understand the words I touched on earlier, 'Even coquettes threescore years old', or in another place: *pur chè porti la gonella, voi sapete quel chè fà.*[29] For Don Giovanni every girl is an ordinary girl, every love affair an everyday story. Zerlina is young and pretty, and she is a woman, that is the peculiarity she shares with hundreds of others, but it is not the uncommon that Don Giovanni desires but the general, what she has in common with every woman. If that is not how it is, then *Don Giovanni* ceases to be absolutely musical, the aesthetic calls for spoken lines; but then since that is indeed how it is, *Don Giovanni* is absolutely musical.

I will throw light on this from another side too, from the inner structure of the piece. For Don Giovanni, Elvira is a dangerous enemy. This is frequently stressed in the dialogue we owe to the Danish translator. Sure enough, it is a mistake to give him spoken lines, but that doesn't mean that the lines might not include the occasional good comment. Thus Don Giovanni is afraid of Elvira. Now presumably some aesthetician thinks he can give a meticulous explanation of this with some longwinded chit-chat about Elvira's being an uncommon girl, etc. This misses the point entirely. She is a danger to him because she has been seduced. In the same sense, exactly the same sense, Zerlina is a danger to him when she is seduced. As soon as she is seduced she is lifted up into a higher sphere, which is a consciousness in her that Don Giovanni himself does not have. Therefore she is a danger. Thus, again, it is not through the accidental but the general that she is dangerous for him.

So Don Giovanni is a seducer; his eroticism is seduction. This says much if understood aright, little if grasped with typical lack of clarity. We have already seen that the concept of a seducer is essentially modified in the case of Don Giovanni, as the object of his desire is the sensual and that alone. This was important for showing the musical in Don Giovanni. In antiquity the sensual found expression in the silent stillness of plastic art; in the Christian world the sensual had to fume in all its impatient passion. Although one can thus truly say that Don Giovanni is a seducer, this expression, which can have a disturbing effect on the weak brains of certain aestheticians, has often occasioned misunderstanding, inasmuch as they have scraped together whatever could be said of such a one and transferred it without further ado to Don Giovanni. At times they have demonstrated their own cunning in running Don Giovannis to earth, at others talked themselves hoarse explaining his intrigues and wiles; in short the word 'seducer' has given everyone the chance to do him down as best they can, to contribute their mite[30] to the total misunderstanding. Of Don Giovanni we must use the word 'seducer' with great caution, in so far, that is, as it is more incumbent on us to say something true than just anything. This is not because Don Giovanni is too good, but because he simply doesn't come within ethical categories. I would therefore rather call him a deceiver, since there is always a greater ambiguity in that word. Being a seducer requires always a certain reflection and consciousness, and once this is present one may talk of cunning and intrigues, and of wily measures. This consciousness is something Don Giovanni lacks. So he does not seduce. He desires, and this desire acts seductively. To that extent he seduces. He savours the satisfaction of desire; as soon as he has savoured it he seeks a new object, and so on endlessly. So he does indeed deceive, though not in such a way that he plans his deception in advance; it is the power of sensuality itself that deceives the seduced, and it is more of a kind of Nemesis. He desires and stays constantly in a state of desire, and he constantly savours its satisfaction. To be a seducer he lacks the time ahead in which to lay his plans, and the time behind in which to become conscious of his act. *A seducer should therefore be in possession of a power* which Don Giovanni does not have, however well equipped he is otherwise – *the power of speech.* As soon as we give him that power he ceases to be musical, and then the aesthetic interest becomes quite another.

Achim von Arnim tells somewhere of a seducer in quite another style, a seducer who falls under ethical categories. Of him he uses a form of expression which, in its truth, boldness and pithiness, can almost match a stroke of the bow in Mozart. He says he could talk with a woman in such a way that, if the devil caught him, he could talk himself free if only he was given a chance to talk with the devil's great-grandmother.[31] This is the real seducer; the aesthetic interest here is also different; namely, how, the method. There is therefore something of profound significance in what has perhaps escaped most people's attention, that Faust, who is a reproduction of Don Giovanni, seduces only one girl, while Don Giovanni seduces hundreds; but then this one girl is, in terms of intensity, seduced and destroyed in quite another way from all those whom Don Giovanni has deceived. Simply because Faust, as a reproduction, has in him the category of spirit. The power of such a seducer is speech, that is to say, lies. A few days ago I heard one soldier speak to another about a third who had deceived a girl. He gave no extensive description, yet the expression he used was quite excellent: 'He were able to do such with lies and such.' This seducer is of quite another kind than Don Giovanni and differs essentially from him, as can be seen from the fact that he and his activity are extremely unmusical and aesthetically belong in the category of the interesting. The object of his desire is therefore, if one has the right aesthetic conception of him, also something more than the merely sensual.

But what is this force with which Don Giovanni seduces? It is the force of desire, the energy of sensual desire. In each woman he desires the whole of femininity, and in this lies the sensually idealizing power with which he at once beautifies and overcomes his prey. The reflection of this gigantic passion beautifies and unfolds the desired, it irradiates a heightened beauty with its refulgence. As, with a seductive glow, the enthusiast's flame illumines even those not concerned, so Don Giovanni transfigures every girl in a far deeper sense, since his relation to her is essential. So for him all finite differences fade away in comparison with the main thing: being a woman. The older women he rejuvenates into womanhood's beautiful middle age; children he practically matures in a twinkling; all that is woman is his prey (*pur chè porti la gonella, voi sapete quel chè fà*). On the other hand, it would be quite wrong to take his sensuality for blindness; instinctively he knows very well how to make distinctions, and above all he idealizes. If for a moment I think back to a preceding stage, to the Page, the reader may recall that already in discussing him I compared some lines of his with some of Don Giovanni's. The mythical Page I let stay, I let the real one go off to the army. If I now imagined the mythical Page having liberated himself, having got going, then I would call to mind a line of the Page's which suits Don Giovanni. For as Cherubino, light as a bird and daring, jumps out of the window, this makes such a powerful impression on Susanna that she almost swoons, and when she recovers she exclaims, 'See how he runs! My, won't he have luck with the girls!' That is quite right of Susanna, and the reason for her swooning is not just the idea of the daring leap, but rather that he had already succeeded with her. The Page is the future Don Giovanni, though this is not to be understood, ridiculously, as though the Page would become Don Giovanni just by growing older. For Don Giovanni not only has luck with the girls, he makes them feel lucky too – and unlucky, but curiously enough, in such a way that they would have it thus, and it was a foolish girl who did not want to be unlucky in order just once to have been lucky with Don Giovanni.[32] In continuing to call Don Giovanni a seducer, therefore, I am not at all imagining him slyly drafting his plans, craftily calculating the effect of his intrigues. His deception is due to the genius of sensuality, whose incarnation it is as though he was. He lacks shrewd circumspection; his life is effervescent like the wine with which he fortifies himself, his life is excited like the tones which accompany his joyous feast, he is always triumphant. He needs no preparation, no plan, no time, for he is always ready, the force is always in him and the desire too, and only when he desires is he in his proper element. He is seated at the table, he raises the goblet, happy as a god – he rises with napkin in hand, ready to attack. If Leporello rouses him in the middle of the night, he wakes up always certain of victory. But this force, this power words cannot express, only music can give us an idea of it, for it is inexpressible in reflection and thought. The cunning of an ethically specified seducer I can clearly present in words, and music would presume in vain to perform that task. With Don Giovanni the converse is the case. What is this force? No one can say. Even if I asked Zerlina before she went to the ball, 'What is this force with which he captivates you?', she would reply, 'No one knows'; and I would say, 'Well said, my child! You speak more wisely than the wise men of India, *richtig, das weiss man nicht*; and the unfortunate thing is that I can't tell you either.'

This force in Don Giovanni, this omnipotence, this gaiety, only music can express, and I know no other description for it than 'exuberant good cheer'. So when Kruse[33] has Don Giovanni say as he comes on stage at Zerlina's wedding, 'Cheer up, children! You are all dressed as though for your own weddings!', he is quite right and perhaps more than he thinks. For the gaiety is something he brings with him, and as far as the wedding goes, it is not insignificant that they are all dressed as though for their own weddings; for Don Giovanni is not just Zerlina's man, he celebrates with sport and song the weddings of all the young girls in the parish. What wonder then that they flock round him, the happy girls! Nor will they be disappointed, for he is enough for them all. Flattery, sighs, bold glances, soft handclasps, secret whisperings, dangerous proximity, tempting withdrawal – and yet these are only the lesser mysteries, the gifts before the wedding.[34] It is a delight for Don Giovanni to look out over such a rich harvest; he takes care of the whole parish, and yet perhaps it does not cost him as much time as Leporello uses in the office.

These considerations bring us back to the main topic of this inquiry, that Don Giovanni is absolutely musical. He desires sensually, seduces with the demonic power of sensuality, he seduces all. The spoken word is no part of him, for that would straightaway make him a reflective individual. He has no substance of this kind but hurries on in a perpetual vanishing, just like music, of which it is true that it is over as soon as it stops playing and only comes

back into existence when it starts again. So if I were now to raise
the question of Don Giovanni's looks – is he handsome, young or
old, about how old? – it is just a concession on my part, and
anything I say on this score can only expect admission here in the
way that a tolerated sect is given room in the State Church. Handsome, not altogether young; if I were to suggest his age, my proposal
would be thirty-three, that being the age of a generation. The
trouble with going into questions of this kind is that one loses the
whole by dwelling on the parts, as if it were through his good
looks, or whatever else might be mentioned, that Don Giovanni
seduces. One sees him then, but no longer hears him, and then he is
lost. If, as it were, to do my bit in helping the reader form a mental
picture of Don Giovanni, I said, 'Look, there he stands, see how his
eyes blaze, his lips curl in a smile, so certain is he of his victory; look
at his regal glance, which demands the things that are Caesar's; see
how gracefully he enters into the dance, how proudly he stretches
out his hand, how happy the one to whom it is offered' – or if I
said, 'Look, there he stands in the shadow of the forest, he leans
against a tree, he accompanies himself on a guitar, and look! there
disappears a young girl among the trees, frightened as a startled
fawn, but he is in no hurry, he knows she seeks him' – or if I said,
'There he rests by the shore of the lake in the pale night, so
beautiful that the moon pauses and relives its youthful love, so
beautiful that the young girls from the town would give much to
dare steal up on him and use the moment of darkness, while the
moon rises up again to illumine the heavens, to kiss him.' If I did
this, the attentive reader would say, 'Look, now he's spoiled everything for himself, he has forgotten that Don Giovanni is not to
be seen but heard.' So I do not do that but say, 'Listen to Don
Giovanni; that's to say, if you cannot get an idea of Don Giovanni
by listening to him, you will never get one. Hear the beginning of
his life; as lightning twists out of the thunder cloud's murk, he
bursts forth from the depth of earnest, swifter than lightning, less
constant than it yet just as measured. Hear how he plunges into
life's diversity, how he dashes himself against its solid dam, hear
these light, dancing tones of the violin, hear the beckoning of joy,
hear the exultation of desire, hear the festive bliss of enjoyment;
hear his wild flight; he hurries past even himself, ever faster, ever

more impetuously; hear the murmur of love, hear the whisper of temptation, hear the swirl of seduction, hear the stillness of the moment – listen, listen, listen, to Mozart's *Don Giovanni*.

2. Other Adaptations of Don Juan, Considered in Relation to the Musical Interpretation

The Faust motif, as we know, has been interpreted in a wide variety of ways; but this is not so with Don Juan. That may seem strange, especially as the latter idea represents a far more universal phase in the development of the individual life than does the first. However, this can easily be explained by the fact that the Faustian motif presupposes a degree of spiritual development that makes interpretation far more natural. There is also the fact, of which I reminded you above, that there is no corresponding Don Juan legend, that people have been dimly aware of the difficulty over the medium until Mozart discovered the medium and the idea. Only since then has the idea acquired its true dignity and again, more than ever, given content to a phase of the individual's life, but so satisfactorily that the need to encapsulate the experience separately in imagination was no longer a poetic necessity.

This, once more, is indirect proof of the absolute classic value of this Mozartian opera. The ideal in this direction having now already found its perfect artistic expression, people could indeed be tempted by it, but not to poetic activity. Tempting Mozart's music has no doubt been, for where is the young man for whom there have not been moments when he would have given half his fortune to be a Don Juan, or perhaps all of it; when he would have given half his lifetime to be a Don Juan for a year, or perhaps the whole of it. But that's how it was; those of a deeper nature who were affected by the idea found everything in Mozart's music, even the gentlest breeze; they found in its passionate grandeur a full-toned expression of what stirred in their own hearts; they sensed how every mood strained in the music's direction, just as the brook hurries on to lose itself in the infinity of the ocean. These natures found in the Mozartian Don Juan as much text as commentary, and while they were thus carried along and down in its music and enjoyed the delight of losing themselves, they also gained the riches of wonder. The music of Mozart was in no way too constricted; quite the contrary, their own moods were broadened, assumed a larger-than-life dimension, as they recaptured them again in Mozart. Those of a lower nature who have no inkling of infinity do not grasp hold of it; of course the dabblers who took themselves to be a Don Juan because they had pinched a peasant girl's cheek, flung their arms round a waitress, or made a little maiden blush, understood neither the idea nor Mozart, nor how to produce a Don Juan themselves, other than a ridiculous monstrosity, a family idol who perhaps might have seemed a true Don Juan, the epitome of all attractiveness, to the dim, sentimental eyes of some cousins. Faust has never been able to find expression in this sense, and, as noted above, never will, because the idea is far more concrete. Though an interpretation of Faust may deserve to be called perfect, a succeeding generation can still give birth to a new Faust; while Don Juan, due to the abstractness of the motif, lives eternally for all ages, and the thought of providing a Don Juan after Mozart cannot but be like wanting to write a post-Homerian Iliad in an even more profound sense.

Now, even if that is so, it by no means follows that individual talents should not have tried their hands at interpreting Don Juan differently. Everyone knows they have, but what no one has perhaps noticed is that the representative type for all interpretations is essentially Molière's *Don Juan*.[35] though again, this is much older than Mozart's, and is a comedy. It is to Mozart's *Don Giovanni* what a fairy-tale in Musaeus's interpretation is to an adaptation of Tieck's.[36] So really I can confine myself to a discussion of the *Don Juan* of Molière and in attempting an aesthetic appraisal of it I can judge the others at the same time. [. . .]

We have already indicated the turning-point in interpreting Don Juan: as soon as we give him spoken lines everything changes, for the reflection which motivates the spoken line refracts him out of the obscurity in which he is audible only musically. For that reason Don Juan might perhaps seem best interpreted as ballet. And people are fairly familiar with the fact that he has indeed been interpreted in that way.[37] One has to praise this interpretation, however, for recognizing what are after all its limitations, something which has led to its confining itself to the final scene, where the passion of Don Juan can be made most easily visible through the pantomimic play of muscles. The result again is that Don Juan is represented not according to his essential but to his accidental passion, and the playbill for such a performance always has more in it than the piece itself; it tells us, for instance, that it is Don Juan, the seducer Don Juan, whereas the ballet for all practical purposes only presents the pangs of despair, whose expression, seeing this can only be panto-mime, Don Juan can have in common with many other despairing persons. What is essential in Don Juan cannot be represented in ballet, and everyone intuitively feels how ridiculous it would be to see Don Juan beguiling a girl with his dance steps and contrived gesticulations. Don Juan is an inward specification and so cannot become visible in this way or reveal himself in bodily forms and their movements, or in sculptured harmony.

Even if we were not to give him spoken lines, we could neverthe-less imagine an interpretation of Don Juan using words as its medium. Indeed we have an example from Byron. That Byron was in many ways just the man to present a Don Juan is clear enough, and one may therefore be sure that the reason for the project's miscarrying lay not in Byron himself but far deeper. Byron has dared to bring Don Juan into existence for us, to tell us of his childhood and youth, to reconstruct him from a context of finite life-circumstances. The result is to make Don Juan into a reflective personality who loses the ideality that is his in the traditional concep-tion. I can detail here right away what changes occur in the idea. When Don Juan is interpreted musically I hear the whole of the infinity of passion in him, but also its infinite power which nothing can resist; I hear the wild craving of desire, but also that desire's absolute triumphancy which it would be in vain for anyone to oppose. You only need to think once of the obstacle to realize that its function is merely to inflame the passion than put up any real resistance; the pleasure is magnified, the victory is certain and the obstacle only an incitement. A life agitated in this elemental way, demonically powerful and irresistible, that is what Don Juan conveys to me. This is his ideality, and this I can take uninterrupted pleasure in, because the music does not represent him to me as a person or individual, but as a power. If Don Juan is interpreted as an individual, that alone puts him in conflict with a world around him; as an individual he feels the pressure and chains of this en-vironment; perhaps as a great individual he overcomes it, but one immediately feels that here the difficulties in the obstacles have a different role. It is on them that interest is essentially focused. But this brings Don Juan within the category of the interesting. Were we to resort to a bombastic show of words in representing him as absolutely victorious, we would feel immediately that this was not satisfactory, since it does not belong essentially to an individual as such to be victorious, and the crisis of conflict is called for.

The resistance the individual has to contend with can be partly an external resistance lying not so much in the object as in the environing world, partly a resistance in the object itself. Most interpretations of Don Juan have been mainly occupied with the former, because the element in the motif that has been retained is the need for him to be erotically victorious. On the other hand, I think that stressing the other side opens up the only prospect of a significant contrast to the musical Don Juan, while any interpretation lying in between is bound to contain imperfections. So that in the musical Don Juan one would then have the extensive seducer, in the other the intensive one. The latter Don Juan is not presented then as possessing his object by a single stroke, he is not the immediate seducer, he is the reflective seducer. What interests us is the astuteness, the cunning with which he can insinuate himself into a girl's heart, the dominion he can acquire over it, the fascinating, systematic, progressive seduction. It becomes a matter of indifference how many he has seduced; what concerns us is the art, the thoroughness, the profound ingenuity with which he seduces. In the end the very enjoyment becomes so reflective that compared with the musical Don Juan's enjoyment it becomes something else. The musical Don Juan enjoys the satisfaction, the reflective Don Juan enjoys the deception, enjoys the cunning. The immediate enjoyment is over, and a greater enjoyment is found in reflecting upon the enjoyment. There is a hint or two of this in Molière's interpretation, only there is no chance of its coming into its own since all the rest of the interpretation interferes. Desire awakens in Don Juan because he sees one of the girls happy in her relation to the one she loves, and he begins by being jealous. This is a point of interest that would not occupy us at all in the opera, precisely because Don Giovanni is not a reflective individual. Once Don Juan is interpreted as a self-aware individual, we can achieve an ideality corresponding to the musical one only by transferring the matter to the psychological domain. Then one attains the ideality of intensity. For that reason Byron's *Don Juan* must be considered a failure, because it expands itself epically. The immediate Don Juan has to seduce 1,003, the self-aware one has only to seduce one, and what occupies us is how he does it. The self-aware Don Juan's seduction is a sleight-of-hand every single little step of which has its special significance; the musical Don Giovanni's seduction is a flick of the wrist, the matter of a moment, quicker done than said. I am reminded of a tableau I once saw. A pretty young fellow, a real ladies' man, was playing with a number of young girls who were all at that dangerous age when they are neither grown-up nor children. Among other things, they were amusing themselves by jumping over a ditch. He stood at the edge and helped them jump by taking them around the waist, lifting them lightly into the air, and then setting them down on the other side. It was a charming sight; I enjoyed him just as much as I enjoyed the young girls. Then I thought of Don Juan. They fling themselves into his arms, these young girls; then he grabs them, and just as briskly sets them down on the other side of life's ditch.

The musical Don Juan is absolutely victorious and therefore, of course, also in complete command of all the means that can contribute to this victory. Or rather, he is in such absolute command of the means that it is as though he had no need to use them; that is, he does not use them as a means. Once he is a reflective individual it appears there is something there called the means. If the poet then grants him this, but also makes the opposition and obstacles so serious as to make victory doubtful, then Don Juan comes within the category of the interesting and in this regard one may think of several interpretations of Don Juan, up to the point where we reach what we earlier called intensive seduction. If the poet denies him the means, the interpretation falls into the category of comedy. I have never seen a perfect interpretation that brings him into the category of the interesting. On the other hand, of most interpretations of Don Juan it can truly be said that they approach comedy [which] can easily be explained by their adherence to Molière, in whose interpretation comedy lies dormant [. . .] Once a passion is portrayed and denied the means of its satisfaction, either a tragic or a comic turn may be produced. You cannot properly produce a tragic turn where the motif appears entirely unwarranted, and that is why the comic is so likely. If I depict an addiction to gambling in some individual and then give this individual five dollars to lose, the effect is comic. This is not quite how it is with Molière's Don Juan, but there is a similarity. If I place Don Juan in financial straits, harassed by creditors, then he immediately loses the ideality he has in the opera, and the effect is comic. The famous comedy scene in Molière,[38] which has great value and also fits very well into the whole, ought therefore never to be introduced into the opera, where it has a totally distracting effect.

That the Molière interpretation aspires to the comic is shown not only by the comedy scene just mentioned, which in isolation would prove nothing at all; the whole plot bears its mark. Sganarelle's first and last lines, the beginning and end of the whole piece, provide more than sufficient evidence of this. Sganarelle begins with a eulogy over a rare snuff, from which one learns among other things that he cannot be all that busy in this Don Juan's service. He ends by complaining that he alone has been wronged. When one then considers that Molière, too, has the statue come and fetch Don Juan, and that despite Sganarelle's also having witnessed this horror Molière nevertheless puts those words into his mouth, as though Sganarelle were saying that since the statue otherwise meddled in the exercise of justice on earth and the punishment of vice, it ought to have been ready to pay Sganarelle the wages due to him for long and faithful service to Don Juan, which his master had been unable to do because of his sudden departure – when one considers this, then indeed anyone will have a sense of the comical in Molière's *Don Juan*. [. . .] The hero of the piece, Don Juan, is anything but a hero; he is a subject of misfortune, who has presumably failed his finals and has now chosen another vocation. True, one learns that he is the son of a very distinguished man, who has also tried to inspire him to virtue and immortal enterprises by impressing upon him the great name of his forefathers, but this is so improbable in relation to the rest of his behaviour that one soon begins to suspect the whole thing of being a pack of lies fabricated by Don Juan himself. His conduct is not very chivalrous; one does not see him sword in hand clearing a path for himself through life's difficulties; he deals out cuffs on the ear to this one and that; yes, he even reaches the point of coming to blows with one of the girls' betrothed. So if Molière's Don Juan really is a knight, the poet is very good at having us forget the fact and does all he can to show us a bully, an ordinary rake, who is not afraid of using his fists. Anyone who has had occasion to observe what we call a rake knows, too, that this class of people has a great predilection for the sea, and he will therefore find it quite as it should be that Don Juan should set eyes on a pair of skirts and then put out after them in a boat on Kallebostrand – a Sunday adventure, plus the fact that the boat capsizes. Don Juan and Sganarelle are almost drowned and are finally saved by Pedro and the tall Lucas, who were earlier betting whether it was a man or a stone, a wager that cost Lucas ten sous, which is almost too much for Lucas and for Don Juan. If all this then strikes one as appropriate, the impression becomes confused for a moment when one learns that Don Juan is also the fellow who has seduced Elvira, murdered the Commendatore, and so on, something one finds quite illogical and must once again explain as a lie in order to restore harmony. If Sganarelle is meant to give us an idea of the passion raging in Don Juan, his expression is such a travesty that it is impossible not to laugh, as when Sganarelle says to Gusman that, to get the one he wants, Don Juan would gladly marry her dog and cat, indeed what is worse, 'and you into the bargain'; or when he remarks that his master has faith neither in love nor in medicine.

Now if Molière's interpretation of Don Juan, regarded as a comic adaptation, were correct, then I should say no more about it here, since I am concerned in this inquiry only with the ideal interpretation and the significance of music for that. I could then be content with calling attention to the remarkable circumstance that only in music has Don Juan been interpreted ideally in the ideality he has in the traditional medieval conception. The absence of an ideal interpretation in the medium of words could then furnish indirect proof of the correctness of my proposition. Here, however, I can do better, precisely because Molière is not correct, and what has prevented him from being so is his having kept something of the ideal in Don Juan that is due to the traditional conception. It will again appear, on my pointing this out, that this could be essentially expressed, after all, only in music, and so I return to my proper thesis.

Right at the beginning of the first act of Molière's *Don Juan*,

Sganarelle makes a very long speech in which he wants to give us a conception of his master's boundless passion and the multiplicity of his adventures. This speech exactly corresponds with the servant's second aria in the opera. The speech has absolutely no other effect than comedy. [. . .] It tries to give us some hint of his power, but the effect fails to materialize; only music can incorporate this factor because it describes Don Juan's behaviour and lets us hear the power of seduction, at the same time as the list is unrolled for us.

In Molière, the statue arrives in the last act to fetch Don Juan. Even if the poet has tried to motivate the statue's appearance by giving advance warning, this piece of stone always presents a dramatic stumbling-block. If Don Juan is interpreted ideally as force, as passion, then heaven itself must be set in motion. If he is not so interpreted, it is always ill-advised to use such drastic means. Really the Commendatore need not have inconvenienced himself. [. . .] It would be quite in the spirit of modern comedy, which has no need of such great forces of destruction precisely because the motivating powers themselves are not so grandiose, to have Don Juan thrown into a debtor's gaol. It would be quite consistent with it to let Don Juan learn the tedious constraints of reality. In the opera it is quite right that the Commendatore should reappear, but then his conduct too possesses an ideal truth. The music immediately makes the Commendatore into something more than a particular individual, his voice is expanded to that of a spirit. So, just as Don Giovanni himself is interpreted with aesthetic seriousness in the opera, so too is the Commendatore. In Molière he comes in with an ethical gravity and weightiness that make him almost ridiculous; in the opera he comes in with aesthetic lightness, metaphysical truth. No power in the piece, no power on earth has been able to coerce Don Giovanni; only a spirit, a ghost, can do that. If this is understood correctly it will again throw light on the interpretation of Don Juan. A spirit, a ghost, is a reproduction; this is the mystery in the return; but Don Giovanni can do everything, can put up with anything, except the reproduction of life, precisely because he is sensual life in its immediacy, the negation of which is spirit.

In Molière's interpretation, Sganarelle becomes an inexplicable figure whose character is extremely confused. What causes the confusion is, again, that Molière has kept something of the traditional idea. As Don Giovanni is altogether a force, this also shows in the relation to Leporello. Leporello feels drawn to him, overwhelmed by him, is absorbed in him, and he becomes merely an instrument of his master's will. This obscure, impenetrable sympathy is exactly what makes Leporello into a musical personality, and we find it quite in order that he does not manage to tear himself away from Don Giovanni. With Sganarelle it is different. In Molière, Don Juan is a particular individual, and so it is as to an individual that Sganarelle relates to him. If Sganarelle then feels indissolubly bound to Don Juan, it is no more than a modest aesthetic requirement to ask how this is to be explained. It is nothing to the purpose that Molière has him say that he cannot tear himself away from Don Juan, for neither reader nor spectator can see any rational ground for this, and a rational ground is just what is in question. Leporello's inconstancy is well motivated in the opera, because compared with Don Giovanni he himself is closer to being an individual consciousness, and in him the Don Giovanni-life is therefore reflected differently, though without his really being able to penetrate it. In Molière, Sganarelle is sometimes worse, sometimes better than Don Juan, but it is unthinkable that he should not desert him when he does not even get his wages. If one were to imagine a unity in Sganarelle corresponding to the sympathetic musical opacity of Leporello in the opera, there would be nothing for it but to let it be a sottish partiality. Here again we see an example of how the musical must be invoked for Don Juan to be interpreted in his true ideality. The fault in Molière is not in interpreting him comically, but in not interpreting him correctly.

Molière's Don Juan is also a seducer, but the piece gives us only an impoverished idea of his role. That Elvira, in Molière, is Don Juan's spouse is undeniably rightly conceived, particularly for its comic effect. We see at once that what we have here is an ordinary person who uses promises of marriage to deceive a girl. Elvira thus loses all the ideal bearing that is hers in the opera, where she appears with no other weapon than that of her affronted womanhood, while here one imagines her wielding a marriage certificate; and Don Juan loses his seductive ambiguity by being both a young man and an experienced husband, that is to say, practised in all his extramarital escapades. How he has deceived Elvira, with what means he has enticed her out of the convent – of this a number of Sganarelle's lines are supposed to enlighten us; but since the seduction scene in the play gives us no opportunity to admire Don Juan's art, our confidence in these bits of information is naturally weakened. Of course inasmuch as Molière's Don Juan is comic, this was hardly necessary. But since he would still have us understand that his Don Juan really is the hero Don Juan, who has deluded Elvira and killed the Commendatore, we readily see where Molière has gone wrong. But we are then forced to consider whether this was not really because Don Juan can never be represented as a seducer except with the help of music, unless, as noted above, one wishes to go into the psychology of it, which it is hard to invest with dramatic interest.

Nor, in Molière, does one hear him deluding the two young girls, Mathurine and Charlotte. The deception takes place off-stage, and since Molière here, too, gives us to understand that Don Juan has made them promises of marriage, again we get but a meagre idea of his talent. To delude a young girl with a promise of marriage is a very inferior art, and it by no means follows from the fact that someone is low enough to do this that he is high enough to be called Don Juan. The only scene which seems to show us Don Juan in his seducing – though scarcely seductive – activities is the scene with Charlotte. But to tell a young peasant girl that she is pretty, that she has sparkling eyes, to ask her to turn round in order to observe her figure, all this betrays nothing exceptional in Don Juan, only that he is a lewd fellow who looks over a girl as a dealer does a horse. One can gladly concede a comic effect to the scene, and if that is all it was intended to have I would not discuss it here. But since this, his notorious attempt, bears no relation to the many affairs he must have had, this scene too, directly or indirectly, contributes to showing the imperfection in the comedy. Molière seems to have wanted to make something more of him, seems to have wanted to preserve the ideal in him, but he lacks the medium, and therefore everything that actually happens falls rather flat. In general, one can say that in Molière's Don Juan it is only historically that we get to know that he is a seducer; we do not see it dramatically. [. . .]

Perhaps, in conclusion, I can elucidate what has been expounded here by considering an often-made remark, that Molière's Don Juan is more moral than Mozart's. However, if properly understood, this is precisely to eulogize the opera. In the opera there isn't just talk of a seducer, Don Giovanni *is* a seducer, and one cannot deny that in its details the music can often be seductive enough. But that is as it should be, and this is exactly its greatness. To say, therefore, that the opera is immoral is a piece of foolishness originating in people who do not know how to grasp a whole but are captured by details. The definitive aspiration in the opera is extremely moral, and the impression it produces absolutely salutary, because everything is big, everything has genuine, unadorned pathos, the passion of pleasure no less than of seriousness, of enjoyment no less than of wrath.

3. The Inner Musical Structure of the Opera

Although the title of this section may be thought self-explanatory, for safety's sake I shall nevertheless point out that it is of course not my intention to give an aesthetic appraisal of *Don Giovanni*, or a demonstration of the dramatic structure in the text. One must always be very cautious in making such distinctions, especially with a classic work. For, as I have already frequently stressed in the foregoing and repeat yet again, Don Juan can only be expressed in music, something I have myself essentially experienced through the music, so I should guard in every way against giving the impression that the music enters from outside. If the matter is treated in that way, then admire the music in this opera as much as you will, you will not have grasped its absolute significance. [. . .] It is not my intention to examine the whole opera so much as the opera *as* a whole, not dealing with its single parts separately, but incorporating these as far as possible in my examination, so as to see them not apart from but in their connection with the whole.

In a drama the main interest centres quite naturally on what we call the hero of the piece; the other characters assume only a subordinate and relative importance. However, the more the drama is penetrated with the discriminatory power of its own inner reflexivity, the more the minor characters, too, assume a relative absoluteness, if I may so put it. This is by no means a fault, on the contrary it is an advantage, just as the view of the world that can take in only single outstanding individuals and their meaning for its development, but not the common man, may in some sense be a higher way of looking at it, but is lower than one that includes what is less in its equally great validity. The dramatist will only succeed in this to the extent that there is no incommensurable remainder, nothing of the mood from which the drama proceeds, that is to say, nothing of the mood *qua* mood, but everything is converted into the sacred coin of the drama: action and situation. To the extent that the dramatist succeeds in this, the general impression his work produces will be correspondingly less a mood than a thought, an idea. The more the total impression of a drama is a mood, the more certain one can be that the poet's own first intimation of it has been in the mood, and he has allowed it progressively to come into being from that and has not seized it in the form of an idea and let this unfold itself dramatically. Dramas of the latter kind suffer from an abnormal preponderance of lyricism. This is a fault in a drama, but by no means in an opera. What preserves the unity in the opera is the basic tone that carries the whole production.

What has been said here about the total dramatic effect applies in turn to the drama's individual parts. Were I to characterize the effect of drama in a single phrase, inasmuch as it differs from that produced by any other literary form, I would say that drama achieves its effect in contemporaneity. In drama I see mutually unrelated factors brought together in the situation, the unity of action. The more then the discrete factors are separated, the more profoundly the dramatic situation is interpenetrated with reflection, the less the dramatic unity will be a mood and the more a definite thought. But just as the totality of the opera cannot be brought fully to consciousness as in drama proper, so too with the musical situation, which though indeed dramatic has nevertheless its unity in the mood. The musical situation has contemporaneity just like every dramatic situation, but the effect of the forces is a simultaneous sound, a concord, a harmony, and the impression made by the musical situation is the unity achieved by hearing together what sounds together. The more the drama is interpenetrated with reflection, the more the mood is transmuted into action. The less action, the more the lyrical element dominates. In opera this is quite as it should be; opera is less concerned with character delineation and action as its immanent goal; it is not reflective enough for that. On the other hand, in opera passion, unreflective and substantial, finds its expression. The musical situation lies in a unity of mood in the distinct voices. It is exactly the characteristic of music to be able to preserve the plurality of voices in the unity of mood.[39] [. . .]

Dramatic interest calls for a rapid forward movement, an excited rhythm, what one might call the immanently increasing tempo of the fall. The more the drama is interpenetrated with reflection, the more uninterruptedly it hurries along. If, on the other hand, there is a bias in favour of the lyrical or the epic element, this expresses itself in a kind of numbness which allows the situation to go to sleep, makes the dramatic procedure and progress slow and laborious. No such haste is inherent in opera; a certain lingering is characteristic, a certain self-expansion in time and space. The action lacks the pre-cipitancy of the fall, or its direction, but moves more horizontally. The mood is not sublimated in character and action. Consequently, the action in an opera can only be immediate action.

Applying the above to *Don Giovanni* gives us an opportunity to see the latter in its true classic validity. Don Giovanni is the hero in the opera, the main interest centres on him. But that's not all: he bestows interest on all the other figures. This is not to be understood, however, in a merely external sense; the very secret of this opera is that its hero is also the force animating the other characters. Don Giovanni's own life is the principle of life in them. His passion sets in motion the passions of the others; it resonates everywhere, it resonates in and sustains the Commendatore's earnest, Elvira's anger, Anna's hate, Ottavio's self-importance, Zerlina's anxiety, Masetto's indignation and Leporello's confusion. As the eponymous hero, as a hero in general, he gives the piece its name. But he is more; he is, if I may so put it, the common denominator. Compared with his, the existences of all the others are merely derivative. If we require of an opera that its unity be a tonality of mood, we see readily that no more perfect project can be conceived for an opera than Don Giovanni. For, in relation to the forces in the opera, this tonality might have been a third force sustaining these. I could mention *The White Lady* as a case in point,[40] but, in relation to opera, a unity of that kind brings in a further lyrical aspect. In *Don Giovanni* the tonality is nothing other than the primitive power of the opera itself; this is Don Giovanni, but again, just because he is not character but essentially life, he is absolutely musical. The other figures in the opera are not characters either but essentially passions posited through Don Giovanni and are, to that extent again, musical. For as Don Giovanni entwines them all, so do they twine themselves round Don Giovanni; they are the outward consequences constantly posited by his life. It is this absolute centrality of the musical life of Don Giovanni which makes this opera exert a power of illusion as no other, makes its musical life transport one into the life of the play. Because of the omnipresence of the musical in this opera, one may enjoy any snatch of it and be instantly transported. One may enter in the middle of the action and instantly be at its centre, because this centre, which is Don Giovanni's life, is everywhere.

Well-attested experience tells us that it is not pleasant to strain two senses at once, and it is often distracting to have to make much use of the eyes when the ears are already occupied. We have a tendency, therefore, to close our eyes when listening to music. This is true of all music to some extent, of *Don Giovanni* in a higher sense. As soon as the eyes are engaged the impression gets confused, for the dramatic unity afforded to the eye is entirely subordinate and defective compared with the musical unity which is heard simultaneously. My own experience has convinced me of this. I have sat close up, I have sat further and further away, I have resorted to an out-of-the-way corner of the theatre where I could hide myself totally in this music. The better I understood it or believed I understood it, the further I moved away from it, not from coolness but from love, for it wants to be understood at a distance. For my own life there has been something strangely puzzling about this. There have been times when I would have given anything for a ticket; now I needn't spend even a penny for one. I stand outside in the corridor; I lean up against the partition separating me from the auditorium and then the impression is most powerful; it is a world by itself, apart from me, I can see nothing, but am near enough to hear and yet so infinitely far away.

Since the main figures in the opera do not need to be so interpenetrated with reflection that, as characters, they are transparent, it also follows, as was stressed in the foregoing, that the situation cannot be completely developed or full-blown but must to some extent be sustained by a mood. The same applies to the action in an opera. What is called an action in a stricter sense, a deed undertaken in the consciousness of a purpose, cannot find expression in music, but only what one might call immediate action. Now both of these are true of *Don Giovanni*. The action is immediate action; here I must refer to the foregoing where I explained in what sense Don Giovanni is a seducer. Because the action is immediate action, it is also quite proper that irony should be so prevalent in this piece, for irony is and remains the taskmaster of the immediate life. Thus, to cite just one example, the return of the Commendatore is a monstrous irony; for Don Giovanni can overcome every obstacle but we all know you cannot kill a ghost. The situation is sustained throughout by the mood. I must remind you in this connection of Don Giovanni's significance for the piece as a whole, and of the relative existence of the other figures in relation to him. I will indicate what I mean by looking at a single situation more closely.

For this purpose, I choose Elvira's first aria. The orchestra performs the prelude, Elvira enters. The passion raging in her breast must have air, and her song helps her find it. This, however, would be far too lyrical really to form a situation; her aria would be like a monologue in a play. The difference would only be that the monologue in effect renders the universal individually, the aria the individual universally. [. . .] In the background we see Don Giovanni and Leporello in tense expectation of the approach of the lady they have already seen in the window. Now if this was a play, the situation would not consist in Elvira's standing in the foreground with Don Juan in the background, it would consist in the unexpected encounter. Interest would hinge upon how Don Giovanni was going to get out of it. The encounter has its importance in the opera too, but a very subordinate one. The encounter is there to be seen, the musical situation to be heard. The unity in the situation is then the blending of voices in which Elvira and Don Giovanni are heard together. It is therefore also perfectly proper for Don Giovanni to stay as far in the background as possible; for he should not be seen, not only by Elvira but even by the audience. Elvira's aria begins. Her passion I know no way of describing other than as love's hatred, a mingled, but full-bodied, resonant passion. Her inmost being is stirred by turbulent emotions, she has found air, for a moment she grows faint as all passionate outbreaks enervate; there follows a pause in the music. But the turbulence in her inmost being is sufficient to show that her passion has not yet found expression enough, the diaphragm of wrath must vibrate still more intensely. But what can call forth this agitation, what incitement? There can be but one thing – Don Giovanni's mockery. Mozart has therefore made use of this pause in the music – would that I were a Greek, for then I would say, quite divinely – to fling in Don Giovanni's jeering laughter. Now passion blazes stronger, rages even more violently within her and bursts forth in sound. Once again it repeats itself; then her inmost soul trembles, and wrath and pain pour forth like a stream of lava in the celebrated run with which the aria ends.

Here then we see what I mean when I say that Don Giovanni resonates in Elvira, that it is no mere phrase-making on my part. The spectator is not meant to see Don Giovanni, is not meant to see him together with Elvira, in the unity of the situation; he is meant to hear him inside Elvira, coming out of Elvira, for although it is Don Giovanni singing, the way he sings is such that the more developed the spectator's ear the more it sounds as though it was coming from Elvira herself. As love fashions its object, so too does indignation. She is obsessed with Don Giovanni. That pause and Don Giovanni's voice make the situation dramatic, but what makes it musical is the unity in Elvira's passion, in which Don Giovanni resonates while it is nevertheless through him that her passion is posited. Musically conceived, the situation is matchless. But if Don Giovanni is a character and Elvira equally so, then it is a failure and a mistake to let Elvira unburden herself in the foreground while Don Giovanni jeers in the background, for that requires me to hear them together yet without my being given the means to do so, quite apart from their both being characters who could not possibly harmonize in that way. If they are characters, then it is the encounter which forms the situation.

It was remarked above that although opera does not call for the same dramatic urgency, the mounting acceleration of events, as drama, the situation can very well expand just a little. Yet this must not degenerate into perpetual stoppage. As an instance of the happy medium I can single out the situation just discussed, though not as if that were the only one in *Don Giovanni*, or the most perfect – quite the contrary, they are all like this and all perfect – but because the reader will remember this one best. And yet here I am coming to a touchy point; for I admit that there are two arias that must go, which, however perfect they may be in themselves, have nevertheless an obstructive, retarding effect. I would gladly make a secret of this but there is no help for it now, the truth must out. If these are removed, all the rest is just as perfect. One of them is Ottavio's, the other Anna's; they are both more like concert pieces than dramatic music, just as Ottavio and Anna are far too insignificant figures to justify holding up the action. When they are removed the musical-dramatic pace of the rest of the opera is perfect, perfect as no other.

It would be well worth the trouble of going through each individual situation individually, not to accompany it with an exclamation mark but to show its significance, its validity as a musical situation. That, however, is beyond the scope of the present little inquiry. What is especially important here is to highlight the centrality of Don Giovanni within the opera as a whole. Something similar recurs with regard to the individual situations.

I shall throw a little more light on this centrality of Don Giovanni in the opera by considering the other figures in the work in their relation to him. As in a solar system, the dark bodies receiving their light from a sun in the centre are always only half illuminated, on the side facing the sun, so too with the figures in this piece. Only that aspect of life, that side, which is turned towards Don Giovanni is illuminated; otherwise these figures are dim and obscure. This must not be understood in the restricted sense as though each of them were one or another abstract passion – as though Anna, for example, were hate, Zerlina frivolity. Here, least of all, is the place for examples of such poor taste. The passion in the individual is concrete, though concrete in itself, not concrete in the figure; or, to express myself more distinctly, everything else in the figure is swallowed up by that passion. That is absolutely right, because here we are dealing with an opera. This obscurity, this partly sympathetic, partly antipathetic mysterious communication with Don Giovanni makes all of them musical, and has the effect of making the whole opera consonate in Don Giovanni. The only figure in the piece who seems an exception is, naturally, the Commendatore; but that too is why it is so wisely planned as to have him lie to some extent outside the piece, or circumscribe it; the more the Commendatore was brought to the fore, the more the opera would cease to be absolutely musical. So he is always kept in the background and as indistinct as possible. The Commendatore is the powerful antecedent and the fearless consequent between which lives Don Giovanni's middle premiss, but the rich content of this middle premiss is the substance of the opera. The Commendatore appears only twice. The first time it is night, it is at the back of the stage, we cannot see him but we hear him fall to Don Giovanni's sword. His gravity, made all the more strongly apparent by Don Giovanni's parodying mockery, is something Mozart has already splendidly expressed in the music; already his seriousness is too profound to be that of a human being; he is spirit even before he dies. The second time it is as spirit that he appears, and the thundering of heaven resounds in his earnest, solemn voice, but as he himself is transfigured, so his voice is transformed into something more than human; he speaks no more, he judges.

Next to Don Giovanni the most important character in the piece is clearly Leporello. His relation to his master is explicable precisely through the music; without music it is inexplicable. If Don Giovanni were a reflective individual, Leporello would become almost a greater scoundrel than him; then it would be inexplicable how Don Giovanni was able to exercise so much power over him, the only motivation left being his ability to pay him better than anyone else – a motivation that even Molière seems not to resort to, since he has his Don Juan financially embarrassed. If, on the other hand, we continue to identify Don Giovanni as the life of immediacy, we easily grasp how he can exercise a decisive influence upon Leporello, that the latter assimilates him so completely that he almost becomes one of Don Giovanni's functioning parts. In a sense Leporello comes nearer to being consciously personal than Don Giovanni, yet to be that he would have to be clear about his relation to the latter; but that he cannot manage, he is unable to break the spell. Here too it is the case that whenever Leporello is given spoken lines he has to be transparent to us. Even in Leporello's relation to Don Giovanni there is something erotic, a power with which he is captivated against his will; but in this ambiguity he is musical and Don Giovanni constantly resonates through him. I shall offer an example later to show that this is no mere phrase-making on my part.

With the exception of the Commendatore, everyone is in some

kind of erotic relationship to Don Giovanni. Over the Commendatore he cannot exercise any power, for he is consciousness. The others are in his power: Elvira loves him, which puts her in his power; Anna hates him, which puts her in his power; Zerlina fears him, which puts her in his power; Ottavio and Masetto go along with him for the sake of brotherhood-in-law, for the ties of blood are tender.

If I look back now for a moment upon what has been expounded, the reader will perhaps see how, here again, the matter has been explicated from many sides: what relation the Don Juan idea bears to the musical, how this relation is constitutive of the whole opera, how this is repeated in the individual parts. I could gladly stop at this point, but for the sake of even greater completeness I shall shed light on the matter by examining some individual pieces. The choice will not be arbitrary. I take the overture, which really lays down for us, in a tightly concentrated form, the tonality of the opera's mood. Next I take the most epic and the most lyrical moments in the work, in order to show how the perfection of the opera is preserved, the musical drama maintained, even at its extremes, and how Don Giovanni sustains the opera musically.

This is not the place for a general account of the part played by the overture in opera. All we can single out here is the circumstance that the fact that an opera needs an overture is enough to show the preponderance of the lyrical, and that the effect thus aimed at is the evocation of a mood, which is something drama cannot take upon itself, since there everything must be transparent. It is appropriate, therefore, that the overture be composed last, so that the artist himself can be properly permeated with the music. So the overture generally affords an opportunity to gain a deep insight into the composer's soul and its relation to his music. If he hasn't succeeded in grasping its centre, if he has no deeper rapport with the basic mood in the opera, this will betray itself unmistakably in the overture; it will then be a random compilation of the salient points based on the association of ideas, but not a totality containing, as it really should, the most profound illumination of the music's content. An overture of that kind is therefore as a rule also entirely arbitrary; it can be as long or as short as it likes, and the collative element, the element of continuity, since it is only an association of ideas, can be made to spin out as long as may be. To inferior composers the overture is therefore often a dangerous temptation, for they are led to plagiarize themselves, pick from their own pockets, something that causes much confusion. While clearly the content of the overture should not be the same as the opera's, neither, of course, should it be anything absolutely different. Its content should be the same but in some other way. It should contain what is central to the piece so that this can seize the listener with all its might.

In this respect, the ever-admired overture to *Don Giovanni* is and will remain a perfect masterpiece, so that if no other proof were afforded of this opera's classic status, it would suffice to single out this fact alone, namely the inconceivability of the one who holds the centre not also holding the periphery. This overture is no mere fabric of themes, it is not a labyrinthine hotchpotch of associations; it is concise, resolute, powerfully structured; and above all it is impregnated with the essence of the whole opera. It is powerful as the thought of a god, stirring as the life of a world, trembling in its earnest, quivering in its passion, crushing in its terrible anger, inspiring in its zestful joy; it is sepulchral in its judgement, strident in its lust; it is unhurriedly solemn in its imposing dignity; it is stirring, shimmering, dancing in its joy. And it has not achieved this by sucking the blood of the opera; quite the contrary, it is prophetic in its relation to the latter. In the overture, the entire compass of the music unfolds; it is as though, with a few mighty wing-beats, it hovered over itself, hovered over the place where it is to alight. It is a contest, but a contest in the higher regions of the air. To someone hearing the overture after making closer acquaintance with the opera, it might perhaps seem as if he had found his way into the hidden workshop where the forces he has come to know in the opera display their primal energy, where they vie with one another with all their might. Yet the struggle is too unequal, one power is already the victor before the battle, it flees and gets out of the way, but this flight is precisely its passion, its burning unrest in its brief moment of delight, the quickening pulse in its passionate heat. It thereby sets the other power in motion and sweeps it along with it. This latter, which seemed at first so unshakeably firm as to be almost immoveable, must now be off, and soon the movement becomes so fast that it seems like a real contest. To express more of this is an impossible task; all one can do here is listen to the music, for the contest is not one of words but a raging of the elements. Except that I must draw attention to what was made clear earlier, that the opera's focus is Don Giovanni, not Don Giovanni and the Commendatore. This is already evident in the overture. Mozart seems to have carefully constructed it in such a way that the deep voice which resonates at the beginning grows gradually weaker and weaker, almost loses, as it were, its majestic bearing, has to hurry to be able to keep up with the demonic haste which eludes it yet almost gains the power to degrade it by dragging it, in the brevity of an instant, into a race for a wager. With this, the transition to the opera itself gradually takes form. Consequently, one must conceive the finale in close relation to the first part of the overture. In the finale the gravity has once more come to itself, while in the course of the overture it is as though it were outside itself. There is no question now of running a race with passion; earnest has returned and has thus cut off every avenue to a new competition.

So, while in one sense independent, the overture is to be regarded in another sense as preliminary to the opera. I have tried in the foregoing to remind the reader of this by refreshing his memory of the progressive diminutions in which the one power approaches the beginning of the opera. Similarly when one observes the other power; it grows progressively larger. It starts in the overture, it grows and increases. What is particularly admirable is the way in which this, its beginning, is expressed. We hear it intimated so faintly, so mysteriously; we hear it but it is gone so quickly, so what we get is exactly the impression of having heard something we haven't heard. It takes an attentive, an erotic ear to catch the first hint given in the overture of the light play of this desire, which is later expressed so richly in all its extravagant abundance. I cannot say exactly to the dot where this place is because I am not expert in music, but then I am writing only for those in love, and they will surely understand me, some of them better than I understand myself. Still, I am content with my appointed lot, with this enigmatic infatuation, and although I usually thank the gods that I was born a man and not a woman, Mozart's music has taught me that it is beautiful and restorative and rich to love like a woman.

I am no friend of metaphors; modern literature has given me a great aversion to them; it has come almost to the point where, every time I come upon a metaphor, I am seized by an involuntary fear that its true purpose is to conceal an obscurity in the thought. I shall therefore not venture upon an indiscreet or fruitless attempt to translate the overture's energetic and terse brevity into long-winded and platitudinous figures of speech; I single out just one point in the overture, and will employ a metaphor to call the reader's attention to it, that being the only means I have for putting myself in touch with him. This point is naturally none other than Don Giovanni's first outburst, the premonition of him, of the power with which he later emerges. The overture begins with distinct, deep, serious, uniform tones; then for the first time, infinitely far away, we hear a hint which nevertheless, as though it had come too early, is instantly recalled, until later, again and again, bolder and bolder, louder and louder, one hears that voice which first slyly and coyly, and yet as though anxiously, gained access but could not force its way through. Thus sometimes in nature one sees the horizon heavy and lowering. Too heavy to support itself, it rests upon the earth and hides everything in its dark night; distinct hollow sounds are heard, yet not in movement but like a deep rumbling within itself – then one sees at the furthest bounds of the heavens, far on the horizon, a flash; swiftly it runs along the earth and is gone in the same instant. But soon it returns, it grows stronger; for a moment it lights up the whole heaven with its flame, the next instant the horizon seems darker than ever; but swifter, even more fiery it blazes up; it is as if the darkness itself had lost its calm and was getting into motion. As the eye suspects in this first flash a conflagration, so the ear in that dying strain of the violin stroke has a presentiment of all the passion. There is an apprehension in that flash, it is as if in the deep darkness it were born in dread – such is Don Giovanni's life. There is a dread in him, but this dread is his energy. It is not a subjectively reflected dread, it is a substantial dread. In the overture we do not have – what we commonly say without realizing what we say – despair. Don Giovanni's life is not despair; it is the full might of sensuality, which is born in dread, and Don Giovanni is himself this dread, but this dread is precisely the demonic joy of life. After Mozart has brought him thus into existence, Don Giovanni's life evolves for us in the dancing tones of the violin in which he lightly, casually, hastens forward over the abyss. As when one skims a stone over the surface of the water, it skips lightly for a time, but as soon as it stops skipping, instantly sinks down into the depths, that is how Don Giovanni dances over the abyss, jubilant in his brief respite.

But if, as indicated above, the overture can be considered a preliminary to the opera, if in the overture one climbs down from these higher regions, the question is where best in the opera to alight, or how to get the opera to start. Here Mozart has seen the only right way: to begin with Leporello. It might seem that there was no great merit in this, inasmuch as practically all adaptations of the Don Juan story begin with a monologue by Sganarelle. However, there is a big difference, and here again one has an opportunity to admire Mozart's mastery. He has placed the first servant-aria in immediate conjunction with the overture. This is a rare practice; here it is entirely appropriate, and it casts a new light on the overture's construction. The overture is trying to set itself down, to find a foothold in the action on the stage. The Commendatore and Don Giovanni have already been heard in the overture; next to them Leporello is the most important figure. He, however, cannot be raised up into that battle in the airy regions, and yet he is more closely involved than any other. So the action begins with him, in such a way that he is linked immediately with the overture. It is quite correct, then, to count Leporello's first aria as belonging to the overture. This aria corresponds to the not-unnoted Sganarelle monologue in Molière. We shall examine this situation a little more closely. Sganarelle's monologue is far from unwitty. [. . .] On the other hand, the situation is defective. [. . .] I say this not to find fault with Molière but to show Mozart's merit. A monologue is always more or less of an interruption in the drama, and when, for effect, the writer tries to do this through the humour in the monologue itself, instead of through the character, then he has irrevocably condemned himself and abandoned the dramatic interest. In the opera it is otherwise. Here the situation is absolutely musical. I have previously drawn attention to the difference between a dramatic and a dramatic-musical situation. In drama no idle talk is tolerated, what are needed are action and situation. In opera the situation contains a breathing space. But then what makes it a musical situation?

It has been stressed earlier that Leporello is a musical figure, and yet
it is not he who sustains the situation. If it were, his aria would be
analogous to Sganarelle's monologue, even though that would show
equally that a quasi-situation of this kind works better in opera than
in drama. What makes the situation musical is Don Giovanni, who
is in the house. The crux of the situation lies not in Leporello who
draws near us, but in Don Giovanni whom we do not see – but
whom we hear. Now one might well object that we do not in fact
hear Don Giovanni. To this I would reply: we do indeed hear him,
for he resounds in Leporello. To this end I shall draw attention to
the transitions (*voi star dentro colla bella*),[41] where Leporello is
obviously reproducing Don Giovanni. But even if this were not
so, the set-up of the situation is such that we get Don Giovanni
anyway, forgetting Leporello who is outside the house because of
Don Giovanni who is inside it. Altogether, Mozart with true
genius has let Leporello reproduce Don Giovanni, thus achieving
two things: the musical effect that wherever Leporello is alone
we hear Don Giovanni; and the parodying effect that when Don
Giovanni is there too, we hear Leporello rehearse him and thereby
unconsciously parody him. As an example I would mention the
close of the ball.

If anyone asks what is the most epic moment in the opera, the
answer is unquestionably Leporello's second aria, the list. We have
already stressed earlier, by comparing this aria with the corresponding monologue in Molière, the absolute importance of the music,
and how, by letting us hear Don Giovanni, letting us hear the
variations in him, the music produces an effect of which the spoken
word or the dialogue is incapable. Here it is important to emphasize
both the situation and its musical aspect. If we now look at the
stage, the scenic ensemble consists of Leporello, Elvira and the
faithful servant. The faithless lover, on the other hand, is not there,
for, as Leporello fittingly puts it, 'he is off'. This is a virtuosity
possessed by Don Giovanni, he is there and then – he is off, and he
leaves the scene as conveniently (that is, for himself) as a Jeronimus
arrives upon it.[42] Now, since it is obvious he is not there, it may
seem strange that I mention him and bring him in a sense into the
situation. But, on second thoughts, we may perhaps see that this is
just as it should be, and see in it an example of how literally we

must take Don Giovanni's omnipresence in the opera. For one could hardly give a more striking indication of this than by drawing attention to the fact that he is there even when he is away. But let him be off now, all the same, so that we can see later in what sense he is present. We look instead at the three figures on the stage. Elvira's presence naturally contributes to forming a situation, for it would not do to have Leporello unroll the list just to kill time. But the position she is in also contributes to making the situation a painful one. The mockery occasionally made of Elvira's love is undeniably close on cruel. Thus in the second act where, at the decisive moment, when Ottavio has finally got the courage in his heart and the sword from its scabbard to slay Don Giovanni, she throws herself between them and discovers that it is not Don Giovanni but Leporello, a difference Mozart has indicated so strikingly with a kind of whimpering bleat. Thus in the situation we are examining there is something painful too, that she should be present to learn that in Spain the number stands at 1,003; what is more, in the German version she is told indeed that she is one of them. This is a German improvement as foolishly indecent as the German translation itself is no less foolishly, ridiculously decent and a total failure. It is to Elvira that Leporello gives an epic survey of his master's life, and one cannot deny that it is entirely proper that Leporello should recite it and Elvira listen, for they are both exceedingly interested. Therefore, as we constantly 'hear' Don Giovanni throughout the entire aria, so too in places we 'hear' Elvira, who is now visible on the stage as an exemplary witness, not because of some accidental merit on her part, but because, since the method remains essentially the same, one example does for all.

If Leporello were a character or person permeated by reflection, it would be hard to imagine such a monologue, but it is just because he is a musical figure, who is submerged in Don Giovanni, that this aria has so much meaning. It is a reproduction of Don Giovanni's whole life. Leporello is the epic narrator. Though such a one should indeed not be cold or indifferent to what he tells, he ought to be able nevertheless to maintain an objective attitude towards it. This is not the case with Leporello. He is totally diverted by the life he describes, he forgets himself in Don Giovanni. So here I have another example of what it means to say that Don Giovanni resonates everywhere. The situation therefore consists not in Leporello and Elvira's preoccupation with Don Giovanni, but in the mood sustaining the whole, in Don Giovanni's invisible, spiritual presence. To give a more detailed account of how this aria develops, of how it begins peacefully, with little agitation, but becomes more and more inflamed as Don Giovanni's life resounds increasingly within it; of how Leporello is more and more distracted by it, wafted away in and rocked by these erotic breezes; of the nuances it contains as the differentiations of womanhood that come within Don Giovanni's scope become audible in it – for here is not the place.

If anyone asks what is the most lyrical moment in the opera, the answer might be more doubtful; while on the other hand it can hardly be open to doubt that Don Giovanni must be conceded the most lyrical moment, and that it would be a breach of dramatic ranking were it granted to a minor character to engage our attention in this way. Mozart, too, has realized this. The choice is thus considerably restricted, and on closer inspection the only possibilities are either the banquet in the first part of the grand finale or the familiar champagne aria. As far as the banquet scene is concerned, this may indeed be regarded as a lyrical moment; the feast's intoxicating cordials, the foaming wine, the festive strains of distant music, everything unites to intensify Don Giovanni's mood, as his own festive gaiety throws a heightened glow over all the enjoyment, an enjoyment so powerful in its effect that even Leporello is transfigured in this rich moment which is the last smile of gladness, the last farewell to pleasure. On the other hand, it is more of a situation than a sheerly lyrical moment. This, of course, is not because there is eating and drinking on stage, for that in itself is very inadequate in terms of a situation. The situation consists in Don Giovanni's being forced out to life's furthest point. Pursued by the whole world, this victorious Don Giovanni now has nowhere to stay except a small secluded room. It is at the extreme tip of life's see-saw that, once again, for lack of lusty companionship, he excites every lust of life in his own breast. If *Don Giovanni* were a drama, then this inner unrest would have to be made as brief as possible. In the opera, on the other hand, it is proper that it is maintained, glorified by every possible exuberance, which only sounds the wilder because, for the spectators, it reverberates in the abyss over which Don Giovanni is hovering.

It is otherwise with the champagne aria. One looks here in vain, I believe, for a dramatic situation. But it has all the more significance as a lyrical effusion. Don Giovanni is wearied of the many intersecting intrigues; on the other hand he is by no means spent, his soul is still as vigorous as ever, he has no need of convivial society, to see and hear the foaming of the wine or to fortify himself with it; the inner vitality bursts forth in him stronger and richer than ever. Mozart constantly interprets him ideally, as life, as power, but ideally in opposition to a reality; here he is as though ideally intoxicated in himself. If all the girls in the world surrounded him at this moment he would be no danger to them, for it is as though he is too strong to want to turn their heads, even reality's most variegated enjoyment is too little for him compared with what he enjoys in himself. Here is the clear indication of what it means to say that the essence of Don Giovanni is music. He dissolves before us into music, he dilates into a world of tones. This has been called the champagne aria, and that is undeniably very apt. But what is especially to be noted is that it stands in no accidental relation to Don Giovanni. This is his life, foaming like champagne. And just as the bubbles in this wine, while it seethes in inner heat, sonorous in its own melody, rise and continue to rise, so the desire for enjoyment resounds in the elemental boiling that is his life. What gives this aria dramatic significance is not the situation, but the fact that here the keynote of the opera sounds and resounds in itself.

PLATITUDINOUS POSTLUDE

Assuming what has been elaborated here is correct, I return once again to my favourite theme, that among all classic works Mozart's *Don Giovanni* stands highest. I shall rejoice once again over Mozart's good luck, a fortune which is truly enviable, both in itself and because it brings fortune to all those who only moderately grasp his good fortune. For myself, at least, I feel indescribably fortunate in having even remotely understood Mozart, and in having gained some intimations of his good fortune. How much more so, then, those who have perfectly understood him, how much more fortunate must they feel with that fortunate man.

3 ANCIENT TRAGEDY'S REFLECTION IN THE MODERN

An Essay in the Fragmentary Endeavour

Read before
Symparanekromenoi[1]

IF someone said the tragic will always be the tragic, I wouldn't object too much; every historical development takes place within the embrace of its concept. At least assuming that what he says makes sense, and that the twice-repeated 'tragic' isn't just a meaningless bracket surrounding a contentless nothing, the meaning must be that the content of the concept didn't turn the concept off its throne but enriched it. But then surely no observer has failed to notice something – what the reading and theatre-going public indeed already thinks it has legal possession of as a dividend for the labours of the culture experts – namely that there is an essential difference between ancient and modern tragedy. If one were to go on and absolutize this difference, and exploit it first stealthily and then perhaps forcibly to separate the ancient from the modern conception of the tragic, this would be no less absurd than in the former case, for one would be forgetting that the foothold one needs is the tragic itself, and that far from their being separable, this was precisely what bound the ancient and the modern conceptions together. And it must be a warning against any such partisan attempt to separate them that aestheticians still constantly invoke Aristotle's apparatus of conditions and criteria as exhaustive of the concept. All the more necessary this warning in that it must seize people with a certain sadness that, however much the world has changed, the concept of the tragic nevertheless remains essentially unchanged, just as weeping still comes no less naturally to man.

Reassuring as this may seem to one who wishes no divorce, let alone a separation, the same difficulty just circumvented reappears in another and even more dangerous form. No one at all familiar with modern aesthetics, and who therefore recognizes how closely Aristotle's principles are adhered to and still constantly apply in modern aesthetics,[2] will deny that we still keep on going back to Aristotelian aesthetics, not just from dutiful observance or force of habit. But when we look more nearly at these principles the difficulties are immediately evident. The criteria are quite general in kind, and one could easily agree entirely with Aristotle and yet in another sense disagree. So as not to anticipate the discussion

that follows by mentioning right at the start the subject that will
provide its content, I shall illustrate what I mean by making the
corresponding point about comedy. If an aesthetician of the past
had said that what comedy presupposes is character and situation,
and that what it gives rise to is laughter, this is something we can
appeal to over and over again; but as soon as one reflects on how
different the things can be that make people laugh, one is quickly
apprised of the criterion's colossal scope. Anyone who has ever
observed others' or his own laughter, anyone who in the course of
such observation has kept his eye less on accidental differences than on
the general features, whoever has noted with psychological interest
how different the things are that each generation finds laughable,
will be readily convinced that this unchanging criterion of comedy
– that it gives rise to laughter – embraces a high degree of change-
ableness respecting how the world consciousness conceives the laughable, yet without the differences being so far-reaching that the
bodily expression of laughter might be weeping. The same, then, is
true of the tragic.

The gist of this little inquiry will, in the main, be not so much
the relation between the ancient and the modern conception of
the tragic, as an attempt to show how the special characteristic of
ancient tragedy can be discerned in the modern, so that the true
tragedy in the latter may come to light. Yet however hard I try to
ensure that it does come to light, I shall refrain from prophecies
about this being what the age demands. Nothing, then, will result
from its coming to light; all the more so that the tendency of the
whole age is rather towards comedy. Human existence is considerably undermined by doubt on the part of its subjects and
isolation is consistently gaining the upper hand, the best confirmation of which is to take note of all the various *social exertions*. By
aiming to oppose the tendency to isolation, such exertions serve
only to confirm it, as far as they do so by adopting such misguided
means. To be isolated is always to assert oneself numerically; when
you assert yourself as one, that is isolation. I'm sure all friends of
association will concur with me in this, even if they are incapable of
seeing that just the same isolation obtains when hundreds want to
assert themselves as nothing but hundreds. To a number itself the
number is always a matter of indifference, whether it is one or a

thousand or the whole world's population specified merely as a number. This spirit of association is therefore in principle just as revolutionary as the spirit it would counteract. When David wanted to savour properly his power and glory, he had his people counted.[3] In our age you might say, on the contrary, that to feel their importance in the face of a greater power, people count themselves. But all these associations bear the stamp of contingency and are usually formed for some accidental purpose or other, naturally that of the association itself.

The numerous associations thus prove the age's dissolution, and themselves help to hasten it. They are the infusoria in the organism of the state which indicate that it is indeed in dissolution. When did political clubs begin to be general in Greece if not just when the state was on the point of dissolution? And hasn't our own age a remarkable similarity to the one which not even Aristophanes could make more ludicrous than in fact it was? Hasn't that invisible and spiritual bond loosened which held the state together politically? Isn't the power of religion, which held fast to the invisible, weakened and destroyed? Haven't the statesmen and clergy this in common, that like the augurs of old they find it hard to look at one another without smiling?[4] Our age certainly has one peculiarity to a greater degree than Greece, namely that it is more melancholy and hence deeper in despair. Our age is thus melancholy enough to realize there is something called responsibility and that it has some significance. So while everyone wants to rule, no one wants the responsibility. It is still fresh in our memory that a French statesman, on being offered a portfolio for a second time, declared that he would accept on the condition that the secretary of state be made responsible.[5] The King of France, we all know, has no responsibility, while his minister has; the minister does not want to be responsible but wants to be minister provided the secretary of state becomes responsible. Naturally, the end result is that the watchmen or street wardens become responsible.[6] What a subject for Aristophanes, this upside-down tale of responsibility! On the other hand, why is it the government and rulers are so afraid of assuming responsibility, if not because they fear an opposition party that seeks to evade responsibility through its own ladder of command? When one imagines these two powers in mutual opposition but unable to come to grips with each other because the one constantly evades the other, because the one only makes its obeisances before the other, a set-up like that would certainly not lack comic effect. This is enough to show that the real bonds of the state have dissolved, yet the isolation thus incurred is naturally comic, and the comedy is that subjectivity wants to assert itself as mere form. All isolated individuals always become comic by asserting their own accidental individuality in the face of evolutionary necessity. There is no doubt that it would be most deeply comical to have some accidental individual come by the universal idea of wanting to be the saviour of the whole world. On the other hand, the appearance of Christ is in a certain sense the deepest tragedy (in another sense it is infinitely more), because Christ came in the fullness of time, and – a point I must particularly stress in connection with what follows – He bore the sins of all the world.

Aristotle, we know, mentions two things, *dianoia* and *ethos* [thought and character], as the source of the action in tragedy. But he remarks also that the main thing is the *telos* [end or completion], and the individuals do not act in order to portray characters but the latter are included for the sake of the action.[7] One quickly notes a departure here from modern tragedy. The peculiarity of ancient tragedy is that the action does not proceed from character alone, that the action is not reflected enough in the acting subject, but has a relative admixture of suffering. Nor is it the case that ancient tragedy has developed dialogue to the point of exhaustive reflection, so that everything can be absorbed in that. In the monologue and the chorus it does in fact possess the separate elements of dialogue. Whether the chorus approaches the substantiality of epic or the exaltation of lyric, it still points in a way to that extra which will not be absorbed in individuality. The monologue, for its part, has more of the concentration of lyric and its extra is what will not be absorbed in action and situation. In ancient tragedy the action itself possesses an epic feature; it is just as much event as action. The reason is of course to be found in the fact that in the ancient world subjectivity was not fully conscious and reflective. Even though the individual moved freely, he still depended on substantial categories, on state, family, and destiny.

This category of the substantial is the authentically fatalistic element in Greek tragedy, and its true peculiarity. The hero's downfall is therefore not the outcome simply of his own action, it is also a suffering, while in modern tragedy the downfall of the hero is really not suffering but action. In modern times, therefore, it is really situation and character that predominate. The tragic hero is subjectively reflected in himself, and this reflection hasn't simply refracted him out of every immediate relation to state, race, and destiny, often it has refracted him even out of his own preceding life. What interests us is some certain definite moment of his life as his own deed. Because of this, the tragic element can be exhaustively represented in situation and words, there being nothing whatever left over of the immediate. Hence modern tragedy has no epic foreground, no epic heritage. The hero stands and falls entirely on his own deeds.

The significance of this brief but adequate account is to illuminate a difference between ancient and modern tragedy which I consider of great importance: the different kinds of tragic guilt. Aristotle, as we know, requires the tragic hero to have *hamartia* [guilt][8]. But just as the action in Greek tragedy is something intermediate between activity and passivity, so too is the guilt, and in this lies the tragic collision. On the other hand, the more the subjectivity becomes reflected, or the more one sees the individual, in the Pelagian manner, left to himself, the more the guilt becomes ethical.[9] Between these two extremes lies the tragic. If the individual is entirely without guilt, the tragic interest is removed, for the tragic collision loses its power. If, on the other hand, he is guilty absolutely, he can no longer interest us tragically. So it is surely a misunderstanding of the tragic that our age strives to have the whole tragic destiny become transubstantiated in individuality and subjectivity. One turns a deaf ear on the hero's past life, one throws his whole life upon his shoulders as his own doing, makes him accountable for everything; but in so doing one also transforms his aesthetic guilt into an ethical guilt. The tragic hero thus becomes bad. Evil becomes the real object of tragedy. But evil has no aesthetic interest, and sin is not an aesthetic element. No doubt this mistaken endeavour has its origin in the whole tendency of our age to work towards the comic. The comic is to be found precisely in the isolation. If you try to let the tragic take effect inside this isolation, you get the evil in all its baseness, not the properly tragic guilt in its ambiguous innocence. It isn't hard to find examples when one looks about in modern literature. Thus that in many ways brilliant work of Grabbe's, *Faust und Don Juan*, is really built around the notion of evil.[10] However, so as not to argue from just a single work, I shall indicate this instead in the general consciousness of the age as a whole. If one wanted to portray someone upon whom an unhappy childhood had had so disturbing an effect that the experiences in question were the cause of his downfall, a thing like that would simply have no appeal for the present age – and not of course because it was badly handled, for I can certainly take for granted that it would be handled with distinction, but because our age sets another standard. It won't listen to such effeminacy; it holds the individual responsible for his own life, without further ado. So if he goes to the dogs it isn't tragic but bad. It leads you to think this must be a kingdom of gods, this generation in which I too have the honour to live. However, that is by no means the case; the energy, the courage, which would thus be the creator of its own fortune, yes, the creator of itself, is an illusion and in losing the tragic the age gains despair. There is a sadness and a healing power in the tragic which truly one should not despise, and when one wants, in the larger-than-life manner of our age, to gain oneself, one loses oneself and becomes comical. Every individual, however original, is still a child of God, of his age, of his nation, of his family, of his friends. Only thus does he have his truth. If in all this relativity he tries to be the absolute, he becomes ridiculous. In language one sometimes finds a word which, used in a particular case because of the construction, ends up by having independence declared on its behalf, if you will, as an adverb in that particular case.[11] For the experts a word like this acquires an emphasis and weakness it never recovers from. Should it seek recognition as a substantive all the same and insist on its right to be inflected in all five cases, it would be truly comic. And so, too, with the individual when, fetched perhaps with difficulty from the womb of time, he wants in this monstrous relativity to be absolute. But if he renounces the claim of the absolute in order to become relative, then *eo ipso* the tragic is his, even if he were the happiest of individuals; indeed I would say that it is only when the individual has the tragic that he becomes happy.

The tragic contains an infinite leniency; really it is what divine love and mercy are, but from the aesthetic perspective on human life; it is even milder, and so I would say it was a maternal love which soothes the troubled. The ethical is strict and harsh. So if a criminal pleads to the judge that his mother had a propensity for stealing, and particularly at the time she was carrying him, the judge secures the Board of Health's opinion of his mental condition and decides that what he is dealing with is a thief and not a thief's mother. Since we are talking about a crime, the sinner can't very well flee to the temple of aesthetics, and yet the aesthetic will put in an extenuating word for him. Still, it would be wrong for him to seek comfort there, for his path leads him not to the aesthetic but to the religious. The aesthetic lies behind him, and it would be a new sin for him now to grasp at the aesthetic. The religious is the expression of a paternal love, since it contains the ethical but in a mollified form. And mollified by what? Precisely by what gives the tragic its leniency: continuity. But while the aesthetic gives this pause before the profound opposition of sin is pressed home, the religious does not give it until after this opposition is seen in all its fearfulness. Just when the sinner is about to sink under the general sin which he has taken upon himself, because he felt that the more guilty he became the better his prospects for salvation – in that same moment of terror, consolation appears in the fact that it is a general sinfulness which has asserted itself, now also in him. But this is a religious consolation, and he who thinks to attain it in some other way, for instance by aesthetic volatilization, has taken this consolation in vain and doesn't really possess it. In a sense, then, it is a very proper tactic of the age to hold the individual responsible for everything. But the unfortunate thing is that the age does not do it deeply and inwardly enough, and hence its vacillation. It has enough conceit of itself to disdain tragedy's tears, but it also has enough self-conceit to dispense with divine mercy. But then what is human life when we take these two things away? What is the human race? Either the sadness of the tragic, or the profound sorrow and profound joy of religion. Or is that not the peculiarity of everything that emanates from that happy people – a melancholy, a sadness, in its art, in its poetry, in its life, in its joy?

In the preceding I have mainly sought to underline the difference between ancient and modern tragedy, so far as this becomes clear in differences in the tragic hero's guilt. This is really the focus from which all other characteristic differences radiate. If the hero is unequivocally guilty, the monologue disappears and with it destiny. The thought is transparent in the dialogue, and the action in the situation. The same can be put from another point of view with regard to the mood evoked by the tragedy. Aristotle, as we know, requires that tragedy should arouse fear and pity in the spectator. I recollect that Hegel aligns himself with this view in his *Aesthetics* and embarks on a double, though not particularly exhaustive, reflection on each of these points.[12] In respect of Aristotle's distinction between fear and pity, one could interpret fear as the mood accompanying the particular event, and pity as the mood forming the definite impression. It is the latter that I have most in mind, because it is this that corresponds to tragic guilt, and so it has the same dialectic as that concept. Now Hegel observes in this connection that there are two kinds of compassion, the ordinary kind concerned with the finite aspect of suffering, and true tragic pity. This, indeed, is correct, but for me of less importance, since the common emotion is a misunderstanding which can just as well apply to ancient as to modern tragedy. What Hegel adds regarding true pity, however, is straight to the point: 'True pity, on the contrary, is sympathy at the same time with the sufferer's justification.'[13] While Hegel considers compassion in general and its differences in individual variation, I prefer to underline differences in compassion as they are related to differences in tragic guilt. To make the point in a trice I shall let the passion in the word 'compassion' be split up and ascribe the sympathy which the word expresses to every man, without saying anything about the mood of the spectator that might be traced to his contingency but in such a way that, in explaining the difference in his mood, I also express the difference in the tragic guilt.

In ancient tragedy the sorrow is deeper, the pain less; in modern tragedy, the pain is greater, the sorrow less. Sorrow always contains something more substantial than pain. Pain always indicates a reflection on suffering which sorrow does not know. It is very interesting, from a psychological standpoint, to watch a child when it sees an older person suffer. The child hasn't sufficient reflection to feel pain, and yet its sorrow is infinitely deep. It hasn't sufficient reflection to have a conception of sin and guilt, so when it sees an older person suffer, it does not occur to it to think about it, and yet when the cause of the suffering is concealed from it, there is a dim presentiment of it in its sorrow. Such too, though in complete and profound harmony, is the Greek sorrow, and that is why it is at one and the same time so gentle and so deep. But when an older person sees someone younger, a child, suffer, his pain is greater, his sorrow less. The more clear the conception of guilt, the greater the pain and the less profound the sorrow. Applying this, then, to the relation between ancient and modern tragedy, one has to say: in ancient tragedy, the sorrow is deeper, and in the corresponding consciousness, too, the sorrow is deeper. For one must always bear in mind that the sorrow lies not in me, but in the tragedy, and that to understand the deep sorrow of Greek tragedy I must enter into the Greek consciousness. Often, then, it is surely only affectation when so many people profess to admire Greek tragedy; for it is obvious that our age has at least no great sympathy with the real character of Greek sorrow. The sorrow of Greek tragedy is deeper because the guilt has the ambiguity of the aesthetic. In modern times the pain is greater. It is a fearful thing to fall into the hands of the living God,[14] that is what one might say about Greek tragedy. The wrath of the gods is terrible, yet the pain is not so great as in modern tragedy, where the hero suffers all his guilt, is transparent to himself in his own suffering of his guilt.

Here, as with tragic guilt, we must show what is the true aesthetic sorrow and what the true aesthetic pain. Now, obviously the bitterest pain is remorse, but remorse has an ethical, not an aesthetic, reality. It is the bitterest pain because it has all of guilt's total transparency, but just because of this transparency it has no aesthetic interest. Remorse has a holiness which obscures the aesthetic. It won't be seen, least of all by the spectator, and it requires quite a different kind of self-activity. True, modern comedy has sometimes presented remorse on the stage, but this just shows lack of judgement on the part of the author. Perhaps it has to do with the thought of the psychological interest one may have in seeing remorse portrayed, but then again, psychological interest is not the aesthetic. This is part of the confusion evident in so many ways in our age: we look for a thing where we ought not to look for it; and worse, we find it where we ought not to find it. We want to be edified in the theatre, to be influenced aesthetically in church, to be converted by novels, to enjoy books of devotion; we want philosophy in the pulpit and the preacher in the professorial chair. This pain is accordingly not aesthetic pain, yet clearly it is this the modern age works towards as its highest tragic interest. The same is true of tragic guilt. Our age has lost all the substantial categories of family, state and race. It has to leave the individual entirely to himself, so that in a stricter sense he becomes his own creator. His guilt is therefore sin, his pain remorse. But the tragic is then done away with. And what is, in a stricter sense, the tragedy of suffering has really lost its tragic interest, for the power from which the suffering comes has lost its meaning, and the spectator cries: 'Heaven helps those who help themselves!' In other words, the spectator has lost his compassion. But compassion is, in an objective as well as a subjective sense, the authentic expression of the tragic.

For clarity's sake, and before going further with this account, I shall identify true aesthetic sorrow a little more closely. Sorrow has the opposite movement to that of pain. So long as one doesn't spoil things out of a misplaced mania for consistency – something I shall prevent also in another way – one may say: the more innocence, the deeper the sorrow. If you press this too far, you destroy the tragic. There is always an element of guilt left over, but it is never properly reflected in the subject; which is why in Greek tragedy the sorrow is so deep. In order to prevent misplaced consistency, I shall merely remark that exaggeration only succeeds in carrying the matter over into another sphere. The synthesis of absolute innocence and absolute guilt is not an aesthetic feature but a metaphysical one. This is the real reason why people have always been ashamed to call the life of Christ a tragedy; one feels instinctively that aesthetic categories do not exhaust the matter. It is clear in another way, too, that Christ's life amounts to more than can be exhausted in aesthetic terms, namely from the fact that these terms neutralize themselves in this phenomenon, and are rendered irrelevant. Tragic action always contains an element of suffering, and tragic suffering an element of action; the aesthetic lies in the relativity. The identity of an absolute action and an absolute suffering is beyond the powers of aesthetics and belongs to metaphysics. This identity is exemplified in the life of Christ, for His suffering is absolute because the action is absolutely free, and His action is absolute suffering because it is absolute obedience. The element of guilt that is always left over is, accordingly, not subjectively reflected and this makes the sorrow deep. Tragic guilt is more than just subjective guilt, it is inherited guilt. But inherited guilt, like original sin, is a substantial category, and it is just this substantiality that makes the sorrow deeper. Sophocles' celebrated tragic trilogy, *Oedipus at Colonus*, *Oedipus Rex* and *Antigone*, turns essentially on this authentic tragic interest. But inherited guilt contains the self-contradiction of being guilt yet not being guilt. The bond that makes the individual guilty is precisely piety, but the guilt which he thereby incurs has all possible aesthetic ambiguity. One might well conclude that the people who developed profound tragedy were the Jews. Thus, when they say of Jehovah that he is a jealous God who visits the sins of the fathers on the children unto the third and the fourth generations,[15] or one hears those terrible imprecations in the Old Testament, one might feel tempted to look here for the material of tragedy. But Judaism is too ethically developed for this. Jehovah's curses, terrible as they are, are nevertheless also righteous punishment. Such was not the case in Greece, there the wrath of the gods has no ethical character, but aesthetic ambiguity.

In Greek tragedy itself we find a transition from sorrow to pain, and as an example of this I must mention the *Philoctetes*.[16] This is, in the stricter sense, a tragedy of suffering. But here, too, there is a high degree of objectivity. The Greek hero reposes in his fate, his fate is unchangeable, there is nothing further to be said about it. This factor furnishes the element of sorrow in the pain. The first doubt with which pain really begins is this: why has this befallen me, why can it not be otherwise? It is true that in the *Philoctetes* there is – and this is something that has always struck me as remarkable and as essentially distinguishing this piece from the immortal trilogy – a high degree of reflection: the masterly portrayal of the self-contradiction in his pain, which contains so deep a human truth while an objectivity still sustains the whole.[17] Philoctetes' reflection doesn't become absorbed in itself, and it is typically Greek that he complains that no one understands his pain. There is an exceptional truth in this, and yet it is just here that the difference shows between his pain and the reflective pain that always wants to be alone in its pain, which seeks a new pain in this solitude of pain.

True tragic sorrow accordingly requires an element of guilt, true tragic pain an element of innocence. True tragic sorrow requires an element of transparency, true tragic pain an element of opaqueness. This I believe best indicates the dialectic in which the categories of sorrow and pain come in contact with each other, as well as the dialectic inherent in the concept of tragic guilt.

Seeing it is contrary to the spirit of our Society to produce closely coherent works or greater wholes. Seeing it is not our purpose to labour upon a Tower of Babel which God in His righteousness can descend upon and destroy. Seeing that we, conscious of the justness of that confusion of tongues, recognize the fragmentary as a characteristic of all human striving in its truth and realize that it is precisely this that distinguishes it from the infinite coherence of Nature, that an individual's wealth consists precisely in his power of fragmentary extravagance, and that the producer's enjoyment is also that of the receiver, not the laborious and meticulous execution, nor the protracted apprehension of this execution, but rather the production and enjoyment of that gleaming transience which for the producer contains something more than the completed effort, since it is the appearance of the Idea, and which for the recipient, too, contains a surplus, seeing that its fulguration awakens his own productivity – since all this, I say, is contrary to our Society's penchant (and since, indeed, even the period just read could well be regarded as a disquieting attack upon the interjectory style in which the idea breaks out but without breaking through, a style which in our Society is accorded official status), then, having called attention to the fact that my conduct still cannot be called rebellious, seeing that the bond holding this period together is so loose that the intermediary clauses stand out in a sufficiently aphoristic and arbitrary manner, I shall merely call to mind that my style has made an attempt to appear to be what it is not – revolutionary.

This Society demands at every one of its meetings a renewal and rebirth, and for the following reason: that its inner activity may be rejuvenated by a new description of its productivity. Let us then describe our purpose as essays in the fragmentary endeavour, or in the art of writing posthumous papers. A fully completed work has no relation to the poetic personality; with posthumous papers one constantly feels, because of their broken-off, desultory character, a need to imagine the personality as being a part. Posthumous papers are like a ruin, and what haunt could be more natural for the interred? The art is therefore artistically to produce the same effect, the same carelessness and contingency, the same anacoluthic flight of thought. The art is to produce an enjoyment which never actually becomes present, but always has in it an element of the past, so that it is present in the past. This is already expressed in the word 'posthumous'. In a sense everything a writer produces is posthumous, yet one would never think of calling a completed work posthumous, even if it possessed the accidental quality of not having been published in his lifetime. Also, it is, I assume, a characteristic of all human productivity, as we have apprehended it, that it is an inheritance, since it is not men's privilege to live in the everlasting sight of the gods. Inheritance [*Efterladenskab*] is therefore what I shall call what is produced among us, an artistic inheritance; negligence [*Efterladenhed*], indolence, I shall call the genius that we appreciate; *vis inertiae*,[18] the natural law that we worship. In saying this I have complied with our sacred customs and rules.

So draw nearer to me, dear *Symparanekromenoi*, gather round me as I send my tragic heroine out into the world, as I give to the daughter of sorrow as her wedding gift a dowry of pain. She is my creation, yet her outline is so vague, her form so nebulous, that each one of you is free to fall for her and to love her in your own way. She is my creation, her thoughts are my thoughts, and yet it is as if I had lain with her in a night of love, as if she had entrusted me with her deep secret, breathed forth both it and her soul in my embrace, and as if the same instant she was transformed before me, had vanished so that her reality could only be traced in the mood that lingered on; instead of the opposite being true, that she was born to greater and greater reality from my own mood. I put words in her mouth, and yet to me it is as though I abused her confidence, she seems to stand reproachfully behind me; yet it is the other way around, in her secrecy she becomes more and more visible. She is my possession, my lawful possession, and yet sometimes it is as if I had crept into her confidence, slyly, as if I must constantly look round to find her behind me; and yet it is the other way around, she is constantly in front of me, she comes into existence only when I bring her forth. She is called Antigone. This name I retain from the ancient tragedy, which in general I shall follow, except that everything will be modern. But first a remark. I use a feminine figure because I really believe that a feminine nature is best suited to showing the difference. As a woman, she will have the substantiality needed for sorrow to be revealed, but as a member of a reflective world, she will have reflection enough to experience pain. In order to experience sorrow, tragic guilt must vacillate between guilt and innocence; what conveys the guilt into her consciousness must always be some substantial feature. But since, in order to experience sorrow, tragic guilt must have this vagueness, reflection must not be present in its infinitude, for then it would refract her out of her guilt, since reflection in its infinite subjectivity cannot allow the element of inherited guilt to which sorrow is due to remain. Since, however, her reflection is awakened, it will not refract her out of her sorrow but into it, at every moment transforming her sorrow into pain.

Labdacus's family, then, is the object of the angry gods' indignation.[19] Oedipus has killed the sphinx, liberated Thebes; he has murdered his father, married his mother, and Antigone is the fruit of that marriage. Thus it is with the Greek tragedy. Here I depart from it. I keep all the facts of the case just as they are, yet everything is different. That he has slain the sphinx and liberated Thebes, we all know. And Oedipus lives honoured and admired, happy in his marriage with Jocasta. The rest is concealed from the eyes of men, and no presentiment has ever summoned this horrible nightmare out into reality. Only Antigone knows it. How she has come to know it falls outside the tragic interest, and everyone is free to concoct his own explanation. At an early age, before she is yet fully matured, vague suspicions of this horrible secret have now and then gripped her soul, until with a single blow certainty casts her into the arms of anxiety. Here, straightaway, I am given my definition of the modern idea of the tragic. For anxiety is a reflection, and in this it differs essentially from sorrow. Anxiety is the organ through which the subject appropriates sorrow and assimilates it. Anxiety is the energy of the movement by which sorrow bores its way into the heart. But the movement is not swift like the arrow's, it is gradual. It is not once and for all, but in constant becoming. As a passionate, erotic glance desires its object, anxiety looks at sorrow in order to desire it. As a quiet, incorruptible glance of love is pre-occupied with the beloved object, anxiety preoccupies itself with sorrow. But anxiety contains something extra which makes it cling even more strongly to its object, for it both loves and fears it. Anxiety has a double function. It is the movement of discovery that constantly touches, and by fingering it, discovers sorrow by going around it. Or anxiety is sudden, positing the whole sorrow in the here and now, yet in such a way that this here and now instantly dissolves into succession. Anxiety in this sense is a genuinely tragic category, and this is where the old saying *quem deus vult perdere, primum dementat*[20] comes properly into its own. The fact that anxiety is a phenomenon of reflection is something language itself indicates; for I always say 'to be anxious about something', thus separating the anxiety from that about which I am anxious; I can never use anxiety to refer to its object. Whereas, if I say 'my sorrow', this, on the contrary, can express what I sorrow over just as much as my sorrow over it. Anxiety, furthermore, always involves a reflection upon time, for I cannot be anxious about the present, only about the past or the future; but the past and the future, holding on to each other so tightly that the present vanishes, are reflective phenomena. Greek sorrow, on the contrary, like the whole of Greek life, is in the present tense, and therefore the sorrow is deeper but the pain less. So anxiety is essential to the tragic. Hence Hamlet is deeply tragic because he suspects his mother's guilt. Robert le Diable asks how he could ever have come to cause so much evil.[21] Hogne, whom his mother had begotten with a troll, happening to see his image in the water, asks his mother how his body acquired such a shape.[22]

The difference is now plain to see. In the Greek tragedy Antigone is not at all concerned about her father's unhappy destiny. This rests like an impenetrable sorrow over the whole family. Antigone lives as carefree a life as any other young Greek girl; indeed the chorus pities her, seeing her death is preordained, because she is to quit this life at so early an age, quit it without having tasted its most beautiful joys, evidently forgetting the family's own deep sorrow. That doesn't at all imply frivolity, or mean that the particular individual stands alone by himself, unconcerned with his relationship to the family. It is authentically Greek. Life-relationships are assigned to them once and for all, just like the heaven under which they live. If that is dark and cloudy it is also unchangeable. It gives the soul a keynote, and that is sorrow, not pain. In Antigone, tragic guilt focuses on a definite point: that she had buried her brother in defiance of the king's prohibition. If this is seen as an isolated fact, as a collision between sisterly affection and piety and an arbitrary human prohibition, then the *Antigone* would cease to be a Greek tragedy, it would be an altogether modern tragic subject. What in the Greek sense provides tragic interest is the fact that, in the brother's unhappy death, in the sister's collision with a single human circumstance, there is a re-echoing of Oedipus's sorry fate; it is, one might say, the afterpains, the tragic destiny of Oedipus, ramifying in every branch of his family. This totality makes the spectator's sorrow infinitely deep. It is not an individual that goes under, but a little world; the objective sorrow, set free, now strides forward with its own terrible consistency, like a force of nature, and Antigone's sorry fate is like an echo of her father's, an intensified sorrow. So when Antigone, in defiance of the king's prohibition, resolves to bury her brother, we see in this not so much a free action on her part as a fateful necessity which visits the sins of the fathers on the children. There is indeed enough freedom here to make us love Antigone for her sisterly love, but in the necessity of fate there is also, as it were, a higher refrain enveloping not just the life of Oedipus, but all his family too.

So while the Greek Antigone lives a life free enough from care for us to imagine her life in its gradual unfolding as even being a happy one if this new fact had not emerged, our Antigone's life is, on the contrary, essentially over. It is no stingy endowment I have given her, and as we say that an aptly spoken word is like apples of gold in pictures of silver, so here have I placed the fruit of sorrow in a cup of pain. Her dowry is not a vain splendour which moth and rust can corrupt,[23] it is an eternal treasure. Thieves cannot break in and steal it; she herself will be too vigilant for that. Her life does not unfold like that of the Greek Antigone; it is not turned outward but inward. The scene is not external but internal, a scene of the spirit.

Have I not succeeded, dear *Symparanekromenoi*, in arousing your interest in such a girl, or must I resort to a *captatio benevolentiae*?[24] She, too, does not belong to the world she lives in; however flourishing and healthy, her real life is clandestine. She, too, though living, has in another sense departed; quiet is that life and hidden, not even a sigh does the world hear, for her sigh is hidden in the privacy of her soul. I need not remind you that she is by no means a weak and sickly woman, quite the contrary, she is vigorous and proud. Perhaps nothing ennobles a human being so much as keeping a secret. It gives a man's whole life a meaning, though one that it has only for him. It saves him from every vain regard for his environment; sufficient unto himself, he rests blessed in his secret — we can almost say that, even if his secret were the most sinister. Such is our Antigone. Proud of her secret, proud that she has been chosen to save in so remarkable a manner the honour and esteem of the house of Oedipus; and when the grateful people cheer Oedipus and applaud him, she is conscious of the role she is playing, and her secret sinks deeper into her soul, even more inaccessible to any living being. She feels how much has been placed in her hands, and this gives her the larger-than-life dimension needed for her to engage us as a tragic personality. She must interest us as an individual figure. More than just a common young girl, she is yet a young girl; she is a bride, but in all innocence and purity. As a bride, woman achieves her destiny, and ordinarily a woman can interest us only to the degree that she is brought into relation to this her destiny. But there are analogies here. One says of a bride of God that it is faith and spirit that provide the substance in which she rests. I would call our Antigone a bride in perhaps an even more beautiful sense, indeed she is almost more than that, she is mother; in the purely aesthetic sense she is *virgo mater*,[25] she bears her secret under her heart, out of sight and undetected. She is silence precisely because she is secretive, but this self-withdrawal, implicit in silence, makes her larger than life. Proud of her sorrow, she is jealous over it, for her sorrow is her love. Yet her sorrow is not a dead, immovable possession: it is constantly in motion, it gives birth to pain and is born in pain. As when a girl resolves to dedicate her life to an idea, when she stands there with the sacrificial wreath upon her brow she is a bride, for the great inspirational idea transforms her and the votive wreath is like a bridal garland. She knows not any man, yet she is a bride; she knows not even the idea that inspires her, for that would be unwomanly. Yet she is a bride.

Such is our Antigone, the bride of sorrow. She consecrates her life to sorrow over her father's destiny, over her own. A misfortune such as has overtaken her father calls for sorrow, yet there is no one who can grieve over it, because there is no one who has knowledge of it. And as the Greek Antigone cannot bear to have her brother's corpse flung away without the last honours, so she feels how cruel it would be should no one come to know of this; it troubles her that no tears should be shed; she practically thanks the gods because she has been chosen as this instrument. Thus is Antigone great in her pain. Here, too, I can indicate a difference between Greek and modern tragedy. It is genuinely Greek for Philoctetes to complain that there is no one who knows what he suffers; it is an expression of a deep human need to want others to realize this. Reflective grief, however, has no such desire; it does not occur to Antigone to wish that anyone should learn of her pain. But she feels it in relation to her father, she feels the justice of having to suffer grief, which is just as proper aesthetically as that a man should suffer punishment if he has done wrong. So while it is the idea of her being about to be buried alive that first wrings from the Antigone of the Greek tragedy this outburst of grief:

> O hapless alien,
> Lodged with neither mortal man nor corpse,
> Not with the living nor yet with the dead,[26]

our own Antigone can say this about herself all her life. The difference is striking; there is a factual truth in the former's assertion that makes the pain less. If our Antigone were to say the same, it would be unreal, but it is this unreality which is the real pain. The Greeks do not express themselves figuratively, precisely because the reflection that goes with this was not present in their lives. So when Philoctetes complains that he lives solitary and forsaken on a desert island, what he says is also an outward truth. But when our Antigone feels pain in her solitude, it is only in a figurative sense that she is alone. Yet just for that reason, her pain is real pain.

As far as the tragic guilt goes, on the one hand it lies in the fact that she buries her brother, but also partly in the context of her father's sorry fate, which is presupposed from the two preceding tragedies. Here again I come to the peculiar dialectic which puts the guilt of Oedipus's house in relation to the individual. This is hereditary guilt. Dialectics is commonly considered fairly abstract; one thinks usually of logical steps. However, one soon learns from life that there are many kinds of dialectic, that nearly every passion has its own. So the dialectic which puts the guilt of the race or family in connection with the particular subject, so that the latter is not just a passive sufferer under it – for that is a natural consequence one would try in vain to steel oneself against – but bears the guilt along with the suffering, participates in it, this dialectic is foreign to us, does not compel us. But if one were to envisage a rebirth out of ancient tragedy, then every individual would have to be concerned about his own rebirth, not just in a spiritual sense, but in the definite sense of a rebirth from the womb of family and race. The dialectic which puts the individual in connection with family and race is no subjective dialectic, for what that does is precisely to remove the connection and take the individual out of the network of relationships. No, it is an objective dialectic. Essentially it is piety, and to preserve piety cannot be considered in any way harmful to the individual. In our time one allows in respect of nature what one is loth to allow in matters of spirit. Still, one would not wish to be so isolated, so unnatural, as not to regard the family as a whole, of which one must say that if one member suffers, then all suffer. This one does involuntarily, and why else should a particular individual fear lest another member of the family brings disgrace upon it, if not because he feels that he, too, will suffer the disgrace? This suffering the individual must obviously take along with him, whether he wants to or not. But since the point of departure here is the individual not the family, this enforced suffering is *maximum*; one senses that mankind cannot be complete master over its natural circumstances, yet still wants to be so as far as possible. If, on the other hand, the individual looks on the natural tie as a factor involved in his own truth, the way to express this in the spiritual world is: the individual participates in the guilt. This is an implication many people would perhaps be unable to grasp, but then neither could they grasp the tragic. If the individual is isolated, he is either absolutely the creator of his own destiny, in which case nothing tragic remains, but only the evil – for it is not even tragic for an individual to be blinded by or engrossed in himself, it is his own doing – or individuals are nothing but modifications of the eternal substance of existence, and so once again the tragic is lost.

Regarding tragic guilt, a difference in the modern version comes readily to view only after the latter has discerned the ancient within it, for only then can we speak of this. The Greek Antigone participates in her father's guilt through filial piety, as does also our modern one. But for the Greek Antigone her father's guilt and suffering is an external fact, an immovable fact, which her sorrow does not alter (*quod non volvit in pectore*);[27] and in so far as she herself, as a natural consequence, personally suffers under her father's guilt, this again is an altogether external fact. With our Antigone it is otherwise. I assume now that Oedipus is dead. Even while he lived Antigone had been aware of this secret but lacked the courage to confide in her father. His death has deprived her of the only means by which she could be freed from her secret. Confiding it now to any living being would be to disgrace her father; the meaning her life acquires for her is in its dedication, through her inviolable silence, to showing him the last honours daily, almost hourly. There is one thing, however, of which she is ignorant. She does not know whether her father himself knew. This is the modern feature; the disquietude in her sorrow, the ambiguity in her pain. She loves her father with all her soul, and this love draws her out of herself and into her father's guilt. The fruit of such love is a sense of alienation from mankind; she feels her own guilt the more she loves her father; only with him can she find rest, so that, equally guilty, they would grieve with each other. But while her father was living she had been unable to confide her sorrow to him, for she did not know whether he knew about it, and so there was a possibility of plunging him into a similar pain. And yet, was he less guilty for not knowing about it? The movement here is constantly relative. Had Antigone not known the circumstances with certainty, she would lack significance, she would have nothing but a suspicion to struggle with, and in that there is too little of the tragic to interest us. But she does know everything; yet even in this knowledge there is still an ignorance which can always keep sorrow in motion, always transform it into pain. In addition, she is constantly at odds with her external surroundings. Oedipus lives in the people's memory as a king favoured by fortune, honoured and fêted; Antigone herself has admired as well as loved her father. She takes part in every celebration in his honour, she enthuses over her father as none other in the realm, her thoughts constantly return to him, she is praised throughout the land as a model of a loving daughter. Yet this enthusiasm is her only way of giving vent to her sorrow. Her father is always in her thoughts, but how is he in those thoughts? – that is her painful secret. And yet she dare not give in to her sorrow, dare not openly fret; she feels how much depends on her, she fears that if anyone saw her suffering, people would pick up the trail, and so from this side, too, what she gets is not sorrow but pain.

Expanded and reworked in this way, I think we can very well find interest in Antigone. I think you will not reproach me for frivolity or paternal partiality when I believe that she might well try her hand at the tragic disciplines and venture an appearance in a tragedy. Hitherto she has only been an epic figure, and the tragic in her only held an epic interest.

Nor is it all that hard to find a context in which she could fit. In this respect we can just as well make do with the one provided by the Greek tragedy. She has a sister living. Let's have her rather older than Antigone and married. Her mother could also be living. That these will naturally always be minor characters goes without saying, as also the fact that in general the tragedy acquires an epic element, as the Greek one does, though it need not be so very conspicuous on that account. Still, the monologue will always play a principal role here, even if the situation ought to come to its assistance. One has to imagine everything united around this one main interest which comprises the content of Antigone's life, and when everything has been put in order, the question arises: how is the dramatic interest to be brought home?

Our heroine, as she has presented herself in the foregoing, is set on wanting to skip over an element in her life; she is on the point of wanting to live in a wholly spiritual manner, something nature does not tolerate. With her depth of soul she needs to love with an extraordinary passion, if she does fall in love. Here, then, I have the dramatic interest – Antigone is in love, and I say it with pain,

Antigone is mortally in love. Here manifestly is the dramatic collision. In general one should be rather more particular about what to
refer to as dramatic collision. The more sympathetic the colliding
forces are, and the deeper but also more homogeneous they are, the
more significant the collision. So she is in love, and the object of her
affection is not ignorant of this fact. Now, my Antigone is no
ordinary woman, and so her dowry, too, is unusual – it is her pain.
Without this dowry she cannot belong to a man, that she feels
would be too high a risk; to conceal it from such an observer would
be impossible; to want to have concealed it would be to sin against
her love. But can she belong to him with it? Dare she confide it to
any human being, even to a beloved husband? Antigone has
strength; the question is not whether to reveal something of her
pain for her own sake, to lighten her heart, for this indeed she can
bear without support. But can she justify this to the dead? She
herself would suffer, too, in a way, by confiding her secret to her
husband, for her own life too is grievously interwoven in it.
This, however, does not trouble her. The only question concerns
her father. From this angle, therefore, the collision is of a sympathetic nature. Her life, formerly peaceful and quiet, now becomes
violent and passionate, always of course within herself, and her
words here begin to fill with pathos. She struggles with herself, she
has been willing to sacrifice her life to her secret, but now what is
demanded as a sacrifice is her love. She wins – that is to say, the
secret wins and she loses. Then comes the second collision, because
in order for the tragic collision to be really profound, the colliding
forces must be homogeneous. The collision described up to now
lacked this quality, for the real collision is between her love for her
father and her love for herself, and whether her own love is not too
great a sacrifice. The other colliding force is the sympathetic love
for her beloved. He knows he is loved, and boldly sues for her
hand. Doubtless her reserve puzzles him, he notes that there must be
some quite special difficulties, but not insurmountable ones. The all-
important thing for him is to convince her how much he loves her,
yes, persuade her that his life is over if he must waive his claim to
her love. His passion becomes at last something almost unreal, but
then only the more inventive because of her resistance. Every assurance of his love increases her pain, with every sigh he buries the dart

of sorrow ever deeper into her heart. He leaves no means untried to persuade her. Like everyone else, he knows how much she loved her father. He meets her at Oedipus's grave, to which she has repaired to ease her heart, where she abandons herself to her yearning for her father, even though this very yearning is mingled with pain, for she knows not how a new encounter with him might be, whether he was cognisant of his guilt. Her lover surprises her and beseeches her in the name of the love with which she enfolds her father; he sees that the impression he is making on her is an unusual one, but he persists, he puts all his hope in this means, and he doesn't know that in doing so he has defeated his own intentions.

What the interest focuses on, then, is his being able to wrest her secret from her. Letting her become momentarily deranged, and so betray it in that way, would not help. The colliding forces hold their own so evenly that action becomes impossible for the tragic individual. Her pain is now increased by her love, by her sympathetic suffering with the one she loves. Only in death can she find peace; thus her whole life is consecrated to sorrow, and it is as though she had set a limit, a dike against the woe that might perhaps have fatally transmitted itself to a succeeding generation. Only in her moment of death can she admit the intensity of her love; she can only admit that she belongs to him at that instant when she does not belong to him. When Epaminondas was wounded in the battle of Mantinea, he left the arrow in the wound until he heard the battle was won, because he knew that the moment it was drawn out he would die. Thus our Antigone bears her secret in her heart like an arrow which life has driven constantly in, deeper and deeper, without depriving her of life, for as long as it remains in her heart she can live. But the moment it is drawn out she must die. Wresting her secret from her is what her lover must constantly strive for, yet this means her certain death. By whose hand, then, does she fall? That of the living or the dead? In a sense of the dead, for what was prophesied of Hercules, that he would not be slain by someone living but by someone dead,[28] is true also of her, in so far as the cause of her death is the memory of her father; in another sense it is by the hand of the living, in so far as her unhappy love provides the occasion for that memory to put her to death.

4 SHADOWGRAPHS

Psychological Entertainment

Read before
Symparanekromenoi

Love may always breach its oath;
Love's spell in this cave does lull
The drunken, startled soul
Into forgetting it pledged its troth.

*

Yesterday I loved,
Today I suffer,
Tomorrow I die.
Yet fain would I think
Today and tomorrow,
Of yesterday.[1]

We celebrate, in this hour, the founding of our Society. We rejoice once more at the recurrence of the happy event of the longest day's passing and the commencement of the victory of night. This long, livelong day we have waited; even a moment ago we were sighing at its length, but now our despair is turned to joy. True, the victory is but trifling and the day will remain in the ascendant yet a while, but the fact that its dominion has been broken does not escape us. So we do not put off our celebrations until night's victory can be seen by all, do not wait until the sluggish bourgeois life reminds us that the day is waning. No, as a young bride impatiently awaits nightfall, we longingly await the first onset of night, the first announcement of its coming victory, and the nearer we approach despair at what to do should the days not shorten, the greater our joy and surprise.

A year has passed and our Society is still in being. Shall we rejoice at this fact, dear *Symparanekromenoi*, rejoice that its survival mocks our teaching that everything must end? Or should we not rather sorrow over the fact that it is still there, and be glad that in any case it has just one more year to go, seeing we decided to dissolve it if it had not vanished of itself before then? – In founding it we have formed no far-reaching plans, for knowing life's misery and the perfidy of existence we are resolved to lend the law of the world a hand and destroy ourselves if it does not get there first. A year has passed and our numbers are still complete, no vacancies have occurred. And none has been made; we are each of us too proud for that, for we all look upon death as the greatest good fortune. Should we rejoice over this and not rather sorrow, and be glad only in the hope that life's tumult will soon separate us, that life's storm will soon snatch us away? Thoughts like these are indeed better suited to our Society, accord best with the moment's celebration, with the whole setting. For is it not a stroke of genius and a matter of significance that the floor of this little room, according to the custom of the land, should be strewn with green as though for a funeral, and does not the nature that surrounds us itself lend its approval if we heed the wild storm raging around us, the mighty voice of the wind? Yes, let us be silent for a moment and listen to the music of the storm, its sturdy course, its bold challenge, the defiant roaring of the ocean, and the anguished sighing of the forest, the despairing creaking of the trees, and the faint-hearted rustling of the grass. It is true men say the divine voice is not in the rushing wind but in the gentle breeze,[2] but our ears are not made to pick up gentle breezes, only to gulp in the din of the elements. And why does it not break forth in still greater violence, making an end of life and the world and this brief speech, which at least has the supreme advantage that it is soon ended! Yes, let that vortex which is the innermost principle of the world, even though people are not aware of it but busily eat and drink and marry and propagate without a heed, let it break forth and in its resentment shrug off the mountains and the nations and the cultural achievements and clever inventions of man, let it break forth with the last terrible shriek, which more surely than the last trump proclaims the overthrow of everything, let it move and whirl away this naked cliff on which we stand, as easily as fluff before the breath of our nostrils.[3] – And yet night is winning and the day is shortening and hope is growing! So fill your cups once more, dear drinking companions; with this goblet I toast you, the eternal mother of all things, silent night![4] From you all things come, to you they all return. Then take pity once more upon the world, open yourself again to gather everything in and protect us all safely in your womb! I toast you, dark night, I toast you as victor, and this is my solace, for you make everything shorter, the day, time, life, and memory's tribulation, in eternal oblivion!

Ever since Lessing, in his famous essay *Laocoön*, resolved the boundary disputes between poetry and art,[5] we may take it that the upshot unanimously accepted by all aestheticians is that the difference lies in the fact that art belongs in the category of space and poetry in that of time, that art represents repose, poetry movement. Whatever, then, is to be an object of artistic representation must have that quiet transparency in which the inner reposes in a corresponding outer. The less this is the case, the more difficult the artist's task becomes, until finally the difference becomes insistent and tells him that the task just isn't his. If we apply the distinction, not propounded here but only loosely acknowledged, to the relation between sorrow and joy, it is easy to see that joy is far easier to represent in art than sorrow. That does not at all mean that art cannot represent sorrow, but only that there comes a point at which the essential thing is to posit an opposition between inner and outer, which makes its representation impossible for art. This stems in turn from the very nature of sorrow. It is of the essence of joy to reveal itself, but sorrow wants to hide, yes, sometimes even to deceive. Joy is communicative, sociable, open-hearted, and wants to express itself; sorrow is reserved, silent, solitary, and seeks to retire into itself. Surely not even life's most casual observer will deny that this is correct. There are those so constituted that under affect their blood rushes to the skin, making the inner movement outwardly visible. Others are so constituted that the blood flows inwards, seeking the ventricles of the heart and the inner parts of the organism. Something of the same difference is to be found in the ways joy and sorrow express themselves. The first type of constitution described is much easier to observe than the second. In the first you see the expression, the inner movement is outwardly visible; in the second the inner movement is intimated. It is as though the outward pallor were the inner's leave-taking, and thought and imagination hasten after the fugitive in its secret hiding-place. This is especially true of the kind of sorrow I shall now consider, what may be termed reflective sorrow. Here the outer contains at most only a hint that puts you on the track, sometimes not even that much. This sorrow cannot be represented in art; since the equilibrium between inner and outer has been revoked, it does not lend itself to spatial specifications. In another respect, too, it is not susceptible of representation in art, since it lacks that inner repose and is constantly in movement. This movement, though it gives no richer content, is nevertheless the essential thing. Like a squirrel in its cage it goes round in itself, though not so uniformly as that animal but constantly varying the combinations of sorrow's inner elements. What prevents reflective grief from being represented in art is that it lacks repose, that it fails to come into accord with itself, does not come to rest in any single definite expression. As the sick person throws himself from one side to the other in pain, so does reflective sorrow toss about, looking for its object and its expression. When sorrow finds repose, then its interior also gradually works its way outwards, becomes visible in the exterior, and so becomes an object of representation for art. If sorrow has calm and composure, it invariably begins its movement from inside outwards; reflective sorrow moves inwards, like the blood that runs away from the surface, giving only a hint of its presence through a sudden pallor. Reflective sorrow brings with it no characteristic outward change; from its very first moment it hastens inwards and only a reasonably careful observer suspects its vanishing; afterwards it takes great care that the exterior obtrude as little as possible.

Seeking its way thus inwards, it finds at last an enclosure, an innermost recess, where it thinks it can stay,[6] and now it begins its monotonous movement. Like the pendulum in a clock it swings back and forth and cannot find rest. It begins always at the beginning and ponders anew, interrogates the witnesses, collates and tests their various statements, as it has already done a hundred times, yet it is never finished. In the course of time monotony has a somewhat numbing effect. As the monotonous drip from a roof, the steady whirl of a spinning-wheel, the monotonous sound of the measured paces of someone walking up and down on the floor above all make us numb, so in the end reflective sorrow finds relief in this movement, which becomes a necessity for it in the form of an illusion of motion. Finally a certain equilibrium emerges. The need for sorrow to break through, to whatever extent it may on occasion have expressed itself, ceases to exist; the exterior is calm and composed, and deep inside, in its little nook, sorrow lives like a well-guarded prisoner in an underground gaol, where it spends year after year in its monotonous movement, walking back and forth in its by-chamber, never wearying of putting sorrow's long or short road behind it.

What gives rise to reflective sorrow can lie partly in the individual's own subjective nature, partly in the objective sorrow itself or its occasion. A pathologically reflective individual will transmute every sorrow into a reflective sorrow, his individual structure and organization make it impossible for him to assimilate the sorrow without further ado. This, however, is a morbid condition of no particular interest, since any accidental happening can undergo a metamorphosis in this way and so become a reflective sorrow. Such is always the case when the objective sorrow has not been dealt with, where it leaves a doubt behind, whatever its nature otherwise. A great multiplicity is immediately offered to thought, the more in proportion to how much one has lived and experienced, or is disposed to employ one's powers of discernment in such experiments. I have no intention, however, of working through all this diversity; I shall bring out just one single aspect as this has revealed itself to my observation.

When the occasion for the sorrow is a case of deception, then the nature of the objective sorrow is such as to beget reflective sorrow in the individual. That a deception really is such is often very hard to ascertain, and yet everything depends on this; as long as it remains disputable, sorrow will find no rest but must continue wandering back and forth in reflection. Moreover, when this deception touches, not something external, but a person's whole inner life, the innermost core of his life, then the probability of the reflective sorrow's persisting becomes greater and greater. But what, indeed, can with greater truth be called a woman's life than her love? So when the sorrow of an unhappy love is rooted in a deception, we have unreservedly a case of reflective sorrow, whether this persists for a lifetime or she overcomes it. Unhappy love is certainly of itself the most profound of sorrows for a woman; but it does not follow that every unhappy love generates a reflective sorrow. Thus when the loved one dies or perhaps she simply finds her love is unrequited, or life's circumstances make it impossible to realize her wish, certainly there is an occasion for sorrow but not for reflective sorrow, unless the individual is already sick, in which case she falls outside the scope of our interest. If, on the other hand, she is not sick, her sorrow will be an immediate sorrow and as such also able to become an object of representation in art, whereas on the contrary, it will be quite impossible for art to express and represent reflective sorrow or the point of it. For immediate sorrow is that immediate copy and expression of the sorrow's impression which is entirely congruent with the original, just like the image Veronica kept on her handkerchief; and sorrow's sacred script is stamped in the external, beautiful and clear, and legible by all.[7]

Reflective sorrow cannot, therefore, be an object of representation in art, partly because it never subsists but is always in the process of becoming, partly because it is unconcerned with and indifferent to the external, the visible. So unless art is to limit itself to the naivety one finds examples of in old books, where a figure is depicted which can represent just about anything while on its breast one discovers a piece of armour in the form of a heart, or some such, on which one can read all about it, especially if the figure by its posture draws attention to itself, or even simply points to it – an effect the artist could just as well have produced by writing 'Please note' above the picture – he will have to give up the idea of representation in this area, leaving it to poets and psychologists.

It is this reflective sorrow I now propose to draw out and render visible, so far as that is possible, in some pictures. I call them 'shadowgraphs', partly to remind the reader by the very designation that I am summoning them from the dark side of life, partly because, just like shadowgraphs, they are not visible straightaway. If I take a shadowgraph in my hand, I gain no impression from it, can form no real idea of it; it is only when I hold it up to the wall and look not at the immediate image but at what appears on the wall, it is only then that I see it. Similarly the picture I want to show here is an inner picture which can also only be detected by looking through the exterior. There may be nothing striking about the exterior, it is only when I look through it that I discover the inner picture, which is what I want to show, an inner picture too refined to be visible on the outside, woven as it is of the softest moods of the soul. If I look at a sheet of paper, to outward observation there may be nothing remarkable about it; it is only when I hold it up to the light of day and see through it that I discover the delicate inner picture which is as though too insubstantial to be seen immediately.

So fasten your gaze, dear *Symparanekromenoi*, upon this inner picture, do not let yourselves be distracted by the exterior, or rather, do not introduce it yourselves, for I shall constantly draw it aside in order the better to view the interior. But that, surely, is something for which this Society, of which I have the honour to be a member, needs no encouragement; for although fairly young, we are all still old enough not to let the outer deceive us or be satisfied with that. Would I be flattering myself with a vain hope, then, were I to believe that you would grant these pictures your attention? Or must these efforts of mine be alien and indifferent to you, not in harmony with the interests of our association, a fellowship that knows but one passion, namely sympathy with sorrow's secret? We, too, form an order; we, too, sally forth now and then into the world like knights errant, each along his own path, although not to fight monsters or to come to the aid of innocence or be tried in adventures of love. None of that occupies us, not even the latter, for the arrow in a woman's glance cannot hurt our hardened breast, and it is not the merry smile of happy maidens that moves us, but the secret beckoning of sorrow. Let others be proud that no girl near or far can withstand the power of their love, we do not envy them; we would be proud if no secret sorrow escaped our attention, no private sorrow were too coy and too proud for us to succeed in probing triumphantly into its innermost hiding-places!

What is the most hazardous conflict, what presupposes the most skill and provides the greatest enjoyment, into that we will not inquire; our choice is made, we love only sorrow, it is sorrow alone we seek out and wherever we find its footprints we follow them, undaunted, unwavering, until it stands revealed. For this battle we arm ourselves, we train ourselves in it every day. And it is true that sorrow steals through the world so very secretively that only someone with sympathy for it succeeds in getting a whiff of it. You walk down the street, one house looks like the other, and only the experienced observer suspects that in that house, at midnight, everything looks quite different: an unhappy person wanders about, unable to rest; he climbs the stairs, his steps echo in the stillness of the night. We pass one another in the street, the one person looks like the other, and the other just like anyone else, and only the experienced observer suspects that, in that head, there lives a lodger who has nothing to do with the world, but lives out his lonely life confined to quiet domesticity. So the outer is the object of our observation, but not of our interest. Thus the fisherman sits and directs his attention unwaveringly on the float, yet the float does not interest him at all, only the movements down on the sea-bed. So the outer does indeed have significance for us, yet not as an expression of the inner but like a telegram telling of something hidden deep within. When you look long and attentively at a face, you sometimes discover that it is as if there were another face within the one you see. This is in general an unmistakable sign that the soul conceals an emigrant who has withdrawn from the outside world to watch over a hidden treasure, and the direction observation must take is intimated by the way one face lies as though inside the other, from which one understands that in order to discover anything one must try to probe inwards. The face, which is ordinarily the mirror of the soul, assumes here an ambiguity which cannot be represented in art, and which usually only lasts for a fleeting moment. It needs a special eye to see it, a special glance to pursue this infallible index of a secret sorrow. This glance is a covetous one and yet so painstaking, disturbing and compelling, yet so sympathetic, persistent and subtle, yet so frank and benevolent; it lulls the individual into a certain pleasant languor in which he finds a sensual rapture in gushing out his sorrow, just like the rapture enjoyed in bleeding to death. The present is forgotten, the outer is penetrated, the past resurrected, sorrow's breathing is made easy. The sorrowing person finds relief, and sorrow's sympathetic knight rejoices at having found what he was seeking. We seek not the present but the past, not joy, for that is always present, but sorrow, because its nature is to pass by, and in the instant of the present one sees it only as one sees a person of whom one just catches sight the moment he turns the corner and disappears.

But sometimes sorrow is even better at concealing itself, and the outer gives us not the least hint of anything. For long it can escape our attention, but when it happens that a look, a word, a sigh, a tone of voice, a twitch of the eye, a trembling of the lips, a fumbled handclasp, treacherously betrays what was painstakingly hidden, then passion is aroused, then the contest begins. Now we have need of vigilance and tenacity and cunning; for what after all is as inventive as private sorrow – a prisoner for life in solitary confinement also has ample time to think up a great deal; and what so quick to hide itself as private sorrow, for no young girl can cover a bared bosom in greater alarm and haste than hidden sorrow when taken by surprise. Unflinching fearlessness is called for in this conflict, then, for one struggles with a Proteus,[8] but if only one holds out it has to give up. Like that old man of the sea, whatever shape it puts on to slip free, twining itself like a serpent around us, terrifying us like a lion with its roar, turning itself into a tree with the wind howling in its leaves, or a foaming lake, or a crackling fire, in the end he still has to prophesy, and the sorrow must finally be revealed.

Behold, these adventures are our pleasure, our pastime, testing ourselves in them is our chivalry. For their sake we get up like thieves in the night, for their sake we risk everything, for no passion is as savage as that of sympathy. Nor need any shortage of adventures be our fear, only that we may encounter opposition that is too hard and unyielding; for as naturalists tell that by blasting huge rocks that have defied the centuries, they have found deep inside a living animal which has supported life undetected, so it should be possible for there to be humans with exteriors as firm as a rock who have safeguarded an eternally hidden life of sorrow. Yet this shall not quench our passion or cool our ardour. Quite the contrary, it will inflame it, for our passion is not indeed curiosity, content with the external and the superficial, but a sympathetic dread which searches hearts and hidden thoughts, evokes through magic and incantation what is secret, even what death has withheld from our gaze. It is said that Saul came in disguise to a witch before the battle,[9] and demanded that she show him the image of Samuel. Surely it was not mere curiosity that drove him, not simply a desire to see Samuel's visible image; it was his thoughts he wanted to learn, and no doubt he waited anxiously until he heard the stern judge's verdict. Neither, then, will it be mere curiosity, dear *Symparanekromenoi*, that moves one or another of you to contemplate the images I shall now present to you. For although I have indicated them by certain poetic names, this in no way suggests that it is these poetic figures alone presenting themselves before you. The names must be regarded as common nouns, and I for my part shall not object should one or other of you feel inclined to call the particular picture by another name, a dearer name, or some name that perhaps comes more naturally to you.

1. Marie Beaumarchais

We make this girl's acquaintance in Goethe's *Clavigo*, which we shall keep to except that we shall accompany her a little further forward in time, to where she has lost her dramatic interest and sorrow's retinue is gradually thinning out. We, however, continue to accompany her; for we knights of sympathy have as much the native gift as the acquired art of keeping pace with sorrow in its progress. Her story is brief: Clavigo was betrothed to her, Clavigo left her. This information suffices for the person who is used to observing life's phenomena as one inspects curiosities in an art cabinet; the shorter the better for the more one can see. One can similarly relate, quite briefly, that Tantalus thirsts and that Sisyphus rolls a stone up a mountain.[10] If one is in a hurry it would only delay matters to dwell further on these things, since one can learn no more than one already knows, which is the whole story. Whatever claims more attention has to be something quite different. One gathers round the tea-table in a familiar cluster, the samovar sings its final refrain, the lady of the house begs the mysterious stranger unburden his heart, to which end she has sugared water and jam brought in, and now he begins: it is a long and complicated story. That's how it goes in novels, and that too is something quite different: a long-drawn-out story with such a short little advertisement. Whether it is a short story for Marie Beaumarchais is another matter; so much is certain, it is not long drawn out, for a long story has after all a measurable length; on the other hand, a short story sometimes has the puzzling property of being longer than the most long-drawn-out one.

In the foregoing I have already remarked that reflective sorrow is not visible in the exterior, that is, does not find its peaceful, beautiful expression there. The inner unrest does not allow this transparency, rather the exterior is consumed by it; to the extent that the inner does proclaim itself in the outer, that would be a morbidity which can never be an object of representation in art, for then it lacks the interest of beauty. Goethe has given us a few hints about this. But even if one were agreed on the correctness of this observation, one might still be tempted to consider it something accidental; it is only when one is convinced by purely poetic and aesthetic considerations that what observation teaches is aesthetically true, only then does one acquire the deeper awareness. Suppose I imagine a reflective sorrow and ask whether it might not be represented in art; immediately it would be evident that in relation to it the exterior is entirely accidental. But in that case the idea of artistic beauty has been abandoned. Whether the subject is large or small, significant or insignificant, beautiful or not so beautiful, none of that matters; to consider whether it would be more correct to let her head incline to one side or to the other or towards the ground, to have her stare in melancholy or fix her gaze sadly upon the ground, all such things are entirely irrelevant – the one is no more adequate at expressing reflective sorrow than the other. Compared with the internal, the external becomes insignificant and of no consequence. The point in reflective sorrow is that the sorrow is constantly in search of its object; the searching is the unrest of sorrow and its life. But this searching is a constant fluctuation, and if the outer were at every moment a perfect expression of the inner, to represent reflective sorrow would require an entire series of pictures and no one picture would acquire genuine artistic value, since it would not be beautiful but true. We would have to look at the pictures as we do at the second hand of a watch; the works themselves are invisible, but the inner movement constantly expresses itself in the constant change in the outer. But this change cannot be represented in art, yet it is the whole point. Thus when unhappy love has its ground in a deception the pain and suffering are this: that the sorrow cannot find its object. If the deception is proved and if the victim perceives that it is a deception, the sorrow does not cease but it becomes an immediate sorrow, not a reflective one. The dialectical difficulty is easy to see, for what does she sorrow for? If he was a deceiver, it was just as well he left her, the sooner the better; she should be glad indeed and sorrow only at the fact that she loved him; and yet it is a profound sorrow that he was a deceiver. But this question of whether it is indeed a deception, that is the unrest in sorrow's *perpetuum mobile*. To establish with certainty the external fact that a deception is a deception is itself very hard, but even that would by no means settle the matter or bring the movement to a standstill. For love, deception is an absolute paradox, and in this lies the necessity for reflective sorrow. The various factors in love could be put together in the individual in very different ways, so that love in the one will not be as in the other. Egoism may be the dominant factor, or sympathy. But however the love may be, in its elements as much as its constitution, a deception is a paradox it cannot think and which it nevertheless wants, in the end, to think. Yes, if either the egoism or the sympathy were present absolutely, the paradox

would be removed; that is, the individual is, on the strength of the
absolute, beyond reflection, does not think the paradox in the sense
of abolishing it through a 'how' of reflection, but is saved precisely
by not thinking it; he does not trouble with the busy deliverances or
confusions of reflection, but rests in himself. Egoistically proud
love, because of its pride, considers deception impossible; it does not
bother to find out what might be said for or against, how the party
in question can be defended or exonerated; it is absolutely sure,
because it is too proud to believe that anyone should dare to deceive
it. Sympathetic love possesses the faith that can move mountains;
for it, every defence is nothing compared with its unshakeable
certainty that there was no deception; every accusation proves
nothing against the witness who testifies that there was no deception,
testifies to it not in this way or that but absolutely. Yet seldom in
life does one see such a love, or perhaps never. Generally love
contains both factors, and this puts it in relation to the paradox. In
the two cases described, the paradox is no doubt also there for love
but does not occupy it; in this latter case the paradox is there before
it. The paradox is unthinkable and love nevertheless wants to think
it, and according to the different factors as they momentarily come
to the fore, it comes near, and often in a contradictory manner, to
thinking it, but does not succeed. This line of thought is infinite and
ends only when the individual voluntarily breaks it off by bringing
something else into the picture, a volitional factor, but in that case
the individual comes within ethical categories and does not concern
us aesthetically. It is by a decision that he reaches what he cannot
reach by way of reflection, namely rest.

This is true of every unhappy love based on a deception. What
must evoke reflective sorrow even more in Marie Beaumarchais is
the fact that it is only an engagement that has been broken off. An
engagement is a possibility, not something actual, yet just because it
is only a possibility, it might seem that the effect of its being broken
off would be less, that it is much easier for the individual to withstand this blow. And sometimes that may well be true. On the
other hand, the fact that it is only a possibility that is destroyed
tempts reflection much more to the fore. When something actual is
brought to an end, generally the break is far more radical, every
nerve is cut asunder and in itself the fracture, regarded as such,

remains complete. When a possibility is broken off, the instantaneous pain may not be as great, but then it often leaves one or another small ligament whole and unharmed, which becomes a constant source of continued suffering. The destroyed possibility appears transfigured in a higher possibility; while the temptation to conjure up such a new possibility is less when it is something actual that is broken off, because actuality is higher than possibility.

So Clavigo has abandoned her; he has faithlessly broken the tie. Used to depending on him, when he rejects her she hasn't the strength to stand, she sinks helplessly into the arms of the environment. That is how it seems to have been with Marie. One could imagine another beginning; one could imagine that from the very first she had the strength to turn her sorrow into a reflective form; that either to escape the humiliation of hearing others talk of her being deceived, or because she still cared so much for him that it would pain her to hear him constantly reviled as a deceiver, she straightaway broke off every connection with others in order to consume her sorrow in her self and herself in her sorrow. We follow Goethe. Those around her are not unsympathetic, they feel her pain with her, and in doing so say it will be the death of her. Now, aesthetically, that is quite right. The nature of unhappy love can be such that suicide is to be considered aesthetically correct, but in that case it must not be based on deception, for then a suicide loses all nobility and implies an admission which pride must refuse to make. On the other hand, if it is indeed the death of her, this amounts to his having murdered her. That expression is in total harmony with the strength of the emotion within her and the idea gives her relief. But it is not often that life adheres closely to aesthetic categories, it does not always obey an aesthetic imperative, and she does not die. This causes those around her embarrassment. They feel that it won't do to keep on repeating the assurance that she is dying when she continues to live; besides, they find themselves unable to proclaim it with the same energetic pathos as at the start; and yet this was the condition on which she was to receive any comfort. So they change their method. He was, they say, a blackguard, a trickster, a detestable person not worth taking one's own life for; forget him, think no more of the matter, it was just an engagement, erase this incident from your memory; you are still young, can still hope. They set her aflame, for this pathos of wrath harmonizes with other moods within her; her pride feeds on the vindictive thought of making nothing of it all; it was not because he was exceptional that she loved him, far from it; she could see his faults very well, but believed him to be a good person, a faithful person, that's why she loved him, it was from pity, and so it will be easy to forget him because she has never actually needed him. The environment and Marie are in unison again and the duet between them proceeds excellently.

For those around her it is not hard to think of Clavigo as a deceiver, for they have never loved him and so it is no paradox; and if there was any fondness for him (something Goethe suggests in connection with the sister), just this interest arms them against him, and this good will, which may have been something more than good will, becomes an excellent incendiary for feeding the flames of hate. Nor does her circle find it hard to erase its memory of him, so it demands that Marie do the same. Her pride breaks out in hatred, the circle adds fuel to the fire, she gives vent to her feelings in strong words and forthright declarations of intent with which she intoxicates herself. Those around her rejoice. They fail to notice, what she will hardly admit to herself, that in the next instant she is weak and faint; they fail to notice the anxious suspicion taking hold of her that the energy she now and then has is an illusion. She assiduously conceals this and admits it to no one. The circle goes on happily with its theoretical exercises, but nevertheless begins to demand evidence of practical results. This fails to appear. Her circle continues to incite her, since her words reveal inner strength, and yet they harbour a suspicion that all is not well. They become impatient, they risk extreme measures, they drive the spurs of ridicule into her flank to spur her on. Too late, the misunderstanding has taken effect. It is no humiliation for those around her that he really deceived Marie, but it is for her. The revenge offered, however, to despise him has little meaning; for he does not love her, and her scorn becomes a bank draft that no one honours. On the other hand, although for the circle there is nothing painful in Clavigo's being a deceiver, there is for Marie; and yet he does not altogether want for an advocate in her heart. She feels she has gone too far, she has given hint of a strength she does not possess. That is not something she will admit to. And what consolation is there in contempt? It is better, then, to sorrow. Besides, perhaps there is some secret note or other in her possession, of great significance for interpreting the text, but also such that it can present him, according to circumstances, in a better or worse light. But she has let no one in on this, nor will she; for if he wasn't a deceiver he might conceivably rue the step and turn back, or perhaps – what would be even more glorious – have no need to rue it. He might justify himself absolutely or explain everything, and then it could be a hindrance were she to make use of it; the old relationship could no longer be evoked, and that would be her own fault, for it would have been she who had made others privy to the most secret growth of his love. Were she really able to convince herself that he was a deceiver, yes, then it would make no difference anyway, and in any case the nicest thing for her to do would be not to make use of it.

The environment has thus been her unwilling assistant in developing a new passion, jealousy over her own sorrow. Her decision is made. On every side the environment lacks the energy to harmonize with her passion; she takes the veil. She does not enter a convent, but she takes the veil of sorrow which hides her from every alien glance. Outwardly she is calm, all is forgotten, her conversation betrays no hint; she takes the vow of sorrow and now begins her solitary, secret life. At that moment everything is changed; before, it seemed at least she could talk to others, but now not only is she bound by the vow of silence wrung from her by her pride with love's connivance, or demanded by her love and assented to by her pride, she simply doesn't know where to begin, or how, and not because new factors have appeared, but because reflection has triumphed. If someone were now to ask her what it was she sorrowed over, she could give no answer, or she would answer in the same way as that wise man[11] who, when asked what religion was, kept on demanding time to think it over and so was perpetually at a loss for an answer. Now she is lost to the world, lost to her surroundings, immured alive; it is with sadness she covers the last opening, for even then she feels it might be possible to reveal herself; the next moment she is removed from them for ever. Yet it is decided, irrevocably decided, and she need have no fear that, as with anyone else walled in alive, once the meagre portion of bread and water provided for her is used up she shall perish, for she has nourishment for a long time; she need have no fear of boredom, she can keep herself busy. Her exterior is calm and peaceful, there is nothing unusual about it, and yet her heart is not the incorruptible being of a quiet spirit,[12] but a restless spirit's fruitless occupation. She seeks solitude or its opposite. In solitude she rests from the effort it always costs to force one's outward appearance into a definite form. In the way someone who has been standing or sitting in a forced position stretches his body with pleasure, as a branch long bowed under pressure joyfully regains its normal position when what binds it is broken, so she too finds her recreation. Or she seeks the opposite – noise, distraction – so that while everyone's attention is directed elsewhere, she can be safely occupied with herself; and what goes on nearest her, the sound of music, the noisy conversation, sound so far away that it is as if she were sitting in a little room by herself, removed from all the world. And if perchance she cannot force back the tears, she is certain to be misunderstood, maybe she is just having a good cry; for when one lives in an *ecclesia pressa*,[13] it is a real joy when one's way of expressing one's worship coincides with the public way of doing so. Only the quieter forms of contact make her anxious, for here she is less unguarded, here it is so easy to make a mistake, so hard to prevent its being noticed.

So outwardly there is nothing to remark, but inside there is ceaseless activity. Here there is an examination which one might quite justly and with special emphasis call interrogation under torture; everything is brought out and carefully examined: his form, his appearance, his voice, his words. In interrogations of this kind it sometimes happens that a judge, captivated by the beauty of the accused, has broken off the examination and found himself unable to carry on. The court expectantly awaits the results of his investigation, but they fail to materialize, and yet not at all because the judge is in neglect of his duties; the gaoler can testify that he comes every night, that the accused is brought before him, that the examination lasts several hours, that in his experience no judge has ever kept going like this. And so the court concludes that it must be a very complicated case. Thus it goes with Marie, not once but again and again. Everything is presented as it occurred, faithfully, justice demands that – and love. The accused is summoned. 'There he comes, he turns the corner, he opens the wicket gate, look how he hastens, he has longed for me, it's as though he threw everything aside so as to come to me as soon as possible, I hear his swift steps, swifter than my own heartbeat, he comes, there he is' – and the interrogation – it is postponed.

'Good Lord, this little phrase! I have so often repeated it to myself, recalled it in the midst of much else, but never before have I noticed what really lies concealed in it. Yes, it explains everything; he is not serious about leaving me, he is coming back. What is the whole world to this little phrase? People wearied of me, I had no friend, but now I have a friend, a confidant, a little phrase that explains everything – he is coming back, his eye is not downcast, he looks at me half reproachfully and says, "You of little faith", and this little phrase hovers like an olive leaf upon his lips – there he is' – and the interrogation is postponed.

In circumstances like these it is natural enough that giving a verdict should be attended with great difficulty. Obviously a young girl is not a jurist, but it by no means follows that she cannot pass judgement, and yet this girl's verdict will always be such that, while at first glance looking like a verdict, it contains something else that shows it is no verdict, and which also shows that the next moment a quite opposite verdict can be given. 'He was no deceiver, for to be that he must have been aware of it from the beginning; but he wasn't, my heart tells me he loved me.' If one raises the requirements of deception in this way, perhaps in the final analysis no deceiver has ever lived. To acquit him on that ground shows a partiality for the accused which is not consistent with strict justice, nor does it stand up to a single objection. 'He was a deceiver, an abhorrent creature who has callously and heartlessly made me boundlessly unhappy. I was content before I knew him. Yes, it's true, I had no idea I could be so happy, or that there was such a wealth of joy as he taught me; but nor did I have any idea I could become as unhappy as I am now, and this too he has taught me. Therefore I will hate him, abhor him, curse him. Yes, I curse you, Clavigo, in the inmost depths of my soul I curse you. But no one must know this, I cannot allow anyone else to do the same, for no one but myself has the right to do so. I have loved you as no one else has, but I hate you too, for no one knows your cunning as I do. Ye

good gods to whom vengeance belongs, grant me it just a while! I
shall not misuse it, I shall not be cruel. I shall then creep into his
soul when he wants to love another, not to kill that love, that
would be no punishment, as well I know, for he loves her as little as
he loved me; he simply does not love people, he loves only the idea,
the thought, his mighty influence at court, his intellectual power,
none of which I can understand how he can love. I take these away
from him, then he will learn to know my pain. And when he is
near to despair I will give it all back to him, but it is me he shall
thank for it – and then I am avenged.

'No, he was no deceiver. He loved me no more and so left me,
but that was no deceit. If he had stayed without loving me, then he
would have been a deceiver, then I would have lived like a pensioner
on the love he once had for me, lived on his compassion, on the
mite he might have thrown to me, though generously, lived as a
burden on him and as a torment to myself. Cowardly, wretched
heart, despise yourself, learn to be great; learn it from him; he has
loved me better than I have known how to love myself. And
should I be angry with him? No, I shall continue to love him,
because his love was stronger, his thought prouder than my weakness and my cowardice. And perhaps he loves me still, yes, it was
out of love for me that he left me.

'Yes, now I see the truth, I am no longer in doubt, he was a
deceiver. I saw him, his look was proud and triumphant, he looked
down upon me with his scornful glance. At his side walked a
Spanish girl, radiantly beautiful; why was she so beautiful? – I could
murder her – why am I not as beautiful? And was I not? I didn't
know it, but he taught me that I was, and why am I no longer?
Who is to blame? A curse upon you, Clavigo! If you had stayed
with me I would have become even more beautiful, for with your
words and your assurances my love grew, and with it my beauty.
Now I am faded, I thrive no more, what power has all the world's
tenderness compared with a word from you? Oh, that I were
beautiful again! Would that I could be pleasing to him again, for
that is the only reason I want to be beautiful. Oh, think if he could
no longer love youth and beauty; then I would grieve more than
before, and who can grieve as I?

'Yes, he was a deceiver. How else could he have stopped loving me? Have I stopped loving him? Is it not the same law for a man's love as for a woman's? Or should a man be weaker than the weak? Or has he perhaps made a mistake, perhaps it was an illusion that he loved me, an illusion that vanished like a dream; does this befit a man? Or was it an instability, is it proper for a man to be unstable? And why did he assure me in the beginning, then, that he loved me so much? If love has no endurance, what then can endure? Yes, Clavigo, you have taken everything from me, my faith, my faith in love, not just in yours!

'He was no deceiver. What it was that snatched him away, I do not know. I am not familiar with this dark power; but it pained him, pained him deeply; he did not want to share it with me, so he made himself out to be a deceiver. Yes, if he had taken up with another girl, I would say he was a deceiver and no power in the world would make me believe otherwise; but he has not done that. Perhaps he thinks that by adopting the appearance of a deceiver he can lessen my pain, arm me against him. That's why he shows himself now and then with young girls, that's why he looked so scornfully at me the other day, in order to make me angry and so set me free. No, he was certainly no deceiver, and how would that voice be capable of deception? It was so calm, yet full of feeling; as if clearing a path through solid rock, that's how it sounded from an interior whose depth I scarcely managed to suspect. Can this voice deceive? What, then, is the voice, is it a movement of the tongue, a noise one can produce at pleasure? Somewhere in the soul it must have a home, it has to have a birthplace. And that it has, it had its home in his inmost heart. There he loved me, there he loves me. True, he had another voice too, one that was cold, icy, it could kill every joy in my soul, stifle every joyful thought, could even make my kiss cold and disgusting to myself. Which was the true one? He could deceive in every way, but this vibrant voice in which all his passion trembles, this I feel was no deception, it is impossible. The other was a deception, or evil powers took control of him. No, he was no deceiver – that voice which has bound me to him for ever, that is not a deception. A deceiver he was not, even if I never understood him.'

She is never finished with the interrogation, nor with the verdict. Not with the interrogation, because it keeps on being interrupted;

not with the verdict, because it is only a mood. So once begun, this movement can continue as long as it will, and no end is in sight. Only a breach can bring it to a close, that is, breaking off the whole line of thought; but this cannot happen, because the will is always in the service of reflection, which gives the momentary passion energy.

When she tries at times to break away from it all, to make nothing of it, this is again only a mood, a momentary passion, and reflection remains constantly the victor. There can be no mediation.[14] If she sets off in such a way that the beginning is in one way or another the result of processes of reflection, she is immediately carried away. The will has to be wholly indifferent, to begin on the strength of its own willing; only then can there be any question of a beginning. If that happens, she may indeed begin, but this falls altogether outside our field of interest; we can then hand her over with pleasure to the moralists or whoever else would take care of her; we wish her an honourable marriage and promise to dance on her wedding-day, where the change of name will also conveniently let us forget that it was the Marie Beaumarchais we have been speaking of.

We return nevertheless to Marie Beaumarchais. The peculiarity of her sorrow, as we noted above, is the restlessness that prevents her finding the object of sorrow. Her pain cannot find calm, she lacks the peace necessary for a life that can assimilate its nourishment and be refreshed by it; no illusion overshadows her with its quiet coolness while she absorbs the pain. She lost childhood's illusion when she gained that of love; she lost that of love when Clavigo deceived her. If she could gain the illusion of sorrow, that would help. Her sorrow would then grow to a man's maturity and she would have compensation for the loss. But her sorrow does not thrive, for she has not lost Clavigo, he has deceived her; it remains ever an infant child with its wail, a child without father and mother; for if Clavigo had been torn away from her, then in the memory of his faithfulness and love it would have had a father, and in Marie's infatuation a mother. And she has nothing on which to rear it, for though the experience was a beautiful one, it had no significance in itself, only as a foretaste of the future. And she cannot hope this child of pain may be transformed into a son of joy, she cannot hope for Clavigo to return, for she would not have the strength to endure a future; she has lost the glad confidence with which she would have followed him undaunted into the abyss, and she has acquired instead a hundred scruples; the most she could do would be to experience the past once again. When Clavigo left her, there stretched before her a future so beautiful, so enchanting, that it nearly threw her thoughts into confusion; it exerted its power dimly over her, her metamorphosis was already begun, then the development was checked. A new life had been hinted at, she had felt its forces at work in her, then it was destroyed and she recoiled, and there is no compensation for her, neither in this nor the future world. The future smiled to greet her so richly and was mirrored in her love's illusion, and still everything was so natural and straight-forward. Now an impotent reflection may sometimes paint her an impotent illusion, with no power to tempt her but able momentarily to soothe her. And so will time pass for her until she has consumed the very object of her sorrow, which was not identical with her sorrow but the occasion that made her constantly search for an object of sorrow.

If someone possessed a letter which he knew or believed contained information concerning what he had to consider his life's blessedness, but the written characters were thin and faded, the handwriting almost illegible, he would read it and reread it, with anxiety and disquiet certainly, but with passion. At one moment he would get one meaning out of it, the next another. When he was quite sure he had managed to read a word, he would interpret everything in the light of that word. But he would never pass beyond the same uncertainty with which he began. He would stare, more and more anxiously, but the more he stared the less he saw; sometimes his eyes filled with tears, but the more that happened, again the less he saw. In due course the writing became weaker and less distinct; finally the paper itself crumbled away and he had nothing left but eyes blinded with tears.

2. Donna Elvira

We make this girl's acquaintance in the opera *Don Giovanni*, and it will be of some importance for our later investigation to take heed of the hints of her earlier life contained in that piece. She had been a nun;[15] it is from the peace of a convent that Don Giovanni has snatched her. This gives some indication of the intensity of her passion. Here was no frivolous hussy from a boarding-school who had learned to love in class and to flirt at dances; there is no great significance in someone like that being seduced. Elvira, on the other hand, has been brought up in the discipline of the convent, yet this has not been able to root out passion, though it has indeed taught her to suppress it and so made it even more violent once it is allowed to emerge. She is a sure prey for a Don Giovanni; he will know how to coax out her passion, wild, ungovernable, insatiable, to be satisfied only in his love. In him she has everything and the past is nothing; if she leaves him she loses everything, including the past. After she had renounced the world, there appeared a figure she could not renounce, and that is Don Giovanni. Henceforth she renounces everything in order to live with him. The more important the life she leaves behind, the more she must cling to him; the more tightly she has embraced him, the more frightful her despair when he abandons her. Already from the beginning her love is a despair; nothing in heaven or on earth means anything to her except Don Giovanni.

In the opera Elvira interests us only so far as her relationship to Don Giovanni has importance for him. Were I to suggest what this importance of hers is in a few words, I would say, 'She is Don Giovanni's epic fate, the Commendatore his dramatic fate.' There is a hatred in her which will seek out Giovanni in every out-of-the-way corner, a flame of fire which will illumine the darkest hiding-place, and should she still not bring him to light, there is a love within her that will find him. She joins in with the others in pursuit of Don Giovanni, but were I to imagine all powers neutralized, the efforts of his pursuers cancelling each other out, so that it was up to Elvira alone and Don Giovanni was in her power, then the hatred would arm her to murder him, but her love would forbid it; not from sympathy, since for that he is too great in her eyes, and so she would constantly keep him alive, for were she to kill him she would kill herself. So if there were no other forces than Elvira turned against Don Giovanni, the opera would never end; for, in order to avenge herself, Elvira would, if possible, prevent the lightning itself from striking him, and yet she would again be unable to take revenge herself. Such is the interest she has for us in the opera; but here we are only concerned with her relationship to Don Giovanni so far as it is significant for her. She is an object of interest to many, but in very different ways. Don Giovanni has an interest in her before the piece begins; the audience bestows its dramatic interest upon her; but we friends of sorrow, we follow her not just to the end of the street, not only for the instant she crosses the stage; no, we follow her upon her solitary way.

So Don Giovanni has seduced Elvira and abandoned her; it is quickly done, as quickly as 'a tiger can snap a lily'.[16] From the fact that in Spain alone there are 1,003, we can see that Don Giovanni is in a hurry and to some extent reckon the speed. Don Giovanni has abandoned her, but there is no environment into whose arms she can helplessly fall; she need have no fear of the environment closing too tightly around her; it realizes, rather, that it should open wide its ranks to make her departure easier. She need have no fear of anyone disputing her loss with her, on the contrary, someone or other may perhaps take it upon himself to try to prove it. She stands alone and abandoned, and there is no doubt that can tempt her; it is clear that he was a deceiver who has taken everything from her and exposed her to shame and dishonour. Aesthetically, however, this is not the worst that can happen; it saves her, for a while, from that reflective sorrow which is certainly more painful than immediate sorrow. The fact here is indubitable and reflection cannot turn it now into one thing, now into another. A Marie Beaumarchais may have loved a Clavigo just as violently, as wildly and passionately; as far as her own passion goes, it may be altogether accidental that the worst has not happened; she could almost wish that it had, for then, after all, there would be an end of the story; she would be much more strongly armed against him; but it has not happened. So in her case the fact is far more doubtful, its reality will always be a secret between her and Clavigo. When she considers the cold cunning, the shabby calculation required so to deceive her that in the eyes of the world it appears something far less serious, and she herself is exposed to the sort of sympathy that says, 'Well now, good gracious, it's not as bad as all that', it can arouse her, she can become practically insane at the thought of the proud superiority in the face of which she has nevertheless meant nothing, which has set her a limit and said, 'thus far and no further'. And yet the whole story can also be interpreted in another way, a nicer way. But as the interpretation changes, so does the fact. Reflection, therefore, straightaway gets enough to do and reflective sorrow is inescapable.

Don Giovanni has abandoned Elvira; at that instant everything is clear to her, and there is no doubt to lure her grief into the seminar room of reflection. She is mute in her despair. Her sorrow courses through her with a single beat of the pulse, and it flows outwardly, the passion shines through her in a blaze and can be seen in her outward appearance. Hate, despair, vengeance, love, all break forth to make themselves visibly revealed. At this moment she is picturesque. The imagination also therefore immediately presents us with a picture of her, and here the external is not rendered indifferent, reflection upon it is not empty, and its activity not without significance, as it proposes and disposes.

Whether she is at this moment an object of artistic representation is another question. But what is certain is that at this moment she is visible and can be seen, not of course in the sense that this or that actual Elvira can actually be seen, which in most cases amounts to her not being seen, but the Elvira we imagine is visible in her essentiality. Whether art is able to provide just that shade in her expression that renders visible the point of her despair I leave open, but she can be described, and the picture which thus appears is not a mere burden for the memory that is neither here nor there, but has its validity. And who has not seen Elvira!

It was early morning when I undertook a journey by foot in one of the romantic parts of Spain. Nature awoke, the trees of the forest shook their heads, and it was as though the leaves rubbed the sleep from their eyes; one tree bent to the other to see if it had arisen, and the whole forest billowed in the fresh cool breeze; a light mist rose from the earth, the sun snatched it away as if it were a carpet under which it had rested during the night, and now looked down like a loving mother upon the flowers and everything that had life, and said, 'Arise, dear children, the sun is already shining.' As I rounded the end of a gully my eye fell upon a monastery high up on the peak of the mountain, to which there led a footpath with many turnings. My thoughts dwelt upon it. Thus it stands there, I thought, like a house of God founded firmly upon the rock. My guide told me that it was a convent famous for its strict discipline. My pace slackened, like my thought; why hurry when so near the monastery? I should probably have come to a full stop had I not been startled by a rapid movement nearby. Involuntarily I turned; it was a knight who hastened past me. How handsome he was, his step so light yet so full of strength, so royal and yet so fugitive! He turned his head to look back, his countenance so captivating yet his glance so uneasy; it was Don Giovanni. Is he hurrying to an assignation or is he coming from one? Yet he was soon gone from my sight and out of my mind, and my glance was fixed on the convent. I sank once more into contemplation of the joys of life and the quiet peace of the convent, when up on the mountain I saw the figure of a woman. She was hurrying headlong down the footpath, but the path was steep and it looked all the time as though she were plunging down from the mountain. She came nearer. Her countenance was pale, only her eyes blazed terribly, her body was trembling, her bosom rose and fell violently, but still she hurried faster and faster, her locks flung about and scattered in the wind, but not even the fresh morning breeze and her hurried pace could bring colour to her cheeks; her nun's veil was torn in shreds and flew behind, her thin white gown would have betrayed much to a profane glance had not the passion in her face attracted even the most depraved person's glance. She rushed by me – I dared not address her, her brow was too majestic, her glance too royal, her passion too high-born. Where does this girl belong? In the convent? Have these passions their home there? In the world? But the costume? – Why does she hurry? Is it to hide her shame and disgrace or to catch up with Don Giovanni? She hastens on to the forest and it closes around her and conceals her, and I see her no more but hear only the forest's sigh. Poor Elvira! Perhaps the trees have found out something – and yet the trees are better than men, for the trees sigh and keep silent; men whisper.

In this first moment Elvira can be represented, and even though art really cannot take the measure of it, because it would be hard to find a unified expression that also contained all the multiplicity of her passion, the soul demands to see her. This I have tried to suggest through the little picture just sketched. The idea of it was not actually to present her but only to suggest that a description of her was in place, that it was not an arbitrary whim on my part but a legitimate requirement of the idea. Yet this is just one moment and we must follow Elvira further.

The most obvious movement is one in time. She maintains herself on that almost picturesque point suggested in the foregoing, through a series of moments in time. This gives her dramatic interest. In the haste with which she sped past me she overtakes Don Giovanni. This, too, is quite as it should be seeing he has abandoned her, but he has drawn her into his own life's pace and she must reach him. If she does reach him, her whole attention is then turned outward again and we still do not get reflective sorrow. She has lost everything, she lost heaven when she chose the world, the world when she lost Don Giovanni. So she has nowhere to seek refuge except with him, it is only by being in his presence that she can keep despair at a distance, either by drowning out the inner voices with the clamour of hate and resentment, which resound only when Don Giovanni is present, or by hoping. This latter indicates that the elements of reflective sorrow are present already but have not yet been able to gather themselves inwardly. 'She must first be cruelly convinced,' reads Kruse's adaptation,[17] but this requirement completely betrays the inner disposition. If what has happened hasn't convinced her that Don Giovanni was a deceiver, nothing will. But as long as she requires a further proof, she can succeed, with a restless, rootless life constantly occupied in pursuing Don Giovanni, in escaping the inner unrest of a quiet despair. The paradox already exists in her soul, but so long as she can keep the soul agitated by external evidences not designed to explain the past but to provide information about Don Giovanni's present condition, she escapes reflective sorrow. Hate, resentment, curses, prayers, imprecations alternate, but her soul is still not turned back on itself in order to rest in the contemplation that she is deceived. So when Kruse has Don Giovanni say:

> 'Are you now disposed to hear,
> To believe my words, you who suspect me;
> Then I might almost say improbable
> Is the cause that compelled,' etc.,

one must be careful not to think that what, to the spectator's ear, sounds like mockery has the same effect upon Elvira. For her the words are a relief, for it is the improbable she wants, and she wants to believe it just because it is improbable.

If we now let Don Giovanni and Elvira come together, we have the choice of letting either Don Giovanni or Elvira be the stronger. If he is the stronger, her appearance on the scene loses all its point. She demands 'proof to be cruelly convinced'; he is gallant enough not to withhold it. But, naturally, she is not convinced and demands a new proof; for demanding a new proof is an alleviation, and the uncertainty is a relief. She then becomes but one witness more to the exploits of Don Giovanni. But we could also imagine Elvira as the stronger. It rarely happens, but we would do it out of gallantry to the sex. She stands, then, in her full beauty still, for though she has wept, the tears have not quenched the lustre in her eye, and though she has sorrowed, the sorrow has not wasted her youthful vitality, and though she has fretted, her fretting has not gnawed away the vitality of her beauty, and though her cheek has become pale, the expression has become for that reason all the more soulful, and though she does not glide with the lightness of childlike innocence, she steps forward with the energetic firmness of womanly passion. This is how she confronts Don Giovanni. She has loved him more than the whole world, more than the blessedness of her own soul, she has lavished everything upon him, even her honour, and he was unfaithful. Now she knows only one passion, it is hate; only one thought, it is revenge. Thus she is as great as Don Giovanni; for seducing all girls is the male equivalent of the woman's letting herself be seduced once with all her soul and now hating, or if you will, loving her seducer with an energy no spouse possesses. This is how she confronts him, she does not lack the courage to dare to have at him, she does not fight for moral principles, she fights for her love, a love she does not base upon respect; she does not fight to be his mate, she fights for her love, and this is not satisfied with a contrite faithfulness, it demands revenge; for love of him she has thrown away her blessedness, and if it were offered her once more she would throw it away again in order to avenge herself.

Such a figure cannot fail to make an impression upon Don

Giovanni. He knows what pleasure lies in sucking in the finest and most fragrant flower of first youth, he knows it is only a moment, and he knows what follows, he has seen these pale figures often enough wither so quickly that one can almost see it happening. But here a miracle has taken place, the laws of life's ordinary course are broken. He has seduced a young girl but her life is not extinguished, her beauty has not faded; she is transformed and is more beautiful than ever. He cannot deny it, she captivates him more than any girl has captivated him, more than Elvira herself has done; for the innocent nun was still, in spite of all her beauty, a girl like many others, his infatuation with her an adventure like many another; but this girl is the only one of her kind. This girl is armed, she does not conceal a dagger in her breast but she has an armour,[18] not visible, for her hatred is not satisfied with speeches and declamations, but unseen, and it is her hatred. Don Giovanni's passion is aroused, she must be his once more; but not so. Yes, if it were a girl who knew his baseness, who hated him although she had not been deceived by him, then Don Giovanni would have won; but this girl he cannot win, all his seduction is powerless. Had the voice been more ingratiating than his own, the approach more insidious than his own, he still would not have moved her; had the angels prayed for him, had the Mother of God been willing to be bridesmaid at the wedding, still it would have been in vain. She will turn, not away from him, as even, in the underworld, Dido turned away from Aeneas who had deceived her, but towards him, even more coldly than Dido.[19]

But this encounter of Elvira with Don Giovanni is only a moment of transition; she walks across the stage, the curtain falls, but we, dear *Symparanekromenoi*, we steal after, for only now does she really become Elvira. As long as she is in the presence of Don Giovanni she is beside herself, when she comes to herself it is time to think the paradox. Thinking a contradiction, in spite of all the assurances of modern philosophy and the foolhardy courage of its young adherents, must always involve great difficulty.[20] A young girl may well be forgiven for finding it hard, and yet this is the task that is set for her, to think that the one she loves was a deceiver. This she has in common with Marie Beaumarchais, and yet there is a difference between the way in which they each come to the paradox.

The fact which Marie had to go on was in itself so dialectical that reflection had straightaway to grasp hold of it with all its appetitive urgency. In Elvira's case the factual proof of Don Giovanni's deception seems so evident that it is not easy to see how reflection can get hold of it. It therefore attacks the matter from another angle. Elvira has lost everything, and yet her whole life lies before her and her soul demands a pittance to live on. Here two possibilities present themselves: either to observe ethical and religious categories or to preserve her love for Giovanni. If she does the former she falls outside our interest; we gladly let her retire to a Magdalene Institution,[21] or wherever else she wants. This, however, will probably strike her as difficult, for to make it possible she must first despair; she has already known the religious once, and a second time it makes great demands. The religious is, altogether, a dangerous power to have anything to do with; it is jealous of itself and will not be ridiculed. When she chose the convent her proud soul may have found a rich satisfaction in it, for say what you will, no girl makes so brilliant a match as she who gives herself in marriage to heaven; now, however, as a penitent she must return in repentance and contrition. Moreover, there is always the question of whether she can find a priest who can preach the gospel of repentance and contrition with the same pith as Don Giovanni preached the glad tidings of pleasure. In order, then, to save herself from this despair she must hold on to Don Giovanni's love, something she finds so much the easier seeing she does after all still love him. Any third possibility is unthinkable; to be able to seek comfort in the love of another would be more frightful still than the most frightful of all. So she must love Don Giovanni for her own sake; self-defence bids her do so. And this is the spur of reflection which forces her to gaze at this paradox of whether she can love him although he deceived her. Whenever despair would take hold of her, she takes refuge in the memory of Don Giovanni's love, and in order properly to come to terms with this refuge she is tempted to think that he is no deceiver, even though she does this in many ways; for a woman's dialectic is remarkable, and only someone who has had the opportunity to observe it can emulate it, whereas even the greatest dialectician who has loved could speculate himself silly trying to produce it. [. . .]

So Elvira cannot bring Don Giovanni to light, and now she has to find her way out of her entanglement alone; she must come to herself. She has changed her environment and so the support that might perhaps have helped to bring her sorrow into the open is also removed. Her new circle knows nothing of her earlier life, suspects nothing, for there is nothing peculiar or noteworthy in her appearance, no marks of grief, no signpost saying 'Here there is sorrow'. She can control her every expression, for this is indeed something the loss of her honour can teach her; and even though she sets no great store by people's judgements, she is at least able to avoid their condolences. So everything is in order and she can reckon fairly safely on going through life without awakening any suspicion in the minds of the inquisitive rabble which as a rule is as dimwitted as it is inquisitive. She is in legal and undisputed possession of her sorrow, and it is only if she is unlucky enough to fall foul of a professional dealer in contraband[22] that she need fear any more penetrating search. What is going on inside her? Does she sorrow? Indeed she does! But how are we to describe this sorrow? I would call it an anxiety about how to support life; for people's lives consist not of food and drink alone, the soul too needs nourishment. She is young and yet her life's supply is exhausted, but it does not follow that she dies. Every day she is in this respect anxious for the morrow. She cannot stop loving him and yet he deceived her, but if he deceived her, then her love has lost its power to sustain. Yes, had he not deceived her, had a higher power torn him away, then she would have been as well supplied as any girl could wish; for the memory of Don Giovanni amounted to considerably more than many a living husband. But if she gives up her love she is reduced to beggary, she will have to return to the convent in shame and dishonour. Yes, if even that could buy back his love! So she lives on. This, the present day, it seems to her she can still last out, she still has some left-over to live on; but the day after, she fears for that. Then she ponders over and over again, she grasps at every expedient yet finds none, and so she can never sorrow consistently and soundly because she is always trying to find out how to sorrow.

'Forget him, that's what I want, tear his image from my heart, ransack myself like a consuming fire, and every thought that belongs to him shall be incinerated; only then will I be saved; it is self-defence, and if I do not tear out every thought of him, even the remotest, I am done for. Only thus can I protect myself. Myself – what is this self of mine? Wretchedness and misery. To my first love I was unfaithful and am I now to try to make up for it by being unfaithful to my second?

'No, I will hate him; only so can I find rest and occupation. I will weave a garland of curses out of all that reminds me of him, and for every kiss I say "A curse on you!", and for every embrace "Ten curses on you!", and for every time he swore that he loved me I shall swear that I will hate him. This will be my work, my task, to this I shall dedicate myself. At the convent I am used to repeating my rosary, and so I shall be a nun after all, praying early and late. Or should I be content that he once loved me? Maybe I should be a sensible girl who didn't throw him away in proud contempt, now that I know he is a deceiver. Perhaps I ought to be a good housewife who knows how to be frugal and make a little go as far as possible. No, I will hate him, for that is the only way I can tear myself away from him and prove to myself that I am not in need of him. But am I not in his debt when I hate him? Am I not then living at his expense? For what else is it that feeds my hate except my love of him?

'He was no deceiver, he had no idea what a woman can suffer. If he had, he would not have left me. He was a man, sufficient unto himself. Is that a consolation for me? Certainly, for my suffering and torment show me how happy I have been, so happy that he has no conception of it. So why do I complain? A man is not like a woman, not as happy as she when she is happy, not as unhappy as she when she is boundlessly unhappy because her happiness knew no bounds.

'Did he deceive me? No! Had he promised me anything? No! My Giovanni was no suitor, he was a wretched poultry thief; a nun does not degrade herself for the likes of that. He did not ask for my hand, he stretched out his own; I grasped it; he looked at me, I was his; he opened his arms, I belonged to him. I went with him, I twined myself around him like a plant, I rested my head upon his breast and gazed into that omnipotent countenance with which he conquered the world, and yet which rested on me as if for him I were the whole world. Like a child at the breast I sucked abundance, wealth and bliss. Can I ask for more? Was I not his? Was he not mine? And if he was not, was I any the less his? When the gods roamed the earth and fell in love with women, were *they* faithful to their loved ones? Yet no one thinks of saying that they deceived them! And why not? Because they will have it that a girl should be proud of having been loved by a god. And what are all the gods of Olympus compared to my Giovanni? And should I not be proud, should I degrade him, should I insult him in my thoughts, let them force him into the narrow, miserable laws that apply to ordinary men? No, I will be proud that he has loved me; he was greater than the gods, and I will honour him by making myself nothing. I will love him because he belonged to me, love him because he left me, and still I am constantly his and will treasure what he squanders.

'No, I cannot think of him. Every time my thoughts approach that hiding-place in my soul where his memory dwells, it is as if I committed a sin. I feel an anguish, an inexpressible anguish, an anguish like that I felt in the convent when I sat in my solitary cell waiting for him, terrified of the thought of the prioress's stern contempt, the convent's terrible punishment, my crime against God. And yet wasn't this anguish part of it? What would my love for him have been without it? After all, he was not consecrated to me, we had not received the blessing of the Church, the bells had not tolled for us, the hymn had not been sung, and yet what were all the music and festivity of the Church? What power could it have to prepossess me compared with my anguish? – But then he came, and the discord of my anguish resolved itself into the harmony of the most blissful security, and only sweet tremblings luxuriantly moved my soul. Am I then to fear this anguish? Does it not remind me of him, does it not announce his coming? If I could remember him without the anguish it would not be him I remembered. He comes, he invites quiet, he is master of spirits which would tear me from him. I am his, blessed in him.'

If I were to imagine someone in distress at sea, unconcerned for his own life, remaining on board because there was something he wanted to save and could not because he was at a loss what it was he should save, I would have a picture of Elvira; she is in distress at sea, her destruction is approaching, but that does not concern her, she does not notice, she is at a loss what it is she is to save.

3. *Margrete*

We know this girl from Goethe's *Faust*. A young, commonplace girl, not, like Elvira, destined for the convent, yet brought up in the fear of the Lord, even if her soul was too childlike to feel the gravity of it, as Goethe so incomparably says:

> Half sport of childhood,
> Half God within thee![23]

What we especially love in this girl is the delightful simplicity and humility of her pure soul. Straightaway, the first time she sees Faust, she feels too inferior to be loved by him, and it is not out of curiosity to learn whether Faust loves her that she plucks the petals of the daisy, but from humility because she feels herself too unworthy to make a choice, and therefore bows to the oracle-myth of a mysterious power. Yes, lovely Margrete! Goethe has told us how you plucked the petals and recited the words, 'He loves me, he loves me not'; poor Margrete, you can just carry on this occupation, only changing the words, 'He deceived me, he deceived me not'. You can cultivate a little plot of ground with flowers of this kind, and you will have employment for the rest of your life.

It has been pointed out how remarkable it is that, while the Don Juan legend tells of 1,003 seductions in Spain alone, the story of Faust tells of only one girl seduced.[24] It is worth bearing this observation in mind, since it will be important for what follows; it will help us to determine the special nature of Margrete's reflective sorrow. At first glance it might seem that the only difference between Elvira and Margrete was that between two distinct individuals who have had the same experience, but the difference is far more essential than that, though based not so much upon the difference in their feminine natures as in the essential difference to be found between a Don Juan and a Faust. There must be a difference from the beginning between an Elvira and a Margrete, inasmuch as a girl who is to have an effect on a Faust must differ in essentials from one who has an effect on a Don Juan; yes, even if I imagined that the same girl occupied the attentions of both, the one would still be attracted by something different from the other. This difference, at the beginning present only as a possibility, will, by being brought into relation with a Faust or a Don Juan, develop into something completely actual. Certainly Faust is a reproduction of Don Juan; but precisely his being a reproduction makes him, even in that stage of his life when he can be called a Don Juan, differ essentially from the latter; for to reproduce another stage means not just to become that stage, but to become it with all the elements of the preceding stage within one. Therefore, even if what he desires is the same as a Don Juan, still he desires it in a different manner. But in order for him to desire it in a different manner, it must also be present in a different manner. There are elements in him which make his method different, just as there are also elements in Margrete which make another method necessary. His method depends in turn upon his liking, and that differs from Don Juan's even if there is an essential similarity between them.

People usually think there is great wisdom in pointing out that Faust ends up becoming a Don Juan; yet it says very little, for the question is in what sense he becomes one. Like Don Juan, Faust is a demonic figure, but at a higher level. The sensual only becomes important for him after he has lost a whole world, but awareness of this loss is not erased, it is constantly there, and therefore what he seeks in the sensual is not so much pleasure as distraction. His doubting soul finds nothing it can rest in and now he grasps for love, not because he believes in it but because it has an element of presenthood in which there is rest for a moment and a striving which distracts and diverts his attention from the nothingness of doubt. Hence his enjoyment does not have the cheerfulness that distinguishes a Don Juan. His countenance is not smiling, his brow is not unclouded, and happiness is not his companion; young girls do not dance into his embrace, he attracts them through fear. What he seeks is not just sensual pleasure, what he desires is the immediacy of spirit. As the shades of the underworld, when they got hold of someone living, sucked the blood from him and lived as long as this blood warmed and nourished them, so Faust seeks an immediate life that can renew and strengthen him. And where better can this be found than in a young girl, and how more perfectly can he imbibe it than in the embrace of love? As the Middle Ages tell of sorcerers who knew how to prepare an elixir for the renewal of youth, and used the heart of an innocent child for that purpose, so his enervated soul needs this strengthening potion, the only thing that for a moment can satisfy him. His sick soul needs what one might call a young heart's first green shoots; and with what else am I to compare an innocent feminine soul's first youth? To call it a bloom would be to say too little; for it is more, it is a blossoming. The good health of hope and faith and trust sprouts forth and blossoms in rich variety, and gentle yearnings move the delicate shoots, and dreams cast their shadow on its fruitfulness. This is how it affects a Faust; it beckons his restless soul like an island of peace in the tranquil sea. That it is transient no one knows better than Faust; he believes in it as little as he believes in anything else; but that it exists, of that he convinces himself in love's embrace. Only the fullness of innocence and childlikeness can for a moment refresh him.

In Goethe's *Faust*, Mephistopheles lets Faust see Margrete in a mirror. His eye finds pleasure in beholding her, but it is not after all her beauty he desires, although he accepts that too. What he desires is the pure, untroubled, rich, immediate happiness of a woman's soul, yet he desires this not spiritually but sensually. In a sense, then, he does desire like Don Juan, but still he desires quite differently. Here perhaps one or another *privatdocent*,[25] convinced he has been a Faust, since otherwise he could never have become *privatdocent*, will remark that Faust requires intellectual development and culture in the woman who is to attract him. Perhaps a considerable number of *privatdocents* will find this an excellent remark, and their respective wives and sweethearts will nod in assent. However, it completely misses the mark, for Faust would desire nothing less. A so-called cultured woman would belong within the same relativity as himself and this, notwithstanding, would have no significance at all for him, would simply be nothing. With her crumb of culture, she might perhaps tempt this old magister of doubt to take her out on the river, where she would then soon despair. An innocent young girl, on the other hand, belongs within another relativity, and is therefore, in a sense, nothing as against Faust, yet in another sense tremendously much, since she is immediacy. Only in this immediacy is she an object of his desire, and that is why I said that he desires immediacy not spiritually but sensually.

All this Goethe has seen to perfection, and so Margrete is a commonplace little girl, a girl one might almost be tempted to call insignificant. Now, since it is important for Margrete's sorrow, we shall consider a little more closely the effect Faust must have had upon her. The individual traits Goethe has emphasized are naturally of great value, yet I believe that for the sake of completeness we must imagine a little modification. In her innocent simplicity, Margrete soon notices that with Faust all is not as it should be in respect of his faith. In Goethe this is brought out in a little catechism scene,[26] which is undeniably an excellent invention by the poet. The question now is what consequences this examination can have on their relation to each other. Faust appears as the doubter, and for want of further evidence it seems that Goethe intended to let Faust remain a doubter also in Margrete's eyes. He has done his best to keep her mind off all such inquiries and to fix it solely on the reality of love. But, on the one hand, I think Faust would find that difficult once the issue had been raised, and on the other, I believe it is incorrect psychologically. It is not for Faust's sake that I shall dwell further on this point but for Margrete's, for if he has not revealed himself to her as a doubter her sorrow contains an additional element. Faust is a doubter, then, but he is no vain dupe who merely wants to feel his own importance by doubting what others believe; his doubt has an objective ground in himself. Let that much be said in Faust's favour.

On the other hand, the moment he wants to implicate others in his doubt, an impure passion can easily become mixed up in it. As soon as the doubt is made to implicate others, an envy is involved that takes pleasure in depriving them of what they take to be certainties. But for this passion of envy to be aroused in the doubter, there must be some question of an opposition on the part of the individual concerned. Where either no such question can arise or it would be inapposite to imagine it, the temptation ceases. This latter is the case with a young girl. Confronted with her, a doubter always finds himself in difficulties. Depriving her of her faith is no task for him; on the contrary, he feels it is only faith that makes her the great thing she is. He feels himself humbled, for there is a natural demand in her that he should be her protector inasmuch as she herself has become hesitant. Yes, a poor wretch of a doubter, a conceited smatterer, might perhaps find satisfaction in depriving a young girl of her faith and pleasure in frightening women and children, since he cannot terrify men. But this is not true of Faust; he is too big for that. We may well agree with Goethe, then, that Faust betrays his doubt a first time, but on the other hand I hardly think it will happen to him a second time.

This is of great importance for our understanding of Margrete. Faust readily sees that Margrete's entire significance depends on her innocent simplicity; take this away and she is nothing in herself, nothing to him. So this has to be preserved. He is a doubter, but as such has within himself all it takes to conceive positively of faith, for otherwise he is a poor doubter. What he lacks is the final conclusion and it is this that makes all the components of his outlook negative. She, on the contrary, has the conclusion; she has childlikeness and innocence. Nothing is therefore easier than for him to equip her. His experience has taught him often enough that what he propounded as doubt seemed to others to be positive truth. So now he finds his happiness in enriching her with the rich content of a view of life; he brings out all the finery of immediate faith; he delights in adorning her with it because it looks well on her and she thereby becomes more beautiful in his eyes. From this he also derives the advantage that her soul clings more and more closely to his. Really she doesn't understand him at all. She clings to him like a child, for what is doubt to him is for her unfailing truth. But while he thus builds up her faith, at the same time he undermines it, for in the end he becomes for her an object of faith, a god and not a man.

Except that I must try to avert a misunderstanding. It might seem that I make Faust out to be a contemptible hypocrite. This is not at all the case. It is Gretchen herself who has brought the matter up; with half an eye he surveys the glory she thinks she possesses and sees that it cannot withstand his doubt, but he does not have it in his heart to destroy it, and now his conduct is even motivated by a certain kindliness. Her love gives her meaning for him and yet she remains almost a child; he descends to her childlike level and finds his joy in seeing how she makes everything her own. For Margrete's future, however, this has the most sorrowful consequences. Had Faust revealed himself to her as a doubter, she might perhaps later have been able to save her faith; she would then in all humility have known that his high-flown and daring thoughts were not for her; she would have kept hold of what she had. But now, on the contrary, she owes him the content of her faith, and yet she realizes, seeing he has abandoned her, that he has not believed in it himself. As long as he was with her, she did not discover the doubt; now that he is gone, everything is changed for her and she sees doubt everywhere, a doubt she cannot control, since she always associates it with the circumstance that Faust himself has been unable to master it.

What it is about Faust that captivates Margrete, according to Goethe, is not the seductive talent of a Don Juan but his immense superiority. Therefore, as she so touchingly puts it, she simply cannot understand what Faust finds in her.[27] Her first impression of him is altogether overwhelming, over against him she becomes nothing at all. She belongs to him, therefore, not in the same sense as Elvira belongs to Don Juan, for that still expresses an independent existence in relation to the latter, but she altogether disappears in him. Nor does she break with heaven to belong to him, for that would give her a claim on him; imperceptibly, without the remotest reflection, he becomes her all. But just as she is thus nothing from the beginning, so, if I may put it in this way, she becomes less and less the more she is convinced of his almost divine superiority; she is nothing and exists only in him. What Goethe has somewhere said about Hamlet,[28] that in relation to his body his soul was an acorn planted in a flower-pot which finally shatters the vessel, is true of Margrete's love. Faust is too great for her, and her love must end by splitting her soul apart. And the moment for this cannot be long awaiting, for Faust no doubt feels she cannot remain in this immediacy; but then he does not carry her up into the higher regions of the spirit, for it is from these that he is fleeing; he desires her sensually – and abandons her.

So Faust has abandoned Margrete. Her loss is so terrible that her circle itself forgets for a moment what it usually finds so hard to forget, that she has been dishonoured. She reclines in a total impotence in which she is unable even to think of her loss; the strength even to conceive her misfortune is taken from her. Were this condition to continue, it would be impossible for reflective sorrow to occur. Yet, little by little, the consolations she can derive from her environment will bring her to herself, give her thought a jolt that sets it in motion again; but once it is mobilized it is clear that she is incapable of holding on to a single one of its considerations. She listens to her thoughts as though they were not addressed to her, and not a word of them halts or accelerates the unrest in her mind. Her problem is the same as Elvira's, to believe that Faust was a deceiver; but it is even more difficult because she is far more profoundly influenced by Faust; he wasn't just a deceiver, but he was indeed a hypocrite; she has not surrendered anything for him, but she owes him everything, and to some extent she still possesses this everything, except that it now proves to be a deception. But then is what he said less true because he himself did not believe it? Not at all, and yet that is how it is for her, for it was through him that she believed it.

It might seem more difficult for reflection to be mobilized in Margrete; what stops it is her feeling that she was absolutely nothing. Yet there is a tremendous dialectical elasticity in this feeling. Were she able to hold on to the thought that she was, in the strictest sense of the word, absolutely nothing, reflection would be excluded. She would then not have been deceived, for when you are nothing there is no relation, and where there is no relation there can be no question of a deception. So far she is at rest. This thought cannot be kept hold of, however, but immediately veers to its opposite. That she was nothing is merely the expression of the fact that all the finite differences of love are negated, and is therefore precisely the expression of her love's absolute validity, and in that in turn lies her absolute justification. His conduct, then, is not just a deception but an absolute deception, because her love was absolute. And here again she will not rest, for since he has been everything to her she will not be able to hold on even to this thought except through him; but she cannot think it through him, because he was a deceiver.

As her environment now becomes increasingly alien to her, so begins the inner movement. She has not merely loved Faust with all her soul, he was her vital force; it was through him she came into being. The effect of this is that while her soul will not be less agitated in its mood than an Elvira's, the individual moods will be less agitated. She is on the way to having a fundamental mood, and the individual mood is like a bubble rising from the depths, without the strength to maintain itself nor yet displaced by another bubble but dissolved in the general mood that she is nothing. This fundamental mood is again a state that is felt, which does not express itself in any individual outburst; it is inexpressible, and the attempt the individual mood makes to give it life, to raise it up, is in vain. The total mood therefore constantly resounds in the particular mood, creating its resonance in the form of impotence and vapidity. The individual mood is expressed but it does not soothe, it does not ease; it is [...] a false sigh which frustrates, and not the healthy exercise of a normal sigh. Nor is the individual mood full-toned and energetic; for that her utterance is too troubled.

'Can I forget him? Can the brook, however far it flows, forget its source, forget its head-spring, cut itself off from it? Then it would have to cease flowing! Can the arrow, however swiftly it flies, forget the bowstring? Then its flight would have to halt! Can the raindrop, however far it falls, forget the sky from which it fell? Then it would have to dissolve! Can I become another, can I be born again of a mother who is not my mother? Can I forget him? Then I would have to cease to be!

'Can I remember him? Can my memory call him forth, now, when he has vanished, I who am myself merely my memory of him? This faded, nebulous picture, is it the Faust I worshipped? I remember his words but I do not possess the harp in his voice! I remember his speeches but my breast is too weak to give them content! They ring out meaninglessly for deaf ears!

'Faust, oh Faust! come back, satisfy the hungry, clothe the naked, restore the faint, visit the lonely! Well I know that my love had no meaning for you, but neither did I demand that. My love laid itself humbly at your feet, my sigh was a prayer, my kiss a thank-offering, my embrace an act of adoration. Is that why you forsake me? Did you not know it beforehand? Or is it not a reason to love me that I love you, that my soul expires when you are not with me?

'God in heaven, forgive me for having loved a man more than you, yet I do so still. I know it is a sin that I speak thus to you. Eternal love, oh! let your mercy sustain me; do not reject me; give him back to me, incline his heart once more to me; have pity on me, oh pity! that I pray thus again!

'Can I curse him, then? What am I, that I should be so bold? Can the earthen vessel presume against the potter? What was I? Nothing!

The clay in his hand, a rib from which he made me! What was I? A lowly plant, and he bent down to me, he caused me to grow; he was everything to me, my god, the origin of my mind, the nourishment of my soul!

'Can I sorrow? No, no! Sorrow broods like a night mist over my soul. Oh! come back, I will give you up, never demand to belong to you; just sit with me, look at me, that I might gain strength to sigh; speak to me, speak of yourself, as though you were a stranger; I will forget that it is you; speak, that the tears may burst forth. Am I then absolutely nothing, unable even to weep without him?

'Where shall I find rest and peace? The thoughts rise up in my soul, the one against the other, the one confounding the other. When you were with me, they obeyed your beck and call, I played with them as a child, I wove garlands with them and placed them on my head; I let them flutter loose like my hair in the wind. Now they coil themselves terrifyingly about me, like snakes they twine about and crush my anguished soul.

'And I am a mother! A living creature demands nourishment of me. Can the hungry satisfy the hungry, the faint slake the thirst of the thirsty? Am I to become a murderer; then? Oh! Faust, come back, save the child in the womb, even if you will not save the mother!'

Thus is she moved, not by moods, but in her mood. But the individual mood does not relieve her, because it dissolves in the total mood she cannot annul. Yes, if Faust had been taken from her, then Margrete would not have looked for relief; her lot would still have been enviable in her eyes – but she is deceived. She lacks what might be called the situation of sorrow, for she is not able to sorrow alone. Yes, if, like a poor Florine in the fairytale,[29] she could find access to some grotto of echoes, from which she knew that every sigh, every complaint, was heard by the loved one, she would not, like Florine, spend only three nights there, she would stay there day and night; but in Faust's palace there is no echo-grotto, and he has no ear in her heart.

I have, perhaps, already held your attention for too long, dear *Symparanekromenoi*; the more so since, however much I have spoken, nothing visible has appeared before you. Yet the reason for this lies

not in the deceptiveness of my presentation, but in the matter itself
and in sorrow's cunning. When the favourable occasion is offered,
the hidden reveals itself. This we have in our power, and in farewell
we shall let these three brides of sorrow come together, let them
embrace one another in a unison of sorrow, let them form a group
before us, a tabernacle where the voice of sorrow does not become
silent, where the sigh does not cease, because they themselves watch
more scrupulously and faithfully than vestal virgins over the observance of the holy rites. Ought we to interrupt them in this occupation? Should we wish them their loss restored? Would that be a
gain for them? Have they not already received a higher consecration?
And this consecration will unite them, and cast a beauty upon their
union, and bring them relief in their union. For only someone who
has been bitten by snakes knows what the victim of a snake-bite
suffers.

5 THE UNHAPPIEST ONE

An Enthusiastic Address to
Symparanekromenoi

Peroration in the Friday Meetings

SOMEWHERE in England is said to be a grave distinguished not by a splendid monument or sad surroundings, but by a small inscription: 'The Unhappiest One'. Apparently someone opened the grave but found no trace of the corpse. What is the more surprising, that no corpse was found or that the grave was opened? Strange, indeed, that someone should have gone to the trouble to find out if there was anyone in it. When you read a name on an epitaph you are easily led to wonder how it went with his life in the world; one would like to climb down into the grave to converse with him. But this inscription, it says so much! A book may have a title which makes you want to read it, but a title can be so evocative, so personally appealing, that you will never read the book. Truly, this inscription is so full of meaning – harrowing or joyful, according to one's mood – for anyone who in the stillness of his heart may have secretly betrothed himself to the thought that he was the unhappiest. But I can imagine someone whose soul knows no such preoccupations, whose curiosity it was that undertook the task of finding out if there really was someone in this grave. And lo and behold the tomb was empty! Has he perhaps risen from the dead, has he perhaps wanted to mock the words of the poet:

> ... In the grave there is peace,
> Its silent dweller not acquainted with grief.[1]

Did he find no rest, not even in the grave; does he perhaps wander restlessly about in the world? Has he forsaken his house, his home, leaving only his address behind? Or is he not yet found, this the unhappiest one, whom not even the furies pursue until he finds the door of the temple and the seat of the humble suppliant; but whom sorrows keep alive, sorrows follow to the grave![2]

If it is true that he is not yet found, then dear *Symparanekromenoi*, let us enter upon a pilgrimage, not to the holy tomb in the happy East, but to this sorrowful grave in the unhappy West. By that empty grave we shall look for him, the unhappiest one, certain to find him; for as the yearning of the faithful longs for the holy tomb, so do the unhappy feel drawn west to that empty grave, each filled with the thought that it is destined for him.

Or should such a consideration not be worthy of our attention? We whose activities are, if I am to conform with the sacred tradition of our society, experiments in aphoristic and accidental devotion, we who do not merely think and speak aphoristically but live aphoristically, we who live *aphorismenoi* and *segregati*,[3] like aphorisms in life, without society of men, not sharing their sorrows and their joys; we who are not consonants sounding together in the noise of life, but solitary birds in the stillness of night, gathered together only now and then, to be edified by representations of life's misery, the length of the day, and the endless duration of time; we, dear *Symparanekromenoi*, who have no faith in the game of happiness or the fortune of fools, we who believe in nothing but misfortune.

See how they press forward in their countless multitudes, all the unhappy! Yet, many though they are who believe they are called, few are the chosen. A distinction is to be established between them – a word, and the crowd vanishes; for excluded, uninvited guests are all those who think the greatest misfortune is death, those who became unhappy because it was death they feared; for we, dear *Symparanekromenoi*, we, like the Roman soldiers, do not fear death; we know of greater misfortunes, and first and last and above all – life. Yes, if there were a human being who could not die, if the story of the eternally wandering Jew were true, how could we scruple to call him the unhappiest? We could then also explain why the grave was empty, to indicate that the unhappiest person was the one who could not die, could not slip down into a grave. The matter would then be decided, the answer easy; for the unhappiest would be the one who could not die, the happy man the one who could; happy the one who died in his old age, happier the one who died at birth, happiest of all the one who was never born. But that is not how it is; death is the common fortune of all men, and therefore, in so far as the unhappiest has not yet been found, it is within these confines he must be sought.

See how the crowd disappeared, how diminished are their numbers. I need not now say, 'Give me your attention', for I know that I have it; nor 'Lend me your ears'; I know they are mine. Your eyes sparkle. You rise in your seats. It is a contest for a wager well worth joining in, a struggle more terrible even than if the issue were life or death, for death we do not fear. But the reward, yes, it is grander than any other in the world, and more certain; for the one who is assured of being the unhappiest, that man need fear no good fortune; he shall not taste the humiliation in his last hour of having to cry: 'Solon, Solon, Solon!'[4]

So we open a free competition from which none are to be excluded, by either rank or age. No one is excluded except the happy man and the one who fears death – every worthy member of the community of the unhappy is welcome, the seat of honour assigned to every really unhappy person, the grave to the unhappiest. My voice rings forth in the world; hear it, all you who call yourselves unhappy in the world yet fear not death. My voice rings back in time, for we will not be so sophistical as to exclude the departed because they are dead; after all, they have lived. I beseech you, forgive me for disturbing your rest for a moment, meet us here at this empty grave. Three times I let the cry ring out high over the world; hear it, you unhappy ones; for it is not our intention to decide the matter among ourselves in a corner. The place has been found where it must be decided before the whole world.

But before passing on to our individual hearings, let us make ourselves qualified to sit here as worthy judges and competitors. Let us strengthen our thoughts, arm them against the charms of the ear, for what voice is quite so ingratiating as that of the unhappy man when he speaks of his own misfortune? Let us make ourselves worthy to sit as judges, competitors, that we do not lose perspective, are not put off by the individuals themselves, for the eloquence of sorrow is infinite and infinitely inventive. We would divide the unhappy into definite groups and let only one speak for each; for this we will not deny, that no particular individual is the unhappiest; it is a class. But we would not scruple for that reason to award to the representative for this class the name 'the unhappiest one', nor hesitate to assign him the grave.

In all Hegel's systematic writings there is a section dealing with the unhappy consciousness.[5] It is always with qualms and palpitations that one approaches the reading of inquiries like this, with a fear that one might learn too much or too little. Brought up casually in conversation, the term 'unhappy consciousness' can practically turn your blood into ice, set your nerves aquiver; seeing it pronounced now so expressly – like that mysterious word in a story of Clemens Brentano's, *tertia nux mors est*[6] – can make you tremble like a sinner. Ah! happy the one who has no more to do with this matter than write a section on the subject, happier still he who can write the next. For the unhappy person is he who has his ideal, the content of his life, the fullness of his consciousness, his real nature in some way or other outside himself. The unhappy man is always absent from himself, never present to himself. But one can be absent, obviously, either in the past or in the future. This adequately circumscribes the entire territory of the unhappy consciousness. For this firm delimitation we would thank Hegel, and now, since we are not simply philosophers looking upon this kingdom from afar, we shall as natives devote attention in detail to the various stages that lie within it. So the unhappy one is absent. But one is absent either when living in the past or when living in the future. The form of expression is important, for it is evident, as philology also teaches us, that there is a tense that expresses presence in the past, and a tense that expresses presence in the future; but the same science also teaches us that there is a pluperfect tense in which there is no present, as well as a future perfect tense with the same characteristic. These are the hoping and the remembering individuals. Inasmuch as they are only hoping or only remembering, these are indeed in a sense unhappy individuals, if otherwise it is only the person who is present to himself that is happy. However, one cannot strictly call an individual unhappy who is present in hope or in memory. For what one must note here is that he is still present to himself in one of these. From which we also see that a single blow, be it ever so heavy, cannot possibly make a person the unhappiest. For one blow can either deprive him of hope, still leaving him present in memory, or of memory, still leaving him present in hope. We now proceed further and see what more detailed description can be given of the unhappy individual.

Consider first the hoping individual. When, as a hoping individual (and of course to that extent unhappy), he is not present to himself, he becomes unhappy in a stricter sense. An individual who hopes for an eternal life is, indeed, in a certain sense an unhappy individual to the extent that he renounces the present, but nevertheless is strictly not unhappy, because he is present to himself in this hope and does not come in conflict with the particular moments of finitude. But if he cannot become present to himself in hope, but loses his hope, hopes again, and so on, then he is absent from himself not just in the present but also in the future, and we have a type of the unhappy. Similarly if we consider the remembering individual. If he finds himself present in the past, strictly he is not unhappy; but if he cannot do that but remains constantly absent from himself in a past, then we have a form of the unhappy.

Memory is pre-eminently the real element of the unhappy, as is natural seeing the past has the remarkable characteristic that it is gone, the future that it is yet to come; and one can therefore say in a sense that the future is nearer the present than is the past. The future, for the hoping individual to be present in it, must be real, or rather must acquire reality for him. The past, for the remembering individual to be present in it, must have had reality for him. But when the hoping individual would have a future which can have no reality for him, or the remembering individual remember a past which has had no reality for him, then we have the genuinely unhappy individuals. The first of these one might think impossible, or consider sheer madness, but that is not so, for though the hoping individual does not hope for something that has no reality for him, he hopes for something he himself knows cannot be realized. For when an individual loses his hope, and instead of becoming a remembering individual, wants to remain a hoping one, then we get this form. When an individual who loses his memory, or has nothing to remember, will not become a hoping one but remains a remembering one, that is a form of the unhappy. Thus were an individual to lose himself in antiquity, or in the Middle Ages, or whatever other period, but in such a way that this was definitely real for him, or if he lost himself in his own childhood or youth in such a way that that was decidedly real for him, then strictly he would not be a genuinely unhappy individual. Were I to imagine, on the other hand, a person who has never had a childhood himself, this age having passed him by without acquiring significance for him, but who now, say by becoming a teacher of children, discovered all the beauty that lies in childhood, and would now remember his own childhood, always look back upon it; then he indeed would be a very fitting example. He wants in retrospect to discover the significance of what, for him, is past and nevertheless remember it in its significance. Were I to imagine someone who had lived without appreciating the joy of life, or its pleasures, and who now at death's door caught sight of it, but didn't die, which would have been the best, but revived though not to live over again, then he could well be considered in the matter of who was the unhappiest.

Unhappy individuals who hope never have the same pain as those who remember. Hoping individuals always have a more gratifying disappointment. The unhappiest one will always, therefore, be found among the unhappy rememberers.

But we proceed further and imagine a combination of the two, strictly speaking, unhappy forms just described. The unhappy hoping individual was not able to be present to himself in his hope, similarly with the unhappy rememberer. The combination can only be this: that what prevents him being present in hope is memory, and what prevents him being present in memory is hope. This is what it amounts to: on the one hand, he constantly hopes for something he should be remembering, his hope is constantly disappointed, but on its being disappointed he discovers that the reason is not that the goal has been moved further on but that he has gone past it, that it has already been experienced, or is supposed to have been, and has thus passed over into memory. On the other hand, he constantly remembers something he should be hoping for; for in thought the future is something he has already taken up, he has experienced it in thought, and that which he has experienced is something he remembers instead of hopes for. Consequently what he hopes for lies behind him, and what he remembers lies before him. His life is not backwards but back-to-front in two directions. He will soon notice his misfortune even if he does not grasp what it really consists in. But to make sure that he really gets the chance to feel it, that misunderstanding comes along which every moment in a remarkable way casts ridicule. He enjoys, for everyday purposes, the reputation of being in his right mind, yet he knows that were he to explain to a single person just how things were with him, he would be declared mad. This itself is enough to drive a person mad, yet he does not become so, and that is precisely his misfortune. His misfortune is that he has come to the world too soon and is therefore constantly arriving too late. He is forever quite close to the goal and the same moment at a distance from it; he now discovers that what it is that makes him unhappy, because now he has it, or because he is this way, is precisely what a few years ago would have made him happy if he had had it then, whereas then he was unhappy because he did not have it. His life has no meaning, like that of Ancaeus, of whom it is customary to say that nothing is known of him except that he gave rise to a proverb: 'There's many a slip 'twixt the cup and the lip',[7] as if this were not more than enough. His life knows no rest and has no content, he is not present to himself in the moment, not present to himself in the future, for the future has been experienced, and not in the past, because the past has still not arrived. Thus is he chased about, like Latona to the Hyperborean darkness, to the bright isle of the Equator, and cannot give birth and is constantly as though just about to.[8] Left to himself he stands in the wide world alone, he has no contemporaneity to attach himself to, no past he can long for, for his past has still not arrived, and no future he can hope for, for his future is already past. Alone, he has the whole world over against him as the 'Thou' with which he finds himself in conflict. For all the rest of the world is to him just one person, and this person, this inseparable, importunate friend, this is the misunderstanding. He cannot become old, for he has never been young; he cannot become young, for he has already become old; in a way he cannot die, for he has never lived; in a way he cannot live, for he is already dead; he cannot love, for love is always in the present, and he has no present time, no future, no past, and yet he is of a sympathetic nature, and he hates the world only because he loves it; he has no passion, not because he lacks it, but because that same instant he has the opposite; he has no time for anything, not because his time is taken up with something else, but because he has no time at all; he is powerless, not because he lacks strength, but because his own strength makes him impotent.

But soon our hearts are sufficiently steeled, our ears plugged if not closed. We have listened to the circumspect voice of deliberation; let us now feel the eloquence of passion – brief, pithy, as all passion is.

A young girl stands there. She complains that her lover has been unfaithful. This we cannot reflect upon. But she loved him, him alone in all the world, she loved him with all her soul, with all her heart, and all her mind – she can remember, then, and sorrow.

Is this a real being or is it an image, a living person who is dying or a dead one that lives? It is Niobe.[9] She lost everything at a single blow; she lost that to which she had given life; she lost that which gave her life. Look up to her, dear *Symparanekromenoi*; she stands a little higher than the world, as a memorial stone on a burial mound. But no hope beckons her, no future moves her, no prospect tempts her, no hope disturbs her – hopeless she stands, petrified in memory. For one instant she was unhappy, the very same instant she became happy, and no one can take her good fortune from her; the world changes, but she knows no fluctuation, and time keeps coming, but for her there is no time to come.

See yonder, what a beautiful union! The one generation extends its hand to the next! Is it in blessing, to loyal solidarity, to the joyous dance? It is the outcast house of Oedipus, and the blow is passed on and crushes the last – it is Antigone. Yet she is provided for; a generation's sorrow is enough for a human life. She has turned her back on hope, she has exchanged its inconstancy for the allegiance of memory. So be happy, then, dear Antigone! We wish you a long life, as full of meaning as a deep sigh. May no forgetfulness deprive you of anything! May the daily bitterness of grief be extended to you in abundance!

A vigorous figure appears, but he is not alone, he has friends, so why does he come here? It is Job, the patriarch of sorrow – and his friends. He lost everything, but not at one blow; for the Lord took, and the Lord took, and the Lord took. Friends taught him to feel the bitterness of the loss; for the Lord gave, and the Lord gave, and the Lord also gave him a foolish wife into the bargain.[10] He lost everything; for what he kept is beyond our interest. Honour him, dear *Symparanekromenoi*, for his grey hair and his misfortune. He lost everything, but he had possessed it.

His hair is grey, his head bowed, his countenance downcast, his soul troubled. It is the prodigal son's father. Like Job, he lost what he cherished most in the world, yet the Lord did not take it but the enemy; he did not lose it, but he is losing it; it has not been taken from him, but it is vanishing. He does not sit at home by the hearth in sackcloth and ashes; he has arisen from his home, he has forsaken everything to seek what is lost; he snatches at him, but his arm does not come near him; he calls out to him, but his voice does not reach him. Still he hopes, if but through tears. He catches sight of him, if but through mists. He catches up with him, if but in death. His hope makes him aged, and nothing binds him to the world but the hope which he lives for. His feet are tired, his eyes dim, his body seeks rest, his hope lives. His hair is white, his body decrepit, his foot halts, his heart breaks, his hope lives. Raise him up, dear *Symparanekromenoi*, he was unhappy.

Who is this pallid figure, listless as the shade of someone dead? His name has been forgotten, for many centuries have passed since that time. He was a youth, he had fervour. He sought martyrdom. In imagination he saw himself nailed to the cross and heaven open; but the reality was too hard for him; the enthusiasm disappeared, he denied his Master and himself. He wished to carry a world, but he broke under the strain. His soul was not crushed, or annihilated, it was broken and his spirit enfeebled, his soul was paralysed. Congratulate him, dear *Symparanekromenoi*, he was unhappy. And yet he became happy, he became what he wanted, a martyr, even if his martyrdom was not, as he had wished, to be nailed to the cross or thrown to the beasts, but to be burned alive, to be slowly consumed by a steady fire.

A young woman sits yonder, so thoughtful. Her lover was unfaithful – this we cannot reflect upon. Young girl, observe the grave countenances of this assembly; it has heard of more terrible misfortunes, so its venturesome soul demands greater still. – Yes, but I loved him with all my soul, with all my heart, with all my mind. – We have heard the like already, do not weary our impatient longing! After all, you can remember and sorrow. – No, I cannot sorrow, for perhaps he was not unfaithful, perhaps he was not a deceiver. – Why, then, can you not sorrow? Come nearer, chosen among girls, forgive the strict censor for wanting for a moment to reject you. You cannot sorrow. Then why not hope? – No, I cannot hope, for he was a riddle. – Well, my girl, I understand you, you stand high on the ladder of unhappiness; look upon her, dear *Symparanekromenoi*, she soars almost to the pinnacle of unhappiness. But you must divide yourself, you must hope by day and sorrow by night, or sorrow by day and hope by night. Be proud, it is never happiness that should make you proud, but unhappiness. You are not indeed the unhappiest, but is it not your opinion, dear *Symparanekromenoi*, that we award her an honourable *accessit*? The grave we cannot award her, but the place next to it.

For there he stands, the emissary from the kingdom of sighs, the elected favourite of suffering, the apostle of sorrow, the silent friend of pain, the unhappy lover of memory, confounded in his memory by the light of hope, deceived in his hope by the shadows of memory. His head is heavy, his knees are weak, yet he rests on none but himself. He is faint, yet how powerful! His eyes seem not to have shed, but to have drunk, many tears; yet a fire burns in them that could consume the entire world, though not one splinter of the sorrow within his breast. He is bent, yet his youth portends a long life; his lips smile at the world that misunderstands him. Rise, dear *Symparanekromenoi*, bow before him, sorrow's witnesses, in this solemn hour! I salute you, great unknown, whose name I do not know; I salute you with your title of honour: The Unhappiest One! Receive a welcome here in your home from the community of the unhappy; welcome at the entrance to the humble and low dwelling which is yet prouder than all the world's palaces! See, the stone is rolled away, the shade of the grave waits you with its pleasant coolness. But perhaps the time has not yet come, long perhaps is the way; but we promise to gather here often to envy you your good fortune. So accept, then, our wish, a good wish: may no one understand you, but all envy you; may no friend attach himself to you, no girl love you; may no secret sympathy suspect your solitary pain; may no eye fathom your distant sorrow; may no ear detect your secret sigh! Or if your proud soul scorns such expressions of sympathy, spurns the alleviation, may the girls love you, may those with child seek you out in their anguish, may mothers put their hopes in you, may the dying look to you for comfort, may the young attach themselves to you, may husbands depend upon you, may the aged one reach out to you as to a staff — may all the world believe you are able to make it happy. So live well, then, you the unhappiest one! But what am I saying, the unhappiest, I ought to say the happiest, for this indeed is a gift of fortune that no one can give to themselves. See, language fails, and thought is confounded; for who is the happiest except the unhappiest, and who the unhappiest except the happiest? And what is life but madness, and faith but folly, and hope but reprieve, and love but salt in the wound?

He vanished, and we stand again before an empty grave. Then let us wish him peace and rest and recovery, and all possible good fortune, and an early death, and an eternal oblivion, and no remembrance lest even the memory of him should make another unhappy.

Rise, dear *Symparanekromenoi!* The night has passed, the day again begins its untiring activity, never weary, it seems, of repeating itself for ever and ever.

6 CROP ROTATION

An Attempt at a Theory of Social Prudence

CHREMYLOS: There is too much of everything.
               Of love,
KARION: Bread,
CHREMYLOS: Songs,
KARION: And candy.
CHERMYLOS: Of honour,
KARION: Cakes,
CHREMYLOS: Courage,
KARION: And figs.
CHREMYLOS: Of ambition,
KARION: Barley-bread,
CHREMYLOS: High office,
KARION: And pease-porridge.
                    Cf. Aristophanes, *Plutus*, vv. 189ff.

PEOPLE of experience maintain that it is very sensible to start from a principle. I grant them that and start with the principle that all men are boring. Or will someone be boring enough to contradict me in this? This principle possesses to the highest degree that power of repulsion one always requires of any negative that genuinely provides the principle of motion.[1] Not merely is it repellent, it is infinitely forbidding; and the person with this principle behind him must necessarily have an infinite momentum to make discoveries with. For if my principle is true, to slacken or increase one's impetus one need only consider with more or less moderation how ruinous boredom is for man; and if one wants to risk doing injury to the locomotive itself by pressing the speed to the maximum, one need only say to oneself: 'Boredom is a root of all evil.' Strange that boredom, so still and static, should have such power to set things in motion. The effect that boredom exercises is altogether magical, except that it is not one of attraction but of repulsion.

How ruinous boredom is everyone also recognizes in relation to children. So long as children are enjoying themselves, they are always well-behaved. This can be said in the strictest sense, since if they sometimes get out of control even in play, really that is because they are beginning to get bored; boredom has already set in, though in a different way. So in choosing a nursemaid one pays attention not just to her sobriety, faithfulness and decency; one also takes into consideration, aesthetically, her ability to amuse the children. And one would not hesitate to dismiss a nursemaid lacking in this qualification even if she possessed all other desirable virtues. Here, indeed, the principle is clearly acknowledged; but so remarkable are the ways of the world, so much have habit and boredom gained the upper hand, that justice is done to aesthetics only in the case of the nursemaid. Were one to demand divorce on the grounds that one's wife was boring, or a king's abdication because he was boring to look at, or a priest thrown out of the land because he was boring to listen to, or a cabinet minister dismissed, or a life-sentence for a journalist, because they were dreadfully boring, it would be impossible to get one's way. What wonder, then, that the world is regressing, that evil is gaining ground more and more, since boredom is on the increase and boredom is a root of all evil.

We can trace this from the very beginning of the world. The gods were bored so they created man. Adam was bored because he was alone, so Eve was created. From that time boredom entered the world and grew in exact proportion to the growth of population. Adam was bored alone, then Adam and Eve were bored in union, then Adam and Eve and Cain and Abel were bored *en famille*, then the population increased and the peoples were bored *en masse*. To divert themselves they conceived the idea of building a tower so high it reached the sky. The very idea is as boring as the tower was high, and a terrible proof of how boredom had gained the upper hand. Then the nations were scattered over the earth, just as people now travel abroad, but they continued to be bored. And think of the consequences of this boredom! Man stood high and fell low, first with Eve and then the Tower of Babel. Yet what was it that stayed the fall of Rome? It was *panis* and *circenses*.[2] What is it people do nowadays? Do they think of ways of diverting themselves? Quite the contrary, they accelerate the ruin. They think of calling a constitutional assembly.[3] Can anything more boring be imagined, as much for the gentlemen taking part as for those who have to read and hear about them! There is a proposal to improve the State's economy through savings. Can anything more boring be imagined? Instead of increasing the national debt, it is proposed to pay it off. From what I know of politics, it would be an easy matter for Denmark to take out a loan of fifteen millions. Why does no one think of that? That some person is genius enough not to pay his debt, that at least is something one hears of now and then; why shouldn't a state be able to do the same if only all are agreed? So we take out a loan of fifteen millions yet use it not to pay our debts but for public pleasure. Let us celebrate the thousand-year reign with joy and merriment. Just as there are boxes everywhere to put money in, so there should be bowls of money everywhere. Everything would be free, people would go to the theatre free, have free access to the streetwalkers, take free drives to the park, be buried free of charge, have someone speak over their coffin free of charge; for when one always has money in hand everything is in a sense gratis. No one need own property. An exception would be made

just in my own case. I personally reserve 100 dollars a day permanently in the Bank of London, partly because I cannot do with less,
partly because it was I who came up with the idea, and finally
because one never knows whether I might not come up with a new
idea when the fifteen millions are used up. What would this affluence
lead to? Everything great would pour into Copenhagen, the greatest
artists, actors and dancers. Copenhagen would become another
Athens. What would be the result? Men of wealth would all settle
in this city, among them very likely the Shah of Persia and the
King of England. So here is my second idea. We kidnap the Shah.
It may be objected that there would then be rebellion in Persia, a
new Shah would be placed on the throne – it has happened so
often before – and the price for the old Shah would drop. In
that case, my idea is we sell him to the Turks; they will know
how to convert him into cash. And then there is something else
our politicians seem entirely to overlook. Denmark holds the balance of power in Europe. No more fortunate existence can be
imagined. I know it from my own experience. I was once the
balance of power in a family and could do as I pleased; it was
never I that suffered, always the others. Oh that my words might
reach your ears, you who sit in high places to advise and rule, you
king's men and men of the people, wise and understanding citizens
of all classes! Have a care! Old Denmark is foundering, what a sorry
fate, and most fateful of all, it is going under from boredom. In
ancient times he who sang the praises of the dead king most beautifully became the new king.[4] In our time he should be king who
comes up with the best witticism, he the crown prince who provides
the occasion for its utterance.

But how you carry me away, beauteous, sentimental enthusiasm!
Is this the way I should be opening my mouth to address my
contemporaries, initiating them into my wisdom? Not at all. For
my wisdom is really not *zum für Jedermann*,[5] and it is always more
prudent to keep one's rules of prudence to oneself. Disciples, then, I
have no wish for, but should someone happen to be present at my
deathbed, and if I was sure it was all over with me, I might perhaps
in a fit of philanthropic delirium whisper my teaching in his ear,
uncertain whether I had done him a service or not. There is so
much talk of man's being a social animal;[6] basically he is a beast of

prey, as one can ascertain not merely by consideration of his teeth. All this talk of sociability and society is in part, therefore, an inherited hypocrisy, in part a calculated deceit.

So all people are boring. The word itself indicates the possibility of a subdivision. 'Boring' can describe a person who bores others as well as one who bores himself. Those who bore others are the plebeians, the mass, the endless train of humanity in general. Those who bore themselves are the elect, the nobility; and how strange it is that those who don't bore themselves usually bore others, while those who do bore themselves amuse others. The people who do not bore themselves are generally those who are busy in the world in one way or another, but that is just why they are the most boring, the most insufferable, of all. This species of animal life, surely, is not the fruit of man's desire and woman's pleasure. Like all lower forms of life, it is distinguished by a high degree of fertility and multiplies beyond belief. Inconceivable, too, that nature should need nine months to produce creatures like these which one would rather suppose could be produced by the score. The other class of men, the select, are those who bore themselves. As remarked above, generally they amuse others, outwardly occasionally the mob, in a deeper sense their fellow initiates. The more profoundly they bore themselves, the more powerful a means of diversion they offer others, when boredom reaches its zenith, either by dying of boredom (the passive form) or (the active form) by shooting themselves out of curiosity.

Idleness, it is usually said, is a root of all evil. To prevent this evil one recommends work. However, it is easy to see from the remedy as well as the feared cause that this whole view is of very plebeian extraction. Idleness as such is by no means a root of evil; quite the contrary, it is a truly divine way of life so long as one is not bored. Certainly, idleness may lead you to lose your fortune, and so on, but of such things the man of noble nature has no fear; what he fears is boredom. The Olympian gods were not bored, they prospered in happy idleness. A beauty who neither sews nor spins nor irons nor reads nor makes music is happy in her idleness, for she is not bored. So, far from idleness being the root of evil, rather it is the true good. The root of evil is boredom, and that is what must be kept at bay. Idleness is not evil; indeed, one can say that any human who lacks appreciation of it proves he has not raised himself to the level of humanity. There is a kind of restless activity that keeps a person out of the world of spirit and puts him in a class with the animals, which from instinct must always be on the go. There are people with an extraordinary gift for transforming everything into business, whose whole life is business, who fall in love and marry, listen to a joke and admire a work of art with the same zealous sense of affairs with which they work in the office. The Latin proverb, *otium est pulvinar diaboli*,[7] is perfectly correct, but when one isn't bored the devil gets no time to lay his head on that pillow. Yet in so far as people think it is characteristic of man to work, idleness and industry are properly opposed to each other. My own assumption is that it is characteristic of man to amuse himself; my opposites are therefore no less correct.

Boredom is demonic pantheism. If we remain in it as such it becomes evil; on the other hand, as soon as it is annulled it is true.[8] But one annuls it only by amusing oneself – *ergo* one ought to amuse oneself. Saying work annuls it is to betray confusion, for though idleness, certainly, can be annulled by industry, seeing the latter is its opposite, boredom cannot, as one also sees that the busiest workers of all, those who in their officious buzzing about most resemble humming insects, are the most boring of all; and if they don't bore themselves, that's because they have no idea what boredom is; but in that case boredom is not annulled.

Boredom is partly an immediate talent, partly an acquired immediacy. Here the English are, on the whole, the paradigmatic nation. One seldom encounters a born talent for indolence, one never meets it in nature; indolence belongs to the world of spirit. Occasionally you meet an English traveller, however, who is an incarnation of this talent, a heavy immovable ground-hog whose linguistic resources are exhausted in a single one-syllable word, an interjection with which he signifies his greatest admiration and most profound indifference, because in the unity of boredom admiration and indifference have become indistinguishable. No other nation but the English produces such natural curiosities; other nationals are always a little more lively, not so absolutely stillborn. The only analogy I know is the apostle of empty enthusiasm, who also journeys through life on an interjection – that is, people who are always making a profession of enthusiasm, everywhere making their presence felt, and whether something significant or insignificant is taking place, cry 'Ah!' or 'Oh!', because for them the difference between significant and insignificant has become undone in enthusiasm's blind and blaring emptiness. The acquired form of boredom is usually a product of a mistaken attempt at diversion. That the remedy for boredom can bring boredom about in this way seems doubtful, but it does so only to the extent that it is incorrectly applied. A misconceived, generally eccentric form of diversion also has boredom within it, and that is the way it finds its way out and proves to be the immediate. As with horses one distinguishes between blind staggers and sleepy staggers, but calls them both staggers, we can also make a distinction between two kinds of boredom which are still united in being specifications of boredom.

Pantheism, in general, contains the quality of fullness; with boredom it is the opposite, it is based on emptiness, but is for that very reason a pantheistic category.[9] Boredom rests upon the nothingness that winds its way through existence; its giddiness, like that which comes from gazing down into an infinite abyss, is infinite. That the eccentric form of diversion mentioned above is based on boredom can also be seen from the fact that the diversion reverberates without making an echo, just because in nothing there isn't even enough to make an echo possible.

Seeing that boredom is a root of all evil, as enlarged on above, what more natural than to try to overcome it? But here, as everywhere, cool deliberation is clearly called for lest in one's demonic obsession with boredom, in trying to avoid it one only works oneself further into it. 'Change' is what all who are bored cry out for. With this I am entirely in agreement, only it is important to act from principle.

My own departure from the general view is adequately expressed in the phrase 'crop rotation'. This phrase might seem to contain an ambiguity, and in wanting to make it commodious enough to cover the general method, I should have to say that the method of rotation consisted in constantly changing the soil. That, however, is not the sense in which the farmer uses it. Still, I will adopt this use for a moment, so as to talk of that 'crop rotation' which depends on the unlimited infinity of change, on its extensive dimension.

This rotation is the vulgar, the inartistic method, and is based on an illusion. One is tired of living in the country, one moves to the city; one is tired of one's native land, one travels abroad; one is *europamüde*,[10] one goes to America, and so on; finally, one indulges in a dream of endless travel from star to star. Or the movement is different but still in extension. One is tired of dining off porcelain, one dines off silver; one tires of that, one dines off gold; one burns half of Rome to get an idea of the conflagration at Troy. This method defeats itself; it is the bad infinite.[11] And what did Nero achieve? No, Antonine was wiser; he says, 'It is in your power to review your life, to look at things you saw before, from another point of view.'[12]

The method I propose consists not in changing the soil but, as in the real rotation of crops, in changing the method of cultivation and type of grain. Here, straightaway, we have the principle of limitation, which is the only saving one in the world. The more you limit yourself, the more resourceful you become. A prisoner in solitary confinement for life is most resourceful, a spider can cause him much amusement. One thinks of one's schooldays. When one is at the age when no aesthetic considerations are taken in the choice of one's teachers and the latter are for that very reason often very boring, how inventive one is! How amusing to catch a fly and keep it imprisoned under a nut shell and watch how it rushes about with the shell! What pleasure one can get by cutting a hole in the desk to imprison a fly in it, and spy down on it through a piece of paper! How entertaining it can be to hear the monotonous drip from the roof! How thorough an observer one becomes, the slightest noise or movement does not escape one! Here we have the extreme of the principle that seeks relief, not extensively, but intensively.

The more inventive one can be in changing the mode of cultivation, the better; but every particular change comes under the general rule of the relation between *remembering* and *forgetting*. The whole of life moves in these two currents, so it is essential to have control over them. Only when one has thrown hope overboard is it possible to live artistically; as long as one hopes, one cannot limit oneself. It is really beautiful to see a man put out to sea with the fair wind of hope; one can use the opportunity to be taken in tow, but one should never have it aboard one's own ship, least of all as a pilot; for hope is a faithless steersman. Hope was therefore also one of the dubious gifts of Prometheus;[13] instead of the foreknowledge of the immortals, he gave men hope.

To forget – all men want to do that, and when they come across something unpleasant they always say, 'If only I could forget!' But forgetting is an art that must be practised beforehand. Being able to forget depends always on how one remembers, but how one remembers depends in turn on how one experiences reality. The person who sticks fast in it with the momentum of hope will remember in a way that makes him unable to forget. *Nil admirari*[14] is therefore the real wisdom of life. Every life-situation must possess no more importance than that one can forget it whenever one wants to; each single life-situation should have enough importance, however, for one to be able at any time to remember it. The age that remembers best, but is also the most forgetful, is childhood. The more poetically one remembers, the more easily one forgets, for remembering poetically is really just an expression of forgetfulness. In remembering poetically, what was experienced has already undergone a change in which it has lost all that was painful. To remember in this way, one must be careful how one lives, especially how one enjoys. If one enjoys without reservation to the last, if one always takes with one the most that pleasure can offer, one will be unable either to remember or to forget. For then one has nothing else to remember than a surfeit one wants to forget, but which now plagues you with an involuntary remembrance. So when you begin to notice that you are being carried away by enjoyment or a life-situation too strongly, stop for a moment and remember. No other expedient gives a better distaste for going on too long. One must keep reins on the enjoyment from the beginning, not set all sail for everything you decide on. One indulges in a certain distrust; only then can one give the lie to the proverb which says that no one can have his cake and eat it too. The carrying of secret weapons is forbidden, indeed, by the police, yet no weapon is as dangerous as the trick of being able to remember. It is a peculiar feeling when, in the midst of enjoyment, one looks at it in order to remember.

Having perfected the art of forgetting and the art of remembering, one is then in a position to play battledore and shuttlecock with the whole of existence.

how to forget

A person's resilience can really be measured by the power to forget. A person unable to forget will never amount to much. Whether a Lethe flows somewhere I do not know,[15] but what I do know is that this art can be developed. Yet it does not at all consist in the total disappearance of particular impressions; for the art of forgetting is not the same as forgetfulness. It is also easy to see what very little understanding people in general have of this art, for usually it is only the unpleasant they want to forget, not the pleasant. This betrays a complete one-sidedness. For forgetting is the proper expression of the real conversion that reduces experience to a sounding-board. The reason for nature's greatness is that it has forgotten that it was once chaos, but this latter thought can recur whenever need be. Since one usually only conceives of forgetting in relation to what is unpleasant, one usually conceives it as an untamed power that drowns things out. Quite the contrary; forgetting is a quiet occupation and ought to be exercised as much in relation to what is pleasant as to what is unpleasant. As something past, indeed precisely as past, what is pleasant contains also an unpleasant side by being able to arouse a sense of privation. This unpleasantness is overcome by forgetting. The unpleasant has a sting, everyone admits that, and it, too, is removed by forgetting; but if one pushes the unpleasant aside altogether, as many of those who dabble in the art of forgetting do, one soon sees what good that does. In an unguarded moment, it often takes one by surprise with all the force of the sudden. This is in absolute contradiction to the well-organized arrangement in a reasonable mind. No misfortune, no hardship, is so hard to approach, so deaf that it cannot be flattered a little; even Cerberus accepted honey-cakes, and it is not just young girls one beguiles.[16] One talks it round and in doing so deprives it of its bite, by no means does one want to forget it; one forgets it in order to remember it. Yes, even with those memories for which one might think eternal oblivion was the only remedy, one permits oneself this cunning, and the deft will succeed in the deception. Forgetting is the shears with which one clips away what one cannot use – though, mind you, under the overall supervision of memory. Forgetting and memory are thus identical, and the skilfully achieved identity is the Archimedean point with which one lifts the whole world. In saying that we consign something to oblivion, we suggest that it is simultaneously forgotten yet preserved.

The art of remembering and forgetting will then also prevent one's sticking fast in some particular circumstance in life and ensure perfect suspension.

So one must be on one's guard against *friendship*. How is a friend defined? A friend is not what philosophy calls 'the necessary other', but the superfluous third. What are the ceremonies of friendship? One thous and thees in a glass, one opens an artery, one mixes one's blood with the friend's. The exact arrival of this moment is hard to determine, but it mysteriously proclaims itself, one feels it, one can no longer use the formal 'You' in addressing each other.[17] Once this feeling has occurred, one can never prove mistaken, as was Gert Westphaler, who discovered that he had been drinking with the public hangman.[18] – What are the infallible marks of friendship? Antiquity answers, *idem velle, idem nolle, ea demum firma amicitia*,[19] and extremely boringly at that. What significance has friendship? Mutual assistance in word and deed. So two friends form a close association in order to be everything for one another, regardless that all the one can be for the other is in the way. Yes, they may help each other with money, on and off with each other's coats, be each other's humble servant, join in a sincere New Year's greeting, likewise in matrimony, birth and burial.

But to abstain from friendship doesn't mean that you are to live without human contact. Quite the contrary, human relationships of the kind may also sometimes take on a deeper surge, except that, although you share the speed of the movement for a time, you always have enough speed in hand to be able to run away from it. One no doubt thinks that such behaviour leaves unpleasant memories, that the unpleasantness consists in the fact that, after having meant something to you, the relation dwindles away into nothing. But this is a misunderstanding. Unpleasantness is a piquant ingredient in the contrariety of life. Besides, the same relationship can acquire significance again in another way. What one must watch out for is never to stick fast, and for that one must have one's forgetting up one's sleeve. The experienced farmer now and then lets his land lie fallow; the theory of social prudence recommends the same. All things, no doubt, will return, but in another way; what has once been taken into rotation remains there but is varied through the mode of cultivation. It is quite consistent, therefore, to hope to meet old friends and acquaintances in a better world; but one does not share the fear of the masses, that they will have changed too much for one to be able to recognize them again. One fears, rather, that they may be unchanged. It is incredible how much significance even an insignificant person can gain through such rational management.

One never enters into *marriage*. Married couples promise each other eternal love. That is all very fine but does not mean very much, for when one is finished with time, one will no doubt be finished with eternity. So if, instead of saying 'forever', the parties said, 'until Easter', or 'until the first May-Day', then at least their words would have meaning for they would have actually said something, something they could perhaps keep to. And how does it go with a marriage? After a little while one party begins to notice that something's wrong; then the other party complains and cries out, 'Faithlessness, faithlessness!' After some time the other party arrives at the same point and a state of neutrality is brought about, in that the mutual faithlessness balances out to the satisfaction and contentment of both. But now it is too late, for there are great difficulties connected with divorce.

Such being the case with marriage, it is not surprising that it has to be stiffened in so many ways with moral supports. When a husband wants to be divorced from his wife, people cry, 'He is contemptible, a scoundrel', etc. How silly, and what an indirect attack upon marriage! Either marriage has reality in it, in which case he is sufficiently punished by forfeiting the latter; or it has no reality in it, in which case it is indeed absurd to abuse him, for he is wiser than others. If a man grew tired of his money and threw it out of the window, no one would say he was a contemptible person; for either the money has reality, and then he is sufficiently punished by depriving himself of it, or it has no reality, and then indeed he is wise.

One must always be careful not to enter into any life-relation in which one can become several. For this reason friendship is already dangerous, even more so marriage. A married couple are indeed said to become one, but this is a very dark and mysterious saying. When you are several you have lost your freedom and cannot order travelling boots when you will, cannot roam aimlessly about. If you

have a wife it is difficult; if you have a wife and may have children,
it is troublesome; if you have a wife and do have children, it is
impossible. We do, indeed, have the example of a gypsy woman
carrying her husband on her back through life,[20] but for one thing
it is a rare occurrence, and for another, in the long run wearisome –
for the husband. Besides, in marriage one falls into extremely fateful
line with practice and custom, and, like wind and weather, practice
and custom are very hard to pin down. In Japan, I am told, it is
practice and custom for the husbands too to lie in childbed. Why
shouldn't the time come when Europe introduces the customs of
foreign countries?

Friendship is already dangerous, marriage still more so, for the
woman is and will remain the husband's ruin as soon as he enters
into a permanent relation with her. Take a young man, ardent as
an Arabian horse, let him marry, he is lost. First of all the woman
is proud, then she is weak, then she faints, then he faints, then
the whole family faints. A woman's love is only dissimulation and
weakness.

But not entering into marriage need not mean that one's life lacks
eroticism. The erotic should also have infinitude, but poetic infinitude, which can just as well be limited to an hour as to a month.
When two people fall in love and suspect they are made for each
other, the thing is to have the courage to break it off, for by
continuing they only have everything to lose and nothing to gain.
It seems a paradox and is so, for feeling, not for understanding. In
this domain it is especially important to be able to use moods; if
one can do that, then one can bring off an inexhaustible variety of
combinations.

One never accepts any *vocational responsibility*. If one does so, one
simply becomes Mr Anybody, a tiny little pivot in the machinery
of the corporate state; you cease to direct your own affairs, and then
theories can be of little help. One acquires a title, and in it is
contained all the consistency of sin and evil. The law one is then in
thrall to is equally boring, whether promotion is rapid or slow. A
title is something one can never be rid of again, it would have to be
lost through some crime which incurs a public whipping, and even
then you are not certain, for you may be pardoned and have your
title restored to you by royal decree.

Though one abstains from vocational responsibility, one should not be inactive but stress all occupation that is identical with idleness; one must engage in all kinds of breadless skills. Yet in this connection one should develop oneself not so much extensively as intensively, and in spite of being on in years, prove the truth of the old proverb that it takes little to please a child.

If, then, in accordance with the theory of social prudence, one to some extent varies the soil – for if one were to live only in relation to one person the rotation method would turn out as badly as if a farmer had only one acre of land, the result of which would be to make it impossible for him to let land lie fallow, which is of the utmost importance – then one must also constantly vary oneself, and this is really the secret. To that end one must necessarily have control of moods. Controlling them in the sense of being able to produce them at will is impossible, but prudence teaches how to make use of the instant. As an experienced sailor always looks out searchingly over the water and sees a squall far ahead, so should one always see the mood a little in advance. One must know how the mood affects oneself, and in all probability others, before putting it on. One strokes the strings first to elicit pure tones and see what there is in a person, and the intermediate tones follow later. The more practice you have, the more readily you will be convinced that often there is much in a person which one never considers. When sensitive people, who as such are extremely boring, become angry, they are often very diverting. Teasing in particular is an excellent means of exploration.

The whole secret lies in arbitrariness. People think it requires no skill to be arbitrary, yet it requires deep study to succeed in being arbitrary without losing oneself in it, to derive satisfaction from it oneself. One's enjoyment is not immediate but is something quite different which one arbitrarily injects. You see the middle of a play, read the third part of a book. In this way one derives a quite different enjoyment from the one the author has been so good as to intend for you. One enjoys something entirely accidental, one regards the whole of existence from this standpoint, lets its reality run aground on it. I will give an example. There was someone whose chatter certain circumstances made it necessary for me to listen to. He was ready at every opportunity with a little philosophical lecture which was utterly boring. Driven almost to despair, I discovered suddenly that he perspired unusually profusely when he spoke. I saw how the pearls of sweat gathered on his brow, then joined in a stream, slid down his nose, and ended hanging in a drop at the extreme tip of it. From that moment everything was changed; I could even take pleasure in inciting him to begin his philosophical instruction, just to observe the sweat on his brow and on his nose.

Baggesen says somewhere of a man that he was no doubt a very decent person, but that he had one objection to make to him: nothing rhymed with his name.[21] It is extremely beneficial to let the realities of life neutralize themselves in this way on an arbitrary interest of this kind. You transform something accidental into the absolute and, as such, into an object of absolute admiration. This works particularly excellently when tempers are aroused. For many people this method is an excellent stimulus. One looks at everything in life as a wager, and so on. The more consistently one can sustain the arbitrariness, the more amusing the combinations. The degree of consistency always shows whether one is an artist or a dabbler, for to some extent people all do the same. The eye with which one looks at reality must constantly change. The Neo-Platonists supposed that those human beings who had been less perfect on earth became, after death, more or less perfect animals, depending on their deserts. Those, for example, who had exercised civic virtues on a smaller scale (retail traders) became civic animals, bees for example. Such a view of life, which sees all persons transformed into animals or plants (Plotinus also thought that some were transformed into plants), offers a rich multiplicity of variations. The painter Tischbein has tried to idealize every human being as an animal. His method has the fault of being too serious, and that it seeks a real resemblance.[22]

To the arbitrariness within oneself there corresponds the accidental outside one. One should therefore always keep an eye open for the accidental, always be *expeditus*[23] if anything should offer. The so-called social pleasures, for which one prepares eight or fourteen days in advance, have no great interest. Through accident, on the other hand, even the least significant thing can become a rich source of amusement. It is impossible here to go into detail, no theory can stretch that far. Even the most comprehensive theory is still but poverty compared with what, in his ubiquity, the genius easily comes by.

7 THE SEDUCER'S DIARY

Sua passion' predominante
È la giovin principiànte.
            Don Giovanni, Act I[1]

I CANNOT conceal from myself, can scarcely master, the anxiety which grips me at this moment, as I resolve for my own interest to make a fair copy of the hasty transcript I was able at that time to secure only in the greatest haste and with much disquiet. The situation confronts me just as alarmingly, but also just as reproachfully, as it did then. Contrary to his custom, he had not closed his escritoire, so its whole contents lay at my disposal; but it is futile for me to gloss over my behaviour by reminding myself that I did not open any drawer. One drawer was pulled out. In it I found a pile of loose papers and on top of them lay a book in broad quarto, tastefully bound. On the side facing up was a vignette of white paper on which he had written in his own hand 'Commentarius perpetuus No. 4'.[2] In vain have I tried, however, to make myself believe that had that side of the book not been turned up, and had the strange title not tempted me, I should not have succumbed to the temptation, or at least would have attempted to resist it. The title itself was curious, not so much in itself as because of its setting. From a quick glance at the loose papers I saw that these contained constructions of erotic situations, some hints about some relationship or other, sketches of letters of a quite peculiar character, with which I later became familiar in their artistically consummate, calculated carelessness. When now, having seen through the designing mind of this depraved person, I recall my situation; when, with an eye open for every artifice, I approach that drawer in thought, it makes the same impression upon me as it must make upon a police officer when he enters the room of a forger, opens his repositories and finds in a drawer a pile of loose papers, handwriting samples; on one there is part of a foliage motif, on another a signature, on a third a line of reversed writing. It shows him clearly that he is on the right track, and his joy over this is mingled with a certain admiration for the study and industry here clearly in evidence.

For me it might have been a little different, being less used to tracking down criminals and not armed with, well, a police badge. The fact that I was following unlawful paths would have been an additional weight on my mind. On this occasion, as usually happens, I was no less at a loss for thoughts than for words. An impression remains with one until reflection reasserts itself and, diverse and speedy in its movements, ingratiates itself with the unfamiliar stranger and talks him round. The more reflection develops, the quicker it can pull itself together; like a passport clerk for foreign travellers, it becomes so used to seeing the most fantastic figures that it is not easily taken aback. But however strongly developed my own reflection, I was at first still greatly astonished. I remember very well that I turned pale, that I nearly fell over, and how that fact alarmed me. What if he had come home, had found me in a faint with the drawer in my hand? At least a bad conscience can make life interesting.

The title of the book in itself made no particular impression on me; I thought it was a collection of excerpts, which to me seemed quite natural since I knew that he had always embraced his studies with enthusiasm. Its contents, however, were of quite another kind. It was neither more nor less than a diary, painstakingly kept; and just as I did not think, from what I knew of him before, that his life was in such great need of commentary, so I do not deny, after the insight I had now gained, that the title had been chosen with much taste and understanding, with true aesthetic, objective mastery of himself and the situation. The title is in perfect harmony with the entire contents. His life has been an attempt to realize the task of living poetically. With a keenly developed sense for what is interesting in life, he had known how to find it, and having found it he had constantly reproduced the experience in a semi-poetic way. His diary, therefore, was not historically exact or a straightforward narrative, not indicative, but subjunctive. Although of course the experience was recorded after it happened – sometimes perhaps even a considerable time after – it was often described as if taking place at the very moment, so dramatically vivid that sometimes it was as though it was all taking place before one's very eyes. But that he should have done this because the diary served any ulterior purpose is highly improbable; it is quite obvious that, in the strictest sense, its only importance was for him personally. And to assume that what I have before me is a literary work, perhaps even intended for publication, is precluded by the whole as well as by the details. Certainly he did not need to fear anything personally in publishing it, for most of the names are so unusual that there is altogether no likelihood of their being authentic. But I have formed a suspicion that the Christian name is historically correct, so that he himself would always be sure of identifying the actual person, while every outsider must be misled by the surname. Such at least is the case with the girl I knew, around whom the chief interest centres, Cordelia – that was her correct name; not, however, Wahl.

How, then, can we explain that the diary has nevertheless acquired such a poetic flavour? The answer is not difficult; it can be explained by his poetic temperament, which is, if you will, not rich, or if you prefer, not poor enough to distinguish poetry and reality from each other. The poetic was the extra he himself brought with him. This extra was the poetical element he enjoyed in the poetic situation provided by reality; this element he took back in again in the form of poetic reflection. That was the second enjoyment, and enjoyment was what his whole life was organized around. In the first case he savoured the aesthetic element personally; in the second he savoured his own person aesthetically. In the first case the point was that he egoistically, personally, savoured what in part reality gave him and what in part he himself had impregnated reality with; in the second case his personality was volatilized and he savoured, then, the situation and himself in the situation. In the first case he was in constant need of reality as the occasion, as an element; in the second case reality was drowned in the poetic. The fruit of the first stage is thus the mood from which the diary results as the fruit of the second stage, the word 'fruit' being used in the latter case in a somewhat different sense from that in the first. The poetic is thus something he has constantly possessed by virtue of the ambiguity in which his life passed.

Behind the world we live in, in the distant background, lies another world standing in roughly the same relation to the former as the stage one sometimes sees in the theatre behind the real stage stands to the latter. Through a thin gauze one sees what looks like a world of gossamer, lighter, more ethereal, of a different quality from the real world. Many people who appear bodily in the real world do not belong there but to this other world. Yet the fact that someone fades away in this manner, indeed almost disappears from reality, can be due to either health or sickness. The latter was the case with this person, with whom I was once acquainted but without getting to know him. He did not belong to reality yet had much to do with it. He was constantly running around in it, yet even when he devoted himself to it most, he was already beyond it. But it was not the good that beckoned him away, nor was it really evil – even now I dare not say that of him. He has suffered from an *exacerbatio cerebri*[3] for which reality afforded insufficient incitement, at best only temporarily. Reality was not too much for him, he was not too weak to bear its burden; no, he was too strong, but this strength was a sickness. As soon as reality lost its power to incite he was disarmed; that is where the evil in him lay. He was conscious of this, even at the moment of incitement, and it was in his consciousness of this the evil lay.

I once knew the girl whose story forms the substance of the diary. Whether he has seduced others I do not know; it does seem so from his papers. He seems also to have been adept at another kind of practice, wholly characteristic of him; for he was of far too spiritual a nature to be a seducer in the usual sense. From the diary we also learn that at times his desire was for something altogether arbitrary – a greeting, for instance – and under no circumstance would accept more, because in the person in question this was what was most beautiful. With the help of his mental gifts he knew how to tempt a girl, to draw her to him, without caring to possess her in any stricter sense. I can imagine him able to bring a girl to the point where he was sure she would sacrifice all, but when matters had come that far he left off without the slightest advance having been made on his part, and without a word having been let fall of love, let alone a declaration, a promise. Yet it would have happened, and the unhappy girl would retain the consciousness of it with double bitterness, because there was not the slightest thing she could appeal to. She could only be constantly tossed about by the most divergent moods in a terrible witches' dance, at one moment reproaching herself, forgiving him, at another reproaching him, and then, since the relationship would only have been actual in a figurative sense, she would constantly have to contend with the doubt that the whole thing might only have been imagination. She would be unable to confide in anyone, for really there was nothing to confide. When you have dreamed, you can tell others your dream, but what she had to tell was no dream, it was reality, and yet, as soon as she wanted to speak of it to another to ease her troubled mind, it was nothing. She herself felt this very keenly. No one could grasp it, hardly even herself, and yet it lay with an unsettling weight upon her.

Such victims were therefore of a quite special nature. They were not unfortunate girls who, social outcasts or thinking themselves such, openly fumed and fretted and now and then, when their hearts became too full, gave vent in hate or forgiveness. No visible change occurred in them; they lived in their normal circumstances, as respected as ever, and yet they were changed, well-nigh inexplicably to themselves, incomprehensibly to others. Their lives were not, as with those others, snapped off or broken, they were bent in on themselves; lost to others, they sought vainly to find themselves. Just as you might say that your path through life left no trace (for your feet were so formed as to leave no footprints – this is how I best picture to myself his infinite self-reflection), so it could be said that no victim fell to him. He lived in far too spiritual a manner to be a seducer in the ordinary sense. Sometimes, however, he assumed a parastatic body and was then sheer sensuality.[4] Even his affair with Cordelia was so complicated that it was possible for him to appear as the one seduced; yes, even the unlucky girl was sometimes in confusion about it; here, too, his footprints are so indistinct that any proof is impossible. The individuals were merely his incitement; he cast them off as a tree sheds its leaves – he is refreshed, the leaf withers.

But how, I wonder, do things look in his own head? Just as he has led others astray, so in my view he ends by going astray himself. It is not in external respects that he has led the others astray, but in ways that affect them inwardly. There is something outrageous in a person's misdirecting a traveller who has lost his way and then leaving him to himself in his error, yet what is that compared with causing someone to go astray in himself? The lost traveller, after all, has a consolation that the country around him is constantly changing, and with every change is born a new

hope of finding a way out. A person who goes astray inwardly
has less room for manoeuvre; he soon finds he is going round in
a circle from which he cannot escape. This, on an even more
terrible scale, I think, is how it will go with him. I can imagine
nothing more agonizing than an intriguing mind which has lost
the thread and then turns all its wits upon itself, as conscience
awakens and the question is one of extricating oneself from this
confusion. It is to no avail that he has many exits from his fox's
earth; the moment his anxious soul thinks it sees daylight appearing, it proves to be a new entrance, and like startled game,
pursued by despair, he is thus constantly seeking an exit and forever finding an entrance through which he returns into himself.
Such a man is not always what we could call a criminal; often he
himself is deluded by his intrigues, and yet he is overtaken by a
more terrible punishment than the criminal, for what is the pain
even of remorse compared with this conscious madness? His
punishment has a purely aesthetic character, for even to talk of
his conscience awakening is to apply too ethical an expression to
him. For him conscience takes the form simply of a higher level
of consciousness which expresses itself in a disquietude that still
fails to accuse him in a deeper sense, but which keeps him awake
with no support beneath him in his barren restlessness. Nor is he
mad; for in their diversity his finite thoughts are not petrified in
the eternity of madness.

Poor Cordelia! For her, too, it will be hard to find peace. She
forgives him from the bottom of her heart, but she finds no rest, for
then doubt awakens: it was she who broke off the engagement, it
was she who caused the disaster, it was her pride that yearned for
the uncommon. Then she repents, but she finds no rest, for then the
accusing thoughts acquit her: it was he with his artfulness who
placed this plan in her mind. Then she turns to hatred, her heart
finds relief in curses, but she finds no rest; she reproaches herself
again, reproaches herself because she has hated, she who is herself a
sinner, reproaches herself because, however sly he may have been,
she will still always be guilty. It is grievous for her that he has
deceived her; it is even more grievous, one could almost be tempted
to say, that he has aroused in her this many-tongued reflection, that
he has developed her aesthetically enough no longer to listen humbly

to one voice, but to be able to hear these many points of view all at once. Then memory awakens with her soul, she forgets the offence and the guilt, she remembers the beautiful moments, and she is numbed in an unnatural exaltation. In such moments she not only remembers him, she understands him with a clairvoyance which only goes to show how far she has travelled. Then she no longer sees the criminal in him, or the noble person; her sense of him is purely aesthetic. She once wrote me a note in which she expressed her feelings about him. 'Sometimes he was so spiritual that I felt myself annihilated as a woman, at other times so wild and passionate, so filled with desire, that I almost trembled before him. Sometimes I seemed a stranger to him, at other times he gave of himself completely; when I then flung my arms around him, sometimes everything was suddenly changed and I embraced a cloud.[5] I knew that expression before I knew him, but he has taught me what it means; when I use it I always think of him, just as every thought I think is only in connection with him. I have always loved music and he was a matchless instrument; always alive, he had a range that no instrument has, he was the epitome of all feelings and moods, no thought was too elevated for him, none too despairing, he could roar like an autumn storm, he could whisper inaudibly. No word of mine was without effect, and yet I cannot say that my word did not fail of its effect, for it was impossible for me to know what effect it would have. With an indescribable but secret, blessed, unnameable anxiety I listened to this music I myself called forth, yet did not call forth; there was always harmony, he always carried me away.'

Terrible for her, it will be more terrible for him; I can infer this from the fact that even I cannot quite control the anxiety that grips me every time I think of the matter. I, too, am carried along into that nebulous realm, that dream world where every moment one is afraid of one's own shadow. Often I try in vain to tear myself away, I follow as a figure of menace, as an accuser who cannot speak. How strange! He has spread the deepest secrecy over everything, and still there is a deeper secret, and it is this, that I am in on it; and indeed I have myself become privy to it unlawfully. To forget the whole thing would be impossible. I have sometimes thought of speaking about it to him. Still, how would that help? He would disavow everything, maintain that the diary was a literary effort, or impose silence upon me, something I could not deny him considering how I came to know of it. Nothing, after all, is so pervaded by seduction and damnation as a secret.

I have received from Cordelia a collection of letters. Whether these are all of them I do not know, although it occurs to me she once let it be understood that she herself had confiscated some. I have copied them and will now insert them in my own clean copy. It is true the dates are missing, but even if they were there it would not help much, since the diary as it proceeds becomes more and more sparing. Indeed, in the end, with the odd exception, it gives no dates, as though the story as it progressed acquired such qualitative importance, and in spite of being historically real, came so near to being idea, that time specifications became for this reason a matter of indifference. What did help me, however, was the fact that at various places in the diary are some words whose significance at first I did not grasp. But by comparing them with the letters I realized that they furnish the motives for the latter. It will therefore be a simple matter to insert them in the right places, inasmuch as I shall always introduce the letter at the point where its motive is indicated. Had I not found these clues, I would have incurred a misunderstanding; for no doubt it would not have occurred to me, as now from the diary seems probable, that at times the letters followed upon each other with such frequency that she seems to have received several in one day. Had I followed my original intention I should have apportioned them more evenly, and not suspected the effect he obtained through the passionate energy with which he used this, like all other means, to keep Cordelia on the pinnacle of passion.

Apart from complete information on his relationship to Cordelia, the diary also contained, interspersed here and there, several small descriptions. Wherever these were found there was an 'NB' in the margin. These depictions have absolutely nothing to do with Cordelia's story but have given me a vivid conception of what is meant by an expression he often used, though previously I understood it differently: 'One ought always to have an extra little line out.' Had an earlier volume of this diary fallen into my hands, I should probably have come across more of these, which somewhere in the margin he calls 'actions at a distance';[6] for he himself admits that

Cordelia occupied him too much for him really to have time to look about.

Shortly after he had abandoned Cordelia, he received some letters from her which he returned unopened. These were among the letters Cordelia turned over to me. She had herself broken the seal, and so there seems no reason why I should not venture to make a transcript. She has never mentioned their content to me; on the other hand, when she referred to her relationship to Johannes she usually recited a little verse, I believe by Goethe, which seemed to convey a different meaning according to her moods and the difference in delivery these occasioned:

> *Gehe*
> *Verschmähe*
> *Die Treue,*
> *Die Reue*
> *Kommt nach.*[7]

These letters go as follows:

Johannes!

I do not call you 'mine', I realize very well you never have been, and I am punished enough by this thought having once gladdened my soul; and yet I do call you 'mine': my seducer, my deceiver, my foe, my murderer, source of my unhappiness, grave of my joy, abyss of my ruin. I call you 'mine', and call myself 'yours'; and as it once flattered your ear, which proudly bent down to my adoration, so shall it now sound like a curse upon you, a curse to all eternity. Don't expect me to pursue you, or to arm myself with a dagger so as to incite your ridicule! Flee where you will, I am still yours; go to the farthest boundaries of the world, I am still yours; love a hundred others, I am still yours; yes, even in the hour of death I am yours. The very language I use against you must prove I am yours. You have presumed so to deceive a human being that you have become everything to me; so now will I place all my pleasure in being your slave – yours, yours, yours is what I am, your curse.

Your Cordelia

Johannes!

There was a rich man who had many cattle, large and small;
there was a poor little girl, she had only a single lamb, which ate
from her hand and drank from her cup.[8] You were the rich man,
rich in all the earth's splendour, I was the poor girl who owned
only my love. You took it, you rejoiced in it; then desire beckoned
to you and you sacrificed the little I owned; of your own you could
sacrifice nothing. There was a rich man who owned many cattle,
large and small; there was a poor little girl who had only her love.

Your Cordelia

Johannes!

Is there no hope at all, then? Will your love never reawaken? I
know you have loved me, even if I do not know what makes me
sure of that. I will wait, however heavy time hangs, I will wait,
wait until you are weary of loving others; your love will then rise
up again from its grave, I will love you as always, thank you as
always, as before, oh Johannes, as before! Johannes! This cold-hearted
callousness against me, is it your true nature? Was your love, your
ample heart just a lie and a falsehood? Are you now yourself again,
then? Be patient with my love, forgive me for continuing to love
you; I know my love is a burden to you, but there will be a time
when you return to your Cordelia. Your Cordelia! Hear that en-
treaty! Your Cordelia, your Cordelia.

Your Cordelia

If Cordelia did not possess the compass she admired in her
Johannes, one still sees clearly that she was not without modal
variation. Each of her letters clearly bears the stamp of her mood,
even though to some extent she lacked lucidity in her presentation.
This is especially the case in the second letter, where one suspects
rather than grasps her meaning, but to me it is this imperfection
that makes it so touching.

April 4th

Caution, my beautiful unknown! Caution! Stepping out of a
coach is not so simple a matter. Sometimes it is a decisive step. I
might lend you a short story by Tieck in which you would see how

a lady, on dismounting from her horse, got so caught up in a tangle that this step became decisive for her whole life.[9] Also, the steps on coaches are usually so badly placed that one has almost to forget about being graceful and risk a desperate lunge into the arms of coachman and footman. Yes, coachman and footman have the best of it! I really think I shall seek employment as a footman in a house where there are young girls; a servant easily becomes privy to the secrets of a little girl like that. But for God's sake, don't jump, I beg you! After all, it's dark; I shan't disturb you; I shall just place myself under this street-lamp so you can't see me, and one is always only bashful, after all, to the extent one is seen, but then again, one is always only seen to the extent one sees. So for the sake of the footman who may not be able to withstand such a leap, for the sake of the silk dress, likewise the lace edging, for my sake, let this charming little foot, whose slenderness I have already admired, let it venture out into the world, dare to depend on it, it will surely find a footing, and should you tremble an instant because it seems as though it sought in vain for something to rest upon, yes, should you tremble even after it has found it, then quickly bring the other foot too, for who would be so cruel as to leave you in that position, who so ungracious, so slow to keep up with the revelation of beauty? Or is it, again, some intruder you fear? Hardly the servant, or me, for I have already seen the little foot, and since I am a natural scientist I have learned from Cuvier[10] how to draw definite conclusions from such details. Hurry then! How this anxiety enhances your beauty! Still, anxiety in itself is not beautiful; it is so only when one sees at the same time the energy that overcomes it. How firmly, now, this little foot stands. I have noticed that girls with small feet generally stand more firmly than the more pedestrian, large-footed ones. – Now who would have thought it? It flies in the face of all experience, one runs not nearly so great a risk of one's dress being caught up when climbing out as when one jumps out. But then it is always risky for young girls to ride in a coach, in the end they come to stay there. The lace and the ribbons are lost and that's the end of that. No one has seen anything; to be sure a dark figure appears, wrapped to the eyes in a cloak. One cannot see where he has come from, the light shines right in one's eyes; he passes you by in a moment, when you are about to enter the street-door. Just at the critical second, a sidelong glance seizes upon its object. You blush, your bosom becomes too full to be able to lighten itself in a single breath; there is exasperation in your glance, a proud contempt; there is a prayer, a tear in your eye; both are equally beautiful, I accept both equally as my due, for I can be just as well the one thing as the other. But I'm mischievous all the same – what is the number of the house? What do I see? A window-display of trinkets; my beautiful unknown, perhaps it is outrageous of me, but I follow the path of light . . . She has forgotten what has passed. Ah, yes, when one is seventeen, when one goes shopping at that happy age, when the thought of every large or small object one lays one's hand on gives an inexpressible joy, one forgets easily. She still hasn't seen me. I am standing by myself, far away on the other side of the counter. A mirror hangs on the wall opposite. She doesn't think of it, but it thinks of her. How true to her image it is, as a humble slave who shows his devotion by being faithful, a slave who, although she means something to him, means nothing to her, who although he dares to grasp her, does not dare to comprehend her. That unhappy mirror, which can capture her image but not her; that unhappy mirror, which cannot hide her image in its secret depths, hide it from the whole world, but must on the contrary betray it to others, as now to me. What agony if a man were so made. And yet aren't there many who are made thus, who own nothing except in the instant when they show it to others, who grasp the surface only, not the substance, who lose everything when the substance itself wants to appear, as this mirror would lose her image if she were, with a single breath, to betray her heart to it? And if a man could not possess a memory image even at the moment of presence, he would always want to be at a distance from the beauty, not too near for the earthly eye to see how beautiful is that which he holds in his close embrace and is lost to the outward eye, though he can always regain it by putting it at a distance, but which he can then also have before him in his mind's eye when he cannot see the object itself because it is too near, when lips are closed on lips . . . Yet, how beautiful she is! Poor mirror, it must be agony! It is well that you know no jealousy. Her head is a perfect oval; she inclines it a little forward, thus heightening her forehead, which rises pure and proud without any phrenologist's signs of

intellect. Her dark hair closes softly and gently about her brow. Her
face is like a fruit, every transition fully rounded. Her skin is transparent, like velvet to the touch, I can feel it with my eyes. Her eyes
– well, yes, I haven't seen them yet, they are hidden behind lids
armed with silken fringes curving like hooks, dangerous to whoever
would meet her glance. She has a Madonna head, pure and innocent
in cast; and like the Madonna she is bending forward, but she is not
lost in contemplation of the One. There is a variation of expression
in her face. What she is considering is the manifold, the multiplicity
of things over which worldly pomp and splendour casts its reflection. She pulls off her glove to show the mirror and myself a right
hand, white and shapely as an antique, without adornment, not
even a flat gold ring on her fourth finger – Bravo! She looks up,
and how changed everything is, yet the same, the forehead a little
less high, the oval of her face a little less regular but more alive. She
is talking with the salesman, she is cheerful, joyful, talkative. She
has already chosen one, two, three things; she picks up a fourth and
holds it in her hand, again she looks down; she asks what it costs;
she puts it to one side under her glove, it must surely be a secret,
intended for – a sweetheart? But then she is not engaged. Alas, there
are many who are not engaged and yet have a sweetheart, many
who are engaged and still have no sweetheart . . . Ought I to give
her up? Ought I to leave her undisturbed in her joy? . . . She wants
to pay, but she has lost her purse . . . presumably she mentions her
address, I don't want to hear that, I don't want to deprive myself of
the surprise; I shall no doubt meet her again in life, I shall recognize
her, and maybe she will also recognize me, my sidelong glance is
not so easily forgotten. When I meet her by surprise in unexpected
surroundings, that's when her turn will come. If she does not
recognize me, if her glance does not immediately convince me
of that, then I can always get a chance to see her from the side. I
promise she shall remember the situation. No impatience, no greed-
iness, everything will be savoured in slow draughts; she is earmarked
and she will no doubt be brought in.

the 5th

I rather like that! Alone in the evening on Østergade. Yes, all

right, I can see the footman following you; don't suppose I think
so ill of you that you would go out all alone; don't think I am
so inexperienced that in my survey of the situation I have not
observed that demure figure straightaway. But why in such a
hurry? One is a little anxious after all; one feels a pounding of
the heart, due not to an impatient longing to get home, but to
an impatient fear which courses through one's entire body with its
sweet unrest, and hence the rapid tempo of the feet. – But still it is
gorgeous, priceless to walk alone like this – with the footman
behind ... 'One is sixteen years old, one has read, that is to say,
read romances. While happening to pass through one's brothers'
room one has picked up a piece of a conversation between them
and their friends, something about Østergade. Later one has whisked
through on several occasions to obtain a little more information if
possible. To no avail! As a big, grown-up girl, shouldn't one know
something about the world? If only it were possible to go out
without the servant behind. Thanks, no! Mother and father would
make peculiar faces, and also, what excuse could one give? There's
no chance of it when one is going to a party, it would be a little
too early; I heard August say nine to ten o'clock. Going home it's
too late, and then usually you must have an escort to drag along.
Thursday evening, on the way back from the theatre, would be a
splendid opportunity, but then one always has to drive in the
coach and have Mrs Thomsen and her dear cousins packed in too;
if one drove alone, one could let down the window and look
about a bit. Still, the unexpected often occurs. Today mother said
to me, "You'll never get that sewing finished for your father's
birthday; to be quite undisturbed, you may go to your Aunt Jette's
and stay until tea-time, then Jens can fetch you!" Really it wasn't
such a very pleasing message, since it is extremely boring at Aunt
Jette's; but then I will walk home alone at nine with the servant.
When Jens comes, he will have to wait until a quarter to ten, and
then off we go. Only I may meet my Mr Broder or Mr August –
that mightn't be such a good idea, presumably I'd be escorted
home – thanks, but I prefer to be free, freedom – but if I could
catch sight of them so that they didn't see me' ... Now then,
my little lady, what is it you see, and what do you think I see?
In the first place, the little cap you have on suits you splendidly,

and harmonizes totally with your hurrying. It is not a hat, nor is it a bonnet, more like a kind of hood. But you can't possibly have had that on when you went out this morning. Could the servant have brought it, or have you borrowed it from Aunt Jette? – Maybe you are incognito. One shouldn't lower the veil completely if one is to make observations. Or perhaps it isn't a veil but just a broad piece of lace? In the dark it is impossible to decide. Whatever it is, it hides the upper part of the face. The chin is really pretty, a little too pointed; the mouth small, open; that's because you are walking too energetically. The teeth – white as snow. That's how it should be. Teeth are of the greatest importance, they are a lifeguard hiding behind the seductive softness of the lips. The cheeks glow with health. – If one inclines one's head a little to the side it might be possible to catch a glimpse under the veil or lace. Watch out! A look like that from below is more dangerous than one from straight ahead. It's like fencing, and what weapon so sharp, so sudden in its movement, and hence so deceptive, as the eye? One points high quart, as the fencer says, and thrusts in second; the quicker the thrust follows the pointing the better. The moment of targetting is an indescribable now. The opponent feels as though slashed, yes, indeed he is struck, but in quite a different place than he thought . . . indefatigably, on she goes without fear and without harm. Watch out! There's a man coming over there; lower the veil, don't let his profane glance defile you. You've no idea – it might be impossible for you to forget for a long time the disgusting dread with which it touched you. – You do not notice, as I did, that he has sized up the situation. – The servant has been picked out as the nearest object. Yes, now you see the consequences of going out alone with a servant. The servant has fallen down. Really, it's quite laughable, but what will you do now? Going back and helping him to his feet is impossible, to go on with a mud-stained servant is disagreeable, to go alone is risky. Watch out! the monster approaches . . . You don't answer me. Just look at me, is there anything in my appearance that frightens you? I make no impression at all on you, I look like a good-natured person from quite another world. There is nothing in my speech to disturb you, nothing to remind you of the situation, no slightest movement of mine that comes too near you. You are still a little anxious; you still haven't forgotten that sinister figure's approach. You conceive a certain kindness towards me, the awkwardness that keeps me from looking at you gives you the upper hand. That pleases you and makes you feel safe. You might almost be tempted to poke a little fun at me. I wager that at this moment you would have the courage to take me by the arm, if it occurred to you ... So it's in Stormgade you live. You drop me a cold and hasty curtsy. Have I deserved that, I who have helped you out of the whole unpleasantness? You are sorry, you return, you thank me for my civility, offer me your hand – why do you turn pale? Isn't my voice unchanged, my bearing the same, my eye as quiet and calm? This handclasp? Can a handclasp mean anything? Yes, much, very much, my little miss. Within a fortnight I shall explain everything to you; until then you must remain in the contradiction: I am a good-natured person who came like a knight to the aid of a young girl, and I can also press your hand in a way that is anything but good-natured. –

April 7th

'On Monday, then, one o'clock at the exhibition.' Very good, I shall have the honour of turning up at a quarter to one. A little rendezvous. Last Saturday I finally cut the matter short and decided to call on my much-travelled friend, Adolph Bruun. To that end I set out at about seven in the evening for Vestergade, where someone had told me he was living. However, he was not there, not even on the third floor, which I reached quite out of breath. As I was about to descend, my ear caught the sound of a melodious feminine voice saying, 'On Monday, then, one o'clock at the exhibition; the others are all out then, but you know I never dare see you at home.' The invitation was not to me but to a young man who was out of the door in a flash, and so quickly that not even my eye, let alone my legs, could catch him. Why is there no gaslight on the stairway? At least I might have seen whether it was worthwhile being so punctual. Still, if there had been a gaslight I might not have heard. What exists is the rational, after all;[11] I am and remain an optimist ... Now, which one is her? The exhibition is swarming with girls, to quote Donna Anna.[12] It is exactly a quarter to one. My beautiful unknown! Would that your intended were in every way as punctual as I; or perhaps you would rather he never came a quarter of an hour too early; as you will, I am in every way at your service ... Bewitching enchantress, witch or fairy, let your cloud vanish, reveal yourself, you are presumably already here, but invisible to me; betray yourself, for I hardly dare expect any other kind of revelation. Could there perhaps be several up here on the same errand as she? Quite possibly. Who knows the ways of man, even when he goes to exhibitions? – But there comes a young girl in the front room, hurrying, faster than a bad conscience after a sinner. She forgets to hand over her ticket and the man in red stops her. Heaven preserve us! What a rush she's in! It must be her. Why such premature impetuosity? It still isn't one o'clock. Do but remember that you are to meet the beloved. Is it no matter at all how one looks on such occasions, or is this what it means to put one's best foot forward? When such an innocent young hot-head keeps a tryst, she tackles the matter like a mad-woman. She is all of a flutter. As for me, I sit here comfortably in my chair, contemplating a delightful pastoral landscape ... She's a devil's child, she storms through all the rooms. You must learn to hide your eagerness a little; remember for example what was said to Lisbeth: 'Does it become a young girl to let it be seen how eager she is to pair?'[13] But of course your meeting is one of those innocent ones ... Lovers usually consider a tryst a most beautiful moment. I myself still remember as clearly as if it were yesterday the first time I hastened to the appointed place, with a heart as full as it was ignorant of the joy awaiting me, the first time I knocked three times, the first time the window was opened, the first time the little door was opened by the invisible hand of a girl who concealed herself in opening it, the first time I hid a girl under my cloak in the light summer night. But much illusion is blended with this judgement. The dispassionate third party does not always find the lovers most beautiful at this moment. I have been witness to trysts where, although the girl was charming and the man handsome, the whole impression was well-nigh disgusting and the meeting itself far from beautiful,

though no doubt it seemed so to the lovers. In a way one gains
something by becoming more experienced; for although one loses
the sweet unrest of impatient longing, one gains a preparedness
to make the moment really beautiful. It can irritate me to see a
man given such an opportunity so bewildered that love alone is
enough to give him delirium tremens. But what does the farmer
know of cucumber salad? Instead of being level-headed enough
to enjoy her disquiet, to allow it to enflame her beauty and kindle
it, he produces only a charmless confusion, and yet he goes
joyfully home imagining it to have been something glorious ...
But what the devil has become of the fellow? It's already two
o'clock. What fine types, these sweethearts! A scoundrel like that
lets a young girl wait for him! Not me, I'm a trustworthy person
of quite different calibre! Maybe it would be best to speak to her
now, since she is passing by for the fifth time. 'Pardon my boldness, fair young lady. You are no doubt looking for your family
up here. You have hurried past me several times, and as my eyes
followed you, I noticed you always stop in the next but last room;
perhaps you are unaware that there is still another room further
in. Perhaps you will find them there.' She curtsies to me; it suits
her well. The occasion is favourable. I am glad the person has
not come; one always fishes best in troubled waters. When a
young girl is emotionally disturbed, one can successfully venture
that which would otherwise be ill-starred. I have just bowed to
her as politely and distantly as possible. I sit down again in my
chair, look at my landscape, and watch her. To follow her straightaway would be too risky; she might find me intrusive and then
immediately be on her guard. Just now she believes I addressed
her out of sympathy, I am in her good books. – I know quite
well there's not a soul in the inner room. Solitude will have a
beneficial effect upon her. So long as she sees many people around
her she is agitated; if she is alone she will be calm. Quite right,
she is still in there. After a while I shall approach her *en passant*; I
have earned the right to make a remark, she owes me at least a
greeting ... She's sitting. Poor girl, she looks so sad. She has
been crying, I think, or at least has tears in her eyes. It is outrageous making a girl like that cry. But be calm, you shall be
avenged, I shall avenge you, he will learn what it means to keep

her waiting. – How beautiful she is, now that the various squalls have subsided and she rests in a single mood. Her being is a harmony of sadness and pain. She really is captivating. She sits there in travelling clothes, yet it wasn't she who was to travel, she put them on so as to journey out in search of joy; now it is a sign of her pain, for she is like someone from whom gladness departs. She looks out, as though constantly taking leave of the loved one. Let him go! – The situation is favourable, the moment beckons. The thing now is to express myself in a way that makes it seem that I believed she was looking for her family or a party of friends up here, and yet warmly enough, too, for every word to be appropriate to her feelings, then I shall have a chance to worm my way into her thoughts. – Now devil take the scoundrel! If there isn't a man arriving who can only be him. No, take me for a bungler, just as I've got the situation as I wanted it. Yes, yes, something can surely be salvaged from it. I must touch upon their relationship, have myself placed in the situation. When she sees me she'll have to smile at my believing she was looking for someone quite different. That smile makes me her accomplice, which is always something. – A thousand thanks my child, that smile is worth much more to me than you think; it is the beginning, and the beginning is always the hardest. Now we are acquainted, and our acquaintance is based upon a piquant situation; it is enough to be going on with. You will hardly stay here more than an hour; within two hours I shall know who you are – why else do you think the police keep census rolls?

the 9th

Have I gone blind? Has the soul's inner eye lost its power? I have seen her, but it's as if I'd seen a heavenly revelation, so completely has her image vanished from me again. Vainly do I call upon all the strength of my soul to conjure forth this image. If ever I saw her again I'd recognize her immediately even if she stood among a hundred. Now she has run away, and my mind's eye seeks in vain to overtake her with its longing. – I was walking along Langelinie,[14] to all appearances unconcerned and without regard to my surroundings, although my watchful glance let nothing go unobserved, when my eye fell on her. It fixed itself unwaveringly upon her, it no longer obeyed its master's will. It was impossible for me to undertake any movement with it and use it to survey the object I would behold; I did not see, I stared. Like a fencer who freezes in his pass, so was my eye fixed, petrified in the direction it had taken. It was impossible for me to look down, impossible to withdraw my glance, impossible for me to see, because I saw far too much. The only thing I can remember is that she wore a green cape, that's all. One can call that catching the cloud instead of Juno;[15] she has slipped away from me like Joseph from Potiphar's wife and has left only her cape behind.[16] She was accompanied by an oldish lady, who appeared to be her mother. Her I can describe from top to toe, even though I never really saw her but at most took her in en passant. So it goes. The girl made an impression upon me and I have forgotten her. The other has made no impression and I can remember her.

the 11th

The same contradiction still blinds my soul. I know I have seen her, but I know also I have forgotten it again, in a way that the residue of memory left over gives no refreshment. With a restlessness and vehemence that put my wellbeing at risk, my soul demands this image, yet it does not appear; I could tear out my eyes to punish them for their forgetfulness. When I have finished impatiently raging, when I become calm, it is as if intimation and memory wove a picture which still cannot take definite shape because I cannot get it to stand still all at once. It is like a pattern in a fine texture; the pattern is lighter than the ground and by itself it is invisible because it is too light. – This is a curious state to be in, yet it has its pleasant side both in itself and also because it proves to me that I am still young. It can also teach me something else, namely that I'm always seeking my prey among young girls, not among young wives. A wife has less of nature in her, more coquetry; the relationship with her is not beautiful, not interesting, but piquant, and the piquant is always what comes last. I had not expected to be able to taste again the first fruits of infatuation. I am over my ears in love, I have got what swimmers call a ducking; no wonder I am a little confused. So much the better, so much the more I promise myself from this relationship.

the 14th

I hardly recognize myself. My mind rages like a sea tossed by the storms of passion. If another could see my soul in this condition, it would look as if, like a boat, it bored its bow down in the sea, as if with its fearful speed it had to plunge into the depths of the abyss. He does not see that high up on the mast there sits a sailor on lookout. Rage, you wild forces, stir your powers of passion! Even if the crashing of your waves hurls the foam to the skies, you will still not manage to pile up over my head; I sit serene as the King of the Cliff.[17]

I can almost not find my footing, like a water-bird I seek in vain to alight on my mind's turbulent sea. And yet such turbulence is my element, I build upon it, just as *Alcedo ispida* builds its nest on the sea.[18]

Turkey cocks puff themselves up when they see red; it's the same with me when I see green, every time I see a green cape; and since my eyes often deceive me, all my expectations are sometimes dashed on seeing a porter from Frederiks Hospital.[19]

the 20th

One has to restrict oneself, that is a main condition of all enjoyment. It doesn't seem I can expect so soon to get any information about the girl who fills my soul and thoughts so much that they keep her loss alive. Now I shall stay quite calm, for this state I'm in, this obscure and undefined but intense unrest, has a sweet side nevertheless. I have always loved, on a moonlit night, to lie out in a boat on one of our lovely lakes. I take in the sails and the oars, remove the rudder, stretch out full-length, and gaze up into the vault of heaven. When the boat rocks on the breast of the waves, when the clouds scud before the strong wind so that the moon vanishes for a moment and then reappears, I find rest in this unrest. The motion of the waves lulls me, their lapping against the boat is a monotonous cradle-song. The swift flight of the clouds, the shifting light and shadow, intoxicate me so that I am in a waking dream. Thus now, too, I lay myself out, take in the sails and rudder; longing and impatient expectation toss me about in their arms; longing and expectation become more and more quiet, more and more blissful, they fondle me like a child; the heaven of hope arches over me; her image floats by me like the moon's, indistinct, blinding me now with its light, now with its shadow. How enjoyable thus to splash up and down on a stormy lake – how enjoyable to be stirred in oneself.

the 21st

The days go by and I am no nearer. Young girls give me pleasure more than ever and still I have no desire to enjoy them. I seek her everywhere. It often makes me unreasonable, blurs my vision, enervates my pleasure. That beautiful season is soon coming now when, in public life in the streets and lanes, one buys up these small favours which, in the winter's social life, one can pay dearly enough for, for although there is much a young girl can forget, she cannot forget a situation. Social life does indeed bring one in contact with the fair sex, but there is no artistry in starting an affair there. In social life every young girl is armed, the occasion is threadbare and repeated over and over again; she gets no voluptuous thrill. In the street she is on the open sea and everything therefore seems more intense; it is as if there were mystery in everything. I would give a hundred dollars for a smile from a young girl in a street situation, but not even ten for a handclasp at a party; these are currencies of quite different kinds. Once the affair is under way, you can then seek out the person in question at parties. You have a secret communication with her that tempts you, and it is the most effective stimulant I know. She dares not speak of it and yet she thinks of it; she doesn't know if you've forgotten it or not; you lead her astray in one way and then another. Probably I shan't collect much this year; this girl preoccupies me too much. In a sense my returns will be poor; but then I have the prospect of the big prize.

the 5th

Damned chance! I have never cursed you for appearing, I curse you because you don't appear at all. Or is this perhaps some new invention of yours, you unfathomable being, barren mother of all that exists, sole remnant of that time when necessity gave birth to freedom, when freedom let itself be duped back into its mother's womb? Damned chance! You, my only confidant, the only being I consider worthy to be my ally and my enemy, always the same however different, always unfathomable, always a riddle! You, whom I love with all the sympathy in my soul, in whose image I form myself, why do you not appear? I am not begging, I do not humbly entreat you to appear in this way or that; such worship would be idolatry, not well-pleasing to you. I challenge you to battle: why don't you appear? Or has the turbulence in the world's structure come to a standstill? Is your riddle solved, so that you too have plunged into the ocean of eternity? Terrible thought, for then the world has come to a standstill from boredom! Damned chance! I am waiting for you. I do not wish to defeat you with principles, or with what foolish people call character; no, I want to be your poet! I'll not be a poet for others. Show yourself! I compose you, I consume my own verse and it is my sustenance. Or do you find me unworthy? As a bayadère dances to the honour of God,[20] I have dedicated myself to your service; light, thinly clad, supple, unarmed, I renounce everything, I own nothing, I have no mind to own anything, I love nothing, I have nothing to lose; but haven't I then become more worthy of you, you who long ago must have wearied of depriving people of what they loved, wearied of their cowardly sighs and prayers? Take me by surprise, I am ready, no stakes, let us fight for honour. Show me her, show me a possibility that looks like an impossibility; show me her in the shadows of the underworld, I shall fetch her up.[21] Let her hate me, despise me, be indifferent to me, love another, I'm not afraid; but stir up the waters, break your silence. It's cheap of you to starve me in this way, you who after all fancy yourself stronger than I.

May 6th

Spring is at hand. Everything is in bloom, including the young girls. Capes are laid aside, and presumably my green one has been hung up. That's what comes of making a girl's acquaintance in the street instead of at a party, where one finds out immediately what she is called, what family she is from, where she lives, whether she is engaged. This last is extremely important for all steadfast and sober-minded suitors, to whom it would never occur to fall in love with a girl who was engaged. Such an easy-paced ambler would be in deadly peril if he were in my place; he would be completely devastated if his efforts to acquire information were crowned with success, with the bonus that she was engaged. But that doesn't worry me much. An engaged girl is only a comic difficulty. I have no fear either of comic or of tragic difficulties; all I fear are the tediously long-drawn-out ones. So far I haven't secured a single piece of information, in spite of surely leaving no stone unturned and often feeling the truth of the poet's words:

> *Nox et hiems longaeque viae, saevique dolores*
> *mollibus his castris, et labor omnis inest.*[22]

Perhaps after all she doesn't live here in town, perhaps she is from the country, perhaps, perhaps – I could go crazy over all these perhapses, and the more crazy I become, the more perhapses. I always have money in readiness for a journey. In vain I look for her at the theatre, at concerts, ballets, and on promenades. That pleases me in a way; a young girl who takes too much part in such entertainments is generally not worth conquering; she usually lacks that originality which for me is a *sine qua non*. One can more easily imagine finding a Preciosa[23] among the gypsies than in the cheap dancing-halls where young girls are put up for sale – in all innocence, of course, Lord preserve us, what else?

the 12th

Yes, my child, why didn't you stay standing quite still at the door? There is nothing at all reprehensible about a young girl's stopping in a doorway when it's raining. I do the same sometimes when I have no umbrella, sometimes even when I have, as for instance now. Besides, I could mention a number of respectable ladies who have not hesitated to do so. You have only to stand quietly, turn your back to the street, so that passers-by can't tell whether you are standing there or are about to go into the house. On the other hand, it is unwise to hide oneself behind the door when it is half open, mainly because of the consequences; for the more you are hidden, the more unpleasant it is to be surprised. But if you do hide, you should stand quite still, committing yourself to the good genie and the custody of all the angels; you should particularly refrain from peeping out – to see if it has stopped raining. If you want to find out, then step out boldly and look earnestly up into the sky. But if you poke your head out a little curiously, shyly, anxiously, uncertainly, and then hurriedly draw it in again – then every child understands that movement; it's called playing hide-and-seek. And I, who always take part, I should of course hold back and not answer when asked . . . Don't think I'm getting any injurious ideas, you hadn't the slightest intention when you poked out your head, it was the most innocent thing in the world. In return you mustn't get ideas about me, my good name and reputation won't stand it. Besides, it was you who started it. I advise you never to tell anyone of this; you were in the wrong. What else can I do other than what any gentleman would – offer you my umbrella? – Where has she got to? Excellent, she has hidden herself in the porter's doorway. – She is a most charming little girl, merry, pleased. – 'Do you know anything of a young lady who just a blessed moment ago poked her head out of this doorway, evidently in need of an umbrella? It is she I am looking for, I and my umbrella.' – You laugh – perhaps you will allow me to send my servant to fetch it tomorrow, or if you ask me to call a carriage – nothing to thank me for, it is only due courtesy. – She is one of the most joyful girls I have seen in a long time, her glance is so childlike and yet so forthright, her nature so charming, so pure, and yet she is curious. – Go in peace, my child, if it were not for a certain green cape, I might have wanted to make a closer acquaintance. – She walks down to Købmagergade. How innocent and trusting, not a sign of prudery. Look how lightly she walks, how gaily she tosses her head – the green cape demands self-denial.

the 15th

Thank you, kind chance, accept my thanks! Straight she was and proud, mysterious and rich in ideas as a spruce, a shoot, a thought, which from deep in the earth sprouts up towards heaven, un- explained and to itself inexplicable, a whole that has no parts. The beech crowns itself, its leaves tell of what has taken place beneath; the spruce has no crown, no history, a mystery to itself − such was she. She was hidden from herself inside herself, she rose up from out of herself, she had a self-contained pride, like the daring flight of the spruce, even though it is fastened to the earth. A sadness poured over her like the cooing of the wood- pigeon, a deep longing that had no want. She was a riddle, who mysteriously possessed her own solution, a secret, and what are all diplomats' secrets compared with this, an enigma, and what in all the world is so beautiful as the word that solves it? How significant, how pregnant, language is: 'to solve' [at løse], what ambiguity it contains, how beautiful and strong in all the com- binations where this word appears! As the wealth of the soul is a riddle, as long as the ligature of the tongue is not loosed [løst], and the riddle thereby solved [løst], so is a young girl, too, a riddle. − Thank you, kind chance, accept my thanks! If I had seen her first in winter she'd have been wrapped in that green cape, frozen perhaps and, in her, Nature's inclemency might have diminished its own beauty. But now, what luck! I saw her first at the most beautiful time of year, in the spring, in the light of late afternoon. True, winter also has its advantages. A brilliantly lit ballroom can indeed be a flattering setting for a young girl in evening dress. But she seldom appears to best advantage here, partly because everything demands it of her, a demand whose effect is disturbing whether she gives in to it or resists, and partly because everything suggests transience and vanity, and evokes an impatience that makes the enjoyment less soothing. At times I would not wish to dispense with the ballroom, I would not forgo its costly luxury, its priceless abundance of youth and beauty, its manifold play of forces; but then it isn't so much that I enjoy myself as gorge myself in possibility. It is not a single beauty that captivates me but a totality; a dream image floats past, in which all these feminine natures form their own configurations among one another, and all these movements seek something, seek rest in one picture that is not seen.

It was on the path between Nørre- and Østerport,[24] about half-past six. The sun had lost its strength, its memory only was preserved in a mild radiance spreading over the landscape. Nature breathed more freely. The lake was calm, smooth as a mirror. The comfortable houses on Blegdammen were reflected in the water, which further out was dark as metal. The path and the buildings on the other side were lit by the faint rays of the sun. The sky was clear and only a single light cloud floated over it unnoticed, best seen by directing your eyes at the lake, over whose shining forehead it vanished from view. Not a leaf moved. – It was her. My eye did not deceive me, even though the green cape had done so. In spite of being prepared now for so long, it was impossible to control a certain excitement, a rising and falling, like the song of the lark that rose and fell in the adjacent fields. She was alone. How she was dressed I have forgotten again, and yet now I have a picture of her. She was alone, preoccupied, evidently not with herself but with her thoughts. She was not thinking, but the quiet pursuit of her thoughts wove a picture of longing before her soul, possessed by presentiment, inexplicably like a young girl's many sighs. She was at her most beautiful age. A young girl does not develop in the sense that a boy does; she does not grow, she is born. A boy begins straightaway to develop, and it takes a long time; a young girl takes a long time being born and is born full-grown. Therein lies her infinite richness; the moment she is born she is fully grown, but this moment of birth comes late. Therefore she is born twice, the second time when she marries, or, rather, at that moment she ceases being born, that is her moment of birth. It is not just Minerva who sprang fully grown from the head of Jupiter, not just Venus who rose from the ocean in all her beauty; every young girl is like this if her womanliness has not been destroyed by what people call development. She awakens not by degrees but all at once; on the other hand, she dreams all the longer, provided people are not so unreasonable as to arouse her too early. But this dream is an infinite richness. – She was preoccupied not with herself but in herself, and in her this preoccupation was an infinite peace and repose. This is how a young girl is rich; encompassing this richness makes oneself rich. She is rich even though she does not know that she owns anything. She is rich, she is a treasure. A quiet peacefulness brooded over her and a little sadness.

She was light to lift up with the eyes, as light as Psyche who was carried off by genies,[25] lighter still, for she carried herself. Let theologians dispute on the Virgin Mary's Assumption; to me it seems not inconceivable, for she no longer belonged to the world; but the lightness of a young girl is incomprehensible and makes mockery of the law of gravity. – She noticed nothing and therefore believed herself unnoticed. I kept my distance and absorbed her image. She was walking slowly, no urgency disturbed her peace or the quiet of her surroundings. By the lake sat a boy fishing, she stopped and looked at the mirror surface of the water and the small river. Although she had not been walking vigorously she sought to cool herself. She loosened a little kerchief fastened about her neck under her shawl. A soft breeze from the lake fanned a bosom as white as snow, yet warm and full. The boy seemed unhappy to have a witness to his catch; he turned to her with a somewhat phlegmatic glance and watched her. He really cut a ridiculous figure, and I cannot blame her for beginning to laugh at him. How youthfully she laughed! If she had been alone with the boy I don't think she would have been afraid of coming to blows with him. Her eyes were large and radiant; when one looked into them they had a dark lustre which, because of their impenetrability, gave a hint of their infinite depth; they were pure and innocent, gentle and quiet, full of mischief when she smiled. Her nose was finely arched; when I saw her sideways it seemed to merge with the forehead, making it a little shorter and a little more spirited. She walked on, I followed. Happily there were many strollers on the path; while exchanging a few words with some of them, I let her gain a little on me and soon overtook her again, thus relieving myself of the need to keep my distance by walking as slowly as she did. She walked in the direction of Østerport. I wished to see her more closely without being seen. At the corner stood a house from which that might be possible. I knew the family and so needed only to call on them. I hurried past her at a good pace, as though paying her not the slightest heed. I got a good lead on her, greeted the family right and left, and then took possession of the window which overlooked the path. She came, I looked and looked while at the same time keeping up a conversation with the tea party in the drawing-room. The way she walked easily convinced me she hadn't taken many dancing lessons, yet it had a pride, a natural nobility, but an artlessness. I had another opportunity to see her that I really had not reckoned with. From the window I could not see very far down the path, but I could see a jetty extending out into the lake, and to my great surprise, I discovered her again out there. It occurred to me that perhaps she belonged out here in the country; maybe the family had summer rooms. I was already on the point of regretting my call, for fear that she might turn back so that I would lose sight of her; indeed, the fact that she could be seen at the extreme end of the jetty was a sort of sign that she was disappearing from my view – when she appeared close by. She had gone past the house; in great haste I seized my hat and cane in order, if possible, to walk past and then lag behind her several times again until I found out where she lived – when in my haste I jostled the arm of a lady about to serve tea. A frightful screaming arose. I stood there with my hat and cane and, anxious only to get away and if possible give a twist to the matter to motivate my retreat, I exclaimed with great feeling, 'Like Cain I shall be banished from the place where this tea was spilled.' But as if everything conspired against me, the host conceived the desperate idea of following up my remarks and declared, loudly and solemnly, that I was forbidden to leave before I had enjoyed a cup of tea; I myself served the ladies the tea I had deprived them of, and thus made good everything once more. Since I was perfectly certain that my host, under the circumstances, would consider it a courtesy to use force, there was nothing for it but to remain. – She had vanished.

the 16th

How beautiful to be in love, how interesting to know one is in love! See, that's the difference! The thought of her disappearing a second time can be irritating but in a sense it pleases me. The picture I now have of her wavers indeterminately between being her actual and her ideal image. I am now evoking it, but precisely because either it is real or it has at least its source in reality, it has its own fascination. I feel no impatience, since she must belong here in town, and for me that is enough for the moment. It is this possibility that makes her image properly appear – everything should be savoured in slow draughts. And should I not indeed be relaxed, I who consider myself the darling of the gods, to whom befell the rare good fortune to fall in love again? That, after all, is something no art, no study, can produce; it is a gift. But since I have succeeded in stirring up a love once more, I want at least to see how long it can be kept going. This love I coddle as I never did my first. Such an opportunity is not given every day, it seems, so it is truly a matter of making the most of it. That's what drives one to despair. Seducing a girl is no art, but it needs a stroke of good fortune to find one worth seducing. – Love has many mysteries, and this first infatuation is also a mystery, even if a minor one – most people who rush into it get engaged or indulge in other foolish pranks, and then it's all over in the twinkling of an eye and they don't know what they have conquered or what they have lost. Twice now she has appeared before me and vanished; that means that soon she will appear more frequently. After he has interpreted Pharaoh's dream, Joseph adds: 'The fact that you dreamt this twice, means that it will soon come to pass.'[26]

Still, it would be interesting if one could see a little in advance those forces whose coming on the scene makes for life's content. She lives her life now in peace and quiet; she has no suspicion I even exist, even less what goes on inside me, less still the certainty with which I survey her future; for my soul demands more and more reality, it is becoming stronger and stronger. When, at a first glance, a girl does not make a deep enough impression upon one to awaken the ideal, then the real thing is usually not particularly desirable. But if she does awaken it, then however experienced one may be, generally one is a little overwhelmed. But for someone uncertain of his hand, his eye and his victory, I would always advise him to chance an attack at this first stage when, just because he is overwhelmed, he is in possession of extraordinary powers. For this being overwhelmed is a curious mixture of sympathy and egoism. On the other hand, he will forgo an enjoyment because he does not enjoy a situation he himself is secretly involved in. What is nicest is hard to decide; what the most interesting, easy. However, it is always good to get as close to the limit as possible. That is the real pleasure and what others enjoy I've no idea. The mere possession isn't much and the means lovers use are generally wretched enough;

they even stoop to money, power, influence, sleeping draughts, and so on. But what pleasure can there be in love when it is not the most absolute self-surrender, that is, on the one side? But that as a rule requires spirit, and as a rule these lovers lack that.

the 19th

So her name is Cordelia. Cordelia! That's a pretty name, which is also important, since often it is very disconcerting to have to use an ugly name in connection with the tenderest attributions. I recognized her a long way off; she was walking with two other girls on her left. The way they walked suggested they would soon be stopping. I stood at the corner and read a poster while keeping a constant eye on my unknown. They took leave of one another. The two had presumably come a little out of their way, since they took an opposite direction. She set off towards my corner. When she had taken a few steps, one of the other girls came running after her, calling loudly enough for me to hear, 'Cordelia! Cordelia!'. Then the third girl came up; they put their heads together for a private conference, which with my keenest ear I tried in vain to hear. Then all three laughed and went off in rather greater haste in the direction the two had taken before. I followed. They went into a house on the Strand. I waited quite a time since it seemed likely that Cordelia would soon return alone. But that didn't happen.

Cordelia! That is really an excellent name; it was also the name of the third of King Lear's daughters, that remarkable girl whose heart did not dwell upon her lips, whose lips were silent when her heart was full.[27] So too with my Cordelia. She resembles her, of that I'm certain. But in another sense her heart does dwell upon her lips, not in words but more cordially in the form of a kiss. How full of health her lips were! Never have I seen prettier.

That I am really in love I can tell among other things by the secrecy, almost even to myself, with which I treat this matter. All love is secretive, even faithless love when it has the necessary aesthetic element. It has never occurred to me to want confidants or boast of my affairs. So it was almost gratifying not to get to know her address but a place that she frequents. Besides, perhaps because of this I have come even nearer to my goal. I can begin my investigations without attracting her attention, and from this fixed point it shouldn't be difficult to gain access to her family. Should that prove difficult, however, *eh bien*; it's all in the day's work; everything I do I do *con amore*; and thus also I love *con amore*.

the 20th

Today I got hold of some information about the house she disappeared into. It's a widow with three blessed daughters. An abundance of information can be got from that source, that's if they have any. The only difficulty is to understand this information when raised to the third power, since all three talk at once. She is called Cordelia Wahl, and she is the daughter of a Navy captain. He died some years ago, and the mother too. He was a very hard and strict husband. Now she lives in the house with her aunt, her father's sister, who is said to resemble her brother but is a very respectable woman besides. So far so good, but beyond that they know nothing of this house; they never go there, but Cordelia often visits them. She and the two girls are taking a course at the Royal Kitchens. She usually goes there in the afternoon, sometimes also in the morning, never in the evening. They live a very secluded life.

So that's the end of the story. There seems to be no bridge by which I can slip over into Cordelia's house.

She has, then, some conception of life's pains, of its darker side. Who would have thought it of her? Still, these memories belong to her earlier years; it is a horizon she has lived under without really noticing it. That's a very good thing; it has saved her womanliness, she is not crippled. It can be useful, on the other hand, for raising her to a higher level, if one knows how to bring it out. All such things usually produce pride, in so far as they don't crush, and certainly she is far from being crushed.

the 21st

She lives by the ramparts; it isn't one of the best localities, no neighbours over the way for me to strike up acquaintance with, no public places from which I could make my observations unnoticed.

The ramparts themselves are hardly suitable: one is too visible. If one goes down to the street, the other side right by the ramparts, that will hardly do, for no one goes there and it would be too conspicuous, or else one would have to go along the side on which the houses front and then one can't see anything. It's a corner house. From the street one can also see the windows to the courtyard, since there is no neighbouring house. That is presumably where her bedroom is.

the 22nd

Today I saw her for the first time at Mrs Jansen's. I was introduced. She didn't seem much concerned, or to take much note of me. I behaved as unobtrusively as possible to be the more attentive. She stayed only a moment, she had merely called to fetch the daughters, who were due to go to the Royal Kitchens. While the two Jansen girls were getting on their wraps, we two were alone in the drawing-room, and I made a few cool, almost nonchalant remarks to her, which were returned with undeserved courtesy. Then they left. I could have offered to accompany them, but that would have been enough to mark me down as a ladies' man, and I am convinced she cannot be won in that way. – I preferred, instead, to leave a moment after they had gone but considerably faster than they and by another street, though still aiming at the Royal Kitchens, so that just as they turned into Store Kongensgade I rushed past them in great haste, without greeting or anything, to their great astonishment.

the 23rd

I have to gain access to the house, and for that I am, in military parlance, at the ready. However, it looks like being a long-drawn-out and difficult affair. Never have I known a family that lived so isolated. There are only herself and her aunt. No brothers, no cousins, not a shred to seize on, no relatives however distant to walk arm-in-arm with. I go about with one arm constantly hanging free; not for the whole world would I take someone by the arm at this time. My arm is a grapnel which must always be kept in readiness;

it is designed for unexpected returns, in case far off in the distance
there should appear a remote relative or friend, whom from that
distance I could take lightly by the arm – then clamber aboard. But
in any case, it is wrong of the family to live so isolated; one deprives
the poor girl of the opportunity to get to know the world, to say
nothing of what other dangerous consequences it may have. It
never pays. That goes for courting too. Such isolation may well
protect one against petty thievery; in a very hospitable house opportunity makes the thief. But that doesn't mean much, for from
girls of that kind there isn't much to steal; when they are sixteen
their hearts are already completed samplers and I have never cared
to write my name where others have already written. It never
occurs to me to scratch my name on a window-pane or in an inn,
or on a tree or a bench in Frederiksberg Gardens.

the 27th

The more I see her, the more I am convinced she is a very
isolated figure. A man should never be that, not even a young one,
for since reflection is essential to his development he must have
come into contact with others. But for that reason a girl should
rather not be interesting, for the interesting always contains a reflection upon itself, just as the interesting in art always gives you the
artist too. A young girl who wants to please by being interesting
really only succeeds in pleasing herself. This is the aesthetic objection
to all forms of coquetry. All the figurative coquetry which forms
part of natural motion is another matter, for instance feminine
modesty, which is always the most delightful coquetry. An interesting girl may indeed succeed in pleasing, but just as she has herself
renounced her femininity, so also are the men she pleases usually
correspondingly effeminate. A young girl of this kind really only
becomes interesting through her relationship to men. Woman is the
weaker sex, and yet for her, much more than for the man, it is
essential to be alone with herself in her younger years. She must be
sufficient unto herself, but what she is sufficient in and through is an
illusion; it is the dowry that Nature has bestowed on her, as with the
daughter of a king. But it is just this resting in illusion that isolates

her. I have often wondered why nothing is more demoralizing for a young girl than constant association with other young girls. Evidently, it is due to that association being neither one thing nor the other. It disturbs the illusion but doesn't bring light to it. Woman's highest destiny is to be a companion to the man, but association with her own sex causes a reflection to focus upon this association, and instead of becoming a companion she becomes a lady's companion. Language itself has much to say in this respect. The man is called Master but the woman is not called Handmaiden or anything of that sort; no, an essential qualification is used, she is a 'companion', not a 'companioness'. If I were to imagine my ideal of a girl, she would always have to stand alone in the world and therefore be left to herself, but especially not have girl friends. True, the Graces were three, but surely it has never occurred to anyone to imagine them conversing with one another; in their silent trinity they form a beautiful feminine unity. In this respect I might almost be tempted to recommend the return of the lady's bower, were this constraint not also injurious. It is always most desirable for a young girl to be allowed her freedom but no opportunity offered her. This makes her beautiful and saves her from being interesting. It is in vain to give a young girl who has spent a great deal of time with other girls a maiden's veil or a bridal veil; on the other hand, a man with enough aesthetic appreciation always finds that a girl who is innocent in a deeper and truer sense is brought to him veiled, even if bridal veils are not in fashion.

She has been brought up strictly; I honour her parents in their graves for that. She lives a very reserved life, and for that I could fall on her aunt's neck in gratitude. She is not yet acquainted with the pleasures of the world, does not have the chattering surfeit. She is proud, she defies what other young girls find pleasure in. That's as it should be; it is an untruth which I shall know how to work to my profit. She takes no pleasure in ceremony and fuss as other young girls do; she is a little polemical, but that is necessary for a young girl with her enthusiasms. She lives in the world of imagination. Were she to fall into the wrong hands, it might bring something very unwomanly out of her, precisely because there is so much womanliness in her.

Everywhere our paths cross. Today I met her three times. I know of her every little excursion, when and where I shall come across her. But this knowledge is not used to secure a meeting. On the contrary, I squander on a frightful scale. A meeting which often has cost me several hours' waiting is thrown away as a trifle. I do not meet her, I merely touch tangentially upon the periphery of her existence. If I know she is going to Mrs Jansen's I prefer not to arrive there at the same time, unless it is important for me to carry out some particular observation. I prefer arriving a little early at Mrs Jansen's, and then if possible meeting her at the door as she is coming and I am leaving, or on the steps where I run unheedingly past her. This is the first net she must be spun into. I do not stop her on the street, or I might exchange a greeting but always keep my distance. She must certainly be struck by our continual encounters; no doubt she notices that a new body has appeared on her horizon, whose movement in a curiously un-disturbing way has a disturbing effect on her own, but of the law governing this movement she has no idea. To look for its point of attraction her inclination is rather to look right and left; that she is herself that point she is no more the wiser than her polar opposite. With her it is as with those with whom I associate in general, they believe I have a multiplicity of affairs; I am continually on the go and say, like Figaro, 'One, two, three, four intrigues at once, that's my delight.' I must get to know her first and her whole state of mind before beginning my assault. Most men enjoy a young girl as they do a glass of champagne, in a single frothing moment; oh, yes! that's really nice, and with many young girls it's no doubt the most one can make of it. But here there is more. If the individual is too frail to stand clarity and transparency, well then, one enjoys obscurity, but she can obviously stand it. The more surrender one can bring into love, the more interesting it becomes. This momentary pleasure is a case of rape, if not in an outward sense at least spiritually, and in rape there is only an imaginary pleasure; it is like a stolen kiss, something with no substance behind it. No, when one brings matters to the point where a girl has just one task to accomplish for her freedom, to surrender herself, when she feels her whole bliss depends on that, when she almost begs to submit and yet is free, then for the first time there is enjoyment, but it always depends on a spiritual influence.

Cordelia! What a glorious name. I sit at home and practise it like a parrot. I say 'Cordelia, Cordelia, my Cordelia, my own Cordelia'. I can scarcely forbear smiling at the thought of the routine with which I will come, at a decisive moment, to utter these words. One should always make preliminary studies, everything must be properly prepared. It is no wonder that the poets always portray this intimate moment, this beautiful moment, when the lovers, not content with being sprinkled (sure enough, there are many who never get further), but descending into love's ocean divest themselves of the old person and climb up from this baptism, only now, for the first time, properly knowing each other as old acquaintances though only an instant old. For a young girl this is always the most beautiful moment, and properly to savour it one should always be a little higher, so that one is not only the one being baptized but also the priest. A little irony makes this moment's second moment one of the most interesting; it is a spiritual undressing. One must be poet enough not to disturb the ceremony yet the joker must always be sitting in ambush.

June 2nd

She is proud; I have seen that for a long time. When she sits together with the three Jansens she talks very little, their chatter obviously bores her, and certainly the smile on her lips seems to indicate that. I am counting on that smile. – At other times she can surrender herself to an almost boyish wildness, to the great surprise of the Jansens. For me it is not inexplicable when I consider her childhood. She had only one brother, who was a year older. She knew only her father and brother, had been a witness to serious scenes which produce a distaste in general for jabber. Her father and mother had not lived happily together; what usually beckons, more or less clearly or vaguely, to a young girl does not beckon to her. She may possibly be puzzled about what it means to be a young girl. Perhaps at times she wished she were not a girl but a man.

She has imagination, soul, passion, in short, all substantial qualities, but not in a subjectively reflected form. A chance occurrence convinced me of that today. I gathered from Jansen & Co. that she did not play the piano, it is against her aunt's principles. I have always regretted that attitude, for music is always a good avenue for communicating with a young girl, if one takes care, be it noted, not to pose as a connoisseur. Today I went to Mrs Jansen's. I had half opened the door without knocking, an impertinence that has often stood me in good stead, and which, when necessary, I remedy with a bit of ridicule by knocking on the open door. She sat alone at the piano – she seemed to be playing on the sly (it was a little Swedish melody) – she was not an accomplished player, she became impatient, but then gentler sounds came again. I closed the door and stood outside, listening to the change in her moods; there was sometimes a passion in her playing which reminds one of the maiden Mittelil,[28] who struck the golden harp with such vigour that milk gushed from her breasts. – There was something melancholy but also something dithyrambic in her execution. – I might have rushed in, seized the moment – that would have been foolish. – Memory is not just a preservative but also a means of enhancement; what is permeated by memory seems doubled. – In books, especially in psalters, one often finds a little flower – some beautiful moment has furnished the occasion for preserving it, and yet the memory is even more beautiful. She is evidently concealing the fact that she plays, or perhaps she plays only this little Swedish melody – has it perhaps a special interest for her? All this I do not know, but the incident is for that reason very important to me. Whenever I can talk more confidentially with her, I shall lead her quite secretly to this point and let her fall into this trap.

June 3rd

I still cannot decide how she is to be understood. I wait therefore as quietly, as inconspicuously – yes, as a soldier in a cordon of scouts who throws himself to the ground to listen for the most distant sound of an approaching enemy. I do not really exist for her, not in the sense of a negative relationship, but of no relationship at all. Still I have not dared any experiment. To see her and love her were the same – that's what it says in romances – yes, it is true enough, if love had no dialectic; but what does one really learn about love from romances? Sheer lies that help to shorten the task.

When I think now, with the information I have gained, back upon the impression the first meeting made upon me, I'd say that my ideas about her have changed, but as much to her advantage as to mine. It isn't quite the order of the day for a young girl to go out so much alone or for a young girl to be so self-absorbed. She was tested according to my strict critique and found: delightful. But delight is a very fleeting factor which vanishes like yesterday when that day is gone. I had not imagined her in the setting in which she lived, least of all so unreflectingly familiar with life's storms.

I wonder how it is with her emotions. She has certainly never been in love, her spirit is too free-soaring for that; least of all is she one of those virgins experienced in theory who, well before the time, can so fluently imagine being in the arms of a loved one. The real-life figures she has met with have been less than such as to confuse her about the relation of dreams to reality. Her soul is still nourished by the divine ambrosia of ideals. But the ideal that floats before her is hardly a shepherdess or a heroine in a romance, a mistress; it is a Jeanne d'Arc or some such.

The question is always whether her femininity is strong enough to reflect itself; or whether it is only to be enjoyed as beauty and charm. The question is whether one dares to tense the bow more strongly. It is a wonderful thing in itself to find a pure immediate femininity, but risking change gives you the interesting; in which case the best thing is simply to saddle her with a suitor. There is a superstition that this would harm a young girl. – Indeed, if she is a very refined and delicate plant with just the one outstanding quality, charm, the best thing for her would be never to have heard of love. But if this is not the case it is an advantage, and I would never have scruples about getting hold of a suitor if none is at hand. Nor must this suitor be a caricature, for then nothing is gained; he must be a respectable young man, if possible even amiable, but too little for her passion. She looks down on such a man, she acquires a distaste for love, she almost despairs of her own reality when she senses what she might be and sees what reality offers. If this is love, she says, it's nothing to get excited about. She becomes proud in her love, this pride makes her interesting, it transfigures her being with a higher incarnation; but she is also nearer her downfall – all of which only makes her more and more interesting. However, it is best to check her acquaintances first to see whether there might not be such a suitor. At home there is no opportunity, for next to no one comes there, but she does go out and there could well be one. Getting hold of one before knowing this is always a risky matter. Two individually insignificant suitors could have an injurious effect by their relativity. I must find out now whether there isn't such a lover sitting in secret, lacking the courage to storm the citadel, a chicken-thief who sees no opportunity in such a cloistered house.

The strategic principle then, the law of all motion in this campaign, is always to involve her in an interesting situation. The interesting is the field on which this conflict must constantly be waged, the potentialities of the interesting are to be exhausted. Unless I am quite mistaken, this is what her whole being is based on, so what I demand is just what she herself offers, indeed, what she demands. Everything depends on spying out what the individual has to offer and what, as a consequence, she demands. My love affairs therefore always have a reality for me, they form an element in my life, a creative period, of which I am fully aware; often they even involve some or other acquired skill. I learned to dance for the first girl I loved; for a little dancer's sake I learned French. At that time, like all blockheads, I went to the market-place and was frequently made a fool of. Now I go in for pre-market purchasing.[29] But perhaps she has exhausted one aspect of the interesting; her secluded life seems to indicate that. Now it is a matter of finding another aspect which seems to her at first sight not at all interesting, but which, just because of this resistance, will become so. For this purpose I select not the poetic but the prosaic. That then is the start. First her femininity is neutralized by prosaic common sense and ridicule, not directly but indirectly, together with what is absolutely neutral: spirit. She comes close to losing the sense of her femininity, but in this condition she cannot stand alone; she throws herself into my arms, not as if I were a lover, no, still quite neutrally. Then her femininity awakens, one coaxes it to its greatest resilience, one lets her come up against something effectively real, she goes beyond it, her femininity attains almost supernatural heights, she belongs to me with a worldly passion.

the 5th

I did not have to go far. She visits at the home of Baxter, the wholesaler. Here I found not only Cordelia, but also a person just as opportune. Edvard, the son of the house, is head over heels in love with her, one needs only half of one eye to see it in both of his. He is in trade, in his father's office; a good-looking young man, quite pleasant, rather shy, which last I suspect does not hurt him in her eyes.

Poor Edvard! He simply doesn't know how to tackle his love. When he knows she is there in the evening he dresses up just for her, puts on his new dark suit just for her, cuff-links just for her, and cuts an almost ridiculous figure among the otherwise commonplace company in the drawing-room. His embarrassment borders on the unbelievable. If it were a pose, Edvard would become a very dangerous rival. Awkwardness has to be used very expertly, but with it one can come a long way. How often have I used it to fool some little virgin! Girls generally speak very harshly about awkward men, yet secretly they like them. A little embarrassment always flatters a young girl's vanity, she feels her superiority, it is change in the hand. Then when you have lulled them to sleep, you find an occasion on which they are made to believe you are about to die of embarrassment, to show that, far from it, you can quite well shift for yourself. Embarrassment deprives you of your masculine importance, and it is therefore a relatively good way of neutralizing sexual difference. So when they realize that it is only a pose, ashamed they blush inwardly, they are very conscious of having gone too far; it's as though they had gone on treating a boy too long as a child.

the 7th

We are firm friends now, Edvard and I; there exists a true friendship between us, a beautiful relationship, the like of which has not occurred since the finest days of the Greeks. We soon became intimates when, having embroiled him in diverse observations concerning Cordelia, I got him to confess his secret. When all secrets assemble, it goes without saying that this one can come along too.

Poor fellow, he has already sighed for a long time. He dresses up every time she comes, then escorts her home in the evening, his heart throbs at the thought that her arm is resting on his, they walk home gazing at the stars, he rings her bell, she disappears, he despairs — but hopes for next time. He still hasn't had the courage to set his foot over her threshold, he who has so excellent an opportunity. Although I cannot refrain inwardly from making fun of Edvard, there is something nice about his childlikeness. Although ordinarily I fancy myself fairly experienced in the whole quintessence of the erotic, I have never observed this state in myself, this lovesick fear and trembling, or not to the extent that it removes my self-possession; I know it well enough in other ways, but in my case it tends to make me stronger. One might perhaps say that in that case I've never been in love. Perhaps. I have taken Edvard to task, I have encouraged him to rely on my friendship. Tomorrow he is going to take a decisive step: go in person and invite her out. I have led him to the desperate idea of begging me to go with him; I have promised to do so. He takes this to be an extraordinary display of friendship. The occasion is exactly as I would have it: we burst in on her in the drawing-room. Should she have the slightest doubt as to the meaning of my conduct, this will once more confuse everything.

Hitherto I have not been accustomed to preparing myself for my conversation; now it has become a necessity in order to entertain the aunt. I have taken on the honourable task of conversing with her to cover up Edvard's infatuated advances to Cordelia. The aunt has previously lived in the country, and through a combination of my own painstaking studies in the agronomic literature and the aunt's reports of her practical experience, I am making significant progress in insight and efficiency.

With the aunt I am totally successful; she considers me a steady, reliable man with whom it is a decided pleasure to have dealings, unlike our dandies. With Cordelia I seem not to be particularly in favour. No doubt her femininity is of too purely innocent a kind for her to require every man to dance attendance on her, yet she is all too aware of the rebel in me.

Sitting thus in the comfortable drawing-room while she, like a good angel, diffuses her charm everywhere, over everyone with whom she comes in contact, over good and evil, I sometimes begin to grow inwardly impatient; I am tempted to rush out from my hiding-place; for though I sit there before everyone's eyes in the drawing-room, I am really sitting in ambush. I am tempted to grasp her hand, to take the whole girl in my arms, to hide her within me in case someone else should take her from me. Or when Edvard and I leave them in the evening, when in taking leave she offers me her hand, when I hold it in mine I find it difficult sometimes to let the bird slip out of my hand. Patience – *quod antea fuit impetus, nunc ratio est*[30] – she must be quite otherwise woven into my web, and then suddenly I let the whole power of love rush forth. We have not spoiled that moment for ourselves with kisses and cuddles, by premature anticipations, for which you can thank me, my Cordelia. I work at developing the contrast, I tense the bow of love to wound the deeper. Like an archer, I slacken the bowstring, tighten it again, listen to its song – it is my martial music – but I do not take aim with it yet, do not even lay the arrow on the string.

When a small number of people often come together in the same room, a kind of tradition soon develops in which each one has his own place, his station; it becomes a picture one can unfold at will, a chart of the terrain. That is also how we unite now to form a picture in the Wahl home. In the evening we drink tea there. Generally the aunt, who until now has been sitting on the sofa, moves over to the little work-table, which place Cordelia in turn vacates. She goes over to the tea-table in front of the sofa, Edvard follows her. I follow the aunt. Edvard tries to be secretive, he wants to whisper, and he usually succeeds so well as to become entirely mute. I make no secrets of my outpourings to the aunt – market prices, a calculation of how many quarts of milk are needed to produce a pound of butter, through the middle-term of cream and the dialectic of the butter-churn; not only do these things form a reality which any young girl can listen to without harm, but, what is far rarer, it is a solid, thorough and edifying conversation, equally improving for mind and heart. I generally sit with my back to the tea-table and the day-dreamings of Edvard and Cordelia. Meanwhile

I day-dream with the aunt. And is Nature not great and wise in her productions, is not butter a precious gift, what a glorious result of Nature and art! Certainly the aunt would be unable to hear what passed between Edvard and Cordelia, provided anything passed between them at all; I have promised Edvard that, and I always keep my word. On the other hand, I can easily overhear every word exchanged between them, hear every movement. This is important for me, for one cannot tell how far a desperate man will venture. The most cautious and faint-hearted men sometimes do the most desperate things. Although I thus have nothing at all to do with these two people, I can readily observe from Cordelia that I am constantly an invisible presence between her and Edvard.

Nevertheless it is a peculiar picture we four make. If I were to look for a familiar analogy, I might think of myself as Mephistopheles; but the difficulty is that Edvard is no Faust. If I were to be his Faust, there is the difficulty again that Edvard is no Mephistopheles. Neither am I a Mephistopheles, least of all in Edvard's eyes. He looks on me as his love's good genie, and so he should, for at least he can be sure that no one can watch over his love more solicitously than I. I have promised him to engage the aunt in conversation and I discharge that honourable assignment with all seriousness. The aunt practically vanishes before our own eyes in sheer agricultural economics; we go into the kitchen and cellar, up to the attic, look at the chickens, ducks, and geese, and so on. All this offends Cordelia. What I am really after she cannot of course conceive. I become a riddle to her, but not a riddle that tempts her into wanting to guess, one which irritates her, yes makes her indignant. She has a strong sense that her aunt is almost being made fun of, yet her aunt is a very respectable lady who certainly doesn't deserve that. On the other hand, I do it so well that she is perfectly aware that it would be useless for her to try to put me off. Sometimes I carry things so far that Cordelia secretly has to smile at her aunt. These are necessary exercises. Not that I do this with Cordelia's connivance; far from it, I would never make her smile at her aunt. My expression remains unalterably earnest, but she cannot keep from smiling. It is the first false teaching; we must teach her to smile ironically; but this smile is aimed almost as much at me as at the aunt, for she simply does not know what to think of me. After all, I might be one of those prematurely old young men; it's possible; there might be another possibility, and a third, and so on. When she has smiled at her aunt she is indignant with herself, I turn around and, without interrupting the conversation with the aunt, look at her quite seriously, then she smiles at me and the situation.

Our relationship is not the tender and loyal embrace of understanding, not attraction, it is the repulsion of misunderstanding. My relationship to her really amounts to nothing at all. It is purely spiritual, which of course to a young girl is nothing at all. The method I am now following has nevertheless extraordinary advantages. Someone who appears as a gallant arouses mistrust and evokes resistance; I am exempt from all that. I am not watched, on the contrary one would rather look upon me as a trustworthy person fit to watch over the young girl. The method has only one fault, it is slow; but for that reason it can be used, and only to advantage, against individuals in whom the prize is the interesting.

What rejuvenating power a young girl has! Not the freshness of the morning air, not the soughing of the wind, not the coolness of the ocean, not the fragrance of wine and its delicious bouquet — nothing else in the world has this rejuvenating power.

Soon I hope to have brought it to the point of her hating me. I have taken on totally the character of a bachelor. I talk of nothing else but sitting at ease, lying comfortably, having a reliable servant, a friend of good standing I can thoroughly trust when on intimate terms. If I can now get the aunt to abandon her agronomic deliberations I shall introduce her to these and so get a more direct opportunity for irony. A bachelor one may laugh at, indeed have some sympathy for, but a young man not without spirit outrages a young girl by such conduct; the significance of her sex, its beauty and poetry, are all destroyed.

So the days pass; I see her, but I do not talk with her. In her presence I talk with the aunt. Occasionally at night it occurs to me to give my love air. Then, wrapped in my cloak, with my hat

pulled down over my eyes, I go and stand outside her window. Her
bedroom looks out over the yard, but since the house is on a corner
it is visible from the street. Sometimes she stands for a moment at
the window, or she opens it, looks up at the stars, unobserved by all
but the one whom she would least of all think was aware of her. In
these night hours I steal about like a wraith, like a wraith I inhabit
the place where she lives. I forget everything, have no plans, no
calculations, throw reason overboard, expand and strengthen my
chest with deep sighs, an exercise I need in order not to suffer from
the system which rules my behaviour. Others are virtuous by day
and sin at night; by day I am dissimulation, at night pure desire. If
she saw me, if she could look into my soul. If!

If this girl would only understand herself, she would have to
admit that I am the man for her. She is too intense, too deeply
emotional to be happy in marriage, it would not be enough to let
her yield to a common seducer; if she yields to me she salvages the
interesting from the shipwreck. In relation to me, she must, as the
philosophers say with a play on words, *zu Grunde gehen*.[31]

Really, she is tired of listening to Edvard. As always happens,
where the interesting is narrowly confined, one discovers all the
more. Sometimes she listens to my conversation with the aunt.
When I see that, there comes a flash on the far horizon intimating a
quite different world, to the surprise of the aunt as well as Cordelia.
The aunt sees the lightning but hears nothing, Cordelia hears the
voice but sees nothing. The same instant everything is as it was
before, the conversation between the aunt and myself proceeds at its
uniform pace, like the hooves of post horses in the still of the night;
it is accompanied by the samovar's sad singing. At moments like
these the atmosphere in the drawing-room can sometimes be unpleasant, especially for Cordelia. She has no one she can talk with or
listen to. If she turns to Edvard, she faces the risk of him doing
something foolish in his embarrassment. If she turns the other way,
to her aunt and me, then the certainty prevailing here, the monotonous hammerblow of our steady conversation, forms the most disagreeable contrast. I can well understand that to Cordelia it must
seem that her aunt is bewitched, so completely does she keep in step

with my tempo. Nor can she take part in our entertainment; for this is also one of the ways I have used to provoke her, that is, by letting myself treat her altogether as a child. Not that I would permit myself any liberties with her on that account, far from it. I know too well what a disturbing effect such things can have, and it is especially important that her womanliness be able to rise up again pure and lovely. Owing to my intimate relation to the aunt, it is easy for me to treat her like a child who is no judge of the world. Her femininity is not offended by this but merely neutralized; for though it cannot offend her femininity that she knows nothing of market prices, it can irritate her that they should be the most important thing in life. With my powerful support, the aunt outbids herself in this direction. She has become almost fanatical, something she has to thank me for. The only thing about me which she cannot stand is that I am not anything. I have now begun the habit, every time something is said about a vacant position, of saying, 'That's a job for me!', and discussing it very seriously with her. Cordelia always notices the irony, which is exactly as I wish.

Poor Edvard! Too bad he isn't called Fritz. Whenever in my quiet thoughts I dwell on my relation to him, I am reminded of Fritz in *The Bride*.[32] Like his prototype, Edvard is also a corporal in the militia. To tell the truth, Edvard is also distinctly tiresome. He doesn't tackle the matter properly, and he is always too well-dressed and stiff. *Entre nous*, for the sake of our friendship I turn up as casually as possible. Poor Edvard! The only thing that pains me is that he is so infinitely obliged to me that he almost doesn't know how to thank me. To let myself be thanked for it, that's really too much.

But why can't you be good children and behave? What have you done all morning except shake my awning, pull at my window mirror and its string, play with the bell-rope from the third floor, push against the windowpanes, in brief, in every possible way proclaim your existence, as if you would beckon me out with you? Yes, the weather is fine, but I have no desire, let me stay at home

... After all, you boisterous, wanton zephyrs, you happy lads, you can go alone, amuse yourselves with the young maidens as usual. Yes, I know, no one can embrace a maiden as seductively as you; she tries in vain to squirm away from you, she cannot untwine herself from your tangle – and she doesn't want to; for, cool and refreshing, you do not inflame ... Go your own way, leave me out ... But then, you say, there's no satisfaction in it, it's not for your own sake ... very well, then, I'll come with you, but on two conditions. Here is the first. There lives on Kongens Nytorv a young maiden; she is very pretty, but she has the impudence not to want to love me, and what is worse, she loves another, and it has got to the point where they go out walking arm in arm. I know he goes to fetch her at one o'clock. Promise me now that the strongest blowers among you hide somewhere in the vicinity when he comes out of the street door with her. The moment he is about to turn down Store Kongensgade, this detachment rushes forward, in the politest possible manner takes his hat from his head, and carries it at an even speed just two feet in front of him, no faster, for then he might turn back home again. He thinks he is always just on the point of catching it, he doesn't even let go of her arm. In this way you bring them through Store Kongensgade, along the rampart to Nørreport, as far as Høibroplads ... How long will that take? I'd say about half an hour. At exactly half-past one I approach from Østergade. When the detachment has brought the lovers out into the middle of the Plads, a violent assault is made on them, in which you also whisk off her hat, tangle her curls, carry off her shawl, while all the time his hat floats jubilantly higher and higher into the air; in short, you bring about a confusion, so that not just I but the entire public breaks out into roars of laughter, the dogs begin to bark, and the watchman to toll his bell in the tower. You make her hat fly over to me, so I become the happy individual who restores it to her. – Secondly: the section following me must obey my every signal, keep within the bounds of propriety, offer no affront to any pretty maiden, take no liberty greater than will allow her to preserve her joy during the whole jest, her lips their smile, her eye its tranquillity, and to stay unanxious. If a single one of you dares behave otherwise, your name will be cursed. – And now off with you, to life and joy, to youth and beauty; show me what I have often seen, and never weary of seeing, show me a beautiful young woman, disclose her beauty for me in such a way that she herself becomes even more beautiful; put her to a test that she will enjoy being put to! – I choose Bredgade, but as you know, I have only until half-past one.

There comes a young girl, all smart and starched; today's Sunday, of course . . . Fan her a little, waft her with your coolness, glide in gentle currents about her, embrace her with your touch! I sense the delicate blushing of her cheek, her lips redden, her bosom lifts . . . It's indescribable, isn't it, my girl, it is a blissful delight to inhale these refreshing airs? The little collar bends to and fro and like a leaf. How deeply and soundly she breathes! Her pace slackens, she is almost carried off by the gentle breeze, like a cloud, like a dream . . . Blow a little stronger, in longer puffs! . . . She gathers herself together, the arms drawn closer to her bosom, which she covers more carefully lest a gust of wind prove too forward and steal softly and coolingly beneath the light covering . . . She assumes a more healthy colouring, her cheeks become fuller, her eye clearer, her steps firmer. All vexation makes a person more beautiful. Every young girl should fall in love with the zephyr, for no man knows so well how to enhance her beauty by struggling against her . . . Her body bends a little forward, she looks towards the tips of her toes . . . Stop a little! It is too much, her figure becomes broader, loses its pretty slenderness . . . Cool her a little! . . . It's refreshing, isn't it, my girl, after being warm to feel those invigorating shivers? One could fling open one's arms in gratitude, in joy over existence . . . She turns her side to the breeze . . . Now quick! a powerful gust, so that I can divine the beauty of her contours! . . . A little stronger! to let the draperies close about her more precisely . . . That's too much. Her posture becomes awkward, the light step is disturbed . . . She turns again . . . Blow, now, blow, try her! . . . Enough, too much! One of her curls has fallen . . . will you kindly keep control of yourselves! – Here comes a whole regiment on the march:

> *Die eine ist verliebt gar sehr;*
> *Die andre wäre er gerne.*[33]

Yes, it is an undeniably bad appointment in life to walk on one's future brother-in-law's left arm. For a girl this is about the same as a

man's being a reserve clerk ... But the clerk can get preferment
and has his place in the office, he is called in on exceptional occasions,
and that is not the sister-in-law's lot. But her preferment, on the
other hand, is not so slow — once she gets promoted and is moved
into another office ... Blow now a little more briskly! When one
has something firm to hold on fast to, one can offer resistance ...
the centre advances vigorously, the wings on either flank were
unable to follow ... He stands his ground firmly enough, the wind
can't move him, he is too heavy for that — but also too heavy for the
wings to be able to lift him from the ground. He thrust himself
forward in order to show — that he is a heavy body; but the more
unmoved he stands, the more the young girls suffer from it ... My
beautiful young ladies, may I not offer a piece of good advice: leave
the future husband and brother-in-law out of it, try to walk alone,
and you will see, you will find it much more satisfactory ... Blow
now a little more softly! ... How they riot in the wind's billows;
soon they will be cutting figures in front of each other down the
street — can any dance music produce a more frolicsome gaiety?
And yet the wind is not exhausting, it gives strength ... Now they
sweep along side by side, in full sail down the street — can any waltz
carry a young woman away more seductively? And yet the wind
does not weary, it supports ... Now they turn round to face the
husband and brother-in-law ... Isn't a little opposition pleasant?
One likes to struggle to gain possession of what one loves; and one
will no doubt succeed, for there is a Providence that comes to the
aid of love, that is why the man has the wind in his favour ...
Haven't I arranged it well? When you have the wind at your back
you can easily steer the loved one past you; but when it blows
against you, you are pleasantly excited, then you seek refuge near
him, and the wind's breath makes you more wholesome and more
tempting, and more seductive, and the wind's breath cools the fruit
of your lips which should preferably be enjoyed cold because it is so
hot, as champagne is said to be when kept near freezing ... How
they laugh and talk — and the wind carries off the words — is there
anything to talk about here now? — and they laugh again and bend
before the wind, and hold on to their hats, and watch their feet ...
Stop now, lest the young girls get impatient and angry at us, or
afraid of us! — That's it, resolutely and vigorously, the right foot in

front of the left ... How bravely and buoyantly she looks about in the world ... Do I see correctly? She is hanging on to a man's arm, so she's engaged. Show me, my child, what kind of present you have received on life's Christmas tree? ... Aha! really it seems to be a very solid fiancé. She's in the first stage of the engagement, then, she loves him — that's certainly possible, and yet her love flutters loosely about him, wide and spacious; she still has the cloak of love which can conceal many ... Blow a little more! ... Yes, when one walks so fast it is no wonder the ribbons on her hat stiffen in the wind, that it looks as if they bore this light body like wings — and her love — it follows too, like a fairy veil that the wind plays with. Yes, when you see love like this, it seems so spacious; but when you are about to put it on, when the veil must be resewn into an evening dress — then one won't be able to afford many puffs ... Lord preserve us! When one has had the courage to take a decisive step for one's entire life, surely one has the heart to walk straight into the wind. Who doubts it? Not I; but temper, temper, my little miss! Time is a hard taskmaster, and the wind is not bad either ... Tease her a little! ... What became of the handkerchief? ... Oh, so you did recover it again ... There went one of the hat ribbons ... it is really quite embarrassing for the intended who is present. A girl friend approaches who must be greeted. It is the first time she has seen you since the engagement; of course, showing that you are engaged is the reason you are here on Bredgade, and moreover are thinking of going on to Langelinie. I believe it is the custom for a newly wedded couple to go to Church the first Sunday after the wedding, but engaged couples, on the other hand, go to Langelinie. Yes, an engagement really also has much in common with Lange-linie ... Watch out now! The wind is taking hold of your hat, hold on to it a little, bend your head down ... What a real shame you got no chance at all to greet your girl friend, not enough calm to greet her with the superior air that an engaged girl ought to assume before the unengaged ... Blow a little more softly now! ... Now come the good days ... how she clings to the beloved; she is just far enough ahead to be able to turn her head back and look up at him, and rejoice in him, her riches, her happiness, her hope, her future ... Oh my girl, you make too much of him ... Or won't you allow that he owes it to me and the wind that he looks so

vigorous? And don't you yourself owe it to me, and to the soft
breezes that now bring you healing and turn pain into oblivion,
that you look so full of vitality, so full of longing, so expectant?

> And I will not have a student
> Who lies and reads at night,
> But I will have an officer
> With feathers in his hat.[34]

One can see it in you at once, my girl, there is something in your
look ... No, a student won't do for you ... But why exactly an
officer? A graduate, finished with his studies, couldn't he do just as
well? ... Just now, however, I cannot help you to either an officer
or a graduate. But I can help you to some cooling breezes ... Blow
a little harder now! ... That's right, throw the silk shawl back over
your shoulder; walk quite slowly, that should make your cheek a
little paler and the eye's lustre more subdued ... That's it. Yes, a
little exercise, especially on a fine day like this, and a little patience,
then no doubt you will get your officer. – There's a couple over
there who are meant for each other. How measured their steps,
what poise their whole appearance presents, built on mutual confidence, what pre-established harmony in all their movements, what
assured solidity. Their carriage is not light and graceful, they do not
dance with each other, no, there is a durability in them, a forthright-
ness, which arouses infallible hope and inspires mutual respect. I will
wager that their view of life is 'Life is a road'. And they also seem
bent on walking with each other arm in arm through life's joys and
sorrows. They are so much in harmony that the lady has even given
up the privilege of walking on the flagstones ... But, my dear
zephyrs, why are you so busy with that couple? They don't seem
worth paying attention to. Is there anything special to take note of?
... But it is half-past one; off to Høibroplads.

One would not think it possible to calculate so accurately a soul's
historical development. It shows how healthy Cordelia is. Truly,
she is a remarkable girl. Although she is quiet and modest, unde-
manding, there is an immense demand lying there unconsciously. –

It was obvious to me today when I saw her coming in from the street. It's as though the slight resistance a gust of wind can offer arouses all her powers but without there being any internal conflict. She is not a little insignificant girl who slips between your fingers, so fragile that you are almost afraid she will go to pieces just by looking at her; but neither is she a showy ornamental flower. Like a physician I can therefore observe with pleasure all the symptoms in this case history.

Gradually I am beginning to close in on her in my attack, to go over into a more direct assault. If I were to describe this change on my military map of the family, I would say that I have turned my chair round so that now I am facing her. I have more to do with her, address remarks to her, elicit answers from her. Her soul has passion, intensity, and though not overblown in absurd and vain reflections, it has a hankering for the unusual. My irony at the foolishness of human beings, my scorn of their cowardice, of their lukewarm indolence, fascinate her. She is fond enough of driving the chariot of the sun across the arch of the heavens, of coming too near to the earth and scorching people a bit.[35] She does not trust me, however. Up to now I have obstructed every approach, even in spiritual respects. She must become stronger in herself before I can let her find her repose in me. It may look in flashes as though it were her I would make the confidante in my freemasonry, but it is only in flashes. She herself must be developed inwardly; she must feel her soul's resilience, she must test the world's weight. From her conversation and her eyes I can easily see what progress she is making. Just once I have seen a destructive anger in them. She must owe me nothing, for she must be free; love exists only in freedom, only in freedom are there recreation and everlasting amusement. For although I intend her to fall into my arms through, as it were, natural necessity, and am striving to bring things to the point where she gravitates towards me, it is nevertheless also important that she does not fall as a heavy body, but gravitates as spirit towards spirit. Although she is to belong to me, it mustn't be just in the unaesthetic sense of resting on me like a burden. She must neither be a hanger-on physically speaking nor an obligation morally. Between the two of us must prevail only the proper play of freedom. She must be so light for me that I can take her on my arm.

Cordelia occupies me almost too much. I am losing my equanimity again, not directly in her presence but when alone with her in the strictest sense. I can yearn for her, not to talk with her but just to have her image float by me. When I know she has gone out I can steal after her, not to be seen but to see. The other evening we all left the Baxter house together. Edvard escorted her. In the greatest haste I left them, hurried off to another street where my servant was waiting for me. In a trice I had changed clothes and met her once more without her suspecting. Edvard was silent as usual. Certainly I am in love, but not in the usual sense, and therefore one must also be very careful; there are always dangerous consequences; and after all one is in love only once. Nevertheless, the god of love is blind and if one is clever one can delude him. The trick is to be as receptive in regard to impressions as possible, to know the impression you are making and the impression each girl makes on you. In this way you can even be in love with many at the same time, because with each particular girl you are differently in love. Loving just one is too little; loving all is being superficial; knowing yourself and loving as many as possible, letting your soul hide all the powers of love in itself, so that each gets its particular nourishment while consciousness nevertheless embraces it all – that is enjoyment, that is living.

July 3rd

Edvard cannot really complain of me. Certainly, I want Cordelia to burn her fingers on him, so that through him she gets a distaste for run-of-the-mill love and in that way goes beyond her own limitations; but for that very reason it is necessary for Edvard not to be a caricature, for that would not help. Now Edvard is a good match, not just in the bourgeois sense of the word, which means nothing in her eyes (things like that do not cross a seventeen-year-old girl's mind), he has a number of attractive personal qualities which I try to get him to show to best advantage. Like a costumier, like a decorator, I fit him out as well as the house's resources stretch. Indeed, I sometimes hang a little borrowed finery on him. Then when we accompany each other to Cordelia's it is quite strange walking beside him. It is as though he were my brother, my son, and yet he is my friend, my contemporary, my rival. He could ever become a danger to me. So, since he is bound to fall, the higher I can raise him the better; the more consciousness it awakens in Cordelia of what she scorns, the more intense her presentiment of what she desires. I help him to adjust, I commend him, in short I do everything a friend can do for a friend. To set my coldness properly in relief, I behave almost as though I were Edvard's ardent admirer. I portray him as a visionary. Since Edvard has no idea of how to help himself, I have to haul him forward.

Cordelia hates and fears me. What does a young girl fear? Spirit. Why? Because spirit constitutes the negation of her whole feminine existence. Masculine good looks, a charming personality, etc. are good expedients, one can also make conquests with them, but never win a complete victory. Why? Because then one is making war upon a girl on her own ground, and there she is always the stronger. With these methods one can make a girl blush, put her out of countenance, but never call forth that indescribable, captivating anxiety which makes her beauty interesting.

> *Non formosus erat, sed erat facundus Ulixes,*
> *et tamen aequoreas torsit amore Deas.*[36]

Everyone should know his own powers. But something that has often disturbed me is that even those who have natural endowments bungle things so. Really one ought to be able straightaway to see in any young girl who has become the victim of another's, or rather of her own love, in what way she has been deceived. The practised murderer uses a definite stab, and the experienced policeman knows the perpetrator as soon as he sees the wound. But where does one meet such systematic seducers, such psychologists? For most men, seducing a girl means seducing a girl, full stop. And yet there is a whole language concealed in this thought.

As a woman she hates me; as a gifted woman she fears me; as a woman of intelligence she loves me. Now for the first time I have produced this conflict in her soul. My pride, my defiance, my cold scorn, my heartless irony tempt her; not as though she might wish to love me – no, there is certainly no trace of such feelings in her, least of all towards me. She wants to compete with me. What tempts her is the proud independence of people, a freedom like that of the Arabs in the desert. My laughter and oddity neutralize every erotic impulse. She is fairly at ease with me, and so far as there is any reserve, it is more intellectual than feminine. Far from her regarding me as a lover, our relation to each other is that of two able minds. She takes my hand, presses it a little, laughs, is attentive to me in a purely Platonic sense. Then when the ironist and the scoffer have fooled her long enough, I shall follow the directions to be found in an old verse: 'The knight spreads out his cape so red, and begs the beautiful maiden to sit thereon.' However, I do not spread out my cape in order to sit with her on the greensward, but to vanish with her into the air on the wings of thought. Or I do not take her with me but set myself astride a thought, wave farewell, blow a kiss, and vanish from her sight, audible only in the murmur of winged words; not, like Jehovah,[37] in his voice more and more visible, but less and less, because the more I speak, the higher I climb. Then she wants to go with me, off on the wings of bold thoughts. Still, that's only for a single moment; the next instant I am cold and impassive.

There are different kinds of feminine blushes. There is the gross brick-red blush; that's the one romantic writers are always so free with when they have their heroines blush all over. There is the refined blush; it is the blush of the dawn's early light. In a young girl it is above all price. The fleeting blush produced by a happy idea is beautiful in the man, more beautiful in a youth, lovely in a woman. It is a flash of lightning, the sheet lightning of the spirit. It is most beautiful in the young, charming in the girl, because it appears in its virginal state, and for that reason has the bashfulness of surprise. The older one becomes, the less frequently this blush appears.

Sometimes I read something aloud to Cordelia; usually something very inconsequential. Edvard must as usual keep the spotlight. So I have drawn his attention to the fact that a very good way of getting on good terms with a young girl is to lend her books. He has also gained considerably through this, for she is directly beholden to him. It is I who gain most, for I dictate the choice of books and remain remote. This gives me broad scope for my observations. I can give Edvard whatever books I wish, since he is no judge of literature; I can risk what I will, to whatever extreme. Then when I visit her in the evening, I make as if to pick up a book by chance, turn over a few pages, read half-aloud, commend Edvard for his attentiveness. Yesterday evening I wanted to assure myself of her mental resilience by an experiment. I was undecided whether to have Edvard lend her Schiller's poems, so that I could accidentally chance on Thekla's song[38] which I'd then recite, or Bürger's poems. I chose the latter particularly because his 'Lenore', however beautiful, is after all somewhat extravagant. I opened it at 'Lenore', read this poem aloud with all the pathos I could muster. Cordelia was moved, she sewed with a rapid intensity as though it were her Vilhelm had come to fetch.[39] I stopped. The aunt had listened without particular concern. She fears no Vilhelms, living or dead – in any case her German is not all that good – but found herself quite in her element when I showed her the beautifully bound copy and began a conversation about the art of bookbinding. My purpose was to destroy in Cordelia the impression of pathos at the very moment of its arousal. She became a little anxious, but it was clear to me that this anxiety had an uncomfortable effect on her, not a stimulating one.

Today my eyes have rested upon her for the first time. It is said that sleep can make an eyelid so heavy that it closes of its own accord; perhaps this glance of mine has a similar effect. Her eyes close, and yet obscure forces stir within her. She does not see that I am looking at her, she feels it, feels it through her whole body. Her eyes close and it is night, but inside her it is broad daylight.

Edvard must go. He is treading on the boundary. Any moment I can expect him to go to her and make a declaration of love. No one can know that better than I who am his confidant, and who diligently maintains this exaltation so that his effect upon Cordelia can be the greater. To let him confess his love is nevertheless too risky. Although I know quite well she will refuse him, that will not be the end of the affair. He will no doubt take it very much to heart. That might move and touch Cordelia. Although in that event I need not fear the worst, that she should change her mind, still, possibly her self-esteem might suffer through this pure compassion. Should that happen, my plans concerning Edvard are altogether wasted.

My relation to Cordelia is beginning to take a dramatic turn. Something must happen, whatever it may be; I can no longer remain a mere observer without letting the moment slip from me. She has to be surprised, that is necessary; but to surprise her one must be on the alert. What would normally cause surprise might have no effect on her. Really she has to be surprised in such a way that the initial cause of the surprise is, to all intents and purposes, that something quite ordinary happens. It has to appear gradually that there was something surprising in it after all. This is always the law of the interesting, and the latter the law in turn governing all my movements with regard to Cordelia. If only you know how to surprise someone, you have always won the game; for a moment you suspend the energy of the one concerned, make it impossible for her to act, and it makes no difference whether one resorts to the ordinary or the extraordinary. I recall with some satisfaction a foolhardy experiment upon a lady of distinguished family. For some time I had been sneaking around her secretly looking for an interesting form of contact, but in vain; then one day I met her on the street. I was certain she didn't know me or know I belonged here in town. She was walking alone. I slipped past her so that I could meet her face to face. I stepped aside for her; she kept to the flagstones. Just then I cast a sorrowful glance at her, I think I almost had tears in my eyes. I took off my hat. She paused. In an agitated voice and with a dreamy look, I said, 'Do not be angry, gracious lady; the resemblance between you and someone I love with all my soul, but who lives far away from me, is so striking that you must forgive my strange behaviour.' She thought me an extravagant dreamer, and a young girl can well put up with a little extravagance, especially when she also feels her superiority and dares to smile at one. Just so, she smiled, which became her indescribably. With aristocratic condescension she bowed to me, and smiled. She resumed her walk. I walked a few steps by her side. Some days later I met her; I presumed to greet her. She laughed at me . . . Patience is a precious virtue, and he who laughs last laughs best.

One could think of several ways of surprising Cordelia. I might try to raise an erotic storm which was capable of tearing up trees by the roots. With its help I could see if I could sweep her off her feet, snatch her from her historic setting, and try in this agitation, by stealthy advances, to arouse her passion. It is not inconceivable that it could be done. A girl with her passion can be made to do anything at all. However, it would be wrong aesthetically. I am not fond of giddiness, and the condition is to be recommended only with girls for whom this is the only way of acquiring a poetic image. Besides, one misses the real enjoyment, for too much confusion is also harmful. On her it will altogether fail of its effect. I might imbibe in a couple of draughts what I could have had the benefit of over a lengthy period, indeed, even worse, what with discretion I might have enjoyed in a way that was fuller and richer. Cordelia is not to be enjoyed in a state of exaltation. It might surprise her in the first instance were I to behave in this way, but she would soon have had enough, precisely because this surprise lay too near her daring soul.

A straightforward engagement is the best of all methods, the most expedient. If she heard me making a prosaic declaration of love, likewise asking her for her hand, she might believe her ears even less than if she listened to my heated eloquence, imbibed my poisoned intoxicant, heard her heart throb at the thought of an abduction.

The damnable thing with an engagement is always the ethical side. The ethical is just as boring in life as it is in learning. What a difference! Beneath the sky of the aesthetic everything is light, pleasant and fleeting; when ethics come along everything becomes hard, angular, an unending ennui. Still, strictly, an engagement has no ethical reality in the way marriage does; its validity is only *consensu gentium*.[40] This ambiguity can be very useful to me. The ethical element in it is just enough for Cordelia at some time to get the impression that she is breaking normal barriers, but not so serious that I will have to fear more critical repercussions. I have always had some respect for the ethical. I have never promised a girl marriage, not even casually; if I seem to be doing so here, it is only a pretence. I shall certainly contrive for her to be the one who breaks off the engagement. My chivalrous pride scorns giving promises. I despise a judge who tricks an offender into a confession with the promise of freedom. A judge like that renounces his own power and ability. Besides, there is the fact that I want nothing in my own practice that is not given freely, in the strictest sense. Let common seducers use such methods! What do they achieve? Anyone unable so to encompass a girl that she loses sight of everything he doesn't want her to see, so to poeticize his way into the girl that it is from her that everything issues, just as he himself would wish it, is and will always be a bungler. I will not envy him his pleasure. A bungler is what such a person is and remains, a seducer, which no one could by any means call me. I am an aesthete, an eroticist, who has grasped the nature and meaning of love, who believes in love and knows it from the ground up. I only reserve to myself the private opinion that no love affair should last more than six months at most, and that every relationship is over as soon as one has tasted the final enjoyment. All this I know; I also know that the highest form of enjoyment conceivable is to be loved, loved more than everything in the world. To poeticize oneself into a girl is an art, to poeticize oneself out of her a masterpiece. Yet the latter depends essentially on the former.

Another method is possible. I could do everything to get her engaged to Edvard. I would become a friend of the family. Edvard would trust me implicitly – after all, I am the one to whom he as good as owes his happiness. In this way I would be better concealed. No, it won't do. She cannot become engaged to Edvard without belittling herself in one way or another. Also, my relationship to her would become more piquant than interesting. The endless prosaicness of an engagement is precisely the sounding-board of the interesting.

Everything is taking on more meaning in the Wahl household. One clearly notes that a hidden life is stirring beneath the daily routine, which must soon proclaim itself in a corresponding revelation. The Wahl household is preparing for an engagement. A mere outside observer might suppose there was to be a match between me and the aunt. What an expansion of agronomic knowledge might such a marriage achieve in a coming generation! I would then become Cordelia's uncle. I am a friend of freedom of thought and no thought is so absurd that I lack courage to grasp hold of it. Cordelia fears a declaration of love from Edvard, Edvard hopes it will decide everything. He may be sure of that. But to spare him the unpleasant consequences of such a step, I shall try to steal a march on him. I am hoping now to be rid of him soon; he really is in my way. I felt it clearly today. Doesn't he look so dreamy and love-drunk that he might suddenly get up, like a somnambulist, and in front of the whole congregation confess his love in such objective terms that he doesn't even approach Cordelia? I looked daggers at him today. I caught Edvard with my eyes, big as he is, as an elephant catches something with its trunk, and threw him over backwards. Although he remained seated in his chair I believe he felt something of the sort in his body.

Cordelia is not showing the same confidence towards me. She always approached me with womanly assurance, now she is a little hesitant. But it is of no great matter and it wouldn't be too difficult for me to bring things back to the old footing. But I won't do that. Just one more exploration and then the engagement. There can be no difficulties there; in her surprise Cordelia will say yes, the aunt a hearty Amen, she will be beside herself with joy over such an agronomic son-in-law. Son-in-law! How everything gets stuck together like pea-straw once one ventures into this area! I don't really become her son-in-law, only her nephew, or rather, God willing, neither.

the 23rd

Today I harvested the fruit of a rumour I had spread, that I was in love with a young girl. With Edvard's help it has also reached the ears of Cordelia. She is curious, she watches me, but she doesn't dare ask; yet it is not unimportant to her to be certain, partly because she finds it unbelievable, partly because she might well see a precedent in this for herself; for if such a cold-blooded scoffer as myself could fall in love, there need be no disgrace in her doing the same. Today I brought up the subject. To tell a story in a way that the point doesn't get lost, I think I'm the man for that, likewise telling it in such a way that the point doesn't emerge too soon.

Holding the listeners in suspense, ascertaining through their small incidental movements what they want the outcome to be, putting them off the track in the course of the narration, that's what I like doing; using ambiguities, so the listeners understand one thing by what is being said and then suddenly notice that the words can be understood in another way, that's my *métier*. If what one wants is an opportunity for making certain observations, one should always make a speech. In conversation it is easier for the other party to escape, using questions and answers to hide the impression one's words are producing. In solemn earnest I began my speech to the aunt. 'Am I to impute this to the good-will of my friends or the malice of my enemies, and who hasn't more than enough of both?' Here the aunt made a remark which I helped her to spin out as well as I could so as to keep Cordelia, who was listening, in suspense, a suspense she could not put an end to, since it was the aunt I was talking to and my mood was serious. I continued: 'Or am I to ascribe it to an accident, a rumour's *generatio aequivoca*'[41] (a word Cordelia evidently did not understand – it only confused her, the more so because I put a false emphasis on it and said it with a sly look as if that's where the point lay), 'that I who am used to living a secluded life have become a talking-point by their insisting I am engaged.' Cordelia quite clearly still felt the need of my interpretation. I continued: 'My friends, since it must be considered a piece of good fortune to fall in love' (she started), 'my enemies, since it would be thought quite laughable for this fortune to fall to my lot' (movement in the opposite direction); 'or accident, since there is not the slightest foundation for it; or rumour's *generatio aequivoca*, since the whole thing must have originated in an empty head's thoughtless self-communings.' The aunt with true feminine curiosity lost no time trying to find out who this lady might be with whom it had pleased gossip to betroth me. Every question in this direction was waved aside. On Cordelia the whole story made quite an impression; I rather think Edvard's stock rose a few points.

The decisive moment is nearing. I could address myself to the aunt, asking in writing for Cordelia's hand. This is indeed the customary procedure in affairs of the heart, as if it were more natural for the heart to write than to speak. But it is precisely its philistinism that would decide me to choose it. By doing so I would miss the real surprise, and that I cannot give up. – If I had a friend he might say to me, 'Have you properly considered the very serious step you are taking, a step that is decisive for all the rest of your life, and for another being's happiness?' That's the advantage of having a friend. But I have none. Whether that is an advantage I leave undecided; on the other hand I see it as an absolute advantage to be free of his advice. Otherwise, in the strictest sense of the word, I have certainly thought the whole matter through.

Now there is nothing on my side to prevent the engagement. I proceed accordingly with my courting, though who could see it in me? Soon my humble person will be seen from a higher standpoint. I cease being a person and become – a match; yes, a good match, the aunt will say. It is the aunt I feel most sorry for, for she loves me with so pure and upright an agronomic love, she practically worships me as her ideal.

Now, I have made many declarations of love during my life, yet all my experience is of no help at all here, for this declaration has to be made in a quite special way. What I must mainly bring home to myself is that it is all just a pretence. I have rehearsed several steps to find out which approach would be the best. Making the moment erotic would be dubious, for it might well anticipate what is to come later and ought to develop gradually. Making it very serious is dangerous, for a moment like this is of such great significance for a girl that all her soul may be focused on it, like a dying man's on his last will. Making it easy-going, slapstick, would not be in harmony with the disguise I have used up to now, nor with the new one I plan to construct and adopt. Making it witty and ironical is too risky. If my purpose were the same here as with people in general on such occasions, where the main thing is to coax out the little 'yes', it would be as easy as pie. This is indeed important for me but not absolutely, for although I have now picked out this girl, although I have devoted much attention, indeed all my interest, to her, there are still conditions on which I will not accept her 'yes'. I am not at all interested in possessing the girl in an external sense, but in enjoying her artistically. So the beginning must be as artistic as possible. The beginning must be as vague as possible, an omnipossibility. If she straightaway sees a deceiver in me she misunderstands me, for in an ordinary sense I am no deceiver. If she sees in me a faithful lover she also misunderstands me. The thing is that in this scene her soul must be as little predetermined as possible. In a moment like this a girl's soul is as prophetic as a dying man's.[42] This must be prevented. My lovely Cordelia! I am cheating you out of something beautiful, but it cannot be otherwise, and I shall compensate you as best I can. The whole episode must be kept as inconsequential as possible, so that when she has given her 'yes', she is unable to throw the least light on what may be concealed in this relationship. This infinite possibility is precisely the interesting. If she can predict anything, then I have gone wrong and the whole relationship loses its meaning. It is unthinkable that she should say 'yes' because she loves me, for she does not love me at all. The best thing for me to do is transform the engagement from an action into an event, from something she does into something that happens to her, of which she can say, 'God knows how it really came about.'

the 31st

Today I have written a love-letter for a third party. This is a constant source of pleasure. In the first place, it is always extremely interesting to enter so vividly into the situation, yet in all possible comfort. I have my pipe filled, hear about the relationship, the letters from the parties in question are produced. It is a matter of constant interest to me how a young girl writes. The man sits there now, infatuated as a rat, reading her letters aloud and interrupted by my laconic remarks: she writes well, she has feeling, taste, caution, she has certainly been in love before, etc. Secondly, it is a good deed. I am helping to bring a young couple together. For every happy couple, I select one victim for myself. I make two people happy, just one unhappy at most. I am honest and reliable, and have never deceived anyone who has confided in me. There is always a little fun among the leavings, after all that's just legal fees. And why do I enjoy this trust? Because I know Latin and attend to my studies, and because I always keep my little affairs to myself. And don't I deserve this confidence? After all, I never abuse it.

August 2nd

The moment had arrived. I caught a glimpse of the aunt on the street, so I knew she was not at home. Edvard was at the tolbooth. Accordingly there was every likelihood that Cordelia was at home alone. And so it proved. She sat at the work-table busy with a piece of sewing. Very rarely have I visited the family before dinner, so she was a little disturbed at seeing me. The situation came close to becoming too emotional. She wouldn't have been to blame for that, for she controlled herself quite easily, but I myself; for in spite of my armour she made an unusually strong impression upon me. How charming she was in a blue-striped, simple calico house-dress, with a fresh-plucked rose on her bosom – a fresh-plucked rose! no, the girl herself was like a freshly plucked flower, so fresh she was, newly arrived; and who knows where a young girl spends the night? In the land of illusions, I believe, but every morning she returns, hence her youthful freshness. She looked so young and yet full-grown, as if Nature, like a tender and copious mother, had just at that moment let her out of her hand. It was almost as though I were witness to that farewell scene; I saw how that loving mother embraced her once more in farewell, I heard her say, 'Go out now into the world, my child, I have done everything I can for you; take this kiss as a seal on your lips, it is a seal that guards the sanctuary; no one can break it unless you yourself wish it so, but when the right one comes, you will know him.' And she pressed a kiss on her lips, a kiss which did not, as a human kiss, take something but was like a divine kiss that gives everything, that gives the girl the power of the kiss. Marvellous Nature, how profound and mysterious you are! You give to the man the word, and to the girl you give the eloquence of the kiss! This kiss was upon her lips, and the farewell blessing on her forehead, and the joyous salutation in her eyes; therefore she looked at once so much at home, for she was after all the child of the house, but at the same time so much a stranger, for she did not know the world but only her fond mother who watched invisibly over her. She was really delightful, young as a child and yet adorned with that noble maidenly dignity that inspires respect. – However, I was quickly dispassionate again and solemnly unemotional, as is fitting when one wants to make something significant occur in a way that makes it seem of no consequence. After some

general remarks, I moved a little nearer to her, and then got on
with my proposal. A person who speaks like a book is exceedingly
boring to listen to; sometimes, however, it is not inappropriate to
talk in that way. For a book has the remarkable property that it can
be interpreted any way you wish. If one talks like a book one's
conversation acquires this property too. I kept quite soberly to the
usual formulas. She was surprised, as I'd expected; that can't be
denied. To describe to myself how she looked is difficult. She
seemed multifaceted; yes just about like the still to be published but
announced commentary to my book, a commentary capable of any
interpretation. One word and she would have laughed at me; another and she would have been moved; still another and she would
have shunned me; but no such word came to my lips. I remained
solemnly unemotional and kept to the ritual. – 'She had known me
for such a short time', dear God, it's only on the strait path of
engagement one meets such difficulties, not on the primrose path of
love.

Strangely enough, when pondering the matter the previous days,
I was rather hasty and quite sure that in the moment of surprise she
would say yes. One sees what all the preparation was good for, for
that's not how things turned out; she said neither yes nor no but
referred me to the aunt. I should have foreseen that. But really I
have luck on my side all the same, for this was an even better
outcome.

The aunt gives her consent. And I hadn't entertained the slightest
doubt about that either. Cordelia follows her advice. As for my
engagement, I do not brag that it is poetic, it is extremely philistine
and petty bourgeois in every way. The girl does not know whether
she should say yes or no, the aunt says yes, the girl too says yes, I
take the girl, she takes me – and now the story begins.

the 3rd

So I'm engaged; so is Cordelia, and I suppose that's just about all
she knows of the matter. If she had a friend she could speak frankly
with, she'd no doubt say, 'What it all means I've really no idea.
Something about him attracts me, but what it is I can't make out;

he has a strange power over me; but love him, no, I don't, and perhaps never will; on the other hand I should certainly be able to endure living with him and can therefore be very happy with him, for surely he doesn't ask too much if only one puts up with him.' My dear Cordelia! perhaps he demands more, and in return less endurance. – Of all ridiculous things, engagement must be the most ridiculous of all. In marriage there's at least meaning, even though that meaning doesn't suit me. An engagement is a purely human invention and reflects no credit at all on its inventor. It is neither one thing nor the other, and has as much to do with love as the strip hanging down the beadle's back has with a professor's gown. I am now a member of this honourable company. That is not without significance, for, as Trop says, it is only by being an artist that one acquires the right to judge other artists. And is not a fiancé also a Dyrehaug's artist?[43]

Edvard is beside himself with indignation. He is letting his beard grow and has hung up his dark suit, which says a lot. He wants to speak with Cordelia, wants to describe my deviousness to her. That will be a scandalous scene, Edvard unshaven, negligently dressed, shouting at Cordelia. So long as he doesn't cut me out with his long beard. I try in vain to bring him to reason; I explain that it is the aunt who has brought about the match, that maybe Cordelia still harbours feelings for him, that I shall be willing to withdraw if he can win her. He hesitates a moment, wonders whether he shouldn't let his beard jut out in some new fashion, buy a new dark suit; the next moment he is abusing me. I do everything to keep up appearances with him. However angry he is with me, I am certain he will take no step without consulting me; he doesn't forget the advantages of having me as mentor. And why should I take from him his last hope, why break with him? He is a good man; who knows what the future may bring?

What I must do now is, on the one hand, prepare everything for the breaking-off of the engagement, so as to ensure a more beautiful and more significant relationship with Cordelia; and on the other, make use of the time as well as I can to delight in all the lovableness that Nature has so abundantly equipped her with, delight in it, though within the limits and with the circumspection that prevents any anticipation. Then when I have brought it to the point of her learning what it is to love, and to love me, the engagement breaks like an imperfect mould and she is mine. Others get engaged when they reach this point, and have good prospects of a boring marriage for all eternity. That's their business.

Everything is still *status quo*. But a fiancé could scarcely be more fortunate than I, no miser who has found a gold piece could be more blissful. I am intoxicated with the thought that she is in my power. A pure, innocent femininity, as translucent yet as profound as the ocean, with no suspicion what love is! Now she will learn what kind of power love is. Like a king's daughter who is raised from the dust to the throne of her forefathers, she shall now be installed in the kingdom that is her own. And it is through me it will happen; she learns to love me in learning to love; in extending her rule, the paradigm gradually increases, and that is me. In feeling her whole significance to lie in love, she expends that significance upon me, she loves me doubly. The thought of my joy is so overwhelming that I almost take leave of my senses.

Her soul is not dissipated or slackened with love's indeterminate stirrings, something that prevents many girls from ever learning to love categorically, energetically, totally. They have in their consciousness an indefinite, hazy picture that is meant to be the ideal against which the actual object is to be tested. From such half-measures emerges something which can help one along one's Christian way through the world. – As love now awakens in her soul, I look through it, heed it as it emerges from her with all love's voices. I ascertain what shape it has taken in her and myself conform to it; and as I am already an immediate part of the story, the love that courses through her heart, so I come to meet her once more, from outside, as deceptively as possible. After all, a girl loves only once.

I am now in lawful possession of Cordelia, I have the aunt's consent and blessing, the congratulations of friends and relations. That should do it. Now all the hardships of war are over, the blessings of peace begin. What tomfoolery! As if the aunt's blessing and the friends' congratulations could in any real sense put me in possession of Cordelia; as if love made such a contrast between wartime and peace, and did not, as long as it lasts, proclaim itself rather in conflict, however different the weapons. The difference is really whether it is fought *cominus* or *eminus*.[44] The more the conflict in a love affair has been *eminus*, the more it is to be deplored, for in that case the less significant the hand-to-hand combat. To the latter belong the handclasp and the touching of the foot, both of which, as we know, were as warmly recommended by Ovid as most jealously disparaged, to say nothing of a kiss, an embrace.[45] Someone fighting *eminus* has usually only his eye to rely on, yet if he is an artist he will be able to employ this weapon with such virtuosity that he accomplishes almost the same. He will be able to let his eye rest upon a girl with a desultory tenderness that affects her in the same way as if he had accidentally touched her; he will be able to hold her as firmly with his eye as if he held her in his embrace. It is always a mistake, however, or a misfortune, to fight *eminus* for too long, for a fight of that kind is not the enjoyment itself, always just an indication. It is only when one fights *cominus* that everything assumes its true importance. When love stops fighting it has come to an end. I have as good as not fought *eminus* at all, and am now therefore not at the end but the beginning; I am bringing out my weapons. True, I do possess her in a legal and petty bourgeois sense, but to me that means nothing at all; I have far purer ideas. True, she is indeed engaged to me, but to infer from this that she loved me would be a deception, for she isn't in love at all. I have lawful possession of her, yet I do not possess her as I might very well possess a girl without having lawful possession.

Auf heimlich erröthender Wange
Leuchtet des Herzens Glühen.[46]

She is sitting on the sofa by the tea-table, I in a chair by her side. This positioning has confidentiality but also an exclusiveness that makes for distance. So very much always depends on the positions; that is, for one who has an eye for it. Love has many positionings; this is the first. How royally Nature has endowed this girl, her pure soft contours, her deep feminine innocence, her clear eyes – everything intoxicates me. – I have paid her my respects. She came towards me cheerfully as usual, though a little embarrassed, a little uncertain; the engagement ought after all to change our relationship, but she doesn't know how. She took my hand, but not with the usual smile. I returned the greeting with a slight, almost imperceptible pressure on the hand; I was gentle and friendly though without being amorous. – She is sitting on the sofa by the tea-table, I in a chair by her side. A beautifying solemnity suffuses the situation, a soft morning radiance. She is silent; nothing disturbs the stillness. My eye glides softly over her, not with desire, that indeed would be shameless. A delicate, momentary blush fleets over her, like a cloud over a meadow, rising and receding. What does this blush mean? Is it love? Is it longing, hope, fear? Because the heart's colour is red? Not at all. She is surprised, she marvels – not at me, that would be too little to offer her; she marvels not at herself but inside herself, she is transformed within. This moment demands stillness, so no reflection must disturb it, no noise of passion interrupt it. It is as though I were not present, and yet my presence is precisely what furnishes the condition for this contemplative wonder of hers. My being is in harmony with hers. In a condition like this, a young girl is to be worshipped and adored, like some deities, in silence.

It is fortunate that I have my uncle's house. If I wanted to give a young man a distaste for tobacco, I would take him to one or other smoking-room at the Regent's.[47] If I want to give a young girl a distaste for being engaged, I need only introduce her here. Just as in the tailors' guildhall one looks only for tailors, so one looks here only for engaged couples. It is a frightful company to fall into and I cannot blame Cordelia for becoming impatient. When we are assembled *en masse* I think we can muster ten couples, besides the supplementary battalions that come to the capital on big festive occasions. Then we betrothed could really enjoy the pleasures of betrothal. I meet with Cordelia at the alarm-post to give her a distaste for these infatuated clinches, these journeyman's bunglings. All evening one constantly hears a sound as of someone going round with a fly-swatter – it is the kiss of the lovers. There is an amiable lack of constraint in this house, one doesn't seek out the dark corners; no! one sits around a big round table. I make as if to submit Cordelia to the same treatment. For that I have to do violence to myself.

It would be really outrageous to let myself insult her profound femininity in that manner. I would reproach myself for this more than for deceiving her. In general, I can guarantee a perfect treatment, aesthetically, of any girl who puts her trust in me: except that it ends in her being deceived; but that is consistent with my aesthetics, for either the girl deceives the man or the man deceives the girl. It would be quite interesting if one could get some literary hack to find out in fairy stories, sagas, ballads and mythologies whether a girl is more frequently unfaithful than a man.

I do not regret the time that Cordelia costs me, although it is considerable. Every meeting requires, often, long preparation. With her I am witnessing the birth of her love. I am myself as though present invisibly when sitting visibly by her side. As when a dance which should really be danced by two is only danced by one, that's how my relation is to her. For I am the other dancer, but invisible. She moves as though in a dream, yet she is dancing with another, and this other, it is I who inasmuch as I am visibly present am yet invisible, inasmuch as I am invisibly present am yet visible. The movements require another person: she bows to him, she gives him her hand, she draws back, she draws near him again. I take her hand, I complete her thought, which is nevertheless complete in itself. She moves in the melody of her own soul, I am only the occasion for her moving. I am not amorous, that would only awaken her; I am flexible, yielding, impersonal, almost like a mood.

What as a rule do engaged couples talk about? As far as I know, they are busily occupied in getting themselves mutually enmeshed in the tiresome connections of the respective families. No wonder the erotic disappears. Unless one can make the erotic the absolute in comparison with which all other history vanishes, one should never get mixed up with loving, even if one marries ten times. If I have an aunt called Mariane, an uncle called Christopher, a father who is a major, etc., all such public knowledge is irrelevant to the mysteries of love. Yes, even one's own past life is nothing. Usually a young girl hasn't so much to report in this respect; if she does, listening to her may be worth while, but not, as a rule, loving. Personally, I am not looking for histories; I have more than enough of them. I am

looking for immediacy. That the individuals first exist for one another in its instant is the eternal element in love.

A little trust must be awoken in her, or rather, a doubt must be
removed. I am not exactly one of those loving people for whom it
is out of respect that they love one another, marry one another,
beget children with one another; yet I am well aware that love,
especially when passion is not yet aroused, requires of the one
concerned that he should not offend aesthetically against morality.
In this regard love has its own dialectic. Thus, while from the point
of view of morality my relation to Edvard is far more reprehensible
than my behaviour to the aunt, it would be much easier for me to
justify the former to Cordelia than the latter. Although she hasn't
said anything, I have nevertheless found it best to explain to her the
necessity of my acting in this way. The caution I have used flatters
her pride, the secrecy with which I have handled everything fascin-
ates her. Certainly, it might seem that I have already betrayed too
much erotic refinement here, that I shall contradict myself if I must
later convey the idea that I have never loved before, but that
doesn't matter. I am not afraid of contradicting myself so long as
she doesn't notice it and I achieve what I want. Let scholarly dis-
putants take pride in avoiding all contradiction; a young girl's life
is too rich for there not to be contradictions in it and so makes
contradiction necessary.

She is proud and also has no real conception of the erotic. While
she now defers to me, to some extent, in spiritual respects, it is
conceivable that when the erotic begins to assert itself, she may take
it into her head to turn her pride against me. As far as I can see, she
is confused about what it really means to be a woman. That is why
it was easy to arouse her pride against Edvard. This pride was quite
eccentric, however, because she had no conception of love. If she
acquires it, then she acquires her true pride. But a residue of the
eccentric pride could remain. Conceivably she might then turn
against me. Although she will not regret having agreed to the
engagement, nevertheless it will be clear to her that I made a rather
good bargain; she will realize that the beginning was improperly
effected on her part. If this should dawn on her, she will venture to

defy me. That's how it should be. I shall know then for certain how
deeply moved she is.

———————

Sure enough. Already, far down the street, I see this delightful
little curly head stretching out of the window as far as it can. This is
the third day I've noticed it ... A young girl certainly doesn't
stand at the window for nothing, she presumably has her own good
reasons ... But for heaven's sake, I beg you, don't stretch out so far;
I bet you are standing on the stretcher of the chair, I can tell from
the posture. Think how terrible it would be to fall on your head –
not on me, for I'm staying out of this affair for the time being, but
on him, him, yes, after all there must be a him ... No, what do I
see over there? If it isn't my friend licenciate Hansen walking down
the middle of the street. There's something unusual in his appearance, the method of transportation is unaccustomed; if I'm right he
approaches on the wings of longing. Can it be that he has the run of
this house? And without my knowledge? ... My pretty miss, you
have disappeared; I imagine you have gone down to open the door
for his reception ... You might as well come back, he is not
coming to your house at all ... How do I know that? I can assure
you ... he said so himself. If the wagon that went past hadn't been
so noisy you could have heard it yourself. I said to him, quite
casually you understand, 'Are you going in here?' To which he
replied no, in so many words ... You might as well say goodbye,
for now the licenciate and I are going for a walk. He is embarrassed,
and embarrassed people tend to be talkative. So I shall talk to him
about the living he is applying for ... goodbye, my pretty miss, we
are going now to the tolbooth. When we get there I shall say to
him, 'Well, damned if you haven't taken me out of my way, I
should be up on Vestergade.' – Look, now we're here again ...
what faithfulness, she's still standing at the window. A girl like that
should make a man happy ... And why then, you ask, do I do all
this? Because I'm a mean-hearted man who delights in teasing
others? Not at all. I do it out of concern for you, my amiable miss.
In the first place, you have waited for the licenciate, yearned for
him, so now when he arrives he is doubly handsome. Secondly,

when he comes in the door now, he says, 'Heavens! We were nearly
caught, that damned man was standing there at the door just as I
was going to visit you. But I was smart, I got him involved in a
long chat about the call I'm applying for, and walked him up and
down and in the end as far as the tolbooth; I give you my word, he
noticed nothing.' And so? Well, you are even more fond of the
licenciate than before, you always thought he had an excellent
mind, but that he was smart . . . well, now you can see for yourself.
And you have me to thank for that. – But something occurs to me.
Your engagement can't have been announced, otherwise I'd know
about it. The girl is delicious and a joy to behold, but she is young.
Perhaps her insight is not yet mature. Isn't it conceivable that she
might go and take a very serious step thoughtlessly? It must be
prevented, I must speak to her. I owe her that, for she is certainly a
very amiable girl. I owe it to the licenciate, for he is my friend. And
as for that, I owe it to her because she is my friend's intended. I owe
it to her family, for it is no doubt a very respectable one. I owe it to
the whole human race, for it is a good deed. The whole human
race! Great thought, inspiring achievement, to act in the name of
the whole human race, to possess such general power of attorney! –
But now for Cordelia. I can always make use of mood, and the
girl's beautiful yearning has really affected me.

———

So now begins the first war with Cordelia, in which I take to my
heels and so teach her to triumph in her pursuit of me. I keep on
retreating, and in this backward movement I teach her to recognize
in me all the powers of love, its uneasy thoughts, its passion, what
longing is, and hope and restless expectation. By my putting on this
show for her, all this develops correspondingly in her. It is a triumphal procession that I lead her into, and I am as much the dithyrambic singer of paeans in praise of her victory as I am the one who
shows the way. She will gain the courage to believe in love, to
believe it is an eternal power, when she sees its dominion over me,
sees my movements. She will believe me, partly because I count on
my art, partly because at the bottom of what I do there is truth. If it
were not so, she would not believe me. With every movement of

mine she becomes stronger and stronger; love awakens in her soul, she is initiated into the meaning of her womanhood. – Up to now, in the petty-bourgeois sense, I have not proposed to her personally; I do it now, I set her free;[48] only thus will I love her. She must never suspect that she owes it to me, for then she loses her self-confidence. It is when she feels free, so free that she is almost tempted to break with me, that the second conflict begins. She has power and passion now, and the conflict has importance for me whatever the immediate consequences. Suppose her pride makes her giddy, suppose she breaks with me; well, then, she has her freedom, but she is going to belong to me nevertheless. Of course, it is tomfoolery that the engagement should bind her; I want only to own her in her freedom. Let her leave me, the second conflict will begin all the same, and in the second conflict I shall triumph as surely as it was an illusion that she triumphed in the first. The greater the power in her, the more there is in it for me. The first war is the war of liberation, it is a game; the second is a war of conquest, it is a matter of life and death.

Do I love Cordelia? Yes! Genuinely? Yes! Faithfully? Yes! – in an aesthetic sense, and surely even that means something. What good would it do this girl if she fell into the hands of a numbskull of a faithful husband? What would become of her? Nothing. It is said that loving such a girl takes rather more than honesty. I have that more – it is duplicity. And still I love her faithfully. Sternly and temperately I keep myself in check, so that everything there is in her, all her divinely rich nature, is allowed to unfold. I am one of the few that can do that, she one of the few who are fit for it; are we then not suited to each other?

Is it wrong of me, instead of looking at the priest, to fix my eye on the beautiful embroidered handkerchief you hold in your hand? Is it wrong of you to hold it that way? ... It has a name in the corner ... Charlotte Hahn, is that what you are called? It is so seductive to learn a lady's name in such an accidental manner. It is as if there were a willing spirit who mysteriously made me acquainted with you ... Or is it not an accident that the handkerchief was folded just right for me to see your name? ... You are troubled, you dry a tear from your eye, the handkerchief hangs down loosely again ... It is obvious to you that I am looking at you, not at the preacher. You look at the handkerchief, you realize it has betrayed your name ... It is really a very innocent matter: it is easy to get to know a girl's name ... Why take it out on the handkerchief, why should it be crumpled up? Why be angry with it? Why be angry with me? Listen to what the priest says: 'No one should lead a man into temptation; even one who does so without knowing has a responsibility, he too owes a debt to the other, a debt he can discharge only by greater good-will' ... Now he has said Amen. Outside the church door there's nothing to stop the handkerchief fluttering loosely in the wind ... or have you become afraid of me? What have I done? ... Have I done more than you can forgive, than you dare remember – in order to forgive?

A double movement will be needed for Cordelia. If all I do is constantly withdraw before her superior strength, the erotic in her might well become too diffuse and relaxed for the deeper womanliness to hypostatize itself. Then, when the second conflict begins, she would be unable to offer resistance. She may certainly sleep her way to victory, indeed that's what she must do; on the other hand she must be constantly awakened. So when it seems to her for a moment as though her victory were wrested from her again, she must learn to want to keep hold of it. In this wrestling her womanliness is matured. I could either use conversation to inflame and letters to cool, or conversely. The latter alternative is in every way preferable. I can then enjoy her most extreme moments. When she has received an epistle, when its sweet poison has been absorbed into her blood, a word is enough to make the love erupt. The next moment my irony and iciness put her in doubt, yet not so much that she cannot constantly feel her victory, feel it increased on receipt of the next the epistle. Nor is irony so easy to deploy in a letter, without running the risk of her not understanding it. It is only in small glimpses that ardour can be deployed in conversation. My personal presence will prevent the ecstasy. When I am there only in a letter, she can easily stand up to me, she to some extent confuses me with a universal being who lives in her love. Also, in a letter it is easier to let oneself go; in a letter I can very well throw myself at her feet, etc., something that would very likely look nonsensical were I actually to do it, and the illusion would be destroyed. The contradiction in these movements will evoke and develop, strengthen and consolidate the love in her, in a word, tempt it. –

Yet these letters mustn't assume too soon a strongly erotic tone. To begin with it is best they bear a more universal imprint, contain a hint or two, remove a doubt or two. There can also be the occasional suggestion of the advantage an engagement has, inasmuch as it enables one to keep people away through mystification. What imperfections it otherwise has there will be no lack of opportunity to observe. I can keep up, in my uncle's house, the continual accompaniment of a caricature. The eroticism of the heart she cannot evoke without my help. When I deny it and let this caricature torment her, she will become wearied of being engaged soon enough, yet without really being able to say that it is I who have wearied her of it.

A little epistle today will give her a hint of the taste of her soul by describing the state of my own. That's the right method. And method is what I have; for that I can thank you dear young girls whom I have loved before. I owe it to you that my soul is so attuned that I can be whatever I wish to Cordelia. I remember you gratefully, the honour is yours; I shall always admit that a young girl is a born teacher from whom it is always possible to learn, if nothing else, how to deceive her – for that's something best learnt from the girls themselves. No matter how old I become, I shall never forget that a man is only finished when he is too old to learn anything from a young girl.

My Cordelia!

You say that you hadn't imagined me like this, but nor did I imagine I could be like this. Isn't the change rather in you? Might it not really be that it wasn't I that had changed but the eye with which you see me. It is in me because I love you, in you because it is you that I love. With the cold, calm light of reason I surveyed everything, proud and unmoved, nothing made me afraid, nothing took me by surprise, even if the spirit had knocked at my door I'd have calmly taken up the candelabrum in order to open it.[49] But there, it wasn't ghosts I opened the door to, not pale, powerless figures, it was you, my Cordelia, it was life and youth and beauty that came to meet me. My arm trembles, I cannot hold the light steady, I back away from you, unable, however, to take my eyes off you, unable not to wish I could hold the light still. Yes, I am changed, but to what, in what way, in what does this change consist? I don't know, I don't know what further description to add, what richer predicate to use than this, when infinitely enigmatically I say of myself: I am changed.

Your Johannes

My Cordelia!

Love loves secrecy – an engagement is a revelation; it loves silence – an engagement is a public announcement; it loves whispering – an engagement is a loud-voiced proclamation. Yet with my Cordelia's art, an engagement will be just what is needed for deceiving the foe. On a dark night there is nothing more dangerous for other ships than to hang out a lamp more deceptive than the darkness.

Your Johannes

She's sitting on the sofa by the tea-table, I sit by her side; she's holding my arm, her head rests on my shoulder, weighed down by many thoughts. She is so near, yet so distant. She gives herself up to me, yet does not belong to me. There is still resistance, but not consciously so; it is the usual resistance of womanhood, for woman's nature is submission in the form of resistance. – She's sitting on the sofa by the tea-table, I sit by her side. Her heart is throbbing but without passion, her bosom moves but not in disquiet, at times her colouring changes but in easy transitions. Is this love? Not at all. She listens, she understands. She heeds the winged word, she understands it; she listens to what another says, she understands it as though it were something she herself had said; she heeds the voice of another as it echoes inside her; she understands this echo as though it were her own voice issuing forth both to her and to another.

What am I doing? Am I deluding her? Not at all, that would be no use. Am I stealing her heart? Not at all, I would sooner make sure that the girl I loved kept her heart. Then what am I doing? I am fashioning for myself a heart in the likeness of her own. An artist paints his beloved, that's his pleasure; a sculptor forms her. That's what I am doing too, but in a spiritual sense. She doesn't know I possess this picture, and that is really where my duplicity lies. I have got hold of it secretly, and in that sense I have stolen her heart, as Rebecca is said to have stolen Laban's heart when she deviously defrauded him of his household gods.[50]

The setting and frame have, after all, a great influence on one, are part of what is stamped most firmly and deeply on the memory, or rather on one's whole soul, and are therefore never forgotten. However old I get, I will never be able to think of Cordelia in other surroundings than this little room. When I come to visit her, the maid generally lets me in from the hall; Cordelia comes in from her room and she opens her door just as I open the door to enter the drawing-room, so our eyes meet straightaway at the doorway. The drawing-room is small, comfortable, hardly more than a closet. Although I have seen it now from many different angles, what I'm most fond of is the view from the sofa. She sits there by my side; in front of me stands a round tea-table, over which a tablecloth is draped in rich folds. On the table stands a lamp, shaped like a flower, which shoots up, vigorous and full-bodied, to bear its crown, over which in turn a delicately cut paper shade hangs down, so lightly that it can never stay still. The lamp's shape reminds me of oriental nature, the movements of the shade of the gentle breezes in those parts. The floor is covered with a carpet woven from some kind of osier, a piece of work that immediately betrays its foreign origin. At times I let the lamp become the motif for my landscape. I'm sitting there, with her outstretched on the ground, under the

lamp's flower. At other times I let the osier rug evoke the idea of a
ship, of an officer's cabin – we are sailing out into the middle of the
great ocean. When we sit far away from the window, we are
gazing straight into heaven's vast horizon. This too adds to the
illusion. Then when I sit by her side, I let these things appear like a
picture fleeting swiftly over reality, as death walks over one's grave.
The setting is always of great importance, especially for memory's
sake. Every erotic relationship should be lived in such a way that
one can easily conjure up an image which possesses all of its beauty.
To succeed, in this, one must pay particular attention to the setting.
If one doesn't find the setting one wants, it has to be come by. In
the case of Cordelia and her love the setting fits perfectly. What a
different picture comes to mind when I think of my little Emilie,
and yet again, how suitable the setting! I can't imagine her except in
the little garden room, or rather it is only there that I want to
remember her. The doors stood open, a small garden in front of
the house obstructed the view, forcing the eye to stop there, to
pause before the boldly trodden highway which disappeared into
the distance. Emilie was delightful, but more insignificant than
Cordelia. The setting was also made for that. The eye remained
earthbound, it did not rush boldly and impatiently on, it rested on
this little foreground; as for the highway, even though it lost itself
romantically in the distance, its effect was more to make the eye
traverse the stretches that lay before one, and turn back to this
garden in order to traverse the same distance once again. The
apartment was on earth. Cordelia's setting must have no foreground,
but the infinite boldness of the horizon. She must not be on earth,
but float, not walk but fly, not to and fro, but everlastingly
onward.

When one gets engaged, one is initiated immediately into all of
engagement's humbug. Some days ago licenciate Hansen turned up
with the attractive young girl he has become engaged to. He
confided to me that she was a delight, I knew that already; he
confided to me that she was very young, I knew that too; finally he
confided to me that it was for that very reason he had chosen her,
to fashion her into the ideal which had always floated before his
eyes. Heavens above! such a silly licenciate – and a healthy, bloom-

ing, joyous girl. Now, I am a fairly old practitioner, yet I never draw near a young girl other than as to Nature's *venerabile* and learn first from her. In so far as I may then have any educative influence on her, it is by teaching her again and again what I have learned from her.

Her soul must be moved in all possible directions, not piecemeal, however, and in sudden gusts, but totally. She must discover the infinite, and find out that this is what comes most naturally to a human being. She must discover this not by way of thought – for her that is a detour – but in imagination, which is the real means of communication between her and me; for what in man is part, in the woman is the whole. Not for her to work her way towards the infinite along the laborious path of thought, for the woman is not born to toil; it is along the gentle path of the heart and imagination that she must grasp it. For a young girl, the infinite is as natural as the idea that all love must be happy. Everywhere, in whichever direction she turns, a young girl is surrounded by infinitude; the transition is a leap, but bear in mind that it is a womanly leap, not a manly one. Why are men generally so clumsy? When they are about to leap they first take a little run-up, make lengthy preparations, measure the distance with the eye, take several running starts, then get afraid and turn back again. Finally they leap and don't make it. A young girl leaps in a different way. In mountain regions one often comes across two towering peaks. A yawning chasm separates them, terrible to gaze down into. No man dares this leap. A young girl, however, so the local inhabitants say, has dared it, and it is called the Maiden's Leap. I am prepared to believe it, as I believe everything remarkable about a young girl, and for me it is an intoxicant to hear the simple inhabitants speaking of it. I believe everything, believe the miraculous, am amazed at it simply in order to believe; just as the only thing that has astonished me in the world is a young girl, the first; and it will be the last. And yet a leap like that for a young girl is only a jump, while a man's leap will always be ridiculous because, however long his stride, his exertion is as nothing compared with the distance between the peaks, though it offers a kind of yardstick. But who could be fool enough to imagine a young girl taking a run-up? Certainly one can imagine her running, but then the running is itself a game, an enjoyment, an unfolding of grace, while the idea of a run-up separates what in a woman go together. For a run-up has the dialectical in it, and that is contrary to woman's nature. And now the leap; who dares be so ungracious as to separate here what go together? Her leap is an effortless floating. And when she reaches the other side, she stands there again, not exhausted by exertion, but more than usually beautiful, fuller in her soul, she throws a kiss over to us who stand on this side. Young, new-born, like a flower sprung up from the roots of the mountain, she swings out over the abyss, so that we almost turn giddy. – What she must learn is to make all the movements of infinitude, to rock to and fro, to lull herself into moods, to exchange poesy and reality, truth and romance, to be tossed about in infinity. Then when she is familiar with this tumult, I put the erotic in place, and she becomes what I wish and desire. Then my good turn is done, my labour; I take in all my sails, I sit by her side, it is under her sail we journey on. And truly, when this girl is first erotically intoxicated, I shall have enough to do in sitting at the helm to moderate the speed, so that nothing comes too early, nor in an unpleasing manner. Once in a while I puncture a little hole in the sail, and the next moment we are foaming along once more.

In my uncle's house Cordelia becomes more and more indignant. Several times she has proposed that we do not go there again. It's no use, I always know how to hit upon subterfuges. Last night when we left she pressed my hand with unusual passion. She had presumably really felt pained by being there, and no wonder. If I didn't always derive amusement from observing the unnatural products of their artifice I couldn't possibly endure it. This morning I received a letter from her in which, with more wit than I had given her credit for, her with, she ridicules engagements. I kissed the letter; it is the most precious I have received from her. Just so, my Cordelia! That's how I want it.

———

By a remarkable coincidence there are two confectioners on Øster-

gade opposite each other. On the first floor on the left lives a little
young lady, or lady's maid. She usually hides behind a venetian
blind which covers the windowpane where she sits. The blind is
made of very thin material, and anyone who knows the girl or has
seen her often will easily be able, if he has good eyes, to make out
every feature; while to anyone who doesn't know her and does not
have good eyes, she appears as a dark shadow. The latter is to some
extent the case with me, the former that of a young officer who can
be seen in the offing every day precisely at noon and who looks up
at this blind. Really what first drew my attention to this beautiful
telegraphic situation was the fact that there are no blinds on the
remaining windows; a solitary blind like this, covering just one
pane, is usually a sign that someone is sitting behind it. One forenoon
I stood at the window in the confectioner's over on the other side.
It was just twelve o'clock. Without paying attention to the passers-
by, I stood looking fixedly at this blind, when suddenly the dark
shadow behind it began to move. A female head appeared in profile
at the next pane, so that it turned, strangely, in the direction in
which the blind was facing. Thereupon the owner of the head
nodded in a very friendly manner and hid herself again behind the
blind. First of all, I inferred that the person she greeted was a man,
for her movement was too excited to be evoked by the sight of a
girl friend; secondly, I inferred that the person the greeting was
meant for usually came from the other direction. For then she had
positioned herself quite correctly so as to see him well in advance,
indeed to greet him while still concealed by the blind. – Quite
right, at twelve precisely comes the hero in this little love scene, our
dear lieutenant. I'm sitting in the confectioner's which is on the
ground floor of the building whose first floor is occupied by the
young lady. The lieutenant has already caught sight of her. Careful
now, my friend, it isn't so easy to bow gracefully to a first floor.
Well, he's not so bad really; well-grown, erect, a handsome figure,
arched nose, dark hair, the tricorn suits him. Now for the dilemma.
The knees begin to chatter just a little from standing too long. Its
impression on the eye can be compared to the feeling one has when
one has toothache and the teeth become too long in the mouth. If
you gather all your strength in the eye and direct it at the first floor,
you take a little too much energy from the legs. Excuse me,

lieutenant, for resting that glance on its Ascension. Yes, I know quite well, it's an impertinence. One can hardly call the glance meaningful, meaningless rather, yet very promising. But these many promises clearly go too much to his head; he totters, to use the poet's words about Agnete, he sways, he falls.[51] That's rough, and if you ask me, it should never have happened. He's too good for that. Really it's fatal, for if you want to impress the ladies as a gallant you must never fall down. If you want to be a gallant you must watch out for things like that. But if you want to appear merely as someone of intelligence, all this is of no consequence; one slumps, one collapses, if one should then actually fall, there is nothing remarkable about that. – What impression can this incident have made on my little lady? It is unfortunate that I cannot be on both sides of the Dardanelles at once. I could of course have an acquaintance posted on the other side, but on the one hand, I always like to make my own observations, and on the other, one can never tell what there might be in this story for me, and in that case it is never good to have a confidant, since one then has to waste time getting out of him what he knows and confusing him. – Really I am beginning to grow tired of my good lieutenant. Day after day he comes by in full uniform. How terribly unflinching! Is that kind of thing fitting for a soldier? My dear sir, don't you carry a sword or a bayonet? Shouldn't you take the house by storm and the girl by force? Yes, if you were a student, a licenciate, a curate living on hope,[52] it would be different. Still, I forgive you, for the girl pleases me the more I look at her. She is pretty, her brown eyes are full of mischief. When she waits for your arrival her appearance glows with a heightened beauty that is indescribably becoming. I infer from this that she must have a great deal of imagination, and imagination is the natural rouge of the fair sex.

My Cordelia!

What is longing [*Længsel*]? Language and the poets rhyme it with the word 'prison' [*Fængsel*]. How absurd! As though only someone sitting in gaol could long for something. As if one couldn't long for something when one is free! If I were set free, would I not long?

But then, of course, I am free, free as a bird, but how much I long! I long when I am on my way to you; I long when I leave you, I long for you even when I sit by your side. Can one long for what one has? Yes, when you consider that the next moment you may not have it. My longing is an eternal impatience. Only after living through all eternity and assuring myself that you were mine every instant, only then would I return to you and live with you through all eternity, and no doubt not have patience enough to be separated from you for an instant without longing, but assurance enough to sit calmly at your side.

Your Johannes

My Cordelia!

Outside the door stands a cabriolet, for me bigger than all the world, since it is large enough for two, hitched to a pair of horses, wild and unmanageable as natural forces, impatient as my passions, bold as your thoughts. If it's your wish, I shall carry you off – my Cordelia! Is it your command? Your command is the password that loosens the reins and sets free flight's desire. I carry you off, not from one lot of people to another, but out of the world – the horses rear, the chaise rises; the horses stand almost vertically over us; we drive heavenwards through the clouds, the wind roars about us; is it we who sit still and the whole world that is moving, or is it our bold flight? Does it make you giddy, dear Cordelia? Then hold on to me; I shall not be giddy. When one thinks only of one thing, one never becomes giddy in a spiritual sense, and I am thinking only of you – nor in a bodily sense, for I look only at you. Hold tight: if the world perished, if our light carriage disappeared beneath us, we would still hold each other in our embrace, floating in the harmony of the spheres.

Your Johannes

It's almost too much. My servant has waited six hours, I myself two, in wind and rain, just to be on the lookout for that dear child, Charlotte Hahn. There is an old aunt of hers she usually visits every Wednesday between two and five. Today she doesn't come, just when I wanted so much to see her. And why? Because she puts me in a quite special mood. I greet her, she curtsies in a way at once indescribably earthly yet heavenly; she almost stands still, it's as though she was about to sink into the earth, yet her look is as of one who could be raised up to heaven. When I look at her, my mind becomes at once solemn yet covetous. Otherwise, the girl does not interest me in the least. All I demand is this greeting, nothing more even if she were willing to give it. Her greeting puts me in a mood which I then lavish on Cordelia. – And yet I'll bet that some way or another she has given us the slip. It is difficult, not just in comedies but in real life too, to keep track of a young girl; one needs an eye in every finger. There was a nymph, Cardea, who meddled in fooling men. She lived in woods, lured her lovers into the thickest brush, and vanished. She wanted to fool Janus too, but he fooled her, for he had eyes in the back of his head.[53]

My letters do not fail of their purpose. They are developing her mentally, if not erotically. For that I have to use notes. The more prominent the erotic becomes, the shorter the notes will be, but all the more certain to grasp the erotic point. Nevertheless, in order not to make her sentimental or soft, irony stiffens her feelings again, but also gives her an appetite for the nourishment most dear to her. The notes give distant and vague hints of the highest. The moment this presentiment begins to dawn in her soul, the relationship fractures. Through my resistance, the presentiment takes shape in her soul as though it were her own thought, her own heart's inclination. It's just what I want.

My Cordelia!

Somewhere in town there lives a little family consisting of a widow and three daughters. Two of these go to the Royal Kitchens to learn to cook. It is spring, about five one afternoon, the drawing-room door opens softly, a reconnoitring glance looks about the room. There is no one, just a young girl sitting at the piano. The door is ajar so one can listen unnoticed. It is no artist playing, for then the door would have been shut. She is playing a Swedish melody, about the ephemeral quality of youth and beauty. The words mock the girl's own youth and beauty; the girl's youth and beauty mock the words. Which of them is right, the girl or the words? The tones are so quiet, so melancholy, as though sadness were the arbitrator who would settle the dispute. — But it is wrong, this sadness! What association is there between youth and reflections of this kind, what fellowship between morning and evening? The keys vibrate and tremble, the spirits of the sounding-board rise in confusion and do not understand one another — my Cordelia, why so vehement! To what end this passion?

How far removed in time must an event be for us to remember it? How far for memory's longing to be no longer able to seize it? Most people have a limit in this respect: what lies too near them in time they cannot remember, nor what lies too remote. I know no limit. What was experienced yesterday, I push back a thousand years in time, and remember it as if it were yesterday.

Your Johannes

My Cordelia!

I have a secret to confide to you, my confidante. Who should I confide it to? To Echo? She would betray it. To the stars? They are cold. People? They do not understand. Only to you can I confide it, for you know how to safeguard it. There is a girl, more beautiful than my soul's dream, purer than the light of the sun, deeper than the source of the ocean, more proud than the flight of the eagle — there is a girl — oh! bend your head to my ear and my words, that my secret may steal into it — this girl I love more dearly than my life, for she is my life; more dearly than all my desires, for she is the only one; more dearly than all my thoughts, for she is the only one; more warmly than the sun loves the flower, more intensely than sorrow the privacy of the troubled mind; more longingly than the desert's burning sand loves the rain — I cling to her more tenderly than the mother's eye to the child, more confidingly than the pleading soul to God, more inseparably than the plant to its root. — Your head grows heavy and thoughtful, it sinks down on your breast, your bosom rises to its aid — my Cordelia! You have understood me, you have understood me exactly, to the letter, not one jot have you ignored! Shall I stretch the membrane of my ear and let your voice assure me of this? Should I doubt? Will you safeguard this secret? Can I depend on you? One hears of people who, in terrible crimes, dedicate themselves to mutual silence. I have confided to you a secret which is my life and my life's content. Have you nothing to confide to me, nothing so beautiful, so significant, so chaste, that supernatural forces would be set in motion if it were betrayed?

Your Johannes

My Cordelia!

The sky is overcast — it is furrowed with dark rain-clouds, like dark brows above its passionate countenance; the trees in the forest stir, unsettled by troubled dreams. You have vanished from me in the forest. Behind every tree I see a womanly being that resembles you; when I get nearer, it hides behind the next tree. Won't you reveal yourself to me, not gather yourself together? Everything is in confusion before me; the single parts of the forest lose their separate outlines, I see everything as a sea of fog, where womanly beings resembling you everywhere appear and disappear. But you I do not see, you are always moving on the waves of intuition, and yet even every single resemblance of you makes me happy. What is the reason? — Is it the rich unity of your being or the impoverished multiplicity of mine? — Is not loving you to love a world?

Your Johannes

It would really be interesting, if it were possible, to keep an exact record of my conversations with Cordelia. But I see very clearly that it is not possible. For even if I managed to remember every word exchanged between us, it would still be impossible to convey the contemporaneity that is really the nerve of our conversation, the element of surprise in the outburst, the animation that is conversation's life-principle. Nor, as a rule, of course, have I prepared myself, which would also go against the real nature of conversation, particularly erotic conversation. All that I have constantly in mind is the content of my letters, and constantly in view the mood these might possibly evoke in her. Naturally, it could never occur to me to ask her if she had read my letter. I can easily prove to myself that she has read it. Nor do I ever talk to her of this directly, but keep up a secretive communication with the letters in my conversations, partly to implant some impression or other more deeply in her soul, partly to take it away from her again and leave her undecided. Then she can read the letter again and get a new impression from it, and so on.

A change has taken place in her, and is taking place. Were I to describe the state of her soul at this moment, I would call it pantheistic daring. Her glance betrays it straightaway. It is bold, almost foolhardy in its expectation, as if every instant it demanded and was prepared to behold the supernatural. Like an eye that sees beyond itself, this glance travels beyond what appears immediately before it and beholds the marvellous. It is bold, almost foolhardy in its expectation but not in its self-confidence; it is therefore something dreaming and imploring, not proud and commanding. She seeks the marvellous outside herself, she prays for it to appear, as if it was not in her own power to evoke it. This must be prevented, otherwise I shall gain the ascendancy over her too soon. She said to me yesterday that there was something regal in my nature. Perhaps she wants to submit; that won't do at all. Certainly, my dear Cordelia, there is something regal in my nature, but you have no idea what kind of kingdom it is I rule over. It is over the storms of moods. Like Aeolus, I keep them shut up in my personal mountain and let now one, now another, go forth.[54] Flattery will give her self-esteem; the difference between mine and thine will become effective; everything is placed on her side. To flatter requires great caution. At times one must set oneself up very high but in a way that leaves room for a place still higher; at times one must set oneself down very low. The former is the more correct in moving in the direction of the spiritual, the latter in moving towards the erotic. – Does she owe me anything? Nothing at all. Could I wish that she did? Not at all. I am too much a connoisseur, and know the erotic too well, for any such tomfoolery. If that were actually the case, I should endeavour with all my might to make her forget it, and hush my own thoughts about it to sleep. In relation to the labyrinth of her heart, every young girl is an Ariadne; she owns the thread by which one can find one's way through it, but she owns it without herself knowing how to use it.[55]

My Cordelia!

Speak – I obey. Your wish is my command. Your prayer is an all-powerful invocation, your every fleeting wish my benefaction; for I obey you not as an obliging spirit, as though I stood outside you. When you command, your will takes shape, and with it myself, for I am a confusion of soul that simply awaits your word.

Your Johannes

My Cordelia!

You know I am very fond of talking to myself. In myself I have found the most interesting of my acquaintances. I have sometimes feared that I might come to lack topics for these conversations of mine; now I have no fear, now I have you. I talk, then, to myself, now and to all eternity about you, about the most interesting subject to the most interesting person – alas! for I am only an interesting person, you the most interesting subject.

Your Johannes

My Cordelia!

You think it is such a short time I have loved you; you seem almost afraid that I may have loved someone before. There is a certain kind of handwriting in which the well-favoured eye immediately suspects an older hand, which in the course of time has been supplanted by empty foolishness. With corrosive chemicals this later writing is erased and the original then stands out plain and clear. Similarly, your eye has taught me, within myself, to find myself; I let oblivion consume all that has nothing to do with you, and then I discover an ancient, a divinely young, elemental hand; I discover that my love for you is as old as myself.

Your Johannes

My Cordelia!

How can a kingdom stand which is divided against itself?[56] How am I going to be able to keep going when I am in two minds? What about? About you, to find rest if possible in the thought that I am in love with you. But how to find this rest? One of the contesting powers wants constantly to persuade the other that it is the one most deeply and heartily in love; the next moment the other does the same. I wouldn't be greatly troubled if I had the struggle outside me, if there was someone else who dared to be in love with you, or dared not to be, the crime is equally great; but this struggle within my own being consumes me, this one passion in its ambivalence.

Your Johannes

Just be off with you, my little fisher-girl; just hide yourself among the trees; just take up your burden, bending down suits you well; yes, even at this moment it is with a natural grace you bend down under the firewood you have collected – that such a creature should bear such burdens! Like a dancer you reveal your beautiful contours – slender waist, broad bosom, burgeoning, any enrolment officer must admit that. Maybe you think it's all unimportant, you think that the fine ladies are far more beautiful. Ah, my child! You do not know how much deception there is in the world. Just begin your journey with your burden into the huge forest, which presumably stretches many, many miles into the country, right up to the blue mountains. Maybe you are not a real fisher-girl but an enchanted princess; you are the servant of a troll; he is cruel enough to make you fetch firewood in the forest. That's how it always is in fairy stories. Why else do you go deeper into the forest? If you are a real fisher-girl, you should go down to the bothy with your firewood, past me as I stand on the other side of the road. – Just follow the footpath which winds playfully through the trees, my eyes will find you; just turn and look at me, my eyes are following you; you cannot move me, no longing carries me away, I sit calmly on the fence and smoke my cigar. – Some other time – perhaps. – Yes, your glance is roguish when you half turn your head back that way; your graceful walk inviting – yes, I know, I realize where this path leads – to the solitude of the forest, to the murmur of the trees, to the manifold stillness. Look, heaven itself befriends you, it hides in the clouds, it darkens the background of the forest, it is as if it drew the curtain for us. – Farewell, my pretty fisher-girl, live well. Thanks for your favour, it was a beautiful moment, a mood not

strong enough to move me from my firm place on the railing, yet
rich in inward emotion.

When Jacob had bargained with Laban about the payment for his
services, when they had agreed that Jacob should watch the white
sheep, and as return for his work should have the speckled lambs
which were born in his flock, he laid sticks in the water troughs and
let the sheep gaze at them.[57] Similarly, I place myself everywhere
before Cordelia, her eye sees me constantly. To her it seems nothing
but attentiveness on my part: for my part, however, I know that
her soul is losing interest in everything else, that there is developing
within her a spiritual concupiscence which sees me everywhere.

My Cordelia!

If I could forget you! Is my love then a work of memory? Even
if time expunged everything from its tablets, expunged even
memory itself, my relation to you would stay just as alive, you
would still not be forgotten. If I could forget you! What then
should I remember? For after all, I have forgotten myself in order
to remember you; so if I forgot you I would come to remember
myself; but the moment I remembered myself I would have to
remember you again. If I could forget you! What would happen
then? There is a picture from antiquity.[58] It depicts Ariadne. She is
leaping up from her couch and gazing anxiously after a ship that is
hurrying away under full sail. By her side stands Cupid with unstrung bow and drying his eyes. Behind her stands a winged female
figure in a helmet. It is usually assumed this is Nemesis. Imagine this
picture, imagine it changed a little. Cupid is not weeping and his
bow is not unstrung; or would you have become less beautiful, less
victorious, if I had become mad? Cupid smiles and bends his bow.
Nemesis does not stand inactive by your side; she too draws her
bow. In that other picture we see a male figure on the ship, busily
occupied. It is assumed it is Theseus. Not so in my picture. He
stands on the stern, he looks back longingly, spreads his arms. He
has repented, or rather, his madness has left him, but the ship carries
him away. Cupid and Nemesis both aim at him, an arrow flies

from each bow; their aim is true; one sees that, one understands, they have both hit the same place in his heart, as a sign that his love was the Nemesis that wrought vengeance.

Your Johannes

My Cordelia!

In love with myself, that is what people say I am. It doesn't surprise me, for how could they notice that I can love when I love only you; how could anyone else suspect it when I love only you? In love with myself. Why? Because I'm in love with you, because it is you I love, you alone, and all that truly belongs to you, and it is thus I love myself, because this, my self, belongs to you, so that if I ceased loving you I would cease loving myself. What then is, in the eyes of the profane world, an expression of the greatest egoism, is for your initiated eyes the expression of purest sympathy; what in the profane eyes of the world is an expression of the most prosaic self-preservation, is for your sacred sight the expression of the most enthusiastic self-annihilation.

Your Johannes

What I feared most was that the whole process might take me too long. I see, however, that Cordelia is making great progress; yes, that it will be necessary to mobilize everything to keep her mind on the job. She mustn't for all the world lose interest before time, that is, before the time when time has passed for her.

If one loves, one does not follow the main road. It is only marriage that keeps to the middle of the king's highway. If one loves and takes a walk from Nøddebo, one doesn't go along Esrom Lake even though really it's just a hunting track; but it is a beaten track and love prefers to beat its own. One penetrates deeper into Grib's Forest. And when one wanders thus, arm in arm, one understands each other; what before vaguely delighted and pained becomes clear. One has no idea anyone is present. − So that lovely

beech tree became a witness to your love; you first confessed it
beneath its crown. You remembered everything so clearly. That
first time you saw each other, when you held out your hands to
each other in the dance, the first time you parted near dawn, when
you would admit nothing to yourselves, least of all to each other. –
It's really rather beautiful listening to these rehearsals of love. –
They fell on their knees under the tree, they swore inviolable love
to each other, they sealed the pact with the first kiss. – These are
fruitful moods that must be lavished on Cordelia. – So this beech
was a witness. Oh yes! a tree is a very suitable witness, but still not
enough. You think, perhaps, the sky was also a witness, yet the sky
in itself is a very abstract idea. But as far as that goes, there is still a
witness. Ought I to stand up, let them see I am here? No, they
might know me and that would ruin things. Should I stand up
when they leave, let them realize there was someone there? No,
there's no point in that. Let silence rest over their secret – as long as
I please. They're in my power, I can separate them when I want. I
am in on their secret; it is only from her or from him that I could
have learnt it – from her, that's impossible – so from him – that's
abhorrent – bravo! yet it's really almost spite. Well, I'll see. If I can
get a definite impression of her in the normal way, as I prefer, but
usually I can't, then there's nothing else for it.

My Cordelia!

I am poor – you are my riches; dark – you are my light; I own
nothing, need nothing. And how could I own anything? After all, it
is a contradiction that he can own something who does not own
himself. I am happy as a child who is neither able to own anything
nor allowed to. I own nothing, for I belong only to you; I am not, I
have ceased to be, in order to be yours.

Your Johannes

My Cordelia!

'Mine': what does this word mean? Not what belongs to me, but
what I belong to, what contains my whole being, which is mine
only so far as I belong to it. My God is not the God that belongs to

me, but the God to whom I belong; and so, too, when I say my native land, my home, my calling, my longing, my hope. If there had been no immortality before, this thought that I am yours would be a breach of the normal course of nature.

Your Johannes

My Cordelia!

What am I? The modest narrator who accompanies your triumphs; the dancer who supports you when you rise in your lovely grace; the branch upon which you rest a moment when you are tired of flying; the bass that interposes itself below the soprano's fervour to let it climb even higher – what am I? I am the earthly gravity that keeps you on the ground. What am I, then? Body, mass, earth, dust and ashes. – You, my Cordelia, you are soul and spirit.

Your Johannes

My Cordelia!

Love is everything. So, for one who loves, everything has ceased to have meaning in itself and only means something through the interpretation love gives it. Thus if another betrothed became convinced there was some other girl he cared for, he would presumably stand there like a criminal and his fiancée be outraged. You, however, I know would see a tribute in such a confession; for me to be able to love another you know is an impossibility; it is my love for you casting its reflection over the whole of life. So when I care about someone else, it is not to convince myself that I do not love her but only you – that would be presumptuous; but since my whole soul is filled with you, life takes on another meaning for me: it becomes a myth about you.

Your Johannes

My Cordelia!

My love consumes me. Only my voice is left,[59] a voice which has fallen in love with you whispers to you everywhere that I love you. Oh! does it weary you to hear this voice? Everywhere it enfolds you; like an inexhaustible, shifting surround, I place my transparently reflected soul about your pure, deep being.

Your Johannes

My Cordelia!

One reads in ancient tales how a river fell in love with a girl. Similarly, my soul is a river which loves you. At one moment it is peaceful and allows your image to be reflected in it deeply and undistorted; at another it fancies it has captured your image, and its waves foam to prevent you getting away; sometimes it softly ruffles its surface and plays with your reflection, sometimes it loses it, and then its waves become dark and despairing. – That's how my soul is: like a river that has fallen in love with you.

                                                    Your Johannes

----

Frankly, without an exceptionally vivid imagination one could conceive of a more convenient, comfortable, and above all more elegant means of transport; riding with a peat-carrier creates a stir only in a metaphorical sense. – But at a pinch one accepts it with thanks. One goes some way down the highway, one sets oneself up on the cart, one rides five miles or so and meets nothing, ten miles and everything's going fine: one becomes calm and secure; really the scenery looks better than usual from this position. One has come almost fifteen miles – now who would have expected, so far out here on the highway, to meet someone from Copenhagen? And it is someone from Copenhagen, you can see that all right, it's no countryman; he looks at you in a quite special way, so assured, so observant, so appraising, and a little scornful. Yes, my dear girl, your position is by no means comfortable; you look as if you were sitting on a serving-tray, the wagon is so flat that it has no hollow for your feet. But it's your own fault; my carriage is entirely at your service. I venture to offer you a much less embarrassing place, unless it would embarrass you to sit by my side. If so, I would leave the whole carriage to you and sit in the driver's seat myself, pleased to be allowed to convey you to your destination. – The straw hat isn't quite adequate protection against a sideways glance. It's no good your bending down your head, I can still admire the lovely profile. – Isn't it annoying, the peasant greeting me? But after all it's quite proper for a peasant to show respect to a distinguished man. – You can't get out of it like that; here's a tavern, yes, a staging-post, and a peat-carrier is in his own way too pious not to attend to his devotions. I'll take care of him. I have an exceptional talent for charming peat-carriers. May I be so fortunate as to please you too! He won't be able to resist my offer, and when he has accepted it he won't be able to resist its effect. If I can't do it, my servant can. There, he's going into the tap-room now; you are alone on the wagon in the shelter. – Heaven only knows what kind of young girl this is. Could she be a little middle-class girl, perhaps a deacon's daughter? If so, for a deacon's daughter she is uncommonly pretty, and dressed with unusual taste. The deacon must have a good living. It occurs to me, might she not be a little thoroughbred who has tired of riding in her equipage, who has perhaps gone for a little hike out to the country house, and now wants to try her hand at a little adventure too? Certainly possible, such things are not unheard of. – The peasant doesn't know a thing; he is a numbskull who knows only how to drink: yes, yes, just drink, old chap, he's welcome to it. – But what do I see in there? Miss Jespersen, no less, Hansine Jespersen, daughter of the wholesaler. God preserve us! We two know each other. It was her I once met on Bredgade, she was sitting on a seat facing backwards and she couldn't get the window up; I put on my glasses and then had the pleasure of following her with my eyes. It was a very confined position, there were so many in the carriage that she couldn't move, and she presumably didn't dare to cause a scene. The present position is just as awkward, to be sure. Clearly we two are predestined for each other. She's supposed to be a romantic little girl; she is definitely out on her own. – There comes my servant with the peat-carrier. He is completely drunk. It's disgusting; they're a depraved lot, these peat-carriers. Yes, alas! Yet there are worse people than peat-carriers. See, now you are going to have to drive anyway. You will have to drive the horses yourself; it is quite romantic. You refuse my invitation. You insist you are a very good driver. You do not deceive me. I can see well enough how sly you are. When you have gone a little way, you will jump off, it's easy to find a hiding-place in the forest. – My horse must be saddled, I shall follow you on horseback. – There, look! now I am ready, now you can feel safe against any assault. – But don't be so frightfully afraid, or I'll turn back immediately. I only want to frighten you a little and provide an opportunity for your natural beauty to be heightened. You don't know, indeed, that it was I who let the peasant get drunk, and I have not permitted myself a single offensive remark. Everything can still be fine; I shall no doubt give the affair a twist which will let you laugh at the whole story. All I want is a little settling of accounts with you. Never believe I would take any young girl off her guard. I am a friend of freedom, and whatever does not come to me freely I do not bother with at all. – 'You will certainly realize that you cannot continue your journey in this manner. I myself am going hunting, that's why I'm on horseback. However, my carriage is ready at the tavern. If you so command, it will catch up with you in an instant and take you where you want. I am myself unfortunately unable to have the pleasure of accompanying you, for I am bound by a hunting promise, and they are sacred.' – But you accept – everything will be arranged in an instant. – Now you see you needn't at all be embarrassed at seeing me again, or at least not more embarrassed than well suits you. You can amuse yourself with the whole story, laugh a little and think a little about me. More I do not ask. It may not seem very much; for me it is enough. It is the beginning, and I am especially strong on rudiments.

Yesterday evening the aunt had a small party. I knew Cordelia would take out her knitting. I had hidden a little note in it. She lost it, picked it up, became excited and wistful. This is how one should always exploit the situation. It is incredible the advantages you can derive from it. A note of no consequence in itself, read in these circumstances, becomes for her infinitely important. She got no chance to talk with me; I had arranged it so that I had to escort a lady home. So Cordelia had to wait until today. That's always a good way of letting an impression bury itself all the deeper in her soul. It looks all the time as if it were I that was showing her attention. The advantage I have is that I am given a place in her thoughts everywhere, surprise her everywhere.

Love, however, has its own dialectic. There was a young girl I was once in love with. Last summer at the theatre in Dresden I saw an actress who bore a deceptive resemblance to her. Because of this I wanted to make her acquaintance, and succeeded, and then convinced myself that there was a quite considerable difference all the same. Today I met a lady on the street who reminded me of that actress. This story can go on as long as you like.

Everywhere my thoughts encircle Cordelia, I place them around her like guardian angels. As Venus is drawn in her chariot by doves, she sits in her triumphal car and I harness my thoughts to it like winged creatures. She herself sits there happy, rich as a child, omnipotent as a goddess; I walk by her side. Truly, a young girl is after all, and remains, a *venerabile* of Nature and of all existence! That's something no one knows better than I. The only pity is that this glory is so short-lived. She smiles at me, she greets me, she beckons to me as if she were my sister. A single glance reminds her that she is my beloved.

Love has many positionings. Cordelia makes good progress. She is sitting on my lap, her arm twines, soft and warm, round my neck; she leans upon my breast, light, without gravity; the soft contours scarcely touch me; like a flower her lovely figure twines about me, freely as a ribbon. Her eyes are hidden beneath her lashes, her bosom is dazzling white like snow, so smooth that my eye cannot rest, it would glance off if her bosom were not moving. What does this movement mean? Is it love? Perhaps. It is a presentiment of it, its dream. It still lacks energy. Her embrace is comprehensive, as the cloud enfolding the transfigured one, detached as a breeze, soft as the fondling of a flower; she kisses me unspecifically, as the sky kisses the sea, gently and quietly, as the dew kisses a flower, solemnly as the sea kisses the image of the moon.

I would call her passion at this moment a naive passion. When the change has been made and I begin to draw back in earnest, she will call on everything she has to captivate me. She has no other means for this purpose than the erotic itself, except that this will now appear on a quite different scale. It then becomes a weapon in her hand which she wields against me. I then have the reflected passion. She fights for her own sake because she knows I possess the

erotic; she fights for her own sake so as to overcome me. She herself
is in need of a higher form of the erotic. What I taught her to
suspect by arousing her, my coldness now teaches her to understand
but in such a way that she thinks it is she herself who discovers it.
So she wants to take me by surprise; she wants to believe that she
has outstripped me in audacity, and that makes me her prisoner.
Her passion then becomes specific, energetic, conclusive, dialectical;
her kiss total, her embrace without hesitation. – In me she seeks her
freedom and finds it the better the more firmly I encompass her.
The engagement bursts. When that has happened she needs a little
rest, so that nothing unseemly will emerge from this wild tumult.
Her passion then composes itself once more and she is mine.

Just as I had already supervised her reading indirectly in the time
of Edvard of blessed memory, so now I do that directly. What I
offer her is what I consider the best nourishment: mythology and
fairy-tales. She is nevertheless free in this as in everything; there is
nothing that I have not learned from her herself. If it isn't there to
begin with, I first put it there.

When the servant girls go to the Zoological Gardens in the
summer, generally the Gardens offer but poor entertainment. The
girls go there only once a year and so feel they must really make the
most of it. They have to put on hat and shawl and disfigure themselves in every way. Their gaiety is wild, unseemly and lascivious.
No, I count then on Frederiksberg Gardens. It's on Sunday after-
noons they come there, and I too. Here everything is seemly and
decent, the gaiety itself quieter and more refined. In general, the
man who doesn't appreciate servant girls has more to lose than
they. The servant girls' motley host is really the most beautiful civil
guard we have in Denmark. If I were king, I know what I would
do – I wouldn't review the regulars. If I were a city alderman I
should immediately move to have a welfare committee appointed
to strive to encourage the servant girls in every possible way, by
insight, advice, exhortation and suitable rewards, to get themselves
up with taste and care. Why should beauty go to waste? Why

should it go through life unnoticed? At least let it appear once a week in the light that shows it to best advantage! But above all, taste, restraint. A servant girl should not look like a lady, so far I agree with *Politivennen*,[60] but the reasons that respectable paper adduces are altogether mistaken. If we could anticipate a desirable flourishing of the servant class in this way, wouldn't this in turn have a beneficial effect on our houses' daughters? Or is it too bold of me to espy a future for Denmark which can truly be called matchless? If only I myself were lucky enough to be that golden age's contemporary,[61] the whole day could be spent with a good conscience in the streets and alleys rejoicing in the pleasures of the eye. What broad and bold, what patriotic daydreams! But here I am in Frederiksberg Gardens where the servant girls come on Sunday afternoon, and I too. – First come the country girls, hand in hand with their sweethearts; or in another formation, girls all in front hand in hand, men all behind; or in another, two girls and one man. This throng forms the frame; they usually stand or sit along by the trees in the big quadrangle in front of the pavilion. They are hale and hearty, just the colour clashes are a little too strong, in their dress as well as their complexions. Inside this frame now come the servant girls from Jutland and Fyn: tall, straight, a little too stalwart, their dress a little confused. Here there would be much for the committee to do. Nor does one want for the occasional representative of the Bornholm division: capable cooks, but not very approachable either in the kitchen or in Frederiksberg; there is something proudly forbidding about them. The contrast their presence offers is therefore not without its effect, and I'd rather not be without them out here, though I rarely have anything to do with them. – Now follow the core troops, the girls from Nyboder. Smaller in stature, plump, with a full figure, delicate complexion, gay, happy, sprightly, talkative, a little coquettish and above all, bareheaded. Their dress can well approximate to a lady's; just two things to notice, they don't have a shawl but a kerchief, no hat but a little smart cap at most, they should preferably be bareheaded. – Why, hello, Marie! Fancy meeting you here! It's been a long time. Are you still at the Counsellor's? – 'Yes' – An excellent situation, isn't it? – 'Yes' – But you are so alone out here, no one to accompany ... no sweetheart, perhaps he hasn't had time today, or you're waiting for him? – What, you aren't engaged? Impossible. The prettiest girl in Copenhagen, a girl in service at the Counsellor's, a girl who is an embellishment and an example to all servant girls, a girl who knows how to dress so prettily and . . . so opulently. What an exquisite little handkerchief you have in your hand, of the finest cambric . . . and what do I see, embroidery on the edges? I bet it cost ten marks . . . you can be sure there's many a fine lady who doesn't own its equal . . . French gloves . . . a silk parasol . . . and a girl like that not engaged? . . . It's absurd. Unless my memory is letting me down badly, Jens was pretty fond of you. You must know Jens, the wholesaler's Jens, on the second floor . . . See, I got it right . . . So why didn't you get engaged? Jens was a handsome fellow, he had a good situation, with the Counsellor's influence he might have made a policeman or fireman in due course; it wouldn't have been such a bad match . . . The fault must definitely be yours, you've been too hard on him . . . 'No!, but I found out Jens had been engaged once before to a girl they say he didn't treat nicely at all.' – . . . No, you don't say; who would have believed Jens was such a naughty rascal . . . yes, these Guards fellows . . . these Guards fellows aren't to be depended on . . . You did quite right, a girl like you is altogether too good to be thrown away on just anybody . . . You can be sure you'll make a better match, I'll guarantee it. – How is Miss Juliane? I haven't seen her for some time. I'm sure my pretty Marie could help me with a little information . . . just because one has been unhappy in love oneself one needn't lack sympathy for others . . . There are so many people here . . . I daren't talk to you about it, I'm afraid in case someone spies on me . . . Listen just a moment, my pretty Marie . . . Look, here's the place, in this shaded walk, where the trees twine round each other so as to hide us from others, where we see no one else, hear no human voice but only a soft echo of the music . . . here I dare to speak of my secret . . . Now, if Jens hadn't been a bad man, you'd have walked with him here arm in arm, wouldn't you, and listened to the joyful music, and enjoyed an even greater happiness yourself . . . why so moved? – Just forget Jens . . . Don't get me wrong . . . it was to meet you I came out here . . . It was to see you that I came to the Counsellor's . . . You surely noticed . . . Whenever I could I always passed the kitchen door . . . You must be mine . . . The banns shall be published

... tomorrow evening I will explain everything ... up the back-stairs, the door to the left, right across from the kitchen ... Goodbye, my pretty Marie ... don't let anyone know you have seen me out here or spoken with me. You know my secret. – She is really delightful, something might be made of her. – If I ever get a foothold in her chamber I'll announce those banns myself. I have always tried to develop that beautiful Greek autarchy and in particular make the priest superfluous.

————————

If I could stand behind Cordelia when she received a letter from me, it might be very interesting. Then I could convince myself more easily how far she had taken them in erotically in the most literal sense. On the whole, letters are and will always be an invaluable means for making an impression upon a young girl; often the dead symbol has far greater influence than the living word. A letter is a secret communication; you are master of the situation, feel no pressure from anyone's presence, and I think a young girl would really rather be quite alone with her ideal, that is, at particular moments, and precisely when it is influencing her mind most strongly. Even if her ideal has found a fairly complete expression in a definite object of love, there are still moments when she feels that there is an excess in the ideal that reality lacks. These great feasts of the atonement must be granted to her; only one must be careful to use them in the right way, so that she does not return to reality from them weakened but strengthened. Here a letter helps; its effect is that one is invisibly but spiritually present at these sacred moments of consecration, while the idea that the real person is the author o the letter creates a natural and easy transition to reality.

Could I become jealous of Cordelia? Damn it, yes! Though in another sense, no! For if I saw that even if I won my fight against the other, her nature would be disturbed and not what I wanted – then I would give her up.

An old philosopher has said that if you accurately record all that you experience, before you know it you are a philosopher. For

some time now I have lived in association with the community of
the betrothed. Such a relationship ought then to bear at least some
fruit. So I have considered gathering material for a book, entitled
Contribution to the Theory of the Kiss, dedicated to all tender lovers. It
is remarkable, besides, that no work on this subject exists. So if I
manage to complete it I will also be fulfilling a long-felt need.
Could the reason for this gap in the literature be that philosophers
do not consider such matters, or is it that they do not understand
them? – I can offer several suggestions right away. The perfect kiss
requires that the agents involved be a man and a girl. A kiss between
men is in poor taste, or what is worse, distasteful. – Secondly, I
believe a kiss comes closer to its concept when a man kisses a girl
than when a girl kisses a man.[62] Where in the course of years the
distinction in this relation is lost sight of, the kiss loses its significance.
This is true of the domestic kiss with which married people, for
want of napkins, wipe each other on the mouth while saying,
'You're welcome.' – If the age difference is very large, the kiss falls
outside the concept. I remember in a girls' school, in one of the
provinces, the oldest class had its own saying: 'to kiss the counsellor', an expression with which they associated an idea that was
anything but agreeable. It began like this: the schoolmistress had a
brother-in-law living in her house. He had been a counsellor, was an
elderly man, and took advantage of his age to kiss the young girls. –
The kiss must be an expression of a definite passion. When a brother
and sister who are twins kiss each other, that is not a proper kiss.
The same is true of kisses that are bonuses from Christmas games,
likewise a stolen kiss. A kiss is a symbolic action which lacks meaning
when the feeling it should indicate is not present, and this feeling
can only be present under certain conditions. – If one wants to try
classifying the kiss, one can conceive of several principles of classification. They can be classified according to sound. Unfortunately, here
language is not adequate to my observations. I don't believe all the
languages in the world have an adequate supply of onomatopoeias
to cover the distinctions I have come to recognize just in my uncle's
house. Sometimes it is clicking, sometimes hissing, sometimes smack-
ing, sometimes popping, sometimes rumbling, sometimes resonant,
sometimes hollow, sometimes like calico, and so on. One can classify
the kiss according to the form of contact, as in the tangential kiss, or

kiss *en passant*, and the clinging kiss. One can classify them with reference to time, the brief and the prolonged. There is also, with reference to time, another classification, and it is the only one I have really cared about. Thus a distinction is made between the first kiss and all others. What reflection focuses on here is incommensurable with what the other classifications bring to light; it is indifferent to sound, touch, time in general. But the first kiss is qualitatively different from all others. Few people consider this; a pity if there were not one who thinks about it.

My Cordelia!

A good answer is like a sweet kiss, says Solomon.[63] You know I am given to asking questions. People almost take me to task for it. That's because they do not understand what I ask; for you and you alone understand what it is I ask, and you and you alone understand how to answer, and you and you alone understand how to give a good answer; for a good answer is like a sweet kiss, says Solomon.

Your Johannes

There is a difference between a spiritual and a physical eroticism. Up to now it is mostly the spiritual kind I have tried to develop in Cordelia. My physical presence must now be something different, not just the accompanying mood, it must be tempting. I have been constantly preparing myself these days by reading the celebrated passage in the *Phaedrus* on love.[64] It electrifies my whole being and is an excellent prelude. After all, Plato really understood love.

My Cordelia!

Latin says of an attentive disciple that he hangs on his master's lips.[65] For love everything is imagery, and the image in turn is reality. Am I not a diligent, an attentive disciple? But then you aren't saying a word!

Your Johannes

If someone other than I were guiding this process, he would presumably have more sense than to let himself be guided. Were I to consult an initiate among the betrothed, he would probably declare with an access of erotic daring, 'I search in vain in these positionings of love for the sound-image in which the lovers tell of their love.'[66] I would reply, 'I'm glad you seek it in vain, for that image just does not come within the scope of the genuinely erotic, not even if you include the interesting.' Love is far too substantial to make do with chat; erotic situations have far too much meaning in themselves to be supplemented by chat. They are silent, still, in definite contours, and yet eloquent as the music of Memnon's statue.[67] Eros gesticulates, he does not speak; or if he does, it is an enigmatic hint, a symbolic music. Erotic situations are always either sculptural or picturesque; but two people talking together about their love are neither sculptural nor picturesque. The solidly engaged, however, always begin with such small talk, which later also becomes the connecting thread in their garrulous marriage. This small talk is also the beginning and promise of the fact that their marriage will not lack the dowry Ovid speaks of: *dos est uxoria lites.*[68] – If there is talking to be done, it is enough that one of them should do it. The man should do the talking and should therefore possess some of the powers that lay in the girdle of Venus, with which she beguiled men: conversation and sweet flattery, that is to say, the insinuative.[69] It by no means follows that Eros is silent, or that it would be erotically incorrect to converse, only that the conversation itself should be erotic, not lost in edifying observations about prospects in life, and so on, and that it be essentially regarded as a respite from the erotic act, a pastime, not as what is most important. Such a conversation, such a *confabulatio*, is in its nature quite divine, and I never weary of talking with a young girl. That is to say, I can get tired of a particular young girl, but never of talking with a young girl. For me, that is just as impossible as getting tired of breathing. What is the real peculiarity of such a conversation is its vegetative flowering. The conversation stays down to earth, it has no essential topic, the accidental is the law of its movement – but 'a thousand joys' is the name of itself and its produce.[70]

My Cordelia!

'My', 'Your' — these words enclose the humble content of my letters like a parenthesis. Have you noticed that the distance between its arms is getting shorter? Oh, my Cordelia! It is beautiful that the emptier the parenthesis becomes, the fuller it is with meaning.

Your Johannes

My Cordelia!

Is an embrace to be at loggerheads?

Your Johannes

Generally Cordelia keeps silent. This has always pleased me. Her womanly nature is too deep to plague one with hiatus, a figure of speech especially characteristic of the woman and which is unavoidable if the man who is to provide the missing consonants before or after is equally feminine. Occasionally a single brief utterance, however, betrays how much there is in her, and then I can lend a hand. It's as though, behind a person making disconnected stabs at a drawing with an unsure hand, there stood someone else who kept on making out of it something bold and rounded off. She is surprised herself, and yet it seems to be her own. I watch over her, therefore, over every accidental remark, every casually dropped word, and when I give it back to her it has always something more significant in it that she both knows and does not know.

Today we were at a party. We hadn't exchanged a word. We were leaving the table when a servant came in and informed Cordelia that a messenger wished to speak to her. The messenger was from me and brought a letter which contained allusions to a remark I had made at the table. I had managed to introduce it into the general table conversation so that Cordelia, although she sat at a distance from me, couldn't avoid overhearing and misunderstanding it. This is where the letter came in. If I hadn't succeeded in steering the conversation in that direction, I'd have been there in person at the appointed time to confiscate the letter. She came back into the room; she had to tell a little lie. Things like that consolidate the erotic secretiveness without which she cannot make headway down the road onto which she has been directed.

My Cordelia!

Do you believe that he who lays his head on a fairy mound sees the image of the fairy in his dreams? I don't know, but I do know this, that when I rest my head on your breast and don't close my eyes but look out beyond, I see the countenance of an angel. Do you believe that the person who reclines his head on a fairy mound cannot lie still? I don't believe so, but I know that when my head bends to your bosom I am roused too strongly for sleep to fall on my eyes.

Your Johannes

Jacta est alea.[71] The turn must now be made. I was with her today, quite taken with the thought of an idea that entirely occupied me. I had neither eye nor ear for her. The idea itself was interesting and fascinated her too. It would also have been incorrect to begin this new operation by being cold in her presence. Now that I have left and the thought no longer occupies her, she will realize at once that I was different from usual. That it is in her solitude she realizes the change makes this discovery much more painful to her, it acts more slowly but all the more forcibly. She cannot immediately flare up, and when the opportunity arises she has already pondered the thing so much that she cannot find expression for it all in one go but always retains a residue of doubt. The unrest increases, the letters cease, the erotic fare is reduced, the love is scorned as ridiculous. Perhaps she goes along with it for a moment, but in the long run she cannot endure it. She wants now to captivate me with the same means I have used against her, with the erotic.

When it comes to breaking off an engagement every little girl is a great casuist, and although the schools hold no courses on the subject, all young girls are excellently informed of the circumstances in which an engagement should be broken off. It should really be a standard question in the final-year school exams, and while I know there is usually very little variety in essay subjects in girls' schools, I am certain there would be no lack of variation here, since the problem itself offers wide scope for a girl's powers of penetration. And why shouldn't a young girl be given an opportunity to prove her sharpness in the most brilliant manner? Or don't you believe she will get a chance here to show that she is mature enough to – be engaged? I once experienced a situation that interested me very much. At a family's where I sometimes visited, the older members were out one day, but the two young daughters of the house had invited a circle of their girl friends for a morning coffee-party. They were eight in all, all between sixteen and twenty. Presumably they hadn't expected any visitors; the maid had probably been given orders to say no one was at home. I went in all the same and saw clearly they were a little surprised. God knows what eight young girls like that really talk about in a solemn synod of this kind. Married women, too, sometimes gather in similar meetings. Then they discuss pastoral theology, taking up in particular the important questions of when it is most proper to let the maid go to the market alone, whether it is better to have an account with the butcher or pay cash, whether it's likely the cook has a sweetheart and how to put an end to this sweetheart skylarking which causes delays with the cooking. – I found my place in this beautiful cluster. It was very early spring. The sun sent a few scattered rays to herald its arrival. In the room itself everything was wintry, and the scattered rays so annunciative for that very reason. From the table came the aroma of coffee – and then there were the girls themselves, happy, healthy, blooming, and exuberant too, for their anxiety had soon been allayed, and in any case what was there to fear? They were in a way manpower enough. – I managed to draw their attention and the talk to the question of when an engagement should be broken off. While my eye diverted itself by flitting from one flower to the other in this garland of girls, entertaining itself by resting now on one beauty, now on another, my outer ear revelled in the pleasant music of the voices, and the inner ear in listening observantly to what was said. A single word was often enough for me to form a deep insight into the heart of a particular girl, and its history. How seductive, after all, is the road of love! How interesting to find out how far down it the individual has come! I continually fanned the

conversation; cleverness, wit, aesthetic objectivity all helped to make
the relationship between us more free, yet everything remained
within the bounds of strictest decorum. As we thus joked in the
free-and-easy atmosphere of conversation, there lay dormant the
possibility of a single word of mine causing the good children an
unfortunate embarrassment. This possibility was in my power. The
girls did not realize it, hardly suspected it. It was suppressed all
along by the easy play of conversation, as Scheherazade put off the
death sentence by telling stories.[72] Sometimes I led the conversation
to the very edge of sadness; sometimes I gave free rein to wanton-
ness; sometimes I tempted them out into a dialectical game. And
what material offers more diversity, all depending on how one
looks at it? I kept on introducing new themes. – I told of a girl who
had been cruelly forced to break off her engagement by her parents.
That unhappy collision almost brought tears to their eyes. – I told
of someone who had broken off an engagement and given two
reasons, that the girl was too large and that he had not gone down
on his knees to her when confessing his love. When I had objected
to him that these couldn't possibly be considered good enough
reasons, he replied, 'Indeed, they are precisely good enough for me
to get what I want, for no one can offer a rational answer to that.' I
presented a very difficult case for the assembly's consideration. A
young girl broke off her engagement because she felt she and her
sweetheart were unsuited to each other. The loved one tried to
bring her to reason by assuring her how much he loved her, to
which she replied: 'Either we are suited to each other and there is
real sympathy, and then you will see that we do not suit each other;
or we do not suit each other, and then you will see we do not suit
each other.' It was amusing to see how the young girls cudgelled
their brains to understand this puzzling story, and yet I could see
clearly that one or two of them understood it very well, for when it
comes to whether to break off an engagement, every young girl is a
born casuist. – Yes, I really think I'd find it easier to dispute with
the devil himself than with a young girl when it's a question of
when one should break off an engagement.

Today I was with her. Quickly, with the speed of thought, I led
the conversation to the same subject I had occupied her with yester-

day, in a renewed effort to arouse her to an ecstasy. 'There was something I should have mentioned yesterday; it occurred to me after I'd gone.' That succeeded. As long as I am with her she enjoys listening to me; when I've gone she realizes she's been cheated and that I am changed. In this way one extends one's credit. The method is sly but very expedient, like all indirect methods. She has no difficulty in explaining to herself that I myself can be occupied with the sort of things I talk about, and indeed at the time they even interest her, yet I cheat her out of the real erotic.

Oderint, dum metuant.[73] As if only fear and hatred belonged together, while fear and love had nothing at all to do with each other, as if it wasn't fear that made love interesting! What kind of love is it with which we embrace Nature? Isn't there a secret fear and terror in it because Nature's beautiful harmony has to work its way out of lawlessness and wild confusion, its security out of faithlessness? But this anxiety is just what is most fascinating. So too with love if it is to claim our interest. Behind it there should brood the deep, fearful night from which the flower of love springs forth. So rests *nymphaea alba*,[74] with its cup, on the surface of the water, while thought fears to plunge down into the deep darkness where it has its root. – I have noticed, she always calls me *mine* when she writes to me but lacks the courage to say it to me. Today I begged her to do that, as insinuatingly and with as much erotic warmth as I could. She began doing so; an ironic glance, more brief and quicker than you can say it, was enough to make it impossible for her, although my lips urged her with all their might. This mood is normal.

She's mine. I do not confide this to the stars, as is custom and practice. I do not really see what interest those distant spheres can have in this information. Nor do I confide it to any human being, not even to Cordelia. I keep this secret all to myself, whisper it, as it were, to myself, in my most secret conversations with myself. The attempted resistance on her part was not particularly strong; on the other hand the erotic strength she is developing is admirable. How interesting she is in this deep passionateness, how great, almost supernatural! How flexible she is in evasion, how supple in insinuating herself wherever she finds an unfortified point! Everything is mobilized, but in this elemental whirl I find myself precisely in my own element. Yet even in this commotion she is by no means unbeautiful, not torn apart in her moods, not split up into her parts. She is a constant Anadyomene,[75] except that she does not rise up in naive grace or unaffected calm, but stirred by the strong heart-throbs of love, though still in unity and equilibrium. Erotically, she is fully equipped for the struggle; she fights with the shafts of her eyes, with the command of her brow, with the secretiveness of her forehead, with the eloquence of her bosom, with the dangerous attractions of the embrace, with the lips' prayer, with her cheeks' smile, with the sweet longing of her whole form. There is a power in her, an energy, as if she were a Valkyrie; but this erotic vigour is in turn tempered by a certain seductive languor which is exhaled over her. – She must not be held too long at this peak, where only anxiety and unrest can hold her steady and prevent her from falling over. With respect to such emotions she will soon feel that the engagement is too narrow, too confining. She herself will become the tempter who seduces me into going beyond the boundary of the normal; in this way she will become conscious of it herself, and for me that's the main thing.

Not a few remarks are being let fall on her part that suggest she is tired of the engagement. They do not go unheeded; they are my operation's scouts in her soul, which give me informative hints; they're the ends of threads with which I wind her into my plan.

My Cordelia!

You complain about the engagement. You think our love does not need an external bond that only gets in the way. In this I recognize my excellent Cordelia immediately! Truly, I admire you. Our external union is after all nothing but a separation. There is still a partition wall separating us, like Pyramus and Thisbe.[76] That people are privy to it is still a disturbing factor. Only in opposition is there freedom. Only when no outsider suspects it does the love acquire meaning. Only when every stranger believes the lovers hate each other is love happy.

Your Johannes

Soon the bond of betrothal will be broken. She is the one who is unloosening it, to see if by this loosening she can't captivate me still more, as flowing locks are more captivating than those that are bound up. Were I to annul the engagement myself, I would miss this erotic somersault which is so seductive to look at and so sure a sign of her soul's daring. For me that's the main thing. Furthermore, the whole incident would cause me some unpleasantness with others. I would be mistrusted, hated, detested – though unfairly, for think of the advantages it would bring many. Many a little maiden would be quite happy, in the absence of a betrothal, to have come almost that far. That's always something, though, frankly, painfully little because once you have elbowed your way to a place on the expectancy list you have no expectations; the higher one rises on the list, and the further forward one gets, the less prospect there is. In the world of love, the principle of seniority for advancement and promotion does not apply. Furthermore, a little maiden like that is tired of retaining undivided possession; she needs to have her life stirred by an event. But what can compare with an unhappy love affair, especially, too, when she can take the whole thing so lightly? So she lets herself and her neighbour believe she is among the deceived, and since she doesn't qualify for enrolment in a Magdalena Institution,[77] she takes up lodging beside it in a tearful story. One is thus in duty bound to hate me. Furthermore, there is still another division, of those who have been wholly, or half, or three-quarters, deceived by another. Here there are many degrees, all the way from those who have a ring to show for it to those who can pin their faith on a handshake in a country dance. Their wounds are reopened by the new pain. Their hatred I accept as a bonus. But naturally, to my poor heart all these haters are like so many secret lovers. A king without a country is an absurd figure, but a war of succession between a host of pretenders to a kingdom without a country – that outdoes everything in absurdity. I ought to be loved and cared for by the fair sex as a public pawnbroker. After all, a real fiancé can only take care of one, but such a comprehensive possibility can provide – that is to say, provide more or less – for as many as may be. Then I'm free of all this finite twaddle and also have the advantage of, afterwards, being able to appear in an entirely new role. The young girls will be sorry for me, sympathize with me, sigh for me; I chime in in just the same key; this is also a way of taking captive.

It's rather strange; I notice at this juncture with dismay that I am getting the symptom that Horace wished on every faithless girl – a black tooth, a front tooth at that.[78] How superstitious we can be! The tooth really disturbs me, I find it quite hard to stand any allusion to it; it's a weak side I have. While otherwise I am fully armed, here even the biggest bungler can administer me a blow that goes far deeper than he thinks when he touches on the tooth. I do everything to make it white, but in vain. I say with Palnatoke:

> I rub it day and night,
> But I do not erase this dark shadow.[79]

Life contains, after all, extraordinarily much puzzlement. A little thing like that can upset me more than the most dangerous assault, the most embarrassing situation. I want it extracted, yet that would interfere with my speaking voice and its power. But I want it out anyway, I want a false one put in; false to the world, that is; it was the black one that was false to me.

It's quite excellent that Cordelia finds an engagement an impediment. Marriage is and remains, after all, an honourable institution, even though it has the boring feature that from its very youth it receives part of the veneration brought by age. But an engagement, on the other hand, is a genuinely human invention, and so important and ridiculous on that account that it is quite all right for a young girl in the whirl of passion to place herself above it on the one hand, yet on the other to feel its importance, to feel her soul's energy, like a higher circulatory system, present everywhere within her. What is needed now is to steer her in such a way that in her bold flight she loses sight of marriage and of the mainland of reality in general, so that her soul, as much in its pride as in its anxiety about losing me, destroys an imperfect human form in order to hasten on to something higher than the ordinarily human. In this respect, however, I need have no fear, for her passage through life is already so floating and light that reality has already to a large extent been lost sight of. Besides, I am constantly on board and can always unfurl the sails.

Woman is and remains, after all, an inexhaustible topic for my reflections, an eternal profusion for my observations. Let the person who feels no urge for this study be whatever he likes in the world; one thing he is not: he is not an aesthetician. The glory and divinity of aesthetics is just this, that it only enters into relation with the beautiful, all it has to do with, essentially, is fiction and the fair sex. It can gladden me and my heart to imagine the sun of feminine loveliness radiating in an infinite diversity, spreading itself in a confusion of tongues where each individual has a small part of femininity's total wealth, yet so that what else she has forms itself harmoniously about that point. In this sense feminine beauty is infinitely divisible. Except that the particular share of beauty must be harmoniously controlled, for otherwise its effect will be disturbing and it will seem as though Nature's intentions for this woman had not been realized. My eyes can never weary of coursing over this multifaceted surface, these diffused emanations of womanly beauty. Every individual feature has its own small part and is yet complete, happy, glad, beautiful. Each has its own: the merry smile, the roguish glance, the longing eye, the pensive head, the exuberant spirits, the quiet sadness, the deep foreboding, the portending melancholy, the earthly homesickness, the unconfessed emotions, the beckoning brows, the questioning lips, the secretive forehead, the inveigling curls, the concealing lashes, the heavenly pride, the earthly modesty, the angelic purity, the secret blush, the graceful step, the lovely swaying, the languishing posture, the wistful dreaming, the unaccountable sighs, the willowy form, the soft outlines, the luxuriant bosom, the swelling hips, the tiny foot, the dainty hand. – Each has its own, what it has the other does not. When I have looked and looked again at, considered and considered again, this worldly multiplicity, when I have smiled, sighed, flattered, threatened, desired, tempted, laughed, wept, hoped, feared, won, lost – I close the fan and the scattered fragments gather themselves into the unity, the parts into the whole. My soul then rejoices, my heart pounds, my passion is inflamed. This one girl, the only one in all the world, she must belong to me, she must be mine. God can keep His heaven so long as I can keep her. I know what I'm choosing – something so great that it can't be to heaven's advantage to apportion things thus, for, if I kept her, what would be left over for heaven? The Muhammadan faithful would be disappointed in their hope were they, in their paradise, to embrace pale, weak shadows; for warm hearts they would not find, since all the warmth of the heart would be concentrated in her breast. Disconsolate, they would despair when they found pale lips, lacklustre eyes, an impassive bosom, a limp handclasp; for all the redness of the lips and the fire of the eyes and the heaving of the bosom and the promise of the handclasp and the foreboding of the sigh and the seal of the kiss and the trembling of the touch and the passion of the embrace – all – all would be united in her who lavished upon me a wealth sufficient for a whole world, both here and in the beyond. That's how I have often thought of this matter. But every time I think in this way I become warm, because I imagine her as warm. Although warmth is usually considered a good sign, it does not follow that this way of thinking will be accorded the distinction of being called 'solid'. So now, for the sake of variety, being myself cold I shall think coldly of woman. I shall try to think of woman categorially.[80] Under what category must she be understood? Under being-for-another. This is not, however, to be taken in the bad sense, as if the one that was for me were also for another. Here, as always with abstract thought, one must refrain from having any regard to experience; for otherwise, in the present case, I would find, most curiously, that experience is both for and against me. Here as always, experience is a most curious character, because it is its nature always to be both for and against. So she is being-for-another. Here again, but from another quarter, one must not be put off by experience, which teaches us that one seldom encounters a woman who is truly being-for-another, since a great many are generally speaking absolutely nothing, either for themselves or for others. She shares this description with Nature, with anything feminine at all. Thus Nature as a whole is only for-another; not in the teleological sense in which the separate links in Nature exist for some other particular link, but in the sense that all of Nature is for-another – for Spirit. Similarly with particular things. Plant-life, for instance, unfolds its hidden charms in all naivety and is only for-another. Likewise a puzzle, a charade, a secret, a vowel, etc. are only for-another. And this can explain why, when God created Eve, He let a deep sleep fall upon Adam; for woman is the man's dream. There is also another way in which this story teaches that woman is being-for-another. For it is said that Jehovah took a rib from the man's side. Had he taken something, say, from the man's brain, woman would no doubt have remained a being-for-another; the idea, however, would not have been to make her a figment of the brain but something quite different. She became flesh and blood, but for that very reason she falls under the description 'Nature', which is essentially being-for-another. It is at the touch of love that she first awakens; before that she is dream. Yet we can distinguish two stages in that dream existence: the first is when love dreams about her, the second when she dreams about love.

As being-for-another, woman is characterized by pure virginity. For virginity is a form of being which, in so far as it is a being-for-self, is really an abstraction and it only appears for another. The same is true of feminine innocence. So one can say that a woman in that state is invisible. And we know there was no image of Vesta,[81] the goddess who most nearly represented authentic virginity. For the form of this existence is aesthetic jealousy of oneself, just as Jehovah is ethically jealous of himself,[82] and it will not allow there to be any image of it or even any notion. It is this contradiction, that what is for-another is not, and only becomes visible as it were with the other. Logically, there is nothing wrong with this contradiction, and no one who knows how to think logically will be put off by it but rejoice in it. Anyone who thinks illogically, however, will fancy that whatever has being-for-another simply is, in the finite sense in which one can say of a particular thing, 'That's something for me.'

This being of woman (for the word 'existence' already says too much, since she does not subsist out of herself)[83] is rightly characterized as charm, an expression suggesting vegetative life; she is like a flower, as the poets are fond of saying, and even the spiritual is present in her in a vegetative manner. She is wholly contained in categories of Nature, and so she is free only aesthetically. She only becomes free in a deeper sense through the man, and that is why we say [in Danish] at frie, and that is why the man 'frees' [frier].[84] Certainly the woman chooses, but if we are thinking of this as the outcome of a long process of deliberation, the choice is unfeminine. That's why it is a humiliation to get a refusal, because the individual in question has thought too well of himself, has wanted to make another free without being able to. – There is a deep irony in this situation. The for-another has the appearance of being the dominant party: the man sues for her, the woman chooses. In terms of her concept a woman is the vanquished one; in terms of the man's he is the victor; and yet this victor bows before the vanquished. Still, that's quite natural and it is only boorishness, stupidity and lack of erotic sensibility to ignore what is immediately presented in this way. There is also a deeper reason. For the woman is substance, the man is reflection. So she doesn't choose, then, without further ado. The man sues, she chooses. But the suing is a question and her choice is just an answer to a question. In one sense the man is more than the woman, in another he is infinitely less.

This being-for-another is pure virginity. If it makes an attempt to be itself in relation to another being which is being-for-it, then the opposition manifests itself in an absolute prudishness; but this opposition, too, shows that woman's essential being is being-for-another. Absolute devotion has as its diametrical opposite absolute prudishness, which is invisible in a converse sense as the abstraction against which everything breaks, but without this bringing the abstraction to life. Femininity then takes on the character of abstract cruelty, an extreme in caricature of authentic feminine refractoriness. A man can never be as cruel as a woman. Consult mythology, fable and folk-tales and you will find this corroborated. If one has to describe a principle of Nature whose mercilessness knows no bounds, then it is a virginal being. Or one reads in horror of a young woman who, unmoved, lets her suitors lay down their lives, something one finds so often in the folk-tales of all nations. A Bluebeard kills all the girls he has loved on the bridal night; but it is not the killing of them that he takes pleasure in; on the contrary, his pleasure has gone before. That is where the concreteness lies; it isn't cruelty for cruelty's sake. A Don Juan seduces them and runs away, but it is seducing them he takes pleasure in, not running away; so it is not at all this abstract cruelty.

Thus I see, the more I reflect on this matter, that my practice is in perfect harmony with my theory. For my practice has always been permeated with the conviction that woman is essentially being-for-another. That is why the moment is of infinite importance here; for being-for-another is always a matter of the moment. The moment may take a longer or a shorter time coming, but as soon as it comes, what was originally being-for-another becomes a relative being, and then it is all over. I am well aware that husbands, in another sense, say something to the effect that the woman is being-for-another, that she is everything to them for the whole of their lives. Of course one must give the husbands credit for that. But really I believe it is something they delude one another into thinking. Every class in society has, as a rule, certain conventional practices, and in particular certain conventional lies. This sailor's yarn must be reckoned among them. To be a judge of the moment is not such an easy matter, and naturally what a person who misjudges it lands himself in for the whole of his life is simply tedium. The moment is everything, and in the moment the woman is everything. The consequences I do not comprehend. Among them is the consequence of having children. Now I fancy that I am a fairly consistent thinker, but even if I were to go crazy I am not a man to consider this consequence; I simply do not understand it; you need a husband for that.

Yesterday Cordelia and I visited a family at their summer home. The party kept mostly to the garden, where we passed away the time in all sorts of physical exercise. Among other things we played quoits.[85] When another gentleman who had been playing with Cordelia had gone, I took the opportunity to take his place. What a wealth of charm she displayed, even more seductive through the becoming exertion of the game! What graceful harmony in the contradictions of her movements! How light she was – like a dance over the meadows! How vigorous, yet unopposed, deceiving the eye until equilibrium resolved everything. How vehement her appearance, how challenging her glance! The game itself naturally held a special interest for me. Cordelia seemed not to notice it. A remark of mine to one of the spectators about the attractive custom of exchanging rings struck down in her soul like a lightning bolt. From that moment a higher radiance pervaded the whole situation, a deeper significance permeated it, a greater energy kindled her. I held both rings on my stick. I paused a moment. I exchanged a few

words with the bystanders. She understood this pause. I tossed the
rings to her again. Soon she caught both of them on her stick. As
though inadvertently, she tossed them straight up into the air, so
that it was impossible for me to catch them. This toss was accompanied by a look full of boundless temerity. There's a story of
how a French soldier who had campaigned in Russia had his leg
amputated at the knee because of gangrene. As soon as the painful
operation was over, he grabbed the leg by the foot, threw it in the
air and shouted: '*Vive l'empereur!*' With the same kind of look, and
more beautiful than ever, she threw both rings into the air and said
to herself: Long live love! I found it inadvisable, however, to let her
run riot in this mood, or to leave her alone in it, for fear of the
languor that so often ensues. I therefore remained quite calm and
compelled her with the help of the presence of those around us to
continue playing, as if I had noticed nothing. Conduct of that kind
simply gives her more resilience.

If one could expect any sympathy these days for such inquiries, I
would pose the prize question: 'Aesthetically, who is the more
bashful, a young girl or a young matron, the ignorant or the
knowledgeable? To which of them dare one grant greater freedom?'
But such things don't concern these earnest times of ours. In Greece
such an inquiry would have aroused general interest; the whole state
would have been in commotion, the young girls and young wives
in particular. No one would believe it nowadays, but nor would
they believe it nowadays if they were told of the famous contest
waged between two Greek girls and the extremely thorough inquiry
it led to.[86] For in Greece one did not treat these things lightly and
irresponsibly. Yet everyone knows that Venus bears a nickname as a
result of this contest, and that all admire the image of Venus which
has immortalized her. A married woman has two periods in her life
when she is interesting: her earliest youth and then again, long after,
when she has become a great deal older. But she has also – this must
not be denied her – a moment when she is even more charming
than a young girl, and inspires even more respect; but it is a rare
moment in life which need not be seen in life itself, and perhaps
never is so. I imagine her, then, healthy, blooming, luxuriantly
developed; she holds a child in her arms, on whom all her attention

is turned, in whose contemplation she is lost. It is a picture one might call the most charming human life has to offer; it is a Nature myth, which may therefore only be seen in art, not in reality. Nor must there be any additional figures in the picture, no setting, for that would only disturb. If one has resort to our churches one has frequent opportunity to see a mother approaching with a child in her arms. Quite apart from the disconcerting wail of the child, and the anxious thoughts the wailing arouses about the parents' expectations for the child's future, the surroundings are in themselves so confusing that, even if everything else were perfect, the effect would be lost. One sees the father, and that is a great mistake since it removes the myth, the enchantment; one sees – *horrendo refero*[87] – the earnest choir of godparents, and one sees – simply nothing. Conceived as a picture for the imagination it is the most charming thing of all. I am not without courage and daring, nor recklessness enough to venture an assault – but if I saw such an image in reality, I would be defenceless.

How Cordelia occupies me! Yet the time is soon over, for my soul constantly requires rejuvenation. It is already as though I heard the cock crowing in the distance. Perhaps she hears it too, but she believes it proclaims dawn. – Oh why is a young girl so pretty, and why does it last so briefly? I could become quite melancholy with this thought, and yet it is no concern of mine. Enjoy, don't chatter. Those who make a business of such reflections generally have no enjoyment at all. However, letting the thought of it come out can do no harm; for generally this sadness, not on one's own but on others' behalf, adds a little to one's male beauty. A sadness which dawns deceptively, like a misty veil, over manly strength is part of the masculine erotic. In the woman the corresponding quality is a kind of melancholy. – When a girl first gives herself totally it is all over. I still approach a young girl with a certain anxiety; my heart throbs because I feel the eternal power latent in her nature. That has never struck me in the presence of a married woman. The modicum of resistance she tries, with artful means, to put up is nothing. It's as if the married woman's cap should make a greater impression than a young girl's uncovered head. That is why Diana has always been my ideal. That pure virginity, that absolute decorousness, has always greatly engaged me. But while indeed occupied by her, I have always looked at her askance. For I take it she really in no way deserved all the praise she reaped for her virginity. She knew the role it played in her life; that is why she preserved it. Also, I have heard mumblings in philological corners that she retained an image of the terrible birth pangs her mother had endured. This is said to have put her off and I can't blame Diana for that, for I say with Euripides: I would rather go to war three times than bear one child.[88] Now I couldn't really fall in love with Diana, but I don't deny I'd give a lot for a conversation with her, for what I might call a straight talk. She had to get used to all sorts of tricks. Obviously my good Diana possesses, in one way or another, a knowledge that makes her far less naive even than Venus. I wouldn't bother spying on her in her bath,[89] not at all, but I'd like to spy her out with my questions. If I were stealing off to a tryst where I feared for my victory, I would prepare myself, arm myself, mobilize all the spirits of love, by conversing with her. –

It has often been a matter of consideration for me what situation, what moment, might be regarded as the most seductive. The answer to this naturally depends on what one desires and how one desires and the way one has developed. I go for the wedding-day and for one moment in particular. When she stands decked out as a bride yet all her magnificence pales before her beauty, and she too turns pale, when the blood stops, when her bosom rests, when the look falters, when the foot is unsteady, when the virgin trembles, when the fruit ripens; when heaven exalts her, when the seriousness gives her strength, when the promise sustains her, when the prayer blesses her, when the myrtle wreath crowns her; when the heart trembles, when the eyes are fixed on the ground, when she hides in herself, when she belongs other than to the world in order wholly to belong to it; when her bosom swells, when the living form sighs, when the voice falters, when the tear quivers before the riddle is explained, when the torch is lighted, when the bridegroom waits – then the moment has come. Soon it will be too late. There is only one step left but it is all that a false step needs. This moment makes even an insignificant girl significant, even a little Zerlina becomes a subject. Everything must be composed, the biggest contrasts united in the moment; if something is missing, especially one of the chief contrasts, the situation immediately loses part of its seductiveness. There is a well-known engraving. It represents a penitent. She looks so young and innocent that one is almost embarrassed on her and her confessor's behalf about what she can really have to confess. She is lifting her veil a little, she is looking out into the world as if seeking something she might on some later occasion have an opportunity to confess, and of course one understands that indeed it is nothing more than obligation out of consideration to – the father-confessor. The situation is really most seductive, and since she is the only figure in the piece, there is nothing to prevent one's imagining the church in which all this takes place being so spacious that several very different preachers could all preach here simultaneously. Yes, the situation is really most seductive, and I have no objection to being placed in the background, especially if the girl has nothing against it. However, it will always be an extremely subordinate situation; after all, it appears that it is not only in her relation to a father-confessor that the girl is a child,[90] and it will take time before the moment comes.

Now have I, in my relationship with Cordelia, been constantly faithful to my pact? That is to say, to my pact with the aesthetic. For that is what makes me strong, the fact that I always have the idea on my side. It is a secret, like Samson's hair, which no Delilah shall wrest from me. Straightforwardly to betray a young girl, that is something I certainly couldn't endure. But the fact that the idea, too, is there in motion, that it is in its service that I act and to its service that I dedicate myself, that makes me strict with myself, an abstainer from every forbidden enjoyment. Has the interesting always been preserved? Yes, in this secret conversation I dare say it freely and openly. The engagement itself was interesting precisely in not offering what is ordinarily understood by the interesting. It preserved the interesting through the outward appearance contradicting the inner life. Had I been secretly bound to her, it would only have been interesting to the first power. This, however, is interesting to the second power, and for that reason interesting for the first time for her. The betrothal bursts, but by virtue of the fact that she herself cancels it in order to raise herself to a higher sphere.[91] So it should be; for this is the form of the interesting which will occupy her most.

September 16th

The bond burst; longingly, strong, daring, divine, she flies like a bird which is allowed now for the first time to stretch its wings. Fly, bird, fly! Truly, if this royal flight were a departure from me, my pain would be infinitely deep. As if Pygmalion's beloved were turned to stone again,[92] that is how it would be for me. I have made her light, light as a thought; shouldn't this, my thought, belong to me? It would be something to despair over. A moment earlier it would not have occupied me, a moment later it will not trouble me, but now – now – this now which is an eternity to me. But she does not fly away from me. Fly, then, bird, fly; rise proudly on your wings, glide through the soft realms of the air, soon I am with you, soon I will be hiding myself with you in that deep solitude!

The aunt was somewhat taken aback by the news. However, she is too much the free-thinker to want to coerce Cordelia, even though, partly to lull her into an even sounder sleep, partly to confuse Cordelia a little, I have made some attempts at getting her to take an interest on my behalf. As for that, she otherwise shows me much sympathy; she has no notion of what good reason I have to deprecate all sympathy.

She has got permission from the aunt to spend some time in the country; she is to visit a family. It is very fortunate that she cannot straightaway surrender to an excess of mood. It means she will be kept in a state of tension for a while yet by all kinds of outside resistance. I keep up a tenuous communication with her with the help of letters; that keeps our relationship alive. She must be made strong now in every way; in particular the best will be to let her have a few flings at eccentric contempt for people and the commonplace. Then when the day of departure arrives, a dependable fellow will turn up as her coachman. They will be joined outside the gate by my highly trusted servant. He accompanies them to the

appointed place and remains with her for her service and assistance
in case of need. Next to myself I know of no one better fitted for
this than Johan. I have myself arranged everything out there as
tastefully as possible. Nothing lacks that can serve in any way to
beguile her soul and reassure it with a sense of luxurious wellbeing.

My Cordelia!

So far the separate family cries of 'Fire!' have not joined in a
general capitoline city-war's confusion.[93] Presumably you have
already had to put up with individual solos. Imagine the whole
assembly of tea-and-rum and coffee mesdames; imagine a lady presiding who forms a worthy counterpart to Claudius's immortal
President Lars,[94] and you have a picture, a conception, and a
measure of what you have lost and with whom: being well thought *lost her*
of by good people.   *virginity*

I enclose the famous engraving which represents President Lars. I
couldn't purchase it separately, so I bought the whole of Claudius,
tore it out and threw away the rest, for how could I venture to
trouble you with a gift that at this moment has no meaning for
you? Why shouldn't I use every means to get hold of what might
give you pleasure just for one moment? Why should I let more get
mixed up in a situation than belongs to it? Nature may be given to
such excesses, and the person who is in thrall to all of life's finite
circumstances. But you, my Cordelia, in your freedom you would
hate it.

                                                         Your Johannes

Spring is the most beautiful time to fall in love, autumn the most
beautiful to reach the goal of one's desires. In the autumn lies a
sadness which is entirely in keeping with the way the thought of a
desire's fulfilment courses through one. Today I have been out at
the country place where in a few days Cordelia will find a setting in
harmony with her soul. I myself do not want to share in her
surprise and pleasure over this; such erotic issues would only weaken
her soul. If she is alone in this, on the other hand, she will pass her
time in reverie over such things. Everywhere she will see allusions,

hints, an enchanted world, but all of this would lose its meaning if I stood by her side; it would make her forget that, for us, the time is past when such things enjoyed in fellowship had meaning. The surroundings must not inveigle her soul like a narcotic, but constantly allow it to rise up out of them by looking upon them as a game of no significance compared with what is to come. I intend in these days that remain to visit this place more often to keep me in the mood.

My Cordelia!

I can now truly call you *mine*, no outward sign reminds me of my possession. – Soon I shall truly call you *mine*. And when I hold you firmly in my arms, when you entwine me in your embrace, we need no ring to remind us that we belong to each other, for is not this embrace a ring that is more than a symbol? And the more firmly this ring closes round us, the more inseparably it unites us, the more freedom, for your freedom consists in being mine, as mine in being yours.

Your Johannes

My Cordelia!

While out hunting, Alpheus fell in love with the nymph Arethusa. She would not grant his prayer but fled constantly before him, until on the island of Ortygia she was changed into a fountain. So bitterly did Alpheus sorrow over this that he was changed into a river in Elis on the Peloponnese. He did not forget his love, however, but united himself beneath the sea with that fountain.[95] Is the time of metamorphosis past? Answer: Is the time of love past? With what should I compare your pure deep soul, which has no ties with the world, except with a fountain? And have I not said to you that I am like a river that has fallen in love? And do I not plunge now beneath the sea, now we are separated, to be united with you? There under the sea we meet again, for it is in these depths that we really belong together.

Your Johannes

My Cordelia!

Soon, soon you are mine. When the sun closes its searching eye, when history is over and the myths begin, then it is not only my cloak I fling about me, I fling the night about me just like a cloak and hasten to you and hearken to find you, not by footfalls but by the beating of your heart.

Your Johannes

These days, when I cannot be with her in person whenever I want, the thought has troubled me that it might occur to her at some moment to consider the future. So far that hasn't happened; I have been too good at drugging her aesthetically. Nothing less erotic is imaginable than this talk of the future, the reason for which is basically that people have nothing with which to fill the present. When I'm there I have no fear of that either, for I can make her forget both time and eternity. If one doesn't know how to put oneself in rapport with a girl, one should never get involved in trying to beguile, for then it will be impossible to avoid the two reefs: questions about the future and a catechism on faith. Thus it is quite right of Gretchen to hold a little examination of this kind for Faust,[96] since he had taken the imprudent step of playing the knight, and against an assault of that kind a girl is always armed.

Now everything is, I think, in order for her reception; she must not want of opportunity to admire my powers of memory, or rather, she must not have time to admire it. Nothing has been overlooked which might have some significance for her, while on the other hand, there is nothing there that could directly remind her of me, while invisibly I am nevertheless present everywhere. But the effect will largely depend on how she comes to see it for the first time. Here my servant has received the most detailed instructions, and he is in his way a complete virtuoso. He knows how to drop remarks carelessly to order; he knows how to be ignorant, in short he is invaluable to me. – The location is as she could wish. If one sits in the middle of the room, in both directions one has a view beyond anything in the foreground, on both sides one has the endless horizon, one is alone in the wide ocean of the atmosphere. If one approaches a row of windows on the one side, there far on the horizon a forest curves in on itself like a wreath, delimiting and enclosing. That's how it should be. What does love love? – an enclosure; wasn't Paradise itself an enclosed place, a garden towards the east? – But this ring closes itself too tightly about one – one comes nearer the window, a calm lake hides humbly amidst the higher ground encircling it. At its edge lies a boat. A sigh from the fullness of the heart, a breath from thought's unrest – it frees itself from its moorings, it glides over the surface of the lake, softly moved by the gentle breezes of inexpressible longing; one disappears into the secretive solitude of the forest, cradled by the surface of the lake, which dreams of the forest's dark depths. One turns to the other side, where the open sea spreads before the unhindered eye, pursued by thoughts with nothing to detain them. – What does love love? Infinitude. – What does love fear? Limitation. – Behind this large salon is a smaller room, or rather a closet; for whatever that room in the Wahl house was on the verge of being, this is it. The similarity is striking. A carpet woven of osiers covers the floor; before the sofa stands a small tea-table, on it a lamp, the image of the one at home. Everything is the same, only more splendid. It's a difference I feel I can permit myself with the room. In the salon stands a piano, a very plain one, but reminiscent of the fortepiano at the Jansens'. It is open; on the music stand a little Swedish melody lies open. The door into the entry stands ajar. She comes in by the door at the back of the room – Johan has been instructed in this. Her eye then takes in the closet and the piano together. Memory awakens in her soul; just then Johan opens the door. – The illusion is perfect. She goes into the closet. She is pleased, of that I'm sure. As her glance falls on the table she sees a book. The same instant Johan picks it up as if to lay it to one side, as he adds casually, 'The master must have forgotten this when he was out here this morning.' From that she first learns that already this morning I have been out there, and then she wants to see the book. It is a German translation of Apuleius's well-known *Cupid and Psyche*.[97] It is no poetic work, but nor should it be; for it is always an insult to a young girl to offer her a piece of genuine poetry, as if she herself were not poetical enough in such moments to absorb the poetry hidden in them before it is consumed by another's thought. This is not something people generally consider, and yet it is so. – She will read this book and thus the purpose is achieved. – In opening it at the place where it was last read she will find a little sprig of myrtle; she will also find that it means rather more than a bookmarker.[98]

My Cordelia!

What fear? When we keep together we are strong, stronger than the world, stronger than the gods themselves. You know, there once lived a race on earth who, though human, were each sufficient unto themselves and did not know the inner union of love.[99] Yet they were mighty, so mighty that they would storm heaven. Jupiter feared them and divided them up so that one became two, a man and a woman. Now it happens sometimes that what was earlier united is brought together once more in love; such a union is stronger than Jupiter. Then they are not merely as strong as was the individual but even stronger, for love's union is an even higher one.

Your Johannes

September 24th

The night is still – the clock strikes a quarter to twelve. – The keeper by the gate blows his benediction out over the countryside. It echoes back from Blegdammen – he goes inside the gate – he blows again, it echoes even further. – Everything sleeps in peace, except love. So rise up, you secret powers of love, unite in this breast! The night is silent – a solitary bird breaks this silence with its screech and the beat of its wings as it skims over the dewy field down the sloping bank to its rendezvous – *accipio omen!*[100] How full of omens all Nature is! I take warning from the flight of the birds, from their cries, from the playful slap of the fish against the water's surface, from their disappearance beneath the depths, from a distant barking of dogs, from a wagon's faraway clatter, from footfalls that echo from afar. No ghosts do I see in this night hour; I do not see what has been, but what shall be, from the bosom of the lake, from the kiss of the dew, from the mist that spreads over the earth and hides its fruitful embrace. Everything is image; I myself am a myth about myself, for is it not rather as a myth that I hasten to this meeting? Who I am has nothing to do with it. Everything finite and temporal is forgotten, only the eternal remains, the power of love, its longing, its bliss. – My soul is attuned as a drawn bow, my thoughts ready as arrows in a quiver, not poisoned yet well able to mingle with blood. How vigorous is my soul, healthy, happy, all-present like a god. – Her beauty came from Nature. I thank you, wonderful Nature! Like a mother you have watched over her. Accept my thanks for your care. She was undefiled. I thank you, you people to whom she owed that. Her development was my handiwork – soon I shall enjoy my reward. – How much have I gathered into this one moment which is now at hand. Death and damnation if I should fail! –

I don't see my carriage yet. – I hear the crack of a whip, it's my coachman. – Drive for dear life, even if the horses drop dead, but not one second before we are there.

September 25th

Why can't a night like that be longer? If Alectryon could put a foot wrong,[101] why can't the sun be compassionate enough to do the same? Still, now it is over and I want never to see her again. Once a girl has given away everything, she is weak, she has lost everything; for in the man innocence is a negative factor, while for the woman it is her whole worth. Now all resistance is impossible, and only when it is there is it beautiful to love; once it is gone, love is only weakness and habit. I do not wish to be reminded of my relation to her; she has lost her fragrance, and the time has gone when, for pain over her untrue lover, a girl is transformed into a heliotrope.[102] I will not take leave of her; nothing disgusts me more than a woman's tears and a woman's prayers, which change everything yet are really of no consequence. I have loved her, but from now on she can no longer engage my soul. If I were a god I would do for her what Neptune did for a nymph: change her into a man.[103]

Nevertheless, it would really be worthwhile knowing whether one couldn't poetize oneself out of a girl, whether one couldn't make her so proud that she imagined it was she who had wearied of the relationship. It could become a quite interesting epilogue, which in its own right might be of psychological interest, and besides that, enrich one with many erotic observations.

PART TWO

CONTAINING THE PAPERS OF B:
LETTERS TO A

Les grandes passions sont solitaires, et les transporter au désert, c'est les rendre à leur empire.

Chateaubriand

1 THE AESTHETIC VALIDITY OF MARRIAGE

My Friend!

These lines your eyes first fall upon were written last. Their aim is to try once more to compress into letter form the extensive inquiry commended to you herewith. They are therefore of a piece with the lines that come last; together these form an envelope and thus indicate externally what you will find many proofs to convince you of within, that it is indeed a letter you are reading. The idea of writing you a letter has been one I have been unwilling to give up, partly because the time at my disposal has not permitted the more careful preparation required of a treatise, partly because I was reluctant to forgo this opportunity to address you in the more admonitory and urgent tones which the form of a letter allows. You are far too adept in the art of speaking in altogether general terms about anything, and without letting yourself be personally affected, for me to tempt you into mobilizing your dialectical powers. [. . .] As a public official I am accustomed to writing in folio. That could have its advantages if it can contribute to giving what I write a certain authority. The letter you hereby receive is of some size: if weighed on the Post Office scales it would have been an expensive one. On the fine scales of cultivated criticism it could prove very insignificant. So I beg you not to use either of these scales: not the Post Office's, for the letter is to be received into your own charge and not for further conveyance; nor that of criticism, since I would hate to see you incur such an uncongenial misunderstanding.

If this inquiry came to any other person's eyes but your own, it would strike them as exceedingly strange and pointless; if it were a married man he might exclaim with the *bonhomie* of the paterfamilias, 'Yes, marriage, that's life's aesthetic.' If it were a young man he might rather vaguely and unreflectingly chime in, 'Yes, love, you are life's aesthetic.' But neither of them would be able to grasp why it should occur to me to want to save the aesthetic reputation of marriage. Indeed, rather than earning the gratitude of actual or aspiring husbands, I would no doubt invite their suspicion. For to defend is to indict. And I would have you to thank for that, since I myself have never been in doubt about it; yes, you who in spite of

all your bizarrerie I love like a son, a brother, a friend, who I love
with an aesthetic love, since perhaps sometime you will find a
centre for your eccentric movements; who I love for your impetuosity, your passions, your foibles; who I love with the fear and
trembling of a religious love because I see in what ways you have
gone astray, and because for me you are something quite other than
mere appearance. Yes, when I see you lunge to the side, see you rear
like a wild horse, starting back and then plunging forward, yes, I
refrain then from any pedagogical frippery but think of a horse that
is unbroken, and see, too, the hand that holds the reins, see the
scourge of an overpowering fate raised above your head. And when
now at last this inquiry has come to hand, perhaps you will say,
'Yes, undeniably it is a monstrous task he has set himself, but now
let us see how he has coped with it.'

Perhaps I speak to you too mildly; perhaps I bear with you too
much, perhaps I should have wielded more of that authority which
for all your pride I do wield over you; or perhaps I should not have
involved myself with you in this topic at all; for you are in many
ways a pernicious person and the more one has to do with you the
worse it becomes. You are not really an enemy of marriage, but
you abuse your ironic glance and sarcastic taunting to make a
mockery of it. I will admit to you that in this respect you are not
tilting at the air, that you strike home, and that you are extremely
observant. But I will also say that this is perhaps what is wrong
with you. Your life will be nothing but approach-runs. You will no
doubt reply that that is better, after all, than to travel on the train of
triviality and lose oneself like an atom in the social throng. As I say,
you cannot say that you hate marriage, for your thoughts have no
doubt never really come that far, at least not without the very idea
scandalizing you, so you will have to forgive me for assuming that
you have not thought the matter through. What you are drawn to
is the first rapture of love. You know how to drown and hide
yourself in a dreamy, love-intoxicated clairvoyance. All around
yourself you spin the finest spider's web and then lie in wait. But
you are not a child, not a waking consciousness, and the look in
your eye means something else; but for you that is enough. You
love the accidental. A smile from a pretty girl in an interesting
situation, a captured glance, that is what you are after, that is a

theme for your idle imagination. You who always make so much of being the observer must put up with being an object of observation in return. I will remind you of a case in point. A pretty young girl who happened (for naturally this had to be stressed, that you had no idea of her social standing, name, age, and so on) to be seated beside you at table was too prim to want to bestow you a glance. You were perplexed for a moment as to whether it was simply prudery or whether there wasn't some embarrassment mixed up with it, which when properly illuminated, might present her in an interesting situation. She sat opposite a mirror in which you could see her. She cast a shy glance at it without guessing that your eye had already taken up residence there; she blushed when your eye met hers. Things like that you preserve as accurately as a daguerreotype and register just as quickly, just half a minute even in the worst weather, as you know.

Alas! you are indeed a strange being. Child one moment, old man the next, at one moment reflecting with tremendous seriousness upon the most exalted scientific problems, on how you will give your life to them, the next a love-struck fool. From marriage, however, you are a long way off, and I hope your guardian angel stops you going astray; for sometimes I seem to detect signs in you of wanting to play at being a little Zeus. You are so exclusive in your love that you no doubt fancy that any girl should count herself lucky to be your sweetheart even for a week. That gives you your studies in the amorous to pursue along with aesthetics, ethics, metaphysics, world-politics, etc. It is impossible really to be angry with you; the evil in your case, as in the medieval conception, has a certain admixture of good nature and the childlike. As for marriage, you have always remained simply an observer. There is something treacherous in wanting only to observe. How often have you not – yes I admit, it amused me – how often have you not also plagued me with your stories of how you have sneaked your way first into the one then into another husband's confidence, in order to see how deeply he had become stuck in the mire of married life. To steal your way into people, that's where you have a truly great gift, I do not deny it, or at the same time that it is a proper entertainment to hear you recount the results and to witness your uncontained joy every time you can bring some really fresh observation to the market. But frankly your psychological interest lacks seriousness and is more like hypochondriacal curiosity.

But now to the matter in hand. There are two things in particular I must regard as my task. To show the aesthetic significance of marriage, and to show how the aesthetic element can be sustained in the face of life's manifold obstacles. However, so that you can devote yourself the more safely to any edification the reading of this little essay might possibly bring you, I will prefix short polemical prologues to the discussion of these points in which due consideration will be given to your sarcastic observations. But in this way I hope also to have paid my dues to the pirate states thus to be left in peace at my vocation, for it is indeed my vocation as a husband to fight for marriage – *pro aris et focis* [for hearth and home]. And I assure you the affair is so close to my heart that I, who otherwise feel little temptation to write books, could really be tempted if I could hope to save even a single marriage from whatever hell it may have plunged into, or to make a few people better able to bring to fruition the most beautiful task set for a person.

To be on the safe side, I will occasionally allude to my wife and my relationship with her, not because I would make so bold as to present our marriage as the exemplary norm, but partly because poetic portrayals plucked out of thin air have, through their gener ality, no particular power to convince, and partly because it is important for me to show how it is possible to preserve the aesthetic even in everyday circumstances. [. . .] One thing I thank God with all my soul for is that she is the only one I have ever loved, the first. And one thing I pray God with all my heart for is that He will give me the strength never to want to love another. This is a domestic prayer in which she joins me; for every feeling, every mood, acquires a higher meaning for me by my making her party to it. All feelings, even the highest religious ones, can acquire a certain spaciousness and ease when one is always agreed in them. In her presence I am at once priest and congregation. And if I should once in a while be so unloving as not to remember this good, so ungracious as not to give thanks for it, she will remind me. For mark well, my young friend! what we have is not the dalliance of the first days of infatuation, or attempts at experimental eroticism, of the kind in which practically everyone in the days of engagement has posed himself and the loved one the question whether she hasn't been in love before or he hasn't loved someone before. It is life's earnest, and yet it is not cold, unbecoming, unerotic, unpoetic. And in truth, that she really loves me and that I really love her, are things I have very much at heart. Not, of course, that our marriage has not in the passage of years become as stable as most others, but for me this is a matter of the continual rejuvenation of our first love. [. . .] This rejuvenation [. . .] is not just a sad backward glance, or the poetic memory of an experience which is really only a way of deluding oneself – all things of that kind sap one's energy. This is an activity. The time when one has to be content with memories can come all too soon; life's fresh spring should be kept open as long as possible. You, on the contrary, really live from theft. You creep up on people unawares, steal from them their moments of happiness, their most beautiful moments, put this phantom-image into your pocket [. . .] and present it whenever you want. [. . .] You think [. . .] they should be grateful to you because from your study of lighting effects and by your captivating turn of phrase you have let them appear transfigured in those exalted moments into something larger than life. Perhaps they *lose* nothing, and one may even surmise that they might possibly retain a memory of these things, which always causes them pain. But *you* lose. You lose your time – your peace of mind – your patience to live; for you well know how impatient you are. [. . .] There is an unrest in you over which your consciousness nevertheless soars light and clear. Your whole soul is gathered at that point. Your mind draws up a hundred plans, everything is prepared for the assault. Should it fail in one direction, instantly your well-nigh diabolical dialectic is ready to explain that away as . necessary part of the new plan of operation. You hover constantl over yourself and however decisive each step you take, you are ready with an interpretation which with a word can change everything. And then there is the whole embodiment of the mood: your eyes sparkle, or rather it is as though a hundred watchful eyes were simultaneously shining, a fleeting blush passes rapidly over your face; you have full confidence in your calculations, and yet still wait with a terrible impatience – yes, my dear friend, I really think that in the final analysis you delude yourself; all this talk of catching a person in his moment of happiness, it is only your own exalted

why its
harmful for
the seducer

mood that you capture. You are so wrought up that you are
fabricating things. That is why I thought it was not so harmful for
others. For you it is absolutely harmful.

And underlying this is there not after all a monstrous breach of
faith? You say people do not concern you yet should thank you for
turning them, through this contact with them, not into swine as
Circe did[1] but from swine into heroes. You say it would be quite
different if there were someone who really confided in you but that
so far you have never met such a person. Your heart is moved, you
melt with inward agitation at the thought of sacrificing everything
for him. Nor will I deny that you have a certain kindly disposition
to help, that the way you support the needy, for example, is truly
beautiful, and that in the gentleness you display now and then there
is something noble. Nevertheless I think that there lurks here a
certain superiority. [. . .] You once told me how while out walking
you came up behind two poor women. Maybe my own account
here of what happened lacks the vividness of yours when you
rushed up to me possessed only of this thought. They were two
women from the poorhouse. They'd perhaps seen better days, but
all that was forgotten and the poorhouse is not exactly the place to
foster hope. While one of them took and offered the other a pinch
of snuff, she said, 'If only someone had five dollars.' Perhaps this
bold wish, which reverberated unanswered over the slopes up to the
ramparts, surprised even herself. You approached. Before taking the
decisive step you had already taken out your wallet and extracted a
five-dollar bill, so that the situation should remain duly flexible and
she should not suspect anything too soon. You approached with an
almost subservient civility, as befits a ministering spirit; you gave
her the five dollars and vanished. You revelled in the thought of the
impression it would have on her, whether she would see this as
some divine dispensation, or whether her mind would rather,
perhaps grown defiant through much suffering, turn almost with
contempt against a divine governance that took on the form here of
pure accident. You told me that this prompted you to consider
whether the wholly accidental fulfilment of such an accidentally
expressed wish could cause someone to despair because of its negat-
ing the reality of life in its deepest roots. Thus what you wanted
was to play the part of fate, what you really revelled in were the

multifarious thoughts you could spin out of the situation. Now I admit you are well suited to the part of fate, to the degree one links this word to the notion of the greatest inconstancy and caprice. For myself, I am content with a less superior appointment in life. Moreover, you can see in this case an example that might enlighten you on just how far you do not harm people with your experiments. It can look as though the advantage were on your side; you have given a poor woman five dollars, fulfilled her highest wish. And yet you yourself admit that its effect on her could just as well be to make her, as Job's wife advised him to do, curse God. You may say these consequences are not under your control, and that if one has to calculate consequences in this way one cannot act. But I will reply, yes, one can indeed act. If I'd had five dollars I too might have given them to her, but I would also have been very much aware of not behaving experimentally; I would remain convinced that divine providence, whose poor instrument I felt myself that instant to be, would surely arrange everything for the best, and that I had nothing to reproach myself for. [. . .]

The eagerness you exhibit can be praiseworthy enough, but can you not see how increasingly clear it is that what you lack, lack entirely, is faith? Instead of saving your soul by putting everything into God's hands, instead of making this short-cut you prefer an endless detour which may never lead you to your goal. To this you will no doubt say, 'Yes, that means you need never act.' I would reply, 'Of course you must, when you know in yourself that you have a place in the world which is yours and where you should concentrate all your activity. But acting as you do borders on insanity.' You will say that if you had just stood by and let God take care of things the woman might not have been helped. I would reply, 'Possibly, but you would have been helped, and the woman too if she entrusted herself to God.' And do you not see that if you really put on your travelling-boots and journeyed out into the world, wasting your time and energy, you would miss the chance of all other activity, which may come to torment you again later on? But, as I said, is this capricious way of living not a breach of faith? It may look as if journeying around the world to find the poor woman showed an extraordinary, an unprecedented degree of constancy, nothing the least egoistic motivated you, it was not as when a lover travels in search of the loved one, not at all, it was pure sympathy. I reply, 'Certainly you should take care not to call that feeling egoism; it is your usual rebellious lack of shame.' Everything established by divine or human law you despise, and to free yourself from it you grasp hold of the accidental, as in this case a poor woman unknown to you. And as for your sympathy, perhaps it *was* pure – for your experiment. [. . .]

As I have said, what you want to be is – fate. But now wait a moment. I do not mean to preach to you, but there is a seriousness in you for which I know you still have an unusually deep respect; anyone with the power to evoke it in you, or enough confidence in you to let it come to the surface, would see in you today, I know, a quite different person. Imagine, to take the highest we can, imagine that the almighty creator of all things, that God in heaven were in this way simply to posit Himself as a riddle for man, were to let the whole human race hover in this fearful ignorance. Would not something deep inside you rebel in resentment against this, could you stand such agony, could you stand the very thought of such a horror, even just for a moment? Yet it is almost, dare one say it, as if God Himself were haughtily to have declared, 'What care I for man?' But that is why it is not so. And when I myself say that God is incomprehensible, it is because my soul is raised to the heights; it is precisely in the most blessed moments that I say the word – incomprehensible – because His love is incomprehensible, incomprehensible because his love surpasses all understanding.[2] [. . .] But bear in mind your life is passing; there will come a time even for you when it draws to its close, when you are offered no further ways out in life, when recollection is all that is left. Yes, recollection, but not in the way you so much love it, this mixture of poesy and truth, but the serious and faithful recollection of conscience. Take care that it does not unroll a personal record, not indeed of genuine crimes, but of wasted possibilities, phantom-images which it will be impossible for you to chase away. You are still young, the suppleness of your spirit is becoming to youth and amuses the eye for a while. One is struck at the sight of a clown whose joints are so pliant as to repeal the necessity of human gait and posture. That, spiritually speaking, is how you are, you can just as well stand on your head as your feet, for you everything is possible and with this possibility you can surprise others and yourself. But it is unhealthy, and for the sake of your own peace of mind I beg you to watch out that your advantage does not become a curse. No one convinced of something can turn himself and everything else upside down at will in this manner. I am warning you, therefore, not about the world but about yourself and I am warning the world about *you*. This much is certain: had I a daughter of an age where there could be any question of her being influenced by you, I would most assuredly warn her, the more so if she were also intellectually gifted. And if there were no reason to warn her against you, then I myself, who nevertheless imagine I might be your match, if not in suppleness then at least in firmness and constancy, if not in the variable and brilliant then at least in steadiness – then I myself, with a certain reluctance, sometimes actually feel that you are corrupting me, that I am letting myself be carried away by your exuberance, by the apparently good-natured wit with which you mock everything, that I am letting myself be borne away into this aesthetic-intellectual intoxication in which you live. In a way, then, I feel to some degree uncertain towards you, at times being too severe, at others too indulgent. However, that is not so strange, for you are the epitome of all possibility; so that one may see in you the possibility at one moment of your own ruin, at another of your own salvation. Every mood, every thought, good or evil, cheerful or sad, you pursue to its farthest limit, yet more in abstraction than concretely, so the pursuit is itself more like a mood from which nothing results except the knowledge of it, though not enough to make it more difficult or easy next time to abandon yourself to that same mood; for you keep it as a constant possibility. So it is almost as though you could be reproached for everything and nothing at all, because it is and yet is not attributable to you. You admit or don't admit, according to circumstances, to having had such a mood. But you are not available for any charge. The important thing for you is that you have had the mood completely, with proper pathos.

But it was the aesthetic significance of marriage I was to deal with. That inquiry might seem unnecessary, to be something everyone would concede as having been sufficiently demonstrated. Haven't knights and adventurers for centuries withstood unbelievable trials and tribulations to end up in the quiet peace of a happy marriage? Haven't novelists and their readers for centuries worked their way through one volume after another to come to a halt with a happy marriage? And hasn't one generation after another endured again and again four acts of trials and intrigues just because there was some likelihood of a happy marriage in the fifth? However, these huge exertions have accomplished very little for the glorification of marriage, and I very much doubt whether there is anyone who has felt that reading such works has qualified him to fulfil the task he has set himself, or felt himself oriented in life. For this is precisely what is pernicious and unhealthy about such writings, that they end where they should begin. After the many twists of fate they have overcome, the lovers finally fall into each other's arms, the curtain falls, the book ends, but the reader is none the wiser. [. . .] What is true in [these works], the properly aesthetic element, is the fact that love is put to work, that this feeling is represented as fighting its way through an opposite. What is false in them is that the struggle, this dialectic, is entirely external, and that love comes out of the struggle as abstract as it entered into it. Once there is a proper appreciation of love's own dialectic, of its pathological struggle, of its relation to the ethical, to religion, there will in truth be no need of hard-hearted fathers, maidens' bowers, or enchanted princesses and ogres and monsters to give love enough to do. Nowadays one seldom meets such cruel fathers or frightful monsters, and to the extent that recent literature models itself on the earlier it is really money that has become the medium of opposition through which love moves, and again we struggle through four acts if there is reasonable prospect of a rich uncle dying in the fifth.

However, performances like these are less frequent, and recent literature is on the whole fully occupied with ridiculing love in that abstractly immediate form found in the world of the romance. [. . .] [But] how far has the age which demolished romantic love succeeded in replacing it with anything better? First I shall offer some criteria of romantic love. One could say, in one word, that it is immediate, that to see her and to love her were one and the same; or, though she saw him just once through a slit in the closed window of her maiden's bower, from that moment she loved him and him alone in the whole world. The immediacy of romantic love is revealed by its dependence on natural necessity. It is based on beauty, in part on sensual beauty, in part on the beauty that can be depicted through, in, and with the sensual, not in the way that some thought-process is needed to bring it to light, but as if constantly on the point of expressing itself on its own, peeping out through the sensual. Though based essentially on the sensual, this love still has a nobility by virtue of the consciousness of the eternal it takes up in itself. For what distinguishes love from lust is its having the stamp of the eternal. [. . .] For the sensual is the instantaneous. [It] seeks instant satisfaction, and the more refined it is, the better it knows how to make the moment of pleasure into a little eternity. [While] the true eternity in love, as in the truly ethical way of life, is what really first delivers love from out of the sensuous. But to bring about this true eternity there must be a determination of the will; of which more later.

The weakness of romantic love is something our own age has grasped very clearly. Its ironical polemic against it has also on occasion been directly amusing; whether it has remedied the defects and what it has put in its place we shall now see. It can be said to have struck out on two paths, one of which is shown at first glance to be a wrong one, that is, an immoral path; the other is more respectable, but to my mind misses the deeper aspects of love. For if love depends on the sensual, then anyone can see quite easily that this immediate knightly loyalty is madness. What wonder, then, that women want emancipation – one of many ugly phenomena in our time and for which men are to blame. The eternal in love becomes an object of scorn, the temporal is retained, but the temporal refined again in a sensual eternity, in the eternal instant of the embrace. What I say here applies not only to this or that seducer slinking about in the world like a beast of prey; no, it befits a numerous chorus of often highly gifted persons, and it is not only Byron who declares love to be heaven, marriage hell.[3] One now sees clearly that what we have here is a reflection, something romantic love lacks. The latter can happily accept the blessing of the Church as one more beautiful celebration, yet without this having any significance for it as such. On the basis of this reflection the love now in question has, with the fearful unfeeling fixity of intellect, come up with a new definition of unhappy love,[4] namely to be loved when one is no longer in love, rather than be in love and not have one's love requited. And in truth, if those who go this way knew just what profundity lies in these few words, they would recoil; for apart from all its experience, shrewdness and sophistication, it also contains an inkling of the existence of a conscience. [. . .] This direction is of course absolutely immoral, but on the other hand it brings us in one way a step nearer our goal, in thought; in a sense it lodges a formal protest against marriage. In a sense this same direction tries to put on a slightly more decent exterior, so it does not just confine itself to the single instant but extends this to a longer period, yet in such a way that instead of taking up the eternal in its consciousness, it takes up the temporal, or entangles itself in this opposition between the eternal and the idea of a possible change in time. It thinks it is possible to put up with living together for quite a while but wants to keep a way out open so that if a happier choice appeared it would still be possible to choose that. It makes marriage into a civil arrangement; one only has to notify the appropriate authority that this marriage is now over and a new one entered into, just as one gives notice of a change of address. Whether this is an advantage for the State, I leave undecided; for the individual it must be a truly remarkable situation. Hence one does not often see it in fact, though the threat is constantly there in the times. Indeed it would require shamelessness of a high degree — I do not think the word is too strong — just as much as it would betray a frivolity bordering on depravity, especially on the part of the female party to this association.

However, there is a quite different tendency of mind which can easily come upon a similar idea, and since it is very characteristic of our time I think I should deal with it here. Such a plan can in fact originate in either an *egoistic* or a *sympathetic melancholy*. There has been enough talk now of the frivolity of our age; I think it high time to speak a little of its melancholy, and I trust that this will make everything clearer. For is not melancholy the defect of our time, is this not what reverberates even in its frivolous laughter, is it not melancholy that has bereft us of the courage to command, the courage to obey, the strength to act, the confidence to hope? And now when the good philosophers are doing everything they can to intensify the actual, will we not soon be so crammed with it that we choke? Everything is cut away except the present; little wonder

then that in one's constant anxiety about losing it one does lose it.
Now, it is true enough that we ought not to vanish in a fleeting
hope, and that this is not the way we are to be transfigured on high;
but for real enjoyment one must have air and it isn't only in the
moment of sorrow that the heavens must be held open, it is important to have an unobstructed view even in times of joy and the
double doors thrown wide. [. . .] If enjoyment were the main thing
in life I would sit at your feet to learn, for in this you are a master.
At one moment you can become an old man in order to suck in
through the funnel of memory, in slow draughts, what you have
experienced, at another you are in the first blush of youth, flushed
with hope; at one moment masculine, at another feminine; now
you enjoy immediately, now you enjoy reflecting on your enjoyment, now reflecting on the enjoyment of others; at one moment
you enjoy abstaining from enjoyment, at another you enjoy abandoning yourself to it; your mind is open, accessible as a city that has
capitulated, reflection is silenced and every step of the intruders
echoes in the empty streets, yet there will always be a little outpost
left over, observing; and then your mind is closed again and you
barricade yourself in, unapproachable and intractable. This is how it
is, and you will see also how egoistic your enjoyment is, and that in
fact you never abandon yourself, never let others enjoy you. [. . .]

Naturally the egoistic kind [of melancholy] fears for itself, and
like all melancholy it is self-indulgent. It has a certain exaggerated
deference for, a secret horror of, a lifelong alliance. 'What can one
count on? Everything can change. Perhaps this being whom I now
almost worship will change; perhaps fate will tie me to another that
is truly the ideal I dreamed of.' Like all melancholy it is defiant and
knows it. 'Perhaps my tying myself irrevocably to one person may
make this being I'd otherwise love with all my soul intolerable,
perhaps, perhaps, and so on.' The sympathetic melancholy is more
painful and also somewhat nobler: it fears for itself for the other's
sake. 'Who can be sure one cannot change? Perhaps what I now
consider good in me may vanish, perhaps what the beloved finds
captivating in me, and which I want to hold on to for her sake, can
be taken from me, and now she stands there, disappointed, tricked;
perhaps a brilliant prospect opens for her, she is tempted, she doesn't
resist the temptation – good God, I'd have that on my conscience; I

have nothing to reproach her for, it is me that has changed, I forgive her everything if only she can forgive me for being so incautious as to let her take such a decisive step. Although I know quite well that far from talking her round I warned her against me, it was her own free decision, but perhaps it was this very warning that tempted her, made her see in me a better being than I am, etc. ...' It is easy to see how this way of thinking is no better served by a ten-year alliance than a five-year one, [...] that such a way of thinking is only too well aware of the meaning of the phrase 'sufficient unto the day is the evil thereof'.[5] It is an attempt to live each day as though that day were decisive, as though every day were examination day. For this reason the widespread tendency today to neutralize marriage is not, as in the Middle Ages, because unmarried life is considered more perfect, but is due to cowardice and self-indulgence. It is also evident that contracting marriages for a definite period is of no avail, since such marriages involve just the same difficulties as do those contracted for a lifetime and, far from bestowing on the parties the strength to live, on the contrary they sap the inner energy of married life, loosen the power of the will, and diminish the blessing of trust that marriage possesses. Also it is already clear, and will later become even more so, that associations of this kind are not marriages, since although contracted in the sphere of reflection they have nevertheless not attained the consciousness of the eternal, as has the ethical way of life, which is what makes the alliance a marriage. This is also something you will entirely agree with, for how often and how unerringly have those mood-tableaux not been the well-deserved targets of your mockery and your irony ('fortuitous love affairs or love's bad infinite')?[6] As when someone with his sweetheart looks out of the window at the moment when a young girl turns the corner into another street, and it occurs to him that 'it is her I'm really in love with'; but as he is about to pick up the trail something interrupts, and so on.

The other expedient, the respectable way, would be *the marriage of convenience*. The very name indicates that one has entered the sphere of reflection. Certain persons, you among them, have always frowned at what is meant here to be a marriage between immediate love and calculating reason – for if one is to respect linguistic usage shouldn't one really call it 'the marriage of reason'? You in particular tend always, with much ambiguity, to recommend 'respect' as a solid foundation for the tie of marriage. That it has to resort to such an expedient as the marriage of convenience shows how thoroughly reflective our age is. To the extent that such an alliance disavows genuine love, it has at least the merit of consistency, but it also shows that it is no solution to the task. A marriage of reason must therefore be looked upon as a kind of capitulation made necessary by life's complications. But how sad all the same that this should be, as it were, the only comfort left for the poesy of our age, that despair should be its only solace. For, clearly, it is indeed despair that makes such an alliance admissible. It tends therefore to be entered into by people who have long since reached the years of discretion and who have learnt that real love is an illusion and its fulfilment a pious wish. Its concern, therefore, is with the prose of life: making a living, social standing, etc. In so far as it has neutralized the sensual in marriage it has the appearance of being moral; but one may ask all the same whether this neutralizing is not as immoral as it is unaesthetic. Or if the erotic is not entirely neutralized after all, then it is disheartened by a prosaic rational consideration that one should be cautious, not too quick to pick and choose, that life after all never gives us the ideal, that it is quite a respectable match, etc. So the eternal which, as was shown above to be part of every marriage, is not really present here, for a rational calculation is always temporal. [. . .]

We have seen now how romantic love was based on an illusion, and how its eternity was based on temporarlity, and that regardless of the knight's remaining fervently convinced of its absolute durability, there was still no assurance of this inasmuch as love's trials and temptations had hitherto been in an entirely external medium. [. . .] We have seen how, when taken up in the consciousness of a reflective age, this immediate, beautiful, but also naive love had to become the object of its scorn and its irony; and we have seen what such an age was reduced to replacing it with. Marriage, too, it took up into its consciousness and declared itself partly in favour of love, to the exclusion of marriage, partly in favour of marriage, disavowing love. [. . .]

With this our little inquiry (as no doubt I'm obliged to call what I'm writing, though first I thought only of a longish letter) has reached the point where marriage can first be viewed in the proper light. That marriage belongs to Christianity, that for all the sensuality of the Orient and for all the beauty of Greece the pagan nations have not perfected it, that in spite of its truly idyllic elements even Judaism has been incapable of that – all this you will surely grant without my having to go into details, all the more so since one only has to recall that the contrast between the sexes has nowhere been made the object of a reflection deep enough to do the opposite sex full justice. But within Christianity, too, love had to suffer many a turn of fate before coming to where it could see the profundity, beauty and truth that lie in marriage. Since, however, the immediately preceding age and to some extent our own have been reflective, it is not such an easy matter to demonstrate it. [. . .]

In so far as it proved a defect of romantic love that it was not reflective, it might perhaps seem proper to let true conjugal love begin with a kind of doubt. That might seem all the more necessary, seeing it is a world of reflection that has brought us to this point. I will not deny that a marriage might be artfully accomplished in accordance with such a doubt, but the question remains whether this is not already to alter the nature of marriage, seeing that it envisages a divorce, after all, between marriage and love. The question is whether it can really be part of marriage to annihilate the possibility of first love through doubt of the possibility of realizing that love, and to make conjugal love both possible and actual through this annihilation [. . .] [or] whether the immediate, the first love can be secured against this scepticism by being taken up into a higher concentric immediacy, so that the conjugal love would not need to plough under the beautiful expectations of the first love, but be itself first love with an admixture of qualities which did not impoverish but enriched it. This is a difficult point to prove, yet of immense importance if we are not to get a rift in the ethical like that in the intellectual sphere between faith and knowledge. And how beautiful, dear friend, you won't deny it for your heart too has, after all, a feeling for love, as your head is all too familiar with doubt – how beautiful it would be if the Christian could call his God the God of love also in a way that what he was thinking of was that inexpressibly blessed feeling, that eternal force in the world – earthly love.

Seeing, then, that in the foregoing I have presented romantic love and reflective love as discursive positions, we are now well placed properly to appreciate how far the higher unity is a return to the immediate, how far the latter contains, besides the 'more', also what lay in the first. It is now sufficiently clear that reflective love constantly consumes itself and stops quite arbitrarily now here, now there; it is clear that it points beyond itself to something higher, but the question is whether the higher cannot straightaway combine with first love. Now, this higher something is the religious, where rational reflection ends, and just as for God everything is possible, so neither for the religious individual is anything impossible. In the religious sphere love finds again the infinity for which as reflective love it sought in vain. [...]

The first thing I must do now is orient myself and particularly you in the essential characteristics of marriage. Obviously, what really constitutes marriage, what is its substance, is love, or if you want to be more explicit, the being in love.[7] Take that away and a shared life is either just a satisfaction of sensual desire or an association, a partnership in the interests of some goal. But love has in itself precisely the quality of eternity, whether the love is of the superstitious, romantic, chivalrous kind or the deeper moral and religious love which is filled with an energetic and vital assurance.

Every estate has its traitors, so too matrimony. Naturally I do not mean the seducers, for of course they have not entered into this holy estate (I trust the mood this inquiry meets you in doesn't cause you to smile at that expression); I do not mean those who have left it through divorce, for they have at least had the courage to be openly rebellious. No, I mean those who are rebels only in thought, who do not even dare let it be expressed in action, these wretched husbands who sit and sigh over the fact that love has long ago evaporated from their marriage, these husbands who, as you once said of them, sit like lunatics each in his matrimonial cell, and tug at the iron bars and fantasize about the sweetness of betrothal and the bitterness of marriage, these husbands who, as you rightly observe, are among those to congratulate, with a certain malicious glee, anyone who gets engaged. I cannot describe how despicable they appear to me, and how much unholy joy it gives me when such a husband confides in you and pours out all his sufferings, rattling off all his lies about the happy first love, and you say with a knowing look, 'Yes, I'll make sure not to get onto thin ice', and he is all the more embittered that he can't drag you with him into a common shipwreck. It is these husbands you so often refer to when you speak of a tender paterfamilias with four blessed children he would sooner see in hell.

Now, if there was any truth in what they say, there would have to be a separation of love and marriage, so that love is assigned to one moment in time and marriage to another, love and marriage remaining incompatible. Then it would not take long to discover to which moment of time love belonged – it would be the engagement, the beautiful time of the engagement. [. . .] If the engagement really were the most beautiful time, truly I fail to see why they and – if they are right – why anyone at all gets married. But still they do get married with all possible petty-bourgeois precision, when it suits aunts and cousins, neighbours and the people across the street, which betrays the same drowsiness and apathy as looking on the engagement as the most beautiful time. [. . .]

The substantial element in marriage is being in love; but which comes first: love, or marriage so that being in love forms the sequel? This latter view has enjoyed no little esteem among narrow-minded advocates of common sense, has been preached not infrequently by shrewd fathers and even shrewder mothers who themselves think they have learnt from experience and, to compensate for the harm done, insist their children should learn from it too. This is the wisdom of dove-fanciers who shut two doves up in a little cage, though they haven't the slightest sympathy for each other, and think they are bound to learn to come to terms. This whole way of thinking is so narrow-minded that I mention it only as a matter of form and also to remind you of much that, in this respect, you have turned your back upon. [. . .]

Marriage, then, is not meant to evoke love; on the contrary it presupposes it, but presupposes it as something present, not past. Yet marriage has an ethical and religious factor; being in love has not. For this reason marriage is based upon resignation; being in love is not. Now unless we are to assume that everyone makes two moves in their lives, first the (if I may so put it) pagan move, where being in love belongs, and then the Christian move which is expressed in marriage, unless one is to say that such love has to be left out by Christianity it will have to be shown that love and marriage are compatible. [. . .]

First, then, an examination of love. Here I shall fasten on an expression which for me, despite your own and the whole world's derision, has nevertheless always had a beautiful meaning: first love (believe me, I am not going to give in and presumably neither will you, so on this point there will be a peculiar discord in our correspondence). When I myself mention this phrase I think of what is among the most beautiful things in life; when you use it, it is the signal for the whole line of your advanced observation-posts to open fire. Yet just as for me there is nothing ludicrous about this phrase, and frankly I only put up with your attack because I overlook it, so is there none of the sadness in it for me that it can no doubt have for some. This sadness need not be morbid, for the morbid is always the untrue and contrived. There is something pleasing and salutary in someone's having had ill-luck in his first love, when he has come to know its pain but still kept true to his love, still kept faith in this first love; there is something nice about it when, in the course of years, he sometimes now recalls it quite vividly, and although his soul has been sound enough to, so to speak, take leave of that kind of life in order to dedicate itself to something higher, there is something pleasing about his then remembering it sadly as something that may have fallen short of perfection but was very beautiful none the less. And this sadness is far more healthy, more beautiful, and nobler than the prosaic reasonableness which has long ago done with such childish pranks, or than this devilish shrewdness of the song-master Don Basilio which fancies itself to be health but is nevertheless the most wasting of sicknesses.[8] For what is a man profited if he shall gain the whole world and lose his own soul?[9] For me there is nothing at all sad in this phrase 'first love', or in any event only a small seasoning of bittersweet. For me it is a battle-cry, and although now a married man of several years, I have still constantly the honour to fight under first love's victorious banner.

For you, on the contrary, its significance, its over- and underevaluation, has a puzzling wave-like motion. At one moment you are altogether enthusiastic about the first love. You are so infused with the energetic concentration implied in it that it is the only thing you want. You are so kindled and inflamed, so burning with love, so dreaming and fertile, as heavy as a rain cloud, as gentle as a summer breeze, you have in short a lively conception of what it means for Jupiter to visit the loved one in a cloud or in rain.[10] The past is forgotten, every restriction removed. You expand more and more, you feel a softness and pliability, every joint becomes supple, every bone a flexible sinew: as a gladiator reaches up and stretches his body so as to exert complete control over it – anyone would think this would deprive him of his energy and yet this voluptuous torture is precisely the condition for his making proper use of his strength. You are now in the state in which you enjoy the pure rapture of complete receptivity. The softest touch is enough to thrill this invisible, fully stretched-out spiritual body through and through. There is an animal which I have frequently pondered upon, the jellyfish. Have you noticed how this gelatinous mass can extend itself into a plane and then slowly sink or rise, so still and firm that one might think one could step on it? Now it observes its prey drawing near, it makes itself hollow, becomes a bag and sinks with immense speed deeper and deeper, using this speed to snatch the prey into – not its bag, for it has no bag, but into itself, for it is itself a bag and nothing more. It can now contract itself so much that it is incomprehensible how it could possibly expand. This is just about how it is with you, and you will simply have to forgive me for having no more beautiful animal to compare you with, as also for the fact that you cannot perhaps quite help smiling at yourself at the thought of being just a bag. At such moments it is 'the first' you are pursuing, that alone is what you want, without suspecting that it is contradictory to want the first constantly to return, and that it follows from this that either you simply cannot have reached the first or you have had the first and what you now see, what you now enjoy, is always merely a reflection of that first; from which we may additionally note that you are in error in believing that the first could be completely present in anything other than the first itself if only one seeks rightly, and that, as far as your appealing to your own practice is concerned, this too is a misunderstanding since you have never practised in the right direction. [. . .]

From you, then, one seeks in vain to learn what lies behind this mysterious word 'first', a word that has had and always will have enormous significance in the world. What significance the word has for the individual is really decisive for his whole spiritual condition, just as its having no significance at all for him is enough to show that his soul is not at all attuned to being touched and thrilled by higher things. For those, on the other hand, for whom 'first' has acquired a significance, there are two paths. Either 'the first' contains the promise of the future, is the propulsive, infinite impulse in their lives; and these are the fortunate individuals for whom the first is nothing but the present, though the present as the first in its constant unfolding and rejuvenation. Or the first does not urge the individual on within; the energy that is in the first does not become the motive power in the individual but the power of repulsion that thrusts away. These are the unfortunate individuals who are continually distancing themselves more and more from 'the first'. This, naturally, can never be something for which the individual himself is totally without blame.

All affected by the idea of the first connect the word 'first' with a solemn conception, and it tends only to be in connection with things at a lower level that 'first' means worst. You are rich in examples in this respect: the first proofs, putting on a new dress coat for the first time, etc. The greater the likelihood something can be repeated, the less significant the first becomes, the less likelihood the more significant; while on the other hand, the more significant whatever proclaims itself for the first time, the less likely it can be repeated. Should there even be something eternal in it, then all likelihood that it can be repeated vanishes. If, then, one has spoken with a certain wistful earnestness of the first love as something that could never be repeated, this is no disparagement of love but the most profoundly-felt extolling of it as the eternal power. [. . .]

So much for the predicate we give love when we call it the 'first'. I now go on to consider *first love* more directly. [. . .] It is surely obvious enough that the philistines who think they have pretty well come to that point in life when the thing to do is listen and look about (perhaps even in a newspaper) for a life partner have already excluded themselves from first love, and that a philistinism of this kind cannot be regarded as the state that precedes first love. It is, of course, conceivable that Eros might be merciful enough to play a trick on such a person by making him fall in love. 'Merciful' indeed, because it shows extraordinary mercy to bestow the highest earthly good upon a person, and that is what first love always is even when it is unhappy; but this will always be the exception and his previous condition will remain just as unedifying. If one is to believe the priests of music (and this is a matter in which one is almost bound to believe them), and if in their company one were also to hearken to Mozart, then surely the state preceding first love must be described by recalling how love makes blind. The individual becomes as though blind, you can almost see it in him, he sinks into himself, looks in upon his own looking, and yet there is a constant striving to look out upon the world. Though the world has blinded him, he still stares out at it. It is this dreaming yet searching state that Mozart has depicted in the Page in *Figaro*, as sensual as it is of the soul. In contrast, the first love is an absolute wakefulness, an absolute watchfulness, and this has to be kept going not to do it injustice. It is directed at a single, definite, actual object which is all there is for it; everything else just does not exist. This one object exists not in vague outline, but as a definite living being. This first love has an element of the sensual, of beauty, in it, yet it is not simply sensual. The sensual as such comes forth first in reflection, but first love lacks reflection and is therefore not simply sensual. This is the necessity in first love. As with everything eternal, it has in itself the twofold character of presupposing itself back into all eternity and forward into all eternity. [. . .]

[First love] is the unity of freedom and necessity. The individual feels drawn to the other with an irresistible power but precisely in this feels his freedom. It is a unity of the universal and the singular, it has the universal *as* the singular, even to the verge of the contingent. But it is not on the strength of reflection that it has all this, it has it immediately. The more definitively first love conforms to this, the healthier it is, the more likely that it is indeed a first love. The two are drawn to one another by an irresistible power and yet they enjoy in this their whole freedom. I have no hard-hearted fathers on hand here, no sphinxes to be dealt with first,[11] I have fortune enough with which to equip them (nor have I taken it on myself, as novelist and playwright, to drag out time to the torment of the whole world, of the lovers, of readers and audience), so in the

name of God let them come together. You see I offer you the noble
father and actually it is really a very attractive role if only we
ourselves had not often made it so laughable. You noted perhaps
that, in the father's style, I added the little phrase, 'in the name of
God'. This you can surely forgive in an old man who may never
have known what first love is or has long since forgotten; but that a
younger man still enthused over first love lets himself make a point
of it, may surprise you. [. . .]

So first love is immediately secure in itself. But the individuals
have also had a religious development. This I have a right to assume,
and indeed I shall, seeing I am to show that first love and marriage
can survive together. It is of course another matter when an unhappy
first love teaches the individuals to *seek* security in God and marriage.
Then the first love is changed even if it may still be possible to
restore it. [. . .] Here it is not in time of sorrow that they seek God,
nor is it fear and dread that impel them to pray. Their heart, their
whole being, is filled with joy; what more natural than to thank
Him for this? There is nothing they fear: outside dangers will have
no power over them, and inward dangers, yes, those are quite
unknown to first love. But this thanksgiving does not alter first
love; it has not been joined by any disturbing reflection, it is assumed
into a higher concentricity. But a thanksgiving of this kind, like all
prayer, is combined with an element of action, not in an external
but an internal sense, in this case to want to hold on to this first
love. This doesn't change the nature of the first love, no reflection
has joined in, its firm-jointedness is not loosened, it still retains its
blessed assurance intact, it is simply assumed into a higher concentricity. Perhaps in this higher concentricity it simply does not
know what it has to fear, perhaps it imagines no dangers, and yet
through this good intention, which also is a kind of first love, it is
lifted up into the ethical. [. . .]

You will of course remind me that I left it quite unclear and
vague which God I was referring to, that it was not a heathen Eros
who would gladly be privy to love's secrets, and whose presence
was then at bottom merely a reflection of the lovers' own mood,
but the Christian God, the God of spirit who is jealous in His
opposition to everything that is not spirit. You would remind me
that in Christianity beauty and the sensual are negated, you would

remark in passing that for the Christian it is indifferent whether Christ was ugly or beautiful; you would beg me to keep away from love's secret meetings with my orthodoxy and in particular from any attempt at mediation, which you oppose even more than the most crass orthodoxy: 'Yes, how cheering for the young girl, how totally in harmony with her mood, to step up to the altar. As for the congregation, it must surely see in her an imperfect being who has been unable to resist the seduction of earthly desire; she is to stand there as though to be chastised or make a public confession; and the priest first reads the text and then perhaps leans over the rail to confide to her, as a small crumb of comfort, that matrimony is, after all, an estate well pleasing to God. All that's worthwhile here is the priest's position, and if the girl were sweet and young I wouldn't mind being in it so I could whisper this secret in her ear.'

My young friend! Yes, matrimony is indeed an estate well pleasing to God: on the other hand I know of no place in the Scriptures which speaks of a special blessing for bachelors – which is after all where all your multifarious love affairs end. But dealing with you is just about the hardest of tasks, for you are capable of proving anything and in your hands every phenomenon can become anything. Yes, certainly, the Christian God is spirit and Christianity is spirit, and a discord is posited between flesh and spirit; but flesh is not sensuality, it is selfishness, and in this sense even the spiritual can be sensual; if for example someone takes his spiritual gifts in vain, then he is carnal. And well I know that for the Christian it is not necessary that Christ should have been an earthly beauty, and if it were, it would be very sad for a different reason from the one you proffer, for if beauty were essential think how the believer would have to yearn to see him. But from all this it in no way follows that the sensual is annihilated in Christianity. First love has in it the element of beauty, and the joy and fullness to be found in the sensual when it is innocent can very well be taken up into Christianity. [...]

So you have found what your soul was yearning for, what in many mistaken attempts it thought it would find; you have found a girl in whom your whole being finds its repose; and even if one might think you a little too experienced, this then is nevertheless your first love, of that you are convinced. 'She's pretty' – naturally;

'sweet' – what else? 'and yet her beauty lies not in the normal, but in the unity of the manifold, in the accidental, the self-contradictory'; 'she has a soul' – I can imagine; 'she can abandon herself to an impression so that it can practically make your head swim; she is light, she can bob like a bird on a twig, she has spirit, spirit enough to illuminate her beauty but not more'. The day has come that is to assure you of the possession of all you own in the world – a possession which for that matter you are certain enough of. You have requested the favour of imparting extreme unction upon her. You have already waited some time in the family dining-room; several times a bustling chambermaid, four or five inquisitive cousins, a venerable aunt, a hairdresser, have hurried past. You are already half indignant at all this. Then the door to the parlour slowly opens, you take a quick look inside, you are delighted there is not a soul there, that she has had the tact to remove all intruders even from the parlour. She is pretty, prettier than ever, there is an animation about her, a harmony whose vibrations resonate even through her. You are astonished; she exceeds even your dreams; you too are transformed but your subtle reflection instantly conceals your emotion; your calm has a still more seductive effect upon her, imparts a desire in her soul which gives interest to her beauty. You approach her. Her finery, too, gives the situation a touch of the uncommon. You still haven't uttered a word. You look at her, yet as though you were not looking, you do not wish to embarrass her with amorous boorishness, but even the mirror comes to your aid. Upon her bosom you fasten a brooch you gave her the first time you kissed her, with a passion which now seeks its confirmation; she has herself kept it hidden, no one has known about it. You produce a little bouquet of flowers of just one sort, a flower of no significance in itself. When you sent her flowers there was always a small shoot of it, but not noticeable, so no one suspected it but her. Today this flower too shall stand up in honour and dignity, it alone is to adorn her, for she loved it. You hand it to her, a tear trembles in her eye, she returns it to you, you kiss it and fasten it to her bosom. A certain sorrow spreads over her. You yourself are moved. She takes a step back, she looks half in anger at the finery that is getting in her way, she throws her arms about your neck, she cannot tear herself away, she embraces you as vehemently as though an enemy power would tear you from her. Her delicate finery is crushed, her hair has fallen down, in the same instant she has vanished. You are left once more to your solitude, which is broken only by a bustling chamber-maid, four or five inquisitive cousins, a venerable aunt, a hairdresser. Then the parlour door opens, she enters, and a quiet earnestness is to be read in her every feature. You press her hand, leave her only to meet her again – yes, at the Lord's altar; you had forgotten that, you who had pondered so much at other times on that too. You forgot it in your infatuation. You had come to terms with the situation as it is for everyone else, but this you had not considered; and yet you have come too far not to see that a marriage is rather more than a ceremony. You are seized by a fear: 'This girl whose soul is as pure as the light of day, sublime as the vault of heaven, innocent as the ocean, this girl before whom I could fall down in worship, whose love I feel could snatch me out of all confusion and give me new birth, it is she I am to lead to the Lord's altar, she who is to stand there like a sinner, of whom and to whom it shall be said that it was Eve who seduced Adam. To her before whom my proud soul bows down, the only one to whom it has bowed down, to her it shall be said that I am to be her master and she subservient to her husband. The moment has come, the Church is already reaching out its arms for her and before giving her back to me it will first press a bridal kiss upon her lips, not that bridal kiss I gave the whole world for; it is already reaching out its arms to embrace her, but this embrace will cause all her beauty to fade, and then it will toss her over to me and say, "Be fruitful and multiply". What kind of power is it that dares intrude between me and my bride, the bride I myself have chosen and who has chosen me? And this power would command her to be true to me; does she then need to be so commanded? And is she to be true to me only because a third party commands it, one whom she therefore loves more than me? And it bids me be true to her; must I be bidden to be that, I who belong to her with all my soul? And this power decides our relation to each other; it says I am to ask and she is to obey; but suppose I do not want to ask, suppose I feel myself too inferior for that? No, I will obey *her*, her hint is my command, but I will not submit to a foreign power. No, I will flee with her afar while there is still time, and I will beg the night to hide us and the silent clouds to tell us fairytales in bold images, as befits a wedding night, and under the immense vault of heaven I will intoxicate myself in her physical charms, alone with her, alone in the whole world, and I will throw myself into the abyss of her love; and my lips are mute, for the clouds are my thoughts and my thoughts are clouds; and I will cry out and implore all the powers of heaven and earth that nothing may disturb my happiness, and I will bind them on oath and let them swear to this. Yes, away, far away, that my soul might be restored to health, that my breast might breathe again, that I shall not stifle in this sickly air – away.' – Yes, away, that is what I would say too: *Procul o, procul este, profani.*[12] But have you also considered whether she will follow you on this expedition? 'Woman is weak', no, she is meek, she is much nearer to God than man is. That is why, for her, love is everything, and she will certainly not disdain the blessing and the confirmation which God would grant her. It has certainly never occurred to a woman to have anything against marriage, and in all eternity it never will, so long as men themselves do not corrupt her, for an emancipated woman might well light upon such a thing. Offence always comes from men; for man is proud, he wants to be everything, he will have nothing above him. [. . .]

The first thing that scandalized you was that you should be solemnly instated as her master. As if that is not what you were and perhaps all too much so, as though your words did not carry that stamp sufficiently. But you will not give up this idolatry, this coquetry, about wanting to be her slave though you sense very well that you are her master.

Second, what made your soul rebel was that your beloved should be declared a sinner. You are an aesthete, and I might be tempted to propose it to your idle head's consideration whether this could not make a woman even more beautiful. [. . .] You can well understand I am not serious in this [. . .] [but] there would be plenty for you to busy yourself with in this respect. You would have thought of the tremulous light which even in the Gospel spreads over the woman that was a sinner, whose many sins were forgiven because she loved much.[13] What I would say, however, is that, once again, it is just a whim of yours to have her stand there as a sinner. For it is one thing to sin *in abstracto*, another to know it *in concreto*. But woman is meek and certainly it has never occurred to a woman to be truly offended at the earnest word of the Church being addressed to her. Woman is meek and full of trust. Who can cast her eyes down like a woman, but who like her can lift them up? So if the Church's solemn proclamation that sin has come into the world should bring about any change in her, it would have to be that she held fast still more strongly to her love. [. . .]

Finally, it upsets you that a third power wants to bind you to being true to her and her to you. For the record, I must ask you to recall that this third power does not impose itself; since the individuals we have in mind are religiously developed, they themselves seek it out, and the question is whether anything in it stands in the way of their first love. You will hardly deny that it is natural for first love to seek corroboration through love being made, in one way or another, into a duty the lovers impose upon themselves in the face of a higher power. Lovers swear fidelity to one another by the moon, the stars, the ashes of their fathers, their honour, etc. If to this you say: 'Yes, such oaths wouldn't mean anything, they're just a reflection of the lovers' own mood, why otherwise should it occur to them to swear by the moon?', I reply that here you yourself have changed the nature of first love; for the beauty of first love is precisely that everything acquired reality for it on the strength of love, and only in the moment of reflection is it clear that swearing to the moon is meaningless [. . .]

We saw, then, how first love could come into relation with the ethical and the religious without the aid of a reflection that changed its nature, since it is simply drawn up into a higher immediate concentricity. In one sense a change has indeed occurred, and it is this I shall now consider, what could be called the lovers' metamorphosis into bride and bridegroom. The way the lovers refer their love to God is by thanking God for it. Here the change is one of refinement. The weakness to which the man is most prone is to suppose he has conquered the girl he loves; this makes him feel superior – but there is nothing at all aesthetic in that. When he thanks God, on the other hand, he humbles himself under his love, and it is in truth far more beautiful to take the beloved as a gift from the hand of God than to have subdued the whole world to conquer her. Add to this that a man really in love will not find rest in his soul until he has thus humbled himself before God; and the girl he loves really means far too much for him to dare take her even in the most refined sense as a prize. And should it please him to conquer and take possession of her, he will realize that the proper thing is daily possession throughout a whole lifetime, not the preternatural power of brief infatuation. Yet this does not occur as though consequent upon some previous doubt, it happens immediately. Thus what is really living in first love remains, while the bitter elements, if I may so put it, are filtered out. It is natural for the other sex to be sensible of the imbalance and submit to it, and if she goes so far as to feel joy and happiness in being nothing, that might well be on the way to becoming something untrue, but if she now thanks God for the loved one, her soul is safe against suffering; being able to thank God means she can put the loved one at just enough distance for her to be able to draw breath. And that occurs not as a result of an anxious doubt. She knows no such thing. It happens immediately.

I have already indicated above that even the illusory eternity in first love made it moral. In now referring their love to God, this thanks which the lovers give for their love will itself give it an absolute stamp of eternity, as also will the intention and the obligation, and this eternity will be based not upon dark forces but upon the eternal itself. The intention is significant in another way too. In it lies the possibility of movement in the love, and so also the possibility of its being freed of the difficulty under which first love as such labours, that it cannot get started. The aesthetic in it lies in its infinitude, but its unaesthetic aspect lies in the fact that this infinitude can be finitized. I shall use a more figurative expression to throw light on how the advent of the religious cannot disturb the first love. The religious is really the expression of the conviction that with God's help man is lighter than the whole world, the same faith that lies behind man's ability to swim. Now assuming there is a swimming belt that can hold one up, we might suppose it would always be worn by someone who had been in mortal danger, but we might also suppose that a person who had never been in mortal danger would wear it too. The latter corresponds to the relation between first love and the religious. First love girdles itself with the religious without any previous painful experience or anxious reflection. Only do not, I pray, press the analogy too far, as if the religious only stood in an external relation to first love. That this is not the case has been shown above.

And let us settle accounts once and for all. You talk so much of the erotic embrace, but what is it compared with the matrimonial! What greater richness of modulation in the matrimonial 'we' than in the erotic! It resonates neither with the merely momentary eternity of seduction, nor with the illusory eternity of fantasy and imagination, but with the eternity of consciousness, the eternal's eternity. What strength in the matrimonial 'my', for will, resolve and intention sound a note of far greater depth. What energy and resilience, for what so hard as will and what so soft! What power of movement! – not the merely confused enthusiasm of dark incitement, for marriage is made in heaven and duty permeates the whole body of the universe to its furthest extremity; it prepares the way and assures us that in all eternity no obstacle is able to disturb the love! So let Don Juan keep his leafy bower, the knight the dark heaven and its stars if he cannot see above it; marriage has its heaven even higher. Such is marriage; and when it is not so, God is not to blame, nor Christianity, nor the wedding, nor a curse or a blessing, but man alone. And is it not a pity and a shame that books are written which confuse people about life, make them bored with it before they begin, instead of teaching them how to live? If they were right, that would be a painful truth, but it is lies. We are taught to sin, and those who haven't the heart for that are made just as unhappy in another way. I myself, alas, am all too affected by the aesthetic not to know that the word 'husband' grates on your ear. But I do not care. Even if the word 'husband' has come into disrepute and is now almost a laughing matter, it is high time one tried to restore it to its place of honour. And if you say, 'You never see anything like that even though you see marriages often enough', that does not disturb me; for seeing marriage every day makes one see the greatness in it less often, not least when one does everything to belittle it. For have you not brought it to such a pass that a girl who offers a man her hand before the altar is thought more imperfect than those heroines in your romances with their first love?

Now that I have listened patiently to you and your outbursts, more angry perhaps than you would rightly admit (but when you confront marriage as a reality you will perhaps see that you have not quite understood these agitations inside you – you will rage inwardly yet presumably again without confiding in anyone), then you may forgive me my small observations. One loves only once in one's life, the heart holds on to its first love – marriage! Hearken to and wonder at this harmony of the different spheres. It is the same thing, just expressed aesthetically, religiously and ethically. One loves only once. To help make this a reality marriage steps in, and if people who do not love one another take it into their heads to get married, then the Church cannot be held responsible. One loves but once, this echoes from the most divergent quarters: from the fortunate to whom each day brings happy proof of the fact, and from the unhappy, of whom there are really only two classes, those continually yearning for the ideal and those not willing to hold on to it. The latter are the real seducers. You meet them less often because there is always something special about them. I knew one, yet he too admitted that one loves only once, but love had been unable to tame his wild lust. 'Yes,' say certain people, 'one loves only once, one marries twice, three times.' Here again the spheres are united; for the aesthetic says no and the Church and clerical ethics look with suspicion on the second marriage. This for me is of the utmost importance; for if it were true that man loved several times, then marriage would come into question; it might look as though the erotic was being injured by an arbitrary rule of religion requiring one to love only once, treating matters of the erotic so carelessly in this way. As if to say, 'You can marry once and let that be an end of it.'

We have now seen how first love came into relation with marriage without being changed. That same aesthetic which is to be found in the first love must therefore also be found in the marriage, since the former is contained in the latter. But the aesthetic aspect of first love lies in its infinitude, its apriority – as explained above. Next, it lies in the unity of opposites which love is: love is sensual yet spiritual; it is freedom yet necessity; it is in the instant, has to a high degree the quality of presence, and yet has an eternity in itself. All this marriage has too: it is sensual yet spiritual, but it is more, for applying the word 'spiritual' to first love amounts to saying it is of the soul, that it is sensuality permeated with spirit. It is freedom and necessity, but also more, for freedom in the case of first love is really rather the freedom of the soul in which individuality has not yet expurgated itself of natural necessity. But the more freedom, the more self-surrender, and only a self-possessed person can be lavish with himself. The religious freed the individuals – he from false pride, she from false humility, and it thrust itself between the lovers who held each other in such a close embrace, not to separate them but so that *she* could give of herself with an abundance she had never before suspected, and *he* not simply receive but give of himself to be received by her. It has in it an inner infinitude even more than first love, for marriage's inner infinitude is an eternal life. It is a unity of opposites even more than first love, for it has one opposition more, the spiritual and thereby the sensual in a yet deeper opposition; but the further from the sensual one gets the greater aesthetic significance it acquires, for otherwise the most aesthetic thing would be animal instinct. But in marriage the spiritual is higher than in first love, and the higher the heaven over the marriage bed the better, the more beautiful, the more aesthetical it is, and the heaven that overarches the marriage is not this earthly one but the heaven of the spirit. [. . .]

Yes, I confess, it may be wrong of me, but often when I think of my own marriage, the thought awakens an inexplicable sadness within me; that it will come to an end, that certain as I am that I shall live in another life with her to whom my marriage united me, she will be given to me there in another way, that the opposition which was one of the conditions of our love will be transcended. Yet it consoles me that I know, that I shall recall, that with her I have lived in the most heartfelt, the most beautiful fellowship that earthly life affords. For if I understand anything of all this, then earthly love's defect is the same as its advantage, that it is preferential love. Spiritual love shows no partiality and goes in the opposite direction, constantly discharging all relativities. In its true form earthly love takes the opposite path and at its best is only love for one single person in the whole world. Herein lies the truth in having to love only one and love only once. Earthly love begins by loving several – the preliminary anticipations – and ends in loving one. Spiritual love opens itself constantly wider, loves more and more, has its truth in loving all. So marriage is sensual but spiritual at the same time, free and also necessary, absolute in itself and also, within itself, pointing beyond itself.

Because it has this inner harmony, marriage naturally has its teleology in itself; it is, in so far as it constantly presupposes itself, and in this respect any question of its 'why' is a misunderstanding. [. . .] I would stress the beauty in those marriages which have as little 'why' as possible. The less 'why' the more love, that is, when one sees what is true in it. For the frivolous there will of course prove to have been a little 'why' in retrospect; for the serious person there will prove, to his joy, to have been a huge 'why'. The less 'why' the better. In the lower classes marriage is usually entered upon without any great 'why', but that is why these marriages resound far less frequently with so many 'hows' – how to make ends meet, how to provide for the children, etc. For marriage there is only marriage's own 'why', but that is infinite and so it is not a 'why' according to the sense I am taking it in here. [. . .] The true 'why' is only one but at the same time has in it an infinite energy and strength which can stifle all 'hows'. The finite 'why' is a totality, a swarm, from which each takes his own, one more, the other less, all as bad as each other. For even if someone could unite all finite 'whys' at the beginning of his marriage, he would be the basest of husbands just for that reason.

One of the seemingly most reputable answers to the 'why' of marriage is that marriage is a school for character; one marries in order to elevate and improve one's character. I shall stick to an actual occurrence which I owe to you. There was a government official you had 'got hold of', as you put it, and that's just like you, for when something becomes an object for your observation you shrink from nothing, you think you are following your vocation. He was, besides, quite a clever fellow and had a particularly good knowledge of languages. The family was gathered round the tea-table. He was smoking his pipe. His wife was no beauty, looked rather simple, and old compared with him, all of which could promptly lead one to suppose, as you remarked, that there must be some very special 'why'. At the table sat a young, rather pale, newly-wed woman, who looked as though she knew another 'why'. The wife herself poured tea. It was passed round by a young girl of sixteen, not pretty but plump and lively – she appeared not yet to

have arrived at any 'why'. In that honourable company your un-
worthiness had also found a place. You, who were present *ex officio*,
who had already on a number of occasions come there in vain,
naturally found the situation far too favourable to let it slip. There
had been talk at the time of a broken engagement. The family had
not yet heard this important piece of local news. The case was
pleaded from all sides, that is to say, everyone was prosecutor; it
was submitted to judgement and the sinner excommunicated. Feelings ran high. You ventured to put in a little word in the condemned
man's favour, which naturally wasn't intended to be to his advantage
but to act as a cue. It didn't succeed, so you continued, 'Maybe the
whole engagement was too hasty, maybe he failed to account
for the important "why" – one might almost say the "but" – which
should precede so decisive a step, – *enfin* why does one marry, why,
why?' Each of these 'whys' was uttered with its distinctive but
equally doubting inflection. That was too much. One 'why' would
already have been enough, but such a comprehensive roll-call, a
general call to arms in the enemy's camp, was decisive. The moment
had come. With an air of good humour that also bore the stamp of
a prevailing common sense, the host said, 'Yes of course, my good
man, I can tell you, one marries because marriage is a good school
for character.' Now the whole thing was in motion. Partly by
opposing, partly by approving, you got him to surpass himself in
absurdity – scarcely to the edification of his wife, to the scandal of
the young married woman, and to the astonishment of the young
girl. Then I reproached you for your behaviour, not for the host's
sake but for the women, for whom you were malicious enough to
make the scene as trying and protracted as possible. Two of the
womenfolk do not need my defence, and it was also only your
customary coquetry which led you not to avert your eyes from
them. But his wife, perhaps she really loved him, in which case
think how dreadful it must have been for her to listen to this. Also
there was something indecent in the whole situation; far from
making marriage moral, common-sense reflection really makes it
immoral. Sensual love has only one transfiguration in which it is
equally aesthetic, religious and ethical, and that is love; common-
sense calculation makes it just as unaesthetic as irreligious, because
the sensual here is not within its immediate rights. So the man who

marries for this or that reason takes a step as unaesthetic as it is irreligious. The goodness of his purpose helps not at all, for the fault is precisely that he has a purpose. Were a woman to marry so as – yes, one has heard of such madness, a madness that appears to give her marriage an immense 'why' – so as to bear a saviour to the world, that marriage would be just as unaesthetic as immoral and irreligious. It's something one cannot make clear often enough. A certain class of common-sense persons look down with enormous contempt on the aesthetic as vanity and childishness, and in their pitiable teleology they imagine they are raised high above such things. But it is the exact opposite: with their common sense such people are as unethical as they are unaesthetic. So one always does best to look to the other sex, which is both the more religious and the more aesthetic. The host's exposition was in any case rather trivial and I do not need to present it. On the other hand, I will conclude these remarks by wishing every such husband a Xanthippe for his wife and as wicked children as possible, so that he can hope to possess the means for attaining his purpose.

The fact that, apart from this, marriage really is a school for character or, to avoid using so philistine an expression, a genesis of character, is something I gladly admit; though naturally I must constantly hold that anyone who marries for that reason should rather be directed to any other school at all than to that of love. Besides, someone like that will never derive any benefit from attending that school. In the first place, he deprives himself of the strength, the consolation, the shiver running through all one's thoughts and limbs which is what a marriage is, for it is indeed an act of daring; but that is what it should be, and far from its being correct to want to calculate, such a calculation is precisely an attempt to enervate it. Second, he has of course let go the great working capital of love and the humility which the religious element in marriage gives. Naturally he is much too super-shrewd not to bring with him a pat conception of how he wants his development to go; this will then be the guideline for his marriage and for the unfortunate being he has been shameless enough to select as his sampler. [. . .]

Or one marries – to have children, to make one's humble contribution to the propagation of the human race upon earth. Imagine he gets no children; then his contribution will be very meagre. True,

States have taken it upon themselves to invest marriage with this purpose, giving out rewards for those who marry and for those with most male children. At times Christianity has done the opposite by giving out rewards for those who avoid marriage. Even if this was a misunderstanding, at least it shows a deep respect for the person, that to this extent the individual is not to be treated as merely an element, but as definitive. The more abstractly the State is conceived, and the less it champions individuality, the more natural such an injunction and such an encouragement become. By contrast, in our own time childless marriage has occasionally been almost extolled. For our age finds it hard enough to summon the resignation needed to enter a marriage; having performed that amount of self-denial, one thinks that that must be enough and one cannot really put up with such extravagances as a flock of children. In novels one often finds, if only idly in a casual aside, but still proffered as a reason for a particular individual's not marrying, the fact that he cannot abide children; in real life one sees this manifested in the most refined countries in the removal of children at the earliest opportunity from their parents' home, their being placed in boarding-schools, etc. How often have you not amused yourself at the expense of these tragi-comic heads of family with four blessed children who in all secrecy they wished far away! How often have you not regaled yourself with the injury done to the superiority of those heads of family by the pettiness life brings with it, when the children have to be spanked, when they spill things, when they scream, when the great man – the father – feels his dauntlessness obstructed by the thought that his children bind him to the earth. How often have you not, with well-deserved cruelty, brought such a father to the highest pitch of suppressed rage when you occupied yourself exclusively with his children, letting fall a few words about what a blessing it is, after all, to have children.

Marrying in order to contribute to the propagation of the race might seem an extremely objective reason and a highly natural one. It is as though one took God's point of view and saw from there the beauty of maintaining the race. Indeed, one might attach a special importance to the saying 'Increase and multiply and replenish the earth'. And yet such a marriage is as unnatural as it is arbitrary and has no support in the Holy Scriptures. For we read that God established marriage because it was 'not good that man should be alone', to make a companion for him.[14] And if to some mocker of religion there might seem something slightly questionable about this companionship which begins with man being cast into perdition, that proves nothing and I would rather appeal to that event as a motto for all marriages; for only after the woman had brought this about was the heartfelt fellowship established between them. Then we also read, 'and He blessed them'.[15] These words are completely overlooked. And when the Apostle Paul in some place exhorts the woman to 'learn in silence with all subjection' and 'to be in silence', and then, having silenced her, to humiliate her even further, adds, 'she shall be saved in childbearing', I would never have forgiven the Apostle this contempt had he not made up for it all by adding, 'if they continue in faith and charity, and holiness, with sobriety'.[16] [...]

But back to [...] those married people indefatigably bent on propagating the race. A marriage of this sort usually covers itself in a more aesthetic wrapping. A noble old family of distinction is about to die out; only two representatives remain, a grandfather and his grandson. It is the venerable old man's only wish that the grandson marry so that the family should not become extinct. Or a man who is of no great importance in his own life thinks back, if not so very far then at least to his parents, whom he has loved so much that he would rather their name should not die out but be preserved in the grateful memories of the living. Perhaps he has some vague idea of how fine it would be to be able to tell the children of their grandfather, long since dead, and let this ideal picture, which is just a memory, give strength to their lives and inspire them to all that is noble and great. Maybe he thinks he can in this way repay some of the debt he feels he owes to his parents. That is all very nice and beautiful but irrelevant to marriage, and a marriage entered into for this reason alone is as unaesthetic as it is unethical. That may sound harsh but it is true. Marriage can only be undertaken with one purpose which makes it ethical and aesthetic in the same degree, but that purpose is immanent; every other purpose separates what belongs together and in doing so turns both the spiritual and the sensual into finitudes. Someone may win a girl's heart by talking in this way, particularly if the sentiments expressed are to some extent genuine, but it is wrong and the fact alters her very being, and it is always an insult to a girl to want to marry her for any other reason than that one loves her.

Although all (to use one of your own expressions) stud-farm purposes are as such irrelevant for marriage, a person who has not become confused about his relationship will find a blessing in the family descent. It is a beautiful thing, after all, for the one person to owe the other as much as possible, but the highest thing, surely, one person can owe another is – life! And yet a child can owe a father even more, for it does not receive life bare and blank, it receives it with a definite content, and when the child has rested long enough at the mother's breast it is laid at the father's, and he too nourishes it with his flesh and blood, with a stormy life's dearly bought experience. And, after all, what possibility there is in a child! I am ready to agree with you in hating all the idolatry practised with children, especially the whole cult of the family and the circulating of children at the dinner-table and supper-table for the family kiss, family adulation and family expectations, while the parents complacently congratulate one another on the troubles they have survived and rejoice in the product of their art. Yes, I admit I can be almost as sarcastic at such tiresome practices as you. But I do not allow myself to be disturbed further by them. Children belong to the innermost and most private life of the family, and it is to this twilight zone of mysteries one ought to direct every serious or God-fearing thought on the matter. But there every child will also be shown to have a halo round its head, and every father will feel there that there is more in the child than it owes to him, indeed with humility he will feel that the child is a trust and that he is in the finest sense of the word its stepfather. [. . .]

As for you, indeed you love possibility, yet the thought of children certainly will not make you glad, for I have no doubt this, too, is a world your inquisitive and vagabond mind has peeped into. That, of course, is because you want to have possibility under your own control. You are very fond of being in the same state children are in when they wait in the darkened room for the Christmas tree to appear. But a child, to be sure, is a possibility of quite another kind, and of so serious a kind that you would hardly have the patience to put up with it. And yet children are a blessing. It is a fine and good thing for someone to think with deep seriousness of what is best for his children, but if he does not at least sometimes remember that it is not just a duty that is imposed upon him, a responsibility, but also a blessing, and that God in heaven has not forgotten what even human beings never forget, to lay a gift on the cradle, then he has not opened his heart, either to aesthetic or to religious feelings. [. . .]

I have seen a poor woman who carried on a small trade, not in a shop or stall – she stood in the open square, she stood there in the rain and wind with a baby in her arms; she herself was clean and tidy and the baby carefully wrapped. I have seen her many times. A fashionable lady came by who practically told her off for not leaving the child at home – all the more so because it got in her way. And a priest passing in the same direction approached her; he wanted to find a place for the child in an institution. She thanked him kindly, but you should have seen the look with which she glanced down at the child. Had the child been frozen, that look would have thawed it; had it been dead and cold, that look would have called it back to life; had it been famished and parched, that look's blessing would have restored it. But the child slept and not even its smile could reward the mother. See how this woman perceived what a blessing a child is! If I were a painter I would never paint anything but this woman. Such a sight is a rarity, like a rare flower which one gets to see only by a lucky chance. But the world of spirit is not subject to vainglory; if one finds the tree it blooms perpetually. Her I have often seen. I showed her to my wife. I did not affect importance, sent no rich gifts as though I had a divine authority to reward; I humbled myself beneath her, in truth she needs neither gold nor fashionable ladies, or institutions and priests, or a poor judge in civil law and his wife. She needs absolutely nothing except that the child will one day love her with the same tenderness, and she wants not even for that, it is the reward she has deserved, a blessing which heaven will not withhold. [. . .]

But children are a blessing also in another sense, for one learns so indescribably much from them. I have seen proud people whom hitherto no fate had humbled, who snatched the girl they loved from out of the family life where she belonged with such assurance that it was as if to say, 'When you have me, that should be enough,

I'm used to defying storms, how much more so now when I have the thought of you to give me heart, now that I have much more to fight for.' I have seen the same men as fathers; a small mishap that befell their children could humble them, a sickness bring prayer to their proud lips. I have seen people who prided themselves for practically despising the God that is in heaven, who were wont to pick on every believer as a target of scorn – I have seen them as fathers take the most pious people into service for the good of their children. I have seen girls whose proud glance brought Olympus to tremble, girls whose vain minds lived only for pomp and finery – I have seen them as mothers endure every humiliation, practically begging like mendicants for what they thought was to their children's advantage. [. . .]

In another way, too, one learns much from children. In every child there is something original upon which all abstract principles and maxims come more or less to grief. One has to begin from the beginning, often with much trial and tribulation. There is a deep significance in the Chinese saying: 'Bring your children up well, and you will come to know what you owe your parents.' And now, the responsibility that rests on the father. One consorts with other people, one tries to convey to them some idea of what one thinks right, perhaps makes several attempts; when it does not help, one stops having anything to do with them, one washes one's hands. But when does the moment come when a father dares, or rather when a father-heart can resolve, to give up any further attempt? The whole of life is lived again in the children; only then does one come to some understanding of one's own life. However, it is really no use talking to you about all this; there are things about which one can never form a living conception if one has not experienced them, among them being a father.

And now finally, the fine way in which one is connected by means of one's children to a future and a past. Although one may not exactly have fourteen distinguished ancestors and a concern for producing the fifteenth in line, one has in fact a far longer genealogy, and indeed it gladdens the heart to see how the race takes on as it were a distinct pattern. The unmarried man, too, can of course make such observations, but he will not to the same degree feel prompted to do so, nor entitled, since to some extent they are the interventions of an intruder.

Or one marries to acquire a home. One was bored at home, one has travelled abroad and was bored, one has returned home and was bored. For the sake of company one keeps a remarkably fine retriever and a thoroughbred mare, but one feels that something is missing. For some time one has been vainly seeking an acquaintance at the restaurant where one meets some like-minded friends. One learns he has married, one becomes soft-hearted, sentimental about one's old age; one feels that everything around one is so empty, no one is waiting for you when you are away. The old housekeeper is basically a very decent woman but she has no idea at all how to cheer one up, how to make things a little comfortable. One marries. The neighbourhood claps its hands, finds that one has acted wisely and sensibly, and then they go on to discuss the most important factor in housekeeping, the supreme earthly good: a well-behaved and reliable cook who can be trusted to go to the market alone, a nimble-fingered chambermaid who is so capable that she can be used for anything. If only a bald-headed old hypocrite like this were content to marry a night-nurse – but usually that is not the case. The best is not good enough, and finally he succeeds in capturing a pretty young girl who is then fashioned into a galley-slave of this kind. Perhaps she has never loved; what a frightful misunderstanding!

You see, I have been giving you the floor. However, you must admit that, particularly among more common folk, one finds marriages entered into for the purpose of acquiring a home which have a rather pleasing effect. These are for men of younger years. Not having been especially buffeted by life, they have accumulated the necessary income and now think of getting married. That is agreeable. I also know it would never occur to you to direct your scorn on marriages like these. A certain noble simplicity lends them a touch of both the aesthetic and the religious. For there is nothing egoistic here in the thought of wanting a home; on the contrary, the notion they attach to it is that of duty, a vocation, which is laid upon them, but at the same time a duty that is dear to them.

One all too often hears married folk console themselves and alarm the unmarried by saying, 'Yes, at least we have a home, and a place of refuge for when we grow older.' They sometimes add with a rare Sunday flourish in the edifying style: 'Our children and

- - --

children's children will one day close our eyes and mourn for us.'
The fate of the unmarried will be the opposite. It is admitted with a
certain envy that for a while, in their younger days, these have the
best of it; one silently wishes that one was not yet married oneself.
Yet it all comes again: like the rich man,[17] the unmarried have
taken their goods in advance.

All such marriages suffer from the defect that they treat one
single factor in marriage as the purpose of marriage, and therefore
they often feel disappointed (especially, of course, the first of the
three) when they have to admit that a marriage, after all, means
rather more than the acquisition of a comfortable, agreeable and
convenient home. But now let us again abstract from the mistake in
order to see what is fine and true. It is not granted to everyone to
extend his activity so very widely, and many who imagine they are
working for something greater, sooner or later catch themselves in
a delusion. I do not at all mean to refer to you, for you of course
are too clever not to get wind of this illusion at once, and your
scorn has been directed at it often enough. You have, in this respect,
an extraordinary degree of resignation and have shown once and
for all a total renunciation. You prefer to amuse yourself. You are
everywhere a welcome guest. Your wit, your ease in company, a
certain good naturedness, likewise maliciousness, all contribute to
the sight of you conjuring up the thought of a pleasant evening.
You have always been, and always will be, a welcome guest in my
house, partly because I am not all that afraid of you, partly because
it will be some time before I have to begin being so: my only
daughter is just three years old, and you surely don't start sending
your messages that early. [. . .] You talk so sensibly, so know-
ledgeably, that anyone not knowing you better must believe you
are a settled man. However, you have by no means reached the
truth. You have come to a halt at the destroying of illusions, and
since that is something you have done in all possible and imaginable
ways, really you have worked your way into a new illusion: the
illusion that one can come to a halt there. Yes, my friend, you are
living in an illusion and you accomplish nothing. [. . .]

It is this thought, that it is a vocation, that must be associated,
first of all, with the idea of a home, so as to be rid of any untrue
and contemptible thought of ease. Even in the man's pleasure there

should be an element of this calling, even if it is not manifested in any single, external tangible act. A man can be active in this respect without its being seen, while the woman's domestic activity is more apparent. But the idea of a home is associated, secondly, with such a mass of small considerations that it is very hard to say anything about them in general. In this respect each house has its own distinctive character, and it could be of some interest to acquaint oneself with a wide variety of these. Naturally, however, the point is whether any such character is permeated with a certain spirit, and I for my part abhor all that separatist nonsense in those families which, from the very first, make a point of showing how special everything is in their house, and which sometimes extends to the family's speaking its own language, or in such enigmatic allusions that one doesn't know what to make of it. What matters is that the family itself has such a distinctive character, the art is to contrive to conceal it.

Those who marry in order to have a home are always complaining that they have no one waiting for them, no one to welcome them, etc. This in itself shows they really only have a home because they think also of an outside. Praise God I have no need at all to be outside, either to remember or to forget that I have a home. [. . .]

What more I could wish to say to you in this matter I would rather say in connection with a particular expression I think can justifiably be applied to you, and one you yourself often use: that you are a 'stranger and an alien' in the world. Young people who have no idea of the cost of experience – and no idea of its unutterable wealth either – could easily let themselves be carried away in the same swirl; your talk may perhaps affect them like a fresh breeze which lures them out onto that infinite ocean you show them; even you yourself can be youthfully intoxicated, almost out of control at the thought of this infinity, which is your element, an element which, like the ocean, changeless, hides everything on its deep floor. Should you not, already an experienced hand in these waters, know how to tell of disaster and distress at sea? Of course, generally there is not much one man knows about another on this sea. Here it is not a matter of large ships that one fits out and launches only with difficulty upon the deep; no, it is a question of very small boats, jolly-boats just for one person; one takes advantage of the instant, one spreads one's sail, one skims along with the infinite speed of restless thoughts, alone on the infinite ocean, alone with the infinite heaven. This life is full of danger, but one is familiar with the thought of losing it, for the real enjoyment is to disappear into the infinite so far that all that is left is enough to savour the disappearance. Seafarers relate how on the great world-ocean one sees a kind of craft called the Flying Dutchman. It is able to spread a small sail and then with infinite speed skim over the surface of the sea. That is pretty much how it is with your voyage over the sea of life. Alone in one's kayak one is sufficient unto oneself, one has nothing to do with anybody except in the instant one wants to. Alone in one's kayak one is sufficient unto oneself – I cannot rightly grasp how one is still able to fill this void, but as you are the only person I have known of whom it can be said with some truth that you do fill it, I know also that you have a person on board who can help you fill the time. You should therefore say: alone in one's boat, alone with one's care, alone with one's despair, which one is craven enough to want rather to keep than submit to the pain of being healed. [. . .] I beg you reflect on the pain, the sadness, the humiliation that lies in being in this sense a stranger and an alien in the world. [. . .]

Think of the hidden life of [a] family when it is clothed in an outward form so beautiful that the seams are nowhere visible, and reflect on your relation to it. Just such a family would be to your taste. And you would perhaps often delight in entering its circle. With your easy ways you would soon be as though intimate with it. I say 'as though' since it is clear that you would not be that, clear that because you will always be a stranger and an alien you never could. You would be looked upon as a welcome guest, they might be kind enough to make everything as agreeable for you as possible, they would be gracious towards you, yes, they would treat you as one does a child one is fond of. As for you, you would be inexhaustible in your attentions, inventive in delighting the family in every way. Very pretty, don't you think? And in one bizarre moment you might be tempted to say that you didn't care to see the family in dressing-gowns, or the daughter in slippers, or the wife without her cap; and yet for you, if you look more closely, there is a colossal humiliation implied by the family's correct behaviour towards you. Every family would have to behave towards you like that, and you would be the one humiliated. Do you not think that the family harbours within itself an entirely different life which is its shrine? Do you not believe that all families still have their household gods even if they don't place them in the ante-room? And in that remark of yours does there not lie a very refined weakness? For if ever you were to marry, I really do not believe that you could bear to see your wife in a négligée, unless this were a decorative garment designed to please you. You think no doubt that you have done much for the family by entertaining them, by spreading over it a certain aesthetic lustre. But suppose the family cared very little for this compared with the inner life it possesses. That is how it will go for you with every family. And however proud you may be, there is a humiliation in it. No one shares sorrow with you. No one confides in you. You no doubt often think they do; certainly you have enriched yourself with a multitude of psychological observations. But this is often a decep-tion; what people like is to talk to you only of this and that, and touch distantly upon, or offer hints of, an anxiety only because the interest it arouses in you eases their pain and already contains that agreeable quality which prompts them to yearn for this medicine even when they don't need it. And if someone approached you just because of your isolated position (you know that people would rather commune with a mendicant monk than with their father-confessor), it would never acquire its true meaning, for you or for him. Not for him because he would sense the arbitrariness in its being you he confided in; not for you because you would be unable altogether to ignore the ambiguity your competence rests on. [. . .]

But now I return to what we were discussing above, to the finite purposes for which people enter marriage. I have mentioned only three because, after all, there did seem to be something to be said for them, seeing that they focus on one or another single factor in marriage, regardless of the fact that in their onesidedness they become as ridiculous as they are unaesthetic and irreligious. I will forbear to mention a host of altogether despicable finite purposes, because one cannot even laugh at them. As when one marries for money, or out of jealousy, or because of the prospects – because there are prospects of her dying soon, or of her living long but being a blessed branch that bears much fruit, so that with her one can pocket the inheritances of a whole line of aunts and uncles. I have no mind to mention all this sort of thing.

As an outcome of this inquiry I can emphasize here that what proved to be the case was that marriage, in order to be aesthetic and religious, must have no 'why'. But precisely this was what formed the aesthetic factor in first love, and so here marriage stands once more on a level with first love. And the aesthetic in marriage is this: that it conceals a multitude of 'why's' which life reveals in all their blessedness.

Since what I took it upon myself to prove in the first instance, however, was the aesthetic validity of marriage, and since what set marriage apart from first love was the ethical and religious element, but again, in so far as the ethical and religious seeks expression in something particular, it finds that most essentially in the marriage ceremony, it is upon this – so as not to appear to treat the matter too lightly, so as not to be guilty of the least thing that could make it seem I was concealing the schism between first love and marriage which you and many others, if for different reasons, try to establish – it is upon this that I will now dwell. [. . .]

What [. . .] does the wedding ceremony do? It offers, first of all, a survey of the genesis of the human race, and thereby fastens the new marriage onto the great body of the race. It offers thereby what is general, the purely human, calls it forth in consciousness. This offends you; you may say, 'It is disagreeable at the moment of uniting oneself so tenderly with another person, so that everything else disappears, to be reminded that *es ist eine alte Geschichte*,[18] something that has been and is and will be.' You want to rejoice in what is peculiar to your love, you want to let all the passion of love blaze up in you, and you do not want to be disturbed by the thought that Peter and Paul do the same: 'It is extremely prosaic to be reminded of one's numerical significance: in the year 1750 Mr N.N. and the virtuous Miss N.N., at ten o'clock; the same day, at eleven o'clock, Mr N.N., Miss N.N.' That sounds perfectly dreadful, but your reasoning conceals a reflection that has disturbed the first love. Love is, as noted above, a unity of the universal and the singular, but the sense in which you want to enjoy the singular shows a reflection that has put the singular outside the universal. The more the singular and the universal permeate each other, the more beautiful the love. The great thing is not to be the singular, either immediately or in a higher sense, but in the singular to possess the universal. So it cannot be a disturbing preliminary to first love to be reminded of the universal. Moreover, the wedding ceremony does more than that. In order to point back to the universal it leads the lovers back to the first parents. So it does not stop with the universal *in abstracto*, but presents it as expressed in the human race's first couple. This is a hint as to how every marriage is. Every marriage, like every human life, is at once this individual thing and yet the whole, an individual and a symbol at the same time. Accordingly it gives the lovers the most beautiful picture of two people who are not disturbed by the thought of others; it says to the individuals, 'Thus you too are a couple, it is the same event that has repeated itself in you, you too now stand here alone in the infinite world, alone before the face of God.' So you see that the wedding ceremony also gives what you ask, but that in addition it gives more, it gives the universal and the singular together.

'But the marriage ceremony proclaims that sin has entered the world, and it grates, after all, just when one feels most pure, to be reminded so forcibly of sin. Further, it teaches that sin entered the world with marriage, and that seems hardly an encouragement to the respective partners; of course the Church can wash its hands if anything unfortunate comes out of it, since it hasn't fostered vain hopes.' But should not the fact that the Church doesn't foster vain hopes be regarded as in itself something good? The Church says that sin entered the world with marriage, but still allows marriage; it says that sin entered with marriage, but it could still be a major question whether it teaches that it was because of marriage that it entered. In any case it proclaims sin merely as the lot of man in general, making no definite application to the individual, and least of all does it say, 'You are now just about to commit a sin.' Indeed it is a very difficult matter to explain in what sense sin entered with marriage. It could look as if sin and sensuality were here being said to be the same; yet it cannot be quite like that, seeing the Church allows marriage. 'Yes,' you will say, 'that's only when it has taken away all that is beautiful from earthly love.' 'By no means,' I would reply, 'at least no word of that is to be found in the ceremony.'

Further, the Church proclaims the punishment of sin, that the

woman shall bear children with pain and obey her husband. But
surely the first of these consequences is such that, even if the Church
were not to proclaim it, it would proclaim itself. 'Yes,' you reply,
'but what is disturbing is that it is asserted to be the consequence of
sin.' You find it aesthetically beautiful that a child is born with pain,
it is a mark of respect for a human being, an emblematic indication
of the significance that lies, after all, in the fact that a human being
enters the world, as opposed to animals which, the lower they are
on the scale, the more easily they bring forth their young. Here I
must stress again that it is proclaimed as the lot of man in general,
and that the fact that a child is born in sin is the profoundest
expression of its highest dignity, that it is indeed a glorification of
human life to refer everything that pertains to it to the category of
sin.

Further, it is said that the woman shall obey the man. Here you
may say, 'Yes that's fine, and it has always appealed to me to see a
woman who, in her husband, loves her master.' But you find it
shocking that it should be a consequence of sin, and you feel called
upon to act as the woman's knight. Whether you do her a service
thereby I leave undecided, but I believe you have not grasped to the
full the inner nature of woman, to which also belongs the fact that
she is at once more perfect and more imperfect than the man. If you
want to say what is purest and most perfect, you say 'a woman'; if
you want to say what is weakest, you say 'a woman'; if you want to
illustrate spiritual ascendancy over the sensual, you say 'a woman';
if you want to illustrate the sensual, you say 'a woman'; if you want
to say what innocence is in all its inspiring greatness, you say 'a
woman'; when you want to say what the dispiriting feeling of guilt
is, you say 'a woman'. So the woman is in a certain sense more
perfect than the man, and the Scriptures express this by saying she is
more guilty. If you now recall again that the Church only proclaims
the lot of woman in general, then I do not see how there can be
anything in this to cause first love disquiet, but only for the reflecting
thought that does not know how to keep hold of her with this
possibility in mind. Besides, the Church does not make the woman
a mere slave, it says, 'And God said, I will make for Adam a
helpmeet for him',[19] an expression possessing as much aesthetic
warmth as it has truth. Therefore the Church teaches that, 'a man

shall leave his father and his mother, and shall cleave unto his wife'.[20] One would almost have expected it to say, 'The woman shall leave her father and her mother and cleave unto her husband', for the woman is after all the weaker. In the Scriptures' expression there lies an acknowledgement of the woman's importance, and no knight could be more gallant towards her.

Finally, as for the curse which fell to the man's lot, the circumstance that he shall eat his bread in the sweat of his brow does indeed seem, in a single word, to cast him out of the honeymoon of first love. The fact that this curse, like all divine curses, as we have often been reminded, conceals within it a blessing, here proves nothing, seeing that the experience of it must always be reserved for a later time. What I would remind you, though, is that first love is not cowardly, that it does not fear dangers, and that therefore it will see in this curse a difficulty which cannot frighten it.

So what does the marriage ceremony do? 'It brings the lovers to a standstill,' you say. Not at all, it lets what was already in motion proceed openly. It brings into the picture the universally human, and in that sense also sin; but all the dread and anguish that wishes sin had not entered the world is based on a reflection unknown to first love. To wish that sin had not entered the world is to take humanity back to something less perfect. Sin has entered, but by humbling themselves beneath it, individuals stand higher than they stood before.

The Church then turns to the single individual and puts several questions to him. Which again appears to prompt a reflection: 'What's the point of such questions? Love contains its own assurance.' But the Church puts the questions not to cause vacillation but to make firm, and to let what is already firm declare itself. Here we meet the difficulty that the Church, in its questions, seems quite unconcerned with the erotic. It asks whether you have consulted God and your conscience and after that your friends and acquaintances. I shall not stress here what great benefit there is in the Church's putting such questions in deep seriousness. The Church, to use one of your own expressions, is not a match-maker.[21] Why then should the parties concerned be put off? In giving thanks they have indeed referred their love to God, and in that sense consulted Him. For even if only indirectly, thanking God is to consult Him.

So the reason why the Church does not ask them whether they love one another is not at all that it wants to destroy earthly love, but because it takes it for granted.

The Church then exacts a vow. We saw above how splendidly love can merge in a kind of higher concentricity. The intention makes the individual free, but as already explained, the freer the individual, the more aesthetically beautiful is the marriage.

Thus I believe it has become apparent that, in so far as one looks for the aesthetic quality of first love in its presentational, immediate infinitude, marriage must be regarded as the transfiguration of first love, and is even more beautiful than it. This I believe is evident from the above, and in the immediately preceding we have seen, too, that all this talk of the Church's belittlement is plucked out of thin air and applies only to the person who has taken offence at religion.

But if that is so, the rest follows of itself. For the question is now whether this love can be realized. Perhaps, having granted everything that has gone before, you will say, 'Marriage is as difficult to realize, after all, as first love.' To this I must answer, no. For in marriage there is a law of motion. The first love remains an unreal *An-sich*[22] which never acquires inner substance because it moves merely in an outer medium; in the ethical and religious intention, marital love has the possibility of inner history and distinguishes itself from first love as the historical from the non-historical. First love is strong, stronger than the whole world, but the instant it occurs to it to doubt, it is annihilated; it is like a sleepwalker who can proceed infinitely surefooted over the most dangerous places, but as soon as you mention his name he plunges down. Marital love is armed; its purpose directs attention not just at the surrounding world, the will is directed inwardly at itself. And now I turn the whole thing around and say, 'the aesthetic lies not in the immediate but in the acquired.' But marriage is precisely the immediacy which has mediacy in itself, the infinity which has the finite in itself, an eternity which has the temporal in itself. Thus marriage proves to be ideal in a double sense, in both the classical and the romantic senses of the word.[23] In saying that the aesthetic lies in the acquired, I do not at all mean that it lies in the mere exertion; for that is negative and the merely negative is never aesthetic. When, on the contrary, an exertion includes its own subject-matter, a conflict its own victory, then in that duality I have the aesthetic. This is something I think I ought to call to mind in view of the passion of despair with which one can nowadays hear the acquired being praised against the immediate, as though the whole point was at bottom to destroy everything in order to build anew. Really it has alarmed me to hear the jubilation with which younger people, like the men of terror in the French revolution, cry: *de omnibus dubitandum*.[24] Perhaps that is narrow-minded of me. Still, I believe one must distinguish between a personal and a scientific doubt. Personal doubt is always about something special, and a passion for annihilation of the kind one so often hears talk of leads at most to a crowd of people venturing out without having the strength to doubt, and failing, or else ending in some half-measures which is certain failure just the same. If the struggle of doubt within a particular individual develops, on the contrary, the strength which again overcomes the doubt, then that sight is an inspiring one by showing what a person is on his own account, but not really a beautiful one; for that it needs immediacy in itself. A development of that kind, brought about in the highest degree by doubt, strives towards what one in an extreme case calls turning someone into a quite different person. Beauty here consists, on the contrary, in the immediate's being acquired in and along with the doubt. I have to stress this against the abstract form in which doubt has been invoked, the way it has been deified, the recklessness with which people have plunged into it, the blind faith with which they hope for a glorious outcome. It should also be remarked that the more spiritual the gain, the more one can extol doubt; but love belongs always to a province where you cannot so much talk of an acquiring as of a giving, and of a giving which is acquired. I have no idea what kind of doubt this should be. Are we to say that the proper situation of a husband is to have had distressing experiences, to have learned to doubt, and that the truly beautiful marriage is the one that proceeded when now, on the strength of this doubt and with great moral seriousness, he married and as a husband was faithful and constant? We would praise him but we would not extol his marriage except as an example of what a human being is capable of. Or, to be a doubter with a vengeance, should he also doubt her love, the possibility of retaining the beauty of this relationship, but yet have enough stoicism to will it? I know quite well how very ready you false teachers are to praise such a thing, just so that your false teaching can find better acceptance; you praise it when it suits your purpose and say, look, that's a true marriage. But you know quite well that in this praise there lurks a censure, and particularly the woman is far from being well served thereby, and so you do everything to tempt her. Therefore you make a distinction according to the old maxim, 'Divide and rule.' You praise first love. It remains, as you tell it, an instant lying outside time, a mysterious something about which one can make up any lie. Marriage cannot hide itself in that way; it takes days and years to unfold. How easy then the opportunity to tear down or build up with perfidious considerations of this kind, so that it needs a despairing resignation to endure it.

This, then, we are agreed on: marital love considered on its own is not only as beautiful as first love, it is even more beautiful because in its immediacy it contains the unity of a larger number of opposites. So it is not true that marriage is a highly respectable personage but a tiresomely moral one, while love is poetry. No, really it is marriage that is poetic. And if the world has so often painfully observed that first love could not be fulfilled, then I will readily join in the grief, but also draw attention to the fact that the mistake lay not so much in what came later as in one's not having begun correctly. For first love lacks the second aesthetic ideal, the element of history. There is no law of motion in it. Were I to treat personal faith as immediate in the same way, then what corresponded to first love would be a faith which believed itself, on the strength of divine assurance, capable of moving mountains, and would then go about working miracles. Perhaps it would succeed, but this faith would have no history, for the check-list of all its miraculous deeds is not its history; on the contrary, the history of faith is the appropriation of faith in personal life. Marital love has this movement, for in the intention the movement is turned inwards. The religious aspect leaves it as though to God to look after the whole world, the intention makes it ready in union with God to strive for itself, to acquire itself in patience. The consciousness of sin contains a conception of human frailty, but in the intention it is represented as overcome. This I cannot sufficiently stress in regard to marital love. I have certainly done full justice to first love and think I am a better judge of it than you, but its fault is to be found in its abstract character. [. . .]

The historical nature of marital love is apparent from its being a process of assimilation; it tries its hand in what it experiences and refers its experience back to itself. Accordingly it is not a disinterested witness of what occurs but essentially a participant; in short, it experiences its own development. Romantic love, too, refers its experiences to itself, as when the knight sends his beloved the banners, etc. won in battle; but even if romantic love could imagine a considerable time being spent on all such conquests, it could never occur to it that the love should have had a history. The prosaic view goes to the opposite extreme; it can well grasp that love should acquire a history, usually a short history, so plain and pedestrian that the love soon acquires feet to walk upon. Experimental love, too, acquires a kind of history, yet is as if without true apriority,[25] also without continuity, and rests merely upon the caprice of the experimenting individual who is his own world and its fate simultaneously. Experimental love is therefore very apt to inquire about its own condition and so has a double joy, one part in its outcome corresponding to the calculation, and another when something quite else transpires. In the latter case it is also content inasmuch as it finds a task for its inexhaustible combinations. Marital love has apriority in itself, but likewise constancy, and the strength in this constancy is the same as the law of its motion, the intention. The intention posits something else but posits it also as that which is overcome; the something else is posited in the intention as something inner, inasmuch as the outer is itself seen reflected in the inner. The historical aspect consists in this something else coming to light, acquiring its validity, but seen precisely in its validity as something that is not about to become valid, so that love emerges tested and purified from this movement and assimilates the experience. For the individual who does not adopt an experimental attitude, how this something else comes to light is not under his control; yet love has, likewise in its apriority, triumphed over the whole thing without knowing it. It says somewhere in the New Testament, 'For every creature of God is good, and nothing to be refused, if it be received with thanksgiving.'[26] Most people are ready to be grateful when they receive a good gift, but at the same time they demand that it be left to them to decide what present is good. This shows their narrow-mindedness. That other gratitude, on the other hand, is truly triumphant and a priori since it contains in itself an eternal health which not even an evil gift can disturb, not because one knows how to hold it at a distance, but because of the boldness, the high degree of personal courage, which dares to give thanks for it. So, too, with love. Here it could not occur to me to reflect on all the Jeremiads you maliciously keep in constant readiness for the edification of concerned husbands; and I hope this time you will restrain yourself, seeing that here you are dealing with a husband who cannot tempt you into amusing yourself by making him still more confused.

But in the course of my pursuit of love from its cryptogamous concealment to its phanerogamous life,[27] I stumble upon a difficulty which you will certainly say is of no little significance. *Posito*, I assume for argument, that I have succeeded in convincing you that those religious and ethical factors which in marital love join first love by no means diminish the latter, that in your heart of hearts you are really deeply convinced of this and now by no means scorn a religious point of departure. You would therefore, alone with the one you loved, be ready to humble yourself and your love under God; you are really much impressed and moved – but watch out now! I mention a word, 'congregation', and immediately, as in the ballad, everything vanishes again.[28] To get beyond the category of inwardness, that I think is something you will never succeed in. 'Congregation, the dear congregation, which in spite of its diversity is still a moral personage; yes, if only, just as it has all a moral person's tiresome qualities, it likewise had the good quality of having but one head on one neck – I know what I would do.'[29] You no doubt know there was a madman whose *idée fixe* was that the room he lived in was full of flies,[30] so that he was in danger of being choked by them. He fought with the fear and the fury of despair for his very existence. Thus you, too, appear to fight for your life against a similar imaginary swarm of flies, against what you call 'the congregation'. Not such a dangerous matter, however, but I will first go over the most important points of contact with the congregation. Before that I would merely remind you that first love can scarcely count it an advantage that it knows no such difficulties; for that fact is due to its being kept abstract and having no contact at all with reality.

You will know very well how to discriminate between those abstract relationships to a surrounding world whose abstraction cancels the relationship. Having to pay a priest and a parish clerk and a functionary of the law, that's something you can put up with, for money is an excellent means of removing any relationship; which is why you also initiated me into your plan never, ever to do anything or ever receive anything, not the slightest thing, without giving or receiving money. Yes, if we look a little at the matter, were you ever to marry, you would be capable of paying a *douceur* to everyone who came to witness your joy in taking that step. It must not surprise you if in that case the congregation grows in numbers, or if what the man with the flies feared actually befalls you. The personal relationships you are afraid of are those which, in inquiries, congratulations, compliments, yes, even presents, aspire to enter into a relation with you that cannot be measured in money, and to show how enthusiastically they share in your joy, though on just this occasion you for your part and that of your loved one would rather they didn't share in it. 'Money, after all, gets you out of a mass of ludicrous situations. With it you can stop the mouth of the church trumpeter who would otherwise make as though to herald the opening of the Royal Assizes, money can get you out of being pronounced a husband, an upright husband, before the whole congregation when you want to limit yourself to being that just for one person.' This is not my invention, this portrait, it is yours. Can you recall how you once fumed on the occasion of a church wedding? You asked, why not let the whole tenderly sharing fraternity bestow a congregational kiss upon the bride and bridegroom, just as clerics present at ordinations come forward to lay their hands upon the ordinand! Yes, you said you were unable to mention the words 'bride' and 'bridegroom' without thinking of the big moment when a dear father or a friend of long standing rises with his glass unctuously to intone those beautiful words 'bride and bridegroom'. For just as you found the whole church ceremony excellently suited to stifling the erotic, so is there as great an absence of decency in the subsequent worldly proceedings as there was an excess of it in the church ceremony; 'after all, wasn't it indecent, ludicrous, tasteless to place such an almost man and wife at a dining-table and convey the partial, untrue, and indelicate thought that it might not be up to the Church to ordain them man and wife'. So you seem to favour a quiet wedding. To that I have no objection, but merely inform you that you will be pronounced a properly married man just as fully there. Perhaps you can bear those words better when no one else hears them. I have to remind you, moreover, that it does not say 'before the whole congregation', but 'before God and the congregation', which is neither discomfortingly narrow nor lacking in boldness.

As for what else you have to say in this respect, that I can more easily forgive even if it comes with the usual intemperance, because it is only the social relationships you attack. [. . .] In my view the great thing is to live in them, to bring something finer out of them if one can; if one can't, to subordinate oneself to them and put up with them. I do not see that love is at all endangered by publishing banns from the pulpit; nor do I believe such publication is harmful for the hearers, as your overwrought severity once led you to divine when you proposed that the announcing of banns be abolished because that is what so many people, especially women, went to church just to hear, so that the impact of the sermon was destroyed. There is something untrue at the bottom of your anxiety, as if all small things of this kind were able to disturb a healthy and strong love. [. . .] Another explanation I can offer of your great anxiety at all this privity and fuss is that you are afraid of missing the erotic instant. You know how to keep your soul as motionless as a bird of prey before it swoops; you realize the instant is not within one's power and that yet it contains the most beautiful experience; therefore you know how to watch out, you do not want to anticipate anything in the restlessness with which you await the instant. But when an event like this is now fixed for a definite time which one knows well in advance, when the preparations constantly remind one of it, one runs the risk of 'missing the point'. From this one sees you have not grasped the nature of marital love and that you cherish a heathen superstition for first love. [. . .]

Every process of becoming, precisely the more healthy it is, always has something polemical about it, and every marital connection has that too, and you know very well that I hate that family laxity, that insipid community of goods which can give a marriage the appearance of being entered into with the entire family. If marital love is a true first love, then there is also something undisclosed about it. It does not want to present itself to view, does not stake its life on mounting guard over the families, does not draw its sustenance from congratulations and compliments or from idolatry, in the way the family can lend itself to. This you know very well – just let your wit make play with all that. In many ways I can well agree with you, and I believe that it would not hurt you or the good cause if occasionally you allowed me, as the experienced, loving forester, to mark the rotten trees for felling, but also in other places to mark a cross.

I have absolutely no reservations, now, in declaring secretiveness to be the absolute condition for the safeguarding of the aesthetic in marriage, not in the way that one should make a point of it, chase after it, take it in vain, place the real pleasure simply in savouring the secretiveness. It is one of first love's pet notions that it wants to run off to an uninhabited island. This has been ridiculed enough, I will take no part in the wild iconoclasm of our time. The fault lies in the fact that first love believes that taking flight is the only way it can be realized. That is a misunderstanding which stems from its non-historical character. The art is to remain in the multiplicity and yet preserve the secretiveness. Here again I might dwell, by way of a prudential maxim, on its only by being among people that the secretiveness acquires its true energy, that it is only with this resistance that its point bores more and more deeply in. But I will not do so, for the same reason as before, and also because I always acknowledge a relationship to other persons as something real. But for that one needs art, and marital love does not run away from these difficulties; it preserves and appropriates them. Besides, marital love has so much else to think about that it has no time to get itself bogged down in a polemic against the particular.

Inwardly this principal condition goes as follows: openheartedness, uprightness, publicity on the largest conceivable scale; for this is the life-principle of love, and secretiveness here is its death. However, this is easier said than done, and truly it needs courage to carry it out consistently; for you no doubt realize that I am thinking of something more than the gabbling prattle which is rife in family marriages. Naturally there can only be talk of publicity where there can be talk of secretiveness; but the more there is talk of the latter, the more difficult the former becomes. It needs courage to reveal oneself as one truly is, it needs courage not to want to purchase one's freedom from a little humiliation when one can do that through a certain secretiveness, not to want to purchase oneself a little addition to one's stature when one can do that by being reticent. It needs courage to want to be healthy, to want the truth in all honesty and candour.

But let us begin with something less momentous. It was in connection with a newly-wed couple who saw themselves obliged to 'limit their love within the narrow confines of three small rooms' that you took a little excursion into the realm of fantasy, though that realm borders so close on your daily residence that one doubts whether it should be called an excursion. You then devoted yourself with the greatest care and taste to decorating your future as you could wish it. [. . .] So you imagined yourself married, happily married, after having delivered your love inviolate from all adversity, and you were now deliberating how you would arrange everything in your home so that your love could preserve its fragrance as long as possible. For that you needed more than three rooms. I granted you this, seeing that as a bachelor you use five. It would be disagreeable for you to have to give up one of your rooms to your wife; as far as that goes you would hand over four of them to her and live in the fifth rather than share one in common. After pondering these inconveniences you continued, 'I take the three rooms in question as my point of departure, but not in a philosophical sense, for I've no intention of returning to them, on the contrary, I intend getting as far away from them as possible.' Yes, such was your aversion to three small rooms that, if you could not have more, you would prefer to live like a vagrant under the open sky, though that in the last resort was so poetic as to require a considerable suite of rooms in compensation. I tried to call you to order by reminding you that this was one of the customary heresies of non-historical first love, and then was very happy to accompany you through the many big, cool, high-vaulted halls in your castle in the air, through the private, half-darkened salons, the dining-rooms illuminated into the farthest corners by lights and chandeliers and mirrors, the small room with double doors opening out onto the balcony where the morning sun fell and a scent of flowers, which breathed only for you and your love, wafted towards us. Here I will not pursue your bold steps further as, like a chamois hunter, you leap from one peak to another. All that I shall discuss a little more closely is the principle behind your arrangement. Your principle was obviously secretiveness, mystification, refined coquetry. It was not just that the walls in your rooms were to be edged with glass, but the world of your consciousness was also to be multiplicated with similar refracted beams of light. Not just everywhere in the room but also everywhere in consciousness you would meet her and you, and you and her. 'But for this to be possible all the riches in the world are not enough, it needs spirit, and a wise moderation controlling the powers of the spirit. So one must be strangers enough to each other for familiarity to be interesting, familiar enough for strangeness to form a titillating resistance. The married life must not be a dressing-gown one makes oneself comfortable in, but neither a corset that hampers one's movements; it must not be a labour that needs strenuous preparation, but not a dissolute indolence either; it must bear the stamp of the accidental, yet in the distance one must discern an art. One doesn't exactly have to stare oneself blind day and night stitching a carpet big enough to cover the floor in the great hall; on the other hand the slightest little curiosity can very well have some small secret sign on its border. One doesn't exactly have to have one's monogram on the cake every day one eats together, yet there can certainly be some small telegraphic allusion. It's a matter of postponing as far as possible that point at which one suspects the movement is circular, that point where repetition begins; and when it can't be postponed altogether, it's a matter of having made adjustments to allow for variation. One has only a certain number of texts, if one preaches oneself out the first Sunday then not only is there nothing left for the whole of the next year, there is not even enough for the first Sunday next year. One should remain to some degree enigmatic to one another as long as possible, and so far as one successively reveals oneself, this must be done with as much use of accidental circumstance as possible, making it relative in a way that allows this, too, to be viewed from many other sides.

One must be on one's guard against all surfeit and after-taste.' So
you want to live on the ground floor of this lordly castle, which
should be situated in a beautiful district but in the vicinity of the
capital. Your wife, your consort, should occupy the left-hand wing
of the first floor. It is something you have always envied princely
people, that man and wife lived separately. But what took the
aesthetic away again from a court life of this kind was a ceremonial
that claimed priority to love. One is announced, one waits a moment,
one is received. That in itself did not lack beauty, but it only assumed
its true beauty when it became a move in the divine game of love,
when it was ascribed a validity in such a way that one could just as
well deprive it of its validity. The love one was in would itself have
to have many limits, but every limit would also have to be a thrilling
temptation to transcend that limit. So you lived on the ground floor
where you had your library, billiard-room, audience-chamber, closet,
bedroom. Your wife lived on the first floor. Here, too, was your
bridal suite, a large room with two closets, one on each side. There
would have to be nothing to remind you or your wife that you were
married, and yet again everything should be such that no unmarried
person could have it thus. You would not be aware of what your wife
was up to, or she of what you occupied yourself with; this, however,
not at all so as to be inactive or to forget one another, but to be able to
give each contact significance, to remove that moment of death when
you looked at each other and, behold, you were bored! So you would
not trudge about in matrimonial procession on each other's arm; for a
long time to come you would follow her with youthful infatuation
from your window as she walked in the garden, you would prepare
your eyes to look out for her, lose yourself in the contemplation of
her image when it vanished from your sight. You would steal after
her, yes, probably on occasion she would also rest on your arm —
after all there was always something beautiful in what had become a
traditional way among people of expressing a particular feeling; and
you would give her your arm, half giving what is beautiful in this
custom its due, half making fun of walking in this way like a proper
married couple. Yet, where should my pursuit of the clever refine-
ments of your ingenious head be able to find its end in this Asiatic
luxuriance, which almost wearies me and makes me wish myself
back with the three small rooms you passed so proudly by!

If there were anything aesthetically beautiful in this whole view, then one should probably look for it partly in the hints you drop of erotic bashfulness, partly in not wanting at any point to possess the loved one as though possession were already gained, but continue constantly to try to gain it. The latter is in itself true and right, but the task by no means set with erotic seriousness, and accordingly so far not solved either. You were clinging constantly to an immediacy as such, to a category of nature, not daring to let it be transfigured in a common consciousness; for this is what I have meant by uprightness and openness. You fear that when the enigma has gone love will cease, while I believe that only when it has gone does love begin. You fear that one dare not altogether know what one loves, you reckon with the incommensurable as an absolutely vital ingredient, while I maintain that only when one knows what one loves does one truly love. Furthermore, all your good fortune lacks a blessing, for it lacks adversity; and since that is a fault it is also, in so far as you were actually to mislead someone with your theory, just as well that it is not true. Let us then turn to the realities of life. In insisting on the part played by adversity, it is far from my intention to let you identify marriage with a catalogue of tribulations. On the contrary, adversity's contribution is already to be found in the resignation contained in the intention, as explained earlier, but without yet having assumed any definite shape or being a cause of anxiety, because in the intention they are looked upon as already overcome. Moreover, the adversity is not seen outwardly but inwardly, as it is reflected in the individual. The secretiveness becomes, as explained above, a contradiction when it has nothing to deposit in its secrecy, a puerility when all its cellar contains are amorous knick-knacks. Only when the individual's heart is truly opened by love, when love has made him eloquent far more profoundly than the usual sense in which love is said to make one that (for even a seducer can have eloquence of that kind), only when the individual has thus deposited everything in the shared consciousness, only then does secretiveness acquire strength, life and meaning. But this calls for a decisive step, and thus courage too; without it married love lapses into nothing, for it is only through this that one shows that one loves not oneself but another. How is one to show that except by being only for the other, yet how can one be only for

another except by not being for oneself? But being for oneself is the
most general characterization of the secretiveness of the individual
life when it remains in itself. Love is to give of oneself, but I can
give of myself only if I go out of myself; how then can it be
reconciled with the concealment that wants precisely to remain in
itself? 'But one suffers loss by revealing oneself in that way'; yes, of
course, anyone who profits by being secretive suffers loss. But to be
consistent, you would have to go much further, you would have to
advise not just against marriage but against every form of personal
approach, and how will your clever head deal with communication
by telegraph? The most interesting reading is that in which the
reader himself is to a degree productive; truly erotic artfulness
would be to make an impression at a distance, an impression which
would be highly dangerous for the person in question just because
there was nothing from which she herself had created her object
and loved now her creation; that is not love but the coquetry of the
seducer. The person who loves is, on the contrary, one who has lost
himself in another; but in losing and forgetting himself in the other
he is revealed to the other, and in forgetting himself he is recalled in
the other. The person who loves is not one who will want to be
mistaken for the other, whether a better or a poorer, and the person
who lacks this deference to himself and to the other does not love.
In general therefore secretiveness has its basis in a pettiness which
would like to add a cubit to its stature. The person who has not
learnt to scorn this has never loved; for if he had he would have felt
that even if ten cubits were added to his stature, he was still too
lowly. [. . .]

First love can wish with supernatural pathos, but this wish can
easily become an 'in case' without content, and our lives are not so
paradisal that our Lord gives every married couple the whole world
to do with as it likes. Married love knows better. Its movements are
not outwards but inwards, and here it is soon aware that it has a
wide world to itself, but also that every little constraint on its self
has a quite other commensurability with the infinitude of love; and
even if it feels pain because there is so much to fight against, so too
it feels courage for this contest. Yes, it is daring enough to outdo
you in paradoxes in practically taking pleasure in sin's having entered
the world; but it has the daring to outdo you in paradoxes in

another sense too: it has the courage to resolve them. For marital love, like first love, knows all these obstacles are overcome in the infinite moment of love. But it also knows that the historical element in it is precisely the gaining of this victory, and that gaining it is not just a game but also a conflict, though also not just a conflict but also a game, as the conflict in Valhalla was a life-and-death struggle and yet still a game, since the contestants continually rose again rejuvenated from the dead. It also knows that this fencing is not an arbitrary duel but a conflict under divine patronage; and it feels no need to love more than one, yet feels a blessedness herein, and no need to love more than once, yet feels an eternity herein. And is it still your belief that this love which has no secrets forgoes something beautiful? Or that it is unable to resist time but must needs be blunted by daily association? Or that boredom overtakes it more swiftly, as though marital love did not possess an eternal content of which one never grows tired, an eternal content which it acquires, and is constantly acquiring, now with a kiss and a jest, now with fear and trembling? [. . .]

Yet not infrequently one sees marriages in which the secrecy system is carried through to perfection. I have never seen a happy one in which that was the case. However, since that may be due entirely to accident, I shall state what reasons there are in general for its being so. This is important for me here, for an aesthetically beautiful marriage is always a happy marriage, so if a happy marriage could be built on that basis my theory would have to be changed. I will shun none of its guises and will describe each as fairly as I can, especially one which, in the house where I saw it realized, was accomplished with a virtuosity which was really fascinating.

Generally, you will admit, the secrecy system proceeds from the husbands, and notwithstanding it is always wrong, this is still more tolerable than the intolerable kind where it is the wife who wields such a *dominium*. The ugliest form is, of course, a pure despotism in which the wife is a slave, a maid-of-all-work in the domestic arrangements. Such a marriage is never happy, even if the years bring a dullness which comes to terms with it. A more becoming form is the very opposite of this, a misplaced solicitude. 'Woman is weak,' they say, 'she cannot endure sorrow and anxiety; the weak and frail must be handled lovingly.' Falsehood! Falsehood! The woman is just as strong as the man, maybe stronger. And do you really treat her lovingly when you thus humiliate her? Who gave you leave to humiliate her? How can your soul be so blind that you take yourself to be a more perfect being than her? Just confide everything to her! If she's weak she can't bear it; but then, of course, she has you to lean upon, you have the strength for that. But look! You can't stand that, that is something you do not have the strength for. So it is you who lacks strength, not her. [. . .]

For a time I frequented a house where I had the opportunity to observe the silence system put into effect in a more artistic and refined manner. The man was fairly young, unusually gifted, with an excellent mind and of a poetic disposition, too lazy to produce anything himself but with an extraordinary flair and sense for making daily life itself poetic. His wife was young, not unintelligent, but of an exceptional character. This tempted him. His ability to arouse and nourish every youthful conceit in her was truly astonishing. Her whole life, their life together, was a tapestry of poetic enchantment. His eye was everywhere; when she looked round, his eye was averted. His finger was in everything, but no more literally or, in a finite sense, really than God's is present in history. Whichever way her thought might turn, he was there beforehand; like Potemkin he knew how to conjure up landscapes,[31] and of just the sort, after a little surprise, a little hesitation, to please her. His domestic life was a Creation story in miniature, and just as everything in Creation focuses on mankind, so was she the centre in an enchanted circle in which she nevertheless enjoyed her full freedom, for the circle would bend to comply with her and had no boundary of which it might be said, 'Here and no further!'. Plunge where she might, whichever way she went the circle gave way but still remained there. She walked as if in a toddler's practice basket, yet not one braided with withies; it was woven out of her hopes, dreams, longings, wishes, fears, in short it was formed out of the whole content of her soul. He himself, in this dream world, moved with great certainty, he surrendered none of his dignity, claimed and asserted his authority as man and lord. She would have been upset had he not done so; it might have aroused in her an anxious suspicion which could lead to the secrecy being dissolved. He seemed, not only to the world at large but to her too, to be such a considerate person; yet inside he knew that every impression she got of him was just as he wished it, and he knew that it was in his power with a single word to dispel the enchantment. All that she might find disagreeable was removed; if anything of the kind occurred, she would receive, whether after being allowed to press her own inquiries or in candid anticipation of these, by way of frank notification an account he had himself drafted, in stronger or weaker terms, according to the impression he had calculated on. He was proud, fearfully consistent, he loved her, but he could not abandon the proud thought, which came to him deep in the still of the night or in an instant outside time, of venturing to say to himself, 'Yes, she owes everything to me.' – You have followed this description with interest, have you not? however imperfectly I have succeeded. Because it conjures up a picture in your soul with which you sympathize, which perhaps you would try sometime to put into practice yourself if you became a husband. Was this, then, a happy marriage? Yes, if you like, yet there hovered a dark fate over that happiness. Suppose he failed, suppose she suddenly suspected something. I do not think she could ever forgive him; her proud soul was too proud to let it be said that he had done it from love for her. There is an old-fashioned expression for the relation between a married couple, of which I will remind you here (in any case I always like to support the revolution, or rather the holy war, in which the plain and simple but true and rich expressions strive to win back the realm from which the novel has expelled them). It is said of married people that they should live on a good understanding with one another. Most often one hears it expressed negatively: a couple does not live on a good understanding, and then one usually thinks of their being unable to stand one another, of their fighting, quarrelling, etc. Take now the positive expression. The married couple described, do they not live on a good understanding? Yes, that is what the world would say, though not you, surely; for how could they live on a good understanding when they do not understand one another? Yet is it not part of the understanding that the one knows how solicitous and loving the other is? Or if he deprived her of nothing else, he deprived her of the opportunity for that degree of gratitude in which her soul would have found repose. Is it not a pretty, a becoming, and an uncomplicated expression: to live on a good understanding? [. . .]

So you see, the secrecy system is by no means conducive to a happy, and thus neither to an aesthetically beautiful marriage. No, my friend; honesty, openheartedness, revelation, understanding, that is the life-principle in marriage; without it marriage is unattractive and indeed unethical, for then it separates what love joins, the sensual and the spiritual. Only when the being I live with in earthly life's most tender association is just as close in spiritual respects – only then is my marriage ethical and therefore also aesthetically attractive. And you proud men who perhaps rejoice silently at this victorious triumph over women, you forget, in the first place, that it is not a good triumph when one triumphs over the weaker, and that the man honours himself in his wife – and the man who does not do that? He despises himself.

So understanding is the life-principle in marriage. One often hears people of experience discussing when one should advise against marriage. Let them discuss these circumstances as thoroughly and interminably as they will: generally what they say amounts to very little. I, for my part, will mention just one case, that is, when the complications in the individual life are such that it is unable to reveal itself. If the history of your inner development contains something unutterable, or if your life has made you privy to secrets – in short, if in one way or another you have gorged yourself on a secret which cannot be dragged out of you without costing you your life, then never marry. Either you will feel tied to a being who has no suspicion of what is going on in you, and your marriage then becomes an uncomely misalliance, or you bind yourself to a being who is anxiously aware of this, who at every instant sees these shadow-images on the wall. She may resolve never to cross-examine you, never to come too close, she will renounce the apprehensive curiosity that tempts her, but she will never be happy, nor you either. [. . .] But having now mentioned secretiveness and understanding as two sides of the same matter, this being the main thing about love as the absolute condition for preserving the aesthetic in marriage, I am no doubt liable to be faced with the objection, on your part, that I seem here to be forgetting 'what I otherwise harp on as insistently as the refrain in a song', namely the historical character of marriage. You yourself have hopes of putting time to the test with the help of your secretiveness and your cleverly calculated relative information, 'but when married folk get down to telling their story, short or long, they soon come to the point where one says, "and that's the end of the story"'. My young friend, what you fail to notice is that it is only because you are not properly placed that you can make such an objection. By virtue of your secretiveness, you have a time dimension in you, and it really is a matter of time being put to the test. Through revelation, however, love has, on the contrary, an eternal dimension, and so all concurrence becomes impossible. Also, it is just a wilful misunderstanding to think of this revelation as a matter of married people spending a fortnight recounting their careers, followed by a deathly silence broken only now and then by a [retelling of] the sufficiently familiar story – 'as is told somewhere in a fairy-tale of a mill that, while all this was happening, went clip, clap, clip, clap'. The historical character of marriage makes of this understanding precisely as much a matter of constant development as an all-at-once affair. It is the same as in an individual life. Just because one has arrived at clarity about oneself, has had the courage to be willing to see oneself, it by no means follows that the story is now over; it is now that it first begins, acquires for the first time a proper meaning through referring each lived moment to this total view. So too in marriage. The immediacy of first love founders upon this revelation, yet is not lost but assumed into the knowledge the marriage shares. With this the story begins, and the particular is referred to this shared knowledge; in this lies its *felicity*, an expression in which again the historical character of marriage is preserved, and which corresponds to the blitheness, or what the Germans call *Heiterkeit*, which first love has.

It is essential, accordingly, for married love to become historical, and because the individuals are now properly placed, the commandment, 'In the sweat of thy brow shalt thou eat bread', is not a terrible and unexpected message. And the courage and strength married love feels corresponds to the romantic need of knightly love for adventurous exploits, and is the element of truth in that. Just as the knight is without fear, so too is married love, notwithstanding the foes it has to contend with are often far more dangerous. Here a broad vista opens up to observation, into which it is not, however, my intention to enter. But if we let the knight say that the man who does not defy the whole world in order to

save his beloved does not know knightly love, then we should let
the husband say the same. Except that I must always remind you
that every victory of this sort that married love wins is more
aesthetically beautiful than the one which the knight wins, because
in winning this victory it also wins its own glorification. It fears
nothing, not even small deviations, it has no fear of minor infatuations, on the contrary, these too serve only to nourish the divine
wholesomeness of married love. Even Ottilia in Goethe's *Elective
Affinities* is ploughed under as but a tender possibility by the serious
marital love; how much more, then, should a deeply religious and
ethically planned marriage have the strength for that! Yes, just what
Goethe's *Elective Affinities* provides is proof of what secretiveness
leads to. That love would not have acquired such power if it had
not been allowed to grow in tranquillity. Had he had the courage
to open himself to his wife it would have been averted, and the
whole story would have become a divertissement in the drama of
the marriage. The fateful part is that Edvard and his wife both have
affairs simultaneously; but this is again the fault of their keeping
silent. The husband who has strength to confide in his wife that he
loves another – he is saved, and so too the wife. But when he does
not have it, he loses confidence in himself, and so what he looks for
is forgetfulness in the love of another. Undoubtedly, it is as much
the pain of not having resisted in time, as true love for the other,
that brings a man to yield. He feels he has lost himself, and when
that feeling first occurs, it takes strong opiates to deaden it.

The difficulties marital love has to contend with I will discuss
only in quite general terms, to show that they are not so important
that marital love has anything to fear from them as far as the
preservation of the aesthetic is concerned. [. . .] I can divide these
difficulties into the external and the internal, though always remembering the relative nature of such a division in the case of
marriage, where of course everything is internal. First, then, the
external difficulties. I am by no means reluctant or afraid to mention
all these depressing, humiliating, vexatious finite afflictions, in short
everything that goes to make up a tearful drama. Here, as everywhere, you and your ilk are exceedingly arbitrary. If a drama of
this kind obliges you to undertake such a peregrination through the
caves of misfortune, then you say it is unaesthetic, snivelling and

tiresome. And you are right. But why? Because you are indignant that something sublime and noble should succumb to the like of this. If you turn to the real world, on the other hand, and there meet a family which has undergone half the adversities a hangman of a playwright has devised for that delicious pleasure, reserved for tyrants, of torturing others, you get the shivers; you think, 'Good-night to all aesthetic beauty.' You show compassion, you are ready to help if for no other reason than to strip away the gloomy thoughts, but you have already long ago given up hope on the unfortunate family's behalf. Yet if it is true in real life, the poet has the right to present it and he is in the right when he does so. When you are sitting in the theatre, intoxicated with aesthetic enjoyment, you have the bravado to require the poet to let the aesthetic triumph over all misery. It is the only comfort left, and, even more effemin-ately, you, whose own strength has not been given a chance to test itself by life, grasp it. [. . .] If it is true, as you teach and proclaim in life, that adversity on a far smaller scale can put a person in thrall, make him walk with head bowed and forgetful that he, too, is created in God's image, then please God let it be your just punish-ment that all playwrights write nothing but lachrymose dramas of all possible terror and ruination, pieces which would not let your effeminacy recline on theatre cushions, nor give you a chance to spread your unnaturally pungent perfume, but which might frighten you into learning to believe in reality what you want only to believe in the form of poetry. I have not, in my own marriage, experienced many adversities of this kind, that I freely admit, so I cannot speak from experience; still, I am convinced that nothing is capable of crushing the aesthetic in a person. It is a conviction so powerful, so felicitous, so heartfelt, that I thank God for it, as for a gift of grace. And when we read in the Holy Scriptures of the many gifts of grace, I would really count among them the frankness, the confidence, the trust in reality and in the eternal necessity with which beauty triumphs, and in the blessedness that lies in the free-dom with which the individual comes to the aid of God. And this conviction is an element in my whole spiritual make-up; I do not permit myself to be convulsed in effeminate and voluptuous tremors by the artificial stimulus of the theatre. All I can do is thank God for this unshakeableness in my soul, but in doing so I would also hope to have exempted my soul from taking it in vain. You know I hate all experimenting, but a person is supposed to be able in thought to have experienced much that he never gets to experience in reality. There are occasional moments of despondency, and when a person does not evoke these arbitrarily, to try his hand at such things, this too is a contest, an extremely serious contest, and in this contest an assurance can be gained which, even if it does not have quite the reality it would have acquired in real life, is still of great importance. Sometimes in life it is a good sign, and a sign of something great, that a person fails like a madman to separate the worlds of poetry and reality but sees the latter *sub specie poeseos*.[32] Somewhere, in one of his sermons where he is speaking of poverty and need, Luther says, 'One has never heard of a Christian person dying of hunger.' With that Luther is finished with the matter and thinks, surely with good reason, that he has spoken of it with much unction and to the genuine edification of his readers.

To the extent, then, that marriage involves such external trials, the thing to do, of course, is to make them internal. I say 'of course' and am pretty free-spoken about all this, but it is to you, and only to you, I am writing, and we two have probably just about the same amount of experience of this kind of adversity. The thing, then, is to turn the external adversity into an internal one. [. . .] It is not at all to be denied, as your quick mind will soon grasp, that this very changing of the external trial to an internal one can make it still harder; but then nor do the gods sell anything great for nothing, and it is exactly here that the educative, the idealizing effect in marriage lies. It is often said that when one stands alone in the world it is easier to bear such things. True enough, to some extent; but often this saying conceals a significant untruth. For how is it that one is able to bear them more easily? By being able to throw oneself away, suffer damage to one's soul without its being anyone else's concern, by being able to forget God, let the storm of despair drown out the scream of pain, by being able to become dulled, and find one's pleasure in living practically like a ghost among people. Of course everyone, even if he stands alone, should mind himself, but only he who loves has a proper conception of what he is and what he is capable of, and only marriage yields historic fidelity, which is every bit as beautiful as the chivalrous kind. For a married man can never behave thus and, however much the world goes against him, if he forgets himself even for an instant and begins to feel so light because despair is about to set him afloat, feel so strong because he has the numbing drink mixed by defiance and despondency, cowardice and pride, so free because the bond which binds him to truth and righteousness is, as it were, loosened, and he now experiences the swiftness which is the transition from good to evil – still, he will soon turn back to the old paths and as husband [*Aegtemand*] prove himself a genuine man [*ægte Mand*].

That must suffice for these external adversities. I am brief about them because I feel no special competence to contribute to the subject, and because to do so properly would require a much fuller treatment. Nevertheless this is the conclusion I reach: if love can be preserved, and so help me God it can, then the aesthetic, too, can be preserved; for love itself is the aesthetic.

The further objections are due mainly to a misunderstanding of the meaning of time and of the aesthetic validity of the historical. They accordingly affect every marriage and can therefore be discussed in quite general terms. That I shall do now, and do my best not to overlook, in this generality, the point of the attack and of the defence.

The first thing you will mention is 'habit, the unavoidable habit, that fearful monotony, the perpetual sameness in the dreadful still-life of married domesticity; nature I love but I'm a hater of second nature'.[33] One must admit you know how to portray with seductive warmth and sadness the happy time when one still makes discoveries, to delineate with dread and horror the time when that is over; you know how to touch in, in laughable and abominable detail, a marital uniformity not even nature can match, 'for there, after all, as Leibniz has already shown, nothing is quite identical; such a uniformity is only reserved for rational creatures, the fruit either of their drowsiness or their pedantry'.[34] Now, I have absolutely no mind to deny to you that it is a beautiful time, an eternally unforgettable time (mark well in what sense I can say this), when in love's world the individual is astonished by, and finds bliss in, what indeed has been discovered long ago, and of which indeed he has often heard and read, but now first appropriates with all the enthusiasm of surprise, with all the depth of inwardness. It is a beautiful time, from the very first inkling of love, the first sight, the first disappearance, of the beloved object, the first chord of this voice, the first look, the first touch of the hand, the first kiss, right up to the first complete certainty of possession; it is a beautiful time, the first uneasiness, the first longing, the first pain because she failed to appear, the first joy because she came unexpectedly – but that is not at all to say that the sequel is not equally beautiful. You who imagine you have such a chivalrous way of thinking, test yourself. When you say the first kiss is the most beautiful, the sweetest, you insult the loved one, for what gives the kiss absolute value here is time and what pertains to that.

But if the cause I defend is not to be harmed, you first owe me a small explanation. For unless you want to proceed in a quite arbitrary manner, you will have to attack first love in the same way that you attack marriage. For, to survive in life, it must be exposed to the same calamities, and it will have nothing like the resources to counter them that married life has in the ethical and the religious. To be consistent, therefore, you must hate all love which wants to be an eternal love. You must stop, therefore, with first love by itself. To have its true meaning, however, first love must have the naive eternity in it. Should that have ever struck you as an illusion, then you have lost everything, unless you took pains to succumb to the same illusion once again, which is a contradiction. Or could it be that your clever head had so conspired with your lust that you could altogether forget what you owed others? Could it be that you thought that, even though it could never be repeated like the first time, there was still a tolerable way out: renewing oneself by experiencing the illusion in others, so that one savoured the infinitude and novelty in its pristine state in the individual whose virginal corset of illusion was not yet loosened? That sort of thing betrays as much desperation as depravity, and since it betrays desperation, it will be impossible here to find enlightenment about life.

The first thing I must now protest against is your right to use the word 'habit' for the recurrence characteristic of every life, and so also of love. 'Habit' is used properly only of what is bad, either through denoting persistence in something which is in itself bad, or through denoting a repetition of something in itself innocent but with an obduracy that makes the repetition bad on that account. 'Habit' therefore designates something unfree. But just as the good cannot be performed without freedom, so neither can one stay in it without freedom; thus with regard to the good one can never talk of habit.

Further, I must also protest when, in portraying marital monotony, you say that even in nature you will find nothing like it. That is very true, but monotony can be the very expression of something beautiful, and mankind can to that extent be proud of being its inventor. Thus in music an even tempo may have much beauty and great effect.

Finally, I would like to say that if such a monotony were unavoidable in marital life, then were you honest you would have to realize that the task was to conquer it, that is, preserve love under it, not to despair. For despair can never be a task; it is a convenience, but only seized upon, I will admit, by those who see the task.

But let us now look rather more closely at this notorious monotony. It is your error, and so too your misfortune, that everywhere, and so also with regard to love, you think too abstractly. You conceive a small summary of love's elements; as you yourself perhaps would say, you conceive the categories of love. In this respect I willingly concede you an exceptional categorial thoroughness. You think of everything concrete in terms of an aspect, and this is the poetic way. Then when you go on to conceive the protractedness of marriage, it seems dreadfully incongruous to you. The mistake is that you do not think historically. Were a systematic thinker to conceive the category of interaction, explain it thoroughly and with sound logic, but then add, 'it takes an eternity before the world can be done with all its eternal interaction', you can hardly deny we would have a right to laugh at him. It is, after all, the meaning of time, and the lot of mankind and of individuals, to live in it. So if all you can say is that it is not to be endured, you will have to look about for another auditorium. Now, this would be a quite satisfactory answer, but to deprive you of the chance of saying, 'We are basically agreed, it's just that you find it best to put up with what can't be altered', I shall try to show not just that one had better put up with it, as it is surely a duty, but that putting up with it is in truth the best.

But let us begin at a place which we can assume to be a point of contact. You are not afraid of the time that precedes the culmination, on the contrary you love it, and often strive with a multitude of reflections to make the moments longer in their reproduction than they were originally, and if someone tried to reduce *your* life to categories at this point, you would be highly indignant. Nor indeed, in that time before the culmination, is it just the big, decisive encounters that interest you, but every little triviality, and you know well enough how to talk of the secret which was hidden from the wise, that the least is the greatest. On the other hand, when the point of culmination is reached, why yes, then everything has changed, everything has shrivelled up into a paltry and unappetizing abbreviation. This, then, you would have us suppose is based in your nature, which is merely to conquer but cannot possess. [. . .]

In insisting 'that's just how you are', you admit that others might be different; more I dare not assert so far, for it might be that you were the normal person, notwithstanding the anxiousness with which you insist on remaining just as you are hardly suggests that. But what do you make of others? When you see a married couple whose union, as it appears to you, drags on in the most fearful boredom, 'in the most vapid repetition of love's holy institutions and sacraments', why yes, a destructive fire rages in you, a flame which would consume them. And this, indeed, is not a piece of capriciousness on your part, you are in the right, you are justified in letting the lightning of irony strike them, the thunder of wrath undo them. You annihilate them, indeed, not because that is your desire, but because they have deserved it. You condemn them. But what does 'condemn' mean, except to demand something of them? And if you cannot demand it, and it is a contradiction to demand the impossible, then it is a contradiction to condemn them. You have committed a blunder, have you not? You have hinted at a law which you yourself will not recognize, and which you have nevertheless enforced upon others. Still, you are not to be put out, you say, 'I don't blame them, I don't reproach them, I don't condemn them, I pity them.' But now suppose the people concerned did not find it boring at all. A self-satisfied smile springs to your lips, you have surprised yourself with a happy thought, which might also surprise the one you address: 'As I said, I pity them; for either they feel the whole weight of boredom and so I pity them, or they do not notice it and then, too, I pity them for being subject to such a pitiable illusion.' That is about how you would answer me, and were several people present, your air of assurance would not fail of effect. But now there are none to hear us, and I can therefore continue the investigation. So you pity them in either case. Only a third possibility remains, namely that one knows this is how it is with marriage and, happily, has not entered into it. But clearly this situation is just as pitiable for the one who has felt love and now sees that it cannot be realized. And finally, the situation of the person who has helped himself as best he may out of this shipwreck by the same egoistic makeshift is also pitiable, for he has set himself up as a robber and troublemaker. It looks, then, as though marriage itself has become the general expression of a happy ending of something, so that marriage's own outcome is not so joyful. Thus general pity is what we arrive at as the true result of this whole investigation. But such a result is in itself a contradiction; it is as if a person were to say that the result of life's development is that one goes backwards. As a rule you are not afraid of concessions and perhaps will say here, 'Yes, it does happen sometimes; when the wind is dead ahead and the going slippery, then often the result of going forward can be to go backwards.'

Nevertheless, I return to the consideration of your whole spiritual make-up. You say that you are by nature a conqueror who cannot possess. In saying this, I take it you do not think you have said anything disparaging; rather the contrary, you feel greater than others. Let us examine this a little more closely. What calls for greater strength, walking uphill or downhill? When the hill is as steep in either case, obviously the latter calls for more strength. There is an innate disposition to go uphill in nearly everyone, whereas most people are somewhat apprehensive about going downhill. Thus, too, I believe far more natures are formed for conquering than for possessing, and in your feeling of superiority in relation to large numbers of married people and 'their stupid brute satisfaction', there may indeed be some truth, but you are not willing to learn from your inferiors either. True art, as a rule, goes in a direction opposite to that of nature, without therefore annihilating the latter, and thus true art will turn out to possess, not to conquer, for possession is conquering in reverse. In these expressions you can see already how art and nature vie with each other. A person who possesses, yes, he too has something that is conquered; indeed, strictly

speaking one can say that it is only when a person takes possession
that he conquers. Now you, too, believe you possess, for you do
indeed have the instant of possession; but it is no possession, for
there is no deeper appropriation. If I were to imagine a conqueror
who had subdued kingdoms and countries, then he would indeed
also possess the provinces he had subdued; he would then have large
possessions; and yet one would describe such a prince as a conqueror,
not a possessor. Only when he ruled those lands wisely in their own
best interests, only then would he possess them. Now this is very
rare in someone whose nature it is to conquer; as a rule he will lack
the humility, the religiousness, the true humanity that is essential to
possession. It was, you see, just for this reason that, in explaining the
relationship of marriage to first love, I stressed the religious element
because this will dethrone the conqueror and let the possessor come
into view. I therefore praised the fact that marriage was constructed
with the highest in mind: lasting possession. I can remind you here
of a saying you are fond of flourishing: 'the great thing isn't the
original but the acquired'; for the urge to conquer, and the fact that
one makes conquests, that is what is really original, while the fact
that he possesses and wants to do that, that is the acquired. To
conquer, one needs pride; to possess, humility. To conquer, one
needs to be violent; to possess, to have patience. To conquer, greed;
to possess, contentment; conquering calls for eating and drinking,
possessing for praying and fasting. Yet all the predicates I have used
here, and surely correctly, to characterize the nature of the conqueror lend themselves to natural man and fit him absolutely; but
natural man is not the highest, for a possession is not a spiritually
null and void, even if legally enforceable, proof of ownership, but a
constant acquisition. Here, once more, you see that the nature of the
possessor has in it that of the conqueror, for he conquers like the
countryman, who does not put himself at the head of his men and
drive away his neighbour, but conquers by digging the earth. Thus
the truly great is not to conquer but to possess. [. . .] When conquering, one constantly forgets oneself, when possessing one remembers
oneself; not as an empty pastime but with all possible seriousness.
When going uphill one has only the other in sight; when going
downhill one must watch over oneself, over the correct relation
between the point of support and the centre of gravity. [. . .]

Nature, a philosopher has said,[35] takes the shortest way. One could say it takes no way at all; it is there all at once, at a stroke; and when I want to lose myself in contemplation of the vaulted heavens, I do not have to wait until the numberless heavenly bodies have taken shape, for there they are all at once. The way of history, like that of justice, is on the contrary very long and hard. Art and poetry then step in and shorten the way for us and have us rejoice in the moment of consummation; they concentrate the extensive in the intensive. But the more significant whatever it is that is to arrive there, the slower the course of history, but then that much more significance, too, in the course itself, that much more that which is the goal proves also to be the way. With regard to individual life, there are two kinds of history, external and internal. These are two kinds of currents, moving in opposite directions. The first in its turn has two sides. The individual does not have what he strives for and history is the struggle in which he acquires it. Or else the individual does have it, but cannot take possession of it because something outside constantly prevents him from doing so; history is then the struggle in which he overcomes those obstacles. The second kind of history starts with the possession, and history is then the development through which the individual obtains the possession. Now since history in the first case is external, and what one strives for lies outside, the history is not truly real, and the poetic and artistic account quite rightly takes steps to shorten it and to hasten to the intensive moment. [. . .] Only internal history is true history, but true history struggles with the life-principle in history – with time, but when one struggles with time, that is exactly when the temporal and every little moment acquire their great reality. Wherever the inner blossoming of the individual has not begun, where the individual is still closed, it is a matter of external history. But as soon as the buds open, so to speak, the inner history begins. Consider what we began with: the distinction between the natures of the one who conquers and the one who possesses. The nature of the conqueror is constantly outside itself, that of the possessor inside itself; so the former has an external history, the latter an internal. But since external history is the one that lends itself without detriment to concentration, it is natural for art and poetry to prefer it for representation, and with it to choose the unopened individual and everything belonging to him. Love opens the individual, it may be said; but not when love is understood in the way that it occurs in Romanticism. The individual is brought only to the point of opening itself, and there one ends; or it is in the process of opening itself but is interrupted. Yet, just as external history and the closed individual are the preferred objects of artistic and poetic representation, so too is everything that makes up the content of such an individual. But that, basically, is everything that pertains to natural man. Here are a few examples. Pride lends itself superbly to representation, for what is essential in pride is not succession in time but intensity in the moment. Humility is hard to represent just because it is indeed successive, and while the observer need only see pride in its culmination, so in the case of humility he really requires what poetry and art cannot provide, to see it in its constant process of becoming, for it is essential to humility that it is present constantly; and if you show it to him in its idealized moment, he feels that he misses something, because he feels that its true ideality consists not in being idealized in the moment but in its being present all the time. Romantic love lends itself superbly to representation in the moment; not so married love, for an idealized husband is not a husband once in his life but is that every day. If I want to represent a hero conquering kingdoms and countries, that lends itself superbly to representation in the moment; but a cross-bearer who every day takes up his cross can never be represented, either in poetry or in art, because the point of it is that he does it every day. If I want to imagine a hero giving his life, that lends itself superbly to being represented in the moment; but not the risking of his life every day, because the main thing is that it happens every day. Courage lends itself superbly to concentration in the moment; not so patience, just because patience struggles against time. You will say that art, after all, has represented Christ as an image of patience, as bearing all the world's sin, that religious poetry has concentrated all the bitterness of life in one chalice and let one individual drain it in a single moment. That is true; but it is because it has been concentrated in an almost spatial way. Anyone moderately informed about patience, on the other hand, knows very well that its real opposite is not the intensive moment of suffering (for then it comes closer to courage), but time, and that true patience is the patience that reveals itself in a struggle against time, or is really long-suffering. But long-suffering does not lend itself to artistic representation, for the point of it is incommensurable with art; neither can it be poetized, for it demands the protractedness of time. [. . .]

In following the development of the aesthetically beautiful, dialectically as well as historically, one finds that the direction of the movement is from the category of space to that of time, and that the perfecting of art depends on art's being able continually to free itself more and more from space and to define itself in temporal terms. Herein lies the transition, and the significance of the transition, from sculpture to painting, as Schelling opportunely indicated. Music has time as its element but gains no persistency in it; its meaning is persistently to vanish in time; it sounds but fades at the same time and has no duration. Poetry, finally, is the most complete of all the arts and therefore that form which knows best how to do justice to the significance of time. It does not need to confine itself to the moment in the way painting does, nor vanish without trace in the way music does. Yet it, too, as we have seen, is obliged nevertheless to concentrate itself in the moment. So it has its limits, and cannot, as was shown above, represent something whose very truth is temporal succession. Still, the fact that justice is done to time detracts in no way from the aesthetic; on the contrary, the more justice is done to it the richer and fuller the aesthetic ideal becomes.

But then what about the aesthetic? If it remains incommensurable even with poetic representation, how can it be represented? Answer: by being lived. In this way it acquires a certain similarity with music, which *is* only because it is constantly repeated, which *is* only in the moment of performance. That is why I drew attention in the above to the pernicious conflating of the aesthetic with what can be presented in the form of poetic reproduction. For, indeed, all that I am talking about here can be represented aesthetically; not, however, through poetic reproduction but by one's living it, realizing it in actual life. This is how aesthetics transcends itself and reconciles itself with life; for just as poetry and art are indeed in one sense precisely a reconciliation with life, so in another they are at enmity with life because they only reconcile one side of the soul.

With this I have reached the highest in the aesthetic. And truly, he who has the humility and courage to let himself be transfigured aesthetically, he who has a sense of being a character in the play written by God, a play where the playwright and prompter are not different people, where the individual, like the trained actor who has made himself one with his part and his lines, is not put off by the prompter but feels that what is whispered to him is what he himself would say, so that he begins almost to doubt whether it is the prompter that is putting the words into his mouth or he putting them into the prompter's; he who in the deepest sense feels himself at once composer and composition, who the instant he feels himself composing has the original pathos of the line, the instant he feels himself composed has the erotic ear that picks up every sound; – he, and only he, has realized the highest in aesthetics. But this history, with which not even poetry proves to be commensurable, this is the internal history. Internal history has the idea in itself and is just for that reason aesthetic. So it begins, as I expressed it, with the possession and its progress is the acquiring of this possession. It is an eternity in which the temporal has not disappeared as an ideal factor, but in which it is constantly present as a real one. When patience acquires itself in this way in patience, it is internal history.

Let us now glance at the relation between romantic and married love, since the relation between the natures of the conqueror and the possessor cannot offer any difficulties. In itself romantic love always remains abstract, and if it is not able to acquire any external history, death already lies in wait for it because its eternity is illusory. Married love begins with the possession and acquires an internal history. It is faithful, so too is romantic love, but now see the difference: the faithful romantic lover can wait, say, for fifteen years, then comes the instant of his reward. Here, very rightly, poetry says that the fifteen years lend themselves superbly to concentration, then it hastens to the moment. A husband is faithful for fifteen years; yet for those fifteen years he has had possession. Accordingly, throughout that long lapse of time he has constantly acquired the faithfulness he possessed, since married love has first love within it and thereby its faithfulness. But an ideal husband of this kind cannot be represented, for the essential thing is time in its extension. At the end of the fifteen years he has apparently come no further than at the beginning, and yet he has lived aesthetically in a high degree. For him his possession has not been a dead property, his possession is something he has constantly acquired. He has fought, not with lions and ogres, but with that most dangerous enemy which is time. But here eternity does not come afterwards as it does for the knight; eternity is something he has had in time, preserved in time. Only he, therefore, has triumphed over time; for it can be said of the knight that he has killed time – as indeed a man always wants to kill time when it has no reality for him – but that is never the real victory. As a true victor, the husband has not killed time but saved and preserved it in eternity. The married man that does this, yes, the life of that man is truly poetical, he solves the great riddle: to live in eternity yet so to hear the parlour clock strike that its striking does not shorten but prolongs his eternity – a contradiction no less profound, but far more glorious, than the one contained in that famous situation in the medieval story of the unfortunate of whom it recounts that he woke up in hell and shouted, 'What time is it?', to which the devil answered, 'An eternity.' [. . .]

Married love, then, has its enemy in time, its victory in time, its eternity in time; so even were I to imagine all so-called external and internal trials gone, it would always have its task. The former, as a rule, it also has, but to grasp them properly one must take note of two things: they are always inward factors, and they always contain a temporal aspect. For that reason, too, it is easy to see that love of this kind cannot be represented. It is constantly drawing itself in, and itself being (in a good sense) drawn along in time, while with anything to be presented in a reproduction it must be possible to coax it out and shorten its time. You will be further convinced of this if you consider the predicates applicable to married love. It is faithful, constant, humble, patient, forbearing, indulgent, sincere, contented, observant, persistent, willing, joyful. All these virtues have the property of being inward specifications of the individual. The individual does not fight external enemies; it is with itself and its love that it fights it out, of its own accord. And they have a temporal qualification, for their truth consists not in applying once and for all, but all the time. And nothing else is acquired by means of these virtues, just the self. Married love is, therefore, at one and the same time what you have often mockingly called the everyday and also the divine (in the Greek sense), and it is the divine through being the everyday. Married love does not come with an external mark, not like the rich bird with a rush and a roar,[36] it is the incorruptible being of a quiet spirit.[37]

Of this, you and all those whose nature it is to conquer have no conception. You are never within yourselves but constantly outside. Yes, so long as your every nerve is a-tingle, whether you steal about softly or make yourself known and the brass band inside you drowns out your consciousness, yes, that is when you think you are alive. But when the battle is won, when the last echo of the last shot has died away, when the swift thoughts like orderly officers hasten back to headquarters to report that the victory is yours – yes, then there is nothing more you know, you do not know how to begin; for only then do you stand at the true beginning.

What you despise, therefore, as unavoidable for marriage under the name of habit, is simply the historical side of it, which to your perverted eye takes on such a terrifying aspect.

But what is it you are used to regard as not only destroyed, but what is worse, profaned by the habit inseparably tied to married life? What you think of, in general, are 'the visible, holy signs of the erotic, which surely, like all visible signs, have no meaning in themselves, but whose meaning is due to the energy, the artistic bravura and virtuosity which is, after all, the natural genius with which they are executed. How disgusting to see the vapidness with which everything of that kind is accomplished in married life, how perfunctorily, how apathetically all that happens, practically on the stroke of the clock, almost like the tribe the Jesuits came upon in Paraguay who were so apathetic that the Jesuits found it necessary to have a bell rung at midnight as an agreeable message to all husbands to remind them of their marital duties. Thus everything happens in *tempo*, the way they've been trained.' Let us now agree not to let the fact that there is much that is ludicrous and absurd in existence put us off in our observations, but just see whether it is necessary, and if it is, then learn from you the way of salvation. I dare not expect much from you in this respect, for you keep on fighting like that Spanish knight,[38] though in another way, for a vanished time. For, in fighting for the moment against time, you are really fighting all the time for what has vanished. Let us take an idea, an expression, from your poetic world, or from the real world of first love: 'The lovers *look* at each other.' This word 'look', how superbly you know how to stretch it out and put an infinite reality, an eternity into it. A married couple who have lived together for ten years and seen each other daily cannot look at each other in that sense; but does that mean they cannot look lovingly at each other? Here we have your old heresy again. You happen to limit love to a certain age, to limit the love of one person to a very short time, and then like all those disposed to conquer you recruit for your experiment. But just that, indeed, is the most profound profanation of the eternal power of love. It is, in fact, despair. However you turn and twist in it, you must admit that the task is to preserve love in time. If this is impossible, then love is an impossibility. Your misfortune is to identify love simply and solely with these visible signs. If these are to be repeated over and over again and, let it be noted, with a morbid concern for their constantly having the reality they had by virtue of the accidental feature of its being their first occurrence, it is no wonder you are afraid and refer these signs and 'gesticulations' to those things of which one dare not say '*decies repetitia placebunt*',[39] for if it was the first time that gave them their value, then a repetition is an impossibility. But healthy love has a quite different worth; it works itself out in time, and is therefore also capable of rejuvenating itself through these outward signs; and – what for me is the main point – it has quite another idea of time and of the meaning of repetition.

I have expanded in the foregoing on how married love has its conflict in time, its victory in time, its blessing in time. In this I have been taking time to be just simple progression. But now it will appear that it is not just a simple progression in which what was there originally is preserved, but a growing progression in which what was there originally increases. You, who are so observant, will no doubt concede the generalization that people divide into two large classes, those who live mainly in hope and those who live mainly in recollection. Both exhibit an incorrect relation to time. The healthy individual lives in both hope and recollection, at one and the same time, and it is only through this that his life acquires true, substantial continuity. Accordingly, he has hope, and unlike those individuals who live only in recollection, he does not want to go back in time. But then what does recollection do for him, since it must surely have some influence? It puts a cross on the note of the instant; the further back recollection goes, the more frequent the repetition and the more crosses. Thus if he has an erotic moment in the present year, it is increased by his remembering one in the previous year, etc. This has come to be beautifully expressed in married life. I do not know how old the world is now, but you and I both know it is customary to say that first there came a Golden Age, then a Silver Age, then a Copper Age, then an Iron Age. In marriage it is the other way round: the silver wedding comes first and then the golden wedding. Or is recollection really the main point of such a wedding? But then the marriage terminology declares these other weddings to be even more beautiful than the first. [. . .] It has often occurred to me, also, to wonder why, according to ordinary ways of talking and thinking, the single state has no such prospects, that one tends instead to think it laughable that a bachelor succeeds in celebrating a jubilee. The reason, no doubt, is that it is generally assumed that the single state can never grasp the true present, which is a unity of hope and recollection, and therefore tends either to lie in hope or in recollection. But this, again, suggests the correct relation to the present that married love has in the popular mind.

However, there is something else in married life that you also indicate with the word 'habit'. 'Its uniformity, its total uneventfulness, its incessant vacuity, which is death and worse than death.' You know there are neurasthenics who are disturbed by the slightest noise, who are unable to think when someone walks softly over the floor. Have you noticed that there is also another kind of neurasthenia? There are people so weak that they need proper noise and distracting surroundings to be able to work. Why if not because they have no command over themselves, only in an inverse sense? When they are alone, their thoughts disappear in the indefinite; on the other hand, when noise and hubbub surround them, this compels them to pit their will against it. It is only when you have opposition that you are within yourself, but then, really, you are never within but constantly outside yourself. The moment you assimilate the opposition, there is quiet once more; so that is something you dare not do. But then you and the opposition are standing facing each other, and so you are not within yourself.

Naturally, the same applies here as before with time. You are outside yourself and therefore you cannot do without the other's opposition. You believe that only a restless spirit is alive, while all men of experience think only a quiet spirit truly lives. For you a turbulent sea is a picture of life, for me the still, deep water. I have often sat beside a small stretch of flowing water. It is always the same, the same soft melody, the verdure on its bed, swaying beneath its tranquil waves, the same small creatures moving about down there, a little fish which glides in under the cover of the flowers, it spreads its fins against the stream, it hides beneath a stone. How uniform, and yet how rich in change! Thus is married domesticity, quiet, modest, murmuring; not many *changements*, and yet, like that water, it is flowing, like that water it has melody, dear to the one that knows it, dear to him just because he knows it. It is without pomp, and yet a lustre sometimes spreads over it though without interrupting its habitual course, just as when moonbeams fall upon that water and reveal the instrument upon which it plays its melody. Such is married domesticity. But to be seen thus and live thus presupposes a property I shall now mention to you. There is a verse of Oehlenschläger's which I know you at least used to set great store by. For the sake of completeness, I transcribe it:

> Yet how much must cohere in the world,
> To conjure forth true love!
> First: two hearts which each other know,
> Then grace, their attendant guide;
> Then the moon with its beam downcast
> Through the branching beech in spring;
> So they can meet alone –
> Then the kiss – and then, too, innocence.

You, too, are in the business of eulogizing love. I will not deprive you of what, indeed, is not yours to own since it belongs to the poet, but of what you have nevertheless appropriated; yet since I, too, have appropriated it, let us be sharers – you get the whole verse, I the last word: and then, too, innocence.

Finally, there is yet another side to married life that has often given you occasion for attack. You say: 'Married love conceals in itself something quite different; it seems so mild and lovely and tender but once the door is closed behind the married couple, and before you know what, out comes the cane and we are told it's a duty. Deck out this sceptre as much as you may, make it into a Shrove-tide rod, it is still just a cane.' I deal with this objection here because essentially it, too, is due to a misunderstanding of the historical aspect of married love. You would have either dark powers or mood to be the constituent factors of love. As soon as consciousness joins in, the enchantment vanishes. But married love has that consciousness. To put it crudely, in place of the conductor's baton, whose movements provide the tempo for the graceful postures of first love, you show us the disagreeable corporal's cane of duty. You have to admit, first of all, that as long as there is no change in the first love which, as we were agreed, married love contains, there can be no question of the strict necessity of duty. So you do not really believe in the eternity of first love. Look, here we have your old heresy again. After all, it is you who set yourself up so often as first love's knight, and yet you do not believe in it, yes, you profane it. Not believing in it, you dare not enter into an alliance which, when you are no longer *volens*, can compel you *nolens* to stay in it. For you, then, love is clearly not the highest thing; for otherwise you would be happy if there were a power capable of compelling you to stay in it. You may say that such an expedient is no expedient; but to that I will remark that it depends on how you look at it. [. . .]

You regard duty as the enemy of love, I regard it as its friend. That assertion may satisfy you, and with your usual mockery you will congratulate me on such an interesting and no less unusual friend. I, for my part, will by no means be satisfied with that, but take the liberty of carrying the war over into your own territory. If duty, once apparent to consciousness, is the enemy of love, then love must look to defeating it; for after all, you would not have it that love was so impotent a being as not to be able to overcome all opposition. On the other hand, you think that when duty comes into view it's all over with love, and also that sooner or later duty does have to come into view, not just in married love but also in romantic love. And really you fear married love because there duty is so much part of it that when it becomes visible you cannot run away from it. Yet you think that is quite all right in the case of romantic love, for the very instant duty is mentioned the love is over, and duty's arrival is the signal for you — with a very polite bow — to take your leave, or, as you once put it, for you to regard it as your duty to take your leave. Here, again, you see how it goes with your eulogizing of love. If duty is the enemy of love, and love cannot defeat this enemy, then love is not the true victor. What follows is that you must leave love in the lurch. Once you have got hold of the despairing notion that duty is the enemy of love, then your defeat is assured and you have disparaged love and divested it of its majesty, just as you have done with duty, and yet that was the last thing you wanted. You see, this is despair once more, and it's that whether you feel the pain of it or try, in despair, to forget it. If you cannot reach the point of seeing the aesthetic, the ethical, the religious as the three great allies, if you do not know how to preserve the unity of the different expressions everything acquires within these different spheres, then life is without meaning and you must be accounted fully justified in your pet theory that one can say of everything: do it or do not do it, you will regret both.

Now, unlike you, I am not under the tragic necessity of having to mount an always unsuccessful campaign against duty. Duty is not for me one climate and love another; duty makes my love into the true, temperate climate, and perfection is this unity. However, in order properly to reveal to you your false doctrine, I will pursue it a little further, begging you to ponder the different ways in which one might feel that duty was the enemy of love.

Imagine someone who has become a husband without ever properly taking into account the ethical factor in marriage. He loves with all the ardour of youth, and is then suddenly, through some outward circumstance, affected by doubt as to whether the one he loves, and to whom he is also bound by ties of duty, might not think that really he only loves her because it is his duty. His case, indeed, is similar to the one indicated above; it seems to him, too, that duty turns out to be opposed to love. But he loves, and for him his love is truly the highest thing, and accordingly his efforts are directed at defeating this enemy. That is, he wants to love her, not because that is what duty enjoins – not according to the poor measure for the necessary minimum duty can yield – no, he wants to love her with all his soul, all his might, and all his fortune. He wants to love her even at the moment, should this be possible, when duty allowed him to refrain. You can easily see the confusion in his train of thought. What does he do? He loves her with all his soul; but that is exactly what duty enjoins, for let us not be confused by the talk of those who think that duty in respect of love is merely a catalogue of rules of etiquette. Duty here is just one thing, truly to love, with the sincerity of the heart, and duty is as protean as love itself, declaring everything holy and good when it is of love, and denouncing everything, however pleasing and specious, when it is not of love. So you see, he too has taken an incorrect attitude; but just because there is truth in him, he does what duty enjoins – seeing it is not just what he wants to do – neither more nor less than what duty enjoins. The 'more' he does is really his doing it; for the 'more' that I can do is always that I can do what duty enjoins. Duty enjoins, it cannot do more. The 'more' I am capable of is doing what it enjoins, and the moment I do that I can say that, in a sense, I am doing 'more'; I translate the duty from the external to the internal and thereby go beyond duty. From this you see what infinite harmony and wisdom and consistency there is in the world of spirit. When one proceeds from a definite position and quite calmly pursues it with truth and energy, it must always be an illusion when all the rest seems to be in contradiction with it; and when someone believes he effectively demonstrates the disharmony, he demonstrates the harmony. So the husband we have been talking of came out of it well; really his only punishment was that the duty teased him a little for his 'little faith'. Duty constantly chimes in with love. If you separate them, as he did, and make one part into the whole, then you are in constant self-contradiction. It is as if one were to separate the 't' and the 'e' in the syllable 'te', and then want no 'e' but claim the 't' is all there is to it. The moment he says it, he says the 'e' too. So it is with true love. It is not something speechless, abstractly inexpressible, but neither is it something soft, ungraspably indefinite. It is an articulate sound, a syllable. If duty is hard, *eh bien*, then love enunciates that fact, it makes it real, and thereby does more than its duty; if love is on the point of becoming so soft that it cannot be kept hold of, then duty sets a limit to it.

Now, if that was what your view that duty is the enemy of love amounted to, if it was nothing but an innocent misunderstanding, then, why yes, your case would be much as that of the man we are discussing. But much as your grasp of the matter is indeed a misunderstanding, it is also a culpable misunderstanding. Hence you disparage not just duty but love; hence duty looks as though it were an insuperable enemy. That is because it is true love that duty loves and it has a mortal hatred of false love, yes, it kills it. If they are in the truth, the individuals will see in duty merely the eternal expression of the fact that the way is prepared for them in eternity, that the way they would gladly go is one along which they are not merely permitted to proceed, indeed they are enjoined to do so. And over that path there watches a divine providence which is constantly showing them the way ahead, putting protective shields at all the dangerous places. And for a person who truly loves, why should he be unwilling to accept a divine authorization just because it expresses itself divinely, and says not merely 'you may' but 'you must'? In duty, everything is put in order for the lovers, and that, I believe, is why the language of duty is in the future tense, to suggest the historical aspect.

Now I am through with this little exposition. Presumably, though, it has made an impression upon you; you feel that everything has been turned around, and you cannot quite harden yourself to the logical rigour of my remarks. Nevertheless, if I had said all this to you in conversation, you would have found it hard not to offer the sarcastic comment that I am 'preaching'. However, you cannot justly accuse my presentation of suffering from that defect, or of being perhaps just as it ought, when one talks to a sinner as hardened as you; and as for your own lecturings and wisdom, these not infrequently remind one of the Preacher's Book,[40] and indeed one might believe you occasionally chose your texts from that source.

But I will let you yourself provide me with an opportunity to illuminate this matter. For as a rule you do not allow people to scoff at ethics, and in fact one has to force you to a certain point before you jettison it. You always keep it on your own side as long as you possibly can. 'I don't by any means despise duty', that is how the more moderate lectures, the more refined assassinations of duty, begin: 'far be it from me, but above all let's keep our consciences clean, duty is duty, love is love, period! and above all, no mishmash. But isn't it the case that marriage is alone in being a monstrosity of that kind, with this hermaphroditic ambiguity? All else is either duty or love. I recognize it is a person's duty to seek a definite position in life, I regard it as his duty to be true to his calling, while if he violates his duty, on the other hand, he well deserves the punishment he suffers. This is duty. I make some definite undertaking,

I can state precisely what it is I promise dutifully to comply with. If I do not do that, I am confronted by a power which can compel me. If I form an intimate attachment to another person, on the other hand, love is everything, I acknowledge no duty. If the love is over, we are through with the friendship. It is reserved exclusively for marriage to base itself on such an absurdity. What does it mean, after all, to pledge oneself to love? Where is the boundary? When have I discharged my duty? How is my duty to be more precisely defined? To what tribunal can I appeal in cases of doubt? And if I fail to discharge my duty, where is the power to compel me? Certainly, the State and the Church have established a certain limit; but may I not still be a bad husband even if I don't overstep it? Who will punish me, who will defend her who suffers under this?' Answer: you yourself. [To resolve] the confusion in which you have ensnared both yourself and me [. . .] [let] us take a look at your classification. [. . .] You think that everything else can be grasped under either the category of duty or its opposite, and that it has never occurred to anyone to apply another criterion: marriage alone is guilty of this self-contradiction. You offer the duty of one's calling as an example and think it an apt illustration of a purely dutiful relationship. This, however, is by no means the case. For if a person simply conceived of his occupation as a sum of appointments he had to keep at definite times and places, he would be degrading himself, his calling and his duty. Or perhaps you think a point of view like that would make for a good official? Where, then, would there be room for the enthusiasm with which one hallows one's calling, where room for the devotion with which one loves it? What forum could keep an eye on these? Or perhaps such things are not required of him as part of his duty? But then would the State not look upon anyone who assumed office without them as a hireling, whose sweat and toil it could exploit and reward, but who in another sense was an unworthy official? If the State does not say so in so many words, that is because what it demands is something outward, something tangible, and when it gets that it presupposes the other. In marriage, on the other hand, the main thing is what is inward, what cannot be pointed at. Yet the precise expression of this is love. I see no contradiction, therefore, in requiring it as a duty; for the fact that there is no one to keep an eye on it is not to the point, seeing the man can, after all, always keep an eye on himself. Should you continue, therefore, to demand such a check, it is either because you want it to help you worm your way out of your duty, or because you are so afraid of yourself that you would gladly have yourself declared legally incompetent; but that is just as wrong and just as reprehensible.

If you bear in mind what I have explained in the foregoing, in the way I have explained it, you will easily perceive that my insisting on the inwardness of duty in love is not done with the hullabaloo one occasionally finds with people whose prosaic common sense has first destroyed the immediate and who now, in old age, have taken to duty; people who, in their blindness, cannot voice their scorn of the purely natural in strong enough terms, nor sing their praises of duty stupidly enough – as though, in this way, it were something different from what you call it. Such a rupture, thank God, is unknown to me. I have not run off with my love into trackless regions and deserts where, in my loneliness, I lose my way, nor exactly have I asked my neighbours and the people across the way for their advice on what I should do. Such isolation and such particularization are equally wrong. I have always had footprints before me in this very region of universal validity which is duty. I have also felt that there are moments when the only salvation is to let duty speak, that it is healthy to let it punish one, not with the dismal effeminacy of a *heautontimoroumenos*,[41] but in all seriousness and emphatically. But I have not been afraid of duty, it has not appeared before me as an enemy which wanted to disturb the crumb of joy and happiness I had hoped to preserve through life; it has appeared as a friend, our love's first and only confidant. But this strength of having the prospect always free, that is the blessing of duty, while romantic love, because of its non-historical character, goes astray or comes to a standstill.

Dixi et animam meam liberavi,[42] not as if my soul had hitherto been trapped and now in this prolix unburdening had got itself air; no, it is merely a healthy drawing of breath in which it has savoured its freedom. Drawing breath in Latin is called *respiratio*, a word which indicates a flowing back of what had first flowed out. In drawing breath the organism enjoys its freedom, the freedom I have every day.

Accept now, well prepared, what is offered to you, well tested. Should you find it all too little to satisfy you, then see if you cannot prepare yourself better, whether you have not forgotten some precaution or other. The Serbs have a legend which tells of an immense giant with an equally immense appetite.[43] He comes to a poor cottager and wants to share the latter's dinner. The cottager puts out what the humble resources of the house afford. The giant's greedy eyes have already devoured it all, and he no doubt reckoned he would be no nearer having his fill had he actually eaten it. They sit down to the table. It does not occur to the cottager that there might not be enough for both. The giant reaches for the dish. The cottager stops him with the words: 'It is the custom in my house first to say a prayer'; the giant complies, and behold! there is enough for them both.

Dixi et animam meam liberavi; for her also, whom I still love, constantly, with the youthfulness of first love, her too have I liberated, not as if she had previously been bound, but she has rejoiced with me in our freedom.

In accepting my loving greeting, accept, too, as usual, a greeting from her, friendly and sincere as always.

It is a long time since I have seen you in our home. I can say this both in a true and a figurative sense; for notwithstanding the fortnight of evenings I have devoted almost entirely to this letter, I have constantly had you with me in a way, and yet I have not, in the figurative sense, really had you in my home, not in my house, in my living-room, but outside my door, from which, with my reproaches, it is almost as though I have been trying to drive you away. For me this has not been an agreeable way of passing the time, nor will you, I know, take my behaviour amiss. However, it will always be, both truly and figuratively, still more agreeable to me to see you in our home both truly and figuratively. I say this with all the husbandly pride of one who feels qualified to use that formula: in our home. I say it with all the humane respect every individual 'in our home' can always be certain of receiving. For next Sunday, then – you receive no standing family invitation 'for ever', i.e. for a whole day. Come when you want – always welcome; stay as long as you want – always the agreeable guest; go when you want – always well commended.

2 EQUILIBRIUM BETWEEN THE AESTHETIC AND THE ETHICAL IN THE DEVELOPMENT OF PERSONALITY

━━━━━━━━━━

My friend!

What I have said to you so often I say once more, or rather I shout it to you: either/or; *aut/aut*. A single *aut* offered as a caution does not make matters clear, since the question here is too important for one to be satisfied with a part and too internally consistent not to be grasped in the whole. There are situations in life to which it would be ridiculous, or a kind of insanity, to apply an either/or; but also, there are people whose souls are too disjointed to grasp what such a dilemma implies, whose personalities lack the energy to be able to say with feeling: either/or. These words have always made a strong impression on me and they still do, especially when I mention them by themselves in this way and out of context; the most frightful conflicts can now be set in motion. Their effect on me is that of an incantation; I become exceedingly serious, sometimes well-nigh shaken. I think back to an early youth when, without properly grasping what it means to make a choice in life, I listened with childlike trust to the talk of my elders and for me the moment of choice became solemn and august, notwithstanding that in choosing I was only following another's instructions. I think of the moment when, later in life, I stood at the crossroads, when my soul was matured in the hour of decision. I think of the many less important, yet for me not indifferent, occasions in life where choice was what mattered. For although there is only one situation where this phrase has its absolute meaning, namely where it points on the one hand to truth, righteousness, and holiness, and on the other to desire and susceptibility, and to dim passions and perdition, it is important to choose rightly even when the choice in itself is harmless; to test oneself so as never to have to begin a retreat to the point one started out from, and thank God for having nothing worse to reproach oneself for than wasting time. I use these words in daily speech as others use them, and it would be foolish pedantry to stop doing so; but there can be times when I catch myself having used them of things that are altogether indifferent. They then take off their humble attire. I forget the insignificant thoughts they disjoin, they appear to me in all their dignity, in their robes. Just as in every-day affairs an official appears in civilian clothes and mingles with the crowd unremarked, so too with those words in everyday speech; for when instead he appears in authority he sets himself apart from everyone else. Like an official of that kind whom I see usually only on solemn occasions, these words appear before me and my soul always becomes serious. And although to some extent my life has its either/or behind it, I know very well that there may still be many a situation, in which its full meaning is yet to be encountered. I hope, however, that these words may at least find me in a worthy state of mind when they make me pause on my way, and that I shall succeed in choosing the right course. But I shall strive in any case to choose with unfeigned seriousness, and then at least I shall dare to comfort myself that I shall return all the sooner to the right path.

And now for you – you certainly use this phrase often enough, indeed with you it has almost become a byword – what does it mean to you? Nothing at all. For you it is, according to your own expressions, a twinkling of the eye, a snap of the fingers, a *coup de main*, an abracadabra. You can produce it at every opportunity, nor without effect. Its effect on you is that of a strong drink on a neurasthenic. You become totally intoxicated in what you yourself call the higher lunacy. 'In it is contained all life's wisdom, but never has anyone expounded it so pithily – as if a god in the guise of a bogle were talking to suffering humanity – as that great thinker and true philosopher of life, who said to a man who had tossed his hat onto the floor. "If you pick it up, you'll get a beating, if you don't pick it up you'll also get a beating, now you can choose!"' You take great delight in 'comforting' people when they appeal to you in moments of crisis. You listen to their explanations and then say, 'Yes, I see quite plainly now, there are two possibilities, one can either do it or not do it; my honest opinion and my friendly advice is as follows: do it or don't do it, you will regret both.' But he who mocks others mocks himself, and it is not a trivial matter but a deep mockery of yourself, a sad proof of how loose the joints of your soul are, that your view of life focuses on a single sentence, 'I say merely either/or.' If you were really serious there would be nothing to be done with you; one would have to put up with you as you were and regret that melancholy or frivolity had weakened your mind. Since, however, one knows very well that that isn't the case, it is tempting not to pity you but to wish, indeed, that the circumstances of your life may some day strap you on their rack and force you to come out with what really dwells within you, that the more rigorous examination that is not satisfied with talk and witticisms should begin. Life is a masquerade, you tell us, and this, for you, is an inexhaustible source of amusement, yet still no one has succeeded in knowing you; for all your revelations are constantly illusions; that is the only way you can breathe and make sure people do not press in on you and prevent you drawing breath. Your activity is designed to keep yourself hidden, and in that you succeed, your own mask is the most enigmatic of all; for you are nothing and exist merely in relation to others, and you are what you are in this relation. To an affectionate shepherdess you languidly offer a hand and, instantly, are masked in every kind of pastoral sentimentality; you deceive a venerable spiritual father with a fraternal kiss, etc. You yourself are nothing, an enigmatic figure, on whose brow is written 'either/or' – 'for that is my slogan, and these words are not, as grammarians think, disjunctive conjunctions; no, they belong inseparably together and should therefore be written as one word, seeing that together they form an interjection which I shout at mankind, as one shouts "Hip" at a Jew'.[1] Now although nothing you say in this vein has any effect upon me, or if it does, the most it can do is provoke a righteous indignation, nevertheless for your own sake I will answer you. Don't you know that a midnight hour comes when everyone has to take off his mask? Do you think life always lets itself be trifled with? Do you think you can sneak off a little before midnight to escape this? And does it not dismay you? I have seen people in real life who deceived others for so long that in the end their true nature could not reveal itself; I have seen people play hide-and-seek for so long that finally, through them, madness forced their secret thoughts upon others as distastefully as hitherto they had proudly kept them to themselves. Or can you imagine anything more frightful than that it might end with your nature dissolving into a multitude, with your really becoming many, becoming, like that unhappy demoniac, a legion,[2] and in that way losing the innermost, the most holy thing in a man, the unifying power of personality? Truly, you should not trifle with what is not only serious but terrifying. There is, in every person, something

which to some degree prevents him from being completely transparent to himself; and this can be on such a scale that he is so
inexplicably woven into the circumstances of life which lie outside
him that he is almost unable to reveal himself. But he who cannot
reveal himself cannot love, and he who cannot love is the unhappiest
of all. And you do the same wantonly, you train yourself in the art
of being a riddle to everyone. My young friend! what if no one
bothered to guess your riddle? What pleasure would you get out of
it then? But, first of all for your own sake, for the sake of your
salvation − for I know of no state of the soul that better deserves to
be called perdition − stop this wild flight, this passion for destruction,
which rages in you; for that is what you want to do, you want to
destroy everything; you want to sate the hunger of doubt upon life.
It is to this end that you cultivate yourself. It is for this that you
steel your mind. For this much you gladly admit, that you are good
for nothing, that all that gives you pleasure is marching seven times
round life and blowing on the horn,[3] and then letting the whole
thing come tumbling down so that your soul may find peace, yes,
sad that you are able to summon forth Echo, for Echo is heard only
in emptiness.

However, I doubt if I can make any progress with you in this
direction; besides, my head is, if you like, too weak to put up with,
or as I prefer it, too strong to find pleasure in, things constantly
swirling before my eyes. So I shall start from another angle. Imagine
a young man at an age when life really begins to have meaning; he
is healthy, pure, joyful, mentally gifted, full of hope and himself the
hope of all who know him; imagine that, yes, it's hard to say this −
imagine that he was mistaken about you, that he believed you were
a serious, tried and experienced person, in whom one could safely
seek enlightenment on life's riddles; imagine that he appealed to
you with that endearing trust which is the ornament of youth, with
that ungainsayable right of claim that is the privilege of youth −
how would you answer him? Would you answer, 'Yes, I say only
either/or'? Hardly. Would you, as you are wont to put it when you
want to indicate your disgust at others' inconveniencing you with
their personal problems, stick your head out of the window and
say, 'Try next door'? Or would you treat him like others who wish
to seek advice or enlightenment from you, whom you dismiss as

you would those who come for the priest's offering, with the words that you are 'only a lodger in life', not a householder and paterfamilias? You wouldn't do that either. A young person, mentally gifted, is something you set too much store by. Yet your relation to him would not be quite as you wished, it wasn't an accidental encounter that had brought you into contact with him; your irony was not tempted. Although he was the younger one, you the older, still, with his noble youthfulness he had made the moment serious. You yourself would like to be young, would you not? To feel that there is something beautiful in being young yet also something very serious, that it is by no means a matter of indifference how one uses one's youth, that one has a choice, a real either/or. You would feel that what is important is not so much cultivating his mind as maturing his personality. Your good nature, your sympathy would be set in motion; it is from this that you would speak to him; you would invigorate his soul, confirm his trust in the world, you would assure him that there is a power in a man which is able to defy the whole world, you would impress very strongly upon him the importance of making good use of time. You can do all this, and when you want to, you can do it handsomely. But mark well what I am going to say to you, young man – for although you are not young, one is always obliged to call you that. What was it you did here? You acknowledged what you otherwise will not acknowledge, the importance of either/or. And why? Because your soul was moved by love for the young man; and yet you deceived him in a way, for it may be that he wants to meet you on other occasions when it is not at all convenient to make this acknowledgement. Here you see a sorry consequence of the inability of a man's nature to reveal itself harmoniously. You thought you were doing what was best, and yet you may have caused him injury; perhaps he would have held out better if confronted with your distrust of life than by finding comfort in the subjective, deceitful trust you imparted to him. Now imagine you met that young man again after a lapse of several years. He was lively, witty, active in thought, bold in expression; but your refined ear could easily detect the doubt in his soul, you formed a suspicion that he, too, had arrived at the questionable wisdom. 'I say only either/or'. You would be sorry for him, would you not? You would

you do things but not want your child to

feel he had lost something, and something essential. But you would not feel sorry for yourself; you are satisfied, indeed you are proud of your questionable wisdom, yes, so proud of it that you cannot let another share in it, you want it for yourself. And yet in another respect you find it deplorable, and it is your sincere opinion that it is to be deplored that this young man has arrived at the same wisdom. What a monstrous contradiction! Your whole nature is in contradiction with itself. But you can only get out of this contradiction with an either/or; and I, who love you more genuinely than you loved that young man, who have experienced in my life the importance of choice, congratulate you on still being young enough, even if there will always be something you miss, young enough, if you have the energy (or rather if you want to have it), to win what is the main thing in life: to win yourself, to take possession of yourself.

Now, if a man could constantly balance on the tip of the moment of choice, if he could stop being a person, if in his inmost being he were only an empty thought, if personality meant no more than to be a goblin which, while going through the motions, remained nevertheless unchanged, if that is how it was, it would be foolish to say it might be too late for a man to choose, for in a deeper sense there could be no question of a choice. Choice itself is decisive for a personality's content; in choice personality immerses itself in what is chosen, and when it does not choose it wastes consumptively away. For a moment it can seem, for a moment it can look as if what the choice is between lies outside the chooser; he has no relation to it, he can sustain an indifference in the face of it. This is the instant of deliberation, but like the Platonic instant, it really has no existence,[4] least of all in the abstract sense in which you would hold on to it. And the longer one stares at it the less it exists. What is to be chosen stands in the deepest relationship to the chooser, and when the choice concerns a problem of life the individual must naturally go on living at the same time; so the longer he postpones the choice the easier it is to modify it, even though he keeps on deliberating and deliberating and thinks, because of that, that he is holding the alternatives properly apart from one another. When one looks at life's either/or in this way, one is not easily tempted to trifle with it. One sees, then, that the inner activity of the personality has no time for thought-experiments, that it hastens constantly on and in one way or another is positing either the one or the other, making the choice in the next instant more difficult because what has been posited has to be retracted. If you imagine a helmsman in his ship when it is just about to tack, then he may be able to say, 'I can either do this or that', but unless he is a pretty poor helmsman he will also be aware that the ship is still maintaining its normal headway, and so there is only an instant when it is immaterial whether he does this or that. Similarly with a human being; if he forgets to take that headway into account, the moment eventually comes when there is no longer any question of an either/or, not because he has chosen but because he has refrained from choice, which can also be expressed in another way: because others have chosen for him, because he has lost himself.

You will also see from this why my view of a choice differs from yours, in the event that I can speak of your having such, for the difference is precisely that yours prevents a choice. The moment of choice is for me very serious, less on account of the rigorous pondering of the alternatives, and of the multitude of thoughts that attach to each separate link, than because there is a danger afoot that at the next moment it may not be in my power to make the same choice, that something has already been lived that must be lived over again. For it is a delusion to think one can keep one's personality blank, or that one can in any real sense arrest and interrupt personal life. The personality already has interest in the choice before one chooses, and if one postpones the choice the personality makes the choice unconsciously, or it is made by the dark powers within it. Then when at last the choice is made, if, as I remarked earlier, one has not gone into complete dissolution, one discovers that there is something that must be done over again, that must be retracted, and that is often very difficult. Fairy-tales tell us of human beings whom mermaids and mermen captivated with their demonic music. To break the spell, says the story, they had to play the same piece backwards without a single mistake.[5] The thought here is very profound but very difficult to put into action, and yet it is so; the errors one has incurred must be eliminated in this way, and every time a mistake is made one must make a fresh start. See, then, how important it is to choose and to choose in time. You, however, have another method

– for I know full well that the polemical side you expose to the
world is not your true nature. Yes, if deliberation were the task for
a human life you would be close to perfection. I will take an
example. To encompass your case the alternatives will naturally
have to be bold ones; either priest/or actor. Here is the dilemma. All
your passionate energy now awakens; reflection with its hundred
arms grasps the thought of being a priest. There is no peace for you,
day and night you think about it; you read all the publications you
can lay your hands on, go to church three times every Sunday,
make the acquaintance of priests, write sermons yourself, deliver
them to yourself; for half a year you are dead to the whole world.
Then you are ready. You are now able to talk with more insight,
and as if you had greater clerical experience, than many who have
been priests for twenty years. Your indignation is aroused when
you meet with such people because they cannot unburden their
hearts with greater eloquence. 'Is this enthusiasm?' you say, 'I who
am not a priest, who am not dedicated to that calling – compared
with them I speak with the voice of angels.' And that could well be
true, but you have not become a priest. Then you proceed in the
same manner with the other problem, and your enthusiasm for art
almost outdoes your ecclesiastic eloquence. Now you are ready for
the choice. However, one may be sure that, in the immense activity
of thought you have been engaged in, much has gone to waste,
many small comments and observations. So just when you are to
make the choice, this refuse begins to come to life, a new either/or
presents itself: lawyer; or perhaps barrister, for that has something
in common with both of the alternatives. Now you are done for.
For at that moment you are, without further ado, barrister enough
to be able to show the propriety of taking the third possibility into
account. So your life goes on. After a year and a half wasted on
these deliberations, having exerted with admirable energy all the
strength of your soul, you have come not one step further. Then
the thread of thought snaps, you become impatient, passionate, you
ravage with sword and fire, and then you go on, 'Or a hairdresser,
or a bank teller, I say only either/or.' Little wonder, then, that for
you this phrase has become 'a stumbling-block and a foolishness',[6]
that to you it seems 'like the arms of the iron maiden whose
embrace is death'. You look down on people. You make a mockery

of them, and you have become what you despise most of all – a critic, a universal critic in all departments. At times I can hardly forbear smiling at you, and yet it is sad that your truly excellent intellectual gifts are dissipated in this way. But here again we have that same contradiction in your nature. For you see the ludicrous very clearly, and God help the one who falls into your hands if he is in a similar case; yet the only difference is that while he may be dejected and broken, you become cheerful and erect and livelier than ever, beatifying yourself and others with the gospel:[7] *vanitas vanitatum vanitas*, hurrah! But that is no choice, it is a case of 'Drop it!',[8] or a mediation, like letting five become an even number. You now feel free, you bid the world farewell:

> Thus I retire into the back of beyond
> Above my cap only stars.[9]

There, now you have chosen – not indeed the better part, that you will agree; but really you have made no choice at all, or you have chosen only figuratively. Your choice is an aesthetic choice, but an aesthetic choice is no choice. In general, the act of choosing is a literal and strict expression of the ethical. Wherever it is a matter of an either/or in a stricter sense, one can always be sure that the ethical is involved. The only absolute either/or there is is the choice between good and evil, but it is also absolutely ethical. The aesthetic choice is either wholly immediate, thus no choice, or it loses itself in multiplicity. Thus if a young girl follows the choice of her heart, this choice, however beautiful, is not a choice in the stricter sense since it is wholly immediate. A person who aesthetically considers a whole range of life-tasks, like you in the above, is more likely to arrive at a multiplicity than an either/or, because here the factor of self-determination in the choice is not given an ethical emphasis, and because, if one does not choose absolutely, one chooses for that moment only and can, for that reason, choose something else the next instant. The ethical choice is therefore in a certain sense far easier, far simpler, but in another sense infinitely more difficult. A person who wants to determine himself ethically in his life's task has usually an insignificant selection to choose from; on the other hand, the act of choice itself signifies far more for him. If you will understand me aright, I could quite well say that in choice it is less a matter of choosing correctly than of the energy, earnest and feeling with which one chooses. The personality thereby proclaims itself in its inner infinitude, and the personality is thereby consolidated in turn. So even if a person chose what was wrong, he would still, because of the energy with which he chose it, discover that what he had chosen was wrong. For inasmuch as the choice is undertaken with all the personality's inwardness, his nature is purified and he himself is brought into immediate relation to the eternal power whose omnipresence interpenetrates the whole of existence. This transfiguration, this higher initiation, is never discovered by someone who chooses merely aesthetically. The rhythm in his soul, despite all its passion, is only a *spiritus lenis*.[10] [. . .]

What is it, then, that I separate in my either/or? Is it good and evil? No, I simply want to bring you to the point where that choice truly acquires meaning for you. It is on this that everything hinges. Only when one can get a person to stand at the crossroads in such a way that he has no expedient but to choose, does he choose what is right. So if you should happen, before you have a chance to read the whole of this somewhat lengthy inquiry, which again is being sent to you in the form of a letter, if you should happen to feel that the moment of the choice has come, throw away the rest, do not bother with it at all, you have not lost anything – but choose, and you shall see what validity there is in it; yes, no young girl can be as happy in the choice of her heart as a man who has known how to choose. Either, then, one is to live aesthetically or one is to live ethically. In this, as I have said, there is no question yet of a choice in a stricter sense; for someone who lives aesthetically does not choose, and someone who, once the ethical has become apparent to him, chooses the aesthetic, does not live in the aesthetic sphere for he sins and comes under the category of the ethical, even if his life must be described as *unethical*. [. . .]

My either/or does not denote in the first instance the choice between good and evil, it denotes the choice whereby one chooses good and evil or excludes them. The question here is, under what categories one wants to contemplate the entire world and would oneself live. That someone who chooses good and evil chooses the good is indeed true, but this becomes evident only afterwards, for the aesthetic is not evil but indifference, and that is why I said that it is the ethical that constitutes choice. It is less a matter, then, of choosing between willing good or evil than of choosing to will but, with this latter, good and evil are posited once again. Someone who chooses the ethical chooses the good, but the good here is wholly abstract; choosing the ethical merely posits it, and from that it does not follow that the chooser cannot choose evil again, notwithstanding he chose good. Here, again, you see the importance of choosing, and that what is crucial is not so much deliberation as the baptism of choice by which it is assumed into the ethical. The more time goes, the more difficult the act of choice becomes, for the soul always finds itself on one side of the dilemma, and it therefore becomes harder and harder to tear oneself away. And yet that is necessary if there is to be a choice, and also of supreme importance if a choice is to mean anything, as I shall show below that it does. [. . .]

Although I am no philosopher, I am obliged at this point to hazard a little philosophical reflection, which I would ask you not so much to criticize as to bear in mind. For the polemical outcome echoing through all your hymns of victory over life bears a remarkable resemblance to the pet theory of recent philosophy, that the principle of contradiction is annulled.[11] I know well enough that the standpoint you adopt is an abomination to philosophy; yet it strikes me that philosophy itself is guilty of the same error; yes, that the reason why this has not been noticed from the start is that philosophy is even less well placed than you are. Your situation is the domain of action, philosophy's is that of contemplation. As soon as one transfers that to the practical domain it must come to the same result as you, though not expressing itself in the same way. You mediate oppositions in a higher lunacy, philosophy does so in a higher unity. You turn to the future, for action is essentially future-oriented: you say, 'I can either do this or do that, but whichever I do is equally wrong, *ergo* I do nothing at all.' Philosophy turns to the past, to the whole of world-historical experience, it shows how the separated elements come together in a higher unity. [. . .] For the philosopher world history is concluded, and he mediates.[12] Thus in our age it is part of the order of the day to be confronted with the distasteful sight of young men able to mediate Christianity and paganism, able to play with the titanic forces of history, yet who are unable to tell a plain man what he has to do here in life, and who do not know any better what they themselves have to do. [. . .]

As truly as there is a future, just as truly is there an either/or. The time in which the philosopher lives is not absolute time, it is itself an element in that, and one should always have misgivings when a philosopher bears no fruit; indeed it should be considered a dishonour, just as in the East it is considered a disgrace to be barren. So time itself is an element, and philosophy itself is an element in time. Our own age in its turn will appear to a later age as a discursive moment and a philosopher of a later age will again mediate it, and so on.[13] To that extent philosophy is within its rights, and it should be considered an accidental error on the part of the philosophy of our own time that it mistook our age for absolute time. But this clearly means that the category of mediation has suffered a significant blow, and that absolute mediation is only possible when history is finished, in other words that the System is in constant process of becoming. But recognition that an absolute mediation exists is what philosophy has retained. This, naturally, is of the utmost importance, since if one abandons mediation one abandons speculation. On the other hand, one has scruples about admitting it, for if mediation is admitted there is no absolute choice, and then there is no absolute either/or. This is the difficulty, yet I believe it to be due partly to a confusion between two spheres, those of thought and freedom. For thought the opposition has no substance, it goes over into the other and the opposites thus come together in a higher unity. For freedom the opposition does have substance, because the one opposite now excludes the other. I am not by any means mistaking *liberum arbitrium*[14] for the true positive freedom, for even the latter has for all eternity evil outside itself, if only as an impotent possibility, and its way of perfecting itself is not by increasingly accepting evil but by increasingly excluding it, and exclusion is precisely the opposite of mediation. Later I shall show that I do not mean by this to assume the notion of a radical evil.

The spheres that are properly the concern of philosophy, those that are properly spheres for thought, are logic, nature and history. Here necessity rules and so mediation has its validity, That this is true of logic and nature nobody will deny; but with history there are difficulties, for here freedom is said to rule. However, I believe that history is viewed incorrectly and that this is the source of the difficulty. For history is more than a product of the free actions of free individuals. The individual acts, but this action enters into the order of things which sustains the whole of existence. What its outcome will be the agent does not really know. But this higher order of things, which, so to speak, digests the free actions and kneads them together in its eternal laws, is necessity, and this necessity is the movement in world history; it is therefore quite right for the philosopher to use mediation, that is to say relative mediation. If I consider a world-historical individual, I can distinguish between the 'works' of which the Scripture says that they 'do follow' him[15] and the works through which he belongs to history. With what might be called inward works philosophy has nothing whatever to do; but inward work is the true life of freedom. Philosophy looks at the outward work and sees it not in isolation but as it is absorbed into and transformed by the world-historical process. It is this process that really forms philosophy's object and philosophy looks at it under the category of necessity. Therefore it keeps at a distance the reflection which would point out that everything might have been otherwise. It looks at world history in a way in which there can be no question of an either/or [. . .] though it cannot occur to any philosopher to deny there is one for the acting individual. Hence the lack of concern, the conciliation, with which philosophy regards history and its heroes, for it considers them under the category of necessity. Hence, too, its helplessness at getting a man to act, its tendency to let everything come to a standstill, for what it really demands is that one act from necessity, and that is a contradiction.

Thus even the humblest individual has a dual existence. Also, he has a history, and this is not just a product of his own free actions. But the inward work belongs to himself and will belong to him in all eternity; this neither history nor world history can take from him, it follows him either to his joy or to his sorrow. In this world there rules an absolute either/or, but it is a world philosophy has nothing to do with. If I imagine an elderly man looking back on an eventful life, he can get a mediation out of it for thought since his history was woven into that of the time. But deep inside he gets no mediation; an either/or is still constantly separating what was separated when he made his choice. If one were to talk here of a mediation, one might say it was repentance; but repentance is no mediation, it does not look with longing upon that which should be mediated, that thing is consumed in its wrath; but this is much like exclusion, the opposite of mediation. Here it is also evident that I do not assume a notion of radical evil when I admit the reality of repentance. Repentance is indeed an expression of conciliation, but it is also an absolutely unconciliatory expression. [. . .]

So it is freedom I am fighting for (partly in this letter, partly and foremost in myself), for the future, for either/or. That is the treasure I plan to bequeath to those whom I love in the world; yes, if my little son were at this moment of an age that he could understand me and my last hour had come, I would say to him, 'I leave you no fortune, no title and honours, but I know where a treasure lies buried which can make you richer than the whole world; and this treasure belongs to you, and you are not even to thank me for it, so no injury is done to your soul through owing a man everything; this treasure is deposited in your own inner being: it is an either/or which makes a man greater than the angels.'

Here I will break off this reflection. Perhaps it does not satisfy you. Your greedy eye devours it without you getting your fill, but that is because the eye gets its fill last,[16] especially when, like you, one is not hungry but merely suffering from an unappeasable craving of the eye.

What stands out in my either/or is the ethical. So far, then, it is not a matter of the choice of some thing, not a matter of the reality of the thing chosen, but of the reality of choosing. It is this, though, that is decisive and what I shall try to awaken you to. To reach this point it is possible for one man to help another, but once he has reached it the importance the one can have for the other becomes more subordinate. I have remarked in a previous letter that the experience of having loved gives to a man's nature a harmony that is never entirely lost; now I want to say that choosing gives to a man's nature a solemnity, a quiet dignity, that is never entirely lost. Many people set extraordinarily great store by having seen one or another remarkable world-historical personage face to face. The impression is one they never forget, it has given to their souls an ideal picture which ennobles their natures. Yet even that instant, however significant, is nothing compared with the instant of choice. When around me all has become still, solemn as a starlit night, when the soul is all alone in the world, there appears before it not a distinguished person, but the eternal power itself. It is as though the heavens parted, and the I chooses itself – or, more correctly, it accepts itself. The soul has then seen the highest, which no mortal eye can see and which never can be forgotten. The personality receives the accolade of knighthood which ennobles it for an eternity. He does not become someone other than he was before, he becomes himself; consciousness unites. Just as an heir, even if he inherits all the world's treasures, does not own them before coming of age, even the richest personality is nothing before he has chosen himself, and on the other hand, even what might be called the poorest personality is everything when he has chosen himself; for the great thing is not to be this or that, but to be oneself; and every person can be that if he wants.

That in a sense it is not a matter of a choice of something, you can see from the fact that what appears on the opposite side is the aesthetic, which is indifference. Yet it is a matter of a choice, yes, an absolute choice; for only through choosing absolutely can one choose the ethical. Through the absolute choice, then, the ethical is posited, but from that it by no means follows that the aesthetic is excluded. In the ethical the personality is centred in itself; the aesthetic is thus excluded absolutely, or it is excluded as the absolute, but relatively it always stays behind. The personality, through choosing itself, chooses itself ethically and excludes the aesthetic absolutely; but since it is, after all, he himself the person chooses, and through choosing himself does not become another nature but remains himself, the whole of the aesthetic returns in its relativity.

So the either/or I have presented is in a sense absolute, for the options are choosing and not choosing. When the choice confronting one is thus absolute, either/or is also that. In another sense, however, the absolute either/or first appears with the choice, for it is now that the options of good and evil appear. But this choice posited by and in the first choice need not detain me here, I would merely press you to the point where the choice proves necessary and after that consider life under ethical categories. I am no ethical rigorist inspired by a formal abstract freedom; once the choice is posited the whole of the aesthetic returns, and you shall see that only then is life beautiful, and that only in this way can a person succeed in saving his soul and gaining the whole world, in using the world and not abusing it.

But what is it to live aesthetically, and what is it to live ethically? What is the aesthetic factor in a person, and what the ethical? To this I would answer: The aesthetic factor in a person is that by which he is immediately what he is; the ethical factor is that by which he becomes what he becomes. Someone who lives in and by and of and for the aesthetic factor in himself lives aesthetically.

It is not my aim here to enter into a more detailed consideration of all that this definition of the aesthetic implies. It would also seem superfluous to want to enlighten you on what it is to live aesthetically, you who are a practitioner of such virtuosity in that area that it is rather I who am in need of your help. Nevertheless, I shall sketch several stages so that we can work our way up to the point where your life really belongs, which is of importance to me if you are not to elude me at too early a stage with one of your favourite digressions. Besides, I do not doubt that there is much I can indeed enlighten you on in regard to what it is to live aesthetically. Although I would send anyone wanting to live aesthetically to you as the most reliable guide, I would not refer to you if, in a higher sense, he wanted to gain insight into what it is to live aesthetically; on that you would not be able to enlighten him because you are yourself caught up in it; it could only be explained to him by someone who stands a step higher, or by someone who lives ethically. You might be tempted for just a second to come up with the quibble that neither could I give a reliable explanation of what it is to live ethically, since I am caught up in that. This, however, would merely give me the opportunity to offer further enlightenment. The reason why someone who lives aesthetically cannot, in a higher sense, give any enlightenment is that he lives constantly in the moment, that his knowing is after all confined constantly to a certain relativity, within a certain boundary. It is not at all my purpose to deny that living aesthetically, when such a life is at its peak, can call for a multiplicity of intellectual gifts, even, indeed, that these may be developed to an unusual degree; but they are fettered and transparency is lacking. Thus one often finds species of animals with senses much keener and of far greater intensity than those of man, but they are bound to the animal's instinct. I would gladly take you as an example. I have never denied your outstanding intellectual gifts, as you will see from the fact that I have often enough reproached you for abusing them. You are witty, ironic, observant, a dialectician, experienced in pleasure, you can calculate the instant, you are sentimental, heartless, all depending on the circumstances. But beneath all this you are all the time only in the moment, your life therefore disintegrates and it is impossible for you to explain it. Now if someone wanted to learn the art of pleasure, it would be quite right to go to you; but if he wants to understand your life, he is addressing himself to the wrong person. With me he would perhaps sooner find what he seeks, although I by no means possess your intellectual gifts. You are caught up, and have as it were no time to tear yourself away; I am not caught up, either in my judgement of the aesthetic or in that of the ethical, just because within the ethical I am raised above the instant, I am in freedom; but it is a contradiction to suggest that one can be caught up in being free.

Every man, however modest his talents, however subordinate his position, feels a natural need to form a view of life, a conception of life's meaning and aim. A person who lives aesthetically has that too, and the general description heard in all ages and from the most diverse stages is this: one must enjoy life. It has, of course, very many variations, accordingly as conceptions of pleasure vary, but in this expression, that one must enjoy life, they are all united. *But the person who says that he wants to enjoy life always posits a condition which is either outside the individual or in the individual but not posited by the individual himself.* I would beg you, regarding this last point, to keep a fairly good hold of the expressions used, since they are chosen with care.

Let us now review these stages quite briefly in order to catch up with you. You are perhaps already a little annoyed at my proposal for a general description of living aesthetically; still, you can hardly deny its accuracy. One hears you often enough scoffing at people for not knowing how to enjoy life, while you think that you, for your part, have studied it from top to bottom. It is quite possible they do not understand it, but in the expression itself they none the less agree with you. Perhaps, then, you suspect that, in this inquiry,

you are to be teamed up with people who are otherwise an abomination to you. Maybe you think I should be courteous enough to treat
you as an artist and pass over in silence those dabblers you have
trouble enough with in life and with whom you wish to
have nothing in common. However, I cannot help you here, for
there is something that you have in common with them after all,
and something very essential at that — namely, a view of life; and in
my eyes that in which you differ from them is unessential. I cannot
help laughing at you; do you not see, my young friend, that it is a
curse that accompanies you, these many brothers in art that you
acquire but whom you have no intention at all of acknowledging?
You are prone to poor and vulgar company, you who are so
superior. I don't deny it must be very disagreeable to have a life-
view in common with every carouser or sportsman. Nor, indeed, is
that altogether the case; for you are placed to some degree beyond
the aesthetic domain, as I shall show later.

Great as the differences within the aesthetic sphere may be, all
stages have the essential similarity that spirit appears not in the form
of spirit but in the form of immediacy. The differences may be
extraordinary, from plain philistinism to the greatest intellectual
refinement, but even at the stage where such refinement appears the
spirit has the form not of spirit but of talent.

I will describe each particular stage quite briefly and dwell only
on what, in one way or another, fits your case, or that I could wish
you would apply to yourself. In its immediate guise, personality has
the form not of the spiritual but of the psychic. Here we have a life-
view which teaches that health is the most precious good, that on
which everything depends. The same view is given a more poetic
expression when beauty is said to be the highest thing. Beauty,
however, is a very fragile good, and it is seldom that one sees this
view of life enacted. One comes across a young girl, often enough,
or a young man, who for a brief period set great store by their
beauty, but it soon lets them down. I remember, however, in my
student days, [. . .] sometimes on my holidays I went to the residence
of a count in one of the provinces. In his younger days he had had a
diplomatic post, but was now elderly and lived quietly on his
country estate. The countess had been exceptionally beautiful as a
young girl; even in her old age she was the most beautiful lady I

have seen. [...] Both of them were highly cultivated, yet the countess's life-view was concentrated on the thought that they were the most beautiful couple in the whole land. I still recall quite vividly an occurrence which convinced me of this. It was a Sunday morning and there was a little festival at the nearby church. The countess did not feel well enough to attend; but the count betook himself there in the morning, dressed up in all his finery, his uniform of gentleman-in-waiting, decorated with his orders. The windows of the great hall opened upon an avenue which led up to the church. The countess was standing at one of them. [...] Far down the avenue the count appeared [...] and when he came near enough to see the countess through the window, with grace and decorum she threw him a kiss, then turned to me and said 'Little Vilhelm, isn't my Ditlev the handsomest man in the whole kingdom? Yes, I can see he looks a little sunken on one side, but no one notices it when I'm walking with him, and when we walk together we are surely the handsomest couple in the whole land.' No little miss of sixteen could be as blissfully happy over her fiancé, the handsome gentleman of the bedchamber, as her ladyship over the already aged lord-in-waiting.

Both life-views agree that one must enjoy life. The condition for doing so lies in the individual, but not in a way that it is posited by the individual.

We proceed. We come across views of life which teach that one must enjoy life but place the condition for doing so outside the individual. This is the case with every life-view which makes wealth, glory, nobility, etc., life's task and content. Here I would also speak of a certain kind of infatuation. Were I to imagine a young girl head-over-heels in love, whose eye knew no pleasure but to see her beloved, whose soul had no thought but for him, whose heart had no desire but to be his, for whom nothing, nothing at all in heaven or on earth, had meaning except him, then here again we have an aesthetic view of life in which the condition is placed outside the individual itself. You, of course, find it foolish to love in that way; you think it is something that only occurs in novels. It is conceivable, however, and one can at least be sure that in the eyes of many, such a love would be regarded as something exceptional. I will explain later why I cannot approve of it.

We proceed. We meet views of life which teach that one must enjoy life but the condition for doing so lies in the individual, though not posited, however, by the individual. In this case personality is presented in general under the category of talent, a practical talent, a mercantile talent, a mathematical talent, a poetic talent, an artistic talent, a philosophical talent. Satisfaction in life, pleasure, is sought in the development of this talent. Perhaps one does not remain with one's talent in its state of immediacy, one can educate it in all manner of ways, but the condition for satisfaction in life is the talent itself, a condition not posited by the individual. Those people in whom one finds this life-view are often among those accustomed to being the constant object of your scorn because of their tireless activity. You think you yourself live aesthetically and will in no way admit it of them. That you have a different view of what it is to enjoy life is undeniable, but this is not what is essential; the essential thing is that one wants to enjoy life. Your life is far superior to theirs, but theirs is also far more innocent than yours.

Now just as all these views have in common that they are aesthetic, so too they resemble one another in having a certain unity, a certain coherence, that is, one definite thing on which everything depends. What they build their lives on is something inherently simple, and so their lives do not split up as those that are built on what is inherently diverse. The latter is the case with the life-view I shall now dwell on a little more closely. It teaches: 'Enjoy life', and interprets this as: 'Live for your desire.' Desire, however, is inherently diverse; it is thus easy to see that a life built on desire splits into an endless diversity, except where in some particular individual desire has, from childhood, become determinate in the form of some particular desire, which then deserves rather to be called a propensity, a bent, for instance for fishing, or hunting, or keeping horses, etc. Inasmuch as this view of life splits into a diversity, it is easy to see that it lies in the sphere of reflection; this reflection, however, is nevertheless always a finite reflection and the personality remains in its immediacy. In desire itself the individual is immediate, and however cultivated or refined the desire, however artful, the individual is nevertheless in it *qua* immediate, in the enjoyment he is in the moment, and whatever diversity he has in this respect, he is still always immediate because he is in the moment. Now, living for the satisfaction of one's desire is to enjoy a very exclusive position in life, and God be praised we seldom see it practised, due to the tribulations of earthly life which give man something else to think about. If that were not so, I do not doubt but that we would be frequent enough witnesses to this terrible spectacle; at least one often hears people complain that they feel inhibited by the prosaic life, which often only means that they long to let themselves go in all the wild folly that desire can whirl a man into. For in order to put this view into practice, the individual must be in possession of a diversity of outward conditions, and this good fortune, or rather misfortune, seldom falls to a man's lot – misfortune because it is certainly not from the merciful gods, but the gods of wrath, that this good fortune comes.

One seldom sees this life-view enacted on any significant scale. On the other hand, one not infrequently sees people who dabble at it a little, and when the conditions cease to exist they think that if only the conditions had been under their own control, then they would certainly have achieved the happiness and joy they craved for in life. In history, however, now and then one meets examples. And since I believe it may be useful to see where this life-view leads, precisely when everything favours it, I will present such a figure, choosing for this end that all-powerful man, the emperor Nero, to whom a world did homage, and who always found himself surrounded by an innumerable host of willing emissaries of pleasure. Once, with your usual recklessness, you said that one could not blame Nero for setting fire to Rome in order to get some idea of the conflagration of Troy, but that one might question whether he really had enough of the artist in him to know how to enjoy it. Now it is one of your imperial pleasures never to shrink from any thought, never to let it appal you. For that one needs no imperial guard, not gold and silver, not all the world's treasures; one can do it quite alone and consummate it privately; it is therefore a wiser pleasure, but no less appalling. Your aim was not to conduct a defence of Nero, and yet there is a kind of defence in your fixing attention not on what he does but on how he does it. Still, I know very well this recklessness of thought is something one often finds in young people, who try it out, as it were, on the world at such moments, and are then easily tempted to extol it themselves, especially when others are listening. I know very well that you and every person, yes, that Nero himself would shrink from such wild folly, and yet I would never recommend that any person credit himself in the strictest sense with enough strength not to become a Nero. For when, to describe Nero's nature, I mention what in my view was its main constituent, it may well strike you as much too mild a word for that, and yet I am certainly no mild judge, even though there is another sense in which I never judge another person. But believe you me, the word is not too mild, it is the right one, but it can also show how near a person is to such a lapse; indeed it can be said that there comes a moment, for every person who does not pass his whole life like a child, a glimpse, if only in the distance, of such a damnation. Nero's nature was *melancholy*. Nowadays it has become something big to be melancholy; in a way I can well see why you find this word too mild; I subscribe to an earlier Church doctrine which counted melancholy among the cardinal sins. If I am right, this to be sure will be very bad news for you, for it turns your whole view of life upside down. But to avoid misunderstanding, I will remark at once that a person can be in sorrow and distress to such an infinite degree that perhaps it pursues him all his life; and although that may be well and true, a person becomes melancholy only by his own fault.

So I imagine the imperial voluptuary. [. . .] I imagine him a little on in years, his youth is past, the lightheartedness has gone out of him, and he is already conversant with every conceivable pleasure, gratified by it to the full. This life, however dissolute, has nevertheless matured his soul, though in spite of all his worldly understanding, his experience, he is still a child, or a youth. The immediacy of spirit cannot break through yet demands a breakthrough, a higher form of existence. But if that is to happen there will come a moment when the splendour of the throne, his power and might, pale, and for this he lacks the courage. So he grabs at pleasure, all the world's ingenuity must think up new pleasures for him, for it is only in the moment of pleasure he finds peace, and when it is over he yawns in ennui. [. . .] He does not have himself; only when the world shivers for him is he appeased, for then at least there is no one who dares seize him. Therefore this anxiety for people, something Nero has in common with every such personality. [. . .] He burns down half of Rome but his torment is the same. Soon such things no longer amuse him. There is an even higher desire; he wants to make people anxious. To himself he is a riddle, and anxiety his being. Now he wants to be a riddle for everyone and to revel in their anxiety. [...] And this anxiety amuses him. He doesn't want to impress, he wants to unsettle. [...] He does not enter proudly, with imperial dignity; weak, impotent, he slinks forward stealthily, for this powerlessness is even more disquieting. [...] He could have the child hewn down before its mother's eyes if only her despair might give passion a new expression that could amuse him. Were he not the Emperor of Rome he might end his life with suicide; for really it is only another expression of the same: that Caligula should want all men's heads on one neck so the whole could be annihilated with one stroke, and for a man to take his own life. [...] Whether this was the case with Nero I do not know, but in personalities of this kind one sometimes finds a certain good-naturedness, and if Nero had that, I have no doubt that his circle were ready to call it condescension. This gives the matter a peculiar twist, but it also provides new proof of the immediacy which through its repression constitutes genuine melancholy. [...]

What, then, is melancholy? It is hysteria of the spirit. There comes a moment in a man's life when immediacy is as though ripened and when the spirit demands a higher form in which it will apprehend itself as spirit. In its immediacy spirit coheres, as it were, with the whole of earthly life, and now the spirit wants to gather itself out of this dispersion, and make itself self-transparent; the personality wants to be conscious of itself in its eternal validity. If this does not happen and the movement halts and is pressed back, melancholy sets in. One can do much to bring it into oblivion, one can work, one can seize more innocent expedients than a Nero, but the melancholy remains. There is something unaccountable in melancholy. A person in sorrow or distress knows why he sorrows or is distressed. If you ask a melancholic what reason he has for his condition, what it is that weighs down on him, he will reply, 'I don't know what it is, I can't explain it.' Therein lies melancholy's infinitude. The reply is perfectly correct, for as soon as he knows what it is, the effect is removed, whereas the grief of the griever is by no means removed by his knowing why he grieves. But melancholy is sin, really it is a sin as great as any, for it is the sin of not willing deeply and sincerely, and this is a mother to all sins. This sickness, or more properly, this sin, is extremely common in our time, and accordingly it is under this that the whole of German and French youth groan. I will not provoke you, I would treat you as considerately as possible. I gladly admit that being melancholy is in a sense not a bad sign, for as a rule only the most gifted natures are afflicted by it. [. . .] People whose souls have no acquaintance with melancholy are those whose souls have no presentiment of metamorphosis. These I do not concern myself with here, for I am writing only of and to you, and to you I think this explanation will be satisfactory, for you scarcely assume, as many physicians do, that melancholy is a bodily ailment, though for all that, remarkably enough, physicians cannot cure it; only the spirit can cure it, for it lies in the spirit, and when the spirit finds itself all small sorrows vanish, those reasons which in the view of some produce melancholy – that one cannot find oneself in the world, that one comes to the world both too late and too early, that one cannot find one's place in life; but for the person who owns himself eternally, it is neither too early nor too late that he comes to the world, and the person who possesses himself in his eternal validity will surely find his significance in this life.

This, however, has been a digression, for which I hope you will forgive me, since really it arose for your sake. I now return to the life-view which thinks one must live to satisfy desire. A prudent common sense readily perceives that this cannot be carried through and that it is therefore not worth starting on. A refined egoism perceives that it misses the point in pleasure. Here, then, we have a life-view which teaches 'Enjoy life', and then expresses itself again thus: 'Enjoy yourself; it is you yourself in the enjoyment that you must enjoy.' This is a higher reflection. Naturally, however, it does not penetrate into the personality itself; this remains in its accidental immediacy. After all, here too the condition for enjoyment is external and not within the individual's control; for although he, as he says, enjoys himself, he still only enjoys himself in the enjoyment, but the enjoyment itself is tied to an external condition. The only difference is that his enjoyment is reflective, not immediate. So even this Epicureanism depends on a condition over which it has no control. A certain callousness of reason then teaches a way out: 'Enjoy yourself in constantly discarding the conditions.' But self-evidently, the person who enjoys himself in discarding the conditions is just as much dependent on them as the one who enjoys them. His reflection turns constantly back on himself, and since his enjoyment consists in the enjoyment's being given as little content as possible, he is, as it were, hollowing himself out, since naturally such a reflection is incapable of opening the personality.

I believe these observations of mine have now given you at least a recognizable outline of the territory of the aesthetic view of life. All stages have in common that one lives for that in which one is immediately what one is; for reflection never grasps high enough to reach beyond that. I have provided no more than a very hasty glimpse, but I have not wished to give more; for me the different stages are not important, only that movement which is unavoidably necessary, as I shall now show, and it is on this I would beg you fasten your attention.

Let me assume, then, that our man who lived for his health was, to use your expression, as quick as ever when he died; that our noble couple danced at their golden wedding and a whisper ran through the hall, just as when they danced on their wedding day; I assume that the rich man's gold mines were inexhaustible, that honours and esteem marked the happy man's pilgrimage through life; I assume that the young girl got the one she loved, that with his connections the mercantile talent hitched all five continents together, and kept all the world's exchanges in his own exchange, that the mechanical talent joined together heaven and earth – I assume that Nero never yawned but a new pleasure surprised him every moment, that every instant our astute Epicurean could enjoy himself by himself, that the Cynic always had conditions [of enjoyment] to discard so as to take pleasure in his own lightness – I assume this, and so all these people were happy. You would probably not say that; the reason why I shall explain later. But this you will readily admit: that many people would in fact think this way, yes, that this or that person would fancy he had said something extremely clever if he added that what they lacked was that they did not appreciate the fact. I will now assume the opposite. None of this happens. So what? They despair. No doubt you would not do that either. Perhaps you will say it isn't worth the trouble. Why you will not admit despair I shall explain later; here I ask only that you recognize that a fair number of people find it right and proper to despair. Let us now see why they despaired. Because they discovered that what they had built their lives on was transitory? But is that, then, a reason to despair, has what they built their lives on changed in any essential? Is it an essential change in what is transitory that it prove to be so? Or is it not rather the case that if it does not prove to be so, then that is what is accidental and unessential? So nothing new has come about that could provide the basis for such a change. If they do despair, then, that must be because they were in despair beforehand. The difference is just that they did not know it, but that indeed is an altogether accidental difference. It turns out, then, that every aesthetic view of life is despair, and that everyone who lives aesthetically is in despair whether he knows it or not. But if one does know it, and you indeed do, then a higher form of existence is an inescapable requirement. [. . .]

It might seem, then, that the correct thing was to undertake the movement by which the ethical emerges. But there is still one stage, however, an aesthetic life-view, the most refined and exclusive of them all, which I shall discuss with the greatest of care, for now it is your turn. Everything I have explained in the above you can calmly go along with, and in a way it is not you I have been addressing; also it would be of little use talking to you thus or informing you of the vanity of life. That is something you know very well and have indeed tried in your own way to adjust to. The reason I have presented it is this: that I want to cover my rear, I want to prevent you from suddenly leaping back. This last life-view is despair itself. It is an aesthetic life-view, for the personality remains in its immediacy; it is the last aesthetic life-view, for it has to an extent admitted to itself a consciousness of the nothingness of such a life-view. However, there is despair and despair. Were I to imagine an artist, a painter, for example, who becomes blind, then if there was any depth in him he might perhaps despair. What he despairs over, then, is this particular thing, and if his sight returned the despair would cease. This is not the case with you. You are far too gifted mentally, and your soul is in a sense too deep for this to happen to you. Nor, in outward respects, has any such misfortune befallen you. You still have in your power all the requirements of an aesthetic life-view. You have wealth, independence, your health is unimpaired, your mind is still vigorous, and you have not yet been made unhappy by a young girl not wanting to love you. Yours is no current despair but a despair in thought. Your thought has hurried on ahead, you have seen through the vanity of everything but you have not come any further. On occasion you duck down into it and in abandoning yourself for a single moment to pleasure you discover also, in your consciousness, that it is vanity. You are thus constantly beyond yourself, that is to say, in despair. This is why your life lies between two huge antitheses: sometimes you are intemperately energetic, at others just as immoderately indolent. [. . .]

Here, then, I have your life-view, and believe me, much in your life will be explicable to you if, with me, you regard it as thought-despair. You are a hater of activity in life; quite right, for before there can be any meaning in activity life must have continuity, and this your life lacks. You occupy yourself with your studies, that is true, you are even industrious. But it is only for your own sake and is done with as little teleology as possible. Otherwise you are unoccupied; like those workers in the Gospel, you stand idle in the market-place.[17] You stick your hands in your pockets and observe life. Then you rest in despair, nothing occupies you, you don't step aside for anything: 'If someone were to throw a tile down from the roof I wouldn't get out of the way.' You are like someone dying, you die daily, not in the profound, serious sense in which one usually takes that word, but life has lost its reality and 'you always reckon your lifetime from one day's notice to quit to the next'. You let everything pass you by, it makes no impression, but then suddenly something comes which grips you, an idea, a situation, a smile from a young girl, and then you are 'in touch'; for just as on some occasions you are not in touch, so at others you are in touch and of service in every way. Wherever something is going on you are 'in touch'. You conduct your life as it is your custom to behave in a crowd, you 'work your way into the thickest of it, trying if possible to be forced up above the others so as to be able to lie on top of them'; if you manage to get up there you 'make yourself as comfortable as possible', and this is also the way you let yourself be carried along through life. But when the crowd disperses, when the event is over, you stand once more at the street corner and look at the world. A dying person possesses, as you know, a supernatural energy, and so too with you. If there is an idea to be thought through, a work to be read through, a plan to be carried out, a little adventure to be experienced – yes, a hat to be bought, you take hold of the matter with an immense energy. According to circumstance, you work untiringly for a day, for a month; you are happy in the assurance that you still have the same abundance of strength as before, you take no rest, 'no Satan can keep up with you'. If you work together with others, you work them into the ground. But then when the month or, what you always consider the maximum, the six months have gone, you break off and say, 'and that's the end of the story'. You retire and leave it all to the other party, or if you have been working alone you talk to no one about what you were doing. You then pretend to yourself and others that you have lost the desire and flatter yourself with the vain thought that you could have kept working with the same intensity if that is what you desired. But that is an immense deception. You would have succeeded in finishing it, as most others, if you had patiently willed it so, but you would have found out at the same time that it needs a kind of perseverance quite different from yours. [. . .]

You are always hovering above yourself, but the higher ether, the more refined sublimate into which you are vaporized, is the nothing of despair and you see below you a multitude of areas of learning, insight, study, observation which for you, though, have no reality but which you quite randomly exploit and combine so as to adorn as tastefully as possible the palace of mental profusion in which you occasionally reside. [. . .] [What] you see below you is a multitude of moods and situations which you use to make interesting contacts with life. You can be sentimental, heartless, ironic, witty; in this respect one must admit you have learning. Thus as soon as something can rouse you out of your indolence you are fully active, with all your passion, and your activity does not lack art, as you are only too well equipped with wit, resilience, and all the seductive gifts of the mind. You are, as you yourself with such complacent presumption put it, never so discourteous as to put in an appearance without bringing with you a small, fragrant, freshly plucked bouquet of wit. The more one knows you, the more one must be astonished at the calculating shrewdness that permeates everything you do in the short time you are moved by passion; for passion never blinds you but only makes you more clear-sighted. You forget your despair and everything else that weighs upon your soul and thought; the accidental contact you have made with a person absorbs you completely. [. . .] [You] exist in the instant, and in the instant you are of supernatural size; you invest your whole soul in it, even by an effort of will, since in the instant your being is absolutely in your power. Someone who sees you only in such an instant is very easily deceived, while someone who waits for the next instant can easily come to crow over you. You may recall the well-known legend from Musaeus about Roland's three pages.[18] One of them acquired from the old witch they visited in the forest a thimble which made him invisible. With it he made his way into the chambers of the beautiful princess Urraca and declared his love for her, which made a strong impression upon her since she saw no one and so presumed it must be a fairy prince, at least, who honoured her with his love. However, she required him to reveal himself. This is where the difficulty lay: as soon as he became visible the fascination had to vanish, and yet he would have no pleasure of his love if he could not reveal himself. As it happens, I have Musaeus's fairy-tale to hand and will transcribe a little passage from it which I would beg you to read for your own true good. 'He agreed, it seemed reluctantly, and the princess's fantasy projected the picture of the most beautiful man whom she thought with eager expectation she was about to see. But what a contrast between the original and the ideal when all that appeared was a common, every-day visage, an ordinary person whose physiognomy betrayed neither the glance of genius nor the soul of sentiment.' What you wish to achieve through these contacts with people, you do achieve, because since you are considerably shrewder than that page, you readily see that it cannot pay to reveal oneself. Once you have passed off an ideal picture of yourself on someone – and one has to admit you are able to appear ideal in any circumstance whatsoever – you carefully withdraw and so have then the pleasure of having fooled someone. What you attain besides is a break in the coherence of your view, and one more point from which to start all over again.

In theoretical respects you are through with the world, the finite cannot sustain itself in your thought; in practical respects, too, you are to some extent through with it, in an aesthetic sense, that is. Nevertheless you have no view of life. You have something resembling a view and this gives your life a certain composure which must not, though, be confused with a secure and refreshing confidence in life. You are composed only in contrast to one who still pursues the prestidigitations of pleasure, *per mare pauperiem fugiens, per saxa, per ignes*.[19] In relation to pleasure you have an absolutely superior pride. That is quite as it should be, for indeed you are through with the whole of finitude. And yet you cannot give it up. You are content compared with those who chase after contentment, but what you have become content with is absolute discontent. To see all the world's glories does not concern you, for in thought you are beyond them, and if the chance were offered you would say, as always, 'Yes, one might well devote a day to them.' It does not trouble you that you have not become a millionaire, and if the chance of that were offered, you would no doubt reply, 'Yes, it might have been really interesting to be that and one could well spend a month on it.' Were it possible to offer you the love of the most beautiful girl you would still reply, 'Yes, for half a year that would be really fine.' I shall not join in the plaintive cry often directed at you, that you are insatiable; I will say rather: in a sense you are right, for nothing finite, even the whole world, can satisfy the soul of one who feels a need for the eternal. Were one able to offer you honour and glory, the admiration of your contemporaries – and that, after all, is your weakest point – you would reply, 'Yes, for a short while it wouldn't be too bad.' You do not really want it and you would not take one step to acquire it. You would perceive that for such recognition to have any meaning your gifts would have to be so outstanding that you deserved it; here, too, your thought sees even in the highest degree of intellectual talent something transitory. So your polemics provide you with an even more extreme expression when, in your inner resentment at the whole of life, you could wish you were the most foolish of men and yet admired and worshipped by your contemporaries as the wisest, for that would be a far more profound mockery of the whole of existence than if the genuinely most capable man were honoured as such. So you desire nothing, wish for nothing, for the only thing you might wish for is a divining-rod which could give you everything, and then you would use it for scraping out your pipe. Thus, you are through with life and 'have no need to make a will since you have nothing to leave'. But you cannot hold out on this extremity, for indeed your thought has taken everything from you but it has given you nothing in its stead. The next instant some little triviality captivates you. You look upon it, indeed, with all the superiority and pride your overbearing thought gives you, you despise it as a worthless toy, you are almost bored with it before you take it in your hand; but still it preoccupies you, and even if it is not the thing itself that preoccupies you – as always – you are still preoccupied with your being willing to stoop to it. In this way, once it is people you have to do with, your nature exhibits a high degree of faithlessness, for which one cannot blame you morally, however, since you are outside the category of the ethical. Fortunately for others you participate very little, so one does not notice it. You come often to my house, and you know you are always welcome, but you know also that it never occurs to me to invite you to participate in the least thing. I would not even take a drive in the woods with you, not because you cannot be very gay and entertaining but because your participation is always a falsehood, for if you really take pleasure one can always be certain it is not in something we others are taking pleasure in, or in the drive, but in something you have *in mente*; and if you do not take pleasure it is not because something unpleasant happens that puts you out of sorts, for that could also happen to the rest of us, but because the moment you climb into the carriage you have already seen the vacuity of this amusement. I am ready to forgive you, for your mind is always too active, and it is true what you often say of yourself, that you are like a woman in confinement and when one is in that 'condition' it is no wonder one is a little different from others.

Yet the spirit is not to be mocked, it takes its revenge on you, it fetters you in the chains of melancholy. My young friend, this is the way to become a Nero, if in your soul there was not an original seriousness, if there was not an innate depth in your thought, if there was no magnanimity in your soul – and if you had become Emperor of Rome. Yet you go another way. There now appears before you a life-view which seems the only one that can satisfy you: it is to immerse your soul in sadness and sorrow. Yet your thought is too healthy for this life-view to stand its test, for to an aesthetic sorrow of this kind existence is just as vain as it is to any other aesthetic view of life. If a person cannot sorrow more deeply, then it is true to say that the sorrow passes just as much as the joy, for everything that is merely finite passes away. And if many find it comforting that sorrow passes, this thought seems to me just as comfortless as the thought that joy passes. So this life-view, too, your thought annihilates, and when one has annihilated sorrow one does indeed retain joy; in place of sorrow you choose a joy which is sorrow's changeling. This is the joy you have now chosen, this laughter of despair. You return again to life, and under this illumination existence acquires a new interest for you. Just as you take a great delight in talking with children in a way they excellently, easily and naturally understand, though for yourself what you say means something quite different, so you delight in deceiving people with your laughter. When you can get people to laugh and shout for joy and be delighted with you, you triumph over the whole world; you say to yourself, 'If only you knew what you are laughing at!'

Yet the spirit is not to be mocked, and the darkness of melancholy thickens about you, and the lightning flash of an insane wit only reveals it to you the more strongly, the more horribly. And there is nothing that distracts you, all the world's pleasure has no importance for you, and though you envy simple people the foolish enjoyment of life, you yourself do not pursue it. Pleasure does not tempt you; and however lamentable your condition, it is truly providential that it does not. It is my intention to praise not the pride in you that scorns pleasure but rather the moderation that holds your thought firm, for if you were tempted by pleasure you would be done for. But the fact that it does not tempt you shows what path you must take, that you must go forward and not turn back. There is another false path no less dreadful, and here again I rely not on your pride but on the moderation that constantly holds you upright. It is true you are proud, and that it is better for a person to be proud than vain; it is true there is a fearful passion in your thought, that you look on it as a claim you have no intention of renouncing, that 'you would rather consider yourself an unpaid creditor in the world than cancel it' – and yet all human pride is but a fragile security.

Take note, then, my young friend, this life is despair; hide it from others if you will, from yourself you cannot hide it, it is despair. And yet in another sense this life is not despair. You are too frivolous to despair; and you are too melancholy not to come in contact with despair. You are like a woman giving birth and yet you are forever putting off the moment and remain constantly in pain. Were a woman in travail to get the idea that she might give birth to a monster, or were she to wonder what it really was she was about to give birth to, her case would be not unlike yours. Her attempt to stay the course of nature would be unavailing, but yours indeed can succeed; for what a person gives birth to in a spiritual sense is a creative urge of the will, and that is in man's own power. What then is it you are afraid of? You are not going to give birth to another human being, you will give birth only to yourself. And yet, as I know well, there is a gravity in this which perturbs the whole soul; to be conscious of oneself in one's eternal validity is a moment more significant than everything in the world. It is as though you were caught and trapped and now could never again escape, either in time or eternity; it is as though you lost yourself, as though you ceased to be; it is as though the next moment you would rue it and yet it cannot be undone. It is a grave and significant moment when one binds oneself for an eternity to an eternal power, when one receives oneself as the one whose memory no time shall efface, when in an eternal and unfailing sense one becomes aware of oneself as the person one is. And yet, one can still let it be! Look: here, then, is an either/or. Let me talk to you in a way I never would if another were listening, because in a sense I have no right to do so and because really I am speaking only of the future. If this is not what you will, if you want to keep on diverting your soul with the vanities and vacuities of wit and *esprit*, then do so; leave your home, travel, go to Paris, give yourself up to journalism, court the smiles of voluptuous women, cool their hot blood with the breeze of your wit, let it be the proud task of your life's activity to drive away an idle woman's boredom or the gloomy thoughts of a flagging sensualist, forget that you were a child, that there was piety in your soul and innocence in your thought, deaden every higher voice in your breast, drowse your life away in the petty brilliance of the soirée, forget that there is an immortal spirit in you,

torment your soul to the last farthing; and when wit falls silent
there is water enough in the Seine and gunpowder in the general
store and travelling companions for any hour of the day. But if you
cannot do that, if you will not – and you neither can nor will –
then pull yourself together, stifle every rebellious thought that
would presume high treason against your better nature, despise all
the pettiness that would envy you your intellectual gifts and which
itself desires them in order to put them to even worse use, despise
the hypocritical virtue which bears life's burdens unwillingly yet
still wants to be honoured for bearing them; but do not despise life
itself on that account, respect every honourable effort, every modest
activity which conceals itself in humility, and above all show a little
more respect for woman; believe me, it is from her that salvation
comes, as certainly as depravity comes from the man. I am a husband
and to that extent partial, but it is my conviction that if ever a
woman plunged humanity into depravity she has also fairly and
honestly made up for it, and still does; for of a hundred men who
go astray in the world ninety-nine are saved by women, one by a
direct divine grace. And since I also believe that it is man's nature to
go astray in one way or another, that this is as true of the man's life
as it is true of the woman's that she should remain in the pure and
innocent peace of immediacy, you readily perceive that in my view
the woman gives ample requital for what she has done.

What then are you to do? Another person might say: 'Get
married; then you'll have something else to think about.' Certainly,
but the question remains whether that would be to your advantage,
and whatever you think of the opposite sex, at least your thoughts
are too chivalrous for you to wish to marry for that reason, and
besides, if you cannot maintain yourself, you will hardly find another capable of doing that. Or one might say, 'Apply for some
office, throw yourself into business life, that's a distraction, and you
will forget your melancholy; work, that's the best thing.' You
might manage to reach the point where it seems as though forgotten,
but forgotten it is not; now and then it will still erupt, more
dreadfully than ever; it might then be able, as hitherto it has not, to
take you by surprise. Besides, whatever you think of life and its
affairs, you will think too chivalrously of yourself to choose a
position for that reason, for it is, after all, a kind of falsehood, just as

marrying on that account. What then are you to do? I have only one answer: 'Despair!'

I am a married man, my soul clings surely and unwaveringly to my wife, my children, to this life whose beauty I shall always acclaim. So when I say 'Despair!' it is no overwrought youth who would have you whirled off into a maelstrom of passions, no mocking demon shouting out this comfort to the shipwrecked; I shout it to you not as a comfort, not as a state in which you are to remain, but as an action requiring all the soul's strength and gravity and self-command, as sure as it is my conviction, my triumph over the world, that any person who has not tasted the bitterness of despair has missed the meaning of life, however beautiful and joy-filled his life has been. You do not commit any fraud upon the world you live in, you are not lost to it, for you have conquered it, as surely as I can count myself an honourable married man even though I, too, have despaired.

When I look at your life in this way I would call you fortunate, for truly it is of the utmost importance that a person does not look amiss at life in the moment of despair; it is just as crucial for him as for someone giving birth that things should not go wrong. The person who despairs over something in particular runs the risk of his despair not being true and profound, of its being a disappointment, a sorrow in that particular respect. You will not despair in that way for you have not suffered any deprivation, you still have everything. If the despairer makes a mistake, if he believes the misfortune lies in the complex world outside him, his despair is not true and it will lead him to hate the world and not to love it; for no matter how much the world gets in your way because it seems as if it wanted to be something else than it can be for you, once you have found your own self in despair you will love it for being the world that it is. If what brings a person to despair is some guilt and offence, a troubled conscience, he may perhaps have difficulty in regaining his good cheer. So, despair, then, with all your soul and mind; the longer you put it off, the harder the conditions become and what is required remains the same, I shout it out to you, like the woman who offered Tarquin a collection of books for sale and, when he refused to pay the sum she asked, she burnt a third of them and demanded the same sum, and when again he refused to give the sum asked, burnt another third and demanded the same sum, until he finally gave the original sum for the remaining third.

The condition for despair in your case is therefore excellent, and yet there is an even better. Imagine a young man, gifted like you. Let him love a girl, love her as much as himself. Let him once ponder in a quiet hour what he has built his life on, and on what she has built hers. The love is something they have in common, and yet he will feel there are differences. She, perhaps, has the gift of beauty, yet for him this is of no importance and is after all so fragile; maybe she has the joyful disposition of youth, yet for him this joy has no real meaning. But the intellectual authority is his and he feels its strength. He truly wants to love her, so it will not occur to him to give that to her and her humble soul will not demand it, and yet there is a difference and he will feel that it must vanish if he is truly to love her. He will then let his soul sink into despair. He despairs not for his own sake but for hers, yet it is also for his own sake, for he loves her as much as himself. The power of despair will then consume everything until he finds himself in his eternal validity, but then he has also found her and no knight will return happier and more joyful from the most hazardous exploits than he from this conflict with flesh and blood and the empty distinctions of the finite, for he who despairs finds the eternally human being and in that we are all equal. The foolish thought of wanting to bring about likeness by deadening his own mind or neglecting its cultivation will not occur to him; he will preserve his mental gifts but in his innermost heart he will be conscious that someone who has them is like someone who does not have them. Or imagine a person with a deeply religious disposition who from a true and inner love of his fellow humans cast himself into the sea of despair until he found the absolute, that point where it is indifferent whether a brow is low or arches more proudly than the heavens, that point which is not indifference but the absolute validity.

You have several good ideas, many odd notions, a mass of silly ones; keep them all. I do not insist, but there is one idea I would beg you to hold on to, an idea which assures me that my own spirit is in kinship with yours. You have often said you would rather be anything else in the world than a poet since a poet-existence is, as a rule, a human sacrifice. I, for my part, would by no means deny there have been poets who have gained their selves before they began to write; on the other hand, it is also certain that a poet-existence as such lies in the obscurity that results from despair's not being carried through, from the soul's constantly shivering in despair and the spirit's being unable to gain its true transparency. The poetic ideal is always an untrue ideal, for the true ideal is always what is actual. So when the spirit is not allowed to vault up into its own eternal world it remains *en route* and revels in the pictures reflected in the clouds and weeps over their transience. A poet-existence is therefore, as such, an unhappy existence, it is higher than the finite and yet not the infinite. The poet sees the ideals but he has to flee the world in order to take pleasure in them; he cannot carry these divine images within him in the midst of life's confusion, cannot quietly proceed on his way unaffected by the caricature appearing all around him, not to speak of having the strength to attire himself in those images. The poet's life is, therefore, often the object of a petty sympathy on the part of those who think themselves safe because they have remained in the finite. You once said in a moment of despondency that no doubt there were already people who had privately made up their accounts with you and were willing to settle on the following condition: that you were recognized as a bright fellow, in return you sank from sight and did not become a useful member of society. Yes, there undeniably exists in the world a pettiness of this kind, which will triumph in this way over everything that protrudes just an inch. But do not let it disturb you, do not defy them, do not scorn them; I would say here, as you usually do, 'It isn't worth the trouble.' But if you do not want to be a poet there is no other way for you than the one I have shown you: Despair!

So then choose despair, since despair is itself a choice, for one can doubt without choosing to, but despair one cannot without choosing to do so. And when one despairs one chooses again, and what then does one choose? One chooses oneself, not in one's immediacy, not as this contingent individual, one chooses oneself in one's eternal validity.

I shall endeavour to cast a little more light on this point in your connection. In recent philosophy there has been more than enough talk about speculation beginning with doubt; on the other hand, so far as I have been able occasionally to occupy myself with questions of that kind, I have looked in vain for information on how doubt differs from despair. Here I shall try to clarify that distinction, in the hope that it will contribute to orienting you and facing you in the right direction. I am far from presuming any real philosophical competence, I do not have your virtuosity in playing with categories, but what in the deepest sense is the meaning of life, that after all must surely be comprehensible to a more simple-minded person. Doubt is a despair of thought, despair is a doubt of the personality. That is why I keep such a tight hold on the category of choice, that being my watchword, the nerve of my life-view, and that is something I indeed have even if I make no claim at all to a system.[20] Doubt is the inner movement in thought itself, and in my doubt I conduct myself as impersonally as possible. Assume now that, doubt having been applied, thought finds the absolute and rests in it; it rests in it not as the result of a choice but following the same necessity according to which it doubted; for doubt itself belongs to the category of necessity, and rest likewise. It is the sublime aspect of doubt, the reason why doubt has so often been praised and extolled by people who scarcely understood what they were saying. But this fact, that it belongs to the category of necessity, shows that it is not the whole personality that is in motion. So there is something very true in a person's saying, 'I'd like to believe it, but I can't; I have to doubt.' That is also why one often sees how a doubter can still possess something positive in himself which lives apart from all communication through thought, that he can be a highly conscientious person who has no doubts whatever about the validity of duty and about the maxim for his action, no doubts whatever about a multitude of sympathetic feelings and moods. On the other hand, especially in our own time, one sees people who have despair in their hearts but have still conquered doubt. This has particularly struck me in considering certain of Germany's philosophers. Their thought is composed, the objective logical thought is brought to rest in its corresponding objectivity, and yet they are in despair even though they distract themselves with objective thinking, for there are many ways a person can distract himself and scarcely any sedative is more effective than abstract thinking, since there it is a matter of conducting oneself as impersonally as possible.

Doubt and despair therefore belong to two quite different spheres, different sides of the soul are set in motion. Still, I am not at all content with this, because doubt and despair would then rank equally and that is not the case. Despair is a far deeper and more complete expression, its movement far more comprehensive than doubt's. Precisely, despair is an expression of the whole personality, doubt only of thought. The reputed objectivity of doubt, what makes it so distinguished, is precisely an expression of its incompleteness. Doubt, therefore, lies in difference, despair in the absolute. It requires talent to doubt, it requires no talent at all to despair; but talent as such is difference and what needs talent to make it effectual can never be the absolute, for it is only for the absolute that the absolute can be absolute as such. The lowliest, least talented person can despair, a young girl who is least of all a thinker can despair, while it is easy for anyone to sense the foolishness of saying of these that they are doubters. The reason why a person's doubt can be assuaged and he can still be in despair, and that this can go on, is that he does not in a deeper sense will despair. In general, one cannot despair at all unless one wants to, but in order truly to despair one must truly want to, but when one truly wills despair one is truly beyond it; when one has truly chosen despair one has truly chosen what despair chooses, namely oneself in one's eternal validity. It is only in despair that the personality is assuaged, though not with necessity, for I never despair necessarily, but with freedom, and only in despair is the absolute attained. I think in this respect our age will make progress, so far as I am entitled to an opinion about our age – that is, seeing I know it only from reading newspapers and the occasional pamphlet, or from our conversations. The time won't be far off when, perhaps at some cost, we will learn that the true point of departure for finding the absolute is not doubt but despair.

But I return to my category, I am not a logician, I have only one such but I assure you it is the choice of both my heart and my mind, my soul's desire and my salvation – I return to the significance of choice. In choosing absolutely, then, I choose despair, and in despair I choose the absolute, for I myself am the absolute, I posit the absolute and am myself the absolute. But, as amounts to exactly the same, I must say: I choose the absolute which chooses me, I posit the absolute which posits me. For unless I bear in mind that this second expression is just as absolute, my category of choice is false; for that category is precisely the identity of both. What I choose I do not posit, for if it were not posited I could not choose it, and yet if it were not posited through my choosing it I would not choose it. It *is*, for if it was not I could not choose it; it *is not*, for it only comes to be by my choosing it, otherwise my choice would be illusory.

But what, then, do I choose? This thing or that? No, I choose absolutely, and I choose absolutely precisely through having chosen not to choose this thing or that. I choose the absolute, and what is the absolute? It is myself in my eternal validity. Anything other than myself I cannot choose as the absolute, for if I choose something else I choose it as something finite, and therefore do not choose it absolutely. Even the Jew who chose God did not choose absolutely, for although he chose the absolute he did not choose it absolutely, and so it ceased to be the absolute and became something finite.

But what, then, is this self of mine? If it is to be a matter of a first glance, a first shot at a definition, my answer is: it is the most abstract thing of all which yet, at the same time, is the most concrete thing of all — it is freedom. Let me here make a small psychological observation. One often hears people giving vent to their discontent by complaining of life, one often hears them making wishes. Imagine such a poor devil, but let us hop over wishes that do not throw light on anything here because they belong entirely to the contingent. He wishes, 'If only I had that man's mind, or his talents,' etc. Yes, at the farthest extreme, 'If only I had that man's firmness.' One hears wishes like this frequently enough, but have you ever heard a person seriously wish that he could become someone else? So far is that from being so, that it is precisely typical of what are called unfortunates that it is they who cling most tightly to themselves, that despite all their sufferings they would not for all the world want to be someone else; which has its reason in the fact that such individuals are very near the truth and have a sense of the eternal validity of personal existence, not in its blessings but in its torment, even if they have kept to themselves this perfectly abstract expression of joy in their eternal validity which says they would rather be themselves than anyone else. As for the man with many wishes, he still thinks of always remaining himself though everything were changed. So there is something in him that is absolute in relation to everything else, something whereby he is the one he is, even if the change he obtains through his wish were the greatest possible. That he is labouring under a misunderstanding I shall show later; here I want merely to find the most abstract expression for this 'self' which makes him what he is. And that is nothing else than freedom. Really it would be possible in this way to offer a highly plausible proof of the eternal validity of personal existence; yes, even a suicide does not really want to do away with his self; he, too, has a wish, he wishes he had another form of his self, and there could well be a suicide, therefore, who was convinced in the highest degree of the immortality of the soul but whose whole being was so confused that he thought to find in this way the absolute form of his spirit.

But the reason why it can seem to an individual that he could constantly change yet remain the same, as if his inmost being were an algebraic entity that could stand for whatever it might be, is to be found in the fact that he has the wrong attitude; he has not chosen himself, he has no conception of doing so, and yet even in his lack of understanding there is an acknowledgement of the eternal validity of personal existence. For someone with the right attitude, on the other hand, things go differently. He chooses himself, not in a finite sense, for then this 'self' would be something finite along with other finite things, but in an absolute sense. And still he chooses himself and not another. This self he thus chooses is infinitely concrete, for it is himself, and yet it is absolutely different from his former self, for he has chosen it absolutely. This self did not exist previously, for it came into existence through the choice, and yet it has been in existence, for it was indeed 'he himself'.

The choice here makes the two dialectical movements at once: what is chosen does not exist and comes into existence through the choice, and what is chosen exists, otherwise it would not be a choice. For if the thing I chose did not exist but became absolute through the choice itself, I would not have chosen, I would have created. But I do not create myself, I choose myself. Therefore while nature has been created out of nothing, while I myself *qua* my immediate personal existence have been created out of nothing, as free spirit I am born of the principle of contradiction, or born by virtue of the fact that I chose myself.

He now discovers that the self he chooses contains an infinite multiplicity inasmuch as it has a history, a history in which he acknowledges identity with himself. This is history of a different sort, for in this history he stands in relation to other individuals of the race and to the race as a whole, and in this history there is something painful, yet he is only the one he is, with this history. Therefore it needs courage to choose oneself, for just when he seems to be becoming most isolated, he is entering more deeply than ever into the roots through which he is linked with the whole. It alarms him, and yet that is how it has to be, for when he awakens to the passion of freedom – and that has been awakened in the choice, just as the choice presupposes it – he chooses himself and fights to possess it as though for his blessedness, and it is his blessedness. He can let go of none of this, not the most painful things, not the most grievous, and yet the expression of this fight, of this acquiring, is – repentance. He repents himself back into himself, back into the family, back into the race, until he finds himself in God. Only on these terms can he choose himself and he wants no others, for only thus can he absolutely choose himself. What, after all, is a human being without love? Yet there are many kinds of love. I love a father in a different way from a mother, my wife in still another way, and every different love has its different expression, but there is also a love wherewith I love God, and there is only one expression for this in language: repentance. If I do not love Him thus I do not love Him absolutely, not from my inmost being; any other love for the absolute is a misunderstanding since – to take what people usually praise so highly and I myself have respect for – when thinking clings to the absolute with all its love it is not the absolute I love, I do not love absolutely since I love necessarily; as soon as I love freely and love God, I repent. And were there no other reason for repentance being the expression of my love of God, there is this reason: that he loved me first. And yet this is an incomplete account, for it is only if I choose myself as guilty that I choose myself absolutely, if ever my choosing myself absolutely is not to be identical with creating myself. And if the sins of the father were inherited by the son, this too he repents, for only in this way can he choose himself, choose himself absolutely. And if the tears are just about to efface him completely, he still keeps on repenting, for only thus does he choose himself. It is as though his self is outside him and is to be taken possession of, and the repentance is his love of it, because he chooses it absolutely, from the hand of the eternal God.

What I have stated here is no rostrum-wisdom, it is something every person who wants to can propound, and which every person can want to when he will. I have not learnt it in the auditorium, I have learnt it in the living-room, or in the nursery if you will, for when I see my little son running across the floor, so joyful, so happy, I think, 'Who knows, perhaps I've had a very damaging influence on him? God knows I take all possible care of him, but that thought doesn't put me at ease.' Then I say to myself, 'There'll come a moment in his life when his spirit too will be matured in the instant of choice, then he will choose himself, then he will also repent whatever guilt of mine may rest upon him. And there's something pleasing about a son's repenting his father's sins, though he won't do it on my account but because it is only in this way that he can choose himself. So let things go as they will; often what one considers best has the most damaging consequences for a person, but all this is nothing after all. I can do a lot for him, that's what I'll strive for, but the highest he can only do for himself.' You see why people have such difficulty in choosing themselves: here absolute isolation is identical with the deepest continuity, and as long as one has not chosen oneself it is as if there was a possibility of becoming something different, in one way or another.

Here, then, you have my humblest opinion on what it is to choose and to repent. It is unseemly to love a young girl as though she were one's mother, or one's mother as though she were a young girl. Every love has its peculiarity; love of God has its absolute peculiarity, its expression is repentance. [. . .] A theologian will be able to base a host of reflections on this point. These I shall not go into further since I am only a layman. I shall try only to throw light on the foregoing with the comment that it is in Christianity that repentance first found its true expression. The pious Jew felt the sins of the fathers weigh upon him, yet he did not feel it nearly as deeply as the Christian, because the pious Jew could not repent it, for he could not choose himself absolutely. The guilt of the fathers weighed upon him, brooded over him, he sank beneath this burden, he sighed, but he could not lift it; only the one who chooses himself absolutely can do that, through repentance. The greater the freedom the greater the guilt, and that is the secret of blessedness, and if not cowardice, it is at least faintheartedness not to want to repent the sins of the fathers; if not to be despised, it is at least petty and devoid of magnanimity.

So then the choice of despair is 'my self', for although when I despair I despair over myself as over all else, the self I despair over is a finitude as every other finite thing, while the self I choose is the absolute self or my self according to its absolute validity. That being so, you will again see why I kept on saying in the above that the either/or I proposed between living aesthetically and ethically is not a perfect dilemma, because there is really only one option. Through choosing it I do not really choose between good and evil, I choose the good, but by virtue of choosing the good I choose the option between good and evil. The original choice is constantly present in every subsequent choice.

So despair, then, and your frivolity shall never more cause you to roam like an inconstant spirit, like a ghost among the ruins of a world which is yet lost to you; despair, and your spirit shall never more sigh in melancholy, for the world shall become beautiful and joyous to you once more, though you now look at it with different eyes, and your spirit, now liberated, shall vault up into the world of freedom.

Here I could break off, for I have now brought you to the point I wished. For this, should you yourself wish it, is where you are. My aim was for you to tear yourself away from the illusions of the aesthetic, and from a dream of half despair, in order to awaken to the earnest of spirit. However, I have no intention of doing that, since I want now to give you, from this vantage-point, a way of looking at life, an ethical life-view. It is only a frugal offering, partly because my talents are in no way commensurate to the task, partly because frugality is a prime characteristic of everything ethical, a characteristic which can be arresting enough for someone coming from the abundance of the aesthetic. Here what matters is *nil ad ostentationem, omnia ad conscientiam*.[21] Breaking off at this point might also seem questionable for another reason: one might easily get the impression that I had ended up in a sort of quietism,[22] where the personality necessarily comes to rest as thought does in the absolute. What then would be the good of having gained oneself, what would be the good of getting a sword which could conquer the whole world if one did nothing with it but thrust it into the scabbard?

But before going on to present such an ethical view of life in more detail, I will indicate in a few words the danger that lies before one in the moment of despair, the reef one can run aground on and be totally shipwrecked. The Scriptures say, 'What is a man profited, if he shall gain the whole world and suffer harm to his own soul?'[23] [. . .] But the expression 'suffer harm to his own soul' is an ethical one, and the person who thinks he has an ethical life-view must also presume to be able to interpret it. One hears the phrase frequently, yet any person who wants to understand it must have felt deep commotions in his soul; yes, he must have despaired, for what are really set before us here are the motions of despair: on the one hand the whole world, on the other one's own soul. You will readily perceive that, if one pursues this phrase, one arrives at the same abstract definition of 'soul' which, in our psychological consideration of the desire to become another, though without becoming another, we reached earlier as the definition of 'self'. For when I can gain the whole world yet suffer harm to my soul, the phrase 'whole world' must also include all the finitudes I possess in virtue of my immediacy. My soul then proves impervious to these. When I can lose the whole world without suffering harm to my soul, the phrase 'the whole world' again includes all those determinations of finitude that are mine in virtue of my immediacy, and yet my soul remains unharmed; it is accordingly impervious to them. I can lose my wealth, my esteem in the eyes of others, my mental powers, and still not suffer harm to my soul. I can gain all these and still suffer harm. What then is my soul, what is this inmost being of mine that can remain unaffected by this loss and suffer harm with this gain? This movement is manifest to the despairer, it is no rhetorical phrase but the only adequate one when, on the one hand, he sees the whole world and, on the other, himself, his soul. In the moment of despair the distinction makes itself apparent, and now it is a matter of how he despairs, for, as I explained above in connection with every aesthetic view of life, it is despair to gain the whole world and gain it in such a way that one suffers harm to one's soul; and yet it is my heartfelt conviction that it is a man's true salvation to despair. Here, again, we have the importance of willing one's own despair, willing it in an infinite sense, in an absolute sense, for such willing is identical with absolute self-surrender. If, on the other hand, I will my despair in a finite sense I suffer harm to my soul, for then my inmost being does not attain its breakthrough in despair; on the contrary, it isolates itself, it is hardened, so that finite despair is a hardening, absolute despair an infinitization. If in my despair I gain the whole world, I suffer harm to my soul by making myself finite, I have my life in that world; when I despair over losing the whole world I suffer harm to my soul, for I make it finite in exactly the same way, since here again I see my soul as posited with finitude. [. . .] Every finite despair is a choice of the finite, for I choose it as much when I lose it as when I gain it; for what lies in my power is not whether I gain it, but my choosing it. Finite despair is therefore an unfree despair. Really despair is not the aim, but finitude, yet that is despair. A person can now hold out at this point, and as long as he stays there I cannot really bring myself to say to him that he has suffered harm to his soul. He stands at a highly dangerous point. At every moment there is the possibility of its happening. The despair is there but it has not yet attacked his inmost being. Only when in a finite sense he hardens himself in the despair, only then does he suffer harm to his soul. His soul is as if anaesthetized in despair, and only when, on coming round, he chooses a finite way out of his despair, only then does he suffer harm to his soul; he has isolated himself, his rational soul is stifled and he is transformed into a beast of prey that shuns no means since everything for him is self-defence. There lies a dreadful anxiety in this thought that a person has suffered harm to his soul, yet everyone who has despaired will have had a presentiment of this false path, this perdition. That a person can suffer harm to his soul in this way is certain; whether it is actually the case with a particular person is impossible to tell, and no one ventures here to judge another. A man's life may look strange and one may be tempted to believe it of him, yet he himself may have quite a different interpretation which assures him of the opposite; on the other hand, a person may have suffered harm to his soul without anyone suspecting it, for this harm lies not on the outside but in the person's inmost being. It is like the rot in the core of the fruit: while the outside can look appetizing, it gives no hint of the inner hollowness.

So when you choose yourself absolutely you easily find out that this self is not an abstraction or a tautology; at the most it may seem so in the moment of orientation when one separates to the point of finding the most abstract expression of this self, but it is still just an illusion that it is altogether abstract and without content, for after all it is not the consciousness of freedom in general, since that is a determination of thought; it is the product of a choice and is the consciouness of this determinate free being which is himself and no other. This self contains a rich concretion, a multitude of determinate qualities, of characteristics; it is, in short, the whole aesthetic self which is chosen ethically. Therefore the more you become absorbed in yourself, the greater sense you will have of the significance even of the insignificant, not in a finite but in an infinite sense, because it is through you that it is posited, and when one chooses oneself in an ethical sense it is not just a reflection upon oneself. To characterize this act, one might recall the word of the Scriptures about giving account of every idle word that men shall speak.[24] For when the passion of freedom is awakened, freedom is jealous of itself and by no means allows it to remain thus indeterminate as between what does and does not belong to it. So while in the first instant of choice the person proceeds apparently as naked as the child from its mother's womb, the next instant it is concrete in itself, and it is only by an arbitrary abstraction that someone can remain at that point. He becomes himself – quite the same as he was before, down to the least significant peculiarity – and yet he becomes another, for the choice permeates everything and transforms it. Thus is his finite personality now made infinite in the choice in which he infinitely chooses himself.

So now he owns himself as posited by himself, that is, as chosen by himself, as free; but when he owns himself in this way, an absolute difference appears, that between good and evil. So long as he has not chosen himself this difference remains latent. How in general does the difference between good and evil emerge? Can we think it – that is, is it something for thought? No. Here the point comes up again that I touched on above, how philosophy could seem actually to have abolished the principle of contradiction, the reason being that it has not yet reached it. Whenever I think, my relation to what it is I am thinking is one of necessity, but that is exactly why the difference between good and evil does not arise. Think anything you like, think the most abstract categories of all, think the most concrete, you never think in the category of good and evil; think the whole of history and you think the necessary movement of the Idea, but you never think in the category of good and evil. You always think relative differences, never the absolute difference. Philosophy, so far as I can judge, may well be justified in claiming it cannot think an absolute contradiction, but it by no means follows that the latter does not exist. In thinking, I make myself infinite, but not absolutely, since I disappear into the absolute; it is only when I choose myself absolutely that I make myself infinite absolutely, for I myself *am* the absolute, for it is only myself that I can choose absolutely, and this absolute choice of myself is my freedom; only when I have absolutely chosen myself have I posited an absolute difference, namely that between good and evil.

In order to abolish the element of self-determination in thought, philosophy says, 'The absolute *is* by virtue of my thinking it.' But since philosophy itself sees that this implies free thought (not necessary thought, which is the one it usually acclaims), it replaces this expression with another, namely that my thought of the absolute is the 'absolute's self-thinking' in me. This expression is not at all identical with the previous one, but on the other hand it is entirely appropriate. For here my thought is an element in the absolute, that is where the necessity of my thought lies, that is where the necessity with which I think the absolute lies. Things are different with the good. The good *is* by virtue of my willing it, and otherwise it has no existence. This is the expression of freedom; similarly with evil, it *is* only by virtue of my willing it. This is in no way to belittle the categories of good and evil or to reduce them to merely subjective determinations. On the contrary, it is to assert the absolute validity of these categories. The good is the in-and-for-itself posited by the in-and-for-itself, and that is freedom.[25]

My use of the expression 'choosing oneself absolutely' may seem questionable, for it might be taken to imply that I chose good and evil equally absolutely, and that both good and evil belonged to me equally essentially. To prevent this misunderstanding I used the expression 'repenting myself out of the whole of existence'. For repentance is the expression of the fact that evil is an essential part of me, and at the same time the expression of the fact that it is not essentially a part of me. If evil were not an essential part of me I could not choose it, but if there were something in me that I could not choose absolutely, then there would be no question of my choosing myself absolutely; I would not be the absolute myself, but only a product.

Here I will break off these reflections in order to show how an ethical life-view looks at the person and life and its meaning. For form's sake I return to some observations made earlier about the relation between the aesthetic and the ethical. We said that every aesthetic life-view was despair; this was because it was built upon what may or may not be. That is not the case with the ethical life-view, for this builds life upon what has being as its essential property. The aesthetic, we said, is that in which a person is immediately what he is; the ethical is that whereby a person becomes what he becomes. This in no way implies that someone who lives aesthetically does not develop, but he develops with necessity, not with freedom; there occurs no metamorphosis in his case, no infinite movement whereby he arrives at the point from which he becomes what he becomes.

When an individual considers himself aesthetically, he becomes conscious of this self of his as a multiple concretion inwardly determined in many ways, but in spite of all the inner diversity it is all still his nature, everything has just as much right to come to light, is just as entitled to demand satisfaction. His soul is like soil from which there spring all kinds of herbs, all equally entitled to thrive; it is in this diversity that his self lies, and he has no self higher than this. Now, if he has what you so often speak of, namely aesthetic seriousness and a little worldly wisdom, he will see that it is impossible for everything to thrive equally. So he will choose, and what decides his choice is a more-or-less, which is a relative difference. Let us now suppose someone were able to live without coming in contact with the ethical; he would then be able to say, 'I have it in me to be a Don Juan, a Faust, a robber chief; I shall now cultivate this trait since aesthetic seriousness demands that I become something definite, that I let the seedling planted in me develop fully.' Aesthetically, that way of looking at personality and its development would be perfectly proper. From this you see what an aesthetic development means: it is a development like that of the plant, and although the individual becomes something, what it becomes is what it is immediately. For someone who regards personhood ethically there is, from the very first, an absolute difference, namely that between good and evil, and if he finds more evil than good, that still does not mean that evil is what has to come to the fore, but that evil is to be suppressed and the good allowed to come to the fore. So when the individual develops ethically, he comes to be what he becomes; for even when he gives rein to the aesthetic in him (which for him means something else than for the one who lives merely aesthetically), it has nevertheless been removed from its throne. [. . .]

It takes much ethical courage not to be distinguished by difference but to be content with the universal. [. . .] Everyone who lives merely aesthetically [. . .] has a secret dread of despairing, for he knows very well that what despair brings out is the universal, and at the same time he knows that his life is based on difference. The higher the individual stands, the more differences he has done away with or despaired over, but he always retains one difference which he will not do away with, on which his life is based. It is curious to see the admirable assurance with which even the most simple-minded discover what one might call their aesthetic difference, however insignificant that may be, and one of life's miseries is the foolish controversy carried on about which difference is more significant than another. Aesthetic minds also express their aversion to despair by saying it is a break. This expression is quite appropriate so far as one supposes life's development to consist of a necessary unfolding of the immediate. If that is not the case, then despair is no break but a transfiguration. Only a person despairing over something in particular suffers a break, but that is just because he does not despair to the full. Aesthetes are also afraid that life will lose the diverting multiplicity it has so long as one looks at it as though every single individual lived under aesthetic categories. Once again, this is a misunderstanding, no doubt fostered by a number of rigoristic theories. In despair nothing is destroyed, all a person's aesthetic qualities remain, it is just that they become ancillary and are preserved for that very reason. Yes, it is indeed true that one does not live in the aesthetic as one did, but it by no means follows that one loses it. It may be true that one uses it otherwise, but it does not follow that it has gone away. All the ethicist does is to carry to its conclusion the doubt which the higher aesthete had already set in motion but which he broke off arbitrarily; for, however great his difference, it is still only relative. And when the aesthetician himself admits that the difference which gives his life meaning is also transitory, but adds that it is still always best to enjoy it as long as one has it, this is really a cowardice in love with a certain kind of enjoyment of ease, under not too high a ceiling, and is unworthy of a human being. It is as though someone were to rejoice in some relationship based on a misunderstanding which, sooner or later, would have to come into the open, and lacked the courage to be cognizant of this or to admit it, but rejoiced in the relationship as long as possible. However, this is not the case with you; you are like someone who has admitted the misunderstanding, broken off the relationship, but then wants to be forever taking leave of it.

The aesthetic view also considers personal existence in its relation to the environment, and the expression of this in its impact on the individual is pleasure. But the aesthetic expression of pleasure in its relation to personal existence is mood. For the person is present in the mood but present only in a shadowy way. A person living aesthetically tries as much as possible to be completely taken up in the mood; he tries to hide himself totally within it, so that there is nothing in him which cannot be bent into conformity with it, for any residue always has a disturbing effect, it is an element of continuity that tries to hold him back. The more his personal being merges into mood, the more the individual is in the moment, and again this is the most adequate expression of aesthetic existence: it is in the moment. Hence the huge oscillations to which the person who lives aesthetically is exposed. A person living ethically also knows mood, but for him it is not the most important thing; because he has chosen himself infinitely he sees the mood beneath him. The remainder that will not fit into the mood is exactly that continuity which is for him what is most important. Someone living ethically has [...] a memory of his life, a person living aesthetically certainly has not. Someone living ethically does not do away with mood, he sizes it up for an instant, but this instant saves him from living in the moment, this instant gives him mastery over desire, for the art of mastering desire consists not so much in doing away with it, or giving it up altogether, as in determining the instant. Take any pleasure you like, its secret, its strength, consists in its being contained absolutely in the moment. True, one often hears people saying that the only way is to abstain altogether. That is a very mistaken way and only succeeds for a while. Take someone who has become addicted to gambling. Desire is aroused with all its passion, it is as though his life were at stake if the desire is not satisfied. If he can say to himself, 'Not just now; in an hour's time', he is cured. This hour is the continuity that saves him. For someone living aesthetically the mood is always eccentric, because he has his centre at the periphery. Personal being has its centre in itself, and someone who does not have himself is eccentric. Someone living ethically, however, has his mood centralized, he is not inside the mood, he is not the mood itself, he has mood and has the mood in him. What he works for is continuity and that is always master over mood. His life does not lack mood, indeed it has a total mood, but it is acquired; it is what one could call equability, but this is no aesthetic mood, and no one has it by nature or immediately.

But he who has now infinitely chosen himself – can he say, 'Now I own myself, I ask nothing more, and to all the world's vicissitudes I oppose the proud thought: I am the one I am'? By no means! If anyone were to express themselves in that way one could easily see they had gone astray. The basic mistake would also lie in his not having chosen himself in the strictest sense; choose himself he may have done, but he has done it from outside himself; he had understood quite abstractly what it was to choose and had failed to grasp himself in his concretion; he had not so chosen himself that, in the choice, he came to be within himself, had not clothed himself in himself; he had chosen himself in respect of his necessity, not of his freedom; he had taken the ethical option in vain, aesthetically. The more truly meaningful the outcome that emerges, the more dangerous are the false paths, and here too, accordingly, there appears a dreadful false path. Once the individual has grasped himself in his eternal validity, this overwhelms him with all its fullness. The temporal vanishes from sight. At first it fills him with an indescribable bliss and gives him a sense of absolute security. If, then, it is this that he begins to gaze one-sidedly upon, the temporal presses its claims. They are rejected. What the temporal has to offer, the more-or-less that presents itself here, is for him so very unimportant compared with what he owns eternally. Everything stops short for him, it is as though he had reached eternity before his time. He becomes lost in contemplation, he gazes at himself, but his gazing cannot fill up the time. It then seems to him that time, the temporal, is his ruin, he demands a perfect form of life, and here again appears a fatigue similar to the languor attending pleasure. This apathy can rest so broodingly over a person that suicide seems the only way out. No power can wrest his self from him, the only power is time, yet neither can this wrest his self from him, but checks and delays him, it detains the spiritual embrace in which he grasps himself. He has not chosen himself; like Narcissus, he has fallen in love with himself.[26] It is certainly not seldom such a situation has ended in suicide.

The mistake lies in the fact that he has not chosen in the right way, not just in the sense that he has been insensible of his errors, but he has seen himself in the category of necessity. Himself, this person with all these multiple characteristics, he has seen as part of the way of the world, he has seen his self over against the eternal power, whose fire has permeated it but without consuming it. But he has not seen himself in his freedom, has not chosen himself in that. If he does that, the very moment he chooses himself he is in motion; however concrete his self is, he has still chosen himself in respect of his possibility, he has purchased his freedom in order to stay in it, but he can only stay in his freedom by constantly realizing it. It is for that reason he has chosen himself, by virtue of that fact he is active.

Here might be the place to say a few words about a life-view which you find most agreeable, particularly as teacher, sometimes also as practitioner. What it amounts to is nothing less than that the real meaning of life, after all, is sorrow, and being the unhappiest is the happiest thing of all. At first glance this does not look like an aesthetic view of life, for its slogan can scarcely be pleasure. Neither, however, is it ethical, but it lies at the dangerous transition between

the aesthetic and the ethical, where the soul is so easily seduced by
one or another version of the theory of predestination. You proclaim
a number of false doctrines, and this is about the worst, but you
know also it is the one most fitted for sneaking your way in upon
people and drawing them to you. You can be as heartless as any,
you can joke about everything, even about man's pain. You are not
unaware that young people are tempted by this, yet this conduct
puts you at some distance from them, for such behaviour repels as
much as it attracts. If it is a young woman you want to deceive in
this way, you cannot but notice that a womanly soul has too much
depth to be captivated permanently by such things; yes, even if you
engaged her attention for a moment, she will soon end up wearying
of it and forming something close to an aversion to you because her
soul is in no need of such titillation. The method is then changed; in
isolated enigmatic outbursts, which only she can understand, you let
it be hinted that it can all be explained by a remote melancholy.
You open yourself only to her, but with such caution that she really
never gets to know anything more; you leave it to her imagination
to depict the details of the profound sadness you hide within you.
Shrewd, one cannot deny you are that, and it is true what a young
girl said about you, that probably you will end up a Jesuit. The
more subtly you can pass them the thread that leads deeper and
deeper into the secrets of sadness, the more joyful you are, the more
sure of drawing them to you. You do not make long speeches, you
do not protest your pain in firm handclasps, or by 'gazing romantically into the romantic eyes of a kindred soul'; you are too smart
for that. You avoid witnesses, and only occasionally let yourself be
taken by surprise. At a certain age, there is no more dangerous
poison to a young girl than sadness; you know that, and this knowledge may, like any other, be all very well in itself; your use of it,
on the other hand, is not something I shall praise. [. . .]

It is part of the whole development in modern times that people
are more disposed to feel sorrow than joy. It is considered a higher
view of life, and so it is, inasmuch as it is natural to want to be
joyful, and unnatural to sorrow. On top of that there is the fact that
being joyful does after all impose a certain obligation on the individual to be thankful, even if his thoughts are too confused for
him to know just whom he should thank; sorrow absolves one

from that and vanity is then better satisfied. Besides, our age has experienced the vanity of life in so many ways that it does not believe in joy, and as it still has to have something to believe in, it believes in sorrow. Joy passes away, it says, but sorrow lasts and anyone who bases his view of life on it builds on a solid foundation.

If we ask now more explicitly what sort of sorrow it is you are talking about, you are shrewd enough to evade ethical sorrow. It is not repentance you mean; no, it is aesthetic sorrow, reflected sorrow in particular. It is based not on guilt but on misfortune, on fate, on a sad disposition, the influence of others, etc. It is something with which you are all too familiar from novels. When you read it there you laugh at it, if you hear others talk of it you mock them; but when you yourself discourse on it, it makes sense and there is truth in it.

Now although the view that takes sorrow to be the meaning of life can seem itself to be sorrowful enough, I cannot neglect to show you, from an angle you perhaps would not expect, that it offers no comfort. [. . .] Someone who says that sorrow is the meaning of life has joy outside him in the same way that someone who wants to be joyful has sorrow outside him. Joy may take him by surprise in exactly the same way that sorrow can take the other. So his life-view is tied to a condition which is not under his control, for it is really just as little under someone's control to refrain from joy as to refrain from sorrow. But any life-view with a condition outside it is despair. And so wanting to sorrow is despair in exactly the same sense as wanting to seek joy, since it is always despair to have one's life centred in something whose nature it is to cease to be. [. . .]

The deeper the source of sorrow, the more it can seem that one might preserve it all one's life, as if there was indeed nothing one need do to make it so, it will stay as a matter of course. If it is some particular event, that will prove very difficult. You yourself are fully aware of that, and so when you want to pronounce on the meaning of sorrow for the whole of life you think mainly of unhappy characters and tragic heroes. It is a feature of the entire spiritual disposition of the unhappy character that he is unable to be happy or joyful, a fate broods over him, and similarly over the tragic hero. So here you are perfectly justified in saying that sorrow is the meaning of life; and this has brought us to plain fatalism, which always has something seductive about it. Here also you encounter your allegation which amounts neither more nor less to the claim that you yourself are the unhappiest man. And yet it is undeniable that this thought is the proudest and most defiant that can arise in a man's brain.

Let me answer you as you deserve. First of all, you do not sorrow. This you know full well, for it is your favourite saying that the unhappiest is the happiest. But this is a falsification more appalling than any other; it is a falsification which turns against the eternal power that governs the world, it is a rebellion against God, like wanting to laugh when you should weep; and yet there is a despair that is capable of it, there is a defiance that pits itself against God. But that is also treason against the human race. True, you too distinguish between sorrows, but you think there is a difference so great as to allow a kind that it is impossible to bear. But if such a sorrow exists, it is not for you to decide which it is, one difference is as good as another, and you have betrayed man's deepest and most sacred right or grace. It is treason against what is great, a mean envy, for what it comes down to is that the great men have not been subjected to the most dangerous trials, have slipped easily into their honours, and that they would also have succumbed had the superhuman temptation you speak of come their way. And is this the way you intend to honour what is great, by belittling it? You mean to bear witness to it by denying it?

And do not misunderstand me now. I am not the kind that thinks one should not sorrow, I despise that petty common sense, and if this is all the choice there is, then I choose sorrow. No, I am aware that to sorrow is beautiful, and that there is mettle in tears; but I also know that one shall not sorrow as one who has not hope. There is an absolute opposition between us that can never be abolished. I cannot live in aesthetic categories, I feel what I hold most sacred is destroyed; I need a higher expression and the ethical gives me that. And this is where sorrow first acquires its true and profound meaning. Do not be shocked by what I am about to say here, do not hold it against me that, while speaking of sorrows which need heroes to bear them, I can talk of children.

It is a sign of a well-behaved child that it is disposed to ask permission without pondering too deeply whether it is in the right or not; and so it is a sign of a magnanimous man of profound soul that he is disposed to repent, that he does not go to law with God but repents and loves God in his repentance. Without that his life is nothing, merely like foam on water. Yes, I assure you that if my own life, through no fault of my own, were so fraught with sorrows and sufferings that I could call myself the greatest tragic hero, revel in my pain, and appal the world by calling attention to it, my choice is made; I divest myself of the hero's apparel and of tragedy's pathos, I am not the afflicted one who can be proud of his suffering, I am the humble one who is aware of his sin. I have only one expression for what I suffer – guilt; one expression for my pain – repentance; one hope before my eyes – forgiveness; and if I find this difficult, ah! I have but one prayer, I will throw myself to the ground and implore the eternal power that governs the world for one grace, early and late, that I be allowed to repent. For I know only one sorrow which can bring me to despair and plunge everything down into it – the sorrow that repentance was a delusion, a delusion not in respect of the forgiveness it seeks, but in the accountability it presupposes.

And do you think that this conduct shows that I fail to give sorrow its due, that I am running away from it? By no means! I deposit it within my being and for that reason I never forget it. By and large it is mistrust of the validity of spirit not to dare to believe that I can have something within me without looking at it at every instant. In everyday life whatever one most wishes to set aside one deposits in a place one does not come to every day; so too in a spiritual sense. I have sorrow within me, and I know that it will continue to be part of my being. I know it far more surely than someone who from dread of losing it takes it out every day.

My life has never been so agitated that I felt tempted by the chaotic wish to throw all existence into confusion, but in my daily life I have often discovered how profitable it is to give sorrow an ethical expression, not to erase the aesthetic factor in sorrow but to master it ethically. As long as sorrow is quiet and humble, I do not fear it; if it becomes vehement and passionate, sophistical so that it deludes me into despondency, I arise, I brook no rebellion, I will have nothing in the world cheat me of what I have from God's hand as a gift of grace. I do not chase sorrow away, do not try to forget it, I repent. [. . .]

Perhaps you see now why I take up this life-view here. Personal being is here again viewed under the category of necessity, and there is only enough freedom left constantly to keep the individual half awake, as in a restless dream, and to lead him astray into the labyrinth of suffering and dispensation where he sees himself everywhere yet cannot come to himself. It is incredible how irresponsibly one sees problems like these dealt with. Even systematic thinkers treat [freedom] as a natural curiosity they have nothing more to say about, but can only describe, without it ever occurring to them that, if there were such a natural curiosity, all the rest of their wisdom is nonsense and illusion. That is why one feels helped quite otherwise by the Christian view than by all the wisdom of the philosophers. It assigns everything to sin, something philosophy is too aesthetic to have the ethical courage to do. And yet this courage is the only thing that can save life and man, unless one is to break off one's scepticism at a whim and join forces with some like-minded persons on what to count as true.

The first form the choice takes is a complete isolation. For in choosing myself I sever myself from my relationship to the whole world until, in this separation, I end in an abstract identity. When the individual has chosen himself in respect of his freedom he is by that very fact active. Yet his action has no relation to any surrounding world, for the individual has completely done away with the latter and is only for himself. The life-view here presented is, however, an ethical view. In Greece it was expressed in a single individual's endeavour to develop himself into a paragon of virtue. As later with the anchorites in Christendom, one withdrew from life's activities, not to steep oneself in metaphysical musings, but to act, not outwardly, but within oneself. This inner action was at once the individual's task and satisfaction, for it was no part of his purpose to cultivate himself the better to be able to serve the State later on; no, in this cultivation the individual was sufficient unto himself and abandoned the life of the State, never to return to it. Really, then, one didn't withdraw from life; on the contrary, one remained within its diversity because contact with it was pedagogically necessary for one's own sake; but civic life as such had no significance for one – through some or other sorcerer's spell one had rendered it harmless, indifferent, unimportant. So the virtues the individual developed were not civic virtues (as the virtues in paganism really were, corresponding to the religious virtues in Christianity), they were the personal virtues: courage, perseverance, temperance, moderation, etc. Naturally, in our own times one very seldom sees this life-view put into practice, since everyone is too much affected by the religious to stay with such an abstract specification of virtue. It is easy to see what the defect is with this life-view. The error is that the individual has chosen himself altogether abstractly, and so the perfection he desired and attained was similarly abstract. It was for that reason I stressed that choosing oneself and repenting oneself are identical, for repentance puts the individual into the most heartfelt connection, and the most intimate cohesion, with the surrounding world.

Analogies to this Greek view have often been seen, even occasionally in the Christian world, except that in Christianity a seasoning of mystical and religious elements makes it richer and more beautiful. Whatever heights of virtuosity a Greek who developed himself into a perfect compendium of all personal virtues might attain, his life is still no less mortal than the world whose temptation his virtue conquered; his blessedness is a lonely self-contentment, transient as everything else. Now, the life of a mystic is far deeper. He has chosen himself absolutely, for although a mystic is less often heard to express himself in this way, although he generally uses the seemingly opposite expression that he has chosen God, it comes to the same as was shown above. For unless he has chosen himself absolutely he is not in any free relationship to God, and the characteristic of Christian piety lies in freedom. In the language of the mystic this free relationship to God is often expressed by saying that He is the absolute Thou. The mystic has chosen himself absolutely, according therefore to his freedom, and consequently is by that very fact active, but his action is inner action. The mystic chooses himself in his complete isolation; for him the whole world is dead and done away with and the weary soul chooses God, or itself. This expression, 'the weary soul', must not be misunderstood, not misused to demean the mystic as if there were something dubious about the soul's choosing God only when it had become weary of the world. No doubt what the mystic is conveying through this expression is his repentance at not having chosen God earlier, and his weariness should not be regarded as the same thing as boredom with life. Here already you will see how little the mystic's life is given to the ethical, since the highest expression of his repentance is to repent that he had not chosen God earlier, before he became concrete in the world, while his soul was merely abstractly defined, that is, as a child.

The mystic, in having chosen, is by that very fact active. But his action is inner action. Inasmuch as he is active his life has a movement, a development, a history. However, a development can be metaphysical or aesthetic to such a degree that it is doubtful whether in any proper sense one should call it a history, since one thinks of that as a development in the form of freedom. A movement can be haphazard to such a degree that one can doubt whether it should be called a development. Thus, if the movement consists in the same factor occurring again and again, undeniably we have movement, indeed one can perhaps discover a law of its motion; but we have no development. The repetition in time is without meaning, and continuity is lacking. This is very largely true of the life of the mystic. A mystic's moanings about the moments of dullness make appalling reading. But when the dull moment has gone there comes the moment of light, and so his life is constantly changing, it has movement indeed, but no development. His life lacks continuity. What really provides that in the life of the mystic is a feeling, namely longing, whether this longing is directed at what has gone or at what is to come. But the fact that what makes up the interval is a feeling shows precisely that cohesion is lacking. A mystic's development is metaphysically and aesthetically determined to such a degree that one can hardly call it history, except in the sense in which one speaks of the history of a plant. For the mystic, the whole world is dead, he has fallen in love with God. The development of his life is then the unfolding of this love. Just as there are instances of lovers bearing some resemblance to one another, even outwardly, in their expression, their physiognomy, so is the mystic absorbed in the contemplation of the Deity, and the latter's image is more and more reflected in his loving soul; thus the mystic renews and revives the lost divine image in man. The more he contemplates, the more clearly this image is reflected in him, the more he comes himself to resemble this image. His inner action consists not, then, in the acquisition of the personal virtues but in the development of the religious or contemplative virtues. Yet even this is too ethical an expression for his life, and his real life is therefore prayer. That prayer is also part of an ethical life I will not deny, but the more ethically a man lives, the more the prayer has the character of an intention, so that there is an element of intention even in the prayer of thanksgiving. With the mystic's prayer it is otherwise. For him prayer means all the more the more erotic it is, the more it is inflamed by a burning love. The prayer is the expression of his love, the only language in which he can address the Deity with whom he has fallen in love. As in earthly life the lovers long for the moment when they can breathe their love to one another, let their souls fuse in a soft whisper, so the mystic longs for the moment when in his prayer he can, as it were, steal into the presence of God. As the lovers experience in that whisper their greatest bliss when really they have nothing at all to talk about, so the mystic in his prayer is all the more blessed, his love all the more happy, the less content there is in it, the more nearly in his sigh he vanishes from before his own very eyes.

Perhaps it would not be too much of a diversion here to bring out more clearly what is untrue in such a life, especially since a person of any profundity is always liable to be impressed by it. Thus you yourself are by no means lacking in what it takes to be a mystic, at least for a while. This is, in general, the area where the greatest contrasts meet, the purest and most innocent souls and the guiltiest, the most gifted and the most simple-minded.

First I will state, quite simple-mindedly, what really offends me in such a life. This is my personal judgement. Later I shall try to show the accuracy of my indications of its dubious sides, as well as the reasons for these and the fearful false paths that lie so close.

In my opinion one cannot exonerate the mystic from a certain importunity in his relationship to God. That a man should love God with all his soul and with all his mind, and not merely should do so but that his actually doing so is blessedness itself, who could deny? However, from this it by no means follows that the mystic should disdain the existence, the reality, in which God has placed him; for in that case he is really disdaining God's love, or demanding another expression of it than the one God wants to give. Here

Samuel's serious saying applies: 'To obey is better than sacrifice, and to hearken than the fat of rams.'[27] But this importunity can occasionally take on an even more questionable form, as when a mystic justifies his relationship to God on the grounds of being the very person he is, and thinks that it is due to some accidental trait that he is the object of God's partiality. For here he debases the Deity and himself: himself because it is always a debasement to be essentially distinguished from others by something accidental; God because he makes the Deity a false god and himself into a favourite at his court.

What next I find displeasing in a mystic's life is the softness and weakness from which one cannot exonerate him. That a man wishes to be assured in his inmost heart that he loves God truly and sincerely, that he many a time feels the need to be properly convinced of this, that he can pray God to let his Spirit bear witness that he does so,[28] who would deny the beauty and truth in that? But from this it by no means follows that at every moment he will repeat this attempt, that at every moment he will put his love to the test. He wants to have greatness of soul enough to believe in God's love, but then he should also have the confidence to believe in his own love, and to continue happily in the situation assigned to him, precisely because he knows that this continuation is the surest expression of his love, of his humility.

Finally, a mystic's life displeases me because I consider it a deceit against the world in which he lives, a deceit against those with whom he is associated or with whom he could enter into relationships had it not pleased him to become a mystic. Generally the mystic chooses the solitary life, but that does not clarify the situation, for the question is whether he has a right to choose it. Inasmuch as it is something he has chosen, he does not deceive others, for this is to say in effect, 'I will have no relationship with you', but the question is whether he has a right to say that, a right to do this. It is especially as a husband, as a father, that I am an enemy of mysticism. My household has also its *adyton*,[29] but if I were a mystic I would also have to have yet another all for myself, and then I would be a bad husband. Now since in my view, as I shall explain later, it is every man's duty to marry, and since it cannot possibly be my view that one should marry in order to become a bad husband, you will easily see that I must have an aversion to all mysticism.

In the end someone who devotes himself one-sidedly to a life of mysticism becomes so much a stranger to everyone that he becomes indifferent to every relationship, even the tenderest and most heart-felt. It is not in this sense that one is to love God more than father and mother;[30] God is not that self-loving, nor is he a poet who wishes to torment men with the most fearful collisions, and you could hardly conceive anything more fearful than that there indeed existed a collision between love of God and love of those human beings our love of whom He has lodged in our hearts. You have surely not forgotten young Ludvig Blackfeldt, with whom we both had so much contact a few years ago, particularly myself. Certainly he had great mental gifts, but his misfortune was to become one-sidedly absorbed not so much in Christian as in Indian mysticism. Had he lived in the Middle Ages, he would undoubtedly have found refuge in a monastery. Our own age has no such expedients. If a person loses his way now he must needs go under unless he is completely cured; we have no such relative salvation to offer him. You know he ended by taking his own life. [. . .] Poor Ludvig was not indeed religiously affected, but he was affected mystically nevertheless; for what is peculiar to the mystical is not the religious but the isolation in which the individual, not heeding any relation with the given reality, would put himself into immediate rapport with the eternal. The fact that the word 'mysticism' naturally and immediately calls something religious to mind has to do with the fact that religion has a tendency to isolate the individual, as the most simple observation can convince you. Maybe you attend church rather infrequently, but you are likely to be all the more observant. Have you noticed that although in a sense one gets the impression of a congregation, the individual still feels isolated? People become strangers to each other, and it is as though one were united again only by way of a long detour. And to what is this due if not to the individual's feeling his God-relationship so strongly, in all its inwardness, that his earthly relationships lose their importance beside it? For a healthy man this instant will not last long, and a momentary distancing of this kind is so far from being a deceit that, rather, it increases the inwardness of the earthly relationships. But what can be healthy as a constituent becomes a most critical sickness when developed one-sidedly.

Not having a theological background, I do not consider myself capable of elaborating on the subject of religious mysticism any further. I have considered it only from my ethical standpoint, and have therefore, correctly I believe, given the word 'mysticism' a much broader meaning than usual. That there is very much that is beautiful in religious mysticism, that the many deep and serious natures who have devoted themselves to it have experienced much in their lives, and were thus qualified to provide counsel and directions and hints of service to others who would venture upon this dangerous path, of that I have no doubt; yet this path is notwithstanding not merely a dangerous path but a false one. There is always an inconsistency implicit in it. Since the mystic has no respect at all for reality, it is not evident why he does not treat with the same distrust that moment in reality when he became affected by higher things.

So the mystic's fault is not that he chooses himself, for in my opinion he does well to do that, his mistake is that he does not choose himself properly; he chooses in respect of his freedom and yet he does not choose ethically. One can only choose *oneself* in respect of one's freedom when one chooses oneself ethically; but one can only choose oneself ethically by repenting oneself, and it is only by repenting oneself that one becomes concrete, and it is only as a concrete individual that one is a free individual. The mystic's mistake does not lie in something later but in the very first movement. If one takes that to be correct, then every withdrawal from life, every ascetic self-torment is simply a further and proper consequence. The mystic's mistake is that in the choice he does not become concrete for himself, and not for God either; he chooses himself abstractly and therefore lacks transparency. For if you believe that the abstract is the transparent, you are mistaken; the abstract is the opaque, the indistinct. Therefore his love for God has its highest expression in a feeling, a mood; in the evening twilight, in the season of mists, he melts with vague movements into one with his God. But when one chooses oneself abstractly, one does not choose oneself ethically. Only when one has taken possession of oneself in the choice, has attired oneself in one's self, has penetrated oneself so totally that every movement is attended by the consciousness of a responsibility for oneself, only then has one chosen oneself ethically, only then has one repented oneself, only then is one concrete, only then is one, in one's total isolation, in absolute continuity with the reality one belongs to.

I cannot return often enough to this proviso that choosing oneself is identical with repenting oneself, however simple in itself it may be. For upon this everything turns. The mystic too repents, but he repents himself out of himself, not into himself, he repents metaphysically, not ethically. To repent aesthetically is detestable because it is effeminate; to repent metaphysically is a misplaced superfluity, for the individual has not created the world after all, and so need not take it so much to heart if the world should really turn out to be vanity. The mystic chooses himself abstractly and therefore has to repent himself abstractly too. This can best be seen from the mystic's judgement upon existence, the finite reality in which he lives. For the mystic teaches that it is vanity, illusion, sin; but every such judgement is a metaphysical judgement and does not define my relation to existence ethically. Even when he says that finitude is sin, what he says is just about the same as when he calls it vanity. If, on the other hand, he were to keep hold of the ethical sense of the word 'sin', he would define his relation to it not ethically but metaphysically, for the ethical expression would not be to run away from it but to enter into it, to abolish it or to bear it. Ethical repentance has but two movements; either it abolishes its object or it bears it. These two movements also indicate a concrete relation between the repenting individual and the object of his repentance, whereas fleeing expresses an abstract relation.

The mystic chooses himself abstractly, and one can therefore say that he constantly chooses himself out of the world; but the consequence is that he cannot choose himself back again into the world. The true concrete choice is that in which in the very moment I choose myself out of the world I choose myself back into it. For when I choose myself repentantly I gather myself together in all my finite concretion, and in thus having chosen myself out of the finite I am in the most absolute continuity with it. [. . .]

The greatest significance [the mystic] can assign to the temporal is to see it as a period of probation in which one must be repeatedly tested without any real result or getting any further than at the beginning. This, however, is to misjudge the temporal, for although it does always retain something of an *ecclesia pressa*,[31] it is at the same time the possibility of the finite spirit's glorification. It is precisely the beauty of the finite that within it infinite spirit and finite spirit are separated, and it is precisely the greatness of the finite spirit that the temporal is assigned to it. So the temporal does not exist, if I may be so bold, for God's sake so that in it He can, mystically speaking, test and try the one who loves; it is there for man's sake and is the greatest of all gifts of grace. For the eternal dignity of man lies in the fact that he can acquire a history, and the divine element in him lies in the fact that he himself can impart to this history a continuity if he will; for it acquires that not by being the sum of all that has happened to or befallen me, but by being my own work, so that even what has befallen me is transformed in me and translated from necessity to freedom. The enviable thing with a human life is that one can come to the aid of the Deity, can understand Him, and again the only way of understanding Him worthy of a man is freely to appropriate all that has fallen to one, both the joyful and the sorrowful. Or does it not seem so to you? That is how it strikes me; yes, I think one would only have to say it aloud to a man to make him envious of himself.

The two standpoints indicated here [the Greek and the mystical] might be regarded as attempts to realize an ethical view of life. The reason why they do not succeed is that the individual has chosen himself in his isolation or has chosen himself abstractly. This can also be put by saying that the individual has not chosen himself ethically. He is therefore not connected with reality, and in that case no ethical life-view can be put into practice. On the other hand, a person who chooses himself ethically chooses himself concretely as this definite individual, and he achieves this concretion by the choice being identical with the repentance which sanctions the choice. The individual is then aware of himself as this definite individual, with these aptitudes, these tendencies, these instincts, these passions, influenced by these definite surroundings, as this definite product of a definite outside world. But in becoming self-aware in this way, he assumes responsibility for it all. He does not pause to consider whether to include some particular trait or not, for he knows there is something far higher that he stands to lose if he does not. At the instant of choice, then, he is in the most complete isolation for he withdraws from the surroundings, and yet is at the same instant in absolute continuity for he chooses himself as product; and this choice is freedom's choice, so that in choosing himself as product he can just as well be said to produce himself. At the instant of choice, then, he is at the conclusion, for his personhood forms a closure; and yet in the same instant he is precisely at the beginning for he chooses himself in respect of his freedom. As product he is pressed into the forms of reality, in the choice he makes himself elastic, he transforms the whole of his outwardness to inwardness. He has his place in the world, with freedom he himself chooses his place, that is, he chooses this place. He is a definite individual, in the choice he makes himself into a definite individual, that is to say, into the same, for he chooses himself.

The individual thus chooses himself as a diversely determined concretion, and chooses himself therefore in respect of his concretion. This concretion is the reality of the individual, but since it is in respect of his freedom that he chooses it, one can also say that it is his possibility, or, to avoid such an aesthetic expression, that it is his task. For the person who lives aesthetically sees only possibilities everywhere; for him it is these that form the content of the future, whereas the person who lives ethically sees tasks everywhere. It is then this real concretion of his that the individual sees as his task, his goal, his aim. But the fact that it is his own possibility that the individual sees as his task expresses precisely his sovereignty over himself, which he never surrenders even though he does not enjoy the highly unencumbered sovereignty that a king without a country always has. This gives the ethical individual a sense of security which someone living merely aesthetically altogether lacks. The person who lives aesthetically expects everything from outside, hence the sickly anxiety with which many speak of the dreadful circumstance of not having found one's place in the world. Who would deny the satisfaction in being fortunate in this respect? But such an anxiety is always an indication that the individual expects everything from the place and nothing from himself. The person who lives ethically will try to choose his place rightly, but if he notices that he has chosen wrongly, or that obstacles arise over which he has no control, he does not lose courage for he never surrenders his sovereignty over himself. He at once sees his task and is therefore instantly active. Similarly, one often sees people afraid that if ever they fall in love they will not get a girl who is exactly the ideal that suits them. Who would deny the satisfaction in getting such a girl? On the other hand, it is after all a superstition that what lies outside a person is what can make him happy. The person who lives ethically also wants to be happy in his choice; however, should the choice prove not quite in accord with his wishes, he does not lose courage, he at once sees his task and knows that the art is not to wish but to will. Many who do, after all, have some conception of what a human life is, wish to be contemporary with great events, to be involved in important situations in life. Who would deny that such things have their validity? It is a superstition, on the other hand, to think that events and situations as such make a man into something. A person who lives ethically knows that in any situation it is a question of what one sees and with what energy one regards it, and that the person cultivating himself in this way in the least significant situations in life may experience more than the person who has been a witness to, indeed a participant in, the most notable events. He knows that everywhere there is a dance floor, that even the lowliest man has his own, that when he himself so wishes, his dance can be just as beautiful, just as graceful, just as expressive, just as moving as that of those who have been assigned a place in history. It is this fencing skill, this suppleness, which is properly the immortal life of the ethical. To the person who lives aesthetically the old saying, 'to be or not to be', applies and the more aesthetically he is allowed to live, the more demands his life exacts, and if only the least of them is not fulfilled he is dead; the person who lives ethically always has a way out even when everything goes against him, even when the storm-filled clouds brood over him so darkly that his neighbour cannot see him, he has not perished, there is always a point he keeps hold of, and it is – himself.

Just one thing I would insist upon: that as soon as the ethicist's gymnastics become an experimentation he has ceased to live ethically. All such gymnastic experimenting is nothing but what counts, in the realm of knowledge, as sophistry.

I want now to recall the definition of the ethical I gave earlier, that it is that whereby a man comes to be what he becomes. So it wants not to make the individual into another but into himself; it wants not to do away with the aesthetic but to transfigure it. To live ethically it is necessary for a person to become aware of himself, so totally that no accidental feature escapes him. The ethical does not want to erase this concretion but sees in it its task, sees from what it must build and what is to be built. People generally consider the ethical altogether abstractly and therefore they have a secret horror of it. The ethical is then looked upon as something alien to personal being, and one shrinks from abandoning oneself to it, for one cannot quite be sure what it may lead to in the course of time. Many are also afraid of death in the same way, because they entertain obscure and confused ideas about the soul passing over in death into another order of things, where laws and customs prevail which are altogether different from those they have learnt to recognize in this world. The reason for such a fear of death is the individual's reluctance to be transparent to himself, for provided one is willing it is easy to see the absurdity of this fear. Similarly with the ethical; a person who fears transparency will always shun the ethical, for really the ethical wants nothing else.

Opposed to an aesthetic view of life which would enjoy life, one often hears talk of another life-view in which the meaning of life is to live for the fulfilment of life's duties. This is meant to be an ethical life-view. However, that is a very imperfect expression of it, and one might almost believe it was invented to discredit the ethical. At all events, nowadays one often sees it used in a way that almost causes a smile. [. . .] The mistake is this, that the individual is placed in an external relation to duty. The ethical is defined as duty, and duty again as a mass of particular propositions, but the individual and duty stand outside each other. A life of duty in this sense is naturally very unattractive and tedious, and if the ethical did not have some much deeper connection with personal being, it would always be very difficult to defend it against the aesthetic. That there are many people who come no further than this I will not deny; but that has to do with the people, not with duty.

It is rather strange that the word 'duty' [*Pligt*] can bring to mind an external relation when the derivation of the word indicates it is an internal relation. For surely what it is incumbent upon me to do, not as this contingent individual but in respect of my true nature, stands in the most intimate relation to me. For duty is not an imposition [*Paalæg*] but something which imposes [*paaligger*].

Seeing duty in this way is a sign that the individual has found his
bearings within himself. Duty will then not be split up into a
multiplicity of particular directives, for that always implies that the
individual stands only in an external relation to it. He has invested
himself in the duty, for him it is the expression of his inmost nature.
When he has thus found his bearings within himself, he is steeped in
the ethical and will have no need to urge himself breathlessly on
into fulfilling his duties. The truly ethical individual has, therefore,
an inner calm and assurance because he does not have duty outside
him but inside him. The more deeply a person imparts an ethical
structure to his life, the less he will feel the need to talk every instant
of duty, to be anxious every instant that he is fulfilling it, to confer
every instant with others about what his duty is. Viewed rightly the
ethical makes the individual infinitely secure within himself; when it
is not viewed rightly it makes the individual completely insecure,
and I can imagine no unhappier and more agonizing life than that
of someone who has got his duty outside him and yet is constantly
wanting to realize it.

If the ethical appears to lie outside one's personal being and to be
in external relation to it, one has given everything up; one has
despaired. The aesthetic as such is despair, the ethical is the abstract
and as such incapable of bringing about the slightest thing. So when
occasionally one sees people with a certain honest zeal struggling
and straining to realize the ethical, which like a shadow keeps
running away as they try to take hold of it, it is both comic and
tragic.

The ethical is the universal and as such the abstract. In its complete
abstraction the ethical is therefore always interdictory. The ethical
thus presents itself as law. As soon as the ethical specifies directives it
already contains something of the aesthetic. The Jews were the
people of the Law. So they had an excellent understanding of most
of the commandments in the Laws of Moses; but the commandment
they seem not to have understood was the one with which Christianity most closely associated itself: 'Thou shalt love God with all thine
heart.' Nor is this a negative commandment, and it is not abstract, it
is positive in the highest degree and concrete in the highest degree.
When the ethical becomes more concrete it passes over into the
specification of moral behaviour. But the reality of the ethical in

this respect lies in the reality of a popular identity, and here the ethical has already assumed an aesthetic element. Nevertheless the ethical is still abstract and cannot be fully realized because it lies outside the individual. Only when the individual himself is the universal, only then can the ethical be realized. This is the secret of conscience, it is the secret the individual life shares with itself, that it is at one and the same time an individual life and also the universal, if not as such in its immediacy, at least according to its possibility. The person who regards life ethically sees the universal, and the person who lives ethically expresses his life in the universal; he makes himself into the universal man, not by divesting himself of his concretion, for then he would be nothing at all, but by clothing himself in it and permeating it with the universal. For the universal man is not a phantom, everyone is the universal man – that is to say, everyone is shown the path along which he becomes the universal man. Someone who lives aesthetically is the accidental man, he thinks he is the perfect man through being the only man. The person who lives ethically works at becoming the universal man. Thus the accidental plays an enormous part for a man who is aesthetically in love, and it is of importance to him that no one has loved with just the nuances that he has. If the person who lives ethically marries, he realizes the universal. Therefore he does not become a hater of the concrete but has one more expression, deeper than any aesthetic expression, inasmuch as he sees in the love a revelation of the universal human. So the person who lives ethically has himself as his task. His self in its immediacy is accidentally specified and the task is to work the accidental and the universal together.

So the ethical individual does not have duty outside him but inside him; this first appears in the moment of despair and then works its way forward through the aesthetic, in and with the latter. One can say of the ethical individual that he is like those still waters that run deep, whereas the person living aesthetically is simply agitated on the surface. So once the ethical individual has completed his task, has fought the good fight,[32] he has reached the point of having become the only man – that is, there is no man just like him – and at the same time of having become the universal man. Being the only man is in itself nothing so great, for that is something all men share with every natural phenomenon. But being it in such a way that at the same time he is the universal, that is the true art of living.

So one's personal being does not have the ethical outside it but inside it, and it breaks forth from this deep. What matters then is, as I said, that it does not do away with the concrete in an abstract and empty storming, but assimilates it. Because the ethical lies deepest in the soul it is not always visible, and someone living ethically can behave exactly like someone living aesthetically so that one can be deluded for a long time; but eventually there comes a moment when it becomes apparent that the person who lives ethically has a boundary not recognized by the other. In this assurance that his life is structured ethically the individual rests securely confident and so does not pester himself or others with captious fears about this or that. For I find it just as it should be that someone living ethically retains a blank space for what is ethically indifferent, and it is precisely a veneration of the ethical not to press it upon every insignificant detail. The attempt to do so, which always fails, is also only to be found among those who do not have courage to believe in the ethical and who lack inner confidence in a deeper sense. There are those whose faint-heartedness is discernible precisely in their inability ever to be finished with the totality just because for them this is a manifold, but these, too, lie outside the ethical, for no other reason of course than weakness of will, which like every other spiritual weakness can be regarded as a form of insanity. The lives of such people are spent in straining at a gnat.[33] They have no conception either of the pure and beautiful earnest of the ethical or of the unconcerned joy of the indifferent. But of course, for the ethical individual the indifferent is dethroned and he can set its boundary at any moment. Thus one believes also in a providence, and the soul rests securely in this assurance, yet one would never think of applying this thought to every accidental happening, nor is one conscious of this belief every minute. Willing the ethical without being disturbed by the indifferent, believing in providence without being disturbed by the accidental, is a healthy condition which can be acquired and preserved if a man himself so wills it. Here, too, the thing is to see the task, to see that when someone tends to be distracted, that task is to summon up resistance, to keep hold of the infinite and not go on a wild goose chase.

Anyone who chooses himself ethically has himself as a task, not as a possibility, not as a plaything for his caprice to sport with. He can only choose himself ethically when he chooses himself in continuity, and so he has himself as a multiply specified task. He does not try to erase the multiplicity or to disperse it; on the contrary, he repents himself firmly into it because this multiplicity is himself, and only by repentantly steeping himself in it can he come to himself, since he does not assume that the world begins with him or that he creates himself. Language has itself branded that idea with contempt and it is always contemptuously that one says of a man: 'he gives himself airs' [*han skaber sig*: lit. 'creates himself']. But when he chooses himself repentantly he is active, not in the direction of isolation but of continuity.

Now let us compare an ethical and an aesthetic individual. The main difference, on which everything turns, is that the ethical individual is transparent to himself and does not live 'out in the blue' as does the aesthetic individual. From this difference everything else follows. The person who lives ethically has seen himself, knows himself, permeates his whole concretion with his consciousness, does not allow vague thoughts to fuss around in him, nor tempting possibilities to distract him with their legerdemain; he himself is not like a witch's letter which, depending on how you turn the pages, gives you first this image, then that.[34] He knows himself. The expression *gnothi seauton* is repeated often enough and one has seen in it the aim of all human striving.[35] Quite right, too, but it is equally certain that it cannot be the goal unless at the same time it is the beginning. The ethical individual knows himself, but this knowledge is not mere contemplation, for then the individual would be specified in respect of his necessity; it is a reflection on himself, which is itself an action, and that is why I have been careful to use the expression 'to choose oneself' instead of 'to know oneself'. In knowing himself the individual is not complete; on the contrary, this knowledge is highly productive and from it there emerges the true individual. Were I to be clever I could say here that the individual knew himself in the same way that, in the Old Testament, it is said that Adam knew Eve. Through the individual's intercourse with himself the individual gets himself with child and gives himself birth. The self that the individual knows is at the same time the

actual self and the ideal self, which the individual has outside him as
an image in whose likeness he has to form himself, yet which he
has, on the other hand, within him since he is that self. Only within
himself does the individual have the goal he must strive for, though
in striving for it he has that goal outside himself. For if the individual
believes the universal man is situated outside him and will come to
meet him from outside, then he is disoriented, he has an abstract
conception, and his method will always be an abstract annihilation
of the original self. Only from within himself can the individual
obtain information about himself. Therefore the ethical life has this
twofold nature, that the individual has himself outside himself within
himself. However, the typical self is the imperfect self, for it is only
a prophecy and therefore not the actual self. However, it constantly
attends him; but the more he realizes it the more it disappears into
him, until finally, instead of appearing in front of him, it lies behind
him as a faded possibility. This image behaves like a man's shadow.
In the morning he casts a shadow in front of him, at noon it goes
beside him almost unnoticed, and in the evening it falls behind him.
When the individual knows himself and has chosen himself, he is on
the way to realizing himself, but since he must realize himself freely
he must know what it is he would realize. Certainly what he would
realize is himself, but that is his ideal self which he can acquire only
from within himself. If one does not insist that it is within himself
that the individual has the ideal self, one's thoughts and aspirations
will be abstract. The person who copies another and the person
who would copy the normal man both become, though in different
ways, equally affected.

The aesthetic individual looks at himself in his concretion and
then distinguishes one thing from another. He sees one thing as
belonging to him accidentally, another as belonging essentially. This
distinction is, however, extremely relative, for so long as a person
lives merely aesthetically everything belongs to him equally accidentally, and if an aesthetic individual insists on the distinction it is
only for lack of energy. The ethical individual has learnt this in
despair, so he has another distinction because he too distinguishes
between the essential and the accidental. Everything posited with his
freedom belongs to him essentially, however accidental it may seem;
everything else he sees as accidental, however essential it may seem.

However, for the ethical individual this distinction is not the product of whim, making it look as though he had absolute power to make himself into whatever he wanted. For although the ethical individual might refer to himself as his own editor, he is at the same time fully aware of his editorial responsibility to himself, in so far as what he chooses has a decisive influence on him personally, to the scheme of things in which he lives, and to God. Looked at in this way I think the distinction is correct, for after all what belongs to me essentially is only whatever I undertake ethically as a task. If I refuse to undertake it, that refusing of mine belongs to me essentially. When a person looks at himself aesthetically he might make the distinction as follows. He says, 'I have a talent for painting, I consider that an accident; but I have wit and acuity, I consider that the essential thing that cannot be taken away from me without my becoming someone else.' To that I would reply, 'This whole distinction is an illusion, for if you do not take this wit and acuity upon yourself ethically, as a task, as something you are responsible for, it does not belong to you essentially, and that is mainly because, so long as you only live aesthetically, your whole life is totally unessential.' The person living ethically abolishes to some extent the distinction between the accidental and the essential, for he takes over every inch of himself as equally essential; but it comes back again since, after he has done that, he makes a distinction, but in such a way that what he excludes as accidental he takes an essential responsibility for in respect of his having excluded it.

In so far as the aesthetic individual sets a task for his life with an 'aesthetic seriousness', really this is absorbing himself further in his own contingency, becoming an individual the like of whose paradoxical and irregular conduct one has never seen, a grimace of a man. The reason why one rarely comes across such figures is that one rarely comes across people with a conception of what it is to live. On the other hand, since many have a decided partiality for talking, one does come across – in the street, at parties, and in books – a great deal of chatter that bears unmistakably the stamp of the craze for originality which, when put into practice, would enrich the world with a mass of artefacts each more ludicrous than the next. The task the ethical individual sets himself is to transform himself into the universal individual. Only the ethical individual renders to himself a serious account of himself and therefore is honest with himself, only he has this paradigmatic dignity and this decorum which are more beautiful than all else. But to transform oneself into the universal man is only possible if I already have this within me *kata dunamin*.[36] For the universal can very well subsist with and in the singular without consuming the latter; it is like the fire that burned in the bush without consuming it.[37] If the universal man is situated outside me only one method is possible, and that is to divest myself of all my concretion. One often finds this straining for unbridled abstraction. There was a sect among the Hussites who thought that being the normal man really meant going about naked like Adam and Eve in paradise.[38] In our own time one not infrequently encounters people offering the same teaching in spiritual respects, that one becomes the normal man by becoming stark naked, which one can do by divesting oneself of all one's concretion. But that is not how things are. The universal man emerged in the act of despair and is then behind the concretion and breaks out through it. A language has many more paradigm verbs than the ones used as examples in grammars. It is a matter of accident that any particular one is offered; any other regular verb would have done as well. So too with men. Everyone can, if he wants, become a paradigm man, not by wiping out his contingency but by remaining in it and ennobling it. But he ennobles it by choosing it.

You will now have perceived that in the course of his life the ethical individual goes through the stages we have previously shown to be distinct. In the course of his life he will develop the personal, the civic, the religious virtues, and his life proceeds through his constantly translating himself from one stage to the next. Whenever a person thinks that one of these stages is sufficient and is prepared to gather himself one-sidedly in that, he has not chosen himself ethically but has overlooked the importance either of isolation or of continuity, and above all has not grasped that the truth lies in the identity of these.

The person who has chosen and found himself ethically has himself as specified in all his concretion. He has himself, then, as an individual who has these abilities, these passions, these inclinations, these habits subject to these external influences, and who is influenced thus in one direction and thus in another. He has himself, then, as a task in a way in which the task in essentials is that of ordering, tempering, kindling, repressing – in short bringing about a proportionality in the soul, a harmony that is the fruit of the personal virtues. The aim of his activity here is himself, though not arbitrarily specified, for he has himself as a task which is set for him even though it has become his through his having chosen it. But although he himself is his aim, this aim is nevertheless at the same time something else, for the self that is the aim is not an abstract self which fits in everywhere, and so nowhere, but a concrete self which stands in living interaction with these determinate surroundings, these conditions of life, this order of things. The self which is the aim is not just a personal self, but a social, a civic self. So he has himself as a task for an activity through which, as this determinate personal being, he intervenes in the affairs of life. Here his task is not to mould himself, but to exert an influence, and yet he does at the same time mould himself, for, as I remarked above, the way in which the ethical individual lives is by constantly translating himself from one stage to another. Unless the individual has originally apprehended himself as a concrete personality in continuity, he will not acquire this later continuity either. If he thinks the knack is to begin as a Robinson Crusoe, he will remain an adventurer all his life. But if, on the other hand, he sees that unless he begins concretely he will never get round to beginning, and that if he doesn't begin he will never end, he will be in continuity simultaneously with the past and the future. From the personal life he translates himself into the civic, from the latter into the personal. The personal life as such was an isolation and therefore incomplete, but by his coming back to his personal being through the civic life the personal life is manifested in a higher form. Personal being proves to be the absolute that has its teleology in itself. Those who take the task of human life to be the fulfilment of duty have often been reminded of the sceptical view that duty itself vacillates, that the laws can be changed. You see readily that with the latter one is thinking mainly of the fluctuations to which the civic virtues are always liable. Still, this scepticism does not apply to negative morals, for they remain unchanged. On the other hand there is another sceptical consideration that applies to every duty, namely that I am quite unable in principle to do my duty. Duty is the universal, what is required of me is the universal, but all I can do is the particular. The great significance of this sceptical argument, however, is that it proves that one's personal being is itself the absolute. But this must be specified in rather more detail. It is interesting that this consideration is highlighted in language itself. I never say to someone that he does duty or duties; I say that he does *his* duty, I say that I do *my* duty, that you are to do *yours*. This shows that the individual is at once the universal and the particular. Duty is the universal, it is required of me; consequently if I am not the universal I cannot do it. On the other hand, my duty is the particular, something for myself alone, and yet it is duty and hence the universal. This is where personal being is manifested in its highest validity. It is not lawless, nor does it give itself its laws, for the category of duty remains, but personal being proves to be the unity of the universal and the particular. That this is the situation is clear, it can be made intelligible to a child, for I can perform duties without doing *my* duty, and I can do *my* duty without performing duties. I am quite unable to see why the world should sink into scepticism on that account, for the difference between good and evil always remains, responsibility and duty likewise; even though it is impossible for another man to say what *my* duty is, it will always be possible for him to say what *his* duty is, and that would not be the case unless the unity of the universal and the particular were posited. It might perhaps be thought that all scepticism has been removed by making duty into something external, fixed and definite, of which it can be said: 'This is duty.' However, this is a misunderstanding, for it is in the external that the doubt lies, not in the internal, not in my relation to the universal. As a particular individual I am not the universal, and it would be absurd to require it of me. So if I am to be able to perform the universal, I must be the universal at the same time as I am the particular, but in that case the dialectic of duty is within me. As I have said, this view implies no danger for the ethical; on the contrary, it emphasizes it. If this is not assumed, the personality will be abstract, its relation to duty abstract, its immortality abstract. Nor does it abolish the difference between good and evil, for I doubt if there has ever been anyone who maintained it is a duty to do evil. That he did evil is another matter, but he tried at the same time to convince himself and others that it was the good. It is inconceivable that he should be able to retain this conviction, since he is himself the universal and so does not have the enemy outside him but inside him. If, on the other hand, I suppose duty to be something external, then the difference between good and evil is indeed abolished, for if I am not myself the universal I can only come into an abstract relationship to it and the difference between good and evil is incommensurate with an abstract relation.

Precisely when one's personal being is perceived to be absolute, to be its own aim, the unity of the universal and the particular, precisely then will every scepticism which takes the historical as its point of departure be overcome. Freethinkers have often tried to introduce conceptual confusion by drawing attention to how people have sometimes held sacred and legal what in the eyes of others was repellent and criminal. Here one has allowed oneself to be dazzled by the external, while in the case of the ethical it is never a question of the external but of the internal. However much the external may change, the ethical content of the action can still be the same. Thus it is certain there have never been people who thought that children should hate their parents. However, to foster doubt, attention has been directed at the fact that, while all cultivated nations have made it a duty for children to care for their parents, it has been the custom among primitives to put their aged parents to death. Perhaps so, but it takes us no further, for the question remains whether in doing this the primitives actually thought they were doing something evil. Ethical consideration lies always in this consciousness, while whether one is accountable for lack of knowledge is another question. The freethinker sees very well that the easiest way to volatilize the ethical is to open the door to historical infinity. And yet there is some truth in his procedure, for if in the final analysis the individual is not the absolute, empirical reality is the only road open to him, and as for where it issues that road has the same property as the river Niger in respect of its source: no one knows its location. If I am shown the road to the finite, it is gratuitous to remain stationary at any particular point. On that road, then, one never arrives at the point of beginning, for in order to begin one would have to have reached the end and that is impossible. When personal being is the absolute it is itself the Archimedean point from which one can lift the world. It is easy to see that being conscious of this cannot lead the individual into wanting to cast off reality, for if that was how he wanted to be the absolute he would be nothing at all, an abstraction. It is only as the particular that he is the absolute, and his awareness of that will save him from all revolutionary radicalism.

Here I will break off my theorizing; I feel keenly that I am not fit for the part, nor wish that I were, but will be quite content if I may be thought an acceptable practitioner. Besides, all theorizing takes so much time. What I can accomplish in an instant as an active agent, or set about straightaway, calls for much fuss and ado before it can be put into words and described. Now I have no mind to expound a doctrine of duty to you and to talk in the customary way of duties to God, oneself and one's neighbour. Not that I by any means repudiate this classification, nor would I have it that what I have to say is too profound to be linked with Balle's textbook,[39] or presupposes more background knowledge than that textbook presupposes; not at all for that reason, but because I believe that what matters with the ethical is not the multiplicity of duty but its intensity. When one has felt in one's personal being the full strength of duty's intensity, one is ethically mature and duty will then break out in one. The main thing, then, is not whether someone can count on his fingers how many duties he has, but that he has had that once-and-for-all experience of the intensity of duty so that his consciousness of it is his assurance of the eternal validity of his being. So I do not at all applaud a strong sense of duty, any more than I would recommend being a bookworm, and yet it is certain that someone to whom the importance of duty has never, in all its infinity, come to light is just as mediocre as the scientist who thinks, after the manner of the people of Mol,[40] that one hits upon wisdom *mir nichts und dir nichts*.[41] Let the casuists be engrossed in hitting upon the multiplicity of duty; the main thing, the only saving thing, is that always, in relation to his own life, a man is not his uncle but his father.

Let me illustrate what I mean through an example. For this I take an impression I have retained from my earliest childhood. When I was five years of age I was placed in a school. That such an event always makes an impression on a child is natural, but the question is what impression. Childish curiosity is absorbed by its various confused conceptions of what this event can really mean. Quite reasonably, that was also the case with me; however, the main impression I received was a quite different one. I made my appearance at school, was presented to the teacher, and was then given as homework for the following day the first ten lines of Balle's textbook, which I was to learn by heart. All other impressions were now wiped from my soul, the only thing that stood out vividly before it was my assignment. As a child I had a very good memory. I soon learned the lines. My sister had heard me several times and assured me that I knew them. I went to bed and before falling asleep tested myself once more. I fell asleep with the firm intention of reading them over again next morning. I awoke at five o'clock, I put on my clothes, got hold of my textbook and read again. Everything still stands before me in that moment so vividly, as though it were yesterday. For me it was as though heaven and earth would collapse if I were not to learn my lines, and on the other hand it seemed as though even if heaven and earth did collapse, that would in no way exempt me from my assignment once I had it, to learn my lines. At that age I had very little idea of my duties; after all, I still had not learned them from Balle's textbook. I had just one duty, to learn my homework, and nevertheless from this impression I can derive the whole of my ethical view of life. I may smile at a small urchin of five like that tackling something with that passion, and yet I assure you, I have no higher wish than that, at any time of life, I may take on my work with the same energy, the same ethical seriousness, as then. It is true that later in life one gets a better idea of what one's work is, but the main thing is still the energy. That this event made such an impression on me I owe to my father's serious-mindedness, and if I owed him nothing else, this would be enough to put me eternally in his debt. In education what matters is not that the child learns this or that, but that the spirit is matured, that energy is aroused. You often talk of how splendid a thing it is to have a good mind. Who will deny the importance of that? And yet, I almost think one makes that for oneself if one wants. Give a man energy, passion, and he has everything. Take a young girl, let her be silly, hysterical, a real chatterbox, imagine her falling deeply and sincerely in love and you will see that the good mind comes of itself, you will see how shrewd and cunning she becomes in finding out if her love is requited; let her be happy in love and you will see ardour bloom on her lips; let her be unhappy and you will hear the cool reflections of wit and understanding. [. . .]

So what matters is the energy with which I become ethically conscious, or rather, without energy I cannot become ethically conscious. I can therefore never be ethically conscious without becoming conscious of my eternal being. That is the true proof of the immortality of the soul. Of course, it is only a fully-fledged proof when the task is congruent with the commitment, but that to which I am eternally committed is an eternal task. The circumstance that the first ten lines of Balle's textbook were given me as an assignment from which nothing else in the world could ransom me was then, in a sense, the first proof produced for me of the immortality of my soul. The incompleteness of the proof lay not in my energy but in the accidental nature of the task.

So I have no intention of initiating you into a consideration of the multiplicity of duties; if I were to express duty negatively that would be easily done; if I were to express it positively it would be very difficult and tedious, indeed beyond a certain point impossible. What has been my intention, on the other hand, and what I have tried to the best of my ability to do, is to illuminate the absolute importance of duty, the eternal validity of the relationship of duty for personal being. For as soon as one's personal being finds itself in despair, chooses itself absolutely, repents itself, one has oneself as one's task under an eternal responsibility, and thus duty is posited in its absoluteness. Since, however, one's personal being has not created itself but chosen itself, duty is the expression of the identity of its absolute dependency and absolute freedom. One will teach oneself the particular duty and seek enlightenment on it from any other man in vain, and yet here too he will be autodidact by virtue of being theodidact,[42] and vice versa. In any case, duty for him will not be something abstract, partly because it is not something outside him, for in that case it is always abstract, partly because he is himself concrete, for in choosing himself ethically he chose himself in all his concretion and renounced the abstraction of the arbitrary.

It remains to show what life looks like when regarded ethically. You and all aestheticists are quite prepared to go shares, you admit the ethical has its importance, you say it is respectable for a man to live for his duties, that it is commendable, indeed you even let fall some innuendos about its being right and proper that there are people who live for their duties, that it is as well the majority do that, and you sometimes run across men of duty good-natured enough to find sense in this talk, in spite of the fact, of course, that like all scepticism it is nonsense. You yourselves, on the other hand, have no wish to embark upon the ethical; that would deprive life of its meaning and above all of its beauty. The ethical is something quite different from the aesthetic, and once it emerges it altogether destroys the latter. – Now, if that were so I would still be in no doubt which to choose. In despair it appears to be like that for an instant, and the despair of someone who has not so felt it has been fraudulent all along and he has not chosen himself ethically. But that is not how it is, and therefore, in the next instant, despair proves not to be a breach but a metamorphosis. Everything returns, but transfigured. So only when life is regarded ethically does it acquire beauty, truth, meaning, substance; only when one lives ethically does one's own life acquire beauty, truth, meaning, security; and only in the ethical view of life can self-directed or other-directed doubts about the meaning of a life be put to rest. Doubts of either kind can only be appeased by one and the same thing, since essentially they are the same doubt. For autopathic doubt is not a manifestation of egoism but a requirement of the self-love that has the interest of its own self at heart in just the same way as it has that of any other. This, I think, is of great importance. If it were not the case that an aestheticist is an egoist, and all conceivable favours were to fall to his lot, he would have to say, 'What my happiness is due to is something another person can't be given in the same way, and something no other person can acquire on his own account.' He would have to be anxious, indeed, in case someone asked him what it was he sought happiness in, since he would in fact have achieved it in order that everyone else should feel that they could not. If such a person had any sympathy he would spare himself no rest until he had found for his life some higher point of departure. Having found it, he would not be afraid to speak of his good fortune, for then if he were to give proper voice to it, he would say something that reconciled him absolutely with every human being, with the whole of humankind.

Let us nevertheless stay a moment with the category which

aesthetics always champion – beauty. Life, you say, loses its beauty once the ethical comes into its own. 'Instead of the joy, happiness, unconcern, beauty that life has when we regard it aesthetically, we get conscientious effectiveness, commendable industry, tireless and unremitting zeal.' If you were here with me now, I would ask you for a definition of the beautiful so as to get started. Seeing you are not, I will permit myself to draw on a definition that you are in the habit of giving: 'The beautiful is that which has its teleology within itself.' You take a young girl, you say, 'She is beautiful, she is joyful, carefree, happy, in perfect harmony, complete in herself, and it is foolish to ask why she exists, for she has her teleology within her.' I won't quibble by objecting that it might not really be to the girl's advantage to have her teleology within her, all alone in this way, or that, if granted the opportunity to expound your view of the divinity of her existence, you might well flatter yourself that she would eventually fail to appreciate the fact and believe she only existed to listen to your ingratiations. You look upon nature and find it equally beautiful, and are ready to anathematize every finite view of it. Neither shall I vex you here with the observation that it might be an essential property of nature to be for-another. You look upon the works of art and poetry and cry out with the poet: 'Procul o, procul este, profani',[43] and understand by profani those who would degrade poetry and art by giving them a teleology that lies outside them. As far as art and poetry are concerned I will remind you of what I have remarked previously, that they give only an imperfect reconciliation with life, and also that when you fix your gaze on poetry and art it is not reality you are looking upon, and that is what we should really be talking about. We return again to that, then, and since you yourself presumably perceive that were you to apply the requirements of art in all their strictness, you would most likely find precious little beauty in life; you are giving the beautiful another meaning. The beautiful you talk of is the individually beautiful. You see each single individual as a little element in the whole, see him precisely in his particularity, and in this way even the accidental, the insignificant, acquires significance and life itself the imprint of beauty. So you look on each person as an element. But the beautiful was supposed to be that which had its teleology in itself, yet when a man is just an element his teleology is indeed not inside but outside him. So even if the whole is beautiful, the parts in themselves are not. [. . .]

When you define the beautiful as that which has its teleology within it and then offer as examples a young girl, or nature, or a work of art, I feel forced to conclude that all this talk of their having their teleology within them is an illusion. To talk of teleology at all there must be a movement, for whenever I think of a goal I think of a movement, and even if I think of someone who has reached the goal I still always think of a movement, for I think of his having got there through a movement. What you call beautiful manifestly lacks movement, for the beautiful in nature exists all at once, and when I look at a work of art and penetrate its thought with mine, really the movement occurs in me, not in the work of art. So you may well be right in saying that beauty has its teleology within it, but in the way you grasp this and apply it, it is really only a negative expression indicating that the beautiful does not have its teleology in something else. Therefore you will not be able, either, to use an apparently synonymous expression, that the beautiful you talk about has an inner teleology or an immanent teleology. For as soon as you use it you require movement, history, and you have thereby gone beyond the spheres of nature and art and are in that of freedom, and so of ethics.

If I say now that the individual has his teleology within him, this cannot be misunderstood as implying that I take the individual to be the central thing, or that the individual in an abstract sense is sufficient unto himself, for after all if he is grasped abstractly I get no movement. The individual has his teleology within him, has an inner teleology, is himself his own teleology, and his self, then, is the goal for which he strives. This self of his is not, however, an abstraction, but absolutely concrete. In the movement towards himself he cannot relate himself negatively to the world around him, for his self would then be an abstraction and remain such. He must open his self in respect of his whole concretion, but to that concretion also belong those factors specifically to do with taking an active part in the world. So his movement will be from himself, through the world, to himself. Also, the movement here is a real movement, for this movement is the work of freedom but at the same time immanent teleology, and it is here, therefore, that there can first be any question of beauty. In that case, the individual comes in a sense to stand higher than any relationship, but it does not at all follow that he is not in this relationship; nor can anything tyrannical be discerned in this, since after all the same applies to every individual. I am a married man and you know I have the deepest respect for this relationship, and I know that with all love I humble myself before it; yet I know that in another sense I am higher than this relationship but I also know that exactly the same applies to my wife. [. . .]

Therefore only when I look upon life ethically do I see it with regard to its beauty, only when I look upon my own life ethically do I see it with regard to its beauty. And if you say that this beauty is invisible, I reply, 'In a sense it is, in another sense it is not since it can be seen in the trace of the historical, seen as when it is said, *Loquere ut videam te.*'[44] True enough; what I see is not the consummation but the struggle, but I do see the struggle all the same, whenever I want to if I have the courage, and without courage I see nothing eternal at all, and consequently nothing beautiful either.

When I look upon life ethically I look at it in respect of its beauty. To me life then becomes rich in beauty, not poor, as it really does for you. I do not have to travel all over the country to discover beauties, or scrape around for them on the streets, I do not have to size up and reject. Well, that is natural, I do not have as much time as you either, for when I have a regard – with pleasure though also with seriousness – for the beauty in my own life, there is always enough for me to do. If occasionally I have an hour free I stand at my window and look at people, and I have a regard for the beauty of each one. However insignificant and humble he may be I see him with a view to his beauty, for I see him as this individual person who is at the same time the universal man; I see him as the one with that concrete task in life; he is not there for the sake of any other person, even if he were the humblest hired waiter; he has his teleology within him, he realizes that task – he triumphs, that's what I see; for the man of courage does not see ghosts, on the contrary he sees conquering heroes; while the coward does not see heroes but only ghosts. He is bound to conquer, of that I am certain, therefore his struggle is beautiful. I am not as a rule much disposed to struggle, not least with others than myself. But you may be sure that for this faith in the victory of the beautiful I will engage in mortal combat, and nothing in the world can wrest it from me. Even if one wished to wrest it from me through prayer, to snatch it from me by force, not for anything in the world would I let myself be deprived of it, for if I lost that faith I would lose the whole world. Through this faith I see the beauty of life, and the beauty I see does not have the sadness and melancholy that are inseparable from all beauty in nature and art, inseparable even from the eternal youth of the Greek gods. The beauty I see is joyful and triumphant, and stronger than all the world. And this beauty I see everywhere, even where your eye sees nothing. [. . .]

Let us now come a little closer to some real-life situations, especially of the kind where the aesthetic and the ethical come into contact with each other, so as to consider how far the ethical view deprives us of any beauty or see if it does not rather bestow on everything a higher beauty. I am thinking of some definite individual, in a sense like anyone else, but in another sense concrete in himself. Let us be quite prosaic. This person has to live, clothe himself, in short has to be able to exist. Suppose he turned to an aesthete to find out how to manage his life. Then information will at least not be something he goes short of. The latter might say to him, 'When one is single one needs three thousand dollars a year to live comfortably, if one has four thousand so much the better; if one wants to get married one needs at least six thousand. Money, after all, is and remains the motivation for doing things, the true that-without-which [. . .] It is the absolute condition of life. As soon as one has no money one is and remains excluded from the numbers of the patricians, one is and remains a plebeian.' [. . .]

If he were to say to the aesthete, 'That's all very well, but I have neither three thousand nor six thousand a year, I have nothing, either in capital or in interest, I have absolutely nothing at all, hardly a hat', the latter would shrug his shoulders and say, 'Well, that's another matter, then there's nothing for it but to put up with the workhouse.' Were he extremely good-natured the aesthete might perhaps beckon again to the poor devil and say to him, 'I wouldn't have you driven to despair without my hazarding the most extreme measures; there are a few makeshifts one shouldn't leave untried before bidding farewell to joy for ever and signing the pledge and putting on the straitjacket. Marry a rich girl, play the lottery, travel to the colonies, spend some years scraping together some money, curry favour with an old bachelor so that he makes you his heir. For the moment our ways separate, get the money and you will always find in me a friend who knows how to forget there was a time when you had none.' But there is something dreadfully heartless after all in such a view of life – murdering in cold blood all joy in life for everyone who has no money. And that is what a moneyed person of this kind does, for at least it is his opinion that there is no joy in life without money. [. . .]

[But] let us now hear how an ethicist would reply to him. His answer would be as follows: 'It is every man's duty to work in order to live.' Had he nothing more to say, you would presumably reply, 'Here we have the same old talk again of duty and duty, everywhere duty; anything more tedious than this astringent which dispirits and amputates everything is unimaginable.' Please recall that our hero had no money [. . .] and unless he wanted simply to think of what he would have done if he did have some, he would have had to be prepared for some other expedient. Note, too, that the ethicist addressed him with all politeness, he did not treat him as an exception, he did not say: 'Good Lord! How unfortunate, you must try to put up with it.' On the contrary, he made the aesthete an exception, for he said, 'It is every man's duty to work in order to live.' In so far, then, as a man need not do so, he is an exception, but [. . .] there is nothing great, only inferior, in being an exception. Therefore if someone wants to look at the matter ethically he will see that having money is a humiliation, for every special favour is a humiliation. [. . .] One could wish that in this respect people had rather more courage, and the reason why one often hears so much of this contemptible clamour about money being the main thing is partly that those who have to work lack the ethical energy to acknowledge the significance of working and have no ethical conviction of its significance. Marriage is not harmed by seducers but by cowardly husbands. So too here. That contemptible talk does no harm, but the good cause is harmed by those who, being compelled to work in order to live, at one moment want their life to be recognized as deserving compared with that of idlers, the next complain and sigh and say, 'The finest thing, after all, is to be independent.' [. . .]

The question whether one might not imagine a world in which it was not necessary to work in order to live is really an idle one, since it concerns not given reality but a fiction. Asking it, however, is always an attempt to belittle the ethical view. For if it were a perfection on the part of existence that work was unnecessary, the most perfect life would be that of someone who did not have to work. It could then only be by attaching to the word 'duty' the sense of a lamentable necessity that one could say it was a duty to work. Duty would then express not the universally human but what is general, and here duty would not express perfection. Therefore I would reply quite properly that it would have to be considered an imperfection on the part of existence that man had no need to work. The lower the level of human life, the less the necessity of work is apparent; the higher, the more obvious it becomes. The duty of working in order to live expresses the universally human, and expresses the universal in another way too because it expresses freedom. It is precisely through work that man makes himself free, through work he becomes master of nature, through work he shows he is higher than nature. [. . .] [What] struggle could be more formative than that of making ends meet! [. . .] I shall not insist so adamantly on my rights as to challenge you to make clear just where in your aesthetics you deal with this matter; I merely leave it to you to consider whether in this struggle life loses its beauty if one does not will it so, or whether it does not gain a higher beauty. To deny that such a struggle exists is madness; to forget it because it passes you by is thoughtlessness, and inasmuch as one pretends to a view of life, callousness or cowardice. [. . .]

So the ethical view that it is every man's duty to work in order to live has two advantages over the aesthetic view. In the first place, it accords with reality and explains something universal in the latter, while the aesthetic proposes something accidental and explains nothing. Second, it construes man in the light of his perfection, sees him in view of his true beauty. This must be regarded as being all that is necessary and more than sufficient on this subject. [. . .]

[But] perhaps [our hero] cannot yet make up his mind to have recourse to the ethicist. He ventures one more attempt. He meets a man who says, 'One must work in order to live, that's just the way life is.' Here it looks as if he had found what he was looking for, since that is just what he thinks too. So this is talk he will listen to: 'One has to work in order to live, that's just the way life is, it is the threadbare side of existence. One sleeps seven hours a day, that's time wasted but it can't be helped. Five hours' work a day gets you your livelihood and once you have that you start living. So one's work had better be as dull and meaningless as possible, as long as one gets a living from it. If one has some special talent one must never commit the sin against it of making it one's means of livelihood. No, one coddles one's talent, it's something one has for one's own sake, and one has greater joy of it than a mother has of her child. One cultivates it, develops it, in the twelve hours of the day, sleeps for seven, is a non-human for five, and so life becomes pretty bearable after all – yes, even quite nice, since the five hours' work don't matter so much, seeing that when one's thoughts are never on the work one is gathering strength for the pursuit in which one's pleasure lies.'

Our hero is again no nearer his goal. In the first place he has no talent with which to fill up the twelve hours at home; second, he already has a more attractive view of what it is to work which he will not give up. So probably he will resolve once more to seek help from the ethicist. The ethicist speaks briefly: 'It is every man's duty to work in order to live.' More he cannot say, for the ethical as such is always abstract and there is no such thing as an abstract vocation for all men; on the contrary, he assumes every person has a special vocation. [. . .] The life-views of the aesthete are always based on difference: some men have talent, others not, yet what distinguishes them is a more-or-less, a quantitative specification. In a way it is arbitrary on the aesthete's part to stop at any particular point, and yet it is precisely in this arbitrariness one finds the nerve of [this] life-view. It therefore divides existence against itself in a way [the aesthetes] find themselves unable to resolve, and in return they seek irresponsibly and callously to arm themselves against it. The ethicist, on the other hand, reconciles man with life, for he says, 'Everyone has a vocation.' He does not do away with differ-ences but says, 'Behind all differences there remains the universal, and it is a vocation. The most eminent talent is a vocation, and the individual who possesses it cannot lose sight of reality, he doesn't stand outside the universally human for his talent is a vocation. The least significant individual has a vocation, he won't be cast out, or sent to live next to the beasts, he doesn't stand outside the universally human, he has a vocation.'

So the ethical proposition that everyone has a vocation implies a rational order of things in which every person, if he wants, fills his place in such a way that he expresses the universally human and the individual simultaneously. Does existence become the less beautiful for this view? One has no aristocracy to rejoice in, whose significance is based on accident and based on that accidentally; no, one has a kingdom of gods. [. . .]

Our hero, then, has got what he was looking for: a work by which to live. At the same time he has got a more significant expression of its relation to his personality: his work is his vocation, consequently accomplishing it is bound up with a satisfaction of his whole personal being. At the same time he has got a more significant expression of the relation of his work to others, for since his work is his vocation he is put essentially on the same footing with all other men, so that in carrying on his work he is doing essentially the same as all others. [. . .]

So the ethical view that everyone has a vocation has two advantages over the aesthetic theory of talent. In the first place what it makes transparent is not something accidental in existence but the universal; second, it displays the universal in its true beauty. Talent is beautiful only when it becomes transparent in a vocation, and existence is beautiful only when everyone has a vocation. That being so, I will beg you not to sneeze at a simple empirical observation which so far as our main topic is concerned you will have the goodness to regard as gratuitous. If a person has a vocation he generally has a standard outside him which, without making him a slave, nevertheless prescribes to some extent what he is to do, apportions his time for him, gives him frequently the opportunity to begin. If for once he should not succeed in his job, he hopes to do it better next time, and this next time is not too far distant. On the other hand, someone who does not have a vocation, if he sets himself a task at all, will usually have to work without a break. He gets no respite that is not also an interruption brought about in himself. If he fails, everything fails, and because the occasion to do so is not there he has extreme difficulty getting going again. So he is easily tempted to become a pedant, unless he becomes a loafer. It is such common practice to denounce people who perform definite functions as pedants. As a rule such a person simply cannot become a pedant. On the other hand, there is a temptation for someone without any definite function to become one in order to put up at least some resistance to that all too great freedom in which he can so easily lose his way. One may therefore be generally inclined to forgive him his pedantry, for it is a sign of something good. On the other hand, it has still to be considered a punishment, because he has wanted to emancipate himself from the common practice. [. . .]

[The ethicist] says, 'What every man does and can accomplish is to do *his* job in life. For if it were the case that there were some people who accomplished something and others who didn't, and the reason for this lay in their contingent abilities, then scepticism would again have the upper hand.' One can therefore say, 'Essentially everyone accomplishes as much as anyone else.' I am by no means preaching indolence, but on the other hand one must be careful how one uses the word 'accomplish'; it has always been a butt of your ridicule. Which is why, as you once put it, you have 'studied integral, differential and infinitesimal calculus in order to reckon what part of the whole was accomplished by a junior Admiralty clerk, reckoned by the whole office a competent worker'. Use your ridicule only upon those who would affect importance in life; never misuse it to confuse people.

The word 'accomplish' indicates a relation between my action and something else outside me. Now it is easy to see that I have no authority over this relation and, to that extent, one can say of the most talented person that he accomplishes nothing, just as one can of the least able. There is no implicit distrust of life in this, on the contrary there is an implicit recognition of my own insignificance and a respect for the significance of every other person. He who has the greatest talent can complete his job, and so also can the least able. Neither can do more. Whether they are to accomplish anything is not in their power, whereas it is indeed in their power to prevent themselves from doing so. I therefore disclaim all that self-importance that calls so much attention to itself in life; I do my job and do not waste my time calculating whether I accomplish anything. So what I accomplish as a result of my work is my good fortune, in which I might well dare to rejoice but which I do not impute altogether to myself. A growing beech forms its crown of leaves and men enjoy sitting in its shade. Were it to become impatient, if it were to say, 'Here where I stand there hardly ever comes a living being, so what good is it that I grow, that I spread out my branches, what do I accomplish by that?', it might merely delay its own growth and perhaps one day there might come a wayfarer who said, 'If, instead of being stunted, this tree had been a leafy beech I could have been resting now in its shade.' Think if the tree had been able to hear! [. . .]

So our hero works for his living; this work is also his pleasure; he follows his vocation, he does his job; in one word, and it is a word that seizes you with dread – he has a living [. . .] What then? You smile, you think I have something up my sleeve. You shudder already at the thought of my unimaginative common sense, for 'now it's going to end up for sure in nothing less than getting him married, yes, please, go ahead, publish the banns for him, I shall have no objection to raise against his and your divine intention. What an incredible rational consistency there is in life [. . .]; with a living comes a wife.' [. . .] [But] you can still hold out hope for a while, just as long as I must remain anxious. Since our hero is no different from anyone else he has some inclination towards the uncommon; he is also a little ungrateful. So before taking refuge with the ethicist he wants to try his luck once more with the aesthetes. He also knows how to put a good face on his ingratitude; he says, 'The ethicist really did help me out of my confusion, I am completely satisfied with the way he got me to look at the reality of my life, its seriousness uplifts me. But as far as love is concerned, there I could well wish to enjoy my freedom, simply follow the impulse of my heart; love does not love this seriousness, it demands the levity and charm of the aesthetic.' [. . .]

Although you never replied to my previous letter, verbally or in writing, you no doubt remember its content, and how I tried there to show that marriage was, by virtue of the ethical, precisely the aesthetic expression of love. Presumably, then, you will give me credit for what was expounded there, in the assurance that to the extent I have succeeded in making it intelligible to you, I will be able, if need be, to explain it to our hero. He has resorted to the

aesthetes and he has departed from them none the wiser what he
should do but rather what he should not. For a little while he has
been witness to a seducer's cunning, has listened to his fawning talk,
but has learnt to despise his art, has learnt to see through him, to see
that he is a liar, a liar when he feigns love, when he puts fresh paint
on feelings which perhaps once had some truth in them when he
belonged in them to another, that he deceives doubly, her to whom
he pretends to cherish them and her to whom they rightly belong, a
liar when he pretends to himself that there is something beautiful in
his desire. He has learnt to despise the clever ridicule that would
turn love into a childish prank at which one should only smile. [. . .]
For a while he has let himself be lulled by the distrust of life that
would teach him that everything is transitory, that time changes
everything, that one dare not build on anything and therefore never
form a plan for one's whole life. A latent indolence and cowardice
found this talk quite acceptable, it was a comfortable costume to
assume and in other people's eyes not unbecoming. Nevertheless, he
has looked closely at this talk, he has seen the hypocrite, seen the
pleasure-lover who came in humble dress, the beast of prey that
came in sheep's clothing, and he has learnt to despise this talk. He
has perceived that it was an insult and therefore ungracious to want
to love a person on the basis of what in his own nature was obscure
and not of what was conscious, to want to love in such a way that
he could imagine it possible that this love should cease and then that
he could bring himself to say, 'So there's nothing I can do, a man
has no power over his feelings.' He has perceived that it was an
insult and therefore ungracious to want to love with one part of the
soul but not with all of it, to treat one's own love as one element
and yet take the whole of another's love, to want to be something
of a riddle and a secret. He has perceived that it would be unseemly
if he had a hundred arms so that he could simultaneously embrace
many; he has but one embrace and wants to embrace only one. He
has perceived that it was an insult to want to attach himself to
another person in the way one attaches oneself to finite and accidental things, conditionally, so that if difficulties later arose one
could make a change. He does not believe it possible that a man
who loves can change, except for the better, and if it did happen he
believes in the power of the relationship to make all well again. He

recognizes that what love demands is, like the temple tribute, a holy tax which is paid in its own currency, and that one does not accept all the world's riches as release from the slightest demand if the stamp is false.

Our hero, you see, is on the right path, he has lost his faith in the aesthetes' callous common sense and in their superstitious belief in obscure emotions that are supposed to be too delicate to be expressed as duty. He has gratefully accepted the ethicist's statement that it is every man's duty to marry; he has understood this correctly, not as saying that it is a sin not to marry, unless it is one's own fault, for then he sins against the universally human with which he is also presented as a task, but as saying he who marries realizes the universal. Further the ethicist cannot bring him, for as we have said, the ethical is always abstract and it can only tell him what the universal is. So, in this case, it can by no means tell him whom he should marry, for that would require close familiarity with all his aesthetic characteristics, but the ethicist does not have that, and if he did he would still be careful not to make nonsense of his own theories by making the choice for him. So when he has made his own choice, the ethical will sanction it and elevate his love, and to some extent it will also help him in his choice by saving him from a superstitious belief in the accidental. [. . .]

However, there is still a sharp corner we must turn before we are safely home. For our hero has heard a man, whose judgement and opinion he respects, express the view that since in a marriage one ties oneself to a person for the whole of one's life, one must be careful in one's choice, it must be an uncommon girl whose uncommon qualities are just those needed to give one security for the whole of one's future. Do you not feel inclined to have some hopes for our hero for just a little longer? I at least feel anxious for him.

Let us deal thoroughly with this question. [Suppose] in the solitary stillness of the forest there dwells a nymph, a being, a girl. Very well then, this nymph, girl, this being, abandons her solitude and turns up here in Copenhagen [. . .] and our hero becomes the lucky man upon whom she bestows her love. [. . .] [He] is in a critical position. About the girl there is but one opinion: this is an uncommon girl. I myself, a married man, say with Donna Clara, 'Here rumour has not exaggerated, she is a prodigy of a child, the beautiful Preciosa.'[45] It is so tempting to lose sight of the common and float in fairy-tale waftings. Yet he has perceived what is beautiful in marriage. What, then, does marriage do? Take something from him? Take from her some of her beauty? Abolish one single difference? Not at all. What it does, however, is make all these look accidental so long as marriage is something outside him; it is only when he gives the difference the expression of the universal, it is only then that he is secure in his possession of it. The ethical teaches him that the relationship is the absolute, for the relationship is the universal. It deprives him of the vain joy of being uncommon in order to give him the true joy of being ordinary. It brings him into harmony with all existence, teaches him to rejoice in it, for as an exception, as the uncommon, he is in conflict with it. Since in this case it was what counted as uncommon that gave him his good fortune, he must feel that his existence vexes what is common, provided there was truth in his good fortune; though surely it must truly be a misfortune to be fortunate in a way that, viewed essentially, one's own good fortune differs from that of all others. For what he does then is win the accidental beauty and lose the true beauty. This he will realize and he will return to the ethicist's principle that it is every man's duty to marry, and he will see that it has not just truth on its side but beauty too. Suppose he gets this prodigy of a child. He need fear no misfortune from gazing too long at the difference. Her beauty, her charm, the wealth of her intelligence and the warmth of her feeling will give him genuine joy in his heart; he will count himself lucky, but essentially he will say, 'I am no different from any other married man, for the relationship is the absolute.' Suppose he gets a less gifted girl. He will be happy in his good fortune, for he will say, 'Even if she is far inferior to others, essentially she makes me just as happy, for the relationship is the absolute.' He will not fail to appreciate the importance of the difference, for as he realized there was no abstract vocation but that each person had his own, so he will realize that there is no abstract marriage. Ethics tells him simply that he must marry; it does not tell him with whom. Ethics makes the universal transparent to him in the difference, and he makes the difference transparent in the universal.

So the ethical view of marriage has several advantages over any aesthetic understanding of love. It highlights the universal, not the accidental. It does not show how two altogether particular people in all their uncommonness could become happy, but how every married couple can become happy. It sees the relationship as the absolute and so does not grasp the differences as guarantees but interprets them as tasks. It sees the relationship as the absolute and therefore looks on love with a view to its true beauty, that is, with a view to its freedom; it understands historical beauty.

Our hero lives, then, by his work; his work is at the same time his vocation and therefore he works with pleasure. Its being his vocation puts him in association with other people, and in carrying out his job he accomplishes what he could wish to accomplish in the world. He is married, content in his home, and time passes excellently for him – he cannot comprehend how time could be a burden for anyone, or be an enemy of his happiness; on the contrary, it seems to him that time is a true blessing. In this respect he admits that he owes a tremendous amount to his wife. It is true – I'm afraid I forgot to mention it – there was a misunderstanding with the nymph from the forest, he did not become the lucky one, he had to make do with a girl just like any other, just as he was a person just like any other. However, for all that, he is very happy, yes, he once confided to me that he thought it rather a good thing he didn't get that prodigy, the task would have been too much for him; where everything is so perfect before one starts it is all too easy to cause harm. But now, however, he is full of courage and confidence and hope, his enthusiasm is complete, he says fervently, 'After all, the relationship is the absolute.' He is convinced more firmly than of anything else that the relationship will have the power to develop this ordinary girl into everything that is great and beautiful; his wife is, in all humility, of the same opinion. [. . .]

My hero – or would you deny him the right to the title? do you not think a courage that dares to believe that it can transform an ordinary girl into a prodigy is truly a hero's courage? – my hero thanks his wife especially for the fact that time has acquired such a beautiful meaning for him, and he attributes this in turn to some extent to the marriage, and in that he and I, we two married men, entirely agree. If he had got that nymph from the forest and had not married, he fears their love would have flared up in single beautiful moments which then left vapid intervals between them.

Then maybe they would only have wanted to see each other on properly meaningful occasions: had that failed several times he fears the whole relationship might gradually have dissolved into nothing. The humble marriage, on the other hand, which made it a duty for them to see each other daily, for richer or poorer, had spread an equitableness and evenness over the whole relationship which makes him so very pleased with his marriage. In its lowly incognito the prosaic marriage had concealed a poet who not only transfigured life now and then but was always at hand and thrilled even the poorer hours with his tones. [. . .]

It happens sometimes that I sit down and inwardly collapse. I have taken care of my work, I have no desire for diversion, and something melancholic in my temperament gains the upper hand. I become much older than my actual years, I become a stranger to my domestic life almost; I see quite well how attractive it is, but I look at it with different eyes than usual; to me it is as if I were an old man, my wife a young sister who was happily married and in whose house I was now sitting. In such hours time itself naturally begins to drag. Now, were my wife a man perhaps the same would happen to her, and maybe both of us would come to a standstill. But she is a woman and on good terms with time. Is it a perfection on the part of woman, this secret rapport with time? Is it an imperfection? Is it because she is a more earthly being than man? Or more because she has eternity within her? You answer, for you have a philosophical mind. When I sit thus abandoned and lost, I look at my wife walk about in the room with light and youthful tread, always occupied, always with something to attend to, involuntarily my eyes follow her every movement and I join in everything she does, and it ends with my finding myself once more in time, with time acquiring meaning for me, the moment again moving swiftly. [. . .] Yes, my good wise man, it is incredible what a natural virtuoso a woman is, she clarifies in the most interesting and beautiful way [this] problem [of time] that has cost many a philosopher his reason. A problem for which in many philosophers, for all their prolixity, one searches for enlightenment in vain, she clarifies without further ado at any time of the day. She clarifies it as she clarifies many others, in a way that arouses the deepest admiration. Though not a husband of any long standing, I believe I could write a whole book on this topic. However, I won't do that, but will recount a story to you which says a great deal to me.

Somewhere in Holland there lived a scholar. He was an orientalist and married. One afternoon he fails to appear at mealtime in spite of being called. His wife waits expectantly with the food, she knows he is at home, and the longer this continues the less she can explain his absence. Finally she decides to go along to him herself and urge him to come. There he is, sitting alone in his study, nobody with him. He is absorbed in his oriental studies. I can picture it. She has bent down over him, put her arm round him, looked down at his book, then looking up at him, said, 'Dear friend, why don't you come along and eat?' The scholar perhaps hardly had time to heed her words, but on seeing his wife he presumably replied, 'Well, my girl, there can be no question of dinner, here is a diacritic I have never come across before – I have often seen the passage quoted but never in this way, and yet my edition is an excellent Dutch edition. Look at this dot here, it's enough to drive one mad.' I can imagine his wife looked at him half smiling, half deprecating, at such a little dot disturbing the domestic order, and the tale recounts that she replied, 'Is that anything to make such a fuss of? It isn't worth wasting one's breath on.' No sooner said than done. She blows, and behold, the diacritic vanishes, for this remarkable dot was a grain of snuff. The scholar hastens happily to the dinner-table, happy that the vowel point had disappeared, even happier in his wife.

Need I draw out the moral of this story? Had that scholar not been married he might have gone crazy, and maybe taken several orientalists with him for I have no doubt that he would have raised an outcry in the literature. That, you see, is why I say one should live on good terms with the opposite sex, for, between ourselves, a young girl clarifies everything and gives not a fig for the whole Academic Senate, and if one is on good terms with her, one is happy in her enlightenment, but if not she makes fun of one. But this story also teaches how one can live on good terms with her. Had the scholar not been married, had he been an aestheticist with all the resources at his disposal, he might have been the lucky one to whom that child prodigy wished to belong. He would not have married; their feelings would have been too exclusive for that. He would have built her a palace and spared no refinement to make her life rich in enjoyment, he would have visited her in her castle, for that was how she wished it to be; with erotic coquetry he would have made the journey to her on foot while his valets followed in a carriage, bringing rich and costly gifts. In his oriental studies he would also have stumbled upon that remarkable diacritic. He would have stared at it without being able to explain it. However, the moment had come to visit the beloved. He would have cast aside this care, for how could he fittingly visit one who loved him with thoughts of anything but her charm and his own love? He would have made himself all amiability, he would have been more fascinating than ever, pleased her beyond measure, because his voice bore the faint echo of many passions, and he had to make gaiety the victor over his despondency. But when at dawn he left her, when he had thrown her the last kiss and sat now in his carriage, his brow was darkened. He came home. The shutters in his study were closed, the lamps lit, he declined to be disrobed but sat on and stared at that dot that he could not explain. Indeed, he had a girl whom he loved, yes, maybe worshipped, whom he could visit when his soul was rich and strong, but not a spouse who came in and called him to dinner, not a wife who could blow the dot away.

Woman has, all in all, an innate talent and a primitive gift for clarifying finiteness, an absolute virtuosity. When man was created he stood there, lord and master of all nature's pomp and splendour, the entire wealth of finiteness awaiting his beck and call, but he did not know what to do with it all. He looked at it, but it was as though everything would vanish at the glance of the spirit, it was as if all would have gone by him were he to take just one single step. Thus he stood, an imposing figure, inwardly thoughtful but comic, for one must indeed smile at this rich man who did not know how to use his wealth, but also tragic because he could not use it. Then woman was created. She was in no embarrassment, she knew straightaway how to tackle the matter, and without fuss or preparation she was ready straightaway to begin. This was the first comfort to be bestowed upon mankind. She drew near to the man, happy as a child, humble as a child, wistful as a child. She wanted only to be his comfort, alleviate his need, a need she did not understand and had no idea she was meeting, the need to make the interval shorter.

And lo and behold, her humble comfort became life's richest joy, her innocent pastimes life's beauty, her childlike play life's deepest meaning. [. . .] Woman clarifies finiteness, man chases after infinity. So it should be, and each has his and her pain; for the woman bears children in pain, but the man conceives ideas in pain, and it is not for woman to feel the anxiety of doubt or the torment of despair. Not that she stands outside the idea, but she has it at second-hand. Yet because woman clarifies finiteness in this way, she is man's deepest life, but a life that must be concealed and clandestine as is always the life of the root. For this reason I hate all that contemptible talk of the emancipation of women. God forbid that it should ever happen. [. . .] But it will not, it must not and cannot. Let evil spirits try it, let stupid people who have no idea what it is to be a man, of what is great or poor in that, no inkling of woman's perfection in her imperfection! Could there really be one single woman simple-minded and vain and pitiable enough to believe that within the category of man she could be more perfect than man, not to perceive that her loss would be irreparable? No base seducer could come up with a more dangerous doctrine for woman, for once he has got her to believe this she is entirely in his power, at the mercy of his caprice, she can be nothing for man but be a prey to his whims, whereas as a woman she can be everything for him. But the poor devils know not what they do, they themselves do not have what it takes to be men, and instead they would corrupt woman and be united with her on condition of remaining what they are, half-men, with woman promoted to the same miserable condition. [. . .]

Let man give up his claim to be lord and master of Nature, let him yield his place to woman; she is its mistress, it understands her and she understands it, it is obedient to her beckoning. That is why she is everything for man, for she bestows finiteness upon him; without her he is an unstable spirit, an unhappy being who cannot find rest and has no place to go. I have often rejoiced to see woman's significance in this light; for me she then becomes a symbol of the congregation in general, and the spirit is greatly embarrassed when it has no congregation in which to dwell, and when it dwells in the congregation it becomes the spirit of the congregation. That is why [. . .] it does not say in the Scriptures that the maiden shall leave the father and mother and cleave unto her husband, as one might expect seeing woman is after all the weaker of the two and seeks protection in the man; no, it says, 'A man shall leave his father and mother and shall cleave unto his wife', for inasmuch as she gives him finiteness she is stronger than he. Therefore nothing can provide as beautiful an image of the congregation as a woman. If one saw it in this way I really believe many a prospect for the beautification of divine worship would open up. Yet what lack of taste it shows in our churches that the congregation, so far as it does not represent itself, is represented by a deacon or a bellringer! It ought always to be represented by a woman. [. . .]

But here I sit and preach, forgetting what I should really be talking about, forgetting that it is to you I should be talking. That's because my new friend [– our hero –] had put you completely out of my mind. With him, you see, I would happily talk about such things – for one thing he is no mocker, and for another he is a married man and only someone with an eye for the beauty of marriage will be able also to see the truth in my remarks.

So I return to our hero. The title is one he certainly deserves, nevertheless from now on I shall not use it but prefer another designation more dear to me, in that with a sincere heart I call him my friend, just as it is my pleasure to call myself his. So life, you see, has provided him with that 'article of luxury known as a friend'. Perhaps you thought I would pass over the subject of friendship and its ethical validity in silence. Or rather, that the topic of friendship is one I would be unable to get round to, seeing it has absolutely no ethical significance and falls entirely within aesthetic categories. Perhaps you are surprised that in discussing it at all I should do so here, for surely friendship is the first dream of youth. [. . .]

You are an observer, and so you will allow the justice of my observation that a familiar character-distinction is marked by whether the period for friendship falls in very early youth or only at a later age. More volatile natures have no difficulty in adjusting to themselves, their selves are currency from the very start and so trade begins at once. For those of a more profound disposition it is harder to find themselves, and so long as they have not done so they cannot wish anyone to offer them a friendship they cannot requite. People of this disposition are partly self-absorbed, partly observers;

however, an observer is no friend. [. . .] To those who seek the relationship of friendship at a very early age it not infrequently happens that, when love begins to assert itself, friendship fades completely. They find that friendship was an imperfect form, break off their earlier relations and focus their whole soul exclusively upon marriage. Others have the opposite experience. Those who have tasted the sweetness of love too early, savoured its joys in the intoxication of youth, perhaps acquired a false view of the opposite sex. Perhaps they became unjust towards the opposite sex. Maybe their frivolity cost them dear, perhaps they believed in feelings on their own part which proved not to be lasting; or believed in the feelings of others which vanished as in a dream. So they gave up love, for them it was both too much and too little, for they had touched upon the dialectic in love without being able to resolve it. So then they chose friendship. Both these configurations must be regarded as abnormal.

My friend is in neither situation. He had made no youthful experiments in friendship before he learnt to know love, but nor had he harmed himself by enjoying the unripe fruit of love too early. [. . .] Precisely because it was in and through his marriage that he learnt to see what is beautiful about having a friend or friends, neither has he for an instant been undecided as to how to regard friendship, or doubted that it loses its significance if not regarded ethically. [. . .]

You treat friendship as you do everything else. Your soul is so little centred in the ethical that from you one can receive opposite accounts of the same thing, and your utterances bear clear witness to the truth of the proposition that sentimentality and callousness are one and the same. Your view of friendship is best compared with a witch's letter and anyone adopting it is bound to become as crazy as one must assume that someone proposing it already is to a degree. When one hears you propounding – should the humour so take you – the divinity of the love of young people, the beauty of the meeting of kindred souls, one almost fears that your sentimentality will cost you your young life. At other times to hear you talk one might almost believe you were an old hand well versed in the hollowness and emptiness of the world. 'A friend,' you say, 'is an enigmatic thing; like fog, he can only be seen at a distance, for it is only when one becomes unhappy that one notices one *has had* a friend.' It is easy to see that you base such a judgement upon friendship on a different requirement from the one you made previously. You spoke earlier of intellectual friendship, of the beauty of a spiritual eroticism, a common passion for ideas; now you are talking of a practical friendship in everyday affairs, of mutual help in the hardships of earthly life. There is some truth in both requirements, but if one cannot find a point of unity for them the best thing is no doubt to conclude in your main result that friendship is nonsense, a conclusion you extract in part from each of your propositions, in part from them both in their mutual opposition.

The absolute condition for friendship is full agreement in lifeview. If one has that, one will not be tempted to base one's friendship on obscure emotions or unaccountable sympathies. Consequently, one will not experience those ridiculous reversals, having a friend one day but not the next. One will not give unexplained sympathy less than its due, for one does not have a friend in the strict sense in everyone with whom one shares a life-view, but neither will sympathy in its mysterious ways by itself be the basis of one's friendships. A true friendship always requires consciousness and that saves it from being infatuation.

The life-view in which one is united must be a positive life-view. As for my friend and I, we do have such a positive view in common. So when we look at each other we do not laugh like those Augurs, we become serious. It was quite proper for the Augurs to laugh since their common life-view was a negative one. That you understand very well, because it is one of your quixotic wishes 'to find a kindred soul with whom you can laugh at it all'; and 'the awful thing, what causes one almost to be worried about life, is that practically no one notices how miserable it is, and of those few who do, it is only a quite rare exception that knows how to hold on to his good humour and laugh at it all'. If your wish isn't satisfied you know how to make the best of that, for 'it is in line with the idea that only one person should laugh; such a one is the true pessimist, there being more of the kind would be proof that the world wasn't completely wretched'. Your thought is now in full swing and knows no limit. You think 'even to laugh is only an imperfect expression of the real ridicule of life. For it to be perfect one ought properly to be serious. The most perfect mockery of life would be if the person who propounded the deepest truth were not a dreamer but a doubter. And that isn't inconceivable, for no one can propound the positive truth as excellently as a doubter, except that he himself doesn't believe in it. If he were a hypocrite the joke would be on him; if he were a doubter who perhaps wanted to believe what he doubted, the mockery would be entirely objective, existence would be mocking itself through him; he would be propounding a doctrine able to explain everything and the whole race could repose in it, but this doctrine could not explain its own founder. Were a person clever enough to conceal the fact of his own madness, he could make the whole world mad.' You see how difficult it is, if this is how you look at life, to find a friend with whom to share a common life-view. Or perhaps you have found such friends in the mysterious society of *Symparanekromenoi* you sometimes speak of? Could it be that you are an association of friends who mutually esteem one another precisely for being clever enough to know how to hide your madness? [. . .]

So friendship requires a positive view of life. But a positive life-view is inconceivable unless it contains an ethical factor. Certainly, in our own time one often meets people who have a system in which there is no room for the ethical. Let them have a system ten times over, they do not have a life-view. In our own time such a phenomenon can be explained very readily, for as it is in so many ways back-to-front, that is what it is in the case of one's being initiated into the great mysteries before being initiated into the lesser ones.[46] So really the ethical factor in the life-view is the starting-point for friendship, and only when one sees friendship thus does it acquire truth and beauty. If one is content with sympathy as something of a mystery, friendship finds its most complete expression in the relation between those lovebirds whose solidarity is so heartfelt that the death of one is also the death of the other. Yet while such a relation is beautiful in nature it is ugly in the world of the spirit. Unity in life-view is what constitutes friendship. If that is present it endures even if the friend dies, for the transfigured friend lives on in the other; if it ceases, the friendship is over even if the friend goes on living.

If one looks at friendship in this way, one looks at it ethically and therefore in the light of its beauty. It thus acquires both beauty and significance. Ought I to cite an authority in my support against you? Very well! How did Aristotle understand friendship? Did he not make it the starting-point of his whole ethical view of life? For with friendship, he says, the concepts of justice are so broadened that friendship and justice come to the same. So he bases the concept of justice on the idea of friendship. Consequently his category is, in a way, more perfect than the modern one which bases right on duty, on the abstract categorical;[47] he bases it on the social. From that one sees that the idea of the State becomes the highest idea, but that again is what makes his category imperfect.

However I shall not presume here to enter into such investigations as the relation between the Aristotelian and the Kantian concepts of the ethical. I cited Aristotle only to remind you that he, too, perceived that friendship contributes to one's winning reality ethically.

The person who looks at friendship ethically sees it as a duty. I might say, therefore, that it is every man's duty to have a friend. But I would rather use another expression which simultaneously conveys the ethical both in friendship and in everything else elaborated in the foregoing and, in addition, brings out sharply the difference between the ethical and the aesthetic: 'It is every man's duty to become revealed.' The Scriptures teach that 'it is appointed unto men once to die, but after this the judgement' when everything shall be revealed.[48] Ethics says it is the meaning of life and reality that man be revealed. So if he is not, the revelation will take the form of punishment. The aesthete, on the other hand, does not wish to give reality meaning, he remains forever concealed because, however often and however much he abandons himself to the world, he never does it totally; there is always something he holds back; if he were to do it totally he would be doing it ethically. But wanting to play hide-and-seek in this way always avenges itself; it does that, of course, through one's becoming a mystery to oneself. Hence all mystics, in not recognizing reality's demand that one be revealed, stumble against difficulties and trials no other knows of. It is as though they discovered quite another world, as though their nature acquired a replica of itself inside. The person who will not fight with reality gets phantoms to contend with.

With that I am through for this occasion. It was never my

intention to propound a theory of duty. What I wanted was to show how, in the mixed regions, far from depriving life of its beauty, the ethical precisely imparts beauty to it. It affords to life peace, assurance and security, for it is constantly crying out to us: *quod petis, hic est.*[49] It saves one from all infatuations that would exhaust the soul and it brings to it health and strength. It teaches us not to overvalue the fortuitous or to idolize good fortune. It teaches one to be happy in good fortune, and this is something the aesthete is incapable of, for good fortune in itself is an infinite relativity. It teaches one to be happy in misfortune.

Just look on what I have written as a trifle, think of it as notes on Balle's textbook; it's of no consequence, yet it has an authority which I hope you will respect. Or do I perhaps seem to have usurped such authority, improperly implicated my official position in this settlement of accounts, behaved as judge and not party? I happily renounce any such claim, I am not even the party opposed to you, for while I readily admit that aesthetics could well give you power of attorney to appear on its behalf, I am far from crediting myself with the qualifications needed to speak on behalf of ethics. I am nothing but a witness, and that is the only sense in which I meant that this letter had some authority; for a person who speaks of what he has experienced always has authority. I am just a witness, and here you have my sworn testimony in legally appropriate form. [. . .]

I perform my services as judge, I am glad to have such a vocation, I believe it is in keeping with my abilities and my whole personal being, I know it makes demands on my powers. I try to mould myself more and more to it, and in doing so I feel that I am developing myself more and more. I love my wife, am happy in my home. [. . .] My work has importance for me, and I think it also has some for others, even though that is something I cannot determine and exactly measure. I feel joy in the fact that the personal life of others has importance for me, and desire and hope that mine also has some for those with whom I am in sympathy in my whole view of life. I love my native country, I cannot imagine thriving properly in any other. I love my mother tongue which liberates my thought, find it an excellent means for expressing what I have to say in the world. Thus my life has importance for me, so much so that I feel joyful and content with it. Meanwhile I live a higher life and when in the respiration of my earthly and domestic existence I occasionally inhale this higher life, I count myself blessed, art and grace come together for me. Thus I love existence because it is beautiful, and hope for one that is more beautiful still.

Here is my testimony. If I were in doubt as to whether to present it, it would be from concern for you, for I fear almost that it will hurt you to hear that life in its simplicity can be so beautiful. However, accept my testimony, let it cause you a little pain, but let it also have a joyful effect on you; it has a property which your life unfortunately lacks – dependability. You can safely build upon it.

Recently I have frequently talked with my wife about you. She is really very fond of you [. . .] and I sympathize with her feelings in this respect, all the more since I believe that part of the reason she is kindly disposed to you is that she sees your weaknesses. She sees clearly that what you lack is some degree of womanliness. You are too proud to be able to give yourself up to anyone. She is not at all attracted by your pride, for she thinks the truly greatest thing is to be able to devote oneself to others. You may not believe it, but I actually plead in your defence against her. She maintains that you reject everyone because of your pride; I try to explain that perhaps it is not quite as she thinks, that you reject people in an infinite sense, that it is the restlessness with which your soul strives for the infinite that makes you unfair to people. That is something she refuses to grasp, and I can well understand that, because when someone is as easily contented as she is – and just how easily contented you can gather from the fact, among other things, that she feels indescribably happy in being tied to me – it is hard not to condemn you. So my marriage, too, has its conflict, and in a way you are to blame for that. We shall get over it and my only hope is that you never become another kind of occasion for marital strife. But you yourself might help to decide the dispute between my wife and me. Do not think I wish to intrude on your secrets, but I have just one question to put to you, which I think you can answer without making too free with yourself. Answer me honestly and without evasion: do you really laugh when you are alone? You know what I mean – I do not mean whether you ever, or even often, happen to laugh when alone, but whether you find this lonely laughter satisfying? If not, I have won the day and I am sure I can convince my wife.

Now whether in fact you do spend your time laughing when alone I do not know; still, it strikes me that it would be rather more than a little strange. Your life may well have evolved in a way that makes you feel a need for solitude, but not, so far as I can judge, a need to laugh. Even the most cursory observation shows that your life is planned to an unusual standard. You seem not at all content to follow the highways but prefer to strike out on your own. One can easily forgive a certain adventurousness in a young man, but it is another matter when this takes the upper hand to such an extent as to make it out to be the normal and the real. One owes it to a person who has gone astray in this way to shout: 'Think of the end!' and to explain that the word 'end' does not mean death, for even that is not a person's hardest task, but life; to explain that the moment comes when the real question is that of beginning to live, and that therefore it is a dangerous thing to be compelled so to split oneself up that it involves the greatest of difficulty to gather oneself together again, yes, that one must do that in such a hurry and haste that one cannot pick it all up, and instead of being a person out of the ordinary one ends up being a defective specimen of humanity.

In the Middle Ages one tackled this matter differently. One broke off life's development abruptly and went into a monastery. What was wrong with that was not going into a monastery but the erroneous conceptions associated with that step. For my part, I can very well reconcile myself to a person's making that decision, indeed I can see something rather attractive in it; but on the other hand I require of him that he can be clear what it means. In the Middle Ages it was thought that in choosing the monastery one was choosing something uncommon and became oneself an uncommon man; from the heights of the monastery one looked down proudly, almost compassionately, upon ordinary people. No wonder people flocked to the monastery when it was possible to be an unusual man at such a reasonable cost! But the gods do not sell the unusual at a bargain price. If those who withdrew from life had been honest and sincere with themselves and others, if they had loved being a human being more than all else, if they had felt with passion all the beauty that lies in that, if their hearts had not been unacquainted with the true, deep feeling for humanity, perhaps they might still have withdrawn into the solitude of the monastery, but they would not have foolishly imagined they had become unusual people except in the sense that they were less perfect than others; they would not have looked down with compassion on the ordinary, but regarded them sympathetically, in wistful joy at having succeeded in perfecting the beautiful and the great in a way that they themselves were not capable of.

In our own time the monastic life has fallen in price; so one rarely sees someone make a clean break with the whole of existence, with all the universally human. On the other hand, if one has some knowledge of people one occasionally finds in a particular individual a heresy which calls the monastic theory vividly to mind. For the record, I will now give you my view of what a man out of the common is. The truly extraordinary man is the truly ordinary man. The more of the universally human an individual is able to realize in his life, the more extraordinary he is. The less of the universal he is able to assume, the less perfect he is. Uncommon he may be, but not in a good sense.

So if a person who wants to realize the task that everyone is assigned – that of expressing the universally human in his individual life – stumbles on difficulties, if it looks as though there is something of the universal that he is unable to assume into his life, what does he do? If the monastery theory haunts his mind, or some aesthetic view quite analogous to it, he will be happy; from the very first moment he feels in all his exclusiveness that he is an exception, an uncommon person, it makes him vain, as childish as if a nightingale which had a red feather in its wing were to rejoice because no other nightingale had the like. If, on the other hand, his soul is ennobled by love of the universal, if he loves man's existence in this world, what then does he do?

He deliberates how far it is true. A man may have himself to blame for this imperfection, or he can have it quite blamelessly, but it can still be true that he cannot realize the universal. If people were in general more energetically self-aware then perhaps many more would arrive at the same conclusion. He will also know how laziness and cowardice can make a person fancy it is true, and make the pain of it into a thing of no consequence by transforming the universal into the particular and preserving an abstract possibility in relation to the universal. For the universal exists nowhere as such, and it is up to me, to the energy of my consciousness, whether I see the universal in the particular or merely the particular.

Perhaps such a deliberation will not strike him as being enough, and he will risk an experiment. He will realize that if the experiment leads him to the same conclusion, the truth will be impressed upon him all the more emphatically, and if he wants to coddle himself perhaps he would do better to desist, since he will come to groan more than ever. He will know that nothing particular is the universal. In order not to delude himself, then, he will transform the particular into the universal, he will see in the particular much more than is contained in it as such; for him it is the universal. He will come to the aid of the particular and give it significance as the universal. Then if he notices that the experiment is failing, he will have arranged everything so that what wounds him is not the particular but the universal. He will watch over himself so that no mix-up occurs, so that it is not the particular that comes to wound him, for its wound will be too light and he will love himself in too serious a way for the most pressing thing to be to receive a light wound; he will love the universal too sincerely to want to replace it with the particular so as to slip away unscathed. He will be on his guard not to smile at the impotent reaction of the particular, he will take care not to look at the matter irresponsibly even though the particular as such tempts him to do so; he will not let himself be distracted by the strange misunderstanding that in him the particular has a greater friend than it has in itself. Having done that, he will go calmly to meet the pain; however much his consciousness is shaken, it does not waver.

Now if it happens that the universal he cannot realize is just the thing he wants, then in a sense, if he is a magnanimous person, that will make him glad. Then he will say: 'I have fought under the most unfavourable conditions possible. I have fought with the particular, I have set my desire on the side of the enemy, and to make it complete I have made the particular into the universal. That all this will make the defeat harder for me is true, but it will also strengthen my consciousness, it will give it energy and clarity.'

Thus he has emancipated himself from the universal on this point.

Not for an instant will he be unclear what such a step means; after all, it was he himself who made the defeat complete and gave it meaning, for he knew where he was vulnerable and how, and he brought the wound upon himself; which the particular in itself could not do. He will then be assured that there is something of the universal that he cannot realize. With this assurance, however, he is not through, because it will engender a deep sorrow in his soul. He will rejoice in the others to whom it was granted to accomplish this thing, he will see perhaps better than they do how beautiful it is, but he himself will sorrow, not in a cowardly and dispirited way, but deeply and frankly, for he will say: 'After all, I love the universal. If it were the happy lot of others to bear witness to the universal by realizing it, very well then, I bear witness to it with my sorrow, and the deeper I sorrow the more significant my witness.' And this sorrow is beautiful, is itself an expression of the universally human, a beating of its heart within him, and will reconcile him with it.

With this assurance that he has won he is still not through, for he will feel that he has laid a great responsibility upon himself. 'At this point,' he says, 'I have put myself outside the universal, I have deprived myself of the guidance, the security and reassurance which the universal gives. I stand alone, without sympathy, for I am an exception.' But he will not become faint-hearted and disconsolate, he will walk his lonely path with poise, for after all he has produced the evidence of the rightness of what he did, he has his pain. He will not be unclear concerning this step, he possesses an explanation which he will be able to proffer at any time; no tumult can confuse it for him, no absence of mind; if he awoke in the middle of the night he would still be able instantly to render himself an account of everything. He will feel that the upbringing that has fallen to his lot is hard, for the universal is a severe master when one has it outside one; it is constantly holding over him the sword of justice, saying, 'Why do you want to be outside?', and even though he says, 'It is not my fault', it still makes him accountable for it and makes its claims on him. He will then return to the same point from time to time, produce the evidence again and again, and then go cheerfully on. He reposes in his hard-earned conviction and will say, 'What in the last resort I rely on is that there exists a righteous rationality and I will place my trust in its compassion, that it is compassionate enough to show justice, for it would not be so dreadful to suffer a punishment I had deserved because I did wrong, but it would be dreadful if I were able to do wrong in such a way that no one punished it, and the dreadful thing would not be that I awoke in my heart's delusion with anguish and terror, but that I could delude my heart in a way that no one could awaken it.'

This whole struggle, however, is a purgatory, of whose horror I can at least form a conception. People should therefore not be so eagerly ambitious to become something out of the common, for being that means something else than a capricious satisfaction of one's arbitrary desire.

The person who, on the other hand, was convinced in pain that he was an uncommon man is reconciled with the universal again through his sorrow at being so; one day he may experience the joy that what caused him pain and made him lowly in his own eyes proves to be an occasion for his being lifted up again and becoming an uncommon man in a nobler sense. What he lost in compass perhaps he gained in inward intensity. For not every person whose life expresses the universal indifferently is for that reason uncommon, for that would be to idolize triviality. For him truthfully to be called uncommon one must first inquire about the intensive power with which he does it. Now, the person we were speaking of will possess that power at the points where he can realize the universal. His sorrow will thus vanish again, it will dissolve into harmony, for he will realize that he has reached the boundaries of his individuality. He knows indeed that every man develops himself with freedom, but he also knows that a man does not create himself from nothing, that he has himself as a task in his concretion; he will be reconciled again with existence in that he perceives that in a sense everyone is an exception, and that it is equally true that everyone is the universally human and at the same time an exception.

Here you have my opinion on what it is to be an uncommon man. I love existence and being a human being far too much to believe that the path to becoming an uncommon man is easy or without temptations. But even if someone is out of the common in this more noble sense, he will nevertheless always admit that it would be more perfect still to take possession of the whole of the universal.

So receive my greetings, accept my friendship, for although I wouldn't go so far as to characterize our relation in that way in the strictest sense, at least I hope that sometime my young friend will be that much older and that I might truthfully use that word. Be assured of my sympathy. Receive a greeting from her whom I love and whose thoughts are concealed in mine, receive a greeting which is inseparable from mine, but also receive one specially from her, friendly and sincere as always.

When you were here a few days ago, probably you didn't think I had such a long letter ready once again. I know your aversion to having people talk to you about your inner history. That's why I chose to write, and I shall never speak to you about it. That you have received such a letter will remain a secret, and I wouldn't want it to have the effect of altering your relationship with me and my family. I know that you have the virtuosity to prevent that if you want, and beg you therefore to do so for your sake and mine. I have never wanted to intrude upon you, and can very well love you at a distance, even though we see one another often. Your nature is too reserved for me to believe that it would help to talk to you, but on the other hand I hope my letter will not be without significance. So when you set to work on yourself in the closed machinery of your person, I thrust in my contributions and am convinced they will join in the operation.

Since our correspondence remains a secret, I observe all the formalities: I wish you farewell as though we were far removed from one another, albeit I hope to see you at my house just as often as before.

3 LAST WORD

PERHAPS you have the same experience with my previous letters as I have: you have forgotten most of what was in them. If so, I trust you are in the same case as myself and able at all times, through shifts of mood, to render account to yourself of the thought and the movement. The expression, the presentation, the embellishment, are the same yet not the same from one year to the next, like a flower, but the bearing, the movement, the stance are unchanged. Were I to write to you now I would perhaps express myself differently. I might even rise to eloquence somewhere in my letters, something I certainly have no pretensions to and which my position in life doesn't demand of me either. Were I to write now I might perhaps succeed in some other way, I don't know, for expression is a gift and 'every age and every year has its own flowering spring'.[1] As for the thought, however, it is and remains, and I hope in the course of time the movements will become easier for me and more natural, unchanged even when they are mute because the flower of expression has been shed.

However, it is not to write you a new letter I take up my pen, but the thought of you was brought vividly to my mind by a letter I myself have received from an older friend who is a priest in Jutland. As far as I know you have never met him. My friendship with him goes back to my schooldays, and although there were five or six years between us, we were on a fairly intimate footing. He was a little, thickset figure, cheerful, light-hearted, and uncommonly jovial. Although a serious soul deep down, his outward life seemed to conform pretty well with the injunction not to 'give a damn'. Learning fascinated him but he wasn't one for exams, and in his theology finals he managed no better than *haud illaudabilis*.[2] About four years ago he was stuck in a little parish on the Jutland moors. Outwardly he had a stentorian voice, inwardly an originality that made him always stand out in the small circle of my acquaintances. No wonder, then, that to begin with he didn't really feel content and thought his work too trifling for him. Now, however, he has regained his contentment, and reading a letter I received from him just recently had a really most encouraging effect on me. 'The Jutland moor,' he says, 'is, after all, a good exercise ground for me and an incomparable study. I go walking there on Saturdays and meditate on my sermons, and everything expands before me. I forget my real audience and gain an ideal one, I manage to become totally self-absorbed, so that when I step up into the pulpit it is as though I were still standing on the moor where my eye can find no one, where my voice lifts itself with all its strength to drown out the storm.'

Still, it isn't to tell you this that I write, but to send you one of his sermons that I found enclosed in the letter. I haven't wanted to show it to you personally, so as not to provoke your criticism, but send you the manuscript to let it make its impression on you in tranquillity. He has not given it yet, but means to do so next year and is confident he will make every farmer understand it. You are not to sneeze at it for that reason, for the beauty of the universal consists precisely in everyone being able to understand it. In this sermon he has grasped what I was saying to you and what I would have liked to say; he has expressed it more felicitously than I find myself capable of. Take it, then, read it; I have nothing to add, except that I have read it and thought of myself, and thought of you.

4 THE EDIFYING IN THE THOUGHT THAT AGAINST GOD WE ARE ALWAYS IN THE WRONG

———————

FATHER in Heaven! Teach us properly to pray, that our hearts may open to you in prayer and supplication, and may hide no secret wish that we know is not well-pleasing to you, but neither any secret fear that you may deny us anything that is truly to our advantage; in order that the labouring thoughts, the restless mind, the anxious heart may find rest in that in which, and through that by which, it alone can be found, by always rejoicing and thanking you as we gladly confess that before you we are always in the wrong.

As it is written in the Holy Gospel according to St Luke, chapter nineteen, from the forty-first verse to the end:

'And when he was come near, he beheld the city and wept over it, saying, If thou hadst known, even thou, at least in this thy day, the things which belong unto thy peace! but now they are hid from thine eyes. For the days shall come upon thee, that thine enemies shall cast a trench about thee, and compass thee round, and keep thee in on every side, and shall lay thee even with the ground, and thy children within thee: and they shall not leave in thee one stone upon another, because thou knewest not the time of thy visitation. And he went into the temple, and began to cast out them that sold therein, and them that bought, saying unto them, It is written, My house is the house of prayer: but ye have made it a den of thieves. And he taught daily in the temple. But the chief priests and the scribes, and the chief of the people sought to destroy him, and could not find what they might do: for all the people were very attentive to hear him.'

What the Spirit had revealed to the prophets through visions and dreams, what in voices of warning they had proclaimed to one generation after another, the repudiating of the chosen people, the dreadful destruction of proud Jerusalem – that was now drawing nearer and nearer. Christ goes up to Jerusalem. He is no prophet proclaiming the future. What he says does not awaken restless anxiety, for that which is still hidden he sees before his eyes. He does not prophesy, there is no more time for that – he weeps over Jerusalem. And yet the city was still standing there in its glory, and the temple still rose as proudly as always, higher than any other building in the world, and Christ himself says: 'If thou hadst known at least, in this thy day, the things that belong to you', but also adds: 'but now they are hid from your eyes.' In God's eternal design its destruction is decided, and salvation is hidden from the eyes of its inhabitants. Was the generation then living more to be damned than the one before it that gave it life? Was the whole nation depraved, were there no righteous in Jerusalem, not a single one who could stay God's wrath, none pious among all those from whose eyes salvation was hidden? And if there were such, was no gate opened to him in that time of anguish and distress when the enemy compassed the city round and kept them in on every side? Did no angel descend and save him even when all the gates were shut? Was no wonder worked on his behalf? But its destruction was appointed; in vain the besieged city searched in its anguish for a way out, the enemy army crushed it in its mighty embrace and no one escaped; heaven remained closed and no angel was sent out except the angel of death who brandished his sword over the city. So, for the sins of the nation it was this generation that had to make atonement, for the sins of this generation every single generation had to pay the price. Shall the righteous then suffer with the unrighteous? Is this the jealousy of God, that He visits the sins of the fathers upon the children unto the third and fourth generations, so that He punishes not the fathers but the children? What should we answer? Are we to say: 'Nearly two thousand years have now gone by since those days; never before has the world seen such a horror and surely it will never do so again; we thank God that we live in peace and safety, that the cry of anguish from those days reaches us only faintly; we would hope and believe that our days and those of our children may pass in peace, undisturbed by the storms of existence! We don't feel strong enough to think of such things, but we would like to thank God that we are not subjected to such ordeals'? Can anything more abject and forlorn be imagined than such talk? Is the inexplicable to be explained by saying it happened only once? Or is not this what is inexplicable, that it did happen? And has not this fact, that it did happen, the power to make everything inexplicable, even the explicable? If it once happened that human circumstances departed essentially from how they otherwise always are, what assurance is there that it cannot recur, what assurance that that was not the truth and what ordinarily happens the untruth? Or is it a proof of what is true that it most often happens? And is it really the case that what those times witnessed does not happen often? Is it not the case, as we have all of us in so many ways experienced, that what happens on a big scale is also experienced on a lesser? 'Suppose ye,' says Christ, 'that these Galileans whose blood Pilate had mingled with their sacrifices, were sinners above all the Galileans because they suffered such things?';[1] 'Or those eighteen, upon whom the tower in Siloam fell, and slew them, think ye that they were sinners above all men that dwelt in Jerusalem?' So some of those Galileans were not sinners above all other men, those eighteen were not guilty above all others who lived in Jerusalem – and yet the innocent shared the lot of the guilty. It was a dispensation of Providence, you will say, not a punishment; but Jerusalem's destruction was a punishment, and it fell with equal severity upon the guilty and the innocent; so you will not alarm yourself by pondering things of that kind, for the fact that someone can suffer adversity and hardship, and like the rain these can fall on good and evil alike, that you can understand – but that it should be a punishment – and yet that is how the Scriptures present it. Is, then, the lot of the righteous like that of the unrighteous; has piety no promise for this life; is every uplifting thought which once made you so rich in courage and confidence an illusion, a legerdemain in which the child believes, the youth hopes, but in which one who is a little older finds no blessing but only mockery and offence? This thought offends, it cannot and must not acquire power to delude you, it must not be capable of dulling your soul. You will love righteousness, practise it early and late, you will even practise it though it has no reward, you sense it, there is a claim in it which sometime, after all, must be satisfied; you will not fall into languor and then decide that righteousness held promises that you had forfeited by not practising it. You will not wrestle with people, but with God you will wrestle, and you will keep hold of Him and not let Him go without His blessing you![2] Yet, the Scriptures say, 'Thou shalt not contend with God.'[3] Is it not this that you are doing? Is this, then, yet another forlorn speech, is the Holy Scripture only given to man to humiliate

him, to annihilate him? By no means! What is meant, when it is
said 'Thou shalt not contend with God', is that you shall not wish
to prove you are in the right against God; the only way you can
contest who is right with God is to learn that you are in the wrong.
Indeed, that is what you yourself ought to want. What the prohibition against contesting who is right with God signifies, then, is your
perfection, and by no means that you are a lowly being with no
meaning for Him. The sparrow falls to the earth, and in a way it is
in the right against God. The lily withers, and in a way it is in the
right against God; only man is in the wrong, only for him is
reserved what to everything else was denied, to be in the wrong
against God. Should I speak otherwise, should I remind you of a
wise saying you have often heard, one that knows conveniently
enough how to explain everything without doing injustice to God
or to men? 'Man is a frail being,' it says, 'and it would be absurd of
God to ask the impossible of him; one does what one can, and if
now and then one is a little negligent, God won't ever forget we are
weak and imperfect beings.' Ought I to admire most the lofty
conceptions of the divine being this shrewdness betrays, or its deep
insight into the human heart, the searching consciousness that ran-
sacks itself and arrives at the comforting and convenient conclusion,
'One does what one can'? Would it be so easy a thing for you, my
hearer, to decide how much one can do? Were you never in such
danger that you exerted yourself almost to despair yet so infinitely
wished you could do more? And perhaps someone else was watching
you with a doubtful and imploring look to see whether it was
possible for you to do more. Or were you never afraid for yourself,
so afraid that it seemed to you no sin was so black, no self-love so
odious, that it might not steal in upon you and as a foreign power
gain mastery over you? Did you not sense this fear? For if you did
not sense it, then you do not open your mouth to reply, for you are
indeed unable to answer what is asked. But if you have sensed it,
then, my hearer, I ask you, Did you find repose in those words
'One does what one can'? Or were you never in fear for others,
have you not seen those wavering in life to whom you were accustomed to look up with trust and confidence, and have you not
heard a soft voice whisper to you: 'If even these could not
accomplish what is great, what is life then but evil affliction, and

faith but a snare that draws us out into the infinity in which we could not live; far better then to forget, to renounce all claims'? – Did you not hear this voice? For if you did not hear it you do not open your mouth to answer, for you are indeed unable to answer what is asked. But if you did hear it, then, my hearer, I ask you, Was this, then, your consolation that you said, 'One does what one can'? Was this precisely not the reason for your disquiet, that you did not know within yourself how much it is a man can do, that at one moment it seemed infinitely much, the next so precious little? Was it not that your fear was so embarrassing because you could not penetrate your consciousness, because the more earnestly, the more sincerely, you wanted to act, the more dreadful became the quandary in which you found yourself, whether you had not done what you could, or had done what you could but no one came to your aid?

Therefore no more serious doubt, no deeper concern is appeased by the saying, 'One does what one can'. If man is sometimes in the right, sometimes in the wrong, to some extent in the right, to some extent in the wrong, who is it then but man who decides; but then again, in the decision may he not be to some extent in the right, to some extent in the wrong? Or when he judges his action, is he a different man from when he acts? Must doubt, then, prevail, constantly discovering new difficulties, and must uneasiness walk at the side of the fearful soul and impress upon it its experiences? Or might we prefer to be always in the right in the way that irrational creatures are? We then only have the choice between being nothing before God and the eternal torment of constantly beginning over again yet without being able to begin. For if we are to decide definitely whether we are in the right at the present instant, this question must be decided definitely concerning the previous instant, and so on, further and further back.

Doubt is afoot again, uneasiness once more aroused; so let us endeavour to set it at rest by considering:

The edifying in the thought that against God we are always in the wrong.

Being in the wrong; can any more painful feeling be imagined? And do we not see that man would rather suffer anything than admit he was in the wrong? We do not approve such obstinacy, either in ourselves or in others, we think it better and more wisely done to admit the fact when we are really in the wrong; and we say that the pain accompanying the admission will be like a bitter pill that makes us healthy; but that it is painful to be in the wrong, painful to admit it, that is not something we hide. So we endure the pain because we know that it is for our own good, we put our trust in managing sometime in the future to put up a stronger resistance, perhaps even coming so far as very seldom really to be in the wrong. This is such a natural point of view, so obvious to everybody. There is, then, something edifying about being in the wrong — that is, inasmuch as by admitting it we improve ourselves with prospects of its occurring more and more rarely. And yet it was not with this consideration that we wanted to appease doubt, but by considering what was edifying in always being in the wrong. But if that first consideration was edifying, which held out the hope in due time of no longer being in the wrong, how can the opposite consideration also be edifying, the consideration that would teach us that we are always in the wrong, in respect of the future as well as the past?

Your life brings you into manifold relationships with other people. Some love right and justice, others seem unwilling to practise these and they do you a wrong. Your soul is not insensible to the suffering they inflict on you in this way, but you search and examine yourself, you assure yourself you are in the right, and you rest calmly and strongly in that conviction. However much they hurt me, you say, they can never take from me this peace of knowing I am in the right and that I am suffering wrong. There is a satisfaction, a joy, in this consideration, which we have no doubt all tasted, and when you continue to suffer wrong you are edified by the thought that you are in the right. This point of view is so natural, so comprehensible, so often tested in life, yet it was not through this consideration that we wanted to appease doubt and cure concern, but by considering what was edifying in the thought that we are always in the wrong. Can, then, this opposite consideration have the same effect?

Your life brings you into manifold relationships with other people. You are drawn more to some by a heartfelt love than to others. Now if such a person who was the object of your love were to do you a wrong, it would pain you deeply, would it not? You would go over it all carefully, but then you would say, I know within me that I am in the right, this thought will put me at ease. Ah! if you loved him it would not put you at ease, you would look into everything. You would be unable to come to any other conclusion than that he was in the wrong, and still that conviction would disquiet you, you would wish that you might be in the wrong, you would try to find something which could count in his defence, and if you did not find it you would find repose only in the thought that you were in the wrong. Or if you were made responsible for the welfare of such a person, you would do everything in your power, and if, notwithstanding, the other showed no appreciation and caused you only sorrow, you would draw up the account, would you not? You would say, I know I have done right by him. – Ah! no, if you loved him, that thought would only distress you, you would grasp at every probability, and if you found none, you would tear up the account in order to be able to forget it, and you would endeavour to edify yourself with the thought that you were in the wrong.

So it is painful to be in the wrong and the more painful the more often one is so, edifying to be in the wrong and the more edifying the more often one is so! It is indeed a contradiction. How can it be explained but by the fact that in the one case you are forced to recognize what you want to recognize in the other? But if the recognitions are nevertheless not the same, how can one's wanting or not wanting help? How can this be explained but by the fact that in the one case you loved and in the other you did not – in other words, that in one case you found yourself in an infinite relationship to a person, in another case in a finite relationship? So wanting to be in the wrong expresses an infinite relationship, wanting to be in the right, or finding it painful to be in the wrong, expresses a finite relationship! So the edifying, then, is to be always in the wrong, for only the infinite edifies, the finite does not!

If, then, there were a human being you loved, even if your love succeeded in piously deluding your thought and yourself, you would nevertheless be in a constant contradiction, because you would know you were in the right but wanted to be – and wanted to believe you were – in the wrong. If, on the other hand, it was God you loved, could there then be any question of such a contradiction? Could what you knew then be anything but what you wanted to believe? Could it be that He who is in heaven is not greater than you who dwell on earth, that His wealth is not more abundant than your sufficiency, His wisdom not more profound than your shrewdness, His holiness not greater than your righteousness? Must you not of necessity recognize this? But if you must recognize it there is no contradiction between your knowledge and your wish. And yet, if you must necessarily recognize it then there is indeed no edification in the thought that you are always in the wrong, for it was said that the reason why it could prove painful on one occasion to be in the wrong and edifying on another was that in the one case one is compelled to recognize what in the other case one wanted to recognize. So you would indeed be freed in your relationship to God from the contradiction, but you would have lost the edification; yet that was precisely what we were to consider: what is edifying in being always in the wrong against God.

Is it really so? Why did you wish to be in the wrong against a human being? Because you loved! Why did you find it edifying? Because you loved! The more you loved, the less time you had to consider whether you were in the right or not; your love had but one wish, that you might always be in the wrong. So, too, in your relation to God. You loved God, and therefore your soul could only find repose and joy in the thought that you must always be in the wrong. So it was not through the trials of thought that you came to this recognition, you were not compelled, for when you are in love you are in freedom. So if thought did convince you that the situation was as you wanted it, that there was nothing for it but that you must always be in the wrong or that God must always be in the right, that followed later, for you did not arrive at the certainty that you were in the wrong from the recognition that God is in the right. It was from love's highest and only wish that you might always be in the wrong that you came to the recognition that God is always in the right. But that wish is a matter of love and therefore of freedom, and so you are by no means compelled to recognize that you were always in the wrong. So you were not made certain that you were always in the wrong by reflection; the certainty came from your being edified by that thought.

It is an edifying thought, then, that against God we are always in the wrong. If this conviction did not have its source in your whole being, that is, in the love that is within you, your reflection would have acquired a different appearance. You would have recognized that God is always in the right, this you would have been compelled to recognize; as a consequence of that, you would have been compelled to recognize that you are always in the wrong. The latter would have already caused difficulties, for although you can certainly be compelled to recognize that God is always in the right, you cannot really be compelled to apply this to yourself, to let your whole being appropriate this recognition. So you would have recognized that God is always in the right and, in consequence of that, that you are always in the wrong, but this recognition would not have edified you. There is nothing edifying in recognizing that God is always in the right, and neither, therefore, in any thought that follows necessarily from it. In that case, when you recognize that God is always in the right, you are standing outside God, and similarly when in consequence you recognize that you are always in the wrong. If, on the other hand, on the strength of no precedent recognition you claim, and are convinced, that you are always in the wrong, you are hidden in God. This is your divine worship, your religious devotion, your reverence for God.

You loved a human being, you wished always to be in the wrong against him; alas! he was unfaithful to you, and however reluctantly, however much it pained you, you were nevertheless shown to be in the right against him, and in the wrong in loving him so dearly. And yet your soul demanded to love in that way, only in that way could you find peace and rest and happiness. Your soul then turned away from the finite to the infinite; there it found its object, there your love became happy. I will love God, you said, He gives the lover everything, He fulfils my dearest, my only wish, that against Him I am always in the wrong. Never shall any anxious doubt tear me away from Him, never will the thought terrify me that I might prove to be in the right against Him, against God I am always in the wrong.

Is it not so? Was this not your only wish, your dearest wish? Was it not the case that a dreadful fear seized you when for a moment the thought could arise in your soul that it was possible you were in the right, that wisdom was not the governance of God but your own plans, that righteousness was not God's thoughts but your own achievements, that love was not God's heart but your own emotions? And was it not your bliss that you could never love as you were loved? This thought, then, that you are always in the wrong against God, is not a truth you are forced to recognize, not a comfort to soothe your pain, not a substitute for something better; it is the joy in which you triumph over yourself and over the world, your rapture, your song of praise, your worship, a proof that your love is happy as is only that love with which one loves God.

That against God we are always in the wrong is, then, an edifying thought; it is edifying that we are in the wrong, edifying that we always are. It proves its power to edify in a twofold way, partly by staying doubt and alleviating its anxieties, partly by inciting to action.

Perhaps you still recall, my hearer, a wise saying we mentioned earlier. It seemed so trusty and dependable, it explained everything so easily, it was ready to give everyone safe conduct through life unmoved by the storms of doubt. 'One does what one can,' it called out to the perplexed. And it is indeed undeniable that it helps just to do that. Beyond that it had nothing to say, it vanished like a dream, or became a monotonous repetition in the doubter's ear. Then when he wanted to use it, it turned out that he could not, that it entangled him in a mesh of difficulties. He could find no time to ponder what he could do, because he had at the same time to be doing what he could. Or if he found time to ponder, the scrutiny gave him a more-or-less, an approximation, but never anything exhaustive. And how is a man to measure his relation to God with a more or less, or with an approximation? He then convinced himself that this wise saying was a treacherous friend which, under the guise of helping him, enfolded him in doubt, frightened him into a perpetual cycle of confusion. What before had been obscure to him but did not cause him worry, now became no clearer but made his mind troubled and anxious. Only in an infinite relation to God could the doubt be allayed; only in an infinitely free relation to God could his trouble be turned into joy. He is in an infinite relation to God when he recognizes that God is always in the right, in an infinitely free relation when he recognizes that he himself is always in the wrong. The doubt is then stayed, for the movement of doubt lay precisely in his being at one moment in the right, at the next in the wrong, being to some extent in the right, to some extent in the wrong, and that was meant to signify his relation to God. But a relation like that is no relation, and that was what gave food for doubt. In his relation to another human being, it was indeed possible to be partly in the wrong, partly in the right, to some extent in the wrong, to some extent in the right, because he himself, like every human being, is finite, and his relation is a finite relation which consists in a more-or-less. He remained in doubt, therefore, so long as doubt made the infinite relation finite, and as long as the wise saying filled the infinite relation with finitude. So whenever doubt makes him anxious with the particular, whenever it teaches him that he suffers too much or is tried beyond his powers, he forgets the finite in the infinite thought that he is always in the wrong. Every time the anxiety of doubt makes him sorrowful, he lifts himself above the finite into the infinite, for this thought that he is always in the wrong is the wing on which he soars over finitude, it is the longing with which he seeks God, it is the love in which he finds God.

So against God we are always in the wrong. But is this not an anaesthetizing thought? However edifying it may be for man, is it not dangerous, does it not lull him into a sleep in which he dreams of a relationship to God which is nevertheless no real relationship, does it not consume the power of his will and the strength of his purpose? By no means! Was the man who wished always to be in the wrong against another man, dull and inactive? Did he not do everything in his power to be in the right and yet wanted only to be in the wrong? Should the thought that against God we are always in the wrong not then be an inspiring one? For what does it express other than that God's love is always greater than our love? Does this thought not make him happy to act? For when he doubts he has no strength to act. Does it not make him fervent in his spirit, since when he makes finite calculations the fire of the spirit is quenched? Then if, my hearer, your only wish were denied you, still you are glad; you do not say, 'God is always in the right', for there is no jubilation in that; you say, 'Against God I am always in the wrong.' If what you wished was what others, and you yourself in a sense, might call your duty, if you were not only to forgo your wish but in a sense be unfaithful to your duty, if you lost not merely your joy but honour itself, still you are glad; 'Against God,' you say, 'I am always in the wrong.' If you knocked but it was not opened unto you, if you sought but did not find, if you laboured but nothing gained, if you planted and watered but saw no blessing, if heaven were closed and the witness failed to appear, still you are glad in your works. If the punishment which the sins of the fathers had called down were to fall upon you, still you are glad, for against God we are always in the wrong.

Against God we are always in the wrong; this thought then stays the doubt and alleviates its anxiety, it puts one in heart and inspires one to action.

Your thought has now followed the course of this exposition, perhaps hurrying on ahead when it followed familiar paths; it gave you the lead, slowly, perhaps reluctantly, when the way was unfamiliar, but nevertheless you must admit this: that it is as it was set forth, and your thought had no objections. Before we part, one more question, my hearer: did you wish, could you wish, that it were otherwise? Could you wish that you were in the right, could you wish that that beautiful law which for thousands of years has borne the human race and every generation of the race through life, that beautiful law, more glorious than that which keeps the stars in their courses across the vault of heaven, could you wish that law breached – more dreadful than if the law of Nature lost its force and everything was dissolved in terrible chaos? Could you wish that? I have no words of wrath with which to terrify you. Your wish must not proceed from dread of the blasphemy of the thought of wanting to be in the right against God. I ask you simply, could you wish that it were otherwise? Perhaps my voice is not strong and warm enough to penetrate to your inmost thought; ah! but ask yourself, ask yourself with the solemn uncertainty with which you would address a person you knew was capable of deciding your life's happiness with a single word, ask yourself even more seriously, for in truth it is a question of salvation. Stay not the flight of your soul, do not sadden what is your better part, do not enervate your soul with half wishes and half thoughts. Ask yourself, and keep on asking until you find the answer, for one can recognize a thing many times and acknowledge it, one can want a thing many times and attempt it, yet only the deep inner movement, only the indescribable motions of the heart, only these convince you that what you have recognized 'belongs unto you', that no power can take it from you; for only the truth that edifies is truth for you.

NOTES

PART ONE

Preface

1. See 'The Fourth Night', verses 629–30, in *The Complaint, or Night-Thoughts on Life, Death and Immortality*, by Edward Young, the eighteenth-century English poet. Kierkegaard's text inverts the lines, here reproduced as in the original.
2. See Hegel's *Logic*, tr. William Wallace, Clarendon Press, Oxford, 1975, paras. 138ff., pp. 196ff.
3. Xerxes is said to have had the Hellespont whipped because his first bridge over it (of boats) was destroyed by a storm (Herodotus, VII, 35).
4. 'Diapsalmata' is the plural Greek form for the Hebrew *selah*, a word that recurs in the Psalms of David at the end of a verse, and which can easily acquire the meaning, as apparently here, of 'refrains', i.e. something (for example a mood) repeated over and over again.
5. 'To himself.' Latin version of the Greek title to the *Meditations* of Marcus Aurelius (A.D. 121–180). The work is regarded as a noble expression of philosophical heathenism.
6. The exploits of the dim-witted people of Mols (*Molboerne*), in Jutland, are legendary in Scandinavia. In one story their plan to farm fish (including, naturally, salt herring) in the village pool was defeated because one of the fish was an eel, which ate all the others. Since burning, hanging, and whipping were too good for it, they decided to drown the eel at sea. On being returned to its element, the eel thrashed its tail joyfully, which the Mols people understood to be its writhing in terrible death pangs. See V. Fausbøll, *Beretning om de vidtbekjendte Molboers vise Gjerninger og tapre Bedrifter*, Fr. Wöldikes Forlagsboghandel, Kjøbenhavn, 1862, pp. 5–6, 45–6. Much the same story is to be found in the English *The Merry Tales of the Wise Men of Gotham*, from the early seventeenth century.
7. April 7th did in fact fall on a Monday in 1834.

8. A Danish opera based on Walter Scott's *The Monastery*.
9. The phrasing is from 1 Corinthians 7.29–31.

1 Diapsalmata

1. By Paul Pelisson (1624–93). It is thought that Kierkegaard got it from Lessing's *Zerstreute Anmerkungen über das Epigramm*:

> Rank, knowledge, renown,
> Friendship, pleasure and means,
> All is but wind, but smoke:
> To say it better, all is nought.

2. Phalaris, ruler of Agrigentum in Sicily from about 570 to 564 B.C., is said to have kept a brazen bull in which he burnt his victims alive, the first being the bull's inventor. Reeds were placed in the nostrils of the bull to turn the cries into music.
3. Dean (Jonathan) Swift, the satirist, died insane in 1745.
4. David Hartley (1705–57), English physician and moral philosopher, whose main works were an *Enquiry into the Origin of the Human Appetites and Affections*, Lincoln, 1747, and *Observations on Man, his Frame, his Duty and his Expectations*, London, 1749 (an abridged version of which was published by his friend, the scientist Joseph Priestley, under the title *Hartley's Theory of the Human Mind on the Principle of Association of Ideas*, London, 1775.
5. In Hebrew grammar a *sheva* is a sign consisting of two dots placed under a consonant letter to indicate the absence of a vowel; a *dagesh lene* is a point placed in a letter indicating that it is unaspirated.
6. Turkish officer whose rank is denoted by the number of horse-tails displayed as symbols of war.
7. Said of the 'hypocrites' in an incorrect (but since Kierkegaard's time corrected) version of Matthew 6.16 in the Danish Bible. According to the text the hypocrites 'have their reward', but (it is ironically implied) not as they suppose.
8. Lynceus was the most keen-sighted of the Argonauts. The giants overcome by the gods (with the help of Hercules) were buried beneath mountains (including Etna) and were the cause of volcanic eruptions. Echo was a nymph who engaged Hera in incessant conversation so that Zeus could carry on with the other nymphs. On discovering this ruse, Hera had Echo turned into an echo, in which state she fell in love with Narcissus but, on her love being unrequited, pined away and remained merely a voice.

9. See Goethe's *Faust*, part 1, stage instruction before verse 968 (English tr. Bayard Taylor, Euphorion Books, London, n.d., p. 61).

10. In the Middle Ages the Roman poet Virgil was thought to have been a sorcerer.

11. 'The same in the same.'

12. The story is found in Athenaeus's *Banquet of the Learned*, a collection of anecdotes, quotations and discussions, from the fifth century (7 vols., Loeb Library). Trophonius's cave was his oracle in the grove of Lebadaea where he had been swallowed up by the earth. Trophonius and his brother, Agamedes, had built the treasury of the king of Boeotia in such a way that they could secretly rob it.

13. The text has *Justitsraad*, a titular counsellor of justice.

14. Fenris or Fenrir, the wolf of sin in Scandinavian mythology, and one of the three children of Loki (the god of strife and spirit of evil). The others were Jørmungand (a monstrous serpent) and Hel (half corpse, half queen). When Fenris gaped, one jaw touched earth and the other heaven. In the *Ragnarok* Fenris swallows the sun and conquers Odin but, on being conquered by Vidar, who thrust his thick shoe into Fenris's gaping jaws, was thrown into Niflheim (the 'mist-home' of those who die of old age or disease), where Loki was confined.

15. Quoted by Kierkegaard from Møinichen, *Nordiske Folks Overtroe, Guder, Fabler og Helte*, Kjøbenhavn, 1800, p. 101. Kierkegaard has 'the bear's grass' where the original (and also Kierkegaard's original manuscript) has 'the bear's sinews'. See also P. A. Munch, *Norrøne gude- og heltesagn*, revised, ed., Anne Holtsmark (ed.), Universitetsforlaget, Oslo, 1967, pp. 50, 53-4.

16. 'Thou art fulfilled, thy nightwatch of my life.' The origin is not known.

17. Cf. *Søren Kierkegaards Papirer* III B 123. The Lüneburger heath is in southern Saxony.

18. See Genesis 2.17, and *The Sickness unto Death*, Penguin Classics, Harmondsworth, 1989, p. 48: 'to die death itself'.

19. Kierkegaard is referring to the Megarian philosopher, Stilpo (*c.*380–*c.*300 B.C.), who denied the possibility of predication. One cannot say 'The man is good', because 'man' does not mean the same as 'good'.

20. A reference to Hegel's *Logic*, tr. William Wallace, Clarendon Press, Oxford, 1975. Hegel gives as examples of infinite judgements: 'The mind is no elephant', 'Mind is mind' (p. 238).

21. Cf. Hegel, ibid., on 'pure being' as 'nothing', 'making the beginning' (pp. 124–6).

22. C. F. Sintenis, German author of a book of devotions called *Stunden für Ewigkeit gelbt* ('Hours Lived for Eternity'), Berlin, 1791.

23. 'Nyboder' is the name of a row of houses built in Copenhagen for families of sailors in the Royal Danish Navy. There was an orphanage attached which was destroyed by fire in 1817, and several children perished. In his description of Elysium, Virgil describes infants weeping at the frontier (*Aeneid*, VI, 426ff.).

24. Exodus 12.23.

2. *The Immediate Erotic Stages*

1. 'Optimates' was the name for the aristocratic party in ancient Rome.

2. Perhaps a reference to Christian H. Weisse, whose *System der Aesthetik* (Leipzig, 1830) Kierkegaard possessed; though perhaps also to the aesthetic views of the local littérateur and Hegelian, J. L. Heiberg.

3. 'Battle of the Frogs and Mice', a mock-epic poem, still extant, formerly attributed to Homer but now thought to be of later origin.

4. A *Receptionsstykke* was the painting artists had to produce for admission to the Art Academy.

5. See Acts 1.9: 'And when he had spoken these things, while they beheld, he was taken up, and a cloud received him out of their sight.' Romulus is also said to have been translated to heaven in a cloud. Cf. *Papirer* I, p. 85.

6. Hegel's expression is *Gestaltung*.

7. There is a continual problem in translating the Danish *Sandselighed*, which covers both 'sensuous' and 'sensual'. But since these two terms are also comparatively ambiguous, and while 'sensuous' can have the neutral sense of what pertains in general to the senses, and 'sensual' conveys fairly clearly the focus on pleasure from sensation relevant in this context, I have consistently chosen the latter. The word translated as 'spirit' here is *Genialitet*, which can also be translated 'genius', but which is also ambiguous. One must be careful to distinguish this from 'spirit' (*Aand*) in the sense that Kierkegaard sharply distinguishes from sensuality. The context should make the meaning clear.

8. An enclitic is typically an unaccented word that can modify the accent of a word it follows.

9. Eros fell in love with Psyche, which gives a point to the remark just below about his love's being based on the psychic, or qualities of soul, rather than the sensual.

10. The 'demonic' in Kierkegaard is conscious fear or hatred of the recog-

nizably good. See, for example, *The Sickness unto Death*, Penguin Classics, Harmondsworth, 1989, p. 103.

11. Whenever Cato (234–149 B.C.) was called upon to vote in the Roman Senate, even if the subject under debate bore no relation to Carthage, he pronounced the words 'Carthage is to be destroyed' (*Delenda est Carthago*) preceded by 'In addition I vote for . . .'.

12. Or 'stranger at the gate'; a Gentile convert to the Jewish faith who did not submit to circumcision but abstained from offering sacrifice to heathen gods and from working on the sabbath.

13. Leipzig, 1819–21, pp. 82ff. Henrich Steffens (1773–1845) was a philosopher, scientist and novelist, born in Stavanger in Norway, and of Danish and German descent. The work in question treats of the relation of sight and hearing to the other, 'lower' senses.

14. The story is told in *Owen Tudor*, *Werke* II, p. 260.

15. This treats of a changeling who puts everything, living or dead, under a spell by his playing. Cf. the brothers Grimm's 'Der kleine Sackpfeifer'.

16. 'Opera seria' is the name applied to Italian opera in the period from about 1650 to 1740, when – especially in the hands of Alessandro Scarlatti – the musical and artistic features were accentuated and given an ever more typical form, including the climactic and general finale.

17. 'And appears to be floating in the air.' Cf. Virgil's *Georgics*, I, 404.

18. In Thor's contest with Urgard-Loke/Loki. See P. A. Munch, *Norrøne gude- og heltesagn*, Universitetsforlaget, Oslo, 1967, pp. 100–102.

19. The original, in Leporello's 'list aria', has '*Delle vecchie fa conquista/Pel piacer di porle in lista*', which can be roughly translated as 'He conquers the old for the pleasure of adding to the list'. Kierkegaard's is from a Danish version.

20. Where the Countess kissed Cherubino when he was disguised as a girl.

21. Julius Caesar's cryptic account to the Roman Senate of his victory (47 B.C.) at Zela, in Asia Minor, over Mithridates' son Pharnaces who had aided Pompey in the civil war.

22. 'The farmer stands waiting, while the river flows by.' Horace, *Letters*, I, 2, 42.

23. 1 Samuel 16.14ff.

24. Perhaps a reference to the Danish poet Hauch's poem, *The Mountain Maiden*. Cf. 'Des Antonius von Padua Fischpredigt' ('St Anthony of Padua preaches to the Fish'), from the anthology *Des Knaben Wunderhorn* (1805–8), familiar in Gustav Mahler's song version.

25. While Kierkegaard refers to the opera as *Don Juan*, this translation adheres to the familiar Italian title. However, in discussing the traditional motif of the opera it is necessary to use the original name of its hero or villain.

26. Kierkegaard employs the Latin forms *sub una specie* and *sub utraque specie*, used in communion at Catholic worship, of the bread alone or the bread and the wine.

27. The Greek word means 'stumbling block' or 'offence'. Here the latter is intended.

28. The mountain of delight and love where Venus holds court and Eckhardt the Faithful warns human beings against entering for fear of perdition.

29. 'If she wears a petticoat/You know what he does.'

30. Cf. Mark 12.41–44.

31. *Armuth, Reichtum, Schuld und Busse der Gräfin Dolores*, *Werke* VIII, p. 25. Kierkegaard goes one better by making Arnim's *Grossmutter* ('grandmother'), a great-grandmother.

32. I have tried to capture the pun here on the Danish *gjör Lykke, det lykkes* ('succeed', 'have success') with *gjör lykkelig* ('make happy'), by using the related English notion of luck and being lucky.

33. L. Kruse arranged the libretto for the Danish version (Copenhagen, 1807).

34. Among the mysteries, or secret cults, the most important were those at Eleusis in honour of Demeter and Dionysus. The Great Eleusinia were preceded by a preparatory celebration, or the lesser mysteries.

35. Molière's *Don Juan ou le festin de pierre* was first produced in 1665.

36. K. A. Musaeus, *Volksmärchen der Deutschen*, Gotha, 1782–6; J. L. Tieck (1773–1853) was a German poet.

37. For example, to Gluck's music (first performed in Vienna in 1761).

38. With the creditor Monsieur Dimanche, Act 4, scene 3.

39. In a sentence omitted here Kierkegaard makes use of an ambiguity in the Danish *Stemmefleerhed* (related to that in the English 'plurality') as between a plurality of voices (more than one) and there being a majority of votes, the Danish word for 'vote' (*Stemme*) being the same as that for 'voice'. The sentence says that in its ordinary use, this notion refers to a unity that is the end result, as is not the case in music.

40. See note 8, p. 610.

41. 'You stay inside with your fair lady.'

42. A reference to Holberg's *Barselstuen*, where Jeronimus turned up when he was most needed.

3 Ancient Tragedy's Reflection in the Modern

1. A Greek expression coined by Kierkegaard, which can be roughly translated as 'the fellowship of buried lives'.

2. Cf. Aristotle's *Poetics*.

3. 1 Chronicles 21.

4. Cf. Cicero, *De divinatione* II, 51; *De natura deorum* I, 71. Kierkegaard confuses the Roman augurs with the Etruscan prophets and sooth-sayers, about whom Cato recounts that he could not understand how they could look at one another without laughing.

5. A Danish newspaper in March 1839 had a report to this effect about Thiers.

6. A street warden (*Gadecommissair* or *Gadefoged*) was responsible for seeing that the streets were clean.

7. See Aristotle's *Poetics*, Chapter 6.

8. ibid., Chapter 13.

9. Pelagius (*c.* 360–*c.* 431), reputedly of British origin, denied the doctrine of original sin, played down the importance of divine 'grace', and rejected the subordination of ethics to religious dogma. His individualistic view ran counter to that of Augustine, who nevertheless held Pelagius in great respect.

10. Chr. D. Grabbe, *Faust und Don Juan: Eine Tragödie*, Frankfurt, 1829.

11. For example the Latin *partim*, an adverb meaning 'partly', was once an accusative of the substantive *pars* ('part').

12. Aristotle, *Poetics*, Chapter 6, and G. W. F. Hegel, *Aesthetics: Lectures on Fine Art*, tr. T. M. Knox, Clarendon Press, Oxford, 1975, vol. II, p. 1197.

13. Hegel, op. cit., p. 1198. Kierkegaard quotes the German.

14. Hebrews 10.31.

15. Exodus 20.5; 34.7.

16. The *Philoctetes* is a tragedy by Sophocles. Philoctetes was the most famous archer in the Trojan War and one of Helen's suitors. He was left on the island of Lemnos because a wound in his foot produced such a stench, and remained there for ten years before being rescued by Ulysses and Diomedes.

17. *Philoctetes*, verses 732ff.

18. The principle of inertia: that by which matter continues in its existing state, whether rest or motion, unless affected by an external force.

19. Labdacus, son of the Theban king, Polydorus, numbered Oedipus, Polynices, Eteocles and Antigone among his descendants (known collectively as Labdacidae).

20. 'Whom the god would destroy, he first makes mad.'

21. Robert, first Duke of Normandy, was given to the devil by his mother before his birth and later lived up to the relevant expectations. The story is found in a thirteenth-century verse romance.

22. In Northern mythology Hogne was the son of Grimhild and a troll.

23. Matthew 6.19–20.

24. An attempt to predispose in favour of one's case.

25. Virgin mother.

26. *Antigone*, verse 850. The present translator's own translation. Kierkegaard quotes the Greek with a German translation in a footnote.

27. 'Which she does not meditate upon in her heart.'

28. Sophocles, *The Trachinian Maidens*, verse 1159. Hercules died from the blood of a centaur which had been poisoned when Hercules killed him with a poisoned arrow.

4 Shadowgraphs

1. Kierkegaard quotes these two poems in German. The second, *Gestern liebt'ich*, is from Lessing's *Song from the Spanish.*, *Sämmtliche Schriften* (Maltzahn) I, p. 240.

2. 1 Kings 19.11–12: 'And he said, Go forth, and stand upon the mount before the Lord. And behold, the Lord passed by, and a great and strong wind rent the mountains, and brake in pieces the rocks before the Lord; but the Lord was not in the wind: and after the wind an earthquake; but the Lord was not in the earthquake: And after the earthquake a fire; but the Lord was not in the fire: and after the fire a still small voice.'

3. Cf. Psalms 18.15: 'Then the channels of waters were seen, and the foundations of the world were discovered at thy rebuke, O Lord, at the blast of the breath of thy nostrils.'

4. In Hesiod's *Theogony* (verses 123ff.) the night is the daughter of chaos and mother of the ether and day.

5. Art here is of course painting and sculpture. Gotthold Ephraim Lessing (1729–81) was a German scholar and critic who, in the essay referred to here, attacked the neo-classical conception of antique beauty. Laocoön was a Trojan priest whose destruction, along with his two sons, by two serpents is the subject of a famous work of ancient art, found in 1506 and now in the Vatican. The effect of Lessing's essay was partly to free art from religious and social pressures and to focus attention on the artistic process itself.

6. For a parallel see Kierkegaard's later work, *The Sickness unto Death*, Penguin Classics, Harmondsworth, 1989, p. 104, where the topic is not sorrow or grief but despair.

7. Veronica is said to have dried the face of Jesus on his way to Golgotha, his image being allegedly left on the cloth. 'Veronica' means 'true image'.

8. In Homer and Virgil, Proteus is the prophetic old man of the sea, whom one could only consult at midday when he rose from the sea and slept in the shade of the rocks. He assumed all possible shapes to slip free and avoid having to prophesy but, as here, told the truth when he saw there was nothing else for it.

9. 1 Samuel 28.7–19.

10. Tantalus, son of Zeus, divulged secrets entrusted to him by the latter, and after death was punished in the underworld by being afflicted with a raging thirst and at the same time placed in a lake whose waters receded every time he tried to drink (Homer, *Odyssey*, XI, 582ff.). Sisyphus, king of Corinth, was also punished in the underworld after his death for fraud and avarice. He had to roll a marble block to the top of a hill, whereupon it constantly rolled down again (Homer, *Odyssey*, XI, 593).

11. The wise man was Simonides. See Cicero, *De natura deorum*, I, 60.

12. See 1 Peter 3.4: 'But let it be the hidden man of the heart, in that which is not corruptible, even the ornament of a quiet and meek spirit, which is in the sight of God of great price.'

13. 'Persecuted church.'

14. 'Mediation' is the Hegelian term for a process of resolving conceptual oppositions or mutual exclusions into higher conceptual unities. For instance, the belief that public service or conformity with public regulations conflicts with personal freedom can be 'mediated' in the realization that, properly understood, the latter depends on the former, so that freedom is merely 'abstract' if not so conceived.

15. In the Danish adaptation. There is no such hint in the original text, though in the final version Elvira says at the very end that she will retire to a convent to end her life there.

16. Adam Gottlob Oehlenschläger's *Aladdin*. Oehlenschläger (1779–1850) was a Danish poet.

17. The Danish adaptation of Lorenzo da Ponte's libretto.

18. As she does in Kruse's version.

19. Virgil, *Aeneid*, VI, 469.

20. This is a gibe at Hegelians who believed all contradictions and either/or's could be 'mediated'. See note 14 above.

21. In Kierkegaard's time the name of homes for the rehabilitation of female moral down-and-outs.

22. Kierkegaard's word is *smugler* ('smuggler').

23. Bayard Taylor's translation, Euphorion Books, London, n.d., Part 1 scene xx, p. 123.

24. The story of Margrete is Goethe's own addition to the Faust legend.

25. *Privatdocent* is an unsalaried academic position paid by attendance.

26. *Faust* Part 1, scene xvi, tr. Bayard Taylor, op. cit., pp. 113–16.

27. 'Dear God! However is it such/ A man can think and know so much? / I stand ashamed and in amaze, / And answer "Yes" to all he says, / A poor, unknowing child! and he – / I can't think what he finds in me!', *Faust*, Part 1, scene xiii, tr. Bayard Taylor, ibid., p. 108.

28. In *Wilhelm Meister's Lehrjahre*, IV, Chapter 13, towards the end.

29. A character in Swedish folklore. Cf. 'The Blue Bird' in Bäckström's *Svenska Folkböcker*.

5   The Unhappiest One

1. Freely translated from Christen Henriksen Pram's allegorical heroic poem 'Stærkodder', Copenhagen, 1785, 77th song, p. 142.

2. Orestes was pursued by the Eumenides (avenging deities or furies) after killing his mother, but took refuge in the temple of Athena, where he was acquitted. They begin to pursue this unhappiest man only when he gets to his 'temple'.

3. Cf. Romans 1.1: 'Paul a servant of Jesus Christ, called to be an apostle, separated [*aphorismenos*] unto the gospel of God . . .'.

4. Herodotus tells (*Histories*, I, 86) how the sage Solon told the victorious Croesus, last king of Lydia (560–546 B.C.), that no man should be considered happy until he had finished his life happily. Later, in defeat and condemned to be burnt to death, Croesus recalled Solon's warning as he stood beside the pyre and called out his name three times.

5. The unhappy consciousness is a form of consciousness that Hegel thought characteristic of the belief that human value is not an inherent possession of humanity but vested in a transcendent God. Christianity, with its belief in the restoration of human value by worship, revelation and grace, is a typical, if not indeed the paradigmatic example. One way of describing the unhappy consciousness is in terms of the fundamental separation of the individual conscious subject (subjectivity) and the eternal scheme of things (substance). Hegel's philosophy made a case for the mutual identity of these in the notion of the absolute, a

case that Kierkegaard devoted much of his earlier writings to attack-
ing.

6. 'The third nut is death.' Clemens Brentano, 'The Three Nuts'.

7. Ancaeus was son of Poseidon and king of Samos. Just as he was about
   to taste a new wine which the oracle had warned him against, he was
   killed by a wild boar. Kierkegaard quotes the proverb in Greek.

8. Latona (Leto), daughter of the Titan Coeus and Phoebe, and mother
   of Apollo and Artemis, by Zeus. Persecuted by Hera for her relation
   to Zeus, she wandered from place to place until she came to Delos,
   then a floating island, where she gave birth to Apollo and Artemis.
   Contrary to the mention of darkness here, the Hyperboreans were
   said to live beyond the North Wind in a land of perpetual sun-
   shine.

9. In retribution for her pride at giving birth to such a large number of
   children (reputedly fourteen), compared with Leto's two (see previous
   note), Niobe's children were all slain by Artemis and Apollo. On
   Mount Sipylus Zeus changed her into a great stone which in the
   summer always shed tears.

10. Job 1.21.

6 Crop Rotation

1. Kierkegaard frequently lampoons the way in which the 'negative', or
   antithesis, in the Hegelian dialectic is made to generate on its own the
   'movement' leading to the resolution of oppositions in a higher unity.
   He writes elsewhere of the 'indefatigable activity' of the negative in
   Hegel's philosophy, and of how it 'gives logical thoughts feet to walk
   on' (The Concept of Dread, tr. W. Lowrie, Princeton University Press,
   Princeton, 1957, p. 12).

2. According to the first-century Roman satirist Juvenal, bread and
   circuses were all the Roman citizen desired (Satires X, 81).

3. Denmark had instituted a legislative assembly, or States General, eight
   years previously.

4. Saxo Grammaticus tells us this in the beginning of Book 6, Gesta
   Danorum.

5. 'For just anyone.'

6. Aristotle (Politics, I, 2, 1253a) says that 'the state belongs to the class of
   objects which exist by nature, and ... man is by nature a political
   animal', by which he means that man's natural habitat is the polis, or
   city-state.

7. 'Idleness is the devil's pillow.'

8. See note 10, p. 613. The 'demonic', for Kierkegaard, is a refusal to acknowledge goodness or truth. Boredom becomes true for someone only when it is opposed or annulled from a point of view that favours industry, or idleness.

9. In Hegelian philosophy a concept contains its opposite, not just in the uncontroversial sense that in order to define, say, 'full' one must also have ('posit') the concept of emptiness, but also in the sense that identifying a case of fullness is somehow to have the opposite concept of emptiness simultaneously and 'interestingly' in mind.

10. 'Tired of Europe.' The expression was a catchword at the time.

11. An expression of Hegel's. The 'bad infinite' is the notion of an endless progression or infinite perpetuation, as against the notion of an infinite that somehow contains all that is finite.

12. Kierkegaard's misreading of a passage from the Emperor Marcus Aurelius's *Meditations* (VI, 2), which says, 'To recover your life is in your power. Look at things as you used to look at them, for in this lies the recovery of your life.' Aurelius was adopted by Pius Antoninus and was commonly called 'the philosopher'.

13. The gifts were fire and blind hope. See Aeschylus, *Prometheus*, verses 250ff. 'Prometheus' means 'forethought'.

14. 'To wonder at nothing.'

15. The river Lethe in Hades from which the shades drank and obtained oblivion.

16. Virgil, *Aeneid*, VI, 417ff. On the advice of the Sibyl, Aeneas gives Cerberus, the three-headed dog that guards the entrance of Hades, drugged honey-cakes to lull it to sleep.

17. *At drikke Duus*, ('to drink thou's') was part of a ceremony of discarding the formal pronoun of address.

18. See Ludvig Holberg's one-act comedy *Mester Gert Westphaler*, scene viii.

19. 'To want the same and not want the same makes for a firm friendship' (Sallust, *Catilina*, 20).

20. As in S. S. Blicher's 'Kjœltringsliv' ('Life of a Scoundrel'). Blicher (see footnote to the motto to the translator's introduction, p. 1 above) was a priest who became a gifted short-story writer whose growing literary preoccupations led to his being defrocked the year before his death (1848).

21. Jens Baggesen (1764–1826) was a Danish poet.

22. J. H. W. Tischbein (1751–1829), the famous German painter and friend of Goethe.

23. 'Ready to march.'

7 *The Seducer's Diary*

1. 'His ruling passion is the young beginner.' From Leporello's 'list' aria.
2. 'Running commentary No. 4.'
3. 'Excitement of the brain.'
4. As Christ, according to the Gnostics, is said to have done. They believed it would be unfitting for the Logos to assume actual flesh and blood, so the body was said to be 'parastatic' (lit. 'near to').
5. Ixion, king of the Lapithae, was taken to heaven by Zeus to purify him after he had killed his father-in-law. But there he attempted to win the love of Hera (Juno), and Zeus created a cloud resembling Hera, by which Ixion fathered a centaur.
6. 'Action at a distance' (with its correlate 'action by contact') is a concept that has been used in natural science to denote phenomena such as magnetism, gravitation, and even human speech, where there is, or has been assumed that there is, no intervening medium in which an action takes place continuously.
7. J. W. Goethe, *Jery und Bätely*, *Werke* XI. 'Go then – scorn fidelity. Remorse will follow.'
8. 1 Samuel 12.
9. In Ludwig Tieck's 'Die wilde Engländerin', in *Das Zauberschloss* (*Schriften*, Berlin, 1853, XXI, p. 238) a beautiful English noblewoman, out riding with a lord, quarrelled with her companion. On dismounting too quickly she had her riding habit torn off, whereupon she hid for a week but then realized she loved the lord and would marry him. The real entanglement, however, was that she had been put off marriage by reading an anatomy textbook as a child and had devoted herself instead to the study of astronomy and other sciences, refusing all suitors. Although a suitor, her companion on this occasion had been allowed to accompany her only because he also had scientific interests.
10. Georges Cuvier, a French scientist, who claimed one could reconstruct a whole animal from a single bone.
11. A parodying reference to Hegel's famous remark, 'What is rational is actual and what is actual is rational'. See *Hegel's Philosophy of Right*, tr. T. M. Knox, Clarendon Press, Oxford, 1952, p. 10. It is often forgotten that by 'real' Hegel meant not just whatever happens to exist, but what is 'actual' in the sense of 'actualized', again in the sense of 'having realized its inherent, even essential, possibilities'.
12. In the Danish adaptation of *Don Giovanni*.

13. In Holberg's *Erasmus Montanus*, Act 5, scene v. This version departs slightly from the original.

14. An esplanade along Copenhagen's seafront.

15. See note 5 above.

16. Genesis 39.7–19. It was Joseph who left his garment in Potiphar's wife's hand.

17. 'Klintekong', or King of the Cliff, was a mythical figure.

18. It was believed in antiquity that the kingfisher built its nest on the sea.

19. The hospital attendants wore green uniforms.

20. A bayadère is a Hindu dancing-girl.

21. As in the story of Orpheus and Eurydice.

22. Ovid, *Ars amandi*, II, 235: 'Night and winter, and long roads and cruel pains, in this unwarlike camp there is all manner of exertion.'

23. *Preciosa* is a lyric drama by Wolff, with music by Weber.

24. Where Øster Voldgade now lies. The path lay behind the fortifications. Kierkegaard often walked here, and sometimes met Regine.

25. In Raphael's painting, Psyche is carried up to heaven by cupids.

26. Genesis 41.32: 'And for that the dream was doubled unto Pharaoh twice; it is because the thing is established by God, and God will shortly bring it to pass.'

27. Shakespeare, *King Lear*, Act I, scene i. Cordelia says: 'I cannot heave my heart into my mouth'. Kierkegaard read Shakespeare only in German translation.

28. The source of the name is not clear.

29. The practice of buying up goods privately before they reach the public market, to enhance the price. The Danish *Forprang* can be translated as 'forestalling', which indeed derives its sense from this context (see OED). *Prang* means unlicensed dealing.

30. 'What before was impulse is now method.' Ovid, *Remedia amoris*, verse 10.

31. Literally 'go aground' and by extension 'go to rack and ruin'. In Hegel, however, the expression is used in the positive sense of something's more nearly reflecting its 'ground' or 'essence'. See *Hegel's Logic*, tr. W. Wallace, Clarendon Press, Oxford, 1975, section 120, p. 175.

32. 'Fritz' was the name of Regine Olsen's second fiancé, who later became her husband. Originally Kierkegaard had used this name instead of Edvard, but for obvious reasons changed it. The reason for the original choice of name is found in this reference to a comedy, *La Fiancée*, with music by Auber and libretto by the influential dramatist A. E. Scribe, translated by J. L. Heiberg, in which Fritz

is jilted by his girlfriend because of his awkwardness or stupidity.

33. 'The one is madly in love,/The other would like to be.' From Joseph von Eichendorff's poem, 'Vor der Stadt'.

34. From a Norwegian peasant song. See A. Caen, *Folke-Visebog*, 1847, Vol. I, pp. 114ff.

35. Phaethon was given permission by his father, the sun god Helios, to drive the chariot of the sun across the heavens for one day, but Phaethon was too weak to control the horses and when they got off track the chariot almost set the earth on fire.

36. 'Ulysses was not handsome, but he was eloquent, and he caused the sea goddesses [Circe and Calypso] to be tormented with love.' Cf. Ovid, *Ars amandi*, II, 123.

37. 1 Samuel 3.4–10.

38. Thekla's song is from Schiller's tragedy *The Piccolomini*. It combines the thoughts of love and death, as does also 'Lenore'.

39. Vilhelm is the dead lover in Bürger's 'Lenore'.

40. 'According to mankind's universal agreement.'

41. 'Spontaneous generation.'

42. Plato's *Apology*, 39c.

43. Trop is a carnival tout in Heiberg's *The Reviewer and the Beast*. Dyrehaug was a summer pleasure-ground whose facilities were transferred in 1843 (the year *Either/Or* was published) to the centre of Copenhagen to form the famous Tivoli.

44. 'Close at hand' or 'at a distance'.

45. Ovid, *Amores*, I, 4, 16 and 44.

46. 'The secretly blushing cheek reflects the glow of the heart.'

47. Student accommodation in the centre of Copenhagen on Købmagergade.

48. A pun in Danish on *at frie til hende* ('to propose to her') and *at frie hende* ('to set her free').

49. As Don Giovanni does when the statue of the Commendatore knocks.

50. A slight confusion on Kierkegaard's part. It was Rachel, not Rebecca, who was involved, and Jacob who 'stole Laban's heart', Rachel only taking over the household gods. See Genesis 31, 9–34. The Hebrew expression is not reproduced in the King James version, as it is in the Danish Bible. One deceived people by stealing their hearts, because the heart was the seat of intelligence.

51. 'Agnete, she swayed, she sank, she fell.' Baggesen, *Agnete fra Holmegaard* (*Danske Værker*, II, p. 195).

52. A reference to Kierkegaard's contemporary, the Danish writer J. L.

Heiberg: 'a curate can become old, and keep himself alive with hope' (*Prosaiske Skrifter*, X, p. 25).

53. Though Cardea, as guardian of door hinges, was the protectress of family life (*Cardo* = 'hinge'), Janus was of course the guardian deity of gates.

54. Aeolus, ruler of the Aeolian islands, to whom Zeus had given charge of the winds, which Aeolus kept locked up in a cave.

55. Ariadne helped Theseus escape from the Labyrinth and the Minotaur with the help of a spool of thread.

56. Cf. Mark 3.24.

57. Genesis 30.28–40.

58. A mural painting from Herculaneum, now in Naples, showing Theseus, who had abducted Ariadne, leaving her on Naxos.

59. As is told of Echo, who fell in love with Narcissus.

60. In 1837 this newspaper (issue 86, pp. 219ff. and 235ff.) published a piece satirizing servant girls for dressing like ladies.

61. A dig at N. F. S. Grundtvig (1783–1872), leader of a populist religious movement who frequently described his own goals as 'matchless' and a 'golden age'.

62. The terminology is self-consciously, and ironically, Hegelian.

63. Proverbs 24.26, following Luther's translation: '*Eine richtige Antwort ist wie ein lieblicher Kuss.*'

64. Plato, *Phaedrus*, Chapters 31ff.

65. '*Pendet ab ore magistri.*'

66. Sound-image (*klangfigur*) or so-called Chladni figure (after their discoverer, the German acoustician, E. F. F. Chladni, 1756–1827), which occurs on, for example, a glass plate, covered lightly with sand and held at one point, when sounded with a violin bow.

67. A huge statue on the Nile which gave out musical sounds when the rays of the morning sun fell on it. The Greeks called 'Memnonium' or 'Memnonia' certain ancient buildings and monuments which they supposed were erected in honour of Memnon, the beautiful son of Tithonius and Eos (goddess of the dawn) and king of the Ethiopians.

68. 'The wife's dowry is quarrels.' *Ars amandi*, II, 155.

69. See Homer, *Iliad*, XIV, 214ff. Venus's (Aphrodite's) magic girdle made anyone who wore it an object of love and desire. The girdle contained 'yearning and bantering speech' and 'the flattering prayer which beguiled even the wise man'.

70. *Tusindfryd* ('a thousand joys') is the Danish name for the English daisy (*Bellis perennis*).

71. 'The die is cast.' Said to be Caesar's words on crossing the river Rubicon, which separated his own province from Italy proper, and so declaring war on the republic.

72. In *The Arabian Nights*, Scheherazade, by enthralling the Sultan with her stories, persuades him to spare her life for a thousand and one nights. The Sultan had vowed to take a new sultana every evening and strangle her the next day, a vow which, out of gratitude to Scheherazade, he eventually revoked.

73. 'Let them hate, so long as they fear', a favourite line of Caligula's.

74. The water-lily.

75. 'Upriser' (from the Greek *anaduomein* – to come or rise up, especially from the sea). The model is Aphrodite.

76. Ovid, *Metamorphoses*, IV, 64ff. The lovers lived in adjoining houses and conversed secretly through an opening in the wall since their parents would not allow them to marry.

77. See note 21, p. 619.

78. Horace, *Odes*, II, 8.

79. From the Danish poet and playwright A. G. Oehlenschläger's *Palnatoke*, Act 5, scene ii. The play concerns the conflict between Christianity and Paganism.

80. In terms of the category most appropriate to her. The passage that follows is a playful but intelligible excursion into Hegelian dialectics, in which the categories of being-for-self and being-for-another are fundamental (see, for example, Hegel's *Logic*, tr. W. Wallace, Clarendon Press, Oxford, 1975, sections 91–6, pp. 135–42).

81. See Ovid, *Fasti*, VI, 292.

82. Exodus 20.5: 'Thou shalt not bow down thyself to them, nor serve them: for I the Lord thy God am a jealous God, visiting the iniquity of the fathers upon the children unto the third and fourth generation of them that hate me.'

83. The original sense of the term 'existence' is something like 'a standing out from', from the Latin prefix *ex* ('out of') and the verb *sistere* ('to stand, place, set'). Existential writers, including Kierkegaard himself in later work, draw on this sense to distinguish the form of *human* being from that of other kinds of entity. Human being is a kind of 'rising up out of' the world of things, which involves a questioning about those things and also a questioning about what to make of human being in particular cases. Here, however, Kierkegaard is exploiting the original sense to make a distinction *within* human being, according to which woman can only 'rise up out of the world' with the help of the man, implying a sense of 'existence' in which

woman-being does not yet amount to 'existence' but is only 'being' (for-another).

84. This passage makes use of the same pun as earlier between *at frie* ('to court', or also, 'to pop the question') and *at frie* (or *at befrie*) ('to set free').

85. Or a version of that game.

86. A beauty contest won by Aphrodite, to whom a temple called Kallipygos ('well put together') was erected in celebration.

87. 'Terrible to relate.' Cf. Virgil, *Aeneid*, II, 204: *Horresco referens*.

88. Euripides, *Medea*, verses 250ff.

89. Actaeon, a famous huntsman, one day saw Diana (Artemis) bathing with her nymphs. She punished him by changing him into a stag, and in that form he was torn to pieces by hounds.

90. The original reads, 'the girl seems in both directions, after all, to be only a child'. The Danish for 'penitent' here is *skriftebarn*, which might be translated 'child confessee', corresponding to *skriftefader* ('father-confessor').

91. An application of the Hegelian notion of *Aufheben*, associated with the 'annulling' or 'cancelling' of an opposition between thesis and antithesis in a 'higher' synthesis which nevertheless preserves the rational aspect of each of the former (see note 4, p. 618). Johannes has made sure that Cordelia's case is not 'dialectical' in a Hegelian sense. Feeling that love and betrothal are incompatible, she simply 'cancels' the second because she has come (been made) to think of it as an inescapable impediment to the free expression of the former.

92. Pygmalion, king of Cyprus, made an ivory image of a maiden which he then fell in love with. Aphrodite granted his prayer to be able to breathe life into it.

93. A surprise attack on the Capitoline Hill by the Gauls was repulsed after the Romans had been alerted to it by the cackling of geese.

94. In a collection of magazine articles by a German writer, Matthias Claudius (1741–1815), a parody of a learned dispute is accompanied by a comic picture of the person presiding over it, Herr Lars Hochedeln. ('*Asinus omnia sua secum portans* oder Sämmtliche Werke des Wandsbecker Bothen', I–II, p. 131) (Vienna, 1844).

95. The Alpheus is the main river of the Peloponnese. In places it runs underground, which led to the story of the river-god Alpheus's pursuit of the nymph Arethusa who was finally changed by Artemis into the fountain of Arethusa in the island of Ortygia at Syracuse. The god continued his pursuit under the sea and tried to join his stream with the fountain.

96. See note 26, p. 619.

97. Apuleius, of Madaura in Africa, was born about A.D. 124. His *Metamorphoses*, known as *The Golden Ass*, is one of the two surviving examples of the Latin novel (the other is Petronius's *Satyricon*). 'Cupid and Psyche' is an episode in this work.

98. Myrtle was sacred to Venus and is an emblem of love.

99. See Aristophanes' speech in Plato's *Symposium*, Chapters 14 and 15.

100. 'I accept the omen.' Cicero, *De divinatione*, I, 103.

101. Alectryon, a friend of Ares (Mars, to the Romans), was meant to keep watch during a tryst between Ares and Aphrodite, but fell asleep so that Apollo (the sun-god) and Hephaestus (Vulcan) took them by surprise.

102. Clytie, a sea-nymph, daughter of Oceanus, was changed into the plant *heliotropum* when the sun-god Apollo was untrue to her. The word means 'turning to the sun'.

103. The Thessalian girl Caenis was changed into a man (Caeneus) by her lover, Poseidon. After many vicissitudes he eventually recovered his female form in the underworld.

PART TWO

1   The Aesthetic Validity of Marriage

1. Homer, *Odyssey*, X, 237ff. Circe, daughter of Helios the sun-god, lived on the island of Aeaea. Odysseus's companions tasted the magic cup Circe offered them and were turned into swine.

2. Philippians 4.7: 'And the peace of God which passeth all understanding, shall keep your hearts and minds through Christ Jesus.'

3. Lord Byron, 'To Eliza', in *Poetical Works*, 1886, I, p. 83: 'Though some women are angels, yet wedlock's the devil.'

4. *Papirer* III, B 41, 5, p. 129 indicates that the reference is to Alexandre Dumas's *Gabrielle de Belle-Isle*, a five-act play performed in Danish translation in 1841–2.

5. Matthew 6.34: 'Take therefore no thought for the morrow: for the morrow shall take thought for the things of itself: sufficient unto the day is the evil thereof.'

6. The 'bad' or 'false' infinite in Hegel's philosophy is the idea of trying to attain the infinite by prolonging a numerical series indefinitely, while the good or true infinite is a whole of which the finite forms the parts. See Hegel's *Logic*, tr. W. Wallace, Clarendon Press, Oxford, 1975, section 94. See note 11, p. 621.

7. The Danish distinguishes love in a general sense (*kjærlighed*) from love in a sense that focuses on its amorous and romantic manifestations (*elskov*). In the following passages the distinction is left largely to the context.

8. In *The Marriage of Figaro*.

9. Matthew 16.26.

10. Jupiter's love for Semele invoked the jealousy of Hera, who (disguised as Semele's old nurse) persuaded Semele to invite Jupiter to appear before her in the same splendour as she herself was accustomed to. Jupiter appeared as the god of thunder and Semele was consumed by the lightning.

11. It was by solving the riddle posed by the Sphinx that Oedipus obtained the kingdom of Thebes and married Jocasta.

12. Virgil, *Aeneid*, VI, 258: 'Away, away, ye unconsecrated.'

13. Luke 7.47: 'Wherefore, I say unto thee, her sins, which are many, are forgiven, for she loved much: but to whom little is forgiven, the same loveth little.'

14. Genesis 2.18.

15. Genesis 5.2: 'Male and female created he them; and blessed them, and called their name Adam, in the day when they were created.'

16. 1 Timothy 2.11ff.

17. Luke 16.1ff.

18. 'It is an old story.'

19. Genesis 2.18.

20. Genesis 2.24.

21. Kierkegaard's expression is 'a Kirsten Gifte-knivs', a character from Ludvig Holberg's *Den forvandlede Brudgom*, and a current term for 'match-maker'.

22. 'In itself.' A reference to Immanuel Kant's notion of the 'thing-in-itself', of which there can be no experience since, as a very condition of the latter, it lies beyond all possible experience.

23. Following Hegel's aesthetics (see Hegel, *Aesthetics: Lectures on Fine Art*, tr. T. M. Knox, Clarendon Press, Oxford, 1975).

24. 'Everything must be doubted.'

25. To be 'a priori' is to be true independently of whatever may be proved or disproved in experience.

26. 1 Timothy 4.4.

27. Phanerogamous plants are flowering plants, while cryptogamous plants (for example mosses and lichens) have no stamen and pistils and so no flowers.

28. A. G. Oehlenschläger's *Skattegraveren* ('The Treasure-Digger'): 'But if you utter one word, it vanishes again.'

29. Caligula is said to have expressed the wish that the Roman people had only one neck, so that they could all be decapitated with one blow.

30. The Emperor Domitian.

31. Catherine II of Russia's minister had false façades of flourishing villages put up near the road she travelled on with him on her inspection of the newly conquered provinces bordering the Black Sea.

32. 'From the poetic point of view.'

33. That custom is second nature (*Vanen er den anden Natur*) is a saying in Danish.

34. Leibniz held that no two things can be alike. This is related to his claim for the identity of things that have all their properties in common, which again is related to the idea that if two things differ, the difference must be present in the nature of the things themselves.

35. Presumably an allusion to Leibniz.

36. Cf. A. G. Oehlenschläger's *Valravnen*.

37. 1 Peter 3.4.

38. Don Quixote.

39. 'When ten times repeated they please.' Horace, *Ars poetica*, 365.

40. Ecclesiastes.

41. 'Self-tormentor.' The title of a Greek comedy by Terence (b. 195 B.C.).

42. 'I have spoken and freed my mind.' Words used by Roman orators to conclude their speeches.

43. *Erzählungen und Mährchen*, Prenzlau, 1826, pp. 323ff.

2 Equilibrium between the Aesthetic and the Ethical in the Development of Personality

1. Originally 'Hep', said to be composed of the initial letters of *Hierosolyma est perdita* ('Jerusalem is lost [to the infidels]') and was the cry of the German knights when persecuting the Jews. Incidentally, 'Hurrah' is said to derive from the Sclavonic for 'On to paradise!'.

2. Luke 8.30: 'And Jesus asked him, saying, What is thy name? And he said, Legion: because many devils were entered into him.' Cf. Mark 5.9.

3. Cf. Joshua 6.

4. In the *Parmenides* (Chapter 19), Plato defines the present instant as the boundary between past and future.

5. P. A. Wolff, *Mythologie der Feen und Elfen*, Weimar, 1828, translated from a work in English.

6. 1 Corinthians 1.23.

7. Ecclesiastes 1.2: 'Vanity of vanities, saith the preacher, vanity of vanities; all is vanity.' The Latin is the title of a poem by Goethe ('Ich hab' mein Sach auf nichts gestellt, Iuchhe').

8. *Lad gaa* ('let [it] go').

9. Goethe, *West-östlicher Divan*, 'Freiheit'. Kierkegaard cites it in the German.

10. 'Weak aspiration.'

11. See note 20, Part 1, p. 618.

12. See note 14, Part 1, p. 618.

13. The Danish *Moment* is translated here as 'element' to avoid confusion with 'moment' as 'instant in time', but I have retained 'discursive moment' – *Trans.*

14. Freedom of the will or 'negative' freedom as distinct from 'positive' freedom, as in Vilhelm's notion of choice of oneself.

15. Revelation 14.13: '... Yea, saith the Spirit, that they may rest from their labours; and their works do follow them.'

16. From a saying that the Lord fills the stomach before the eyes.

17. Matthew 20.3: 'And he went out about the third hour, and saw others standing idle in the market-place.'

18. *Volksmährchen der Deutschen*, Gotha, 1787, I, pp. 164ff; here, p. 220.

19. Horace, *Letters*, I, 46: 'Fleeing poverty, over the sea, over the rocks, through fire.'

20. That is, a philosophical system, like Hegel's science of the spirit.

21. 'Nothing for appearances, everything for conscience.'

22. Quietism is a form of religious mysticism involving contemplation and inactivity.

23. Matthew 16.26. The Authorized Version has 'lose his soul'.

24. Matthew 12.36: 'But I say unto you, That every idle word that men shall speak, they shall give account thereof in the day of judgment.'

25. The for-itself is conscious being, the in-itself is substantial being. In Hegelian philosophy the Absolute is the in-and-for-itself, or the identity of substance and subjectivity. Kierkegaard here appropriates the language to assert the not merely subjective, that is the substantial character, of good.

26. Ovid, *Metamorphoses*, III, 407ff. The beautiful Narcissus, unable to love, was caused by Nemesis to see his own image reflected in a fountain. He fell in love with the image and pined away in his infatuation, until changed into the plant that bears his name.

27. 1 Samuel 15.22.

28. Romans 8.16: 'The Spirit itself beareth witness with our spirit, that we are the children of God.'

29. 'Innermost sanctuary' or 'Holy of holies'.

30. Matthew 10.37: 'He that loveth father or mother more than me, is not
     worthy of me: and he that loveth son or daughter more than me, is
     not worthy of me.'

31. 'Persecuted church.'

32. 2 Timothy 4.7: 'I have fought a good fight, I have finished my course,
     I have kept the faith.'

33. Matthew 23.24: 'Ye blind guides, which strain at a gnat, and swallow
     a camel.'

34. *Hexebrev*, or 'witch's letter', is a bound collection of truncated pictures
     of people or animals, from which, by turning the pages and combining
     the different parts, new images can be constructed.

35. 'Know thyself': the inscription on the temple in Delphi.

36. 'In terms of possibility', a phrase in Aristotle's philosophy.

37. Exodus 3.2: 'And the angel of the Lord appeared unto him in a flame
     of fire out of the midst of a bush, and, behold, the bush burned with
     fire, and the bush was not consumed.'

38. The Adamites. A sect, or sects, in Middle Europe in the fifteenth and
     sixteenth centuries, founded in 1400 by one Picard, of Bohemia, self-
     styled 'Adam, son of God', and dedicated to a state of primitive
     innocence. Apart from going naked, they had wives in common, and
     claimed there was no distinction between good and evil.

39. A primer of morals for the young by the conservative theologian
     Bishop Nicolaj Edinger Balle (1744–1816), used in primary schools,
     both in Denmark and Norway.

40. See note 6, p. 610.

41. 'Without further ado.'

42. 'Taught by God.'

43. See note 12, p. 629.

44. 'Speak, so that I can see you.'

45. See note 23, p. 623.

46. The mysteries were secret cults of purification in honour of the Greek
     gods. The 'greater' mysteries (the Great Eleusinia) took place in Sep-
     tember.

47. Kant's categorical imperative, or the idea that moral duties are absolute
     and not conditional upon some goal.

48. Hebrews 9.27.

49. 'What you are seeking is here.' Horace, *Letters*, I, 2, 29.

3 Last Word

1. A. G. Oehlenschläger, *Ludlams Hule, Samlede Værker* XVII, p. 176.
2. 'Not unpraiseworthy', a mediocre examination grade.

4 The Edifying in the Thought that Against God
We Are Always in the Wrong

1. Luke 13.1–4.
2. Genesis 32.24–30. Jacob wrestled with God.
3. Cf. Job 40.2.